D1318143

Praise for *Understanding Virtual Reality: Interface, Application, and Design*

"*Understanding Virtual Reality* is the definitive, authoritative, and exhaustive exploration of the field by two insiders and practitioners, Sherman and Craig. Virtual reality, a uniquely viewer-centric, large field-of-view, dynamic display technology has evolved over the past decade in many physical formats, driven by many software applications using a variety of operating systems, computers, and specialized libraries. Sherman and Craig capture them all in this substantial volume.

Most writing about virtual reality involves summarizing and interpreting interviews and demos, with massive doses of the speculative and the spectacular, and lots of historical fuzziness. Sherman and Craig, however, lived (and, indeed, still live) in the world of actual VR production at the National Center for Supercomputing Applications at the University of Illinois at Urbana-Champaign, where corporate researchers, educators, scientists, and artists make use of this technology in their daily work. They have personally suffered with VR tech and benefited greatly from access to it as well as to amazing amounts of computing, engineering, and scientific talent. They were held to real deadlines of corporate contracts, scientific conference demonstrations, and the design of IMAX productions. While they were doing all this, they were also writing this book. As a result, Understanding Virtual Reality has the integrity and feel of a long-term, eyewitness account and a personal journal, because these production-oriented researchers were documenting the times contemporaneously, rather than trying to reconstruct the details years later.

Understanding Virtual Reality is truly the most complete reference book to emerge from the past ten years of VR."

—Tom DeFanti
Distinguished Professor of Computer Science
Electronic Visualization Laboratory
University of Illinois at Chicago
Co-inventor of the *CAVE*

"*Understanding Virtual Reality* is the introduction to the medium of VR that we have all been desiring for our beginning courses. The text starts off by defining VR and all its variant terms, moves on to the necessary hardware technology, discusses rendering and interaction in the virtual world, and then finishes by discussing the VR experience and how we would apply VR to real-world problems. The text does not bury one in arcane mathematics but rather points the reader to the original source material for more information—an excellent decision on the part of the authors. Systems details and networked virtual environments are not covered, but supplemental reading material can easily be found for such topics. Sherman and Craig have staggered to the finish line with this notable tome and we suggest you all run out and get one as soon as possible!"

—Michael Zyda
Director, The MOVES Institute

Understanding Virtual Reality

INTERFACE, APPLICATION, AND DESIGN

The Morgan Kaufmann Series in Computer Graphics and Geometric Modeling

Series Editor, Brian A. Barsky,
University of California, Berkeley

Understanding Virtual Reality
William R. Sherman and Alan B. Craig

Texturing and Modeling:
A Procedural Approach, Third Edition
David S. Ebert, F. Kenton Musgrave, Darwyn Peachey,
Ken Perlin, and Steven Worley

Geometric Tools for Computer Graphics
Philip Schneider and David Eberly

Jim Blinn's Corner: Notation, Notation, Notation
Jim Blinn

Level of Detail for 3D Graphics: Application and Theory
David Luebke, Martin Reddy, Jonathan D. Cohen, Amitabh
Varshney, Benjamin Watson, and Robert Huebner

Digital Video and HDTV Algorithms and Interfaces
Charles Poynton

Pyramid Algorithms: A Dynamic Programming Approach
to Curves and Surfaces for Geometric Modeling
Ron Goldman

Non-Photorealistic Computer Graphics:
Modeling, Rendering, and Animation
Thomas Strothotte and Stefan Schlechtweg

Curves and Surfaces for CAGD:
A Practical Guide, Fifth Edition
Gerald Farin

Subdivision Methods for Geometric Design:
A Constructive Approach
Joe Warren and Henrik Weimer

Computer Animation: Algorithms and Techniques
Rick Parent

The Computer Animator's Technical Handbook
Lynn Pocock and Judson Rosebush

Advanced RenderMan:
Creating CGI for Motion Pictures
Anthony A. Apodaca and Larry Gritz

Curves and Surfaces in Geometric Modeling:
Theory and Algorithms
Jean Gallier

Andrew Glassner's Notebook:
Recreational Computer Graphics
Andrew S. Glassner

Warping and Morphing of Graphical Objects
Jonas Gomes, Lucia Darsa, Bruno Costa, and Luiz Velho

Jim Blinn's Corner: Dirty Pixels
Jim Blinn

Rendering with Radiance:
The Art and Science of Lighting Visualization
Greg Ward Larson and Rob Shakespeare

Introduction to Implicit Surfaces
Edited by Jules Bloomenthal

Jim Blinn's Corner: A Trip Down the Graphics Pipeline
Jim Blinn

Interactive Curves and Surfaces:
A Multimedia Tutorial on CAGD
Alyn Rockwood and Peter Chambers

Wavelets for Computer Graphics: Theory and Applications
Eric J. Stollnitz, Tony D. DeRose, and David H. Salesin

Principles of Digital Image Synthesis
Andrew S. Glassner

Radiosity & Global Illumination
François X. Sillion and Claude Puech

Knotty: A B-Spline Visualization Program
Jonathan Yen

User Interface Management Systems:
Models and Algorithms
Dan R. Olsen, Jr.

Making Them Move: Mechanics, Control, and
Animation of Articulated Figures
Edited by Norman I. Badler, Brian A. Barsky,
and David Zeltzer

Geometric and Solid Modeling: An Introduction
Christoph M. Hoffmann

An Introduction to Splines for Use in
Computer Graphics and Geometric Modeling
Richard H. Bartels, John C. Beatty, and Brian A. Barsky

Understanding Virtual Reality

INTERFACE, APPLICATION, AND DESIGN

William R. Sherman
National Center for Supercomputing Applications
University of Illinois at Urbana-Champaign

Alan B. Craig
National Center for Supercomputing Applications
University of Illinois at Urbana-Champaign

MORGAN KAUFMANN PUBLISHERS

AN IMPRINT OF ELSEVIER SCIENCE

AMSTERDAM   BOSTON   LONDON   NEW YORK
OXFORD   PARIS   SAN DIEGO   SAN FRANCISCO
SINGAPORE   SYDNEY   TOKYO

Publishing Director	Diane D. Cerra
Publishing Services Manager	Edward Wade
Senior Development Editor	Belinda Breyer
Project Management/Copyedit	Yonie Overton
Cover and Interior Design	Ross Carron Design
Composition/Art Management	Proctor-Willenbacher
Additional Editorial Illustration	Laurie Wigham
Additional Technical Illustration	Tony Davis
Proofreader	Carol Leyba
Indexer	Barbara Kohl
Printer	The Maple-Vail Book Manufacturing Group

Morgan Kaufmann Publishers
An imprint of Elsevier Science
340 Pine Street, Sixth Floor
San Francisco, CA 94104-3205
www.mkp.com

07 06 05 04 03   5 4 3 2

Library of Congress Control Number: 2002107270
ISBN: 1-55860-353-0

This book is printed on acid-free paper.

Dedicated to Theresa, Danielle, Cindy, and Sheryl
for their love and support through the years

—Bill

Dedicated to my wonderful parents Bradford and Mary,
my brother Stephen, and my sister Elaine, with all my love

—Alan

Contents in Brief

Contents

Preface

What This Book Is

The aim of this book is to explore the use of virtual reality as a means of sharing information and experiences among people—as a medium of human communication. We have sought to provide a comprehensive overview of the medium of virtual reality, including the technology required to produce the physically immersive effect and the interface design necessary to provide useful and meaningful content.

Research in virtual reality (VR) is turning the corner from being focused primarily on technology to an increasing focus on what can be done using VR—content is now driving the application. The earlier focus on technology wasn't because researchers lacked interest in what could be done with the emerging medium, but because the technology itself was lacking in many ways. Researchers like Fred Brooks at the University of North Carolina at Chapel Hill aimed their work at usable applications, but recognized that significant advances would be required in the fields of computer graphics, display, and tracking devices among others, and thus were compelled to extend their research in all these directions.

As the required technology has become widely available and of adequate quality, the medium of virtual reality has become a feasible tool for accomplishing research, and not just a topic of research for its own sake. Beginning in the late 1980s and early 1990s, enough technological advancement had taken place that more centers of research (in business and academia) could afford to experiment with VR. Now we are on the verge of technology being inexpensive enough not only for larger research facilities, but for the mass market as well. Once this occurs, using and creating VR content will become cost effective at the consumer level. This book explores what is required to develop virtual reality applications for real-world uses in areas such as science, industry, art, education, and medicine.

Much like the entertainment industry has driven the development of computer graphics, so movies, arcades, and the home entertainment market have been among the first to exploit the commercial possibilities of VR. These forces are what will help bring prices into a reasonable range for more widespread application. Among some niche audiences, many viable scientific, industrial, medical, educational, and artistic applications have already emerged.

Our goal in writing this book is to provide a comprehensive volume on the medium of virtual reality, how it can be used, and how to create compelling virtual reality applications. Our coverage of this new medium also briefly examines its origins, what comprises a VR system, and the methods of interfacing human participants with virtual worlds. We explore choices of systems and techniques for the creation of VR experiences designed for use by specific populations of society.

Throughout the book, examples are taken from real-world VR applications, ranging from science, manufacturing, business, medicine, education, sports, arcade entertainment, art, and the military. Four in-depth VR application case studies are presented in Appendices A–D. Each application is explored with respect to why it was needed, what had previously been done, how VR was incorporated, what was accomplished, and where future trends will lead.

Our study of the medium of virtual reality ranges from the design and implementation of the hardware that enables VR systems to be built, through how the medium can be used as a new tool, to (hopefully) how to provide greater understanding, productivity, and interest in VR. As the goal of this book is to investigate and report on the latter, we will briefly discuss the types of virtual reality systems and the differences between them, without going into great detail on the hardware technology. Advances in technology are too rapid to be covered in this volume, and there are other resources available for obtaining this information.

What This Book Is Not!

This book is not a tutorial on how to implement a VR system with today's technology. We will presume that the readers of this book will be approaching VR on a content level. The goal is to have a book which will be useful beyond the technologies of today. There are many resources available for those who need to learn the ins and outs of low-level VR device interfacing. The reference section can help you get started in this direction.

Neither does this book cover the programming aspects of virtual reality or computer graphics. Rather, the focus is on issues of content, interaction, system integration, and usability. However, it has been successfully utilized as a text in a VR programming course through integration with VR programming tutorials available online.

Wherever possible, we will try to aid the reader in acquiring factual, practical information and in separating the pragmatic from the gimmicky. VR has been accused of being merely a technological novelty, something overly promoted by the press into a false sense of importance. While there is some truth to VR being hyped in the press, the authors believe (and hopefully demonstrate in the chapters that follow) that VR is a useful new medium, one that cannot be ignored. Astute readers will recognize the power of the new medium and work to harness it in ways that are constructive in their own applications.

Who This Book Is For

This book is intended to be useful as a textbook in a course on virtual reality. It is an appropriate text for graduate or undergraduate courses on VR aimed at providing a broad background in VR systems and content. The intended audience includes students from a variety of disciplines, ranging from computer science, engineering, psychology, medicine, education, science, and the arts.

This book is also intended to be of interest to anyone with a forward-looking view—those in business, as well as scientists, engineers, educators, and artists—who want to go beyond the hype and learn about how VR is being applied to solve problems today. The target reader is technically knowledgeable but may be unaware of how to apply VR to their particular area of interest.

This book is designed to be a useful source of information for anyone who wonders whether VR can benefit them, whether as a tool to explore information and convey ideas or to develop a full virtual reality application. Often VR conjures up the notion of games and complicated science. To investigate how virtual reality can be applied in a variety of fields, we examine general virtual reality interface techniques in Part II.

How to Use This Book

The first part of this book is intended to give the reader the terminology and background required to understand the application of VR. Later chapters focus on technical issues, interaction techniques, content choice, and representation concerns that require attention when designing VR applications. The book concludes with a look at where the future may lie for virtual reality systems and applications.

To gain an understanding of the basics of the field and what has been done with virtual reality in a variety of application areas, the reader may well read this book from cover to cover. However, usage of this book can be tailored to a variety of different university-level courses. A technically oriented course may focus less on the initial chapters, which emphasize VR as a communication medium, and more on the technical and systems chapters; a media studies course, or any course where the interest is primarily at the content level, may de-emphasize the technical issues of VR systems, and focus instead on the usage of virtual reality. A VR programming course can touch on the technology and usability aspects of this book, in particular by taking advantage of the additional online material we provide at *www.mkp.com/understanding-vr*.

This material consists of a link to an open source VR programming system with tutorials that supplement the text and VR case studies in addition to those found in Appendices A–D.

A thorough glossary of virtual reality and related terms is also provided online. Because virtual reality is still a developing field, there are often misunderstandings among researchers regarding what is meant by a particular term. We hope that our online glossary will serve as a resource that the VR community can use to reduce such confusion. Of course, our glossary reflects how we use terms in this text, but we have made every attempt to adhere to the more scholarly definitions of VR terms used by the majority of the VR community.

Quirks of Authorship

VR is a medium that can only truly be experienced live, and it can be difficult to understand certain concepts without prior familiarity with the medium. Thus, in keeping with the visual nature of VR, we use a considerable number of photographs and diagrams to enhance the text. The reader may notice that many of our images utilize the *CAVE* VR system. We did this because it is easier to witness a participant interacting in a virtual reality experience in a stationary VR display and because a CAVE system was at our ready disposal.

However, we have also used many head-based systems and recognize that they are the most appropriate display choice in many circumstances. So our discussion of display technologies attempts to strike a good balance between stationary and head-based displays (HBDs). Accordingly, we also include several photographs of head-based display systems provided by other members of the VR community.

Because there is no set standard for how to implement genderless singular pronouns in the "world" of English, we include our choice as one of our quirks. We have chosen to use *they/them/etc.* as our solution. We think this works the best, and much like *you/your/etc.* were once used only in plural situations (versus *thy/thine/etc.*), it is certainly possible for *they/them/etc.* to make the same leap. Here we boldly offer the precedent found in the works of William Shakespeare, William Caxton, and Jane Austen.

It is not the objective of this book to provide a detailed look at today's rapidly changing technology. We hope the information presented here will continue to be of use when today's hardware is suitable for display in a museum as the object *on* display rather than the means *of* display. There are already many useful sources of information covering the intricacies and implementations of current VR technology. Indeed, references at the end of this book include several texts that address state of the art technology at the time of their publication.

Acknowledgments

A large number of people have contributed to the creation of this book. The first contribution was from Audrey Walko, who put us in contact with Mike Morgan and thus initiated our journey. Another early contribution was provided by Mary Craig, who transcribed portions of our first drafts from dictation.

Ideally, we would like to individually acknowledge each person who has shown and discussed with us their virtual reality work, including hosting us during our visits to many VR facilities around the world. Our initial focus was on how virtual reality has been applied to a wide variety of disciplines and topic areas. Thus, our authorial journey began with an exploration of as many virtual reality applications as we could find, experience, and discuss with the creators. Our discussions with the people responsible for more than 50 virtual reality applications have certainly helped shape our view of what is involved in creating a good VR experience.

As the book progressed and expanded to include material on the medium of virtual reality, it became unwieldy, and we elected to remove much of the material we wrote about existing VR applications from this particular publication. Portions of that effort remain in the images used to exemplify many concepts and in the application case studies that make up the four appendices. Thus we acknowledge many of our contributors directly in the captions and appendices. However, it is our ongoing goal to acknowledge individually the many people whose generosity we encountered in our initial surveys, by working to make much more of that material available.

Of course, there are many people who literally shared their virtual reality work with us by allowing us to run their applications at our facility. Again, their generosity is most amply evident through our use of many of these applications in our photographs of how various VR techniques are implemented, and we acknowledge these individuals in the photograph captions. We would like to especially thank Dave Pape for directly or indirectly making many of the *CAVE* applications available and for allowing us to use the Crayoland House, which we transplanted into many example scenarios.

We would also like to acknowledge the many people we have had the opportunity to collaborate with at NCSA. Certainly this includes all the people who've done visualization work at NCSA, with a special mention of those involved in the visualization group representation project. The representation project introduced us to a lot of the underlying concepts of visualization, including perception, presentation, mapping, symbology, and cognition. Even when our day to day tasks keep us focused on technology, our primary aim is to use technology for the purposes of communication and to gain insight. We hope we have been able to present some of the concepts explored during those insightful sessions in such a way as to make them accessible to the reader.

NCSA has also provided us ample opportunity to work with research scientists interested in pursuing visualization and sometimes VR as tools for investigating their science. Our work has also put us in contact with businesses interested in putting VR to use, as a manufacturing design tool, promoting safety, and visualizing retail data. We have worked with professors who provide novel teaching environments through the medium of virtual reality. NCSA management has contributed through their support of the NCSA virtual reality facilities, beginning with a Fakespace *Boom,* VPL and Virtual Research HMDs, and a single screen projected display in 1991, to the *CAVE* we now use on a regular basis. Also, NCSA's collaboration with the Electronic Visualization Lab at the University of Illinois at Chicago, headed by Tom DeFanti and Dan Sandin, has been a great source of information, technology, and inspiration over the years.

Given the number of iterations through which this book has progressed, it is not surprising that we have a large number of reviewers to thank for their comments. In alphabetical order, they include Colleen Bushell, Toni Emerson, Scott Fisher, George Francis, Kurt Hebel, Andy Johnson, Mike McNeill, Robert Moorhead, Carla Scaletti, Steve Shaffer, Audrey Walko, and Chris Wickens. Three reviewers in particular provided us with detailed comments for several of the chapters: Bill Chapin, Rich Holloway, and Holly Korab. And there have been a few anonymous reviewers whom we would like to thank just as much for pushing the book to be better than it might have been.

We would also like to thank Mike Morgan and his crew at Morgan Kaufmann— in particular, our editor Diane Cerra, series editor Brian Barsky, and Belinda Breyer. Mike and Diane had the patience to allow us to iterate over the design and implementation of various aspects of the book as we honed in on the current product. Belinda's contributions included a complete review and edit of the book to help make sure all the necessary information was included and ordered for readers new to the field.

We would like to thank Beverly Carver for developing many of the line drawings. We would also like to thank Yonie Overton for helping us further shape the prose and for overseeing the design and production process. Her efforts helped make the final product better.

And finally, we would like to thank our families: Bill's wife Sheryl, who took on more of the home load and was supportive through the marathon this book became. And Cindy and Danielle for behaving as best as kids can be expected to for Mom, even though Dad wasn't around as much as he or they would have liked. And Theresa for waiting to arrive long enough for us to get the final edits completed. And Alan's friends and family for encouragement and expertise in any number of technical areas.

PART I

What Is Virtual Reality?

C hapter 1 begins with our description of what is meant by *virtual reality* (VR). We begin with the dictionary definitions of *virtual* and *reality* and consider how these individual words combine to describe a unique means of human communication. We go on to define other key terms and offer a brief history of the origins of VR.

Chapter 2 examines how knowledge about previously existing media can be applied to the medium of virtual reality and looks at the media from which VR has evolved. We compare the characteristics of virtual reality with other media for human communication and explore how VR is used to convey models of virtual worlds.

CHAPTER 1

Introduction to Virtual Reality

Human history is marked by a progression of media used to convey and experience ideas. Perhaps the most recent step in this progression is the use of *virtual reality*. Recorded history begins with people painting on cave walls to express the happenings of the hunt and sharing stories to chronicle the history of a community or tribe. It was the importance of communication that raised the storyteller to a position of high esteem in the community.

The first cave paintings transcend the physical experience they depict (FIGURE 1-1). These paintings were a primitive medium for conveying the artist's concept. They were a method for communicating ideas, useful facts, and events among people. Viewers then superimposed their own interpretations on the painter's manifested expression.

Starting with the first pigment spread on cave walls, new technologies have developed and evolved, leading in turn to new media (FIGURE 1-2). Along the way, humans have explored ways to utilize each new medium to best express their ideas. Virtual reality is a new medium brought about by technological advances in which much experimentation is now taking place to find practical applications and more effective ways to communicate.

FIGURE 1-1 *Cave paintings were an early medium for storytelling. A virtual world could be conveyed from one person to another via the technology of pigment on stone (Image courtesy of Benjamin Britton).*

Defining Virtual Reality

Because virtual reality is a *new* medium, its definition is still in flux. The researchers and users of VR naturally have their own points of view. Those less familiar with the field may have slightly different interpretations. The definition we use in this book reflects what is generally meant by practitioners and scholars of the field of VR—which is not always how the term is used by marketing departments and the mass media.

Webster's New Universal Unabridged Dictionary [1989] defines *virtual* as "being in essence or effect, but not in fact." This usage has been applied to earlier concepts in computing; for example, when a computer system requires more RAM (primary storage) than is available, memory is expanded *virtually* by use of disk storage (secondary, cheaper storage). The resultant, seemingly enlarged RAM capacity is referred to as *virtual memory*.

What is meant by *reality* is more complicated, and trying to define it completely can result in complex philosophical discussions. *Webster's* defines reality as "the state or quality of being real. Something that exists independently of ideas concerning it. Something that constitutes a real or actual thing as distinguished from something that is merely apparent." To simplify things for our purposes, let's say it is a place that exists and that we can experience.

Four Key Elements of Virtual Reality Experience

The key elements in experiencing virtual reality—or any reality for that matter—are *a virtual world, immersion, sensory feedback* (responding to user input), and *interactivity.*

Key Element 1: Virtual World

A virtual world is the content of a given medium. It may exist solely in the mind of its originator or be broadcast in such a way that it can be shared with others. A *virtual world* can exist without being displayed in a *virtual reality system* (i.e., an integrated collection of hardware, software, and content assembled for producing virtual reality experiences)—much like play or film scripts exist independently of specific instances of their performance. Such scripts do in fact describe virtual worlds. Let's carry the analogy further. We can refer to the script of a play as merely the description of a play. When that description is brought to life via actors, stage

Imagination
Dance
Music
Storytelling (oral tradition)
BEGIN RECORDED HISTORY
Cave painting
Written language
Sculpting (e.g., totem poles)
Musical notation
Books (hand written)
Books (printing press)
Newspapers (periodical information)
Telegraph
Photography
Stereoscope (Wheatstone)
Stereo photography
Recorded audio
Animated images
Motion pictures (mass visual presentation)
Telephone
Radio
Television (mass visual presentation)
Digital computer (ENIAC)
flight simulation
Computer graphics (sketchpad)
First HMD (Sutherland)
Video games
Picture phone
Video teleconferencing
Internet (telnet, ftp, sockets, etc.)
Color frame buffers for computers
Computer graphics animation
Networked computer discussion forums (USENET) etc.
Stereo computer graphics
Interactive computer graphics
MUDs, etc.
Immersive interactive computer display (i.e., VR)
The CAVE (a theater-like VR venue)
The World Wide Web

FIGURE 1-2 *From painting cave walls to sharing computer-generated images on the screens of a virtual CAVE and beyond, the history of human-kind has been marked with a progression of new media.*

sets, and music, we are *experiencing* the play's virtual world. Similarly, a computer-based virtual world is the description of objects within a simulation. When we view that world via a system that brings those objects and interactions to us in a physically immersive, interactive presentation, we are experiencing it via *virtual reality.*

> **virtual world** **1.** an imaginary space often manifested through a medium. **2.** a description of a collection of objects in a space and the rules and relationships governing those objects.

Key Element 2: Immersion

Considering the user must be *immersed* within some other, alternate reality, an admittedly simplistic definition of VR might be

> Immersion into an alternate reality or point of view.

But what does this mean? Where do you go to get immersed into an alternate reality or point of view? What in fact *is* an alternate reality or point of view? According to our simple definition, a medium qualifies if its participants are able to perceive something other than they would have without an external influence. This definition acknowledges the possibility of perceiving something besides the world you are currently living in in two ways: you can either perceive an alternate world or the normal world from another point of view.

An alternate world might be a representation of an actual space that exists elsewhere, or it could be a purely imaginary environment. Alternate worlds are often created in the minds of novelists, composers, and other artists and creative individuals.

Imagine for a moment that you are empowered with the magical ability to live in a world other than the one you currently inhabit. You are given new powers, objects have different properties, perhaps there is no gravity. Other human and non-human beings inhabit this space. Space may or may not exist in the same way it does in our universe. Perhaps the shortest distance between two points is not a straight line. Is such a scenario possible?

If you are able to imagine such a place then it is, indeed, possible. Imagination is where virtual worlds begin and how numerous virtual worlds are experienced. The power of imagination can allow us to dwell where we choose, when we choose, and with whom we choose. We are limited only by what we can imagine and our ability to communicate it.

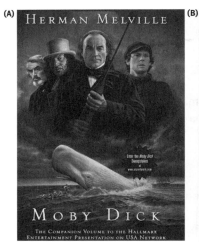

It is often important to manifest the ideas of our imagination into some *medium.* By doing so, we are able to share our world with others and to partake in the creations of others. A novel, for instance, can take us to exotic places and into a life other than our normal daily existence, as can motion pictures, radio, television, and animation (FIGURE 1-3). However, each of *these* media produce only one-way communication: from creator to audience. The point of view is preselected. The dialog is predetermined. The outcome of the story is preordained. However, each member of the audience will likely have a different reaction, perhaps in ways unexpected by the creator.

Depending on a writer's ability to pull the reader into the story—this is called *mimesis,* a term indicating how real or at least consistent with itself a story world is—a novel might qualify as an alternate world that *immerses* the reader. Perhaps you have found yourself empathizing with the characters in a radio, motion picture, or television show. Your *suspension of disbelief* makes the content of these media seem real. None, however, provide direct interaction between the viewer or listener (the recipient) and the world. Furthermore, these media often present their worlds from a third person point of view (POV).

In virtual reality the effect of entering the world begins with *physical,* rather than mental, immersion. Because physical immersion is a necessary component of virtual reality, our simple definition is not specific enough and many other media meet its parameters.

Physical and Mental Immersion

We have already indicated that the term *immersion* can be used in two ways: mental immersion and physical (or sensory) immersion. In discussions of most media, "being immersed" generally refers to an emotional or mental state—a feeling of being involved in the experience. In the medium of VR, however, we also refer to physical immersion as the property of a VR system that replaces or augments the stimulus to the participant's senses.

The state of being mentally immersed is often referred to as having "a sense of presence" within an environment. Unfortunately, there is not yet a common understanding of precisely what each of these terms mean, how they relate to one another, or how to differentiate between them. (We have found one book in which chapters written by different authors give exactly the opposite definitions for immersion and presence.) Let's define what *we* mean by these three terms and how they are used in *this* book.

> **immersion** sensation of being in an environment; can be a purely mental state or can be accomplished through physical means: physical immersion is a defining characteristic of virtual reality; mental immersion is probably the goal of most media creators.
>
> **mental immersion** state of being deeply engaged; suspension of disbelief; involvement.
>
> **physical immersion** bodily entering into a medium; synthetic stimulus of the body's senses via the use of technology; this does not imply all senses or that the entire body is immersed/engulfed.

We will generally use the terms *mental immersion* and *physical immersion* to discuss these phenomena. However, the VR community has also embraced the term *presence* (probably because of prior use of the term *telepresence*) to represent this concept.

Perhaps a better term to express the meaning we wish to convey is *sense of presence,* rather than simply presence. To avoid confusion, we will consider this concept to be the same as mental immersion.

> **presence** short for sense of presence; being mentally immersed.

Key Element 3: Sensory Feedback

Unlike more traditional media, VR allows participants to select their vantage point by positioning their body and to affect events in the virtual world. These features help to make the reality more compelling than a media experience without these options.

Without getting into that philosophical discussion of what reality is, we will consider that there can be more than the reality we experience firsthand with our unaided senses. We refer to the latter as *physical reality*. *Imagined reality* refers to the experiences we have in our thoughts and dreams or that we experience second-hand in novels, films, radio, and so on. In imagined reality, we imagine ourselves within the world presented through the medium—also known as the *diegesis*. The diegesis of a world presented through a medium includes places and events that are not directly presented but are implied to exist or to have occurred. Virtual reality is the medium through which we can experience an imagined reality with many of our physical senses; that is, we use less of our imagination during the experience and rely more on the imagination of the content creator. In other words, virtual reality is a medium that allows us to have a simulated experience approaching that of physical reality. VR also allows us to purposefully reduce the danger of physical reality and to create scenarios not possible in the real world.

Sensory feedback is an ingredient essential to virtual reality. The VR system provides direct sensory feedback to the participants based on their physical position. In most cases, it is the visual sense that receives feedback, although virtual reality environments do exist that display exclusively haptic (touch) experiences. Achieving immediate interactive feedback requires the use of a high-speed computer as a mediating device.

In order to base the sensory output of the VR system on the position of the participant, the system must track their movement. A typical VR system will track the head of the participant and at least one hand or an object held by the hand. Advanced systems may track many of the major body joints. There are a variety of technologies that can be used by a VR system to accomplish tracking. These technologies are described in Chapter 3. A good definition of *position tracking* is the computerized sensing of the position (location and/or orientation) of an object in the physical world—usually at least *part* of the participant's body.

Key Element 4: Interactivity

For virtual reality to seem authentic, it should respond to user actions, namely, be *interactive*. Thus, another necessary component in the full definition of virtual reality is *interactivity*. Interactivity comes more readily with the addition of the computer to the equation. Alternate realities supported by computers include games, computer simulations of natural and unnatural phenomena, and flight simulation.

It should be noted that computer graphics are not required for any of these alternate realities. The classic computer games *The Oregon Trail, Adventure,* and *Zork* (originally called *Dungeon;* see FIGURE 1-4) render their worlds via text description. Each world responds to commands typed by the player, giving the player the sense of being involved with these worlds. The player interacts with objects, characters, and places in these imaginary worlds. The medium of authored, text-based interactive worlds is now often referred to as *interactive fiction* (IF).

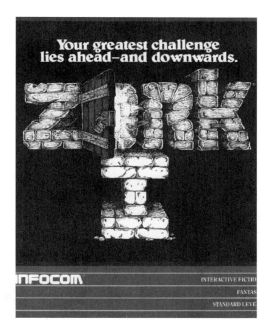

FIGURE 1-4 *The digital computer provided a platform for new media. By allowing a participant to interact with a story delivered in text in a computer program, interactive fiction provides a powerful communication mechanism.* Zork *was one of the first commercially successful interactive fiction programs. Recognizing the power of the medium and the creativity of the consumer, Infocom, Inc. showed a human brain in their advertising and boasted: "We stick our graphics where the sun don't shine!" (Image courtesy of Infocom, Inc.).*

The ability to affect a computer-based world describes one form of interactivity. Another form is the ability to change one's viewpoint within a world. Interactive fiction can be defined in terms of the user/player's ability to interact with a world by changing locations, picking up objects and setting them down, flipping switches, and so on. Virtual reality is more closely associated with the ability of the participant to move physically within the world, obtaining a new vantage point through movements of the head. IF and VR may be defined by one particular form of interaction, but we should note that each medium can make use of the other form. It is true that many VR experiences are constructed with static worlds that cannot be changed by the participant; however, many more are dynamic and do allow modification.

Artificial realities constructed through computational simulation model a portion of a world. These models generally result in a large collection of numbers that represent the state of that world over a period of time. One example might be a scientific simulation of a thunderstorm, wherein the mathematical equations that describe the storm are solved based on the current weather conditions, and the resulting numbers are transferred into imagery.

In FIGURE 1-5, the first image is a photograph of the natural phenomenon of the clouds of a developing thunderstorm. Mathematics allows researchers to manipulate abstract weather concepts to gain further understanding. Most computers don't directly solve analytical mathematical expressions, so the information must be represented in a form the computer can interpret. The result of the execution of the computer program is an array of numbers that describes the physical aspects of the storm. However, a display of millions of numbers is not the best representation for a scientist or any other person to interpret. Instead, the numbers can be transformed into visual images that are more readily understood by humans.

Flight simulation, to take another example, is a computational simulation of various airfoils (wings, propellers, turbines, rudders) interacting with surrounding air, as different flight controls are applied to these surfaces. Output of such a simulation need not be a visual representation of the out-the-window view from the cockpit, but might be simply a representation of the cockpit instrument displays.

Although today we consider flight simulation both a subset and a precursor of virtual reality, early examples of computer-based image generation for flight simulation consisted primarily of displays of dots on the screen. By today's standards, this would probably not be considered very immersive, although it worked well for night landings due to its similarity to the real-world equivalent of runway, taxi, and city lights that dot a pilot's nighttime view. Due in large part to the need to improve the image-generation capabilities for flight simulation, graphics workstations became very powerful and well suited to virtual reality applications. Later, the desire for better visual quality in games led to similar advances for home computers.

Collaborative Environment

The *collaborative environment* is an extension of the interactive element and refers to multiple users interacting within the same virtual space or simulation. Users can perceive others within the simulation, allowing for mutual interaction. The users' representations are referred to as their *avatars*.

> **collaborative environment** multiple users interacting within a virtual world that enables interaction among participants; not necessarily manifested in virtual reality; a collaborative VR environment can be referred to as multipresence or multiparticipant.

Of course, this is a very important feature for many VR applications, including those in combat simulation/practice and the VR game industry, which can involve

PHENOMENAL

MATHEMATICAL

PROCEDURAL

NUMERICAL

GRAPHICAL

FIGURE 1-5 *This image depicts different ways that information about a thunderstorm can be represented (Image courtesy of Matthew Arrott and Bob Wilhemson).*

team play and human opponents. By being unpredictable, other participants make an environment more challenging.

It is important for other uses of VR as well. In virtual prototyping, designers at different locations can interact with one another across large distances. In telepresence surgery, multiple surgeons can watch an operation from the same vantage point, and perhaps hand off control to another participating surgeon in a particular situation. (In Appendix D, we discuss the *Placeholder* application as an example of a collaborative virtual reality application.)

When experiencing a space with other human participants, it is often important to be able to sense their presence in the world—where they are located, which way they are looking/pointing, and what they are saying. The Hindi word *avatar* (which means the worldly incarnation of a deity) is used to denote the concept of representing users in a virtual world. Sometimes a live video image of the person is used as part or the whole of an avatar representation.

> **avatar** **1.** a virtual object used to represent a participant or physical object in a virtual world; the (typically visual) representation may take any form. **2.** the object embodied by a participant. **3.** adapted from Hindi, meaning the earthly embodiment of a deity.

Although we consider multipresence to be a special feature of the VR medium, there are also non–VR situations where multipresence occurs. If you consider a telephone call to be an audio-only virtual environment, then it would also be considered a multipresence environment, because there are two or more participants. This phenomenon produces a technology-mediated space now referred to as *cyberspace* (which we discuss later in this chapter).

Combining the Elements

Taking all of these ingredients into account yields the more suitable definition:

> **virtual reality** a medium composed of interactive computer simulations that sense the *participant's* position and actions and replace or augment the feedback to one or more senses, giving the feeling of being mentally immersed or present in the simulation (a virtual world).

This definition is both narrow enough to discard many misleading uses of the term virtual reality and broad enough to include the wide variety of devices used by practitioners of the medium.

The scenarios described by the definition can be met by modern computer systems through additional hardware devices to provide user position sensing, sensory display, and programming of suitable interaction.

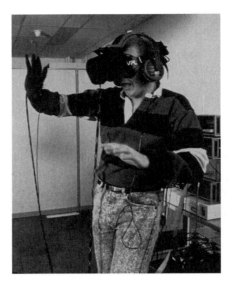

FIGURE 1-6 *The head-mounted display allows a participant to be physically immersed in a computer-generated synthetic environment (Photograph courtesy of NCSA). See color plate 1.*

One such device is a helmet, or *head-mounted display* (HMD), which may or may not allow a view of the outside world (FIGURE 1-6). Graphic images are displayed on a screen or a pair of screens (one for each eye) in the helmet. A tracking sensor attached to the participant's head tells the computer system where the participant is looking. The computer quickly displays a visual image from the vantage point appropriate to the participant's position. Thus, the participant is able to look about a computer-generated world in a manner similar to the real world (within the limits of current technology), making this a natural, intuitive interface. Additional devices can be added to such a system to allow the participant to interact with the world beyond simply looking around. Devices include a voice recognition system that allows them to interact with the world using voice and/or a glove connected to the computer that allows them to grasp and move objects in the world.

Another mechanism for manifesting a virtual reality experience involves placing the participant within a roomlike space that is surrounded by computer-generated imagery. Typically, this is carried out through rear screen projection of computer graphics onto large stationary display screens. The *CAVE* system from the Electronic Visualization Lab at the University of Illinois at Chicago (FIGURE 1-7) is a popular example of such a device [Cruz-Neria et al. 1992]. Such an experience can be compelling even when the imagery only partially surrounds the participant.

A VR system is not necessarily primarily visual. A surgeon might interact with a virtual patient by manipulating medical instruments connected to a computer. The physician's hands are tracked, and the computer provides information to devices that provide haptic feedback (resistance and pressure) to the doctor's hands, simulating the feel of the instruments on the organs (FIGURE 1-8).

FIGURE 1-7 *The CAVE provides another mechanism for supporting virtual reality experiences (Photograph courtesy of NCSA).*

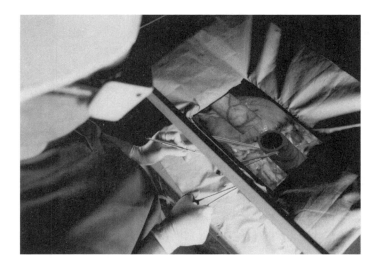

FIGURE 1-8 *Some virtual reality systems use technology to provide feedback to senses other than, or in addition to, the visual sense. This surgery simulator provides both visual and haptic information, which allows users to experience what a surgeon would see and feel with a live patient (Photo courtesy of Boston Dynamics, Inc).*

Artificial Reality

Artificial reality is another term used to describe synthetic environments in which a user may interactively participate. Myron Krueger coined the term to describe his research, giving a definition of artificial reality that coincides with what is now generally referred to as virtual reality. In his book *Artificial Reality II* [Krueger 1991], he discusses many issues of how artificial reality relates to art and technology and indeed brings the two closer together. In his glossary, Krueger defines artificial reality in the following way (and we quote):

> **artificial reality** an artificial reality perceives a participant's action in terms of the body's relationship to a graphic world and generates responses that maintain the illusion that his or her actions are taking place within that world.

Virtual

Because of the hype that has come to be associated with virtual reality, the word *virtual* is often co-opted to imply that VR technology is involved. However, calling something virtual does not necessarily mean it falls within the scholarly definition of virtual reality.

We have mentioned that *virtual* can be added to the name of a computing system to indicate that some component of the system is an extension of the hardware, emulating the real thing through another source. Another use is in simulated virtual worlds where objects exist virtually in that world. Because these objects are merely images of the physical objects they represent, the word *virtual* can be appended to the name of each object to indicate this. We can describe a virtual table in a virtual kitchen, both existing in a virtual world. In a related usage, the domain of optics employs the phrase *virtual image* to refer to objects that appear to exist through a lens or mirror, a use very similar to its meaning in virtual reality.

Virtual World

Virtual worlds and *virtual environments* are a couple of other terms that are often used and confused. How does the term *virtual reality* relate to virtual world and virtual environment?

The term virtual environment is often used as a synonym for both virtual reality and virtual world. However, use of the term virtual environment actually predates the phrase virtual reality. Virtual environment is ambiguous in that it can be defined as a virtual world or as a world presented in a particular virtual reality hardware configuration. In the mid-1980s, researchers at NASA's Ames Research Lab frequently used virtual environment to describe their work in creating an interface that allowed a person to experience a computer-generated scene from a first person point of view (POV)—describing what we would now call their VR systems.

> **virtual environment** **1.** a virtual world. **2.** an instance of a virtual world presented in an interactive medium such as virtual reality.

Cyberspace

Cyberspace is another concept that is related to these terms and which is important to understand. Historically, technology (such as the telephone) has provided a means for people to communicate as if they were in the same location. In the process, a new virtual location was created: cyberspace. The term *cyberspace* was popularized in 1984 by William Gibson, in his novel *Neuromancer;* it described the vast space existing in the computer network of the future that allowed the denizens of this space to locate, retrieve, and communicate information.

Cyberspace is not the same as virtual reality. While we can certainly use virtual reality techniques to interact in cyberspace, such an interface is not required. There are many examples where simple text, voice, or video creates cyberspace. The Internet provides many additional examples of locations that exist only in cyberspace, such as live chat forums, MUDs (multiuser dimensions/dungeons), newsgroups, and the like. Some non-Internet examples include the telephone, CB radio, and video conferencing.

> **cyberspace** a location that exists only in the minds of the participants, often as a result of technology that enables geographically distant people to interactively communicate.

An interesting aspect of this new space is that it is often treated much like a physical location. This is particularly noticeable in people's use of the words *here* and *there*. For example, in a live chat forum, when asking if a particular person is participating, the question asked is "Is Beaker here?"—*here* being the space created by the forum. This same phenomenon can be witnessed in television interviews, when the host will say something like, "Here with us now is an expert in the field of virtual reality, Dr. Honeydew." Yet, often that person is not physically in their studio but at another location and displayed on a large television monitor.

Augmented Reality

Some virtual reality applications are designed to combine virtual representations with perception of the physical world. The virtual representations give the user additional information about the physical world not perceived by unaided human senses. This type of application is referred to as *augmented reality* (AR). In AR, the use of special display technology allows a user to perceive the real world with an overlay of additional information (FIGURE 1-9). This term stems from *Webster's* [1989] definition of augment: "to make larger; enlarge in size or extent; increase." With augmented reality, we are *increasing* the amount of information available to the user in comparison to their normal perception.

FIGURE 1-9 *This image of a multiuser augmented reality application shows one person's view of the world, including another user manipulating a virtual object (Image courtesy of Columbia University).*

Augmented reality can be considered a type of virtual reality. Rather than experiencing physical reality, one is placed in another reality that includes the physical along with the virtual.

Typically, it is the visual sense that is being augmented. For example, contractors who need information about the mechanical systems of a building might display the location of pipe and ductwork on the computer-connected goggles they wear as they walk through the building. Physicians might use AR to see the internal organs of a patient while simultaneously maintaining an external view of the patient's body.

> **augmented reality** a type of virtual reality in which synthetic stimuli are registered with and superimposed on real-world objects; often used to make information otherwise imperceptible to human senses perceptible.

Many possible AR applications focus on the concept of repairing the internal components of a living or mechanical system (FIGURE 1-10). An example of one application of augmented reality to medicine might be providing information about where cancerous tissue is located within a patient. A second medical use of AR might supply information to a surgeon on where to make an incision. A third application might describe to a medical student the proper procedure for making an incision.

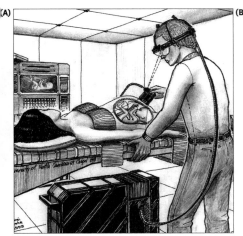

FIGURE 1-10 *Augmented reality can be used to view systems that require investigation or repair.* **(A)** *A physician is able to view 3D representations of ultrasound data of a baby as though it were in the correct position in its mother.* **(B)** *A jet maintenance engineer is shown which parts need to be investigated and can refer to the documentation without moving away from the work area (Drawings courtesy of Andrei State).*

I See, I Cut, I Sew

On September 7, Jacques Marescaux and Michel Gagner became the Charles Lindberghs of the medical world. Hands on joysticks and eyes glued to video monitors, these doctors at Mount Sinai Medical Center in New York City used telesurgery to remove the gallbladder of a 68-year-old woman lying on an operating table in Strasbourg, France.

This first transatlantic operation combined two other remarkable medical technologies: laparoscopy and robotic surgery. Laparoscopy, developed in the late 1970s, uses a minute camera and microsurgical instruments to access the body through tiny incisions, providing a finer degree of accessibility to the surgeon and eliminating the risk of large, open surgical areas. The size of the incision reduces cutting, pain, bleeding, and recovery time. In robotic surgery the operator sits at a computer console, observing the surgical field on a monitor, while using instruments that resemble joysticks to manipulate miniaturized instruments inside the body via data transfer over computer cables. Telesurgery is essentially robotic surgery performed with very long cables—in this case, a sophisticated fiber optic system specially engineered by France Telecom.

Two hurdles stood in the way of telesurgery: how to transmit robotic movements and how to trim time lags in data transfer. "Even a delay of one-fifth of a second—less than half the time it takes to blink—can be fatal if an artery is nicked," says Gagner. "By the time you realize what's happened, blood will have obscured your view, increasing the time it takes to repair the artery. A patient can bleed to death." The new technology, designed by Computer Motion of Santa Barbara, California, allowed surgeons to work in near real time. Although the $750,000 per hour price tag still prohibits bringing bandwidth bedside on a large scale, Gagner foresees a global network of wired hospitals as the costs of data transmission decrease. "This will make the expertise of any doctor available to any patient," he says. "Eventually it could even be used on astronauts." Maybe telehousecalls will be next.

—Jocelyn Selim, *Discover Magazine* (January 2002)

Similar examples can be devised for repair of mechanical systems, such as jet aircraft.

Augmented reality typically requires the use of a movable visual display, especially if the user is to move around in the augmented world. This display is usually a head-mounted display, but it can also be a palm-based display. The critical requirement for AR is that the virtual overlay be aligned to the real world onto which it is mapped. This is referred to as *registration*. The details of AR systems are covered in Chapter 4.

Telepresence

Telepresence utilizes technology closely related to that of VR. Telepresence is a medium in which transducers such as video cameras and microphones substitute for the corresponding senses of the participant. The participant is able to see and hear with the aid of remote sensing devices in a remote location from the first person point of view. The user is able to interact and affect the remote environment by their actions. Telepresence differs from the general case of virtual reality by representing the physical world as opposed to representing a world that is entirely computer generated.

Telepresence is an application that uses VR technology to virtually place the user somewhere else in space—whether in an adjoining room or on a neighboring planet. Perhaps the primary reason the term *presence* is used by so many VR practitioners is because *telepresence* had been an established term in the related domain of remote control operations prior to the advent of VR. *Tele* means distant and *present* is the state of being present or here. Examples of telepresence include remote manipulation of probes in the deep sea, working with dangerous chemicals, and controlling operations on a space probe.

Problems of magnitude can be addressed through the use of telepresence. A doctor might perform an operation using minimally invasive techniques, where the operation can be watched via small video cameras placed inside the body. The doctor performs the operation with tools that translate the doctor's motions outside the patient's body to relatively small cutting and sewing operations inside.

> **telepresence** the ability to directly interact (often via computer mediation) with a physically real, remote environment from the first-person point of view; there are no restrictions on the location of the remote environment, and there are no restrictions on the size of the device used to carry out the user's commands at the remote location.

The definition of telepresence assumes that the user views the remote world from the vantage point of the remote device. In contrast, the term *teleoperation* refers to cases where the operator uses a remote device to interact with the environment, while viewing that device from another perspective—watching the device from an external camera.

Teleoperation is different than television, where the participant merely watches the remote environment and does not interact. Thus the requirement for viewing the world "live" (i.e., synchronously) that characterizes teleoperation is not met. Telepresence in general is considered an inside-out view of a world, whereas teleoperation generally provides an outside-in view. (Inside-out versus outside-in is discussed in Chapter 7.)

The difference between telepresence and teleoperation can be further illustrated by the control of a model airplane (FIGURE 1-11). With telepresence, the operator sees and interacts with the environment just as they would if they were physically present inside the airplane, whereas simple remote (*tele*) operation is when the view and interaction come from an outside (second person) point of view. In this example, flying a radio-controlled airplane, one typically stands on the ground and watches as the airplane performs the command sent to it from a position external to the craft itself. To make this operation telepresence, a camera would need to be mounted inside the craft, allowing the user to view the flight from the point of view a pilot would have (compare with FIGURE 1-12).

(A)

(B)

FIGURE 1-11 *Telepresence can be differentiated from teleoperation by the point of view and the mechanism for control.* (A) *In normal remote control operation, the point of view is from outside the plane (Image courtesy of Bruce Stenulson of the South Park Area RC Society).* (B) *A radio-controlled model airplane can be considered a telepresence application if the point of view and control are as if from inside the cockpit (Image courtesy of Chris Oesterling [N8UDK] of the Detroit Amateur Television Club).*

(A)

(B)

(C)

(D)

FIGURE 1-12 *A remotely operated robot equipped with
video cameras, speakers,
and a shotgun allow police
to virtually put themselves into
potentially dangerous situations for conflict resolution
and enable them to communicate with the parties at the
other end (Image courtesy
of ZMC Productions). See color
plate 2.*

Are vision-enhancing devices like binoculars telepresence or teleoperation systems? While binoculars allow the user to view a scene as if they were much closer, this is only a one-way communication link and the user does not have the ability to interact with the remote environment.

Virtual Reality, Telepresence, Augmented Reality, and Cyberspace

Terms for the forms of computer-mediated interfaces to real and virtual worlds are frequently confused. Although we have defined the terms virtual reality, augmented reality, telepresence, and cyberspace, it is worth a summary look at how these closely related expressions are similar and different.

Augmented reality and telepresence can be considered close relatives of virtual reality. Augmented reality mixes the physical world with computer-generated information. The user is able to interact and affect the remote environment by their actions. In augmented reality, the physical reality is *here* (proximal). In telepresence, the physical reality is *there* (distal). Telepresence differs from the general case of virtual reality by taking input from the physical world as opposed to one that is entirely computer generated.

The relationship between cyberspace and virtual reality is more complicated. Their features seem to intersect with each other. The major difference is that cyberspace does not imply a direct sensory substitution for the user. Virtual reality does not always fit our definition of cyberspace, in that the interaction is not necessarily among multiple people, but rather between a person and a virtual world (which may not include other people).

Both are examples of interactions with a virtual world or community mediated by technology. Cyberspace implies mental immersion with other humans. Virtual reality implies sensory immersion within a computer-mediated virtual world.

Cyberspace is not a medium per se but a feature of many different media. FIGURE 1-13 demonstrates that the characteristics a medium must have to create a

FIGURE 1-13 *Is it cyberspace?*

CHARACTERISTICS / MEDIA	Where?			Who?		Physical immersion?		Mental immersion?		Computer required?		Interactive?	
	Real world here	Real world there	Virtual world	Me	We	Yes	No	Yes	No	Yes	No	Yes	No
Virtual reality ✦			X	X	X	X		?		X		X	
Augmented reality	X			X	X	X				X		X	
Telepresence		X		X		X					X	X	
Teleoperation		X		X			X				X	X	
Telephone ✦			X		X		X	X			X	X	
Novel			X	X			X	X			X	X	
Interactive fiction			X	X			X	X		X		X	
Online chat ✦			X		X		X	X		X		X	
Live TV documentary		X		X	X		X	X			X		X
TV situation comedy			X	X	X		X	X			X		X
Cyberspace			✦		✦			✦				✦	

cyberspace are existence in a virtual world, multiple participants (the "we"), interactivity, and the potential for mental immersion. Of the media shown in the figure, virtual reality, the telephone system, and online chats have the necessary characteristics.

A History of VR: Where Did Virtual Reality Technology Come From?

Although this book is primarily about the content of virtual reality, it is important to have an overview of the history of the technologies from which this new medium has evolved. By exploring some of the milestones that have led to the advent of virtual reality technology, the source of many current interface ideas becomes evident. We look at how content has sometimes been driven by technology and technology by content. The rapid progression of technology has increased our expectations of what will be possible with VR in the not-so-distant future.

The sections that follow—from 1916 to 2001—represent a brief timeline in the development of VR. To understand the forces that have come to bear on the field of VR and drive it forward, we highlight each stage with an icon to indicate whether a particular milestone was

 Technology driven,

 Market driven,

 A conceptual advance, or

 Due to market forces.

1916

 U.S. Patent 1,183,492 for a head-based periscope display is awarded to Albert B. Pratt (FIGURE 1-14).

1929

After several years of flight training via "penguin" trainers (aircraft with shortened wings unable to generate enough lift to get off the ground), Edward Link develops a simple mechanical *flight simulator* to train a pilot at a stationary

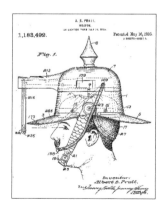

FIGURE 1-14 *The first head-mounted display is patented in 1916 (Image courtesy of United States Patent & Trademark Office).*

(indoor) location (FIGURE 1-15). The trainee can learn to fly and navigate using instruments via instrument replicas in the cockpit of the Link Trainer.

FIGURE 1-15 *Flight simulation was an early adoption of virtual reality technology. Pilots can train in a synthetic environment that behaves as if they were actually flying. Early simulators used mechanical linkages to provide control and feedback. Although flight simulators predated the modern digital computer, today they use highly sophisticated computers, simulation programs, tracking, and display technology (Photo courtesy of the Roberson Museum and Science Center).*

1946

The first electronic digital computer, the ENIAC developed at the University of Pennsylvania, is delivered to the U.S. Army.

1956

Inspired by Cinerama (a very wide screen motion picture format) Morton Heilig develops *Sensorama*. *Sensorama* is a multimodal experience display system. A single person would perceive the prerecorded experience (e.g., a motorcycle ride through Manhattan), via sights, sound, smell, vibration, and wind.

1960

Morton Heilig [1960] receives a U.S. patent for a Stereoscopic-Television Apparatus for Individual Use, which bears a striking similarity to HMDs of the 1990s and even included mechanisms for the display of aural and olfactory sensations as well as visual (U.S. patent 2,955,156—see CG v. 28, n.2—May 1994).

1961

Philco engineers Comeau and Bryan [1961] create an HMD for use as a head-movement-following remote video camera viewing system. They went on to start the company Telefactor Corp. based on their research in telepresence. (FIGURE 1-16.)

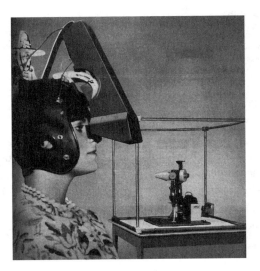

FIGURE 1-16 *Early example of an HMD–based and a telepresence system (Image courtesy of Electronics, VNU Business Publications, New York).*

1963

MIT Ph.D. student Ivan Sutherland [1963] introduces the world to interactive computer graphics with his *Sketchpad* application. Sutherland's seminal work uses a light pen to perform selection and drawing interaction, in addition to keyboard input.

1964

General Motors Corporation begins research on the DAC (design augmented by computer) system, an interactive package for automotive design [Jacks 1964].

1965

Ivan Sutherland [1965] explains the concept of the *ultimate display* in his presentation to the International Federation for Information Processing (IFIP) Congress. Sutherland explains the concept of a display in which the user can interact with objects in some world that does not need to follow the laws of physical reality: "It is a looking glass into a mathematical wonderland." Sutherland's display description includes kinesthetic (haptic) as well as visual stimuli.

1967

Inspired by Sutherland's ultimate display concept, Fred Brooks begins the GROPE project at the University of North Carolina at Chapel Hill to explore the use of kinesthetic interaction as a tool for helping biochemists "feel" interactions between protein molecules [Brooks et al. 1990].

1968

Evans and Sutherland Computer Corp. is founded in 1968 by University of Utah computer science professors David Evans and Ivan Sutherland.

In his paper "A Head-mounted Three-Dimensional Display," Ivan Sutherland [1968] describes his development of a tracked stereoscopic head-mounted display at Harvard University (FIGURE 1-17). The display uses miniature cathode ray tubes (CRT), similar to a television picture tube, with optics to present separate images to each eye and an interface to mechanical and ultrasonic trackers.

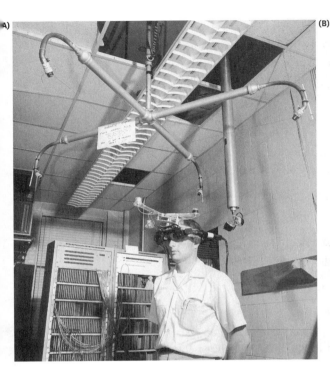

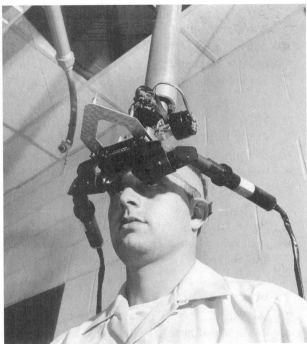

Sample virtual worlds include a stick representation of a cyclohexane molecule and a simple cubic room with directional headings on each wall.

FIGURE 1-17 *Ivan Sutherland created a viable head-mounted display in 1968. The display provided stereoscopic visual images, mechanical or ultrasonic tracking, and a demonstration of the potential of virtual reality (Photographs courtesy of Ivan Sutherland).*

1972

Developed by Atari, *Pong* brings real time, multiperson interactive graphics to the public (FIGURE 1-18). (Magnavox beat Atari to the home market with their *Odyssey* system, but Atari's coin-operated version of *Pong* was the game that started it all.) In 1981, Atari would create a Research Labs division under Alan Kay, bringing together a cast of many future VR pioneers: Fisher, Bricken, Foster, Laurel, Walser, Robinett, and Zimmerman, among others.

FIGURE 1-18 *Atari brought interactive computer graphics to the mass market with the introduction of their* Pong *game (Photograph courtesy of Atari Historical Society).*

1973

Evans and Sutherland Computer Corp. (E&S) delivers their first digital computer image-generation system for flight simulation, *Novoview*. *Novoview* was capable of simulating only night scenes, limited in its display to a single shaded horizon and up to 2,000 light points.

1974

At the University of Utah, Sutherland student Jim Clark (future founder of Silicon Graphics, Inc.) submits his Ph.D. thesis on his head-mounted display research.

1976

Myron Krueger's [1982] *Videoplace* prototype is completed. *Videoplace* uses cameras and other input devices to create a virtual world controlled by the untethered motions of the participant.

1977

The *Sayre Glove* is developed at the Electronic Visualization Lab at the University of Illinois at Chicago. This glove uses light-conductive tubes to transmit varying amounts of light proportional to the amount of finger bending. This information is interpreted by a computer to estimate the configuration of the user's hand [DeFanti et al. 1977].

Commodore, Radio Shack, and Apple introduce personal computers for off-the-shelf use at home.

1979

Eric Howlett develops the LEEP (Large Expanse Enhanced Perspective) System for implementing the optics to deliver a wide field of view from a small display. This technology is later integrated into early HMDs developed at NASA (e.g., the *VIVID* display) and thereafter into commercial products from VPL, Fakespace, Virtual Research, and LEEP System, Inc.'s own *Cyberface* HMD product line.

At AT&T Bell Labs, Gary Grimes [1981] develops a "digital data entry glove interface device." This glove also uses light to sense the amount of bending in the fingers and other hand postures, as well as the overall orientation of the hand.

1981

 Silicon Graphics, Inc. is founded by Stanford professor and former Sutherland student Jim Clark and six of his students to produce high-speed, cost-effective graphics workstations used in many VR facilities today.

 Under the direction of Tom Furness [1986] at Wright Patterson Air Force Base, the *Super Cockpit* becomes operational (featured in *Aviation Week* 1985). The *Super Cockpit* includes a see-through, head-based display mounted to the pilot's helmet. As pilots look in various directions, their vision is augmented with different information. For example, looking at the wing displays which missiles are still available for firing.

 At MIT, the stereoscopic workspace project team begins work on an early augmented reality display that allows users to explore subject matter such as 3D drawing, architectural visualization, and 3D layout of computer chips. The device uses a half-silvered mirror to superimpose a computer image over the real hands and other body parts of the user. Team members include Chris Schmandt, Eric Hulteen, Jim Zamiska, and Scott Fisher.

1982

 In her doctoral thesis, Sara Bly [1982] explores the use of *sonification* (sound to represent large datasets). She lays out a classification of nonordered multivariate datasets from which she creates discrete auditory events. She then maps a number of parameters within the dataset to specific parameters of sound. This early work in sonic representation lays the groundwork for using computer-generated and computer-controlled sound in virtual reality.

1983

 At MIT, Mark Callahan develops an early HMD which is one of the first university research projects involving HMD–style VR outside Sutherland's work at Utah.

1984

 Dave Nagel, chief of the NASA Aerospace Human Factors Research Division, hires Scott Fisher to create the Virtual Interface Environment Workstation (VIEW) lab. Many VR companies receive early funding through work with the VIEW lab, including VPL, LEEP System, Inc., Fakespace, Inc., and Crystal River Engineering.

 The term *Cyberspace* is popularized by William Gibson in his novel *Neuromancer.*

 VPL Research, Inc. is founded by Jaron Lanier to create a visual programming language. The company soon drops this work to create the *DataGlove* and *EyePhones* (in 1985 and 1989, respectively) under grants from the NASA VIEW lab. The *DataGlove* is an instrumented glove that reports the posture of the wearer's hand to the computer. *EyePhones* are an HMD that use a pair of LCD displays in conjunction with LEEP optics.

1985

 VPL is contracted by Scott Fisher at the NASA VIEW lab to build a dataglove to his specifications. Design work is done at VPL by former Atari collaborator Tom Zimmerman, with whom Fisher had discussed the concept while at Atari.

1987

 Jim Humphries, lead engineer for the NASA VIEW project, designed and prototyped the original *BOOM,* which would be commercialized by Fakespace, Inc. in 1990. The *BOOM* was one of many head-based displays designed and prototyped by Humphries for the VIEW project.

Scott Fisher and Elizabeth Wenzel at NASA contract Scott Foster to create a device to simulate the phenomenon of sound seeming to emanate from a specific location in 3D space, using an algorithm developed at the University of Wisconsin at Madison. This work led to the creation of Crystal Rivers Engineering, Inc. in 1988, which then introduces the *Convolvotron* system, a special-purpose hardware device used to implement sound manipulations such as 3D placement of sound.

 Polhemus, Inc. (founded in 1970 to produce navigation system devices) introduces the *Isotrak* magnetic tracking system, used to detect and report the location and orientation of a small, user-worn sensor.

1989

 On June 6, VPL announces a complete Virtual Reality system—*RB-2* (*Reality Built for 2*)—introducing the phrase *virtual reality.*

 Also on June 6, Autodesk, Inc. announces their *CyberSpace* project, a 3D world creation program for the PC.

 Division, Ltd. begins marketing VR hardware and software. They later drop their transputer hardware design efforts and license the *Pixel Planes* technology from the University of North Carolina at Chapel Hill. Division later sold the hardware component to Hewlett Packard to concentrate development on their software toolkit.

 Mattel introduces the *Powerglove* glove and tracking system for the *Nintendo* home video game system. It fails as a video game product, but becomes a popular device for low-cost VR facilities and "garage" VR enthusiasts.

1990

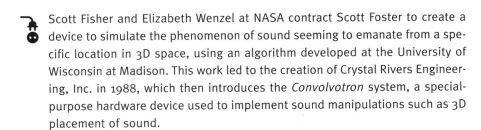 W-Industries launches the first public venue VR system, coining it *Virtuality.* It is a dual player VR arcade system that includes an HMD, hand-held prop, and ring platform for each participant. Interactive computer games graduate to a new level of sophistication. The initial game, *Dactyl Nightmare,* involves two players in a simple multilevel world where they attempt to shoot one

another (FIGURE 1-19). In 1993, W-Industries changes their name to Virtuality Group plc, and in 1997 they sell their assets as part of a filing for Chapter 11 bankruptcy.

FIGURE 1-19 Dactyl Nightmare from Virtuality plc provides 3D worlds and a VR interface via a tracked head-mounted display. An early example of multiperson virtual reality, multiple players compete against each other in the same virtual world. Participants can see each other as graphical representations referred to as avatars. (Image courtesy of Virtuality Group plc).

 Stanford Ph.D. graduate Jim Kramer founds Virtual Technologies, Inc. to commercialize the *CyberGlove*. The *CyberGlove* is a glove device that uses strain gauges to measure the relative position of the fingers with respect to the wrist.

 Ascension Technology Corporation introduces its magnetic tracking system, the *Bird*.

 NASA VIEW lab employees Mark Bolas and Ian McDowall form Fakespace, Inc. Initially hired by Fisher at the VIEW lab to build a more robust version of the *BOOM* for the NASA Computational Fluid Dynamics group, Fakespace later expands into input devices and projection-based stationary VR displays, including the *RAVE*, and *CAVE* systems (the latter upon merging with Pyramid Systems).

 Telepresence Research becomes an early VR application development firm. It is founded by Scott Fisher and Brenda Laurel.

1991

 Virtual Research Systems, Inc. releases their *VR-2 Flight Helmet.* The *Flight Helmet* is perhaps the first reliable HMD priced under $10,000, making it quite popular in university research labs.

 CyberEdge Journal, the first commercial newsletter for the VR community, is published.

 Senator Al Gore of Tennessee chairs the U.S. Senate Subcommittee on Developments in Computer Technology: Virtual Reality.

 The SIGGRAPH computer graphics conference introduces a new venue, *Tomorrow's Realities,* that demonstrates significant progress in the application and technology of virtual reality. A public demonstration of the UNC *Pixel Planes 5* graphics hardware and room-size ceiling tracker is held.

 Rend386 open source renderer for the "garage" VR enthusiast is created by Bernie Roehl and Dave Stampe at the University of Waterloo. *Rend386* is later superseded by Roehl's *AVRIL* VR library.

1992

 Projection VR is introduced as an alternative to the head-based paradigm at the SIGGRAPH '92 computer graphics conference in Chicago. The main attraction of the Showcase '92 venue at SIGGRAPH is the *CAVE* (FIGURE 1-20), developed by the Electronic Visualization Lab at the University of Illinois at Chicago with a variety of scientific and artistic applications demonstrating the technology [Cruz-Neira et al. 1992]. On the SIGGRAPH exhibition floor, Sun Microsystems, Inc. introduces a similar

FIGURE 1-20 *The CAVE, on display for the first time at the SIGGRAPH '92 computer graphics conference in Chicago, generated long lines of people eager to see the new technology (Image courtesy of the Electronic Visualization Lab at the University of Illinois at Chicago).*

display, *The Virtual Portal.* A major difference between these two displays is that the *Virtual Portal* was designed for a single person to be immersed in the experience, whereas the *CAVE* allows up to 10 people to share the visuals, with one person at a time having the optimal view.

1993

 The first two academically oriented conferences specifically for the VR community are held: the VRAIS '93 conference in Seattle and the Research Frontiers in Virtual Reality IEEE Workshop in San Jose. The two groups would merge in 1995, forming the IEEE VRAIS conference, later to be known simply as IEEE VR.

 SensAble Devices (now SensAble Technologies, Inc.) is formed and sells the first *PHANTOM.* The *PHANTOM* is a low-cost force-display device developed by MIT student Thomas Massie and Professor Kenneth Salisbury.

1994

 The *VROOM* venue at the SIGGRAPH convention in Orlando demonstrates over 40 applications running in *CAVE* VR systems.

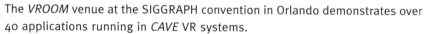 The *Responsive Workbench* is introduced by the German National Research Center for Information Technology (GMD) at SIGGRAPH '94 in Orlando.

1995

 Virtual I/O breaks the $1,000 price barrier for an HMD with the VIO displays. These displays include an inertial tracking system providing rotational information of the wearer's head.

 EVL introduces *ImmersaDesk,* a single-screen projection VR system that works with the *CAVE* library, allowing applications to migrate easily between the *ImmersaDesk* and *CAVE* systems.

 The *CAVE* and *ImmersaDesk* are brought to market by Pyramid Systems, Inc.

 The *Responsive Workbench* is marketed by Fakespace, Inc. as the *Immersive Workbench.*

1996

Ascension Technologies Corporation introduces the *MotionStar* wireless magnetic tracking system at SIGGRAPH '96 in New Orleans. The initial product is focused on the motion capture industry, with receivers for 14 separate body parts.

Fakespace, Inc. introduces a system to allow two people to have separate views from the same projection system. The *Dual User Option* (DUO) system is demonstrated on an *Immersive Workbench* at Supercomputing 1996 in Pittsburgh.

Virtual Space Devices delivers a prototype of their *Omni-Directional Treadmill* to the Naval Postgraduate School.

1997

Virtual Technologies, Inc. introduces their *CyberGrasp* hand-based force feedback device. This display allows the VR system to restrict the ability of the wearer to close individual fingers, enhancing the sense of touching and grasping in a virtual world.

1998

Disney opens the first of their DisneyQuest family arcade centers, which feature numerous VR attractions using both HMD and projection-based visual displays.

Fakespace, Inc. splits into two organizations: a products-oriented company named Fakespace Systems, Inc. and a research and development company named Fakespace Labs, Inc. *CAVE* licensee Pyramid Systems merges with Fakespace Systems, retaining the Fakespace Systems name.

The first six-sided *CAVE*-style display is inaugurated at the Swedish Royal Institute of Technology, Center for Parallel Computers. The *VR-CUBE* is constructed by the German Company TAN Projektionstechnologie GmbH & Co. KG.

1999

The *ARToolKit,* a free, open source tracking library designed for augmented reality, is released from a collaboration between the University of Washington, Seattle, Human Interfaces Technology Laboratory (HITLab), and ATR Media Integration & Communication in Kyoto, Japan. Although designed for AR, the *ARToolKit* provides a method of video tracking that makes it possible (and relatively inexpensive and easy) to do position tracking with just a personal computer equipped with a camera input.

2000

The first six-sided *CAVE* in North America is installed at Iowa State University.

The German company TAN demonstrates their *Infinitec* technology, which allows anaglyphic stereo over a wide band of colors at the SIGGRAPH conference in New Orleans.

2001

The DisneyQuest center located in Chicago closes. The planned third center for Philadelphia remains on hold.

Chapter Summary

The defining features of virtual reality are:

- It is a medium of communication.
- It requires physical immersion.
- It provides synthetic sensory stimulation.
- It can mentally immerse the user.
- It is interactive.

Knowing these features, we can now proceed with a more detailed study of each component: the medium (Chapter 2), physical immersion technology (Chapters 3 and 4), virtual world presentation (Chapter 5), and interaction (Chapter 6). In Chapter 7 we will look at the overall experience and in Chapter 8 the design of experiences in virtual reality. Finally, in Chapter 9 we explore the future potential of virtual reality.

Terminology: Tip of the Iceberg

The terms defined in this chapter cover those that are used (and confused) most often in discussions of virtual reality. The terminology of VR is still young and evolving rapidly, and many words and phrases are used inconsistently even by the VR community (most notably by those trying to market the technology).

In this book, we adhere to more scholarly definitions of the terms common to VR. Related terms, specific to a particular discipline, will be defined as they arise. In addition, you can find an online glossary of VR–related terms at *www.mkp.com/ understanding-vr.*

History: Further Reading

Other sources for the history of virtual reality are Howard Rheingold's journalistic coverage of VR in *Virtual Reality* [1991], and Myron Krueger's coverage of the beginnings of VR in *Artificial Reality II* [1991]. These books give a good overview of VR from the beginnings of the concepts and various technologies through the time when VR was popularized by the mass media and subsequently many more people began to look at this medium as a way to express their ideas.

CHAPTER 2

VR: The Medium

Virtual reality is a medium. Therefore, we can begin to understand the potential of VR in the communication and exploration of ideas by examining how it relates to other media of human communication.

The focus of this chapter is on both the nature of communications media and the role of virtual reality within the larger whole. This is an important topic for the development of effective VR experiences. It isn't sufficient to understand only the technology of the medium if you will be architecting any portion of the experience. (In Part II, we proceed with how VR technology and interface designs are fashioned into a workable system.)

Being literate in the medium is essential for good communication. This is important at both the creator and the recipient ends of the transmission, though a greater onus is naturally put on the creator. To increase our literacy in a medium, it is important to study its history, language, narrative forms, genres, and interfaces.

After our look at how media in general are used in support of human communication, we focus on what conventions and devices have been created to enhance communication through the medium of VR.

Communicating Through a Medium

As a communication medium, virtual reality shares properties with more traditional media, especially those with which it has a common heritage. We believe it is important for the VR developer (and user) to realize the importance of understanding the deeper aspects of the medium in which they work.

In its broadest sense, the word *medium* refers to something that is in between two or more things. From this definition, anything through which something can be passed from one point to another is generally referred to as a medium. That something may be an idea or it may be physical material and/or energy. Thus a metal pipe is a medium that can transfer fluid from one end to the other, and it also has the properties of transferring sound and heat. A novel is a medium that can pass ideas and concepts. We will refer to media that transfer physical matter/energy as *carrier media* and media for transferring ideas/concepts as *human communication media.*

A medium must be able to store its contents until they are delivered. Some media can store the contents indefinitely, while others are intended only as delivery mechanisms. A bucket, to take a very simple example, can be used to store water (in this case a bucket is a storage medium), or the water can be carried in the bucket (now the bucket is a carrier medium). A pipe, however, is intended to deliver its contents rather than store them and is thought of strictly as a carrier medium. Furthermore, there is a point of access through the boundary to the contents; we refer to this access point as the *interface.*

Virtual worlds can be contained in a variety of storage media, such as a super-computer, a book, a floppy disk, a videotape, or even the human brain. Information about virtual worlds is passed from one "container" to another via a communications medium: supercomputer to brain via a workstation, book to brain via written language, or brain to brain via spoken language.

A Medium's Content: A Virtual World

One of the most important aspects of any idea-transmitting medium is the content itself. As elaborated in Chapter 1, the contents of the human communications media we are concerned with are called *virtual worlds*. This term is used because the ideas transmitted are generally brought to life by describing a world in which the recipient experiences the places, objects, and denizens of the world. Thus, while the content of a virtual reality application is indeed called a virtual world, not all virtual worlds are created specifically to be presented via a VR interface.

This section focuses on virtual worlds independent of their medium. Here we will examine how virtual worlds are created, presented, and explored. We will look at where a virtual world comes from and where it exists.

Virtual worlds are not a new concept. Since its beginning, humankind has sought to shape its environment. In addition to manipulating the world in which they live, people have created their own concepts of alternate worlds. These alternate worlds are subject only to the rules of their human creators. The creator has total dominion. Such a virtual world might exist solely in the mind of its originator or be manifested through a medium whereby it can be shared with others.

Of course, the real world influences the virtual world. While virtual worlds are imaginary spaces, it can sometimes be unclear where the real world ends and the virtual begins. This is especially true when the virtual world is a model of some place or experience intended to mimic a specific real-world counterpart.

A virtual world is a real *representation* of some world that may or may not exist in the physical world. Even in the physical world, it is not always obvious whether something encountered is real or a representation. René Magritte demonstrates this in his famous painting *The Treachery of Images* (FIGURE 2-1). Although it is a very realistic painting of a pipe, it is not an actual pipe but a painting. The painting itself is quite real yet there is no confusion between a pipe and a painting of one. However, most people if asked "What is this?" would probably answer "It's a pipe" and not "It's a painting."

FIGURE 2-1 *Surrealist painter René Magritte addresses the complex issue of image versus reality in* The Treachery of Images, *in which he juxtaposes the image of a pipe with the caption "This is not a pipe." (© 2002 C. Hersovici, Brussels/ Artists Rights Society (ARS), New York. The Treachery of Images (This is Not a Pipe), circa 1928–1929, by René Magritte (museum number 78.7), Los Angeles County Museum of Art. Purchased with funds provided by the Mr. and Mrs. William Preston Harrison Collection. Photograph © 2002 Museum Associates/LACMA.).*

A virtual world can be thought of as a simulation of a domain manifested in some medium where the simulation is driven by rules of behavior—programmed or imagined, simple or complex. These rules can be implemented as a computer program, rules of a board game, colors in a still image, or even the imagination of a child. The domain is the extent of the space, participants, objects, and rules of the virtual world.

In short, we reiterate:

The content conveyed by a medium is a virtual world.

Some examples of virtual worlds implemented in various media include

Human Communication Medium	Virtual World
Imagination	Daydream/mental model
Imagination/toys	Child playing with a doll
Storytelling	Legends
Cave painting	Lascaux

Human Communication Medium	Virtual World
Novel (noninteractive)	*Moby Dick*
Maps	London tube system map
Illusions (of magic)	Pulling a rabbit out of a hat
Song	"Early Morning Dreams"
Motion picture (noninteractive)	*Citizen Kane*
Animation	*Fantasia*
Puppetry	*The Muppet Show*
Ham radio/CB	Roundtable discussion
Interactive fiction (via book)	*Zork: The Cavern of Doom*
Interactive fiction (via computer game)	*Adventure*/Zork™
Email	Memos, messages, general correspondence
Newsgroups (via Internet)	Question & answer/chat (culture)
Multimedia interactive fiction	*Myst*/*Virtual Nashville*
MUDs, MOOs	Games/chat space/office emulation
Board games	Chess/Clue/Risk
Video games	*Pong*/*Donkey Kong*
The World Wide Web (WWW)	*www.yahoo.com*
Flight simulation	Boeing 747 training system
Virtual reality (game)	*Dactyl Nightmare*
Virtual reality (design)	Caterpillar virtual prototyping system
Online game world	*Everquest*

It may not be obvious that all of these examples are, indeed, virtual worlds. Pulling a rabbit out of a hat, for example, is a simulation of a world where magic exists and a rabbit can be conjured from "thin air." The element of believing that which is *not* is an important aspect of virtual reality. Each of the media in our list is actually a mechanism to support the passage of ideas from one person to another or to aid oneself in refining one's own ideas.

Suitability of Virtual Worlds for a Particular Medium

Some virtual worlds are designed with a particular medium in mind, and some are designed to be experienced through more than one medium. Some virtual worlds are especially suited for and designed to be implemented using a virtual reality interface. Obvious candidates for VR presentation include worlds in which movement through physical space is an important component of the experience. For example, an architectural walkthrough can take advantage of the user's sense of three-dimensional space and distance. We will look at other types of virtual worlds that are and are not well suited for representation in VR in Chapter 8.

One of the primary features of VR as a medium of expression lies in its mediation via computer. Concerns such as resolution, speed, and interface are all issues that must be considered when working with the computer as the carrier medium, since these issues can have significant effects on the outcome. Computing technology is rapidly improving, so we can look forward to better capabilities in the not-too-distant future.

How Are Ideas Transmitted?

The progress and culture of humankind are built on the ability of people to ponder and relay ideas among one another. Much of the way we circulate these ideas is based on man-made technology.

The communication process begins when, somehow, a person conjures up an idea. An idea may be private or one may intend to pass on an idea to others. For the purposes of clarity, we will refer to the communicant (or creator) and recipient (or participant) of a mental model as if they were separate individuals, even though this may not always be the case.

With an idea in mind, the communicant begins creating a physical manifestation using some technology—scratching marks in the sand with a stick or applying color onto a surface. Other examples of how an idea can be manifested in a physical form can be found in FIGURE 2-2. It is important to remember, however, that choices exist even within a single medium. For example, a painter can choose to apply color using a variety of different transfer media: oil on canvas, pigment on a wall, bits in computer memory. A poet can communicate thoughts through a recitation, a manuscript, or lyrics.

The flow of ideas from communicant to recipient through a selection of media depicted in FIGURE 2-2 hid some details. Most media involve performance as part of how a composition is brought to life for the recipient to experience (FIGURE 2-3). And, if we consider the acts of painting and a computer following instructions to be performances, then basically every medium has a stage where the work must be performed. So a similar flow takes place in a virtual reality experience: the computer acts as the "performer" and the recipient participates with the work to generate the experience.

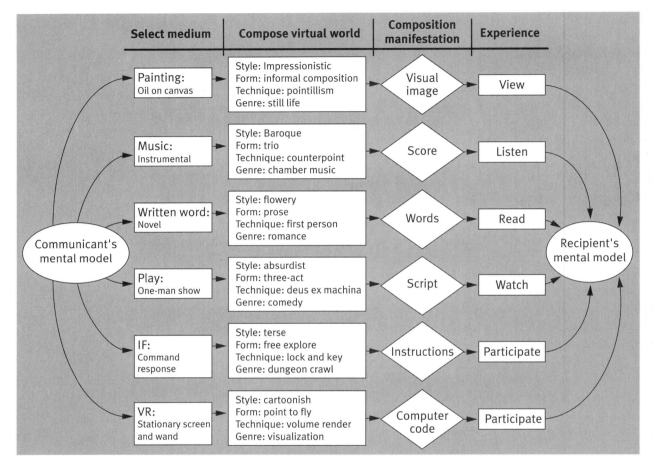

Select medium	Compose virtual world	Composition manifestation	Experience

Painting: Oil on canvas — Style: Impressionistic, Form: informal composition, Technique: pointillism, Genre: still life — Visual image — View

Music: Instrumental — Style: Baroque, Form: trio, Technique: counterpoint, Genre: chamber music — Score — Listen

Written word: Novel — Style: flowery, Form: prose, Technique: first person, Genre: romance — Words — Read

Play: One-man show — Style: absurdist, Form: three-act, Technique: deus ex machina, Genre: comedy — Script — Watch

IF: Command response — Style: terse, Form: free explore, Technique: lock and key, Genre: dungeon crawl — Instructions — Participate

VR: Stationary screen and wand — Style: cartoonish, Form: point to fly, Technique: volume render, Genre: visualization — Computer code — Participate

Communicant's mental model → Recipient's mental model

FIGURE 2-2 *This diagram depicts various ways in which ideas are communicated via particular media for human communication. Note that there is nothing that restricts the communicant and recipient from being the same person.*

As information passes from one phase to the next (i.e., communicant's mental model, physical representation, presentation, and recipient's mental model), it is created in or carried by some transfer medium (FIGURE 2-4). For example, paintings are created by an action such as applying oil paints to canvas, which transfers an artist's vision into the physical object. A symphony's performance might be recorded to compact disc (CD), or a video recording might be made of a play's stage production. In these cases, the carrier medium also acts as a storage medium. The storage medium allows the recipient to perceive the performance at a later time.

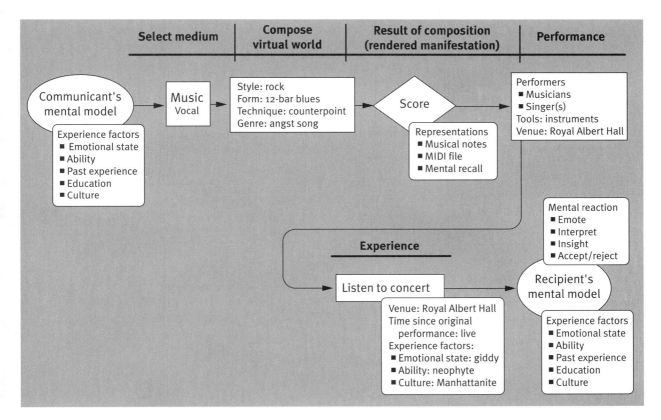

FIGURE 2-3 *This diagram focuses on one particular medium, music, to demonstrate how performance figures into the experience.*

While storage media generally provide a convenient means for a larger number of people to access particular content, the storage medium itself can have an additional influence on how the work is perceived.

When a virtual world is physically manifested via a medium, there are several confounding factors that can influence the reception of the ideas presented. The first factor is the quality of the physical representation: how successful has the communicant been in converting the idea to the chosen medium? Then there are the limitations of the carrier and storage media. The quality of a "live" recording is limited by such constraints as resolution, dynamic range, and other perceptual losses (e.g., depth, field of view) that interfere with the information capture and transfer.

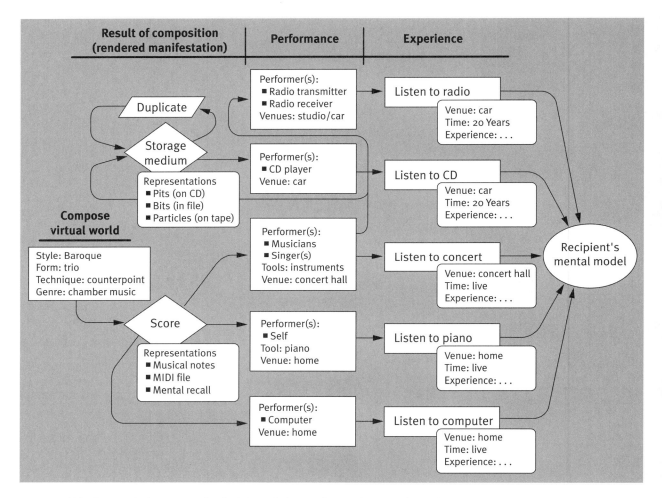

FIGURE 2-4 *This diagram depicts a more detailed view of what can happen between the perform-ance and experience stages of the music medium. During the act of composition, the composer's ideas are generally manifested in some sort of a score. This might be traditional music notation, a MIDI file (instructions telling a computer how to perform), or as the composer's own mental notes on how to perform the piece. The score can be performed by the composer, a computer, or other musicians. The results of that performance can be listened to directly by a live audience, broadcast over a transfer medium such as radio, or recorded on a storage medium such as CD, which itself can then be duplicated, listened to directly, or broadcast.*

The venue in which we experience the creation affects how we perceive it. We perceive a play very differently when viewed live within a group than when viewed alone in a small room. We have a very different experience when viewing an original painting in a gallery than when viewing it as a digital copy on a desktop workstation.

Additionally, a recipient's experience can be affected by numerous external and internal influences. External influences may include the venue and the time since the work was originally performed (in terms of the "freshness" of its appeal). Internal influences may include the recipient's state of mind, prior experiences, and culture. These influences, along with the work itself, contribute to a recipient's mental reaction and can result in such things as a surge of emotion, a change of behavior, a flash of insight, or even confusion or rejection of the message. The work's composition and performance can be affected by similar experience factors influencing the communicant and the performers.

Finally, some media allow the recipient to interact with the virtual world, producing a *feedback loop* to the performer (FIGURE 2-5). In the traditional performing arts, the audience's response to a live performance can greatly influence the remainder of the performance. In an interactive computer-mediated medium—again, the computer can be considered the performer—the audience has an even more profound effect on the outcome. Depending on the level of interactivity, the audience becomes a coauthor of its own experience.

For media in which interactivity plays a vital role, a crucial element is lost when one attempts to transfer the experience to a storage medium. It is simply impossible with current technology to capture every aspect of the original experience. With the interactive element lost, the nature of the experience is altered (FIGURE 2-6).

However, there are instances where very little is lost by the transference of an idea via some carrier medium. For example, if the words of a novel are transmitted via floppy disk and then printed, or even viewed on a computer screen, the story does not lose its soul. In fact, it loses very little, although certainly many people would still prefer to hold a book in their hands while they read. The medium of the novel benefits from the fact that words can easily be transmitted without any critical loss of information. However, layout, typeface, illustrations, and paper quality can be radically changed.

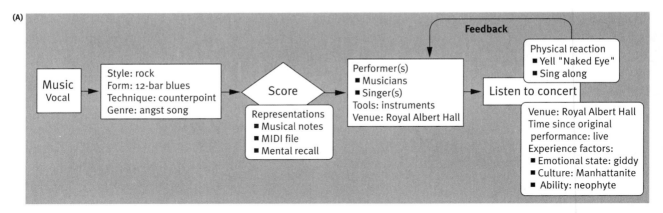

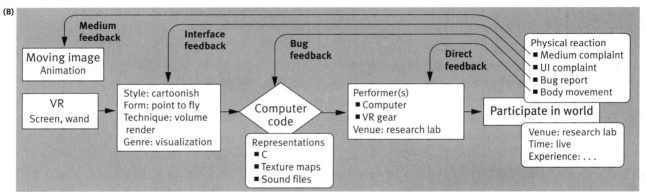

FIGURE 2-5 (A) *This diagram demonstrates how a recipient's physical reaction to an experience can affect the presentation through feedback. In a live performance, audience feedback can often affect the performance itself; for instance, at a music concert, the enthusiasm of the audience can affect how and what the musicians play.* **(B)** *Feedback is one of the key elements of virtual reality. For VR, it is imperative that the virtual reality system be affected by the participant's physical reactions. Feedback can occur at many levels in a VR experience. Interactive feedback occurs when a participant moves their head, resulting in updated sensory images being presented by the computer. Another level of feedback occurs when a participant reports a bug in the code the computer is performing, or they may report that a certain element of the application is difficult to understand, leading to a modification of the design of the virtual world.*

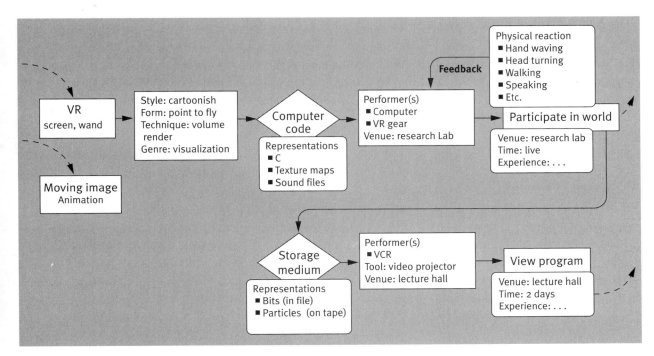

FIGURE 2-6 *As with musical experiences, virtual reality experiences can be recorded to a storage medium, but in the case of VR that medium is the moving image. Unfortunately, watching a video recording of a VR experience is very far removed from the original experience.*

Common Issues of Human Communication Media

Although there is a wide variety of media used for communication, there are a number of issues common to all. The first concern centers on authorship. Who is the *author* of a VR experience: the creator of the experience or the idea recipient? Other issues that developers and critics of a medium must study include language, interfacing with the virtual world, presentation forms, classes of experiences (genres), narrative possibilities, the nature of experience versus information, and exploring the range of a medium. We will draw from a cross section of human communication media to discuss these topics. We will look at some of the features and issues unique to virtual reality as a new medium and explore these issues as they apply to media in general.

What Is Special about Virtual Reality?

Artists working in any given medium seek to exploit the specific qualities of that medium in their work. Virtual reality has many features that combine to make it a truly unique medium. These features include the ability to manipulate the sense of time and space, the option of interactivity and of multiple simultaneous participants, and the potential for participants to drive the narrative flow of the experience. VR brings all of these components together into a single medium, creating the opportunity for a dynamic relationship between the recipient (participant) and the medium.

Authorship (Versus Creatorship)

Depending on the medium, the question of who is the *author* of an experience as received through some medium can be elusive. Of course, the first issue to address is what is meant by the word *experience*. In this case, we are discussing the participatory form of experience described in Chapter 1. So, when the participant feels some particular emotion, who created that feeling? Or, when the participant has an epiphany about the nature of some phenomenon aided by what was presented in the medium, who created that revelation? The answers are not clear cut.

The author of a work can be considered to be the person (or persons) who constructs the content presented through some medium. However, because interpretation occurs in the observer/receiver, they too can claim credit for some amount of authorship—of the experience, not of the content (i.e., the virtual world presented to the participant).

An author of a book is of course the person who writes the words. Arguably, the experience of reading the book belongs both to the writer-of-words and to the reader, making both coauthors of the experience. To broaden the consideration, many cases involve a third party: the person/persons/entities/events that placed the original idea into the head of the writer-of-words.

When a medium allows some form of interactivity—when the recipient chooses to travel a certain path and utilize a tool within a virtual world—the recipient has a more participatory role in creating their experience and the question of authorship becomes even more muddled. But even for media without an interactive interface, when the recipient mulls over the presentation, they are in a way interacting with the presented material.

The Interface to the Virtual World

Regardless of the medium in which ideas are manifested, we need to be able to access the contents. A virtual world has an interface associated with it by which the recipient can access the content. For example, a novel is presented to the reader as words on pages that have a sequential order. The participant interacts with the virtual world at the boundary between the self and the medium. This access point is called the user interface.

> The access point through the boundary between the recipient and the virtual world is the user interface.

Information must go between the communicant and the recipient via the interface of the medium; in our current example, between the novelist and the reader.

The term *user interface* does not necessarily mean the use of a computer (though it is often implied). The medium in which a virtual world is manifested dictates a set of possible interfaces through which the virtual world can be accessed. A novel might be read via a book interface or by using a computer display and mouse. Sometimes the interface is technological (as in a television set or a radio), and sometimes it is not (as a dance performance or a sculpture). Also the interface can be affected by circumstance: is the recipient participating directly with the medium or is the experience being transmitted through a carrier medium? The user interfaces to VR will be discussed in detail in Chapter 6. Here we discuss the relationship between the user interface, the medium, and the virtual world.

As the user's connection with a virtual world, the user interface affects the design of the virtual world. Ideally, this access point will allow for as smooth a transmission as possible, allowing ideas to move freely toward the recipient. Considerable effort has been put into the study of good user interface design for many media, and virtual reality will require no less effort.

Many theorists consider the ultimate goal of VR to be a medium without a noticeable interface, an interfaceless medium. That is, a VR experience would be designed so well that the boundary between user and virtual world would be seemingly nonexistent. The user interface would mimic precisely how the user experiences the real world. This is considered by many to be the ultimate interface. We should always keep in mind, however, that even if the interface is invisible, it still exists.

Therefore, it seems clear that the constraints and capabilities of a particular medium can be best exploited by choosing an *appropriate* interface. The creator can choose to design a virtual world with a specific interface in mind or can make efforts to allow the virtual world to be accessed meaningfully via a variety of user interfaces. Writing for a specific medium or interface has both advantages and disadvantages.

When writing for a particular medium, the communicant can exploit the strengths and flexibility it provides. For example, in writing a novel, the novelist can assume that the reader has encountered all the previous pages and has the required background and context to understand the current chapter. In a more interactive medium, the creator may not be able to make such an assumption. Likewise, the constraints of a particular user interface may allow the creator to ignore certain aspects of the world that would not be advisable when using a different interface. In a world presented in a full virtual reality environment, many visual aspects, such as the effects of gravity on unsupported objects, must be incorporated. In a world presented in text-based media, such as novels and interactive fiction, it is not typically important to incorporate an object falling to the floor. When such an event is significant to the story, it is dealt with specifically.

When creating for multiple media, such as a novel and a work of interactive fiction, extra effort is required to ensure the creation is designed to support the different possibilities offered by the interface to each medium. A virtual world designed for multiple media will likely have a broader range of potential venues and audiences.

To support multiple interfaces, certain aspects of the world must be more thoroughly defined; that is, the world must provide for all the possibilities allowed by each potential interface. At the same time, the combination of constraints from each interface must be considered when designing the world. In the example of creating a world for both a novel and an interactive fiction, the author must create *all* the possible interactions for the participant of the interactive fiction, which would not have been required for the novel. For the novel, the writer must *choose* the path the participant will take.

Often, virtual worlds that were designed for one specific medium and interface are adapted to accommodate a different user interface. The success of the transformation depends largely on the suitability of the virtual world for the new interface and/or the skill of the translator. The adapted work may not achieve the same level of quality as the original, or (less likely) it may actually be improved. Not all content is appropriate for use in VR systems. It is important to select the most appropriate medium for any given content and goal.

Language

Language is not just an artifact of the spoken or written word. According to *Webster's*, language is "any system of formalized symbols, signs, gestures, or the like, used or conceived as a means of communicating thought, emotion, etc." Because each medium through which humans communicate has different attributes associated with it, each develops its own language, which people can utilize to communicate more effectively. Each medium develops a somewhat standardized set of tools and methods, which the creator can use to communicate concepts (e.g., music uses notes and rhythms, painting uses color and texture).

Each new medium goes through a process in which its language evolves from the chaos of all that has gone before. This chaos contains the language of other mediums related by technology or interface. Virtual reality inherits language elements from computer graphics, video games, interactive fiction, and so on (FIGURE 2-7).

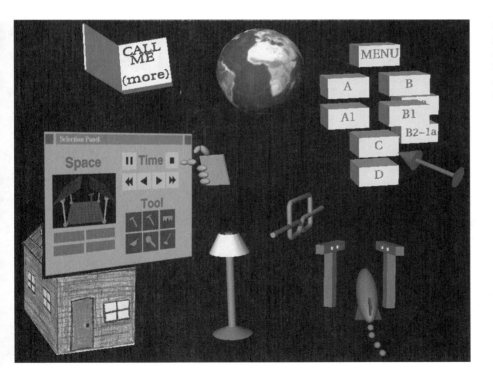

FIGURE 2-7 *Menus, avatars, pointers, and other graphical representations are visual language elements found often in virtual reality experiences.*

Because a new medium hasn't had a chance to develop its own language, it will often be looked down upon by artists working in the "classical" idiom. In *Understanding Comics,* Scott McCloud [1993] states that the bane of all new media is "the curse of being judged by the standards of the old."

Before their significance can be reasonably evaluated, the languages of new media must be given time to evolve into effective means of communication. VR developers and researchers must examine VR's relationship to other media and explore the new possibilities.

In *Understanding Media,* Marshall McLuhan [1964] says that "any study of one medium helps us to understand all the others." Thus, we would be wise to examine how other media evolved and the languages they utilize. The written word extended the symbols of spoken words to a language of symbols that represent the sounds of spoken words. In the process, communication gained persistence. Later generations are able to read, learn from, and enjoy those same words. However, the written word does not support the ability to directly provide information via timing and the *intonations* available with the spoken word. Each new medium brings forth a new means of human communication, with tradeoffs against the old.

Why Discuss Language?

Although it is often possible to understand some of the content of a medium even if you aren't versed in its language, you miss much of the message transmitted by the medium itself. While general audiences may feel they are getting the intended message, recipients who are literate in the language of the medium may be receiving deeper levels of meaning communicated by the communicant. To take full advantage of the medium, one must study both the creative elements (the "writing") and the interpretive elements (the "reading") of the medium's language.

The language of each medium also evolves along with its underlying technology. Let's take motion pictures as an example. When motion pictures were first developed as a way to store and replay moving images, the content was generally a documentation of an event as it was experienced in day to day life. This event might have been a stage play (an established medium) with a stationary motion picture camera set up to simply record the play from the perspective of the audience. Later, filmmakers discovered that they could bring the camera into the action, providing a new way to relay the story. Using the camera as a tool to enhance the story introduced camera technique as a language element in filmmaking.

Methods involving camera placement, sequence of cuts, and the overall mise-en-scène were then combined with greater control of the action in the scene (via actors) to give the filmmaker an increased ability to influence the understanding and emotional response of the audience. Through experimentation, the language of movie making has continued to evolve. The cut, for example, can be used to change views during a dialogue between two characters, or it can be used to make an event more significant by extending the duration of the scene. The number of cuts can also be manipulated and has ranged from none, in Hitchcock's 1948 movie *Rope,* to the fast cut in which dozens of cuts are used in a short period of time (often referred to as MTV–style).

The Idiom of VR

VR is at a point in its development when language elements are still being created. Even though an audience may be unaware of these elements, they may still be affected by them. To be a fully participating VR recipient requires learning the language of the medium.

Language elements can differ within the same medium as is amply exemplified by the medium of painting. For example, a painting can be created in an abstract style using watercolors or in a photorealistic style using computer-based painting software. Likewise, the language rules in any given medium can evolve along differing lines in different social cultures—witness the musical scales used in Chinese music as compared with those used in European music.

Consequently, the medium of virtual reality has a language of symbols and syntax that are combined to present a message to the audience participating in the experience. This language is very young and immature and is evolving with each new application. Many of the elements in the current language of VR have their roots in other related media and need to be adapted to the idiom of VR.

Examples of current symbols found in a variety of VR experiences include artifacts such as the virtual door knob (object) and the 3D cursor (selection icon).

Some elements brought to VR from other media include the "menu" and "widget window." Some symbols of the VR language extend beyond the visual and aural display to physical reality. Randy Pausch and Ken Hinckley call these physical objects (or symbols) that directly correlate with virtual symbols *props* [Hinckley et al. 1994]. For example, a simple ball and a piece of plastic equipped with position sensors (the props) can be used to indicate the user's desire to display certain

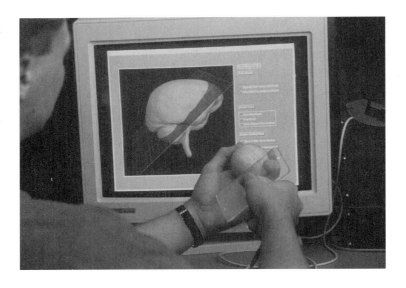

FIGURE 2-8 *A researcher uses generic objects (ball and plastic plane) as props to indicate the location of the cross section of the brain representation displayed on the computer monitor (Photograph courtesy of Ken Hinckley).*

medical information from an MRI (magnetic resonance imaging) scan to the computer (FIGURE 2-8). Moving the plastic in relation to the ball results in a display of information about that part of the brain that corresponds to the position of the plastic piece on the ball.

Language Element of Time and Space

As with other media that are conveyed over time (e.g., movies, comics, computer games), virtual reality has a great deal of flexibility in how time and space can be treated. The control of time can range from having no concept of it (viewing a static scene or object), to holding time constant, to letting it flow at the same rate as our regular daily experience. VR can even allow the user to manipulate time in both direction and speed or allow them to jump to a particular point in time.

Similarly, a VR application can treat space in a variety of ways: space can be limited to a small area, such that anything the user might want to manipulate or observe is within range of the tracking technology, or space can be vast, literally unlimited. Finally, space can literally be given a different shape than in our universe. In larger spaces, users might be able to traverse the space in different ways, perhaps indicating desired motion by pointing their finger in the direction they want to go (point to fly).

Space traversal also has an element of time, in that each method of travel can allow movement through the domain at different rates. An abstract method of moving through space would be to allow the user to simply point to a location on a map and go there instantly, with no passage of time in the real or virtual worlds.

One example of a new concept and symbol in the language of VR is the representation of self. Some media display or describe the environment to the recipient, taking on the role of their eyes and ears. In VR the environment is presented directly to the participants, who use their own senses to perceive the world. This style of presentation, combined with interactivity, requires that the user be represented in the virtual world. The "hand in space" symbol is a specific example of this. The hand can also be represented as any tool that the user is controlling with the hand. Typically, in single-user experiences, only the limbs are displayed rather than the entire body, and often just one hand. Experiences involving a shared world demand a more complete representation of the body. No matter how much of the physical body is represented, these representations of self are still referred to as the user's avatar (FIGURE 2-9).

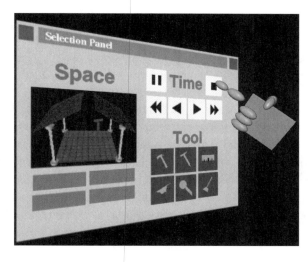

FIGURE 2-9 *A very simple avatar can be a representation of the participant's hand in the virtual world. The avatar helps the user sense their own body in the space and can aid the user in performing tasks.*

The avatar can be simple, to conserve computational expense—a *T* shape with eyes to show orientation and direction of view, or a simple polygon with a still image of the user mapped onto one side (FIGURE 2-10). The avatar can be complex, perhaps a full 3D body scan of the user with a mouth that reshapes itself according to the user's speech patterns. Of course, there is no constraint to accurately represent the user. Any representation can be designed—providing an alter ego or a depiction of the user as they would *like* to be seen. The VR action/adventure *Snow Crash* describes one possible future scenario of avatars in a VR universe: the "multiverse" [Stephenson 1992].

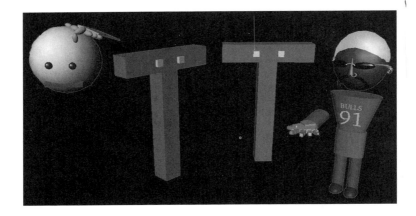

FIGURE 2-10 *Full body avatars can be as simple as a T representation or as complicated as a full body rendering that communicates many aspects of the participant, such as facial gestures, mood, and actions. The hand avatar can be useful not only to the owner of the hand it represents, but to other users sharing the same virtual world, helping them to sense their neighbor's location, actions, and body language (Rodman avatar courtesy of Jim Costigan).*

In their paper on the *Placeholder* experience (Appendix D), Laurel, Strickland, and Tow specifically discuss their efforts to find new representations (avatars) and to explore new ways for participants to interact with the environment [Laurel et al. 1994].

Technological limitations often led early VR application creators to use head (i.e., gaze) direction as the factor determining the direction of travel. Laurel and her colleagues noticed that this tended to make people keep their heads pointing forward. In order to "give people back their necks," they decided to place an additional tracking device on the torso and use the orientation of the user's body to determine the direction of travel. They also chose to replace another technique that was becoming traditional in VR, the point to fly method of travel. To find a new interface, people were surveyed about how they fly in their dreams. They did not get a consistent response, but noticed in their early tests that when people took on the persona of a crow, they tended to flap their arms. So this gesture was made the indicator for crow flight in the *Placeholder* application.

Narrative: Immotive Versus Interactive

In event-based media (fiction, moving pictures, etc.), the creator of the work presents sequences of events that occur in various settings to some set of characters. We call these sequences *stories,* and the unfolding of the story a *narrative.*

Not all narrative is fiction, of course. In the book *Film: Form and Function,* Wead and Lellis [1981] give four roles that a movie can have: (1) realist: documenting the world as closely as possible; (2) persuasive: influencing the viewer toward a particular point of view; (3) personal: conveying the filmmaker's vision of the world; and (4) esthetic: a means of innovative artistic expression. These roles involve the expression of some truth that the creators wish to present. These roles can and do tend to intermingle. And, these same four roles can be applied to virtual reality content. In fact, most VR works will have at least some element of persuasiveness, if not of the other roles as well.

In VR, the creator can also choose the method of conveying information. Non-fiction narrative is certainly an avenue available to virtual reality experience creators. In fact, probably most applications thus far in time have focused on using VR to examine information, although most people have experienced VR only as a game. As VR applications become more abundant, we are likely to see some focused on conveying information and others focused more on creating an experience. The *visualization* and *location walkabout* genres of VR allow the user to explore a space (and information associated with the space) in a sort of free-form narrative that puts as few constraints as possible on the participant. Such freedom allows a more unbiased presentation of the underlying information. The story being experienced might be of the creation of the universe from the perspective of the equations of a particular scientist, as interpreted by a complex computational simulation, or as life inside a child's crayon drawing, governed by the child's own laws of nature (FIGURE 2-11).

The creator constructs a *plot,* or related sequence of events, and possibly subplots that expose different aspects of the virtual world. In standard fiction, the creator has a choice of narrative presentation. They can tell stories in a forward linear manner or backward through time. They can also use the *flashback* to jump back in time, and in some media they have the option to incorporate audience choice (interaction) to help determine the direction of the narrative.

The degree of choice given to the recipient in a narrative can range from entirely passive—or *immotive*—to fully interactive. As interactivity increases, the amount of authorial control kept by the communicant diminishes and shifts to the recipient, resulting in a less static and more explorative experience.

Interactivity, Participation, and Multipresence

Many other media are not as flexible as virtual reality. For example, music exists primarily in time and painting exists primarily in space. Dance and motion pictures exist both in time and space, and the choreographer and director influence the pacing through both dimensions. In VR, the user generally controls how they pass through space and time. The ability of the user to physically alter their vantage point

(A)

(B)

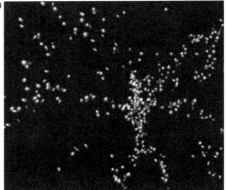

FIGURE 2-11 **(A, B)** *Margaret Geller of Harvard University uses VR to study the placement of galaxies in the universe (Photos courtesy of NCSA).* **(C)** *Danielle and Cindy explore the fantasy world of Crayoland, developed by Dave Pape from the Electronic Visualization Lab at the University of Illinois at Chicago (Application courtesy of Dave Pape; photograph by William Sherman).*

(C)

is a new element in the medium of VR. A virtual world may have a center of action, but the participant is free to turn their head (and attention) to other facets of the virtual world. This freedom presents a challenge to developers of directed narratives, which we will discuss in more detail in the sections that follow.

This touches on another important element that is basically new to VR: the presence of multiple participants in the same experience, each with an interactive avatar occupying space within the virtual world. The avatar of each participant may act upon the others. Sometimes this adds a sense of cooperation, and sometimes the participants compete with one another.

The ability of the user to control time and space—to look and move within the world—and the presence and actions of others in the virtual world all have a significant effect on the level of participation. The more control a VR experience gives the user, the greater the feeling of involvement in the virtual world. Virtual reality is one of the first media that allows such a high degree of participant interactivity.

Narrative Flexibility: Directed and Undirected Narratives

As with most media that play out over time, VR can be used as a storytelling vehicle. There are some peculiarities to storytelling in VR, many similar to the concerns of interactive fiction. First, should you force the participant to stay along a specific linear story line (*directed* narrative)? If you do, aren't you limiting VR to be little more than a 3D movie? If you don't and the participant has complete control of the outcome (*undirected* narrative), how do you guarantee that the viewer will get to see all parts of the narrative? Or *should* everything be seen?

A *directed* narrative is the type typically provided by plot-based works, oriented toward one (or a small number of) predetermined goal(s) or denouement(s). With such an immotive narrative, all that is necessary for the participant to reach the denouement is to continue the experience until it plays out. Not all directed narratives are immotive, however; interactive fiction experiences are also typically directed, but as we've discussed, the experience can be continued by jumping to other points in time and proceeding in different directions.

Josephine Anstey's *The Thing Growing* (FIGURE 2-12) is a virtual reality experience with a directed narrative [Anstey et al. 2000]. During the experience, the participant is confronted with the choice of whether to kill the Thing's cousins and eventually the Thing itself (FIGURE 2-13). The exact denouement of the experience varies, depending on the actions of the participant, but all participants are eventually directed to the climactic scene where the decision to kill or not to kill is made, unless, of course, the participant elects to leave the experience entirely (always an option in other media, as well).

When the participant of a directed narrative VR experience fails to experience a necessary element, the content creators must devise ways of either adjusting the narrative or preventing it from proceeding until the participant does witness or interact with the critical event or characters of the story. This is the same challenge presented to creators of interactive fiction. In virtual reality the experience developer

FIGURE 2-12 The Thing Growing *VR application allows a participant to come in contact with virtual beings in the context of an interactive narrative* (The Thing Growing *application courtesy of Josephine Anstey). See color plate 32.*

FIGURE 2-13 *In* The Thing Growing, *the participant has some freedom in the virtual world, but is eventually directed to make a climactic decision (Application courtesy of Josephine Anstey; William Sherman, photographer).*

is faced with the added difficulty of figuring out how to determine just what the participant has witnessed.

The effect of interactivity on the outcome of the narrative is a major consideration in deciding what degree of interactivity is most appropriate. In an event-based experience, the participant may not find their way to the ultimate denouement (outcome) if they make suboptimal choices along the way, and the end result may prove unsatisfying. In media where this occurs frequently, the common course of action is for the player/participant to make new choices based on what their past experiences have taught them of the virtual world. They can begin the experience again or jump back to some midpoint in the experience.

On the other hand, maybe it isn't wise to present a directed narrative through the medium of virtual reality. According to Mike Adams of Virtuality Group PLC [Adams 1995], VR content doesn't exist as a storyline, but rather as a place to be explored. Laurel, Strickland, and Tow's *Placeholder* (Appendix D) meets this definition. In their research effort purely to investigate new methods of using VR as a narrative paradigm, the developers provided a space for the participants to explore, but also had active elements that interacted with them. Some entities could talk about themselves and allow the users to take on their persona.

Such a world provided for the participant to explore, with no preplanned or predescribed story, is called an *undirected* narrative. Thus, by their nature, all undirected narratives allow some form of interactivity. The narrative evolves entirely from the user's—that is, the audience's—actions. An undirected narrative may have elements of story (setting, characters, plot devices), may be just a place or object to examine, or may be a tool that can be used to create a virtual world. The *NICE* VR experience (Appendix A) is one example of an undirected narrative with components of a story. In contrast, the *Placeholder* experience is an example of a world being constructed by a user and is an undirected narrative without elements of story.

In an undirected narrative, the goal is to allow the participant to construct an independent experience, in which case the narrative may take on far less importance:

```
The user put a wall at (0,0,5 to 0,10,5).
The user put a table at (5,5,7).
The user said the table is brown.
etc.
```

However, the end result of the experience may be highly satisfying to the user. In this case, user satisfaction has more to do with how well the user interface was designed than with the quality of the experience as a narrative. If the user was able to easily recreate *their* mental model, then the interface was properly designed.

One obvious benefit of increased interactivity is increased involvement by the participant. Participants can gain pride and satisfaction in making the decisions that ultimately lead to denouement. On the other hand, a better story might be told by the creator using an immotive narrative experience. This improved story can make the audience interested in the characters, want to figure out what motivates them, and curious about what might happen next in the story.

Our discussion on the narrative interactivity spectrum has focused primarily on the extremes. However, it is also possible to introduce varying degrees of inter-activity. Interaction may be included to further the narrative, without changing it in any significant way. Limited interaction can be used to present subplots in a different order or to experience the prescribed events from different perspectives before arriving at the final denouement.

Finally, given a mechanism for improvisational creation (via computation or human imagination), an interactive story can be created by beginning with a premise but taking narrative detours based on input from the audience.

Form and Genre

Form and *genre* are two terms often used to evaluate and discuss the content of media. Form is related to how the narrative is constructed and presented to the audience. A classic example of form from the movie *Citizen Kane* is the use of flash-backs to tell the story. Genre is a way to categorize style: science fiction or mystery, opera or symphony, abstract or representational are all genres of particular media.

Just as other media have their forms, in virtual reality there are different presentation and interaction styles which combine to make up the forms of VR. The elements of a created work are built around a basic structure that can take any number of forms (i.e., literary or interface styles). The *form* of an experience is manifested in the style of interface chosen for the experience; thus in VR the form is for the most part the interface. In essence, the interface is the way things are presented, the shape of the narrative.

In VR we typically associate genre with the class of problem being addressed and form as the method of interaction and presentation. One form (of interaction) is the *walkthrough*. This form is a somewhat simple application interface that allows the participant to experience some model of a location through an undirected interactive narrative. Participants are allowed to move throughout the modeled virtual world. A common genre that makes use of this form is the architectural or site walkthrough, often based on a real-world location or plan, where the user can perhaps test accessibility of doors, sinks, and cabinets. However, not much else typically takes place in these spaces. One doesn't pass by the water cooler and see a conversation taking place, or hear a fire alarm, watch as people walk calmly to the nearest exit, and see them vacate the building (although one could).

In addition to the walkthrough, there are many common VR interface forms, which we describe in Chapter 6. Of course, the form of a VR experience is not limited to how the user travels through the virtual world. Form also includes how they interact with the objects in the world. For example, to select and move an object, the user might be required to make a fist near the object, move their hand to the desired location, and release their fist. An alternate form of this operation might be to point at the object with a wand, press a button, point to the new location, and release the button.

Along with these various classes of presentation/interaction styles (the forms), there is also a set of narrative styles and prototypical settings (the genres). Some virtual reality genres have begun to emerge and, as with other aspects of VR, many are derived from other media. Examples of today's VR genres include games, scientific visualization, manufacturing procedure analysis and training, product prototyping, interactive story experience, and historical site recreations.

The choice of genre and form is orthogonal; that is, the selection of a particular genre does not (necessarily) put limitations on what form may be used. In practice, however, there may be certain combinations frequently used together; certain genres go hand in hand with specific forms. Similar forms can be used in different genres, however, as we see in the use of the newsreel and flashback in both the dramatic genre film *Citizen Kane* and the comedic genre film *Zelig*.

Experience Versus Information

As with other communication media, VR experiences can be designed for different purposes. Media as a means of communication are used to convey many different types of information (FIGURE 2-14). A sign painter who creates a sign stating that it is 5 miles to Homer has the goal of conveying a piece of factual information through a very simple virtual world. An artist may draw sketches in a courtroom trial, documenting

(A)

(B)

(C)

(D)

FIGURE 2-14 *VR applications can be built for different purposes, much like paintings can be created for different goals. In these examples:* **(A)** *A sign painter creates a factual "world" through signage.* **(B)** *A courtroom artist captures the intensity of a real-life dramatic moment.* **(C)** *An impressionist painter evokes a quiet moment.* **(D)** *A cubist captures motion. (Images:* (A) *Photograph by Alan Craig.* (B) *Sketch by Charlotta McKelvey.* (C) *In the Loge, by Mary Cassatt. Courtesy, Museum of Fine Arts, Boston. Reproduced with permission © 2002 Museum of Fine Arts, Boston. All Rights Reserved.* (D) *Nude Descending a Staircase. © 2002 Artists Rights Society (ARS), New York/ADAGP, Paris/Estate of Marcel Duchamp.).*

the event for the benefit of those not present. An impressionist painter may strive to create an image which evokes a feeling of tranquility. A cubist painter may try to indicate movement, imply multiple perspectives, or evoke emotion.

This same range of motivations and goals is available to the communicant who uses the medium of VR. There are applications developed specifically to pass on factual *information* to the user, for instance, an application created to teach students about the 3D structure of a molecule or to show clients the design of a building through an architectural walkthrough. VR applications can evoke emotion or allow the user to *experience* an environment, as in a simulated roller coaster ride or an environment simulated from the POV of a person with a physical or mental disability.

Objects and events in a VR application must be encoded as information. How, then, can emotion be denoted by a series of information bits? In the medium of *dance,* it is not possible to pass the experience from the mind of one individual directly to another, even another dancer. Consequently, notation methods are used to indicate a dancer's motions, thereby allowing the performer to replicate the virtual world and present it to the audience (FIGURE 2-15). The same is true for the medium of virtual reality. Although not typically referred to as notation, actions and other elements of an experience are "passed" to the medium of VR by being embedded in a computer program.

Just as with any transmission of information, filtering occurs in the transmission of a VR experience. There is no guarantee that the receiver will have the same experience as the communicant; in fact it is highly improbable. The more experiential information that can be transmitted, the greater the degree of fidelity experienced by the recipient.

The real question is how to transmit a virtual world such that the communicant's model is experienced by the participant. This is what artists in all media have been grappling with for centuries (with varying degrees of success), within the limitation that no virtual world can be transmitted entirely.

(A) 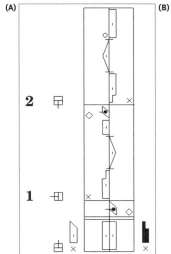 (B)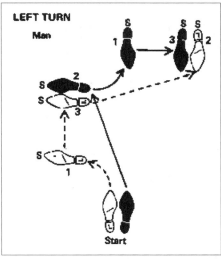

FIGURE 2-15 *Information in a media application must be encoded in some fashion.* (A) *Here, the Laban standardized dance notation depicts the steps, arm movements, and other actions a dancer should perform to create a particular waltz step.* (B) *In this component of the notation, a simple foot placement diagram shows the basic movements of the feet, but does not reveal the complete movements of the body (Image courtesy of Rebecca Nettle-Fiol, Professor of Dance, University of Illinois at Urbana-Champaign).*

The Role of Artists and Technologists

Often, advancement of a medium occurs when two forces approach each other from different viewpoints—from an artistic viewpoint and an engineering viewpoint, for instance. Technologists (engineers) often provide the basis for the (carrier) medium and *push* to improve the medium itself. Artists approach a medium as a way to express their ideas or simply as a place to explore the representation of ideas. Artists drive the content forward by making it more interesting to an audience. If a technology becomes inadequate to allow artists to express themselves as they desire, the demand for improvement in the technology creates a requirements *pull* [Furness 1995]—necessity becomes the mother of invention.

As the technology of a medium becomes more complicated, it is more difficult for a single person (or even a small group) to be able to make it all work *and* be responsible for the message. Many art forms require (or once required) the artist to be familiar with the technology, as well. Painters were required to understand how to mix pigments to make their paints; stone sculptors are still required to master a hammer and chisel; photographers typically develop their own film. By having control at each step of the creative process, an artist can experiment at each stage, giving them more flexibility to find the best way to present their message.

The motion picture medium is one where a large team is generally required to realize the virtual world. This team consists of both artists and technologists with a variety of specialties: camera operator, director, screenwriter, lighting specialists, actors, film developers, cinematographers, and so on. To varying degrees, all of these people affect how the movie looks and how well the message is conveyed to the audience. So, an important factor for how "good" a movie will be is how well the team can work together, by understanding each other's requirements and being able to communicate with one another.

Because virtual reality relies on the use of complicated devices, software, and often several computers linked together, it is similar to motion pictures in that its creation requires a team effort. The *Placeholder* VR experience (Appendix D) is certainly an example of a good-sized team effort in this medium [Laurel et al. 1994]. The VR experience *Detour: Brain Deconstruction Ahead,* by artist Rita Addison and programmer Marcus Thiebaux (a student of both art and computer science), is an example of a small team working to create a powerful piece of work [Addison 1995]. Since the technologist in the latter case is also a student of art, the communication between team members was made easier. Mutual understanding is important in any collaborative effort, so we think it is important for both technologists and artists to think about the issues presented here.

It is important to recognize that in true collaborative efforts, the technologist is not viewed as merely an implementor of the artist's ideas. Rather, the technologist, being expert in the carrier medium, may indeed bring insightful ideas to the message itself by exploiting the nuances of the medium. Conversely, it is essential for the technologist to recognize that they may not be the expert in communication. A synergistic relationship develops when all team members recognize and respect both their own contributions and those of the other group members.

Chapter Summary

Virtual reality is a medium. Having compared the features of VR to those common among other media for human communication, we can now begin to study ways to make use of VR, and best take advantage of the specific features it offers.

The world of ideas is a virtual one. The access point through the boundary between the ideas contained in a virtual world and the recipient is manifested in the interface. Without careful implementation, an interface can impede the flow of ideas. To study the many possibilities of this interface is to learn how to best move ideas from the creator to the audience, who together author the experience.

We now move from a general discussion of how virtual reality fits within the context of all human communication media to an exposition of the technology interface choices available in the creation of a VR experience.

PART II

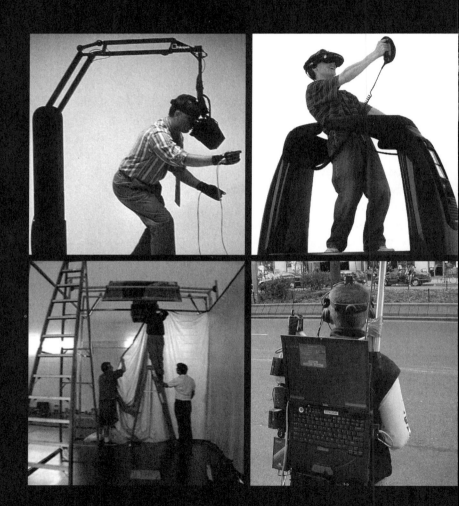

Virtual Reality Systems

Before we can reasonably discuss methods of using VR, we first must have a basic understanding of what this medium is all about and an overview of the technology involved. In Part II of this book, we present the basics of VR technology and experience. We discussed in Part I a variety of possible media used to access virtual worlds. Indeed, the user interface is how the user communicates with the constructed world and, conversely, how the world is mani-fested in a way to be perceived by the senses. In Part II, we explore the many levels at which the user interacts with a virtual world using the medium of virtual reality.

We begin by considering the physical level of the interface—the hardware (input in Chapter 3 and output in Chapter 4). In Chapter 5, we look at how the world is pre-sented to the user. In Chapter 6, we take an in-depth look at user interfaces (UIs) for interacting in the medium of virtual reality. We will then look at the components of the virtual world and the experience it conveys to the user (Chapter 7), and at the overall design of a VR experience (Chapter 8). Finally, we'll take a look at the future of VR (Chapter 9).

Recall from Chapter 1 that we spoke of mental immersion and the role of technology and synthetic imagery to fool the senses as aids in achieving this state. The chapters in this section focus on the many ways in which a user is involved with the VR experience, from the physical interface and the controls used to manipulate and travel through the experience to the methods by which the experience is presented to the user.

A virtual reality experience is the summation of all the elements presented in Part II. FIGURE II-1 illustrates the relationship between the two levels of user interface, how the virtual world is authored, the impact of the previous life experience of the user,

and the fact that the UI is as much a part of the content of virtual reality as is the virtual world. Each

component of this diagram is described in detail in the indicated chapters, beginning with the more

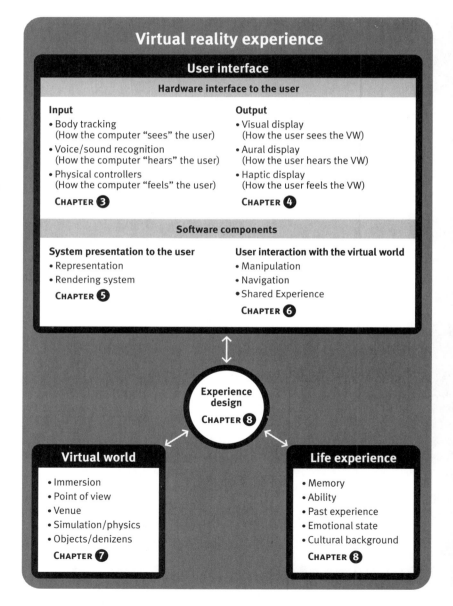

FIGURE II-1 *A virtual reality experience is the culmination of several factors, including the user interface, the components of the virtual world, and the life experience of the participant.*

hardware/ technically oriented chapters, and moving toward software user interface possibilities and overall experience design.

We can distinguish between the user interface to the system that supports the virtual world and the UI within the world, which the immersed participant can manipulate (compare FIGURES II-1 and II-2). An example of one component of the system UI is the visual display system. The UI within the world itself includes components such as the controls and menus used to affect the world.

FIGURE II-2 shows the flow of information within a typical VR setup. A virtual world is mapped into a representation that is then rendered and fed to the user via display devices. The rendering process takes into account the movements of the user to create the immersive point of view. In addition, the user can affect the virtual world through inputs programmed to interface with certain aspects of the world. For augmented reality systems, rendering of the virtual world is mixed with a view of the real world.

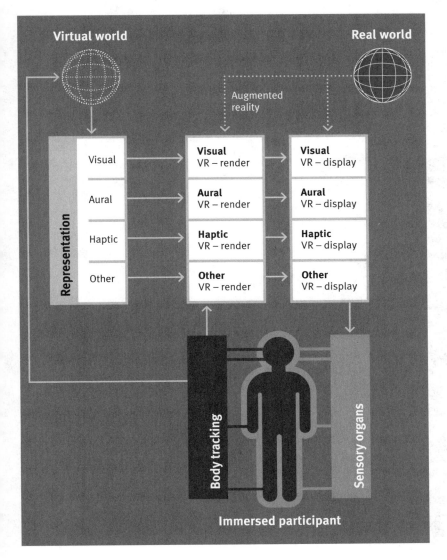

FIGURE II-2 *This chart depicts the flow of information within a VR system. Information feeds back via active and passive user interactions sensed by the system.*

Virtual reality experience

User interface

Hardware interface to the user

Input
- Body tracking
  (How the computer "sees" the user)
- Voice/sound recognition
  (How the computer "hears" the user)
- Physical controllers
  (How the computer "feels" the user)

CHAPTER 3

Output
- Visual display
  (How the user sees the VW)
- Aural display
  (How the user hears the VW)
- Haptic display
  (How the user feels the VW)

CHAPTER 4

Software components

System presentation to the user
- Representation
- Rendering system

CHAPTER 5

User interaction with the virtual world
- Manipulation
- Navigation
- Shared Experience

CHAPTER 6

Experience design
CHAPTER 8

Virtual world
- Immersion
- Point of view
- Venue
- Simulation/physics
- Objects/denizens

CHAPTER 7

Life experience
- Memory
- Ability
- Past experience
- Emotional state
- Cultural background

CHAPTER 8

Interface to the Virtual World — Input

Our definition of virtual reality allows for many possibilities by which a user might interact with a virtual environment. These categories of interaction, although implemented in widely different ways and perceived by different senses, still incorporate most of the basic features of VR: immersion, interaction, collaboration, and flexible narrative.

This chapter enumerates many types of physical VR interfaces that have been utilized to date. We will discuss the components and interface issues associated with each area, as well as the hardware and properties of each modality (hearing, seeing, feeling, etc.).

Although it is not our objective to look at today's technology in detail, we will use examples of existing technology to illustrate specific points and lend context to our discussions on implementation. While the specific products that are used in the examples may come and go in today's rapidly changing technology, the concepts behind them remain the same and will provide a solid foundation to your understanding of VR.

Our definition of virtual reality states that physical immersion and highly interactive simulations are key components of the medium. Thus, the VR system needs hardware devices that monitor the user in order to provide the user information necessary to make a display physically immersive. Inputs from the user also enable them to interact with the virtual world. Many VR applications also require some form of input to gather nonparticipant information about the world (real or virtual), which the user might want to investigate or interact with. In this chapter, we will discuss these two basic distinctions of input to a VR application: *user monitoring* and *world monitoring*.

User monitoring is the real-time monitoring of the participant's actions in a VR experience. Without the ability to accept input from the user, a computer-generated display is not interactive, much less a virtual reality system. In fact, virtual reality systems require not just a means for the user to tell the system what they want but a means to track at least some part of their body. User monitoring includes the continuous tracking of both user movements and user-initiated actions, such as pressing a button or issuing a voice command to the system. Continuous tracking of the user's movements is what allows the system to render and display the virtual world from a user-centric perspective—providing the effect of physical immersion.

When a user interacts with a virtual world via a VR experience, they often both *receive* information and sensations and *transmit* them via input devices to the computer (sometimes, through the same device). There are several components by which input is collected and fed to the VR system.

In user monitoring there are active ways the user inputs information into the system; these can include the use of spoken commands, physical controls like wands, joysticks, steering wheels, dashboards, and keyboards, props, and platforms. In user monitoring, there are also passive ways in which information is supplied to the computer. Passive methods tell the computer how and where the participant is moving and where they are looking. These methods include tracking of the body (including hands, eyes, and feet) and position tracking that tells the computer the participant's location and orientation.

World monitoring—our second category of input to the virtual world—supplies real-world input and information about change in the virtual world, brought about through time or user manipulation. In world monitoring, information can be gathered and brought into the experience from sources not directly related to the participant. The world being monitored might be the real world or a *persistent virtual world* (a virtual world that evolves over time, with or without participants). Sometimes monitoring is necessary because a server and multiple user interfaces are being used, and information needs to go between them. A virtual world server may contain the position of other active participants and/or the current state of the virtual world.

Real-world input is sometimes used to create portions of the virtual world in real time. This type of information is gathered by *transducers* (equipment that gathers information and translates data), which report information about a portion of the real world. Examples of this type of input are data from a weather-monitoring station or satellite imagery contained in a simulation. In this way, real-world data become part of a virtual world. In augmented reality systems, which overlay real and virtual worlds, some input capability of this kind is required even if it is nothing more than a video feed of the physical world.

User Monitoring (User Input to the Virtual World)

VR systems have various ways of monitoring a participant's interaction with a virtual world. The systems vary in how the computer tracks the participant and how the user inputs control interaction with the virtual world. Both movement and user input are important parts of a truly immersive virtual environment—although the body tracking component is the only one mandated by our definition of virtual reality. We can differentiate between these two types of input by referring to them as *passive input* (events triggered by the system monitoring of the participant) and *active input* (events specifically triggered by the user). Another way to think about them is as inputs that passively sense attributes such as the position of the user versus inputs the user must specifically activate.

Position Tracking

A *position sensor* is a device that reports its location and/or orientation to the computer. Typically there is a fixed piece at a known position and additional unit(s) attatched to the object being tracked. Often position sensors are used to track the participant's head and one of the participant's hands.

The position sensor is the most important tracking device of any VR system. Position tracking tells the VR system where the users are located within a VR space. There are several types of position sensors, each with its own benefits and limitations. In this section, we will discuss electromagnetic, mechanical, optical, videometric, ultrasonic, inertial, and neural position-sensing devices.

Position sensors impose limitations on the system. Of course, limitations vary with the type of sensor employed, but in general, limitations arise from the technology used to determine the relationship from some fixed origin and the sensor. For example, some trackers require an uninterrupted line of sight between a transmitter and a sensor. When the line of sight is interrupted (i.e., something comes between the transmitter and the sensor), the tracking system cannot function properly.

In position-sensing systems, three things play against one another (besides cost): (1) accuracy/precision and speed of the reported sensor position, (2) interfering media (e.g., metals, opaque objects), and (3) encumbrance (wires, mechanical linkages). No available technology, at any cost, provides optimal conditions in all three areas. The system designer must consider how the VR system will be used and make the optimal tradeoffs. One consideration is simply the ability of the system to produce an acceptable experience. Noise and low accuracy in the position sensor reports and lag time decrease the realism or immersiveness of the experience and can lead to nausea in some participants.

Of the tracking methods we describe, the first six are commonly found in current VR systems. The seventh method is less commonly used:

1. Electromagnetic

2. Mechanical

3. Optical

4. Videometric

5. Ultrasonic

6. Inertial

7. Neural

Electromagnetic Tracking

A commonly used VR tracking technology is *electromagnetic tracking* (FIGURE 3-1). This method uses a *transmitter* to generate a low-level magnetic field from three orthogonal coils within the unit. In turn, these fields generate current in another set of coils in the smaller *receiver* unit worn by the user. The signal in each coil in the receiver is measured to determine its position relative to the transmitter. The transmitter unit is fixed at a known location and orientation so that the absolute position of the *receiving* unit can be calculated. Multiple receiving units are generally placed on the user (typically on the head and one hand), on any props used, and sometimes on a handheld device.

Electromagnetic tracking works because the coils act as antennae and the signal weakens as the receiving antennae move away from the transmitting antennae. Signals are sequentially pulsed from the transmitter through each of the coil antennae. The strength of the signal also changes based on the relative orientation between transmitter and receiver coils. Each receiving coil antenna receives a stronger signal when its orientation is the same as that of the transmitting antenna; for example, a vertical transmitting antenna is picked up optimally by a vertical receiving antenna. By analyzing the signal strength in each of the receiving coils, the system can determine the full 6-DOF position of each receiving unit with respect to the position of the transmitter: where the receiving units are (*x, y, z* location) and

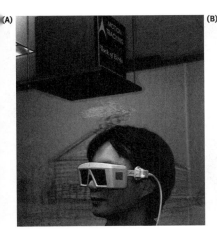

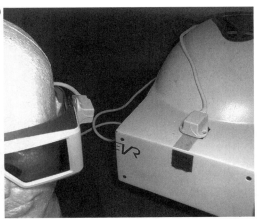

FIGURE 3-1 *Electromagnetic trackers are small and convenient to mount on various devices. Here, the receiver unit of the tracking system is mounted to shuttering glasses* **(A)** *and a head-mounted display* **(B)** *to provide information about the direction and orientation of the user's gaze. The larger transmitter is visible above the participant's head in* (A) *(Photographs by William Sherman).*

how they are oriented (*roll, pitch, yaw*). See this chapter's sidebar, Degrees of Freedom, for further detail on these location and orientation parameters.

One of the limitations of electromagnetic tracking systems is that metal in the environment can cause magnetic interference. Another limitation is the short range of the generated magnetic field. The receivers will operate with reasonable accuracy only within 3–8 feet of the transmitter, depending on the specific model. The accuracy drops off substantially as the user moves toward the edge of the operating range. Using multiple transmitters to extend the range is possible, but difficult to implement.

The major advantage is that electromagnetic systems have no line of sight restriction. The absence of this restriction allows the users to move about in a space that might have multiple visual or sonic obstacles between them and the transmitter—obstacles that can interfere with other types of tracking devices. Another advantage is that wireless systems have become available, reducing encumbrances on the participant. It should be noted, however, that these wireless systems are currently designed for motion capture systems and thus tend to include many more receivers than typically used in a VR system, making them bulkier and more costly than necessary.

Mechanical Tracking

Tracking may also be accomplished through *mechanical* means. For example, an articulated armlike boom may be used to measure the head position. Users can strap part of the device to their heads, or they can just put their face up to it and grasp the

Degrees of Freedom

A degree of freedom (DOF) is a particular way in which a body may move in space. This may be a rotation about some axis or sliding along a straight line (the latter is referred to as a *translation*). In mechanical devices, these movements can be combined to allow the body a wider range of movement and, accordingly, more freedom to maneuver. The constraints of the mechanics still impose some limitations, so additional movements (degrees of freedom) can be added to allow a body to approach total freedom. A standard joystick device allows the stick to be moved around two independent axes and thus is a 2-DOF input device. A knob (such as the volume knob on a radio) allows only one rotation and is a 1-DOF input device. The mechanics of an entire human hand require tracking 22 movements and thus the hand is a 22-DOF system.

When a body can move independently of any mechnical linkages, then any possible movement can be stated in terms of six degrees of freedom. These six degrees are specified as three rotational and three translational degrees, about and along three orthogonal axes (FIGURE 3-2). We can speak of the rotational movements as *roll, pitch,* and *yaw* and the translational as simply location along the *x, y,* and *z* axes.

For user monitoring, most VR position-tracking systems report the complete 6-DOF positions of receivers mounted on parts of the user's body and on mobile devices. However, there are occasions when only the three rotational DOF (which define orientation) or only the three translational DOF (which define location) are required. Also, not all position-tracking devices are capable of determining the complete 6-DOF position and thus report only one set or the other.

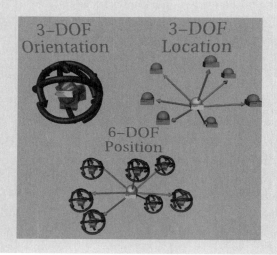

FIGURE 3-2 *Position sensors can track either just the 3-DOF orientation, the 3-DOF location, or the complete 6-DOF position of an object.*

handles. The boom follows their movements within a limited range; each elbow joint and connecting link of the boom is measured to help calculate the user's position.

The rotational and linear measurements of the mechanical linkages can be made quickly, accurately, and precisely. Using straightforward matrix mathematics, accurate and precise position values can be quickly calculated. Some devices, such as the BOOM by Fakespace Systems, Inc. (FIGURE 3-3A), also make use of the boom linkages to help support the physical weight of the visual display system.

In addition to position trackers, motors can also be connected to the boom linkages to create a force display (a sense of touch or haptic display that provides pressure and resistance effects), as in the SensAble Technologies, Inc. *PHANTOM* devices (see FIGURE 3-3B).

The primary disadvantage of this type of system is that the physical linkages restrict the user to a fixed location in the world. The joints in the boom arm are flexible and allow user movement in the area within reach of the boom arm. There are some residual effects, because the inertia of a heavy display can take some effort to move fluidly—especially when a large mass (like a pair of CRT displays) is attached to the linkages. In addition to being a tracking device, this type of system is generally used for the head as a visual display or for the hands as a haptic I/O device, but can't be used for both head and hands; thus, a second tracking system is usually required if both head- and hand-tracking are important.

(A)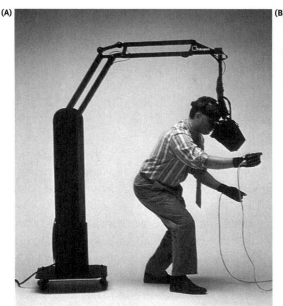

(B)

FIGURE 3-3 *Mechanical tracking has the advantage of being very fast and accurate. The Fakespace FS2 device* (A) *and the SensAble Technologies* PHANTOM *device* (B) *are equipped for mechanical tracking. Each joint in the arm reports a value position by sensing the rotation of each joint via optical encoders. In some cases potentiometers (variable resistors) are used instead of optical encoders to report how much the joint has rotated, but these wear out, get dirty, and become electrically noisy. The results from the various joints are integrated to provide the input position. (FS2 photograph courtesy of Fakespace Systems, Inc.; PHANTOM photograph by William Sherman).*

Optical Tracking

Optical tracking systems make use of visual information to track the user. There are a number of ways this can be done. The most common is to make use of a video camera that acts as an electronic eye to "watch" the tracked object or person. The video camera is normally in a fixed location. Computer vision techniques are then used to determine the object's position based on what the camera "sees." In some cases, light-sensing devices other than video cameras can be used.

When using a single sensing device, the position of the "watched" point can be reported in only two dimensions; that is, where the object is in the plane the sensor sees, but without depth information. Watching multiple points or using multiple sensors allows the system to triangulate the location and/or orientation of the tracked entity, thereby providing three-dimensional position information.

Single-source, 2-D optical tracking is typically used in *second person VR,* in which the participants watch themselves in the virtual world, rather than experiencing the virtual world from the first person point of view (see Chapter 6 for further discussion). The video source (the incoming picture signal from a video camera) is used both to determine the user's position within the video picture and to add the user's image to the virtual world.

Another single-source video-tracking method uses a small camera mounted near a desktop monitor (such as one used for desktop video teleconferencing). This camera can roughly calculate the user's position in front of the monitor by detecting the outline of the viewer's head (given that the distance of the user's head from the screen generally falls within some limited range). This system can then be used as a crude, untethered optical tracker for a VR system based on a desktop monitor (also known as *Fishtank VR* because of the display's resemblance to peering into a fishtank).

Multiple visual input sources can be combined by the VR system to garner additional position information about the participant. Using three visual inputs, such as three video cameras in different locations, a full 6-DOF position can be calculated by triangulation. By judiciously aiming the cameras, one can track multiple objects, or multiple body parts (such as each of the hands and the feet) of a participant. However, techniques for enabling the system to keep track of which object is which are complex.

A limitation of optical tracking is that the line of sight between the tracked person or object and the camera must always be clear. Keeping the tracked object within the sight of the camera also limits the participant's range of movement.

Videometric (Optical) Tracking

An alternate method of optical tracking is referred to as *videometric tracking.* Videometric tracking is somewhat the inverse of the cases just described in that the camera is attatched to the object being tracked and watches the surroundings, rather than being mounted in a fixed location watching the tracked object. The VR system analyzes the incoming images of the surrounding space to locate landmarks and derive the camera's relative position to them. For example, the camera could be mounted on a head-based display to provide input to the VR system, which would be able to determine the locations of the corners of the surrounding room and calculate the user's position from this information.

For a videometric tracking system to work, the location of the landmarks in the space must be known or be discernible from other data in order to determine the absolute position of the sensing device. Thus, the extent of computational resources needed to do the image analysis for locating landmarks becomes a consideration. The amount of computation can be significantly reduced by placing distinct landmarks at known locations. By making the landmarks distinct in shape or color, the computer vision algorithm can readily track multiple points and distinguish them from surrounding objects. These fiducial landmarks act as known reference points in the world.

Different approaches have been taken for creating distinct landmarks. Researchers [Welch and Bishop 1997] at the University of North Carolina at Chapel Hill (UNC) have taken two separate approaches based on the goal of the task. To allow 3D position tracking over a large room-sized space, infrared light sources have been placed throughout the ceiling to be sensed by multiple infrared-sensitive cameras mounted on the tracked object—in this case, an HMD, as shown in FIGURE 3-4. The light sources are activated and deactivated, providing distinct patterns of light that act as landmarks in locations likely to produce good tracking results. A single camera can determine its own 6-DOF position by using multiple reference points; however, multiple cameras are often used because there can be times when a single camera does not have any landmarks in view. In the UNC work, the infrared light sources act as reference points. This results in a fast, accurate determination of the location and orientation of the tracked object.

An alternate approach for creating landmarks places easily distinguishable patterns in places that are likely to fall within the camera's view. In work done at UNC for ultrasound diagnosis using augmented reality, four bright colors were chosen to be placed in two concentric circles, with different colors in each circle [State et al. 1996]. This approach

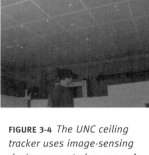

(A)

(B)

FIGURE 3-4 *The UNC ceiling tracker uses image-sensing devices mounted on a user's head* **(A)**, *and other tracked objects, to measure their location by doing image analysis of the views of a grid of light sources* **(B)** *positioned on the ceiling (Images courtesy of University of North Carolina at Chapel Hill).*

is often used in augmented reality systems that employ the video see-through method of overlaying the synthetic world onto the real world.

Ultrasonic Tracking

Ultrasonic tracking uses high-pitch sounds emitted at timed intervals to determine the distance between the transmitter (a speaker) and the receiver (a microphone). As with optical tracking, three transmitters combined with three receivers provide enough data for the system to triangulate the full 6-DOF position of an object.

Because this method of tracking relies on such common technology as speakers, microphones, and a small computer, it provides a fairly inexpensive means of position tracking. Logitech, a manufacturer of this technology, has even embedded ultrasonic trackers directly in the frame of shutter glasses, providing an economical system for monitor-based (also called *fishtank*) VR systems (FIGURE 3-5; fishtank VR systems are discussed in detail in Chapter 4).

Properties of sound do limit this method of tracking. Tracking performance can be degraded when operated in a noisy environment. The sounds must have an unobstructed line between the speakers and the microphones to accurately determine the time (and therefore distance) that sound travels between the two. Trackers built around this technology generally have a range of only a few feet and are encumbered by wires attached to both the transmitter and receiver. Because the emitter technology (speakers) is low cost, it is possible to cover a large area economically, and adding more microphones and transmitters can extend the range.

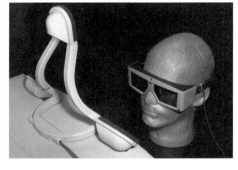

Another limitation of ultrasonic tracking is that triangulating a position requires multiple, separate transmitters and receivers. These transmitters and receivers must be separated by a certain minimum distance. This is not generally a problem for transmitters, which can be mounted throughout the physical environment, but can be a problem for receivers. One aim in designing a receiver unit is to make it small and light to be as unencumbering as possible.

FIGURE 3-5 *Logitech provides an example of a tracking system that utilizes ultrasound technology. A very high-pitched sound travels from the speakers on the unit fixed atop the monitor to the microphones on the glasses. The triangular arrangement of the speakers and microphones allows the system to compute the location and orientation of the glasses relative to the base unit. Because ultrasound is a line-of-sight medium, the microphones must face the base unit. Thus the range of motion in which the glasses can be tracked is less than 100% (Photograph by William Sherman).*

Inertial Tracking

Inertial tracking uses electromechanical instruments to detect the relative motion of sensors by measuring change in gyroscopic forces, acceleration, and inclination [Foxlin 1996]. These instruments include accelerometers which are devices that measure acceleration. Thus accelerometers can be used to determine the new location of an object that has moved, if you know where it started. Another instrument is the inclinometer, which measures inclination, or how tipped something is with respect to its "level" position (the tilt of a person's head, for instance). It is very much like a carpenter's level except that the electrical signal it provides as its output can be interpreted by a computer.

Inexpensive transducers that provide angular rates using gyroscopes, combined with angular and linear accelerometers and inclinometers, can be used separately or together to provide small self-contained tracking systems. This technology has been used in highly accurate, large-scale systems as a means of maritime and flight navigation via inertial navigation systems (INS).

Inertial tracking operates with the same technique by which the inner ear aids in determining the head's orientation. A fluid tends to remain motionless while the surrounding structure rotates. Sensors within the structure relay information about the location of the structure relative to the fluid. The brain uses this information to calculate orientation and changes in orientation.

The inertial tracking device is a small sensor that is attached to the object being tracked. It is coupled to the computer via a connecting wire. Often there is an intermediate "black box" to which the sensor is coupled to convert the signals to appropriate levels and digital communication protocols. It is possible to replace the wire linkages with wireless transmission technology, such as radio.

Although full 6-DOF position changes can be measured using sensors that rely on gyroscopes (for orientation information) and linear acceleration (for computing distance from the starting point), there are a few technical issues that one must consider. Because accelerometers provide relative (rather than absolute) measurements, errors accumulate in the system over time, leading to inaccurate information.

Thus, in practical applications of virtual reality, these tracking systems are typically limited to orientation-only measurement. This tracking of orientation alone is referred to as a *strapdown inertial navigation system* or as an *attitude and heading reference system* (AHRS).

The degradation of accuracy over time (drift) is a concern with 3-DOF orientation tracking systems, but it can be reduced using filters and by incorporating information from multiple sensors [Foxlin 1996]. Without a separate tracking system against which the inertia-based tracking values can be compared, the system will occasionally need to be manually realigned. Manual realignment is accomplished by moving the tracked object to a fixed orientation and calibrating it using this fixed reference. The amount of time before significant drift causes the tracking to be unsatisfactory varies, based on the quality of the system and whether a filtering algorithm is used on the incoming data stream.

Inertial tracking is seldom used in conjunction with stationary visual displays, because knowledge of the user's head location is required. Inertial tracking by itself does not provide enough information to determine location.

Despite these limitations, inertial trackers offer some significant benefits. The primary benefit is that they are self-contained units that require no complementary components fixed to a known location, so there is no range limitation. They move freely with the user through a large space. They work relatively quickly compared with many of the other tracking methods and, therefore, introduce little lag into the system. Units of reasonable quality are fairly inexpensive and have been incorporated directly into some inexpensive head-based displays (HBDs). We should note here that an HMD is a subset of HBDs. Not all head-based displays are head mounted (e.g., the BOOM in FIGURE 3-3A). We use HBD unless we are specifically referring to an HMD, as when talking about the weight of an HMD, for instance.

Inertial tracking systems can be combined with other tracking systems to provide the best of both methods. For example, in a VR system using an HBD, low-latency tracking is particularly important to increase immersion and reduce the likelihood of simulator sickness. An inertial tracker can provide this low-latency tracking information for the orientation of the HBD, allowing the system to update the proper direction of view quickly. Other tracking methods, such as magnetic tracking, can provide the location movement at a somewhat slower pace and can also be used to correct for the drift in the inertial system.

Neural (Muscular) Tracking

Neural or *muscular tracking* is a method of sensing individual body-part movement, relative to some other part of the body. It is not appropriate for tracking the location of the user in the venue, but it can be used to track movement of fingers or other extremities. Small sensors are attached to the fingers or limbs, with something like a Velcro strap or some type of adhesive to hold the sensor in place (FIGURE 3-6). The sensor measures nerve signal changes or muscle contractions and reports the posture of the tracked limb or finger to the VR system.

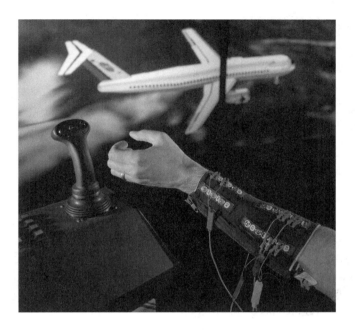

FIGURE 3-6 *NASA researchers have prototyped a device that measures muscle contractions in the arm and can determine the approximate movement of the fingers (Image courtesy of NASA).*

This type of tracking measures the electrical skin response to determine nervous and muscular activity in a certain area. It certainly does not imply information gathering of the "direct brain-tap" sort described in science fiction stories, although some experimentation is being done with brain wave information gathered via EEG transducers. By monitoring electrical impulses in specific areas of the skin, it is possible to determine the triggering of the muscles that control finger flexion and similar movements. This technology has been tested in prosthetic devices to control movements in the prosthesis by monitoring nerve stimulus farther up the limb.

These types of sensors have been shown to be useful for tracking muscle-oriented activities such as the bowing of a virtual violin. Because a violinist uses the muscles of their full arm to achieve different bowing effects, the end result can be more satisfying than simply measuring the position of the point of contact with the virtual bow. However, there aren't yet straightforward software routines to map muscle information into useful information. So a developer must determine what muscular information is needed and how to synthesize the multiple sources into information that is meaningful to the VR application. This form of VR system tracking has not been deeply explored. There have been some experiments with inexpensive skin transducers for controlling virtual worlds using relatively inexpensive off-the-shelf technology. In the following section, we move to tracking on a larger scale.

Body Tracking

Body tracking is the VR system's ability to sense position and actions of the participants. The particular components of movement that are tracked depend on the body part and how the system is implemented. For example, tracking head movement might consist of just 3-DOF location, just 3-DOF orientation, or full 6-DOF position information. Another example is tracking finger movement with a glove device, which might measure multiple joints of finger flexion or might measure just contacts between fingertips. Any component of the body can be tracked in one or more degrees of freedom, assuming a suitable tracking mechanism is available in an appropriate size and weight and is attached to the system.

The requirements of the VR experience determine how much body tracking is to be done, although equipment limitations might force an implementation that substitutes tracking of some body parts with other forms of interaction. There are many degrees to which the user's body can be instrumented. Sometimes only the user's head is monitored by the VR system, sometimes a head and a hand or both hands with a torso.

Body Posture and Gestures

In monitoring the user, the system determines the current position of the user or some part of the user's body. The static position of a body part or group of parts, such as an extended index finger or a clenched fist, is referred to as *posture*. The system can also maintain information on user movement over time. A specific user movement that occurs over time is referred to as a *gesture*. Gestures can be used effectively as intuitive interfaces (though not all gestures are intuitive). An example of an intuitive gesture is to make a grasping motion (clenching the fist) to indicate your desire to grab an object. Perhaps less intuitive is a signal to fly through the world, since we have no experience in the real world on which to base such an action. One method of travel control uses the fingers in a pointing posture. Extending the index finger initiates flying mode, with the direction of the finger indicating the direction of travel. Arm flapping is an example of travel control that uses an active gesture to signal the desire to fly.

Postures and gestures provide an expanded repertoire from which input commands can be derived. However, their intuitiveness varies greatly from user to user, and users might require training in the gesture recognition system.

The body parts and techniques of body tracking commonly used in VR applications include

■ Tracking the head

■ Tracking the hand and fingers

■ Tracking the eyes

■ Tracking the torso

■ Tracking the feet

■ Tracking other body parts

■ Indirect tracking

The Head

The head is tracked in almost every VR system, although not always the full 6-DOF. Most VR systems need to know something about the user's head orientation and/or location to properly render and display the world. Whether location or orientation information is required depends on the type of display being used.

Head-based displays require head orientation to be tracked. As users rotate their heads, the scenery must adapt and be appropriately rendered in accordance with the direction of view, or the users will not be physically immersed. Location tracking, while not essential, enhances the immersion quality of these VR experiences. Location tracking helps provide the sense of *motion parallax* (the sense that an object has changed position based on being viewed from a different point). This cue is very important for objects that are near the viewer. Some VR experiences avoid the need for location tracking by encouraging or requiring the user to continuously move (virtually) through the environment. This movement through space also provides depth information from motion parallax. There may be other interactions that benefit from tracking head location, so applications that lack head location tracking might be harder to use.

Stationary VR visual displays, such as a computer monitor or a projection screen, must determine the relative position between the eyes of the user and the screen. Since the screen is stationary, its position does not need to be tracked. A good approximation of eye position (the bridge of the nose) can be made from the head location data. For the display of monoscopic images, this information is enough, but for the proper display of stereoscopic images, the system must have the location of each eye to render the appropriate views. Unless a separate tracker is located near each eye, the system will need information about head orientation as well as head location to calculate the location of each eye.

Hand-based VR displays, those that can be held in the hand, similar to PalmPilots and Gameboys, are like stationary displays in that the location of the user's head is more important than its orientation. Again, the relative position between the screen and the eyes must be known. Since the display is also mobile, both the head and display must be tracked to determine the viewing vector.

The Hand and Fingers

Tracking the hand, with or without tracking the fingers, is generally done to give the user a method of interacting with the world (FIGURE 3-7). In multiparticipant spaces, hand gestures can also provide communication between participants. A hand can be tracked by attaching a tracker unit near the wrist or through the use of a tracked handheld device. If detailed information about the shape and movement of the hand is needed, a glove input device is used to track the positions of the user's fingers and other flexions of the hand. In this case, the hand position tracker is generally mounted directly on the glove.

While glove input devices provide a great amount of information about a key interactive part of the user's body, they have a few disadvantages. First, they are hard to put on and take off, which is especially a problem in systems that otherwise encourage the sharing of interactive control of the world. Usually there is only a glove or two, and certainly only one or two are connected to the system at any given time. Consequently, to change control of the system requires that the first person remove the glove, the new control person don the glove, and in most cases go through a calibration routine with the glove. The calibration routine consists of striking a number

(A)

(B)

FIGURE 3-7 *Information gained by tracking the user's hand can also be used to control a hand avatar in the virtual world. The representation gives the user a sense of presence within the virtual world (Photographs by William Sherman).*

of hand poses and having the computer take data with each new pose. It takes several minutes. Gloves are also generally hard to calibrate and, worse, to keep calibrated so that the system has an accurate measure of the user's current hand posture. This is much more intrusive than simply handing your collaborator a handheld input device.

Many applications that employ the use of data input gloves do not actually utilize the full information of the hand's shape. Most gloves report information about each joint in the hand, but often are used only to signify a limited selection of commands to the application. Alternatives to measuring the full relative movement of the fingers include the use of limited input gloves and handheld devices (see Props later in this section). Gloves that only sense the contact between the fingertips of one or two hands provide information about a set of discrete events that are more easily sensed and more easily dealt with by the VR system [Mapes and Moshell 1995]. The use of buttons or joysticks on a handheld prop can also be considered a form of limited finger tracking (a finger is either pushing a button or it is not).

Whether to track both or just one of the hands is a choice that must be considered in the design of a VR experience. It is, of course, easier and cheaper to provide the hardware for only one hand, with or without finger tracking. The question is whether tracking one hand is sufficient for the desired result. Specific interactions that can benefit from the use of bimanual input will be discussed in the section on manipulation in Chapter 6.

The Eyes

Technology for tracking the direction in which the user's eyes are looking relative to their head has only recently become practical for use with virtual reality and, consequently, has not been tried in many applications. There are two basic areas in which eye tracking can be useful. One is monitoring the direction of the gaze to allocate computer resources. The scene displays a higher degree of detail in the directon of the tracked eye's gaze. Eye tracking could be used as part of the interface with the world itself. Objects might be selected or moved based on the movement of the eyes.

The Torso

Very few VR applications actually track the torso of the participant, although when an avatar of the user is displayed, it often includes a torso with certain assumptions made about its position, based on head and hand positions. However, the torso is actually a better indicator of the direction the *body* is facing than are either the head or hands. The torso's bearing might be a better element to base navigational direction on than head or hand positions (see the *Placeholder* application in Appendix D).

The benefit of using the torso's bearing for travel direction correlates with the user's experience level in moving through an immersive virtual world. Novice users may adjust better to moving in the direction of their gaze (i.e., nose direction). However, limiting movement to the direction of gaze limits the user's ability to look around. While moving, the user can only look in the direction they are traveling. There are some applications in which torso tracking plays a crucial role in the user's ability to interact with the world. If jumping or leaning are important parts of interacting with the world, more complete tracking of the body is necessary (especially the torso movement) for determining these body movements. For example, a skiing or other sport-related application might require such movements, and thus the torso must be tracked.

The Feet

Some work has been done to provide a means for tracking the feet of the user. Tracking the feet provides an obvious means of determining the speed and direction a user wishes to travel. The obvious method of determining feet movement is to track the position of each foot. The most common way to do this is to use electromagnetic trackers. The tracker is attached to the foot with a wire connecting that device to the computer or to a body pack (containing a radio transmitter). Optical tracking is another method and uses cameras to "watch" the feet. This doesn't require any sensors on the foot or attached wires. Tracking the feet this way, though, is tricky. You would most likely want to put a very high-contrast spot or sticker (a fiducial marker) on the foot to give the camera a very specific reference for which to "look." Other less encumbering methods have been used as part of what are called *platform input devices*. These platforms basically are places to stand or sit while using the VR application. The platforms often have integrated input and output devices. Platforms that track the feet include stationary bicycles and stairsteppers. Tracking the feet can also be combined with a standard or omnidirectional treadmill, with the system causing the treadmill to move in accordance with the participant's steps.

Other Body Tracking

Other body parts can be tracked and used to control various aspects of a virtual world. These items include body functions, such as temperature, perspiration, heart rate, respiration rate, emotional state, and brain waves (FIGURE 3-8). These functions might be measured simply to monitor the participant's condition as they experience a world, or they might be used to control the world—to determine what experiences are most relaxing, for instance, and use that feedback to guide the user down a calmer path [Addison et al. 1995].

Indirect Tracking

Indirect tracking refers to the use of physical objects other than body parts to estimate the position of the participant. These physical objects are usually props and platforms. For example, the movement of a hand-held device, such as a wand or a steering wheel mounted on a platform, are good indicators of the position of one of the participant's hands.

FIGURE 3-8 *Here the user wears a body suit, which provides a means for the computer system to monitor the wearer's physiological attributes, such as respiration rate, heart rate, blood pressure, and blood oxygen saturation. Data from the suit can be used to modify the user's VR experience (Image courtesy of Vivometrics, Inc.).*

Improving Tracking

Each tracking method has its limitations, but all of these limitations can be reduced, eliminated, or avoided. Some ways of overcoming these limitations include the use of predictive analysis and other filtering techniques, system calibration, a combination of tracking methods, and self-calibration using objects (props) in the real world.

Predictive analysis is a computational process that can be used to effectively increase precision while reducing latency. By analyzing the motion of the tracking unit, it is sometimes possible to determine the path it is likely to take and thus supply values for where it is expected to soon be. Predicting an object's location allows the display system to have a reasonable position value for a given point in time, rather than only the latest reported value. Its effectiveness relies on the tracked object moving in a predictable fashion, of course. During times when the object is moving unpredictably, the system will not be able to return accurate and timely results.

Calibrating the system for operation within a specific environment can help reduce errors, such as those caused by certain metals when near a magnetic tracking system, for instance. Regardless of the environment, you have to calibrate all tracking systems in some way before they are useful at all. In some cases, calibration is simply a matter of telling the system where it is originally. Other systems require (or allow) calibration at will. Still others do on-the-fly calibration. Regardless of what the tracking system inherently allows, the signals it puts out can always be altered (i.e., corrected) in the computer code that calculates the tracker position with respect to the VR application.

One form of calibration done for electromagnetic systems is to create a correction (lookup) table. The tracking sensor is put in a very specific place. You can see if the tracking system reports that it is in that exact spot. If it does not, you *tell* the system that it is *really* in the spot you know it is in. You keep doing this by moving the tracking sensor and measuring, thereby building a lookup table that the system can use to correct the values it is reporting. In other words, once you've built the lookup table, the system can always apply those corrections to the reported values. Furthermore, it can interpolate for any positions between the reference locations in your lookup table. For example, say I put the sensor at position 3 ft., 4 ft., 5 ft, but the system reports that the sensor is at 4 ft., 5 ft., 6 ft.; we build into the code that if the sensor reports (4, 5, 6), recalibrate it to (3, 4, 5) before delivering it as a final value.

Let's take another example: an electromagnetic tracker in a *CAVE* display built with a metal framework will report increasingly inaccurate results the closer it gets to the frame. To recalibrate, you take measurements to describe how the frame is affecting the reported tracker positions, and the computer code uses these measurements to correct for the errors introduced by being near the frame. The precise measurements can be made by attaching the receiver to a mechanical tracking device or by using other forms of measurement [Ghazisaedy et al. 1995]. And, again, the resulting lookup table can then be used by the system to correct for errors in location tracking.

As exemplified in the section on Inertial Tracking earlier in the chapter, *combining* tracking methods can sometimes provide favorable results by taking advantage of the good qualities of each method to overcome the limitations of another. For example, in applications that use a video see-through visual display (described in Chapter 4), the system can use videometric tracking based on what the HBD camera sees. If one attaches another form of tracking to that HBD, such as an electromagnetic tracker, information from each tracker can help to calibrate the other. This effectively combines tracking methods, tracking the position of an HBD via both magnetic tracking and videometric tracking.

Other Physical Input Devices

In addition to user tracking, *physical devices* are another part of the interface between the user and the virtual world. Devices range from simple handheld objects to large cockpit-style platforms in which the user can sit. These devices are often designed specifically for a particular application, although some are designed to be a generic, standard interface to many different applications.

A person interacting with a physical device is able to sense physical properties, such as weight, surface texture, and so on. It provides some form of haptic feedback for the user. When the device is grasped or moved, the user senses that they are interacting with something that has solidity, mass, a center of gravity, and perhaps some limitations on how it can be moved (e.g., a platform steering wheel will only move in a circular motion about the center). In this section, we will describe features of physical platforms and props as a means of providing input to the system or, from the system's perspective, as a means of monitoring the user.

Physical Controls

Physical controls are the individual buttons, switches, and valuators (sliders and dials) that allow users to actively provide input directly into the VR system. These devices can be designed generically, allowing them to be used in multiple applications. They can also be designed as specific interfaces with a primary use, such as for musical or puppetry performance. Physical controls can be mounted on a platform used by a VR system (analogous to an automobile gear shift), mounted on a handheld prop tracked by the system, or located elsewhere within the venue. Virtual representations of physical controls are also used in some VR experiences, as we discuss in the manipulation section in Chapter 5.

The simplest type of control device is one that has a small number of discrete positions or states. A basic *button* is such a device with two positions: depressed or released. *Switches* can have two or more positions to which they can be set. Multiple buttons are often mounted on handheld props, allowing a participant to trigger an event based on where they are pointing the prop or on other criteria.

Valuators are simple controls that have a range of continuous values to which they can be set. A dimmer control for a light fixture is a well-known example of this. Valuators can be used individually, such as a slider or dial, or combined so that several related degrees of control can be manipulated at once, such as happens with a joystick (2-DOF).

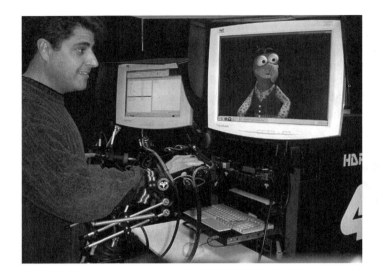

FIGURE 3-9 *One needs to learn puppetry to be an effective puppeteer, but one also needs to master the tools involved. Here, a puppeteer uses a waldo hand-input device to control the computer graphics representation of* Gonzo *(*Henson Digital Performance Studio *and* Gonzo *images courtesy of The Jim Henson Company.* © The Jim Henson Company. *The Jim Henson Company, Henson Digital Performance Studio,* and the Gonzo *characters and elements are trademarks of The Jim Henson Company. All Rights Reserved.). See color plate 3.*

Multiple devices can be consolidated into a single input device. This device can be a generic input controller such as the *CAVE* wand, which has three buttons and a pressure stick. This wand is similar to a 2-DOF joystick, but instead of the stick moving physically, the user merely applies pressure to the stick in the direction of the desired action. Input controllers designed for specific tasks might include many buttons, switches, and valuators. A computer keyboard contains approximately 100 input keys. Other examples include musical instrument interfaces, such as piano keyboards, wind instruments, and character performance devices like the puppetry waldo—a hand device used by puppeteers to control multiple aspects of a puppet such as mouth, eyebrows, eyelids, and so on (FIGURE 3-9).

Props

Like a prop in a film, a user interface prop is a physical object used to represent some object in a virtual world. In a VR experience, a small weighted cylinder might represent a light saber, or a doll's head might represent the head of a patient.

Our definition of a prop includes generic input devices such as the wand and the 3D mouse. Like the standard 2D mouse, a 3D mouse can move in two directions on a flat surface; however, a 3D mouse can also report height information. It can be lifted and used in all three dimensions. In addition to these typical input devices, objects used to represent specific objects in the virtual world, such as a doll's head, are also props. Some props are merely simple shapes (spheres, cones, planes, etc.) that can roughly approximate any number of objects [Hinckley et al. 1994].

> **prop** a physical object used as an interface to a virtual world; a prop may be embodied by a virtual object and might have physical controllers mounted on it.

The physical properties of a prop often suggest its use in a VR experience. These properties include shape, weight, texture, center of gravity, and solidity—all of which provide some haptic information to the user. For example, the use of a real golf putter as a prop provides the texture of the grip and the proper mass and center of gravity that give the realistic momentum necessary to manipulate a virtual putter. These same characteristics are not inherent in glove or wand devices. Props are often custom built for a specific purpose in an application [Hinckley et al. 1994; Fitzmaurice et al. 1995]. FIGURE 3-10 shows examples of both generic and customized props.

Representing a virtual object with some physical manifestation also enhances the user's ability to perform simple physical operations. It becomes a fairly simple task to switch a device from one hand to another—the user does what comes naturally. Creating such an interaction for a device that is represented only virtually is complex, requiring not only specific programming to perform the operation, but design analysis to construct the interface through which the user indicates to the system their wish to transfer control from one hand to the other.

Props allow for more flexible and more intuitive interactions with virtual worlds. The ability to simply determine relative spatial relationships between two props, or a prop and the user, provides strong perceptual cues that the user can take

FIGURE 3-10 *Some virtual reality systems make use of generic control devices that provide buttons, joysticks, and tracking information.* **(A)** *One example of such a device is the wand from Pyramid Systems, Inc. This wand has a 6-DOF electromagnetic tracking sensor mounted at the base (Photograph by William Sherman).* **(B)** *Other systems use customized prop devices created by adding trackers, buttons, and the like to everyday items. Here, a doll head and plastic plane are tracked. The relative position of the plane to the doll head indicates to the system what part of the brain to display on the screen (Photograph courtesy of Ken Hinckley).*

(A)

(B)

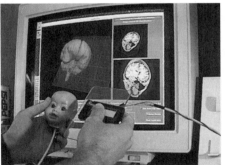

advantage of to better understand the virtual world. The specific nature of the use of props has been researched and utilized in a neurosurgical visualization application developed at the University of Virginia [Hinckley et al. 1994].

First, let's discuss props as passive input devices, that is, as interfaces to the computer that neither contain any physical inputs (like buttons or sliders) that the user must actively engage nor provide active haptic feedback.

In their paper entitled "Props for Neurosurgical Visualization," Hinckley and his colleagues [1994] list the following benefits of *passive interface props*:

- Familiarity
- Direct actions
- Obvious use
- Palpability
- No tool moding (a single interface doesn't have different "modes" for different operations, thus each prop has exactly one function)
- Feedback
- Two-handed interaction
- Pragmatic design (providing props cast as familiar tools whose use and physical constraints are intuitive to the user)
- New tool uses (innovative and unforeseen ways to make use of a tool as demonstrated by the participant)

The goal in the use of props is to create an interface that the user manipulates in a natural way. This seamless interface (the *ultimate* interface we introduced in Chapter 2) is in fact an overarching goal for VR as a whole. An interface so natural that users feel as if they are interacting directly with some virtual world, barely noticing the existence of the intermediating interface, is the ultimate goal of the VR experience.

Another benefit of props is that by making a specific object in the virtual world seem more real by giving it realistic haptic properties (such as a smooth or fuzzy surface), the rest of the virtual world may seem more real to the participant. This is called *transference of object permanence* and is discussed further in the section on immersion in Chapter 7. A VR application for treating fear of spiders would offer an interesting example of transference: the user reaches out to touch a virtual spider, and they actually feel a fuzzy spider prop.

Platforms

As the name suggests, platforms are larger, less mobile physical structures used as an interface to a virtual world. Like props, platforms can be used to represent some part of the virtual world by using real-world objects with which a participant can physically interact. In general, the platform of a VR experience is the place where the participant sits or stands during the experience. Platforms can range from a generic space to a specific control interface station (FIGURE 3-11).

> **platform** the part of the VR system where the participant is situated; a platform can be designed to mimic a real-world device found in the virtual world or simply provide a generic place to sit or stand.

There are many examples of platform interface devices for virtual reality. The platform allows the participants a natural interface to the system. With varying degrees of difficulty, many of these platforms also can provide sense-of-balance (vestibular) feedback by mounting them on a motion base. A motion base is an active floor or cockpit that is moved by hydraulics.

FIGURE 3-11 *Some VR systems use elaborate platforms to provide a realistic feel to the virtual world. For example, this platform provides an actual ship's wheel as an input device to a virtual world where the user pilots a ship (Photograph of Cutty Sark display courtesy of Randy Sprout).*

The following sections describe a number of VR platforms, the most common types being ring platforms, kiosks, ambulatory platforms (treadmill, bicycle, wheelchair), vehicle platforms (cockpit), and stationary VR displays (large-screen room, drafting board).

Ring Platform. A *ring platform* is a generic platform that is generally used in occlusive head-based display experiences to prevent the participant from becoming entangled in cables or tripping over objects in the environment that they can't see. A typical ring platform has a waist-high rail surrounding the participant, which they can lean against and/or touch to help them keep their bearings (FIGURE 3-12). Of course, this railing limits the participant's freedom of movement. Handheld props are the most common form of user input device associated with ring platforms.

FIGURE 3-12 *A simple ring platform provides the participant with a sense of security while wearing a head-mounted display. The ring provides something to hold onto or lean against to maintain balance, limits the amount of physical freedom the participant has, and protects them from tripping or colliding with real objects (Photograph courtesy of Virtuality, Inc.).*

Kiosk Platform. A *kiosk platform* is a boothlike structure in which a participant stands to access a VR experience. Kiosk platforms are typically associated with stationary visual displays, allowing the participant to see the screen and sometimes manipulate controls integrated into the kiosk. Kiosks are often designed to be transportable (FIGURE 3-13).

Ambulatory Platform. *Ambulatory platforms* are designed to provide seemingly realistic travel through a virtual world that requires the users to move their bodies (ambulate) in order to traverse the space.

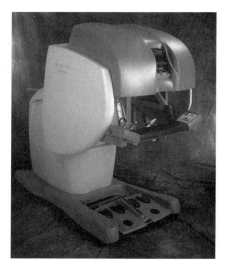

FIGURE 3-13 *The da Vinci surgery kiosk from Intuitive Surgical, Inc. is designed for use in teleoperation surgery (see Chapter 1 sidebar, I See, I Cut, I Sew). A surgeon uses teleoperation for more precision than they might obtain through direct manipulation of the instruments (Photograph courtesy of Intuitive Surgical, Inc.).*

These platforms include devices that allow the participant to walk naturally, ride a bicycle, or propel a wheelchair.

Treadmills or stair-stepping machines provide users with the illusion that their own movement is propelling them through the virtual world. This effect is achieved through kinesthetic feedback, that is, feedback from nerve endings in the muscles and tendons that inform the body about its position. A similar method creates a frictionless interface between the participant's feet and the ground. In this system, the feet movements are tracked while fixing the user's position with a restraining device [Iwata and Fujii 1996].

A wheelchair input device portrays how someone in a wheelchair might maneuver through a virtual world (FIG-URE 3-14). A wheelchair, though, is affected by environmental factors such as inclines and momentum; therefore, a realistic wheelchair simulation must be able to automatically rotate the wheels according to the physics of the virtual world.

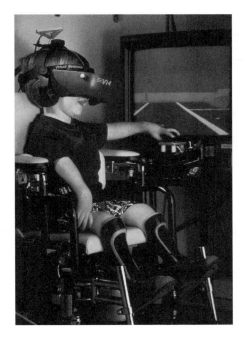

FIGURE 3-14 *A child learns how to control his wheelchair with the aid of a virtual reality system (Image courtesy of the Applied Computer Simulation Labs).*

Vehicle Platform (Cockpit). In *vehicle platforms,* you can either sit or stand to control a virtual vehicle. Most often the user is presented with realistic looking controls and accoutrements while the virtual world is displayed around the cockpit. Most people are familiar with the use of vehicle platforms in flight simulation; in fact, we sometimes refer to their use as the cockpit VR paradigm. In a flight simulator, the platform includes all the controls and displays necessary for the user to pilot a virtual aircraft.

In other instances, a user might enter a room designed like the control room of a vessel. Because the platform affects how the participant sees and interacts with the virtual world, it has a major effect on the way the experience is perceived, as well as on the cost of the application and the space it requires.

FIGURE 3-15 *Caterpillar, Inc. combines the real world with a virtual world by providing an interface to the virtual world made of actual machine components (Photo courtesy of Kem Ahlers). See color plate 4.*

A driving simulator might put the user in an actual car, while the controls provide input to the VR system instead of actually driving the car. Caterpillar, Inc. creates platforms from parts of actual tractors, such as seats, steering wheels, pedals, and control levers (FIGURE 3-15).

Theme park or location-based entertainment (LBE) VR systems often use a cockpit or an entire room as the input platform. Sometimes they are large, such as an elaborate cockpit dressed up to look like the bridge of a ship. Each user is assigned a specific role in the experience and a seat from which to carry out their duties. The user playing the role of the ship's captain may be given a seat at the center with some form of radar display. The pilot will be seated at the steering controls. Many entertainment VR applications use cockpit-based platforms and may be equipped with hydraulic motion devices (FIGURE 3-16).

Stationary VR Display Platform. A *stationary VR display* can also be considered a type of generic platform. For displays that envelop the participant, such as the *CAVE* (a 10 ft. x 10 ft. room display space surrounded by large projection screens), the user is surrounded by the display device and interacts with the virtual world via handheld props or voice command; in some instances, a vehicle platform positioned inside the display provides the controls.

FIGURE 3-16 *Some VR applications provide a cockpit in which the participant sits to "pilot" the virtual vehicle by using devices such as steering wheels, joysticks, pedals, and the like. Here a room of X-21 Hornet cockpits mounted on motion platforms gives the participants a real sensation of sitting in the cockpit of a fighter jet (Photograph courtesy of Fightertown USA).*

For table displays such as the *Responsive Workbench* from GMD [Krüger and Frölich 1994] or the *ImmersaDesk* from Fakespace Systems, Inc., the participant stands or sits in front of the display. As with larger stationary displays, handheld props are often used for interaction. Here, however, applications are sometimes designed using the table-top surface as an integral part of the interface by locating menus and other virtual controls on the screen.

Platform Summary. The use of a platform for input to the VR system is not limited to a particular visual display paradigm. There are examples of platforms in both head-based displays and stationary screen/projection displays. However, some platforms may be designed with a specific type of visual display in mind. Most arcade-style VR experiences use a combination platform/HMD system. Caterpillar, Inc.'s virtual prototyping system has been used with both HMD and *CAVE* VR displays with a cockpit-style platform.

Speech Recognition (Audio Input)

As speech recognition systems become increasingly practical, they provide an excellent opportunity for natural communication with computer systems. This is especially true with VR applications, where the goal is to provide the most natural form of interface possible. The ultimate speech recognition system would understand context and use it to interpret speech, and it would be able to process a steady stream of speech from any speaker. Although many recognition systems have some of these features, this ultimate system has not yet been developed. Therefore, the application designer must choose which features are most important and make a choice that works within the constraints of the current technology.

In general, a speech recognition system works best when it is "trained" by the particular speaker who will be controlling the application and when it is interpreting each word as a discrete utterance rather than continuous speech. Obviously, the right type of voice input system must be combined with the goal of the application. If the application is meant for many users who will not have time to train the system to understand their voice, then it will be necessary to use a system that does not depend on training by the user. If the application has a large, complex vocabulary but will be used by only a few specialists, then a speaker-trained system will work better.

At present, speech recognition systems generally map audio sounds to text strings. These strings are then matched with a set of preprogrammed possible responses.

Control of Speech Recognition Systems. One of the design considerations that must be addressed in any voice-controlled application is deciding when the recognition system should attend to what the user is saying. The simplest solution might be to always have the system listening to the user. However, a constantly listening system might cause problems when the user is speaking with people nearby. The system will continue to try to parse the conversation as commands, possibly resulting in unwanted operations. It is often wiser to allow selective attention to the user's voice.

Three methods of activating selective listening by the voice recognition system include (1) push to talk, (2) name to talk, and (3) look to talk.

Push to Talk. The *push to talk* method is implemented by using a button on a handheld device or a microphone on/off switch to activate the speech software. There are many non–VR situations where push to talk is required. This method works well in scenarios that replicate those situations, for example, the scenario of an officer controlling a ship by verbal command to the pilot [Zeltzer and Pioch 1996].

Name to Talk. In the *name to talk* method, the user says an activation word followed by an instruction. It is as if the user is addressing the computer (an invisible, omnipresent agent in the virtual world) by name. An example might be: "Computer, exit application" or "Computer, please calculate a course to the Ford Galaxy." Because the

FIGURE 3-17 *In this scenario, speech recognition is enabled when the user addresses a computer-generated avatar. Note the small, boom microphone near the participant's mouth. Other systems use a permanently mounted overhead microphone or a handheld microphone* (NICE *application courtesy of Maria Roussos; photograph by William Sherman*).

VR system is always listening for commands, it is effectively omnipresent in the world.

Look to Talk. The *look to talk* method works by addressing a visible agent in the virtual world. This requires that there be an object in the virtual world that represents each of the one or more computer agents. The user signifies when they want an agent to perform an operation by looking at the visual representation of the agent, much like humans can tell who is being addressed based on direction of gaze. This object is effectively the recognition system's avatar, and must be in the vicinity of the user for them to give commands (FIGURE 3-17).

Speaker-Dependent Versus Speaker-Independent Recognition. General speech recognition systems are still largely speaker/situation dependent. Often seemingly subtle changes can affect the ability of the system to recognize commands. Differences, such as the choice of microphone or the number of people in a room, can interfere with some voice systems. It can be difficult to create or even predict the environment in which a VR experience will be run, making it difficult to train the voice system under the same circumstances in which it will need to perform.

Good speaker-independent recognition is achievable, however, if some restrictions are placed on the voice commands. Restrictions can be either a small vocabulary or a limited, well-defined grammar. The latter is often an option in applications designed to emulate military communications, which are often "by the book."

Pros and Cons of Speech Recognition. The advantage of voice communication is that it is a natural, nonencumbering form of communication. Speech recognition technology continues to improve so that it is increasingly feasible in many more situations. However, due to the nature of speech, there are many tasks and situations in which a voice recognition system is not the best solution.

As an auditory communication channel, voice input exists over time. Speech input for control is not as instantaneous as using devices like buttons and valuators. Tasks that require precisely timed inputs, including those that are to be correlated to other physical movements, work best with physical control devices.

Another disadvantage of speech control is that speaking a command can interfere with the task being performed. This is especially true when that task requires listening or holding one's head absolutely still. On the other hand, in situations where hands need to remain still and subsecond timing is not essential, speech recognition is advantageous because the user can trigger a command while holding their hands still.

However, because people are accustomed to conversing with intelligent beings, they might then assume that they are doing so when communicating with artificial entities in a virtual world, even though it is unlikely that an underlying natural language understanding process is evaluating the incoming communication stream and parsing the semantics of the request. Or, they might believe that computers can easily understand our languages, as portrayed in popular science fiction.

Speech can be a very beneficial form of interaction because in *CAVE*-like devices, there usually isn't a keyboard available to enter commands. It is also impractical to use a keyboard when wearing a head-mounted display since the keyboard cannot be seen.

Speech Recognition Summary. Overall, speech recognition systems can play an important role in making a VR experience more immersive and natural to use. However, until systems become capable of perfect recognition of continuous speech, the choice of system will need to be tailored to the particular task. Also, despite how good recognition systems might become, there will be interface tasks for which speech input is not appropriate.

World Monitoring (Input to the Virtual World)

This section examines ways in which a dynamic environment is monitored and included as part of a VR experience. Just as the real world is dynamic and changes over time, a *persistent virtual world* is one that exists and evolves whether or not it is currently being experienced via VR or another medium. Changes in both the real world and persistent virtual worlds that share many of the same qualities may be monitored.

Persistent Virtual Worlds

The separate existence of persistent virtual worlds has several implications. In a non-persistent world, each time a VR application is experienced, it will start from the same initial conditions. User manipulations in a persistent world can remain intact until another user (or agent) comes along and changes them. Persistent worlds can evolve over time and changes can continue to take place, even when no one witnesses them.

A persistent world can be useful in a variety of applications, because it allows for *asynchronous communication*. Asynchronous communication is that which takes place outside of real time, such as leaving a voice mail that is retrieved later. Speaking on the telephone is an example of synchronous communication. Communicating by leaving messages on answering machines is an example of asynchronous communication. With asynchronous communication, users can go through an interactive design process to develop products or spaces without having to be present in the space at the same time. An example of using asynchronous communication in a VR application is the CALVIN application developed at the Electronic Visualization Lab (EVL) at the University of Illinois at Chicago [Leigh et al. 1996]. Using the CALVIN application, room designers can assist each other remotely in laying out the interior of a room. As each designer enters the space, they can readily see the results of what a previous designer has done. Other VR applications use visual or verbal annotations in the world to leave explanations or other information for future participants, as we see implemented in the *Placeholder* application in Appendix D. Asynchronous communication is further discussed in Chapter 6.

Multiuser dimensions/dungeons (MUDs) are persistent text-based virtual worlds that individual users can modify and leave for future participants to find.

Similar to how MUDs are implemented, persistent virtual worlds for VR are often manifested using a client/server model. In this arrangement, the virtual world is a computer simulation that resides on a central server unit, and the interface(s) are accessed through remote client units.

The virtual world database maintains the congruency between copies of the worlds, as well as updates the world to reflect ongoing actions and evolutions that are independent of participant actions. When an individual VR experience is executed, it connects to the server using shared memory or network protocols. Via this connection, each copy of the VR monitors the events in the world (including the movement of other users), and it relays user modifications to the world server. A benefit of maintaining the virtual world separately from the VR experience interface is the freedom to access the world via other media. In the educational application *NICE* (also developed at EVL and included in Appendix A), a vegetable garden is maintained on a separate server and can be manipulated not only through the VR experience client stations, but also via a World Wide Web (WWW) interface, allowing others to view and interact with the fully immersed participants.

Moving large amounts of data between the world server and the user's client stations can cause time lag in world interactions. One strategy to overcome this type of lag is to maintain part of the world database on the local VR system. In an architectural space, the descriptions of objects (chairs, tables, lamps, etc.) can be stored on the VR experience application, while the position of each object is stored at the server and only communicated over the network when moved. Another strategy is to download the entire database of the world to the client site when an application is initiated, and then communicate incremental changes to the server as they occur. By downloading the entire database at the beginning of the experience and only communicating changes with the server, the participant only experiences the communication delay at the very beginning of the experience. Once the initial database is loaded, the amount of communication is minimal and communication lag is reduced.

Bringing the Real World into the Virtual World

Some applications benefit by the integration of real-world information. Real-world data can be gathered by video cameras and other measuring devices. There are several applications where the inclusion of real-world data may be advantageous.

Broadly speaking, including real-world data in a VR application is most helpful in the following scenarios:

- *Analyzing and exploring acquired scientific data.* For example, a real-time system for data acquisition allows a scientist to use various scientific visualization tools to explore a severe weather system as it unfolds. Or, a traffic engineer might need to observe traffic flow at a busy intersection using tools in VR.

- *Preventing users from colliding with objects in real world.* Integrating real-world data into the virtual world is important in order to avoid artifacts of the real world hindering the VR experience—for example, a wireless HBD application in which the user freely walks about in a room. A real-world obstruction would be represented in the virtual world coincident with the object to let the participant know they should not go there.

- *Preparing for a real-world dangerous task.* By becoming familiar with a dangerous location, the user can minimize the actual danger when navigating for the first time in the physical world—as might be useful for rescue and mining operations.

- *Planning for modifying or using real-world space.* Exploring an existing space via the medium of VR can also serve to give the user an opportunity to visualize how the space can be modified or used effectively.

- *Educational experiences.* For those without the immediate opportunity to visit the locale first hand, it would be possible to experience an existing historic or otherwise culturally interesting location for research or personal edification.

Transducers

Transducers are used to retrieve real-world data. A transducer is any device that senses a phenomenon in the physical world and translates it into another form—in VR the form is an electric signal that a computer system can process. According to *Webster's* [1989], a transducer is "a device that receives energy from one system and retransmits it, often in a different form, to another." Transducers include such devices as microphones, weather stations, LIDAR (light detection and ranging), video cameras, and electromagnetic position sensors.

As with accessing persistent virtual worlds, information gathered via transducers can be retrieved over a network. Machines local to the source gather information and send it to a central server. The server or individual machines operate in a client/server fashion, the server responding to information requests from a variety of client machines.

Transducers can be used in VR systems to help create a richer virtual world. They can provide an accurate representation of the real world, such as an application where the user flies over terrain. They can collect data (sometimes acquired by satellite) to create a realistic view of the earth. If the goal is to examine the weather over a region of the earth, then live feeds from monitoring stations can be read by the system and transferred to appropriate representations.

An augmented reality application might use an ultrasonic sensor to determine a patient's internal structures in real time, or a space might be captured with a video camera and then processed to create a computer-based polygonal/textural representation of the space, which would in turn be integrated into a virtual reality application. A LIDAR system can scan a physical location used for filming a movie. The captured data of the physical space can then be recreated as a virtual world, which can be manipulated via computer for special effects or for planning actor and camera placement.

Effect on the Virtual World

Input from the real world can help make a virtual world more *realistic*. On the other hand, the application designer can choose to manipulate the real-world information in unnatural ways. If the application is designed to help visualize aspects of a natural system for the purpose of scientific study—for example, regional weather or a bay ecosystem—information such as temperature and wind/water flow can be represented with standard scientific visualization techniques in addition to or in replacement of realistic representation [Sherman et al. 1997].

Using real-world data in a virtual world is particularly helpful in applications providing situational preparedness training. In such experiences, participants benefit by experiencing the world as accurately as possible. Teleconferencing in virtual reality is also more effective if the avatars are more lifelike, because participants are better able to read facial and body inflections. FIGURE 3-18 shows some examples of how real-world data can be incorporated in a virtual reality experience.

FIGURE 3-18 *Real-world data can be visualized in a VR application to study nature* (A), *or it can be used to recreate an existing real-world space for training purposes* (B) *(CAVE5d application in* (A) *courtesy of Bill Hibbard, photograph by William Sherman; image* (B) *courtesy of David Tate, Naval Research Lab).*

Chapter Summary

The way participants interact with a virtual reality system greatly influences their experience with the virtual world. The modes of interaction affect how easy the system is to use, how mentally immersed the participant feels, and the range of possible user actions.

A participant in a virtual reality experience influences the virtual world through the system's input interface. For virtual reality, a key input component is the position tracker, which can be used to monitor the body position and movements of the participant, as well as other physical objects (props) accessible to them. There are a variety of technologies available to do position tracking. Each technology has its own benefits and drawbacks. It is possible to combine technologies to improve tracking performance.

A significant portion of the input process consists of monitoring the user's actions. Tracking the participant's physical position and movements allows greater integration in the virtual world. A typical VR system will track the head and one hand of the participant. Other methods of user input include buttons, joysticks, props that are themselves position-tracked, and platforms that help define the space the user will occupy during the experience as well as provide a means of input. Occasionally, a VR system may include a method for voice input to provide a natural means of communicating with the virtual world.

Some inputs are used to monitor the real world or a persistant virtual world, gathering data about the dynamic qualities of the world that change over time. These inputs are called transducers, because they retrieve real-world information and translate it into an electrical signal that the computer can process. Sometimes real-world data is used to create portions of the virtual world.

The input devices chosen for any given application set the stage for how the participant will interact with the system and should be chosen carefully. Many input devices can be used generically for multiple purposes and some are specialized, custom-made devices. Some input devices simultaneously provide an output mechanism. For example, a tracked golf putter, although primarily an input device, also serves to provide haptic feedback to the participant and aids them in putting.

Input is only half the story of how a VR system interfaces with the human participant. For a participant to know how their input has affected the virtual world, they must be able to sense how the world looks, sounds, and perhaps feels. Chapter 4 details a number of display options, the relative advantages and disadvantages of different technologies, how display devices interact with each other, and other factors important in the selection of the most appropriate *output* device for a given VR application.

Virtual reality experience

User interface

Hardware interface to the user

Input
- Body tracking
  (How the computer "sees" the user)
- Voice/sound recognition
  (How the computer "hears" the user)
- Physical controllers
  (How the computer "feels" the user)

CHAPTER 3

Output
- Visual display
  (How the user sees the VW)
- Aural display
  (How the user hears the VW)
- Haptic display
  (How the user feels the VW)

CHAPTER 4

Software components

System presentation to the user
- Representation
- Rendering system

CHAPTER 5

User interaction with the virtual world
- Manipulation
- Navigation
- Shared Experience

CHAPTER 6

Experience design
CHAPTER 8

Virtual world
- Immersion
- Point of view
- Venue
- Simulation/physics
- Objects/denizens

CHAPTER 7

Life experience
- Memory
- Ability
- Past experience
- Emotional state
- Cultural background

CHAPTER 8

CHAPTER 4

Interface to the Virtual World— Output

A key component of a virtual reality experience is how the user *perceives* the environment. Their physical perception of the virtual world is based entirely on what the computer displays. We use the term *display* broadly to mean a method of presenting information to any of the senses. The human perceptual system has at least five senses providing information to the brain. Three of these senses—visual, aural, and haptic—are commonly presented with synthetic stimuli in a VR experience. VR systems fool the senses by output of computer-generated stimuli rather than natural stimuli to one or more of these senses.

We will not rank the importance of individual senses to the quality of a VR experience; however, we will say that the inclusion of additional senses almost always improves immersiveness. On the other hand, it is generally easier to implement a system that limits the number of sensory displays. In this chapter, we discuss the VR system's output display devices as directed toward the visual, aural, and haptic senses. We discuss the properties of visual, aural, and haptic displays and explore different modalities for each of them, including their components, features, and interface issues.

We will note display differences and similarities and the impact of display choice on application development decisions. For example, if it is necessary for the participant to see an appendage such as a hand in the application, then the designer must either choose a display that does not occlude (hide) the real hand or track the hand and represent it as an avatar. The choice of visual displays depends on the features most needed for the application and the environment in which the VR system will be housed.

There are three basic arrangements for all sensory displays: stationary, head-based, and hand-based. *Stationary* displays (like rear projection screens and audio speakers) are fixed in place. In a VR system, the output is rendered to reflect the changing position of the user's input sensory organs. *Head-based displays* (HBDs) are worn on or in some way attached to the user's head and move in conjunction with the head. Consequently, no matter which way the user turns their head, the displays move, remaining in a fixed position relative to the body's sensory inputs (in this case, their eyes and ears). Thus, visual screens remain in front of the user's eyes and headphones on their ears. HBDs work well for the sensory organs that are located on the head. *Hand-based displays* (such as palm-top style and glove devices) move in conjunction with the user's hand. Not all senses can receive stimuli from all types of displays.

Visual Displays

Most VR systems include some type of physically immersive visual display (FIG-URE 4-1). The head-mounted display (HMD) system is the most well known; however, it is not necessarily the best visual display for all types of applications. There are a variety of visual displays, each with unique characteristics and technologies for implementation.

We describe five categories of visual display stemming from our three display paradigms:

1. *Stationary displays*
   - Fishtank VR
   - Projection VR

2. *Head-based displays*
   - Occlusive HMDs
   - Nonocclusive HMDs

3. *Hand-based displays*
   - Palm VR

Visual Depth Cues

Before we can discuss visual displays, it will be helpful to have a basic understanding of how our eyes work and some familiarity with the terminology that we'll be using throughout this section on visual displays. Humans perceive information regarding the relative distance of objects in a host of ways; these indicators of distance are called *depth cues*. For the scope of our discussion, we will list the different depth cues and give a brief explanation of each. For those more interested in the subject, there are many books on human perception that can provide detailed information about how these cues work and their relationship to one another.

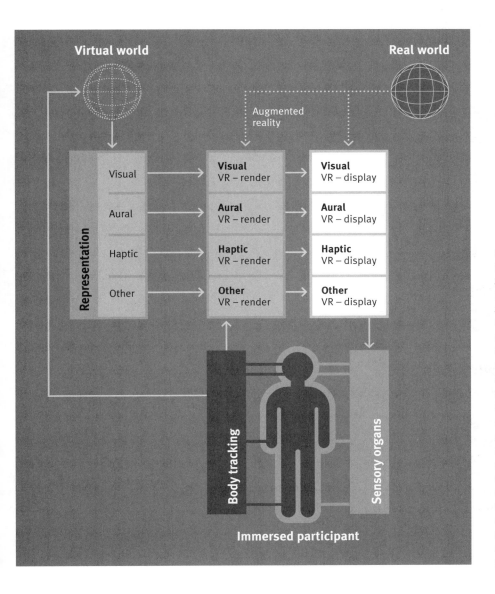

FIGURE 4-1 *This diagram depicts the flow of information in a VR system. Elements of the virtual world are mapped into representations appropriate for visual, aural, and haptic display. Body-tracking information is integrated with virtual world information to render displays from the point of view of the participant. Typically, body-tracking information (including button presses, grab gestures, etc.) feeds directly to the system that renders the various sensory displays. Tracking information is also fed to the virtual world to aid in determining collisions, selections, and other aspects of the world that are dependent on the participant's posture.*

In the sections that follow, we'll describe four varieties of visual depth cues, along with a dozen or so ways in which we can visually perceive relative distance. These are

1. Monoscopic image depth cues
   - Interposition
   - Shading
   - Size
   - Linear perspective
   - Surface texture gradient
   - Height in the visual field
   - Atmospheric effects
   - Brightness

2. Stereoscopic image depth cue (stereopsis)

3. Motion depth cues

4. Physiological depth cues
   - Accommodation
   - Convergence

Monoscopic Image Depth Cues

Monoscopic image depth cues are those that can be seen in a single static view of a scene, as in photographs and paintings (FIGURE 4-2). *Interposition* is the cue we receive when one object occludes our view of another. We've learned from experience that if one object masks another, then it is probably closer. *Shading* gives information about the shape of an object. Shadows are a form of shading that indicate the positional relationship between two objects. We compare the *size* of objects with respect to other objects of the same type to determine the relative distance between objects (i.e., the larger is presumed closer). We also compare the size of objects with our memory of similar objects to approximate how far away the object is from us.

Linear perspective is the observance that parallel lines converge at a single vanishing point. The use of this cue relies on the assumption that the object being viewed is constructed of parallel lines, such as most buildings, for instance. *Surface*

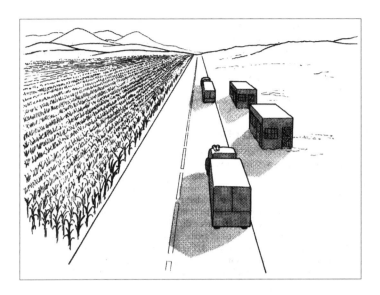

FIGURE 4-2 *This simple drawing provides a number of monoscopic image cues. Interposition and shadows help define the size and location of the buildings. Size, height in the visual field, and shadows provide geometric information about the trucks. We can observe from the road the linear perspective as it recedes from the observation point. The brightness of the road's center line as well as a texture gradient give clues about the stretch of road ahead. A texture gradient is also seen in the corn field. Haze in the atmosphere makes the observation of details of the mountains hard to discern (Image from Engineering Psychology and Human Performance 3/E by Wickens/Hollands, © 2000. Reprinted by permission of Pearson Education, Inc., Upper Saddle River, NJ).*

texture gradient is apparent because our retinas cannot discern as much detail of a texture at a distance as compared with up close. When standing in a grassy field, the high detail of the grass's texture at your feet changes to a blur of green in the distance.

Height in the visual field derives from the fact that the horizon is higher in the visual field than the ground near our feet; therefore, the further an object is from us, the higher it will appear in our view. *Atmospheric effects,* such as haze and fog, cause more distant objects to be visually less distinct. *Brightness* provides a moderate depth cue. Barring other information, brighter objects are perceived as being closer.

Stereoscopic Image Depth Cue (Stereopsis)

Stereopsis is derived from the parallax between the different images received by the retina in each eye (binocular disparity). The *stereoscopic image depth cue* depends on parallax, which is the apparent displacement of objects viewed from different locations. Stereopsis is particularly effective for objects within about 5 m. It is especially useful when manipulating objects within arms' reach.

Motion Depth Cues

Motion depth cues come from the parallax created by the changing relative position between the head and the object being observed (one or both may be in motion). Depth information is discerned from the fact that objects that are nearer to the eye will be perceived to move more quickly across the retina than more distant objects. Basically, the change in view can come about in two ways: the viewer moves or the object moves. When the viewer's body moves, they receive proprioceptive feedback telling them how far they moved. This information helps give a more precise determination of distance. Parallax from object movement or from non–self-propelled movement (e.g., riding in a car) does not afford as much information about the object's relative rate of movement as with viewer-originated movement (FIGURE 4-3). When viewers cannot determine the rate of the relative movement between themselves and the object, their judgment is less precise.

(A)

(B)

FIGURE 4-3 *The perception of depth of objects (and thus the 3D nature of the world) can be enhanced by the relative motion between the user and the world. This relative motion can be initiated by the user or perceived passively while riding in a vehicle. In this image, the user moves his head slightly to better understand the shape and relationship between the objects (Photograph by William Sherman).*

Physiological Depth Cues

Physiological depth cues are generated by the eye's muscle movements to bring an object into clear view. *Accommodation* is the focusing adjustment made by the eye to change the shape of its lens. The amount of muscular change provides distance information for objects within 2 or 3 m. *Convergence* is the movement of the eyes to bring an object into the same location on the retina of each eye. The muscle movements used for convergence provide information to the brain on the distance of objects in view.

Visual Depth Cues Summary

Not all depth cues have the same priority. Stereopsis is a very strong depth cue. When in conflict with other depth cues, stereopsis is typically dominant. Relative motion is perhaps the one depth cue that can be as strong or stronger than stereopsis. Of the static monoscopic image depth cues, interposition is the strongest. The physiological depth cues are perhaps the weakest. Accordingly, if one were to eliminate stereopsis by covering one eye, attempting to rely only on accommodation would be rather difficult [Wickens et al. 1989]. Some depth cues are ineffective beyond a certain range. The range of stereopsis extends about 5 m, and accommodation extends up to 3 m. So, for more distant objects, these cues have very low priority.

A VR designer can introduce depth cues as needed in an experience. Similar effects are used in animated cartoons. For instance, shadows are typically not employed when the character is walking on the ground. In the absence of a shadow, the viewer makes the assumption that the character is on the ground and therefore uses height in the visual field to determine the character's location. By introducing a shadow when the character leaves the ground, the animator indicates the character's height above the ground. This intermittent use of shadows is an example of the language of the medium that works between the animator and the audience.

Properties of Visual Displays

There are visual presentation and logistic properties associated with all visual display devices, but many of these properties vary from one display system to another. Perhaps the only thing all visual displays have in common is that each has a method for transmitting the visual image to the participant. The strengths and weaknesses among display methods can have an effect on the quality of the visuals themselves and on the ergonomic logistics of the hardware, as we summarize in the following two lists.

Visual Presentation Properties

- Color
- Spatial resolution
- Contrast
- Brightness
- Number of display channels
- Focal distance
- Opacity
- Masking
- Field of view
- Field of regard

- Head position information
- Graphics latency tolerance
- Temporal resolution (frame rate)

Logistic Properties
- User mobility
- Interface with tracking methods
- Environment requirements
- Associability with other sense displays
- Portability
- Throughput
- Encumbrance
- Safety
- Cost

Visual Presentation Properties of Visual Displays

The visual properties of a display device are a significant factor in the overall quality of a VR experience. Careful consideration of these optical properties must be made based on the requirements of the intended application. In general, each of these properties is a continuum; however, there is typically a tradeoff in monetary cost that must be measured against the needs of the participant's quality of experience. For example, the ability to see details such as the veins in the arm of a human form might be very important in a medical application but less so in a game world.

Color. The options for displaying *color* vary among display systems. Most displays provide trichromatic color (triplets of primary colors blended to create a range of colors), typically by combining red, green, and blue sources. Monochromatic displays are also available, though they are less common. Monochromatic displays are sometimes preferable in augmented reality systems, because they can be brighter and have more contrast. Greater brightness allows the user to better see the data augmenting the real world.

For trichromatic displays, a single color can be created by placing specific combinations of the three colors in very close groups. Another method overlays the three colors in the same location and displays each color at separate times. This approach is known as *field-sequential color display*. Field sequential displays provide a much clearer image when viewed from very close range.

Spatial Resolution. A visual display's *spatial resolution* is often given by the number of pixels, or dots, presented in the horizontal and vertical directions. One way to measure resolution is the number of dots per inch (dpi). The size of the screen also affects how well the pixels blend together—that is, how discernible the individual dots are. A smaller screen with a given number of pixels will look much crisper than a larger screen with the same number of pixels (FIGURE 4-4).

    The distance from the eye to the screen also affects perceived resolution. In head-based displays, the screens are usually very close to the eyes; thus the pixels must be very dense to become indistinguishable. In a stationary display, as the viewer changes location and distance, the apparent resolution will vary.

    The type of technology used in a particular display also affects resolution. Liquid crystal display (LCD) technology, common in laptop and flat panel desktop monitors, often has lower pixel densities than standard cathode ray tube displays (CRTs, or the typical television picture tube) of the same size and in the same price range. Field sequential CRTs—similar to standard CRTs with the added ability to overlap colors and provide crisper images—can display even higher pixel density.

Contrast. *Contrast* is a measure of the relative difference between light and dark. A high contrast range makes it easier to distinguish the various components of the displayed information (i.e., they stand out more). The amount of contrast varies among display technologies and devices. LCDs tend to be low contrast, whereas CRT displays can provide much higher contrast. There are other qualities against which contrast must be balanced, including field of view, cost, weight, and safety. Displays such as field sequential CRTs, with their higher pixel densities, also help increase the apparent contrast by allowing colors to change rapidly between neighboring pixels.

Brightness. *Brightness* is the measure of overall light output from a display source. A high level of brightness is desirable in any visual display, but there are some technologies for which brightness is a critical factor. Images projected onto a screen, for example, become dimmer as the size of the screen increases and the light is spread over a larger surface. See-through augmented reality displays require brighter displays so that the information stands out with respect to the real-world view.

(A)

(B)

(C)

(D)
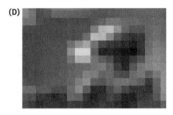

FIGURE 4-4 *This image illustrates the effect of differing levels of spatial resolution on an image. In general, higher resolution conveys more information but requires more computing power, displays with higher spatial resolution, and higher bandwidth connections from computer to display (Photograph by Tony Baylis).*

Number of Display Channels. The *number of simultaneous channels* (or paths of information) of a visual display is usually two. A visual display channel is a presentation of visual information displayed for one eye. Two visual display channels with separate views are required to achieve stereopsis, or visual 3D effects (FIGURE 4-5). The brain fuses the pair of images into a single stereoscopic image. There are a number of ways to achieve a 3D stereoscopic visual display. Multiplexing permits the simultaneous transmission of two or more signals through the same channel. Different visual multiplexing methods can transmit two image signals simultaneously to create a stereoscopic display.

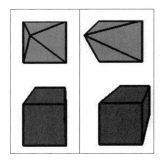

FIGURE 4-5 *Here, two separate visual channels are rendered, providing a stereoscopic image to the viewer. The left image is presented to the viewer's left eye, and the right image to the viewer's right eye.*

Spatial multiplexing consists of positioning separate images in front of each eye, either by using two small separate screens or by using a filter to separate the views. Temporal multiplexing, or time interlacing, presents different images for each eye using *shutter glasses,* which shutter the view for one eye (in a coordinated, timed sequence) to prevent it from seeing the other eye's view. The normally opaque lens shutters become transparent for one of the eyes during the time the proper view for that eye is presented.

Polarization multiplexing is accomplished by overlaying two separate image sources filtered through oppositely polarized filters—for example, by displaying one channel through a horizontally polarized filter and the other through a vertically polarized filter. The participant wears a pair of glasses with a horizontal polarized filter over one eye and a vertical polarized filter over the other; each eye sees only the information intended for it.

Spectral multiplexing, or *anaglyphic stereo,* displays the view for each eye in a different color. Special glasses neutralize the view for the incorrect eye, because each lens correlates to one of the colored views and in effect washes it out. You might recall from childhood those glasses with one green plastic lens and one red one (FIGURE 4-6).

You can actually have more than two channels if more than one viewer requires an independent stereoscopic display, but as we've said most systems only have two channels. What's more, the presence of two channels does not always indicate that a stereoscopic image is being presented. A stereoscopic (3D) image consists of two *distinct* views of the virtual world, each specific for a particular eye. Some systems display a single (monoscopic, or 2D) view to both eyes and are called *binocular monoscopic* displays. It is important to note that the focal and convergence depth cues can still be controlled in binocular monoscopic displays through the use of optics and image offsets.

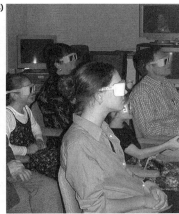

FIGURE 4-6 **(A)** *An early (and inexpensive) form of viewing 3D images utilized red/green (anaglyphic) stereo glasses to provide a 3D viewing experience.* **(B)** *Today, shuttering glasses provide a higher quality, albeit more expensive, 3D technology (Photographs by William Sherman).*

There are some uses for monocular (single-eye) displays in virtual reality. In particular, they are useful for augmented reality displays, where the augmented view is presented to only one eye.

Creating good stereoscopic displays is difficult, and doing it improperly can cause distress in the viewer (which often takes the form of headaches or nausea). Rendering stereoscopic images takes about twice the computational resources, requiring either twice the graphics hardware, a reduction in frame-rate, or a reduction in image complexity.

How useful stereopsis is to the task at hand is another primary factor in determining whether to display images stereoscopically. For tasks that require close-up, hands-on manipulation, stereopsis is beneficial and sometimes required. Stereopsis is much less important for tasks in which the primary view of the world is from a distance of 5 m or more [Cutting and Vishton 1995].

Some projected VR displays, in which two users will be viewing the same screen, offer four-channel visual display (e.g., the Fakespace *DuoView* product). This is generally accomplished by multiplexing four separate views—one for each eye (for each participant). Another technique to create four channels combines spectral and temporal multiplexing; for example, participant A wears one pair of shutter glasses with a green filter over both eyes and participant B wears another pair with red filters. This combined time and spectral multiplexing produces four channels: a left and right eye view for two participants. This allows two people to be tracked in a stationary VR system so that each receives their own personal 3D view of the world.

A single display using filters can allow each eye to see a different image without the need to wear any eyegear. This is considered an *autostereo* display, because the user can see the stereoscopic display without wearing any devices. One product, the *SynthaGram Monitor* from StereoGraphics Corporation, uses an LCD panel as the primary visual display and an integrated lenticular lens placed over the LCD panel to ensure that each eye sees the correct image. The result is that the viewer is able to see stereoscopic imagery from that display without the use of any encumbering technology.

Autostereoscopic displays are still in the early phase of research and development and have not yet been widely applied in VR systems. Two promising methods still in the experimental phase involve the use of holograms and volumetric displays.

Focal Distance. The *focal distance* of a display is the apparent distance of the images from the viewer's eyes. With current display technology, all images in a scene are on the same focal plane regardless of their virtual distance from the viewer. The eye muscles adjust for the focal distance of objects by reshaping the lenses of the viewer's eyes. The use of the eye muscles to determine focal distance is called *accommodation*.

Generally, our ability to judge depth is much weaker at a distance than close up. Beyond 3 m, little relative depth information can be gained using focal accommodation, and depth perception becomes a product of many different cues. When you watch something move from one position to another at a great distance, your eye muscles move very little to accommodate the change. On the other hand, if you are looking at something close up and you move it, your eye muscles move a fair amount to refocus on the object. All of the other cues we listed earlier under Visual Depth Cues—interposition, shading, size, linear perspective, and so on—are more important for depth perception at a distance. Think about looking at a group of hot-air balloons aloft in the distance. It is difficult to tell which is closest to you. Only if one balloon passes in front of another do you get a sense of relative position.

Incongruity between depth perception cues causes conflict in visual perception. This conflict can lead to headaches and nausea in the viewer. Confusion of depth perception cues can cause objects to have an ethereal appearance, which causes some people to reach out with their hands to touch the object.

Let's take an example (FIGURE 4-7): for virtual objects that appear to be located at or near the surface plane of a VR display screen, the depth perception cues will match, because the focal distance for the objects is right at the screen. If the screen is 4 feet away from you, the focal distance is 4 feet. Your brain tells you that

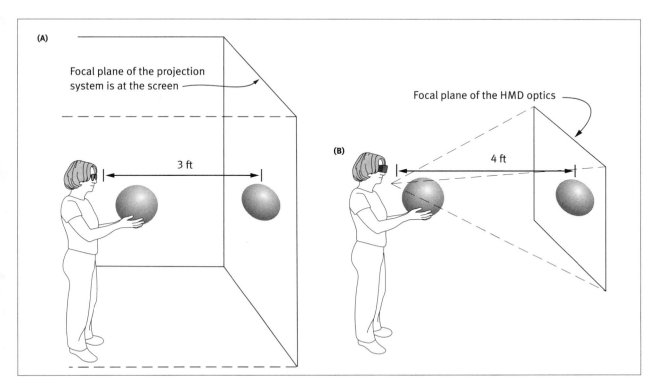

(A)

Focal plane of the projection system is at the screen

Focal plane of the HMD optics

(B)

3 ft

4 ft

FIGURE 4-7 *Focal distance is the measurement between the participant's eyes and the virtual image. In a projection display* (A) *the focal distance is usually the distance to the display screen (e.g., 3 ft. in this diagram). HBD optics* (B) *create a virtual image at some distance beyond the physical display (e.g., 4 ft. in this diagram).*

the focal distance for an object that is drawn so as to appear right on the screen is indeed 4 feet. Stereopsis, perspective, and other visual cues all confirm this perception and are thus in agreement. This creates a stronger sense that those objects actually exist.

On the other hand, if the object is drawn to appear as though it is between you and the screen (say, 2 feet from you), the focal distance cue still tells you the object is at 4 feet. However, stereopsis, perspective, and your other visual senses tell you the object is at 2 feet, resulting in visual conflict. In a head-mounted display, focal distance is controlled by the HBD optics; however, no currently marketed display allows the focus to be automatically adjusted by the VR system.

Opacity. There are two basic options for the *opacity* of a visual display. The display can hide, or occlude, the physical world from view or it can include the physical world. Stationary screen and desktop displays cannot mask out the real world and thus are nonopaque; that is, the rest of the world can still be seen. Most, but not all, head-based displays are opaque and thus occlude the outside world from the user.

The opacity of the display affects both the safety and the collaborative potential of a VR system. Occlusive displays can be dangerous, because the user can trip over something in the real world that they cannot see. Precautions must therefore be taken in how the venue is arranged. Communication between the participant and nearby onlookers is also reduced, because the display acts to isolate the participant from the real world. This isolation results in less dialog between the immersed participant and the rest of the group, which can be detrimental to applications for which open discussion is important.

Some head-mounted displays provide a view of the real world combined with the virtual world. Often referred to as a see-through HMD, this type of display is generally used for augmented reality [Rolland, Holloway, and Fuchs 1994].

Masking. In stationary displays, physical objects such as the user's hand occlude, or *mask,* virtual objects. This is quite acceptable when the hand is closer than the virtual object, in which case the hand should block the object from view. However, masking becomes a problem when a virtual object comes between the viewer's eyes and a physical object. In this case, the virtual object should occlude the hand, but it doesn't.

See-through head-based systems are able to mask part of the real world. Masking is necessary when virtual objects come between some physical object and the viewer's eyes or when a physical object should appear in front of a virtual object. At times, a viewer should see a virtual object occlude a physical object. To do this, one simply renders the complete virtual object and the physical object will not be seen. On the other hand, a physical object positioned such that it *should* mask some virtual object can easily be addressed: one simply doesn't render the virtual object in the region where the physical object should be visible. This assumes that the location of the physical object is known by the computer rendering system. To solve this problem, the computer needs to track physical objects that are likely to be in positions where they would mask virtual objects.

In occlusive head-based displays, none of this is a concern, because all visible objects are rendered by the computer system, even if they represent some real-world physical object located in the VR venue.

Field of View. The normal horizontal *field of view* (FOV) for a human is approximately 200 degrees, with 120 degrees of binocular overlap [Klymento and Rash 1995]. The display's field of view is a measure of the angular width of a user's vision that is

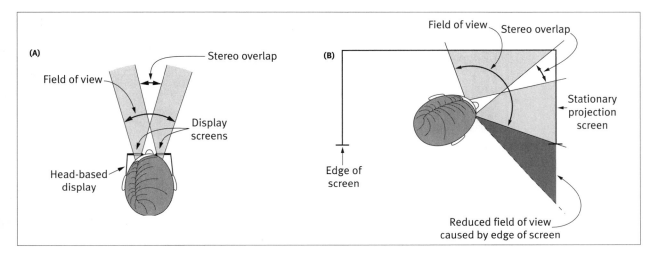

covered by the display at any given time (FIGURE 4-8). In a three-sided *CAVE*, the field of view is 100% when the user faces forward; when the user turns and the open side of the CAVE impinges on the view, the display's field of view is reduced. The measurement can be a percentage of the user's visual field or can be the display's angles of horizontal and vertical coverage. A display with 60 degrees of horizontal FOV provides the equivalent of tunnel vision; this is found in some head-based displays that provide high resolution (high pixel density) at the expense of FOV. Displays that provide 100–120 degrees FOV begin to cover a reasonable portion of the human visual range. However, as an indicator of quality this number alone can be somewhat misleading. The stereo overlap FOV is quite important. Stereo overlap can vary in HMDs in which the two screens are more or less widely separated. If the overlapping FOV for both eyes is as small as 30 degrees, it will be difficult to perceive stereopsis. One major advantage of large projection displays is the larger field of view.

Field of Regard. A display's *field of regard* (FOR) is the amount of space surrounding the user that is filled with the virtual world or, in other words, how much the viewer is enveloped by the visuals (FIGURE 4-9). For example, in head-based displays with unlimited range of motion, the FOR is 100%, because the screens are always in front of the users' eyes. No matter which direction the viewers look, the virtual world is displayed in front of their eyes. For stationary displays, however, the FOR is usually less than 100%, because the virtual world cannot be displayed in the space without screens.

FIGURE 4-8 *Display field of view is the amount of the viewer's visual field covered by a display. Head-based displays* **(A)** *tend to have smaller, fixed FOV angles compared with those possible in projection-based displays* **(B)***; although, when the viewer turns their head in a projection display, they may lose a partial view of the screen, effectively reducing their FOV. The area of stereo overlap is important to note and take advantage of when rendering stereoscopic visual images.*

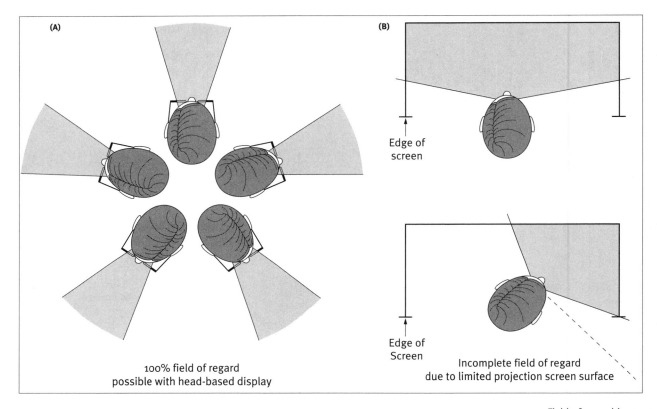

(A)

Edge of screen

100% field of regard possible with head-based display

(B)

Edge of screen

Edge of Screen

Incomplete field of regard due to limited projection screen surface

FIGURE 4-9 *Field of regard is a measure of the amount of coverage a given display provides when head motion and other factors are considered.* **(A)** *Head-based displays can easily provide a 100% FOR, whereas* **(B)** *stationary displays are limited to the area of the screens.*

The FOR is independent of the field of view. You can have a very narrow field of view in a head-mounted display and still have 100% field of regard, because you can look in all directions and see the virtual world (albeit through a narrow field of view). On the other hand, you can have a 1,000 ft. × 1,000 ft. display screen (which gives you a very wide FOV) but a very limited FOR (unless the screen wraps around you), because if you face away from the screen, you can't see the virtual world. The only way to get 100% FOR in a projection-based system is to completely surround the users with screens. This creates the logistic problem of having to create a screen that participants can stand on or somehow providing a means for users to "hover" inside the display. (Surrounding the user with screens has been done at some VR facilities, such as the Royal Institute of Technology in Stockholm, Sweden.)

In displays with a less than complete FOR, stereopsis can be lost when a nearby object is only partially in the display. Partially viewed objects that are (virtually) behind the screen are not a problem, because they would naturally be occluded by the edges of the screen (which acts as the proscenium). Problems arise when a virtual object located between the screen and the viewer is cut off by the edge of the screen (compare FIGURES 4-10 and 4-11). The depth cues of stereopsis and motion parallax conflict with the depth cue of occlusion, which indicates that the object must

FIGURE 4-10 *The effect of the boy appearing to be closer to the user than the screen is spoiled, because he crosses the boundary created by the structure of the VR display device (Photograph by William Sherman).*

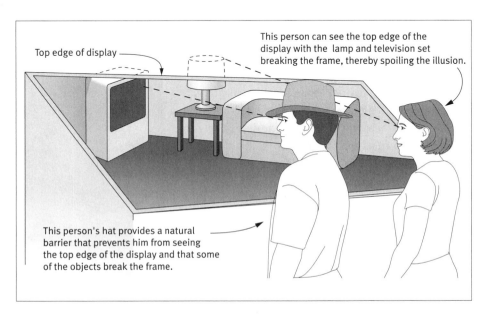

This person can see the top edge of the display with the lamp and television set breaking the frame, thereby spoiling the illusion.

Top edge of display

This person's hat provides a natural barrier that prevents him from seeing the top edge of the display and that some of the objects break the frame.

FIGURE 4-11 *When the user can see the edge of the display, the frame is broken and the illusion of being surrounded by the virtual world is reduced. One solution is to have the user wear a hat, which naturally limits their upper sight line. They cannot see the top of the screen and won't notice when virtual objects (like the television and lamp) are inelegantly lopped off at the top, whereas the user without a hat has a less immersive experience.*

be behind the screen. This problem is referred to as *breaking the frame.* (Breaking the frame is also a concern with other stereoscopic display media, such as 3D movies and the children's stereoscope product, the *GAF Viewmaster.*)

The general occlusion problem can be solved by having the virtual world simulation avoid the condition in the first place. Since the system is capable of locating the position of the viewer and, most likely, the location of control devices and the frame of the screen as well, the simulation can be written in such a way as to keep virtual objects from coming between the physical objects and the viewer in the first place. The breaking the frame problem can be reduced by positioning the object in question so that it naturally hides the frame (or part of the frame).

Head Position Information. As we discussed in the Position Tracking section of Chapter 3, some tracking methods are only capable of determining a subset of an object's complete 6-DOF position in the world. In those cases, the subset is typically either the object's 3-DOF location *or* the object's 3-DOF orientation. While complete positional information is beneficial to producing accurate views of the virtual world, different visual displays rely more heavily on different subsets of positional information.

In the case of stationary visual displays (projection and fishtank), calculations to produce an accurate view are based on the location of the eyes with respect to the screen. In fact, the direction the eye is looking is unimportant to this calculation; the location of the eye is all that matters. Because the location of the eyes can be approximated from the location of the head, the 3-DOF location of the user's head is more important than orientation for stationary displays.

However, for proper stereoscopic viewing of stationary displays, full 6-DOF tracking information is required, because calculating the location of each eye individually requires information about how the head is oriented. A small monitor (fishtank) display might provide an acceptable rendering by making some assumptions about the viewer's head orientation. These kinds of assumptions are less likely to succeed in larger systems. It is important to remember that when multiple people view a large-screen stereoscopic display, stereopsis is calculated based on tracking just one particular person; therefore, if that person's head rotates, then the other participants will experience improper stereoscopic cues, which can lead to eye fatigue.

In the case of head-based visual displays, head orientation is the most important positional cue for proper scene rendering. For example, when we turn our head to the left, we expect to see what is to the left of us. Without orientation tracking, the system won't know when we turn our head. Our view of the world doesn't change very much when our heads move only a few inches, especially if most of the objects in view are far away. Because virtual reality applications that use HMDs are often encumbered by cables and such, they limit how far a user can physically travel; a few inches is often the limit. It is common for these applications to augment the user's ability to travel in the virtual world with a variety of input devices.

Hand-based displays use head position data in much the same way as stationary VR displays. Again, the user's head does not have a fixed relationship to the screen. As with fishtank displays, hand-based displays can provide an acceptable rendering by using assumptions about the user's head orientation. As with stationary displays, calculating the vector from head to handheld screen requires a knowledge of screen position. Because of their portability, hand-based screens need to be tracked to monitor their position in relationship to the head. User location is the most important factor, but input on head position helps to orient the image display in respect to the angle from which it is being viewed.

It is easy to tell if rotating a head-mounted display results in the appropriate rotation of the rendered scene. However, when testing the tracked glasses of a stationary display, things move differently depending on whether they are on the near or far side of the screen. What's more, they don't move at all if they are virtually located on (i.e., coincident with) the screen. The effects of head movement on a stationary display image can seem counterintuitive. This provides particular challenges for projection-based displays.

An object in the virtual world changes on the screen in one of three ways based on its relative location to the user and the screen (FIGURE 4-12):

1. If the virtual object appears to be located on one of the physical screens, then it will not move relative to the screen no matter how much the tracked head moves.

2. If the virtual object appears to be on the near side of a screen, then it will move along the screen in the opposite direction of the tracked head.

3. If the virtual object appears to be on the other side of the screen, it will move in the same direction. If a virtual object is considerably far away on the other side of the screen, then it will appear to move in exact correspondence with the tracked head.

We refer to this as the *moon effect,* because the farther an object is from the viewer, the more it seems to follow them, just like the moon. This occurs because

FIGURE 4-12 *Objects rendered on a stationary display respond differently to the user's movement, depending on which side of the screen the objects appear to be located. Here, when the participant moves from in front of the left window pane to the right, the floor lamp (a close-up object) appears to move in the opposite direction; whereas, the moon (representing a distant object) seems to follow the user.*

the relationship between the viewer and the object is not altered significantly when the viewer moves, but the two are separated by great distances.

Graphics Latency Tolerance. Most VR systems suffer from some amount of lag time between user movements and the update of the display. The amount of apparent lag, or *latency,* varies among displays. Latency is another cause of stress on the viewer's perceptual system, which often manifests itself as nausea or headaches. Nausea often occurs when users turn their heads, and the view before their eyes lags behind the motion of their head.

Latency is more apparent in some displays than in others. In a stationary display like the *CAVE* the view is already drawn; you just don't see it until you turn and look at it. This is especially true in a multiwall stationary display like a *CAVE,* in which you compute and display a lot of the scene that *may* never be viewed. The payoff here is that the image is already visible on the side screen when the user turns their head.

In an HBD, there is no preexisting side image, so the user must wait for the computer to draw a new view when they turn their head. Computing and drawing only what is actually being viewed saves on computer and display resources but at the cost of the introduced lag. Thus, a tradeoff exists between cost and immediacy. Graphics latency tolerance is much lower for augmented reality systems, because high latency causes the view of the real world to lose sync with the virtual world images.

Temporal Resolution (Frame Rate). The rate at which images are displayed is called the *frame rate* and is reported as the number of frames per second (FPS); the same measurement can be expressed in Hertz, which is a unit of frequency generally representing occurrences per second. Frame rate is generally not a function of the type of visual display used but of the ability of the graphics rendering hardware and software and the visual complexity of the virtual world.

The frame rate can have a great effect on mental immersion. Certain frame rates can be used as standards, but faster is better, of course. Modern motion picture film captures 24 frames per second or 24 Hz; standard video is 30 Hz. Twenty-four frames per second for a movie is adequate in most cases, but to realistically capture something very fast (like a hummingbird flying), you need a higher temporal resolution. Above 30 FPS is very good, although some VR experience developers have attained twice that rate [Pausch et al. 1996]. A rate of 15 Hz is considered marginally acceptable, although rates of 15 Hz and below can cause nausea in some viewers. Below 10 Hz, the brain begins to perceive the stream of images as a sequence of individual images, rather than as continuous motion.

Logistic Properties of Visual Displays

In addition to visual display specifications, there are a number of logistical factors related to displays used in various applications. A *CAVE* requires a significant amount of physical space to house the projectors, mirrors, and other devices. This floor space requirement is a constraint in smaller venues. In contrast, a typical head-based display requires very little in the way of floor space. However, the weight, opacity, number of attached cables, and other specifics may prove more or less appealing in different situations. These are logistical concerns that have nothing to do with the actual visual output of the display, but nevertheless affect the user's experience. This section addresses many of the common, practical concerns with different types of visual displays.

User Mobility. *Mobility* can affect both the immersiveness and usefulness of a user's VR experience. Most visual displays place certain constraints on the user. These constraints come in the form of cables tethering the user to the system, tracking systems with limited range, and stationary displays that do not allow the user to move beyond the location of the display. The increasingly widespread availability of portable computers foreshadows the availability of portable virtual and augmented reality displays.

Interface with Tracking Methods. The type of visual display can also influence the selection of *tracking methods*. Many tracking systems have an operating range of only a few feet and require the use of cables, which limit a user's movement. Visual displays, which carry their own constraints to user movement, can use any of these tracking systems without adding further constraints if the system is put together with these inherent limitations in mind. For instance, a mobile VR display would require a mobile tracking system with a very large operating range.

Most head-based displays have specific points for mounting a tracking system. Some consumer-oriented HBDs have simple tracking technology built into the display itself; for example, some systems have built-in accelerometers that provide orientation-only tracking. However, mounting common tracking systems onto stereoscopic glasses can be more difficult. Some shutter glasses can be purchased with built-in microphones for ultrasonic tracking. This combination works well for a desktop VR display but not for larger surround-screen projected VR, because of the range limitations of this type of ultrasonic tracking. A magnetic tracker receiver must be carefully placed on HBDs or shutter glasses containing electronics to avoid interference caused by the electronics.

Environment Requirements. The *environment* in which the VR system is used can affect the choice of visual display. For instance, projection-based displays generally require a low-light environment so that the projected images can be seen more easily. An opaque head-based system shrouds the user's head; therefore, background lighting is less important. Of course, the environment needs to be lit sufficiently so that people can move safely and freely about the room. The size of the venue can also limit which displays are appropriate. To take an extreme example, a training system used onboard a submarine obviously needs to fit in a small, enclosed space.

Associability with Other Sense Displays. Although we have contained our discussion of display logistics to each of the senses, in the applied world there are issues of *associability* between multiple senses and the display. For example, head-based visual displays make using head-based aural displays an easy extension. With a stationary visual display, use of a stationary speaker system is more common, although use of headphones is certainly a possibility. With a speaker system, the sound quality of 3D spatialization is more difficult to implement, especially when we consider the logistics of the stationary visual display system on the acoustics. The complexity of haptic display systems is likely to put constraints on the visual display; this is particularly true of stationary haptic displays that have a limited operational area.

Portability. The importance of *portability* depends on who will be using the VR system and how far the system will have to travel. The smaller head-mounted and handheld displays are clearly easy to transport and simple to set up with the attachment of a few cables. Large projection displays require a theater-like production effort to take on the road. It takes days to assemble a *CAVE,* align its projectors, and verify the entire system is functioning properly (FIGURE 4-13). Another day is needed to pack everything back up. When the time for local disassembly and reassembly plus travel time are considered, taking a *CAVE* on the road can mean several weeks of disruption at the home site.

Potential disruption was a motivating factor in the development of the ImmersaDesk, a smaller projection-based VR display that folds up into a wheeled structure that fits through doorways, can be easily pushed down hallways, and loaded onto a truck. The ImmersaDesk II is constructed in a flight case that will fit in the cargo hold of commercial air carriers.

FIGURE 4-13 *Assembling a* CAVE *is a complicated task, requiring several people over a span of about three days (Photographs courtesy of Tom Coffin).*

(A)

(B)

Kiosk-style displays are often used for VR systems designed to travel from venue to venue. While kiosks may still require semitrailers or specially designed trucks for transportation, a good kiosk display will require minimal setup time once unloaded and moved into place. Hiram Walker Distillers created a traveling VR experience to raise product awareness of their Cutty Sark whiskey (see FIGURE 3-11).

Throughput. The display's effect on *throughput* (the number of people able to partake in an experience in a given amount of time) should be considered in relation to the type of venue in which a VR system will be used. For instance, it takes longer to put on and take off most head-mounted displays than it does for most other visual displays. In public venues, where throughput is a particular concern, the amount of time required to suit up and unsuit can be an important factor when choosing a display device.

Encumbrance. Head-based displays of the mounted variety tend to have more encumbrances than other visual displays. Stationary display systems don't have these encumbrances. A head-mounted display also weighs considerably more than a pair of glasses. The longer a heavy device is worn, the more tired the users will become. Further, HMDs usually require cables to carry the video and audio signals to and from the display. Tracking systems often have cables as well, so HMDs have a large cable burden. Cables limit the movement of the user, allowing them to walk only a short distance or rotate no more than one full turn.

Neither HMDs nor the shuttering glasses associated with most stationary displays fit all users' heads, although they are designed to fit the majority of adult heads. These devices present a particular problem when the primary audience is children. It is hard to find HMDs or shutter glasses that fit a child's head well.

The Fakespace *BOOM* and other displays that use a mechanical linkage are designed to give the benefits of head-based displays (e.g., high resolution and brightness) but still allow users to engage or disengage from the viewing device with ease. In the future, glasses will probably replace head-mounted devices in HBDs, solving many of the existing encumbrances of HMDs, although there will still be cable requirements, at least initially.

Safety. There are many *safety* issues involved with visual displays. The most obvious problem in wearing an HBD is tripping over real-world objects. Eye fatigue can be a problem; the longer you stare at any screen without resting your eyes, the greater the ill effects. Eye strain can be more significant for HBDs, because they do not afford much opportunity for wearers to rest their eyes. The weight of the display can lead to neck fatigue and strain.

It is difficult to perform long-term analysis of extended use of possibly hazardous devices. One concern about using HBDs with cathode ray tube (CRTs) mounted on the side is the possible long-term effect of having high-voltage electromagnetic devices near the brain for extended periods of time.

Nausea is a potential short-term effect of viewing VR displays (especially using HBDs). In addition to the disparity of depth perception cues, nausea can result from the lag between head movement and scene update. Another safety concern is short-term effects on vision and balance that can temporarily impair a participant's ability to drive, including dizziness, blurred vision, and vertigo. An interesting phenomenon can occur once your body acclimates to the lag in the system, or to the offset of the visual input when using a video see-through system. When you leave the VR environment, your body is still accounting for that lag/offset for a period of time. This can lead to impairment of your temporal/spatial judgment. The U.S. Navy has a test that can be administered to verify whether a user has the capacity for operating a vehicle following exposure to such effects [Kennedy et al. 1993].

Cost. The *cost* of visual displays varies greatly. HBDs tend to be lower priced than large-screen projection systems (similar to movie screens, computer monitors, and projection-TV–like devices). In general, a head-based display is cheaper than a stationary display of comparable quality. In reality, when you are doing stationary VR, it is with multiple screens using multiple rear projectors. Projectors that are capable of time-interlaced stereo display are very expensive. Although projectors have uses besides VR displays, they are generally more expensive to manufacture than low-end HMDs, which make use of consumer technology such as small LCD screens designed for portable TVs and small CRT displays used for camcorder viewfinders.

Nevertheless, there is a wide range in cost and quality in HBDs. Most of the tradeoffs among displays arise from the amount of available resolution, field of view, contrast, and durability. For example, HBDs that use small CRTs with NTSC resolution (the same resolution as standard television video) are more reasonably priced and widely available, because of the camcorder's mass market. However, for mega-pixel resolution with high-contrast field sequential CRTs, the market is much smaller and the cost considerably higher.

Projection-based displays are often most costly, because they need multiple projectors to create a surround-screen display and/or to produce left and right eye views for stereoscopic display using polarized glasses. The large space required to cast an image from the projector onto the screen also raises the expense. For some organizations, adequate space can be more difficult to acquire than money.

Now that we have covered the qualities that differentiate visual display devices from one another, we can look at the five major visual display types:

1. Fishtank

2. Projection

3. Head-based (Occlusive)

4. Nonocclusive head-based

5. Handheld

Monitor-based—or Fishtank—VR

The simplest form of VR visual display utilizes a standard computer monitor and is called monitor-based VR, or more often, *fishtank VR.*

The name *fishtank* comes from the similarity of looking through an aquarium glass to observe the 3D world inside (FIGURE 4-14). Viewers can move their heads from side to side and up and down to see around, over, and under objects, but they cannot actually enter the space. This is the norm in fishtank VR; however, since this is *virtual* reality, the creator needn't adhere to this constraint—objects can be displayed on the other (near) side of the screen! When this is done, care must be taken to avoid the screen edge cutting off these objects and breaking the frame. (Recall from the Field of Regard section that breaking the frame ruins

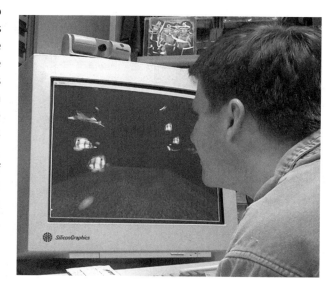

FIGURE 4-14 *Fishtank VR (monitor-based) provides a display paradigm that is similar to peering into a fishtank. The participant is able to see and look about a 3D world that appears to exist within the confines of the monitor (Photograph by William Sherman).*

our illusion of the stereoscopic depth cue by breaking the rules of occlusion from the natural world.)

Fishtank VR differs from generic interactive 3D graphics displayed on a monitor, because a VR system tracks the user's head, and the rendered scene changes in response to the tracked head movement. The fishtank paradigm is classified as *stationary display VR* because, even though a computer monitor is somewhat portable, it is unlikely that the monitor itself would move during use.

Components of Fishtank VR

A fishtank VR display requires only a few components in addition to the computer. A standard computer monitor is usually adequate, but sometimes a different setup is required for better resolution or displaying stereoscopic images. Sometimes a multi-screen approach is desirable, requiring not only more screens but more computer power.

Tracking is an important part of any VR display. A benefit of single-screen stationary displays is that the orientation of the viewer's head is less important than its *location* for appropriate scene rendering. Because one can assume that a user is looking at the monitor in a fishtank VR system, a monitor-top video camera can be used to perform user head tracking (which you may have noticed in FIGURE 4-14). Image processing is used to determine the location of the user's head. Other tracking technologies can also be employed with fishtank systems, but this type of tracking approximation allows the use of less expensive and cumbersome tracking devices, like a video camera, which might already be part of the computer system.

Another important component of fishtank VR is the use of binocular stereoscopic display. The standard method of generating a stereoscopic view on a monitor display is with shutter glasses that use liquid crystal display (LCD) lenses. Alternatively, it is possible to use a special filter over the monitor screen to create an autostereo effect, eliminating the need to wear glasses. Most autostereo displays currently require the user to remain directly in front of the screen, thereby restricting the user's range of movement.

Features of Fishtank VR

Because it requires few components other than a basic computer capable of displaying 3D interactive computer graphics, fishtank VR is the least expensive of the visual VR display paradigms. Most of its technology is mass produced, making it cheap and readily available. Even the necessary stereoscopic display hardware is widely available. It is also easy to suit up for fishtank VR. Typical stereo glasses are not much more difficult to put on than standard eyeglasses. This is especially true if the tracking is done using a video camera or is embedded in the glasses.

The drawbacks of this visual display method are twofold: the user must face in a particular direction to see the virtual world, and the system is generally less immersive than most other VR systems. Decreased immersiveness arises because the real world takes up most of the viewer's field of regard and only a small region is filled by the virtual world. Of course, it can certainly provide an accurate representation of a world that is something like a real fishtank; then, too, people may become engaged in watching a real fishtank but they probably seldom feel immersed (so to speak).

Interface Issues of Fishtank VR

Since fishtank VR is generally an extension of a simple desktop computer setup, it has at its disposal many of the same interface devices. The real world is still visible to users, so a keyboard is still practical. The same applies for the standard mouse, trackball, or 6-DOF pressure stick (e.g., the Spacetec Spaceball). Other physical controls are also easy to see and interact with, but there is a tradeoff in immersiveness since the user is always aware of the "frame" of the virtual world, which makes these devices seem like external controls acting on the world as opposed to tools within the world.

We've discussed the importance of having stereoscopic depth cues, and these cues are satisfied with fishtank VR. Other important 3D cues come from observing changes in the scene when we move our heads (motion parallax cues). While motion parallax cues are present in fishtank VR, they are certainly more limited than with display models that allow the user to walk all the way around virtual objects. For applications where the goal is to get a feel for the space, the inability to physically "walk about" that space makes fishtank VR a less acceptable option.

Summary of Fishtank VR

Fishtank VR provides an inexpensive, unobtrusive means of creating a fairly compelling virtual world on a workstation screen. For applications in which the metaphor of peering through a window is appropriate, this paradigm can provide an effective experience. It is also a good means for testing VR applications that are under development. It is relatively inexpensive, easy to use, and has higher visual resolution than low-cost HMDs. On the downside, it is less immersive than most other VR visual displays, providing only a limited field of regard.

Projection-based VR

Projection-based visual displays are stationary devices. The screen may be much larger than the typical fishtank VR display, thereby filling more of the participants' fields of view and regard and allowing them to roam more freely. The size of the display influences the interface to the virtual world. Although large display walls can be created by setting several CRT monitors side by side, projection systems can create frameless adjoining displays, making the scene more seamless. Most projection VR systems are rear-projected to avoid the participants casting shadows on the screen.

In the future, rear-projection screens and projectors will likely be replaced by large, flat monitors (flat panel displays) thin enough to hang against a wall. Flat panel displays have higher resolution, require less maintenance, and take up less room than typical rear-projected systems. They do not require the additional projector or the distance between the projector and the screen necessary in rear-projected systems. However, projectors and screens will continue to be more economical than flat panel displays for some time to come.

Projection-based VR displays are not usually the display paradigm that leaps to mind when most people discuss virtual reality. As we discussed in Chapter 1 in our brief history of VR, head-based displays were the first method used to put a viewer into another world [Sutherland 1968] and head-mounted displays are more frequently portrayed in the popular media. However, the use of projection-based display for applied virtual reality is growing. Myron Krueger has been using projection displays in his virtual environments for decades [Krueger 1982], but their widespread use began in about 1992 when the EVL *CAVE* and Sun Microsystems' *Virtual Portal* were demonstrated at the 1992 SIGGRAPH computer graphics conference in Chicago. (Of course, flight simulators had been using projector technology for decades but were not then considered a VR display.) Thereafter, several single-screen displays were introduced: (1) a table-top configuration, the *Responsive Workbench;* (2) a drafting table style, the *ImmersaDesk;* and (3) a high-resolution, single-screen, multiple-projector system, the *Infinity Wall.* FIGURE 4-15 shows two projection VR displays: EVL's *CAVE* and the *ImmersaDesk.*

Again, size requirements of the various stationary displays influence the venue in which they are typically experienced. We discuss venues further in Chapter 7; it is enough to say here that desktop displays can generally be placed in an office environment, allowing access without time constraint during the day. Larger, single-screen displays move into the domain of scheduled resources, leading to less frequent use. Nevertheless, these displays are not excessively obtrusive and can be

(A)

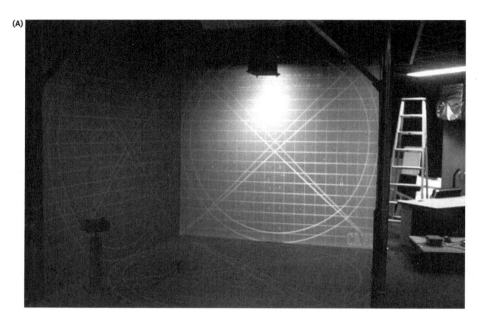

(B)

FIGURE 4-15 (A) *The* CAVE *Automatic Virtual Reality Environment is an example of a projection VR display that provides high resolution and field of view and, depending on the number of screens utilized, a high field of regard.* **(B)** *The* ImmersaDesk *is similar to the* CAVE *in that it is projection based, but it trades field of regard for lower cost and greater portability. It is suitable for applications that do not require much physical movement on the part of the participant (Photographs by William Sherman).*

added without too much difficulty to research environments, museum displays, and like venues.

Large, surround-projected displays, like EVL's *CAVE,* tend to be more of "an architectural statement," as co-creator Tom DeFanti likes to point out, often literally requiring architectural changes to accommodate them. Accordingly, surround-projected displays are more of a limited-access device, at least until large-scale flat panel displays become available. However, many research facilities accustomed to providing state-of-the-art laboratories for their researchers find this type of display is a valuable research tool.

Components of Projection VR

The major difference in required components between desktop and walkabout stationary displays is in the choice of tracking systems. Desktop systems have the advantage of needing less information about orientation. Walkabout systems require a greater range of tracking, plus head-orientation data (particularly important for the proper display of stereopsis on nonvertical surfaces).

Projectors often need alignment. This is especially important in systems with multiple projectors, which also need to be aligned with one another. Multiple projectors also require multiple image rendering. So, an additional component for multiple-screen displays is a computer capable of providing multiple graphical outputs, each from the proper viewpoint, or multiple computers with hardware that can keep them synchronized.

When screens are arranged at angles near 90 degrees, their reflectivity begins to present a problem. Often bright images on the edge of one screen reflect off the nearby side screen. Darker screen material can help reduce this effect but can often result in screens with uneven coloring.

The two common methods of creating stereoscopic imagery on a projected VR display use either shutter glasses or polarized glasses. The use of shutter glasses is easier to implement, because most high-end graphical displays already include the necessary hardware, other than the signal transmitter and the glasses themselves. Polarized glasses require either a single, specialized projector or two regular projectors equipped with filters to polarize left and right images for the appropriate eye. The participant wears a pair of glasses also equipped with polarizing filters.

Using two projectors offers the benefits of a brighter, higher-resolution image, due to their combined effect against a single screen. Polarized glasses are less expensive and need less maintenance than shutter glasses, but require the expense of a second projector for each screen. The polarized glasses that the participants wear have a vertical filter for one eye and a horizontal filter for the other. This is satisfactory for watching a 3D movie on a screen, because it's safe to assume that the viewer's head will always be oriented vertically with respect to the screen. In VR systems, however, this is not a valid assumption, since the viewer's head can be oriented in any direction with respect to the screen, particularly if screens are used on the floor or ceiling. Thus, in VR systems, it is more appropriate to use *circular polarization,* in which one image is polarized circularly (clockwise) and the other image is polarized in a counterclockwise fashion. The viewer must wear glasses with circularly polarizing filters.

Features of Projection VR

Perhaps the primary feature of current large-screen VR displays is the amount of floor space required to house the VR system. Multiscreened projection venues are the biggest consumers of space, generally requiring about a 30 ft. × 30 ft. room. The *ImmersaDesk* occupies a much smaller floor space, occupying only 6 ft. × 7 ft. when fully deployed.

A nice feature of projection VR is that it generally occupies a larger portion of the viewer's field of view than either Fishtank VR or most head-based displays. However, there is still the reduced field of regard experienced in smaller, monitor-based displays to accommodate: the viewer must face the direction of the stationary screen(s) to see the virtual world. Often this affords sufficient quality in projection systems, especially in those that provide multiscreened views.

Because projectors generally spread the image over a larger space, a more powerful computer is required to create a high-resolution image. The cost of projection-based VR graphics rendering systems is often high—considerably higher than fishtank systems that reside on the desktop and get their imagery from a moderately powered PC or a high-powered UNIX desktop workstation (although PCs are rapidly converging on the workstations in terms of power).

Although it might be easier to use a costlier system for image generation, in general the desired applications and venue will have more influence on the selection of computer. For example, museum or "hall of fame" venues will often use a much less expensive computer system.

Multiscreened displays obviously require more graphics rendering capability. Rendering images on multiple screens enhances the experience, because the apparent graphics latency is reduced. This benefit and those of an increased FOR and FOV must be weighed against the additional cost and space required by multiscreened displays.

Larger views allow the option of other participants observing the world alongside the tracked viewer. If the kibitzers are not standing *near* the tracked viewer (the "driver"), they may notice strange distortions, particularly at the corners of multiscreen displays (because the images are computed correctly for the specific POV of the driver). The closer they follow the movement of the tracked viewer, the less distortion they will see. Some systems (e.g., the Fakespace *DuoView*) use extra hardware to allow the presentation of more than two visual channels on a single screen. This allows multiple tracked viewers to have independent 3D views of the world, the tradeoffs being reduced brightness and the cost of the extra hardware. The brightness is reduced because there is twice as much shuttering going on with the addition of a second viewer.

Unlike most head-based displays, in a projection-based system the viewer is not isolated from the real world. There are advantages and disadvantages to this, many of which relate to the type of application. For applications in which collaboration with coworkers is beneficial, being able to see them next to you is a big plus. Not being isolated from the real world also means that the viewers can see themselves and any control devices they are manipulating, thus alleviating the need to render avatars, which can have registration discrepancies from their real-world positions.

A potential negative effect of seeing the real world is the occurrence of occlusion errors. When an object in the virtual world is displayed closer to the viewer than some real-world object (e.g., their hand or a control device), then the occlusion of the virtual object by the real object overrides the other depth cues presented. This can be very confusing to the user's visual system and should be avoided if possible.

Because the viewer(s) of projection-based VR displays generally stand 2 feet or more from the screen, there is less eye strain than from displays that put the screens inches from the eyes. This allows users of this type of VR display to stay immersed longer, increasing the practicality of certain applications. There is also an interesting effect gained from viewing nonvertically arranged screens. The *Immersa-Desk* and *Responsive Workbench* use slanted and horizontal screens, which move the focal point away from the eye as the gaze travels to the top of the screen (FIGURE 4-16). When combined with a scene that goes off into the distance, the focal length increases as the viewer looks further into the world, which creates more natural cues.

As with monitor-based displays, not much physical gear is required to be worn to enter a virtual world via a projection system. The typical requirement is a pair of glasses to create the stereoscopic views and a tracking device, which can easily be mounted right onto the frame of the glasses. The viewer is then encumbered by only

FIGURE 4-16 *In some projection VR displays, focal distance is not constant for the entire screen. As objects recede to the horizon, they appear on the further portion of the screen, matching the viewer's changing focal distance. Here, when the user looks from the house to the mountains, her focus adjusts to the further distance of the screen as her gaze shifts from the bottom to the top.*

a small wire that connects the tracker to the computer system. And, once someone markets a good wireless tracking device suitable for VR application, we'll be left with only the glasses. A handheld control and/or glove is usually provided for interaction but, strictly speaking, these are not part of the *visual* display paradigm.

Interface Issues of Projection VR

A basic capability of most VR systems is the ability to move our head and change our view of the virtual world. In the larger projection systems, viewers are able to physically walk around in a region of the space, enhancing their visual perception of the environment. This ability is limited by the fact that users cannot safely pass their heads through the surface of the screen. With nonstationary displays, the screens are moved by the viewer within the limits allowed by the tracking and video cables.

The ability to see the physical world while in an environment is not completely necessary to enable the use of physical devices for controlling the virtual world, but it can make it easier. Complicated devices, such as a traditional (QWERTY) keyboard are more usable when they can be seen and felt. It is unlikely that people will bring their own keyboard with them into a *CAVE* or other display, but there are devices commonly used in VR environments whose many buttons and other controls are difficult to operate without a *physical* representation of the device, which could be afforded by a Palm Pilot (FIGURE 4-17), for instance. Another consideration is whether the participants in a given application will need to switch between a number of devices, say, as carpenters might do in a virtual training display. If so, a shelf of control devices might be necessary.

A decision must be made about the number of screens to use for projection VR. To fully envelop the user with flat screens requires at least six screens arranged in a cube. Employing six screens is expensive and a logistical problem because the floor must be raised above the room's floor to create a space for the projector. (This has been done at only a handful of research facilities to date.)

For some applications, a single screen is adequate; others require more. Many applications make use of either the floor or the ceiling. If floor projection is required, but not the ceiling, a projector can be placed above the environment and projected directly on the floor. It's interesting to note that most *CAVEs* that project on the floor (but not the ceiling) project from above. Since the projection is straight down and the user is typically standing, there is just a little shadow around their feet and most people don't even notice it. Since your body's "footprint" when viewed from directly above is so small and the shadow is cast directly at your feet, user occlusion is not much of a problem. For location walkthroughs, displaying on the floor can greatly enhance the sense of immersion. An astronomy application would likely benefit more from a screen placed above the participant. Each application warrants thought as to the quantity and best use of each projection device.

In Chapter 3, we discussed how control widgets and menus that exist in the virtual world can be placed in relationship to the user. One method places the (virtual) controls in a fixed position relative to the real world, giving the appearance of the control being located right on the screen. This location matching gives the things that appear on the screen an accommodation depth cue that does not conflict with convergence and stereopsis cues. A side benefit is that those things will look clear to any bystander not wearing the tracked glasses. With location matching, the virtual control will always be displayed at the same location on a screen. If the control is flat, the left and right eye views will be identical, thus allowing the control to be seen without stereoscopic glasses. This eliminates any error, lag, or jitter due to head tracking, making control of the widget easier. (However, it would still be necessary to any hand device that might be used to manipulate the virtual control.)

FIGURE 4-17 *Handheld computers such as the PalmPilot (Palm, Inc.) can be used as interface devices in a projection VR system. They are more convenient to use than a keyboard in a* CAVE *display (Photograph by William Sherman).*

Second Person Projected Realities

VR systems typically present the virtual world to the participant from the first person point of view—through their own eyes. However, some VR systems display the world from a second person point of view—observation from an apparent distance. Projection-based displays that present the virtual world from a second person POV have specific interface issue(s).

Two prominent examples of such displays include Myron Krueger's *Video Place* (and its descendants) and the *Mandala* devices marketed to a wide variety of entertainment venues (FIGURE 4-18). These displays use optical cameras (such as a video camera) to track the participant by watching their outline against a constant (or at least consistent) background, allowing the participant to move about the space without any encumbrance whatsoever.

A common way to interact in experiences written for these displays is for the edge of the participant's image to trigger events in the environment by passing over them on the screen. So, for example, one of the *Mandala* applications displays a set of drums that can be played by passing the hand over one of many drum heads pictured on the screen, causing the computer to make an associated sound. Or, movement up the screen might be caused by the flapping of the participant's arms. Because the interface is based on a 2D image of the user, the environments are often only 2D in nature.

(A)

(B)

(C)

FIGURE 4-18 **(A)** *Pioneering work by Myron Krueger uses video tracking to create a VR experience with a second person POV. This image shows one person lifting the video image of another participant; each participant sees the composite display (Image courtesy of Myron Krueger).* **(B)** *The* Mandala *display device superimposes a video image of the participant "into" a computer-generated virtual world. The participant observes their actions from a second person POV, interacting with the virtual world on a display screen (Image courtesy of The Vivid Group). See color plate 5.* **(C)** *Blue-screen and green-screen backdrops are often used in conjunction with video cameras as a means of capturing a user's gestures in second person POV VR systems (Photograph by William Sherman).*

Summary of Projection VR

In a nutshell, the projection-based paradigm expands on monitor-based displays by making them bigger, thus increasing the field of view. Because they cause less eye strain and are more suitable for collaboration, projection-based VR displays permit users to remain in the virtual environment for longer periods. On the downside, they often require more equipment and maintenance than other paradigms and their larger size makes tracking range a greater concern.

The effective combination of many of the features of this paradigm (resolution, field of view, etc.) can make for very immersive experiences. Despite this, many in the VR field categorize projection displays as nonimmersive VR. We have witnessed that this simply isn't true; in fact, to us, the qualification creates an oxymoron. To us, an experience *must* be physically immersive to some degree to qualify as VR in the first place. True, immersion can be impeded by improper occlusion cues or incomplete field of regard, but these situations can be avoided, with the result that users find themselves no longer thinking in terms of a virtual object or a projected scene, but simply interacting with the world as they experience it.

Head-based VR

As we've discussed, head-based VR visual displays are probably the equipment that most people associate with virtual reality. In this section, we will talk about occlusive head-based VR—displays that block out the real world in favor of the virtual.

Unlike fishtank and projection visual display paradigms, the screens in head-based displays are not stationary; rather, as their name suggests, they move in conjunction with the user's head (FIGURE 4-19). Styles of head-based displays include

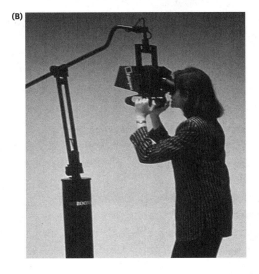

(A)

(B)

FIGURE 4-19 *The head-mounted display* (A) *and* BOOM3C (B) *devices provide display screens that are very near the participant's eyes (Photographs courtesy of William Sherman and Fakespace Systems, Inc., respectively).*

head-mounted displays (HMDs), counterweighted displays on mechanical linkages (e.g., the *BOOM*), small screens designed to display a virtual image several feet away (e.g., the *Private Eye*), experimental retinal displays (which use lasers to present the image directly onto the retina of your eye), and slightly movable, nickelodeon-type displays that the user puts their head up to (e.g., the Fakespace *PUSH* discussed in the next sidebar). Ultimately, this type of display will shift to hardware that is more appropriately referred to as *head-worn* rather than *head-mounted*—approaching something on the order of a device similar to a pair of glasses in weight and size, yet conveying high resolution and wide field of view.

Components of Head-based VR

The screens of head-based VR displays are typically small and lightweight since they are worn or held by the user. Counterweighted systems, of course, allow for slightly heavier displays, but weight is still a factor in trying to control the arm's motion. Most of these systems allow for stereoscopic image depth cues. Stationary displays typically use time interlacing to provide left- and right-eye views (resolved by using shutter glasses), while head-based systems use dual visual outputs (one for each eye).

A wide selection of tracking systems is available for head-based displays. Some have the tracking system built right into the display unit. Others are un-equipped with any type of tracking, and the system developer must choose from the many possible tracking methods. Because the *BOOM* system incorporates mechanical linkages to support the display, it is natural to simply measure the joint angles of the linkages to determine the position of the screens. Such a method provides fast and precise measurements but is not typically used for other types of head-based displays, because of the physical linkage required.

One exception exists in systems where users have a limited range of movement because they are seated in a cockpit, which allows for a combination of the head-based display with mechanical tracking. Head-based displays rely primarily on orientation cues to respond to user motions. If the application developers decide that the experience won't suffer from lack of location tracking, then the sole use of self-referential trackers, such as inertial devices, becomes a reasonable possibility.

Features of Head-based VR

A prominent drawback of head-based displays is that any lag in the tracking and image-generation systems causes a noticeable problem for the viewer. When the view of the scene lags behind the movement of the user's head, it causes visual confusion, often leading the user to oscillate their head. This lag is one of the leading causes of *simulator sickness* in VR.

The field of view of a typical head-based display is very limited. There is some tradeoff between resolution and FOV, and many systems opt for higher resolution. The resolution itself can vary from the relatively few pixels offered in early systems (160×120 color pixels per eye) to very high resolution (over $1,000 \times 1,000$ pixels per eye) with an extremely high pixel density and therefore very sharp images. An easy way to increase FOV is to spread these pixels across the visual field, at the expense of reducing the pixel density.

HMDs can be somewhat encumbering. They are hard to don and can be uncomfortable to wear. HMDs don't accommodate all eyeglasses well, and the weight of many HMDs also leads to fatigue and neck strain, even when worn briefly. The cables that are often attached to HMDs effectively limit the user's freedom of movement. Of course, many of these physical constraints will subside as head-based displays evolve toward a pair of simple glasses.

HMDs can also be difficult to use over an extended period of time due to the conflict between the depth cues of stereopsis, accommodation, and convergence. This conflict can lead to eye strain and other negative effects. Since the HMD has a fixed focal point, the accommodation cue tells your brain that all the objects are at that distance. However, the stereopsis, parallax, perspective, and other cues can conflict with accommodation, telling your brain the objects are at distances other than the focal distance.

There are also many positive features of head-based displays, most notably, the field of regard covers the entire sphere surrounding the viewer. Unlike most stationary displays, there are no gaps in imagery regardless of which direction the user looks. Many head-based displays are more portable than most stationary displays, and they take up very little floor space.

The ability to mask the real world from the user is important in some applications. Because occlusive head-based displays hide the physical world from view, they can be operated in a wider range of venues than projection systems, which require certain lighting conditions to operate. Of course, their use must be limited to protected areas, because people wearing these displays cannot see potential hazards in the real world.

Interface Issues of Head-based VR

Head-based VR visual displays are primarily suited for first person point of view. They display the world directly through the viewpoint of the user's eyes. This capability provides the very intuitive interface of "look left, see left." And, if head location is tracked in addition to orientation, the ability to see another side of an object simply by walking to the other side and looking provides a very natural interface. For simplicity and economy, many VR systems do not track the location of the head and so require some other type of interface to allow the user to virtually move through the space.

Since head-based displays visually isolate the user from the real world, anything the users see must be generated by the computer—*anything,* including their own body. Even in single-person applications, a user's avatar must be rendered, or at least the parts that are important for the user to see. In fact, many props and controls require rendered avatars in order to be used properly in an occlusive head-based display system. This requirement is not all bad; since the actual device cannot be seen, it can be represented as any object. Typically, the device and virtual object will be similar in shape, mass, and center of gravity. A real flashlight might become a virtual *Star Wars* light saber, or a small plastic plate might become a virtual clipboard or a cutting tool able to reveal the interior of objects.

More complex objects like a computer keyboard rely on the user's ability to have fine registration between what they see and where they touch. This registration

The PUSH Display

The *PUSH* display from Fakespace, Inc. is a typical head-based display in many respects, but with one striking difference—it doesn't move with the head. Tracking is built into the device, but is very constrained. The viewer mechanism can be pushed slightly forward or back, but cannot rotate. In this respect, it shares some features of stationary displays, but it doesn't allow side to side head movement.

With the *PUSH* display, users step up to the viewing device, which resembles a nickelodeon (FIGURE 4-20). Inside the device are two very high-resolution images, providing a compelling binocular view. The display is mounted atop three semi-flexible columns, allowing the user to twist, pull, and push the display toward and away from them. There are handles with buttons on either side of the viewer that provide the user interface to the world.

The method for participant travel within the virtual world is left open for the system designer to create. There are a limited number of ways that make sense. The common method is generally based on the notion that pushing the device moves the user forward in the virtual world and pulling it moves them backward. The buttons are used to rotate about the yaw (side to side) and pitch (up and down) axes. With both hands occupied with the display, though, there is not much allowance for interaction with the world. The *PUSH* is perhaps best suited to the walkthrough form of application.

This is not to say that the high resolution and other features of the *PUSH* can't lead to a very *mentally* immersive experience. Combined with ruggedness and navigational ease of use, it is well adapted for use in public venues where many people will be using the system and where movement through a space is a central story element.

FIGURE 4-20 *The Fakespace, Inc.* PUSH *device resembles a nickelodeon. Viewers put their head up to the device and interact with the virtual world by pushing different buttons and "steering" with the hands. The device requires very little time to "suit up" and is particularly useful in public venues (Photograph courtesy of Fakespace Systems, Inc.).*

is difficult to achieve in an occlusive head-based display, so devices with several buttons or other complexities are harder to use when only their avatars are visible to the user.

Summary of Head-based VR

Head-based displays are the more widely recognized forms of visual display for virtual reality. Inexpensive models, with only monoscopic images and orientation tracking, enable many people to experiment with VR, using standard business and home computing platforms.

Although they provide complete FOR, their limited resolution and FOV and encumbrance constraints currently lead many designers of visualization and product design applications to avoid this type of display. In future, some or all of these limitations may be overcome.

See-through Head-based Displays

See-through head-based displays are primarily designed for applications in which the user needs to see an augmented copy of the physical world—augmented reality (AR). There are two methods used to implement the "see-through" effect of these displays—via optics or video. The optical method uses lenses, mirrors, and half-silvered mirrors to overlay an image from a computer onto a view of the real world. The video method uses electronic mixing to add a computer image onto a video image of the real world, which is generated by cameras mounted on the head-based display [Rolland, Holloway, and Fuchs 1994].

FIGURE 4-21 illustrates one example of a common class of augmented reality application, the *Magic Lens* effect [Bier et al. 1993], which allows the user to see information about objects not visible in normal viewing (e.g., relative surface temperature, what's inside, what's behind.)

Annotating the real world is another type of augmented reality application. The annotation can be simple text boxes with pointers to particular parts of an object, more detailed instructions that explain the next step of a task, arrows or other graphics showing where parts should be placed, and so on. These effects can be useful for training or during actual procedures.

Components of See-through Head-based Displays

The components of a see-through HBD include those items needed for occlusive head-based displays plus additional equipment to capture or pass through the real world via video or optics and to register the virtual world to the real-world view. This

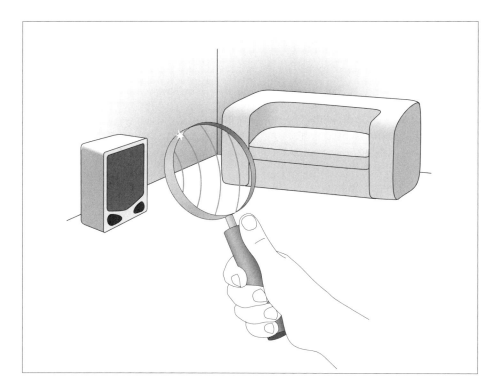

FIGURE 4-21 *The* Magic Lens *paradigm enables the viewer to get additional information about the object under the "lens." In this image, a Magic Lens is used to visualize sound waves within a room.*

requires improved tracking systems able to achieve better registration with the real world and a model or partial model of the real world in which the system will be operating (FIGURE 4-22). Often, these two requirements are interrelated. One method of improving tracking is to use what is known about the real world and match it to what is seen in a video input of the world. It is possible to add special *fiducial markers* (landmarks or reference markers) to the real world to improve the accuracy of the task [State et al. 1996].

The only other additional major requirement for augmented reality is complete 6-DOF positional tracking of the head. This follows from the fact that registration between the virtual and real worlds requires knowing exactly how the eyes are positioned in the real world.

For the computer to create a view of information about the real world that the user cannot see with the unaided eye, it must have an internal model of that information. This model can be pre-stored. For instance, if the application is an aid to look at the electrical, pipe, and duct work in the infrastructure of a building, information

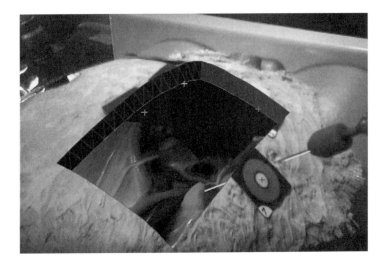

FIGURE 4-22 *See-through video displays allow computer-generated imagery to be registered and superimposed on a view of the real world. In this example, ultrasound imagery is superimposed on a real-world view of a patient, allowing a physician to see the relationship between the sensor data and the patient's body. The circular pattern to the right of the inside view is a fiducial marker used to give better tracking registration (Image courtesy of UNC Chapel Hill). See color plate 6.*

can be gained from the CAD database of the building. A real-world model can also be created on the fly. In an AR application developed at the University of North Carolina at Chapel Hill, called the *Ultrasound Visualization* project [Bajura et al. 1992; State et al. 1996], a model of a patient's internal organs is constructed from data collected by a medical ultrasonic scanner. FIGURE 4-23 illustrates the use of a laser image range finder system, developed by 3rd Tech, to capture a real-world space.

Features of See-through Head-based Displays

In see-through HBDs, the fact that the real world is part of the environment means that the constraints of the real world will affect what can be done in the virtual world. Some aspects of the world can be manipulated, others cannot. Physical laws such as gravity cannot be disabled. Time cannot be stopped, slowed, or reversed. Opaque objects can be made to appear transparent with enough knowledge of the real world and proper rendering techniques. (Scale and distance can be manipulated as parameters of a *telepresence* operation; see the sidebar, Telepresence, later in this chapter for more detail).

Accurate occlusion of objects can be difficult in an AR system. Sometimes virtual objects located in the combined world are (virtually) behind real objects in the world. Determining the proper interposition of objects in the rendered scene is not a trivial problem, particularly when moving real-world, untracked objects (which is to say objects not tracked via any additional means other than the camera(s)

integral to the see-
through display itself).

When a see-
through display is used,
there are generally only a
few objects that present
potential interposition
problems with virtual ob-
jects. One solution is to
track these objects and
render a shadow mask
based on knowledge of
their position. The real object will then be replaced by
avatars of the masked objects and rendered appropriately
in the scene. Because the avatars are part of the virtual
world, their interposition will register appropriately in the
scene.

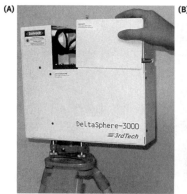

Interface Issues of See-through Head-based Displays

The only new interface issue that arises when using augmented reality versus basic virtual reality is interfacing
with the real world. Otherwise, most of the interface possibilities and concerns are similar to those of occlusive
HBDs, although the tolerances may be a little tighter, especially when registering the
real and virtual worlds.

When using an optical method to create the AR view, the user sees the
physical world directly via lenses and mirrors. Thus, there is no time lag between the
users' movements and their view of the real world. However, the virtual world still
relies on tracking and computer graphics technologies that will probably cause a
delay between the users' movements and the response of the display. Consequently,
the registration between real and virtual worlds will not match perfectly.

When using a video method, the delay from the video input can be matched
to the delay of the virtual world display. The video method also makes it easier to use
clues from the real-world input to more precisely register the virtual world to the real
world. However, the likelihood for uncomfortable lags in the display system increases,
because now even the real world—which we *expect* to behave normally—will lag.

FIGURE 4-23 *Although not yet a real-time process, laser image range finder systems* **(A)**—*devices that "look" at the world, create an image, and provide data about the distance of the objects—are now suitable for capturing real-world spaces, such as this garage scene* **(B, C)** *(Images courtesy of 3rd Tech).*

Another negative effect of the video method is that without additional optics to compensate, the cameras employed to capture the real world will be offset from the actual location of the users' eyes, thereby distorting their view of the world. This offset makes maneuvering in an environment difficult. A user can usually adapt to such a situation, but will need to readapt to the unimmersed way of seeing after exiting the display. (User adaptation is also a factor in optical see-through displays, where the view of the real world may pass through a series of mirrors.)

In addition to system response lag, the difference in lag between the real-world view and the computer-generated view (lag differential) can cause user interface problems. Lag differential itself is a source of registration problems. When the augmented display lags behind the real world, then the overlapping virtual and real views will be spatially displaced. However, lag differential can generally be reduced to the problem of basic lag. In an optical see-through display, the user sees the real world directly, so there is only lag in the augmented display. In a video see-though display, lag can be added to the real-world imagery, so that it matches the lag of the augmented information. In this way, the lag differential is reduced to zero even though the entire view now lags behind the user's movement.

The use of props in a see-through system poses some additional issues. There is an interface benefit from being able to see the props. In AR, it is simpler to implement a multiprop interface, because the user can see where the controls are located. On the other hand, it is harder to disguise the real-world prop.

Disguising the props requires displaying graphics that are viewed instead of the prop; after all, the point of the AR display is to render graphics in place of at least a portion of what the viewer sees. For example, unless masked out by a computer graphics avatar, a flashlight used to represent a light saber will appear as a flashlight. In an optical see-through display, complete masking is more difficult, because the computer-generated image must occlude the real-world object.

Because AR provides a mediated view of the real world, it can become a simple matter to provide an interface to a part of the real world that is geographically separated from where the user is. In this scenario, effecting a change of scale in the viewed world becomes possible. This overlapping technology with AR is called *telepresence*.

Summary of See-through Head-based Displays

Augmented reality is an important subclass of virtual reality. In AR a user can manipulate and see the real world in ways not feasible without the aid of VR. Modified versions of VR head- and hand-based displays are used to create augmented displays, but tracking registration becomes even more important than with basic VR, due to the importance of mapping virtual information onto the real-world view.

The see-through paradigm also allows for some other interesting possibilities. It is possible to implement an AR display that maps one virtual world onto another. Such a system could be created by implementing a projection-based VR display and then using a head- (or hand-) based AR display within that environment. This technique has been used in human factors research at the University of Illinois by Michelle Yeh and Chris Wickens (FIGURE 4-24). In their experiment to evaluate the possible benefits of see-through HMDs, the external terrain is projected on a *CAVE* display [Yeh et al. 1999].

FIGURE 4-24 *Augmented reality can be combined with another virtual reality display, augmenting a virtual world rather than the real one. In a human factors experiment by Michelle Yeh, possible AR soldiering aids are tested using a* CAVE *display to provide the surrounding environment (Application courtesy of Professor Chris Wickens, Director of the University of Illinois Aviation Research Lab; photograph by William Sherman).*

Handheld VR

Another visual display paradigm that works well as an augmented reality display is the handheld or palm-VR display. As the name suggests, a *handheld* VR display consists of a screen small enough to be held by the user. Of course, for it to be considered virtual reality, the image on the screen must react to changes in the viewing vector between it and the viewer; that is, it must be *spatially aware* [Fitzmaurice 1993].

The handheld display paradigm is largely undeveloped. However, as computing devices become increasingly miniaturized and as people continue to take their computers on the road, palm VR displays will probably become more common, particularly for augmented reality applications (see *Boeing* application in Appendix C).

The Chameleon project at the University of Toronto has produced some prototype applications for such a handheld device [Buxton and Fitzmaurice 1998]. The primary purpose of these applications is to use physical objects as anchors in an information space, serving as retrieval cues for the user. One example is to use a simple wall map of Canada for viewing weather or demographic data by holding the palm display over the region of interest (FIGURE 4-25). The palmtop display becomes a Magic Lens from the physical world into a virtual information space.

Another use of a handheld display is to augment the terrain surrounding a user. A farmer in the field might check the display for information on that particular field. A soldier could access information about what's over the next ridge. Basically, the user can determine what activity is occurring in the direction the display is pointed.

Components of Handheld VR

Three items necessary to create a handheld VR display are a screen, some form of tracking, and a method of transferring imagery to the screen. The screen can be of the same type used in portable TVs, a 3- or 4-inch LCD display. In fact, by using a small portable TV, the video can easily be sent to the display

FIGURE 4-25 *Handheld display devices can be used to superimpose additional data on a view of the real world. Here the user can hold the display over a particular region of Canada to see weather-related information about that region (Photograph courtesy of George Fitzmaurice).*

via a short-range television signal transmitter, eliminating the need for a wire to carry the signal. Palm display screens are bright enough to see in a lit room, but resolutions do not yet afford a large amount of detail or text.

Tracking for handheld displays presents a difficult challenge. Standard VR tracking methods will work, but they place the same mobility constraints on handheld VR as they do with the basic HMD. Moreover, applications that would make good use of a handheld display system are more likely to require mobility. For instance, a building inspection application would require that the display be usable from anywhere in the building. Standard tracking technology is currently not capable of this.

Outdoor mobility can be a problem, because the application designer might not have control of the environment in which the system will be used. For open spaces, the global positioning system (GPS) can provide a crude form of location tracking. GPS provides latitude, longitude, and elevation information for any location in the world. However, the update rate is only a few updates per second and the accuracy is limited, especially for civilian models.

Although satellite-based GPS can't penetrate all areas where a user might need to be tracked, an alternative or supplemental GPS system can make use of differential GPS (DGPS). In this system, additional ground-based transmitters can send a beacon capable of extending into remote areas, such as a mining pit, for instance.

By constraining the user interface, some applications can be made to work reasonably well without determining the exact view vector between the user and the screen. Such a system might incorporate a tracking system capable of determining latitude, longitude, and orientation, such as a GPS combined with inertial trackers. If the application is one in which the user would typically view the display from an arm's length and with a perpendicular view angle, then the view vector can be approximated. For instance, such a display might lend itself to an application in which the user is in an outdoor space and is using the display to access a database to help locate the direction of distant objects.

Features of Handheld VR

The characteristic feature of a handheld display is its see-around functionality. The user can look at the information provided by the display or ignore it by looking directly at the physical world. Thus, it would fit the needs of many potential augmented reality applications.

The ability to augment not only the physical world but other virtual reality displays, particularly nonocclusive VR displays, presents an interesting prospect. One could imagine using such a display in an architectural design application within a *CAVE* environment. While the *CAVE* screens project a realistic representation of a planned layout of a new building, the palm-VR display could show the electrical and HVAC systems behind the virtual walls. This technique can be more compelling than simply projecting imagery onto a generic tablet prop.

Interface Issues of Handheld VR

The interface issues of handheld displays include their use as a "magic lens" into a space associated with the physical (or virtual) world in which the display is manipulated. This metaphor works both as a means of acquiring X-ray vision and as a means of using a physical space as a navigation tool to information stored in a database.

In either a physical or a virtual world, the magic lens metaphor can be extended to tools such as virtual binoculars (or telescopes), providing the user with a closeup view of objects. In a virtual world, this tool might simply be used to replicate the virtual environment, but by pressing a button the user can take a digital snapshot of the virtual world.

Summary of Handheld VR

Particularly suitable for augmented reality applications, handheld displays work well as a magic lens into the real world. This interface method can even be applied within other VR applications.

Telepresence

Telepresence is similar to AR but is not a subset. Telepresence does not always provide an augmented view of the world; sometimes it only provides a displaced view (and a displaced manipulation interface). This displacement can be in spatial location, in scale of the world, and in relative control/power. Telepresence technology might be used to control a large machine to crush blocks of concrete, or it might give the user the superfine control necessary to perform delicate operations.

Let's use the scenario of a robotic exploration submarine controlled from the surface to demonstrate the difference between augmented telepresence and nonaugmented telepresence. Say the operator sits in a cockpit that emulates the submarine cockpit and views the ocean floor as if actually seated behind the steering controls of the submarine; this would be an example of nonaugmented telepresence. This same display could

Handheld displays have not yet been used outside of experimental applications; however, their portability and potential as an easy-to-use display for augmenting reality is promising, particularly for outdoor applications. Specifically, they show potential for farming and soldiering.

Summary of Visual Display Paradigms

For most applications, vision is the primary sense used to immerse a participant into a virtual world. The choice of visual display paradigm is ideally influenced by the goals of the application. The main categories of visual displays are stationary (fishtank and projection-based), head-based (occlusive or see-through), and hand-based.

There are many factors that go into deciding which type of visual display to use for an application. Often that choice is simply what is already available to the user; a research lab may already have a CAVE available to any of its scientists, for instance.

Many of the current forms of head-based displays, especially HMDs, are not easy to don or wear, making them impractical for many applications. However, as the technology progresses toward displays that are as lightweight and easy to use as a pair of glasses, usage will increase. Experience has shown that people are more willing to create a VR application for repeated use when less encumbering display paradigms are available.

The following are checklists of the benefits offered by each of the three categories of visual displays. A designer of a VR experience must take these into account when choosing a visual display, modified by other factors such as current availability, demands of the venue, genre of the experience, and so on.

Benefits of Stationary Displays (Fishtank and Projection)

- Higher resolution (than most HMDs)
- Wider field of view
- Longer user endurance (i.e., can stay immersed for longer periods)
- Higher tolerance for display latency
- Greater user mobility (fewer cables)
- Less encumbering
- Lower safety risk
- Better for group viewing
- Better throughput

Telepresence (continued)
be augmented with a map of the ocean terrain, such as mountains, volcanos, and other features, making it an example of augmented telepresence. A similar scenario could take place with a telepresence-driven vehicle in a factory warehouse, where the operator is able to "see inside" the boxes and other entities in the warehouse— clearly an augmented reality experience.

Nonaugmented telepresence does not require a digital computer to mediate the presentation of the information. Many implementations of telepresence can be accomplished with video, analog electronics, and mechanical linkages. In these instances, telepresence does not overlap with AR. There is no notion of a virtual world and no information augmentation about the situation with which the user is interacting. Without the need to overlap virtual information onto the real world, the registration problem does not exist.

Benefits of Head-based Displays (Occlusive and Nonocclusive)

- Lower cost (for lower resolution models)
- Complete field of regard
- Greater portability
- Can be used for augmenting reality
- Can occlude the real world (required in some situations, e.g., as when using haptic [touch] displays in which the participant shouldn't see the haptic hardware).
- Less physical space required (compared with multiscreened stationary displays)
- Less concern for room lighting and other environmental factors

Benefits of Hand-based Displays

- Greater user mobility
- Greater portability
- Can be combined with stationary VR displays

Aural Displays

As in the previous section on visual displays, in this section we'll first discuss the common properties of aural displays—their localization cues and presentation and logistical qualities—and then proceed to the specific categories of aural display systems. Like visual displays, aural display systems typically fall into one of the two general display categories we've been discussing: stationary displays and head-based displays.

Headphones are analogous to head-mounted visual displays. Headphones may be constructed to isolate the participant from sounds in the natural world or to allow real-world sounds to overlap with virtual sounds. Speakers allow multiple participants to hear the sounds.

High-fidelity audio devices are much less expensive than video display devices, a fact that can be exploited when creating virtual reality systems. Often, the addition of high-quality sound can help in creating a compelling experience, even when the quality of the visual presentation is lacking.

Virtual Binoculars
Binocular fieldglass displays are another type of handheld visual display (FIGURE 4-26). Although they share some features in common with the palmtop screen display, such as holding the display up in front of an object to act as a Magic Lens, there are some significant differences.

The primary difference lies in its functionality; when held up to the user's eyes, it functions more as an occlusive head-based display in contrast to the typical see-around style of a palm screen.

Like a palm screen, however, the display can be used as any type of "magic lens," including X-ray vision, simulation visualization, and long-distance viewing simulations. The user interface is intuitive, drawing on the users' past experience using real binoculars and requires no explanation.

Binocular displays share an interesting characteristic with other handheld displays. They

Aural Localization Cues

Before we discuss the varieties and methods of aural display, it will be helpful to present some of the ways that our hearing system works and how we can capitalize on these to enhance the performance of aural VR displays.

Because virtual worlds are often represented as 3D environments, it is important that the sound in that space also have a 3D character. In the real world, we are surrounded by sounds on all sides, and those sounds aid us in understanding the nature of the environment we are in.

Localization is the psychoacoustic phenomenon in which a listener can determine the direction and distance from which a sound emanates, whether in the real world or a virtual world. The brain analyzes the set of cues that indicate where a sound is coming from, and the participant perceives the location of the sound. Localization of sound is analogous to the visual depth cues described in the previous section. The term *spatialization* describes the act of creating the illusion that a sound is emanating from a specific 3D location.

Transfer functions are mathematical transformations that can be applied to a signal to alter the signal in some specific desired way. Transfer functions are used in devices such as the *Convolvotron* which give the virtual reality application developer a method of simulating these phenomena to create the illusion of directional sound. The basic principle of the *Convolvotron* is that a set of transfer functions is determined for sounds from a variety of locations. These functions are predetermined through techniques in which microphones are placed inside the subject's ears, and the filtering effect (i.e., how the sound frequency spectrum is altered, or *filtered,* as it passes through the outer ear and around objects in the environment) is determined for sounds from a variety of locations. The transfer function for the desired location is then applied to the sound, causing it to be spatialized, or appear to the participant to be from a particular location. If the sound display is head-based (i.e., headphones), extra processing must be done to compensate for the user's movement. In order for the location of a sound to appear fixed with respect to the world, the position of the participant's head must be incorporated in the sound computation.

Once these filtering functions are determined for a large number of different locations around the person's head, that information can be used in a VR experience in real time by loading those mathematical functions into a sound spatialization device like a *Convolvotron*. Then, in real time in the VR experience, if the developer wants to make it appear that a sound is coming from a specific place, they pass the sound through the specific filtering function for that particular place. The participant

Virtual Binoculars (continued)

can easily be used within a VR environment displayed on a stationary visual display, providing an intuitive method for users to look more closely at distant objects in the virtual world.

FIGURE 4-26 Virtual Binoculars *by n-vision, inc. can be used to provide a VR display that can be carried in the hand (Image courtesy of n-vision, inc.).*

then perceives that the sound came from the location the VR application designer intended. All of this is assuming that the head position is in a fixed, known location. In a VR application, however, the participant is likely moving around; thus the head position must be tracked and that information integrated with the sound spatialization function.

Convolvotrons aren't used that much anymore, because computers are now much faster. Increasingly, these computations are done on a standard (general purpose) computer.

The transfer functions used by the *Convolvotron* are referred to as *head-related transfer functions,* or HRTFs. An HRTF is specific to each individual, but research has been done to find HRTFs that are sufficiently generic to be useful to a variety of individuals, providing an effect that is "good enough."

There are additional cues that aid the participant in determining the location of sound. One such cue comes from the *ventriloquism effect*. The ventriloquism effect exploits the psychoacoustic phenomenon (learned from experience) that sound is likely to be coming from where it *looks* like it should be coming from. This is a very strong localization cue. Thus, if someone hears a voice and sees a mouth moving in synchronization with the voice, they are likely to perceive the direction of the sound as coming from the mouth. Likewise, in a virtual world, the visual presence of a drum is likely to aid the participant in believing that a drum sonic image is coming from the direction of the drum visual image.

In general, humans are not as skilled in localizing sound as might be expected—in either the real world or the virtual world. Thus, it is important to aid the participant with compelling cues. These cues can be provided by using devices such as the *Convolvotron* or by any other means that cause sound to seem to be located in a specific place. Other rendering possibilities are computer-controlled delay units, reverberation, and so on.

Three-dimensional sound fields can be recorded or created. Recording a 3D sound field can be done by recording separate channels, one for the left and one for the right ear, each positioned such that it receives filtering similar to that created by the body of a listener. This filtering can be accomplished by actually putting the microphones in the ear canal of a human subject or on a mannequin head that sufficiently models the shape of the human head and ears. Another way to create a 3D sound field is to computationally generate one by spatializing multiple sound sources into different locations in the environment.

Properties of Aural Displays

Choices for aural display are few in comparison with visual display options. However, there are still many issues involved in the decision to use speakers or headphones. Several properties of aural displays affect a given VR experience. Only a few presentation properties are specific to aural displays, whereas the logistic properties are about the same as for visual displays, as the following summaries demonstrate.

Aural Presentation Properties

- Number of display channels
- Sound stage
- Localization
- Masking
- Amplification

Logistic Properties

- Noise pollution
- User mobility
- Interface with tracking methods
- Environment requirements
- Associability with other sense displays
- Portability
- Throughput
- Encumbrance
- Safety
- Cost

Aural Presentation Properties

In general, sound is created and processed with much less computation than for 3D computer graphics. Thus, latency and lag are less of a concern with the audio component of a VR display. On the other hand, our ears are much more sensitive to minute dropouts (interruptions) and minor inconsistencies in synchronization than our eyes are. Therefore, it is still important that sound be computed quickly and delivered exactly in synchronization with the associated visual information. Due to the low cost of producing high-fidelity sound, it is usually straightforward to provide high-quality sound at an appropriate level of both temporal and dynamic resolution.

Sound has other characteristics that one must consider when selecting a suitable sonic display. The noise in the vicinity of the VR system can be obtrusive, and the sound from the VR system can be intrusive in the area surrounding the system. There are several presentation properties, which we describe in the sections that follow, that are important to a VR system. These include the number of display channels, the sound stage, localization, masking, and amplification.

Number of Display Channels. Because we have two ears, it is possible to present the same information (monophonic) or different information (stereophonic) to each ear. Because of the space between the ears, each ear typically receives slightly different information. The signals travel different paths before reaching the ears. These signal differences help the brain to determine the source of the sound.

Stereophonic headphones can be used to deliver sound signals that replicate these cues; however, a stereophonic sound source that is not produced based on the user's position within the environment can be misleading, because those stereophonic signals will provide spatial cues that will not correlate with the virtual world visuals.

Sound Stage. The *sound stage* is the source from which a sound appears to emanate relative to the listener (FIGURE 4-27). If not modified to adjust to user movement, the sound stage seems to remain fixed (world-referenced) to the line between the two speakers in stationary speaker displays. In contrast, the sound stage is mobile (head-referenced) in unmodified head-based headphone displays. Headphones can also produce a world-referenced sound stage if the sound is modified to compensate for the user's movement. Either world-referenced or head-referenced sound stages are fine for ambient sounds or nonimmersive listening, but for sounds embedded in an immersive environment, the user will generally expect the sound stage to have a fixed position in the virtual world and not move around with the user.

For example, if you are in your living room listening to a CD, the music sounds spread out in the stereo field (the singer seems to be between the speakers, the violin may be to the right, etc.). If you walk around the room, those instruments sound like they stay in the same place (if the violin is on your right, by your recliner, and you turn around, the violin sounds like it is *still* in that same spot by the recliner). However, if you are wearing headphones and you turn, the violin is always to *your* right. If you are facing forward, it is by the recliner, but if you turn around, it is now

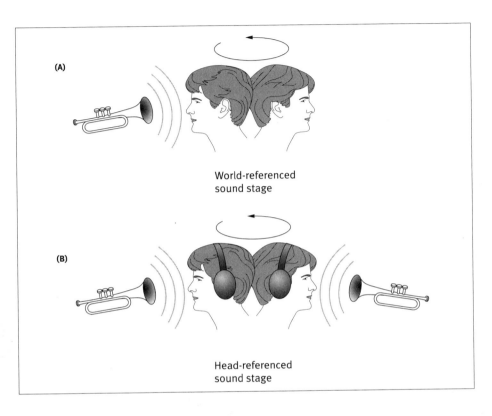

(A)

World-referenced
sound stage

(B)

Head-referenced
sound stage

FIGURE 4-27 **(A)** *In a world-referenced sound stage, the source of the sound remains fixed with respect to the world.* **(B)** *In a head-referenced sound stage, the source of the sound appears to move when the participant moves their head.*

on the opposite side of the room from the recliner. So, in order to have it *always* seem like it is by the recliner while wearing headphones, you need to track the head and use that information to do computations on the sound to make it stay in an absolute spot rather than in a spot relative to your head.

Localization. In the real world, we are able to perceive the three-dimensionality of sounds through a variety of sound characteristics, cues from the world itself, and our own hearing system. In general, our brains are able to perceive the location of a sound by compiling a set of cues, including interaural delay (the difference in time it takes for sound to reach each of our ears), the difference in amplitude (volume) of the signal between our two ears, echoes and reverberation, filtering of the sound based on the material the sound passes through or over, the body's occlusion of certain frequencies, and the filtering provided by our pinnae (outer ears). The feat of perception, of being able to figure out where sound is coming from, is called *localization*.

In a room with some furniture and a television, a listener can close their eyes and still determine where the television is relative to their position. When they hear the sound, they are not only hearing it come directly from the TV, they also hear many reflections of the sound that bounce off the furniture and walls of the room before being received by their ears. Each of the different surfaces the sound bounces off also filters the sound in a particular way. After all this, the sounds are affected by the listener's own body. Their torso and head will act as additional filters, followed by the folds of the outer ear. Finally, the sound arrives at each eardrum at slightly different times. The listener's brain can integrate the timing and characteristics of the filtered sound to determine the location of the TV.

By tracking the listener's head, sounds can be processed by filtering algorithms and displayed to their ears through speakers or headphones. The process of making a sound seem to come from a particular location in space is called *spatialization*. Individual sounds can be processed by a computer and made to seem to come from the appropriate spot. Spatialized sounds can also be directly recorded by placing microphones within a mannequin head's ear canals. Without further processing, when playing back sounds recorded in this manner through headphones, this 3D sound field will be head-referenced, just like any other unprocessed sounds.

A head-referenced 3D sound field can be effectively overlayered with monophonic sounds, as discovered by the creators of Disney's interactive VR experience *Aladdin,* based on the movie of the same name [Pausch et al. 1996]. For example, for a market scene in the *Aladdin* experience (FIGURE 4-28), a general 3D sound field of ambient market noises was recorded and combined with the spatialized voice of important characters in the scene [Snoddy 1996].

A 3D effect can be faked using sound-effect processors with reverberation and delay effects. Reverb effects can be used to create a perceptual cue indicating the size of the space the participant is in—longer delays in the reverberation make the space sound larger.

FIGURE 4-28 *Ambient stereo sounds that provide background atmosphere, such as marketplace voices, can be combined with spatialized sounds, such as character voices, that seem to emanate from a specific location (Image courtesy of Walt Disney Engineering).*

Headphones present sound directly to the ear, whereas speakers present a combination of direct and reflected sound. Thus, in headphones, it is much easier to control exactly what sound is presented to each ear, and it is easier to determine the relative placement between the display and the ear. The greater proximity of the headphone display makes it much easier to create 3D sound fields through headphones than through loudspeakers. Sounds presented through loudspeakers cannot be controlled to ensure that each ear hears only the information intended for it. Sounds from speakers reflect off of other things in the environment, the participant's body, projection screens, and so on. With headphones, the participant hears only the direct sound presented to them, and information can be presented exactly as needed for a particular effect. Certain effects, such as causing the sound to appear to come from within the head of the listener, are feasible only by using headphones.

Masking. *Masking* of sound occurs in two ways. A loud sound can mask a soft sound. This kind of masking can occur with both headphones and speakers. The other type of masking occurs when a physical entity like a pillow or a projection screen blocks the path of sound from the speaker to the ear.

Because sound carries around corners and through some materials, these occluding objects do not completely block sound; however, they do filter it. For example, placing a pillow in front of a speaker muffles the sound coming from that speaker in a certain, characteristic way. In this example, higher frequency (pitch) sounds will be muffled more than lower frequency sounds. A more likely scenario in a VR system is that a projection screen might be located between a speaker and the participant.

Real-world sounds within the environment cannot always be fully masked by speaker systems. Headphones, however, can be used to deliberately occlude sounds from the real world. In particular, closed-ear headphones (the kind that cover the entire ear) are designed to prevent the passage of sound from the outside world to the participant's ear. Likewise sounds from the headphones are occluded from passing to the outside. There are also open-ear headphones, designed to allow outside world sounds to enter. As long as the headphone sound is not too loud, a person wearing open-ear headphones can also hear sounds from the outside world.

In some VR experiences, participants communicate with one another via microphones, sometimes with each voice processed by specific filters to alter the sonic characteristics of their voice (e.g., to make their voice sound like that of a child). Loud, ringing feedback noise may result if open-ear headphones are used by applications that use microphone voice input. Feedback is caused by the sound looping from the speaker or headphones through to the microphone.

When headphones are used by the participant, onlookers should have headphone or speaker access to the system. If speakers are used in the virtual world, onlookers may have access to the participant's speakers. In general, though, it is likely that additional speakers will need to be provided for the onlookers to produce the best sound for both participants and onlookers.

Amplification. Regardless of whether headphones or speakers are used, an *amplifier* is required to boost the audio signals to appropriate levels. The amplifier need not be as powerful for headphones as for speakers. Systems using a greater number of speakers may require multiple amplifiers. Additionally, room size and volume requirements may demand more amplifier power. Multiple amps are mainly an issue of distribution to multiple speakers. Hooking up more and more speakers to a single amp can lead to low power levels, impedence mismatches, and ultimately harm to the amplifier. Some amps are built to do that, some aren't.

Logistic Qualities

In much the same way that visual displays have logistic and ergonomic qualities that can affect the choice of display unit, audio displays have similar practical, logistic considerations. This section describes some of the more important considerations.

Noise Pollution. It is important to consider the environment in which the audio is displayed. In a VR experience, noises from the real world can pollute the VR experience and vice versa. For experiences that alter participant voices before presenting them to the other participants, the real voices of the participants are unwanted sounds and hence a source of *noise pollution*.

Sounds from the speakers may be objectionable to others in the area who are not involved in the experience. In contrast, headphones allow one to listen without the sounds being overheard by others. Systems using speakers require an environment that is reasonably quiet and echo free.

User Mobility. Headphones typically have a cable connecting them to the amplifier. This can restrict the participant's movements. Wireless versions are available that use radio or infrared transmission of the audio signal. Speakers do not inhibit the movements of the participant, but the sound does appear fainter when farther from the speakers, so one must stay within the audible range of the speakers (although this can be overcome somewhat by automatically adjusting speaker amplification based on the user's position).

Interface with Tracking Methods. Headphones and speakers both utilize magnets that can interfere with electromagnetic tracking sensors. Headphones generally have smaller magnets but are typically located closer to the head tracking sensor. Speakers can have an adverse effect on some sonic tracking systems by overwhelming (masking) the sound pulses used by the tracking system to measure distances; this can be a particular problem with high-frequency sound signals. Usually, the same tracking technology is used to provide position information for creating both the audio and visual display. That is, there is no need for an additional tracking unit for audio if there is already one provided for the visual display. Tracking only comes into play for the audio system when one must create a world-referenced sound stage in a headphone display, when creating spatialized sounds, and for any other sound display that is dependent on the participant's position (e.g., when sounds must be changed as the participant moves about the space).

Environment Requirements. The room itself can bounce sound waves and generate cues that may not be intended for the VR experience. The room that the system is in has more impact on a speaker display than on a headphone display. A projection system like the *CAVE*, with squarely aligned surfaces (the screens), can create problems for an audio display. One problem is echoes created by sound reflections within the *CAVE*. All of the normal problems of acoustics in cubical rooms (standing waves, constructive and destructive interference, flutter echoes, etc.) are problematic in a cubical display environment. These can create unexpected or uncontrollable results. Other room noises—from the computing system or air conditioning, for instance— can also adversely affect speaker and open-ear headphone audio presentation.

Associability with Other Sense Displays. In general, headphones are associated with head-based visual displays and speakers with projection displays. Headphones are easily combined with head-based visual displays (especially HMDs) so that both visual and aural senses are handled by one device. Also, both HMDs and headphones are associated with private viewing and listening, whereas projection displays and speakers work well for group presentations. There may be particular applications that benefit from the use of headphones within a projection-based visual display or from speakers with an HMD. In general, anytime one desires spatialized audio, headphones are most likely the best choice.

Because of visual and aural masking, it can be difficult to place speakers in a projection visual display system. If the speakers are placed in front of the projection screen, they can occlude the visual display. If the speakers are placed behind the screen, the screen can occlude the passage of sound to the participant.

Portability. Certainly, headphones are more portable than speakers. If it is important to be able to move the entire system frequently (as in a road show), headphones may be logistically easier to transport from one venue to the next. They require no stands and are generally easier to set up and pack away.

Throughput. Headphones take time to don and doff. This time can be significant in venues where throughput is a major concern. Each person who needs to hear requires a pair of headphones. If there are more people than available headphones, then headphones would need to be shared among listeners. With speakers, everyone can listen at once. Thus, for large crowds, speakers can lead to faster throughput.

Encumbrance. It is often more comfortable to listen to speakers for greater lengths of time than headphones, which can be both uncomfortable and fatiguing due to their weight.

Safety. While hearing damage can occur with either speakers or headphones, the fact that headphones are held tightly against the ears leads to a greater possibility of hearing damage if the volume is accidentally turned too high. Also, the cables connecting the headphones to the amplifier can be a tripping hazard. And, there are hygiene concerns whenever any device is passed from individual to individual.

Cost. In general, high-quality headphones are lower in cost than equivalent quality speakers. Speakers require a more powerful, more expensive amplifier. The tradeoff is that every participant requires a pair of headphones. One pair of headphones may cost less than a pair of speakers, but a dozen pairs may cost more than the price of a speaker system.

Head-based Aural Displays—Headphones

Similar to the head-based visual display, head-based aural displays (headphones) move with the participant's head, are for one person only, and provide an isolated environment. As with head-based visual displays, one can seal off the real world using *closed-ear* head-phones, or allow real-world sounds to be heard along with synthetic sounds with *open-ear* (hear-through) headphones (FIGURE 4-29). Because headphones generally are dual-channel displays located near each ear, the presentation of stereophonic and 3D spa-

FIGURE 4-29 *Closed-ear head-phones (right) shut out sounds from the real world, whereas open-ear headphones (left) allow real-world sounds to be heard (Photograph by William Sherman).*

tialized sounds is much easier to accomplish with headphones than with speakers.

Headphones display head-referenced sounds by default. When sounds in a 3D virtual world should appear to come from a particular location, it is important to track the head position of the participant so that spatialization information reflects the changing location of the listener's ears. Unlike wearing headphones to listen to stereophonic music, in a virtual reality experience, the sound stage should stay registered with the virtual world. This requires tracking the participant's head and filtering the sound appropriately.

Stationary Aural Displays—Speakers

Speakers are the stationary aural display system. Although speakers generally correspond more closely with projection visual displays, both work well as group presentation devices so it is possible to use speakers with head-based visual displays.

One problem encountered with the combination of speakers and projection screens is that one display will often mask the other. If speakers are placed behind the projection screen, then the sound will be muffled; however, if the speakers are placed in front of the screen, then the visuals are blocked. If the visual display is not a 100% field of regard system, then speakers can be moved to the region with no display, but this may make the creation of spatialized sound difficult.

The stationary nature of speakers makes the sounds they produce world-referenced, which is advantageous, because the world-referenced sound stage is generally preferred in VR systems. However, creating spatialized sounds using speaker technology can be more difficult than with headphones.

Ambisonics is the presentation of 3D spatialized sound using multiple stationary speakers. Research on ambisonics continues to move forward and may result in a usable system in the future [Gerzon 1992], but the fact that both ears can hear the sounds from each of the speakers makes this a difficult feat to accomplish.

Combining Aural Display Systems

It is also possible to combine the two types of aural display systems. For instance, very low bass sounds are nondirectional and do not require that separate information go to each ear. The sound waves are long enough (low frequency) that we don't get the same cues we get from high-frequency sounds. Research shows that people are much worse at localizing sound than one might expect, particularly for low frequencies. What we are best at localizing are high-frequency impulses. Low bass sounds are also often emitted loudly, creating a rumbling sensation. These bass sounds could be displayed via a subwoofer speaker, while the rest of the virtual world sounds are displayed via headphone.

Summary of Aural Displays

Aural displays can be added to a VR system fairly easily and inexpensively. Neither headphone- nor speaker-based systems cost very much when compared with the cost of visual displays. Considering the added information and immersive benefits of sound, the addition of aural display can be very cost-effective.

Benefits of Stationary Displays (Speakers)

- Works well with stationary visual displays
- Does not require sound processing to create a world-referenced sound stage (i.e., one that remains stable to the virtual world)
- Greater user mobility
- Little encumbrance
- Multiuser access means faster throughput

Benefits of Head-based Displays (Headphones)

- Works well with head-coupled visual displays
- Easier to implement spatialized 3D sound fields
- Masks real-world noise
- Greater portability
- Private

In the real world, we gain a significant amount of information via sound. Sound often tells our eyes where to look. Since our ears are open channels (we have no "earlids"), we use our hearing to keep us constantly aware of the world around us. Given the importance of sound in the real world and its relatively low cost to implement in the virtual world, it behooves VR application designers to consider how sound might be used to positive effect in the applications they build.

Haptic Displays

When it comes to believing something is "real," the haptic sense (our sense of touch and proprioception) is quite powerful. By coming into physical contact with an object, its existence is verified. Haptics are hard to fool, which means that creating a satisfactory display device is difficult.

Haptic, from the Greek, relates to physical contact or touch. The nature of the haptic interface dictates that it is a form of both input and output: as output it is physical stimuli *displayed* by the computer, and because of its physical connection to the participant, it is also an input device *to* the computer. (However, we should note that there are cases where it is used strictly as input or output; for example, a Braille display would be output only.)

We loosely refer to haptic perception as the sense of touch but, more specifically, haptic perception involves the combined sensations of *kinesthesia* and *taction*.

Kinesthesia is the perception of movement or strain from within the muscles, tendons, and joints of the body. The term *proprioception,* which means stimulation from within the body, is often used as a synonym of kinesthesia, as is the term *force feedback* or *force display.* In fact, proprioception also refers to an individual's ability to sense their own body posture, even when no forces are acting upon it, but this ability is entirely internal and is not affected by external devices.

Taction is the sense of touch that comes from sensitive nerve sensors at the surface of the skin. Tactile display includes stimuli for temperature on the skin (thermoreception) as well as pressure (mechanoreception). Mechanoreceptor information is filtered by the nervous system, such that the brain receives information about both immediate and long-term changes in pressure. Mechanoreception enables the brain to sense such things as when an event is occurring or how the surface texture of an object feels as the skin rubs over it.

In the human, separation of kinesthetic and tactile reception is nearly impossible. However, for computer display, the two have rarely been combined. It is likely that in future devices, combined tactile and proprioceptic output will be more common.

Some VR applications augment the benefits of haptic feedback by *transference of object permanence*. By making one object in the virtual world seem very real (using haptics), the rest of the world seems more real as well.

Overall, VR applications use haptic displays less often than visual and aural displays. Although some forms of haptic display have been researched for several years in teleoperations, its use has been applied to just a handful of VR applications.

Use of haptic display in VR is on the rise in applications that involve training or evaluation of manual tasks, such as medical operations or serviceability testing of mechanical equipment. An example of the latter is a virtual wrench constrained—by the haptic display system—to only those movements possible in the real world.

Sometimes haptic display is extremely effective. Ouh-Young and colleagues [1989] have found that scientists can better analyze forces involved in molecular docking by including haptic display in their simulated environment. Molecules interacting with other molecules have a number of attracting and repelling forces at play between them. By being able to feel the attractions and repulsions, scientists are able to understand different configurations of molecule pairs. This study shows that the addition of the haptic display increased the performance of this task in a way that is statistically significant.

Haptic displays are significantly more difficult to create than are visual or aural displays, because our haptic system is bidirectional. It not only *senses* the world, it also *affects* the world. If I touch something, it also moves. This is in sharp contrast to listening to something or looking at it, which has no effect on the object itself. Touch is the only bidirectional sensory channel and, apart from gustation (taste), it is the only sense that cannot be stimulated from a distance. Herein lies part of the difficulty: the display requires direct contact with the human body.

Despite the difficulties, haptic feedback can be very beneficial to any number of virtual reality applications. One method to make haptic display more feasible is to analyze the task to determine whether any constraints can be placed on user movement without altering the effectiveness of the application. It is a lot easier to have a haptic display that only involves one kind of motion or motion in a small area, for example, than to worry about the whole general sense of haptic feedback. For example, in minimally invasive surgery, the surgeon is limited in what movements they can make in controlling the instruments by the nature of the task. These constraints make surgery simulations with haptic VR displays very useful as training devices. The use of simple non–computer-interfaced props and platforms can also provide beneficial haptic effects.

It is more difficult to differentiate haptic displays based on the three general display categories—stationary, head-based, and handheld—because the user interacts with most haptic displays via the hand. Generally, humans do not receive much haptic sensation through their heads. Most haptic input comes through the hands and arms, as well as the legs and feet (especially when locomoting). Most haptic displays are in some way *hand-based*. A few belong to the *foot-coupled display* category. Objects that are passive haptic representations—that is, static materials that represent, say, a wall or a ledge—may be considered stationary VR displays. Such objects are often part of a platform device, where the user is located when immersed in the experience.

The primary methods of haptic interface used in and researched for applicability to virtual reality experiences can be divided into four categories (although the last category is less robust because it isn't interactive):

1. *Tactile displays* provide information to the user in response to touching, grasping, feeling surface textures, or sensing the temperature of an object.

2. *End-effector displays* (including locomotive displays) provide a means to simulate grasping and probing objects. These displays provide resistance and pressure to achieve these effects.

3. *Robotically operated shape displays* use robots to present physical objects to the user's fingertips or to a fingertip surrogate. These displays provide information about shape, texture, and location to the user.

4. *3D Hardcopy* is the automated creation of physical models based on computer models, which provides a haptic and visual representation of an object. Since the model is a static object, it functions only as an output system.

Most tactile displays focus specifically on the fingertips. Most force displays focus on the limbs as a whole, such as a manipulation arm, a stairstepper, or a unicycle device. Seldom have the different modes of haptic display been combined, although they could be.

Properties of Haptic Displays

As with visual and aural display paradigms, there are a number of factors that affect the quality of display, which we summarize in the following lists.

Haptic Presentation Properties

- Kinesthetic cues
- Tactile cues
- Grounding
- Number of display channels
- Degrees of freedom
- Form
- Fidelity
- Spatial resolution
- Temporal resolution
- Latency tolerance
- Size

Logistic Properties

- User mobility
- Interface with tracking methods
- Environment requirements
- Associability with other sense displays
- Portability
- Throughput
- Encumbrance
- Safety
- Cost

Haptic Presentation Properties

Haptic devices vary in what kinds of cues they provide, how responsive they are, how they are connected to the body, and in terms of logistics. This section addresses a number of haptic display qualities and illuminates how those qualities are important to different applications.

Kinesthetic Cues. *Kinesthetic cues* are the combination of nerve inputs sensing the angles of the joint, muscle length, and tension, plus resistance to muscle effort (force). Kinesthetic cues are used by the brain to determine information about the world, such as the firmness and approximate shape of objects and physical forces like strong wind and gravity exerted by the world on the participant. There are 75 joints in the entire body (44 in the hands alone), all of which are capable of receiving kinesthetic cues, making it very difficult for a single display to engage each possible point of force on the user.

Tactile Cues. *Tactile cues* are those that use sensory receptors at the skin to gather input about the world. Mechanoreceptors in the skin are used to gain detailed information about the shape and surface texture of objects. Thermoreceptors sense the rate of transfer of heat between an object and the skin. Electroreceptors sense electrical current flow through the skin. Tissue damage pain is sensed by the nociceptors.

Grounding. Force/resistance displays require an anchor or grounding point to supply the base against which pressure can be applied. Grounding can be categorized into self-grounded and world-grounded systems. A self-grounded system creates or limits motion against itself, such as preventing an arm from being fully extended. Imagine a computer-controlled linkage between your hand and your chest. This system can affect how you move your arm. There are a set of motions your arm is constrained to, but you can still walk around. All the force display is derived from your own body and no force is derived from the world in an absolute sense. It is *self-grounded* because it is not tied directly to anything other than your body. Self-grounded systems can be portable but are limited in the types of forces that can be displayed.

Now consider that linkage as if it were anchored between your hand and the wall. Now it restricts your arm movement to an *absolute* set of positions. This is called *world-grounded*. A world-grounded system creates resistance, limits motion between the user and some external body like a point in the floor or ceiling, or exerts force against the user.

Number of Display Channels. Haptic displays can consist of a single feedback channel—to one hand or joint depending on the device—or can be used in tandem to accomplish tasks requiring two hands.

Degrees of Freedom. There are six *degrees of freedom* in unconstrained, free movement. The number of DOF in a haptic display can vary from one to six. A common method of force display provides three degrees of movement in the three spatial dimensions. A 3-DOF device allows users to probe a space as they would with a stick or a single fingertip. 2-DOF movement restricted to a line can be useful in systems where a device is inserted into a tube. A mouse or joystick equipped with force display can provide two-dimensional movement. Movements in space combined with rotational feedback provide up to six degrees of movement, as seen with the JPL/Salisbury *Force Reflecting Hand Controller* in FIGURE 4-30 [Bejczy and Salisbury 1983].

Form. The *form* of a haptic display device is the shape of the physical unit with which the participant interacts. The form of the haptic display can be (1) a prop used to represent a particular shape, such as a stick, ball, or plane; (2) a prop in the shape of a real-world object, such as a handgun; or (3) an amorphous form that changes according to the needs of the display, such as a glove or a pin display.

> FIGURE 4-30 *One example of what a multi-DOF force feedback device looks like is the JPL/Salisbury* Force Reflecting Hand Controller *(FRHC). It was designed by Kenneth Salisbury and John Hill in the mid-1970s at the Stanford Research Institute in Menlo Park, California, under contract from NASA JPL. It is a 6-DOF force-reflecting master device that has found use in telerobotic and VR research (Photo courtesy of NASA and Ken Salisbury).*

When specialized instruments are required in a training task, the instruments are usually equipped with tracking sensors. In medical training applications, the use of actual needles, arthroscopic instruments, and sutures duplicates the feel of the actual task, while the device displays force or some other type of haptic sensation. As a secondary benefit, it is easier to implement applications that use mechanized and sensor-equipped instruments. The constraints and nuances of controlling an instrument are built into the instruments themselves and require less software simulation.

The prop style of input device (discussed in Chapter 3) can be felt by users in their hands and thus can be considered a limited haptic display in that it employs

a *form* with which the user interacts. We refer to the use of inactive props for their haptic properties as *passive haptics*. The only thing you feel is the form of the object; there are no active force elements.

Fidelity. There are many tradeoffs involved in determining the *fidelity* of a haptic display. First and foremost is safety. It is generally undesirable for a VR experience to accurately duplicate the forces involved in jumping from a five-story building. High-fidelity systems often require unsafe levels of power, which if programmed incorrectly could be very hazardous. The size of a display also affects fidelity, as the inertia of the device itself makes it harder to finely control forces. With a temperature device, a measure of fidelity is how rapidly it can change from one temperature to another and what range of temperatures it can display. One must also consider safety when using temperature devices to avoid burning the user.

Force devices can be rated by a maximum stiffness measurement taken in Newtons/meter (Nt/m). (A Nt is a unit of measure for force, and Nt/m is a unit of measure for stiffness). Tan and colleagues [1994] report that most users will accept a stiffness of 20 Nt/cm as a solid immovable wall. The maximum force that can be exerted by a human finger is about 40 Nt; however, performing precise manipulations rarely exceeds 10 Nt.

Spatial Resolution. The brain's ability to discriminate closely spaced tactile stimuli (the *just noticeable difference* or JND) varies by region of the body. On the back, stimuli up to 70 mm apart are felt as occurring in one place; on the forearm this distance falls to 30 mm; and on the fingertip, it drops to only 2 mm. This information tells us that high-resolution devices are necessary for displaying textures to the fingertips, but less resolution is required to display to the forearm. These differences in spatial resolution determine how fine a texture can be rendered, either as a direct tactile sensation or through the tip of a stylus display like the *PHANTOM*.

Temporal Resolution. In a force display system, low *temporal resolution* (frame rate) can adversely affect the feel of simulated objects. For example, an object may feel softer than intended, or the user may experience vibrations as they "touch" an object. Temporal resolution also measures how quickly a temperature display can be updated to new temperatures. If the frame rate on a force display is too low, it will either feel "mushy" or "shaky" or vibrate irratically. Shimoga [1992] provides a chart indicating the rates at which our bodies can sense and/or react to various stimuli. In developing the *PHANTOM* device, Thomas Massey found that running a frame rate at 1,000 Hz produced haptic effects that felt correct, with only minimal improvement at higher rates [Massie 1993].

Latency Tolerance. Longer lag time, or *latency,* between actions and the system's response can degrade the illusion of the displayed world's solidity. Because haptic displays usually involve hand–eye coordination tasks, reduction of the latency in the visual display system becomes increasingly important. In applications where multiple participants are sharing a virtual world and are interacting together via haptic display, delays between systems can be catastrophic for the simulation. This can be avoided if the participants need not interact simultaneously with each other or with a single object. For example, in a tennis match, only a single user has any haptic interaction between the ball and their virtual racket at any given time; however, if both participants are trying to pick up a large object, lag time must be minimal.

Since haptic displays require physical contact with the participant, the participant's motion can be tracked mechanically. This type of tracking has lower latency and higher accuracy than many other body-tracking systems.

Size. The *size* of the force display device plays a large role in what types of interactions can be simulated. A larger display generally allows a larger range of motion, thus enabling more tasks. However, a larger system can be a greater safety concern. Smaller, table-top displays work well for applications that emulate tasks such as surgical tasks done in a limited work area.

Logistic Properties

Haptic display devices range from small units that sit on the desktop or are worn on the hand to large robotic devices capable of lifting a man off the ground. Because there are so many different aspects to haptic feedback (taction, proprioception, thermo-reception, electroreception, etc.) and so many different body parts that the display can be coupled with, haptic displays have a very wide range of logistic qualities. Compared with visual and aural devices, haptic devices tend to be more specifically tied to particular applications. This section addresses some of the logistic qualities of haptic devices.

User Mobility. World-grounded haptic displays require the user to remain near the display device, which limits *user mobility.* For applications where the participant is stationary, this is not so detrimental. Self-grounded systems can be worn by the user and are thus more mobile; however, the necessary cables present an additional encumbrance.

Interface with Tracking Methods. Because of the low-latency, high frame-rate requirements of haptic displays, the associated *tracking method* must be equally responsive to achieve a realistic display. Fortunately for force display systems, the tracking is often built into the display using fast and accurate devices.

For systems where high-quality tracking is required, some object is used to mediate between the user and the virtual world. For example, the user might probe the simulated world using a stick-like device. This device is basically a surrogate finger. The surrogate is tracked with an accurate, high-speed method, allowing the virtual world to seem more realistic. Tactile displays mounted on a glove can be less effective, since hand tracking is usually performed by slower, less accurate tracking.

Environment Requirements. Large force displays will generally *require* a specialized room in which to operate. The room might be equipped with hydraulic or pneumatic pressure pumps. Smaller force displays might be built right into a kiosk platform suitable for operation in any room. An example of the kiosk platform display is shown in FIGURE 4-31.

Associability with Other Sense Displays. A drawback to most force display systems is that they can be seen. Unless the display device itself is also part of the virtual world, some effort is required to mask it from view. The simplest solution is to use an occlusive head-based display for the visual system. Another method is to locate the visual display between the force display and the eyes. The Boston Dynamics, Inc. suture trainer hides the force display system using a mirror. The University of Colorado *Celias Plexus Block* (a medical procedure) simulator [Reinig et al. 1996] hides the entire robotic display inside a simulated human body.

Portability. Small haptic displays can be *transported* between sites without too much difficulty. Larger force displays may be more difficult to take on the road if they require significant equipment for generating hydraulic or pneumatic pressure. Systems that are physically mounted to a floor or ceiling are further limited in portability.

Throughput. Wearable devices like gloves and other self-grounded displays can slow the exchange among participants. Some displays necessitate wearing backpack-like devices to support the force display, requiring significant time to don and doff the equipment.

Encumbrance. Only larger, exoskeleton-style devices usually involve much *encumbrance* of the user. Small force displays and glove devices are less encumbering.

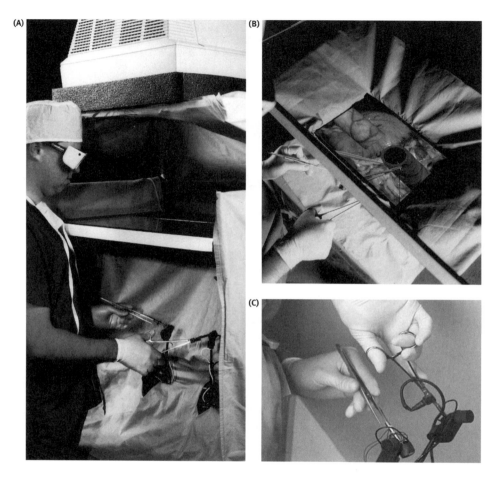

(A)

(B)

(C)

FIGURE 4-31 *These images show a surgeon using a virtual reality surgical trainer built into a kiosk display. Image (C) is a close-up showing the use of actual medical instruments coupled to force feedback devices (Images courtesy of Boston Dynamics, Inc.). See color plate 7.*

Safety. *Safety* is obviously a significant concern when working with large robotic force displays. Large robots can deliver fatal blows to humans, and exoskeleton devices can entrap the body. To increase the level of safety when working with such systems, a "drop-dead" switch is generally placed in the loop. Usually these switches must be pressed with the foot for the machinery to operate. As soon as the foot releases the switch, power is cut off from the system. Thus, if the user senses that the system is doing or about to do something harmful or if the user is knocked over, the system immediately stops. Incorporating a drop-dead switch in smaller displays is often a wise decision in the event of a malfunction, because even though the forces are not strong enough to injure a person, the device may damage itself.

Cost. Haptic displays are *costly*. Part of the reason for this is that they are not widely used and therefore do not benefit from mass market pricing. In addition, haptic displays are more complicated to manufacture than other elements of a VR system, because they contain several moving parts.

Tactile Haptic Displays

Tactile displays focus on the skin's ability to interpret stimuli. The categories of skin (dermal) stimuli are pressure, temperature, electricity, and pain. The two methods most commonly used to "attach" the user to the display are to affix actuators to a participant's hand or have the user grasp a wand, joystick, or steering wheel device. Even if there is no active force feedback, you can still feel the object, which constitutes a certain kind of haptic feedback. A steering wheel without force feedback still feels more realistic and is easier to manipulate than a virtual one.

Components of Tactile Displays

In this section we discuss available actuators for tactile displays, including inflatable bladders, vibrators, pin arrangements, temperature-regulating devices, and specialized pressure devices, such as a chest thumper (a low-frequency speaker worn on the chest that provides thumps and rumble effects). We also consider handheld input devices like props as simple tactile displays.

Bladder actuators are pockets that can be expanded and contracted by controlling the flow of air (pneumatic) or liquid (hydraulic) into and out of the pockets. Strategic placement of the pockets creates the sensation of pressure on different areas of the participant's hand and body. Although no longer available, the *Teletact Glove* from the Advanced Robotics Research Lab (ARRL) had 30 bladders distributed across the palm and on the front and back of the fingers (FIGURE 4-32).

Inflatable bladder technology has inherent difficulties. First, as with creating a data input glove, it is difficult to design a device that works well with many users. Second, the hardware is cumbersome to use, difficult to maintain, and fairly delicate. The response time of filling and vacating the bladders can be slow, especially in pneumatic-based systems. These inherent drawbacks might explain why the *Teletact Glove* is no longer available.

Vibrator actuators can be integrated with a glove input device or with a handheld prop (FIGURE 4-33). Typically, only a few vibrators are integrated into the display—one for each finger, placed on a prop, or located at one or two different locations. Vibrator actuators are more robust and easier to control than bladders, so they are often used to display the sensation of pressure. The pressure of a virtual

(A)

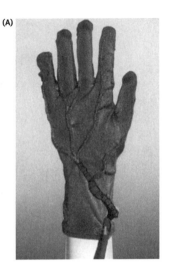

(B)

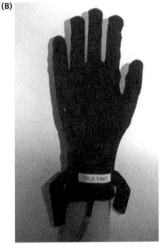

FIGURE 4-32 *The* Teletact Glove *(no longer available) provided haptic feedback using 30 bladders which expanded or contracted under computer control. When a bladder expanded the person wearing the glove sensed pressure (Photographs courtesy of Bob Stone).*

(A)

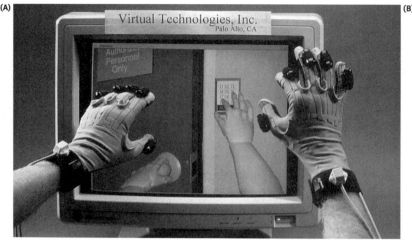

(B)

FIGURE 4-33 *Some gloves and props use vibrator actuators for tactile display. Often vibrations are used in a VR application as a sensory substitute for pressure from contact with a solid object. The* Cyberglove **(A)** *and* Cricket *prop* **(B)** *are equipped with vibrators (Photographs courtesy of Virtual Technologies, Inc. and Digital Image Design Inc., respectively).*

tennis ball can be represented by vibrations in the fingertips. As the ball is squeezed, the amount of vibration increases to indicate increased pressure on the fingers.

Low-frequency speakers (subwoofers) can also be used as a vibratory display. Such speakers can be placed under the floor, attached to a chair, concealed in a garment, or simply put in the room with the user(s). One such example is a chest thumper in use at the University of Houston for the *NewtonWorld* environment of *ScienceSpace* (FIGURE 4-34). This application uses very low-frequency sounds to generate a thump effect on the chest. In the *NewtonWorld* example, the participant

FIGURE 4-34 ScienceSpace *(developed by the University of Houston and George Mason University) teaches children physics concepts. In the* NewtonWorld *application shown here, participants collide with other objects. To heighten the sensation, the participant dons a vestlike garment equipped with a chest thumper, which provides physical feedback when they are involved in a collision (Image courtesy of Bowen Loftin).*

collides with a particle with a thump. The magnitude of the thump is based on the mass and velocity of the objects in the collision.

 Pin actuator technology is still being researched and has not been used in many applications. A pin-based system is used for the display of surface textures. Many pins are arranged in arrays that can move in and out of contact with the skin (FIGURE 4-35). Systems with small, square arrays placed on each finger are being

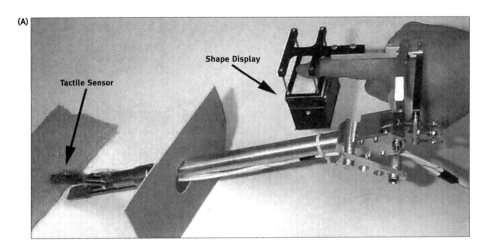

(A)

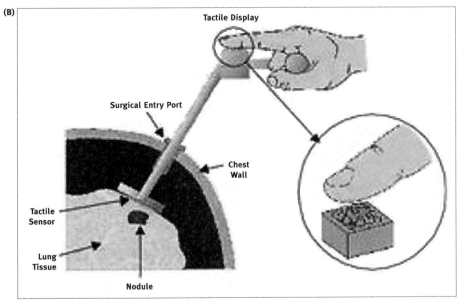

(B)

FIGURE 4-35 **(A)** *While not yet commonly used, pin actuators can provide surface texture display by varying pin pressure on the fingertips.* **(B)** *In this prototype device, a doctor can feel inside a patient's body during a minimally invasive surgical procedure (Images courtesy of William Peine, Harvard Biorobotics Laboratory).*

investigated, as are pins aligned on a rotating cylinder. Surface textures are detected by pressure variations across the fingertip over time.

Temperature actuators (thermo-actuators) are available that can very rapidly present temperature fluctuations, typically to the fingertips. These devices can become sufficiently hot or cold to damage human tissue. Thus, safety is a great concern. One solution is to display only a relative change in temperature to the finger, indicating that an item is "hot" or "cold," but not the exact real-world temperature. This solution is sufficient in many cases. Although thermal displays could be readily integrated into applications for which the temperature of virtual objects is important, they are still seldom used in virtual reality systems.

Features of Tactile Displays

The skin is the largest single organ of the human body. Consequently, full sensory coverage, or 100% tactile field of regard, is not yet feasible. Most tactile displays focus on the fingertips, where the majority of the tactile nerve endings are located and which we depend on for tasks requiring manual dexterity.

Interface Issues of Tactile Displays

The purpose of most tactile displays is to provide information in response to the participant's touching or grasping something or feeling its surface texture or temperature. The common display techniques used to generate these sensations are global pressure, multiple local pressures, vibration, and heat transfer.

When we touch or grasp an object, we feel the pressure of the object on our hand. A simple tactile display can produce a similar effect with expandable bladders. When a virtual object is grasped, the bladder fills with air or fluid by some amount proportional to the resistance of the object it represents. Currently, bladder systems are not widely available, so other technologies are commonly used. One technique mounts vibrators on the fingertips, usually on a data input glove, and adjusts the amount of vibration based on the pressure. This is an example of sensory substitution, because it tells the participant that they've touched something, but doesn't replicate real-life sensation.

Reproducing the surface texture of an object is more complicated. Sensing surface texture relies on the high density of pressure sensors (mechanoreceptors) in the fingertips and on the movement of the finger(s) over the surface. Generating virtual textures requires the fast and accurate sensing of participants' finger movements and rapid feedback from many pressure-sensing elements (e.g., pins).

Props as Tactile Displays

Props provide a basic method of tactile display. As a handheld device, a prop automatically provides the user with tactile sensations. The user can feel not only the shape but the weight, surface texture, and center of gravity, all of which enhance the sense of reality in an application—especially one that links the prop to a virtual device with similar characteristics. This is known as *transference of object permanence,* which we describe in more detail in Chapter 7.

In general, props are tactile displays that provide a sense of form only. Props such as *The Cricket* have an additional, integrated tactile actuator (in this case a vibrator). Other actuators could be incorporated, such as a temperature or pin texture display.

A primitive low-resolution method of surface texture display can be accomplished by moving a finger surrogate over the virtual surface and feeling the bumps. This method is easier to implement than displaying the texture directly to the fingers, because there is only a single point of contact between the surface and the probe. Also, the texture sensation comes mostly from kinesthetic feedback (devices for which are commercially available) rather than through fingertip displays.

Summary of Tactile Displays

Most tactile displays focus on presenting stimuli to the hands, particularly the fingers. This is because we usually use our hands and fingers when manipulating the world. Also most of our tactile nerve sensors are located in the fingertips.

Compared with most visual and aural display systems, tactile displays are not very advanced. The market for these devices is small, so less research is done on them. The most common actuators are simple vibrators, which often substitute for other types of tactile sensation such as pressure.

End-effector Displays

According to *Webster's* [1989], an *effector* is "an organ that becomes active in response to stimulation." Thus, an *end-effector* is a device mounted at the end of a robot arm that can be used to respond to stimulation. *End-effector displays* are force displays in which the user's extremities (hands and/or feet) grasp or otherwise contact a device that they can manipulate. In turn, this device can become active and respond to the user's actions with resistance and force. Examples of end-effector displays include multijointed hand grips, such as the *Argonne Remote Manipulator (ARM)* (FIGURE 4-36), desktop point controls such as the *PHANTOM* (see FIGURE 3-3B), resistive push pedals, resistive rotate pedals like the *Sarcos Uniport* system (FIGURE 4-37), and hand-motion limiters like the *Rutgers Masters I* and *II*.

Components of End-effector Displays

End-effector displays require both a means of sensing the user's movements and a means of supplying resistance at the point of contact with the user. Because these displays are mounted on a mechanical device, mechanical user-tracking can usually be integrated directly into the device, providing a fast and accurate response.

The means of affecting user movement is generally provided via one of two mechanical systems: electric motors or hydraulics/pneumatics. Electric motors can generate or resist rotational movement. Usually an additional motor is added for each

FIGURE 4-36 *An early example of the use of robotics to provide force feedback is the* Argonne Remote Manipulator (ARM) *device used in the GRIP project at UNC. The ARM device provides 6-DOF feedback for molecular docking and other applications (Image courtesy of the University of North Carolina at Chapel Hill). See color plate 8.*

degree of freedom of the display. By combining motors with mechanics, these rotational motions can be converted into translational motion (i.e., back and forth, up and down, left and right). Electric motors can also be used to control the movement of string attached to a thimble or to another end device. By attaching multiple strings to the device, the thimble's location within a confined working area can be controlled by the orchestration of the motors. Conversely, hydraulic and pneumatic pressure systems generally provide translational force, which can be mechanically converted into rotational forces.

FIGURE 4-37 *The* Sarcos Uniport *device measures foot activity and provides feedback based on how difficult the pedals should be to rotate on the simulated landscape: the pedals offer greater resistance when traveling uphill than down. (Photograph courtesy of Naval Postgraduate School and Sarcos Inc.).*

Features of End-effector Displays

Essentially, an end-effector display is a mechanical device that provides a force to the user's extremities. Generally, it also operates as an input device, potentially providing resistance to input controls. In fact, most end-effector devices act as both input and output devices. Let's take the *PHANTOM* as an example. A pen is used to probe around in the world, so the pen is acting as an input device: it is telling the system where you want to touch. It is also acting as an output system: it provides forces that are like the forces you would get if you were touching that spot with a pen. You can drag the pen around (input) and sense what the surface feels like (output). Resistance and movements by the system can then be used by the participant to *interpret* some aspect of the virtual world. For example, a pedaling device that becomes more resistive to the user's exertion implies that they are going up a hill or are using a higher gear-ratio.

Some end-effector displays are world-grounded. These displays include the ARM, which is ceiling mounted, and the *PHANTOM,* which either rests on the desktop or is built into a kiosk or stationary visual display. Self-grounded force display devices are worn by the user to restrict and to create movement with respect to some part of their body. One example of a self-grounded restrictive finger device is the *Rutgers Dextrous Master* (FIGURE 4-38), which prevents the user's hand from closing when it is grasping a virtual object; however, the device cannot prevent the user from moving their hand to any location.

Mechanical movement sensors are generally incorporated directly into the system. This is a beneficial feature because mechanical tracking is generally very fast and accurate—two requirements for a good haptic display system.

The examples presented here take advantage of these features in different ways. In the example of the GRIP project, the user explores the docking mechanism between two molecules by grasping one molecule and moving it with the *Argonne Remote Manipulator (ARM)* force device [Brooks et al. 1990]. The *ARM* display then responds to the user's movements by allowing the user to feel attractions and repulsions between the molecules in various orientations. How the *ARM* responds is based on a real-time molecular model that calculates the forces acting between the two molecules.

In a VR training application developed by the Naval Postgraduate School (NPS) on infantry maneuvers, soldiers practice carrying out a mission by making several decisions about the route they will take. Decision making is based on required effort, speed, and safety. The key piece of equipment used in the application is a

(A)

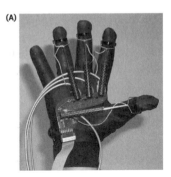

(B)

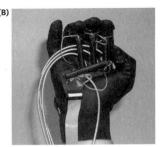

FIGURE 4-38 *The* Rutgers Dextrous Master *(model RMII-ND shown here) prevents the user's hand from closing when grasping a virtual object (Photographs courtesy of Grigore Burdea).*

Sarcos Uniport system (FIGURE 4-37), which uses unicycle pedals to measure foot activity and resistance appropriate to the topography of the simulated landscape.

In a simulation without haptic feedback, the soldier would likely take the shorter route with the least danger. However, this course might take the soldier up and down several hills that, in the real world, would require a fair amount of physical exertion. In a simulation with haptic feedback, the solder might choose a course to circumvent steep hills, even if it entails a longer, more dangerous route.

Interface Issues of End-effector Displays

End-effector displays typically operate with respect to a single point in the virtual world. The number of degrees of freedom in an end-effector display can vary from one to six. An example of a 1-DOF system might be an insertion device (e.g., a camera or other tool used in minimally invasive surgery).

A second degree of freedom could be added to such a system, allowing the operator to twist the tool as it is inserted. For manipulating objects in 3D space, either 3-DOF or 6-DOF displays are used, depending on whether the participants need to orient their grasp or direction of force. The *ARM* is a 6-DOF device. The smaller *PHANTOM* only affects the location of its point of contact (3-DOF), though it does track the user in 6-DOF. Immersion Corp.'s *Laparoscopic Engine* is a 5-DOF input/output device (FIGURE 4-39).

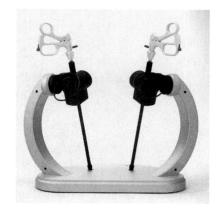

FIGURE 4-39 *This input/output device is specifically constructed to mimic the interface for laparoscopic surgery. Each controller provides the user with 5 DOF: x and y translation, insertion depth (i.e., z movement), pivoting about the insertion point, and width of the device opening (Photograph courtesy of Immersion Corp.).*

As demonstrated in our examples, end-effectors can be used to interface with objects in the virtual world to discover how properties of that world affect the object. End-effectors can simulate resistance and require the user to exert effort to accomplish a task.

Grasping requires that at least two parts of the user's body have separate interfaces to the haptic display. Two or more fingers can wear separate world-grounded end-effectors, or motion between the fingers can be limited with an exoskeleton device. When an object is handheld (e.g., a tennis ball), there is no difference between body-grounded and world-grounded methods. However, body-referenced systems are less appropriate for grasping or pushing on an object that is not free-floating in the world (e.g., a stalled car). An exoskeletal system device can be used in such cases (i.e., grasping or pushing an object fixed to the world); however, if the user is not attached to some immovable object in the real world, they will still be able to walk freely, even though the VR system indicates they are pushing on an immovable object. The user effectively makes the exoskeletal system world grounded by keeping their body position fixed with respect to the world. If the users do not keep the exoskeletal display at a fixed-world position, they can create an impossible circumstance, such as holding onto a fixed virtual object yet moving their hands away from the object's fixed position.

End-effector displays can also be associated with a tactile display or provide simple tactile emulation. Tactile displays such as temperature actuators and vibrator actuators can be mounted at the point of contact between the user and the end-effector. Conversely, the end-effector itself can generate some tactile effects. For instance, the end-effector could generate a vibration effect; or, as the user moves the effector along a virtual surface, it can generate movement that emulates the surface's texture.

Summary of End-effector Displays

An end-effector display basically provides a means for a participant to physically grasp or probe objects in a virtual world. Depending on the mechanism used, these displays can provide a significant amount of resistive pressure, which creates the sensation of physical contact with objects.

The primary characteristic of end-effector displays is whether they are world-grounded or body-grounded systems. World-grounded systems are physically mounted in the real world at a specific location from which forces can be applied. In the body-mounted systems, force and resistance can be generated only between body parts, such as between two fingers or from the shoulder to the hand.

Robotically Operated Shape Displays

Robotically operated shape displays (ROSD) refer to haptic display devices that use robots to place physical objects in front of the user's reach. This display typically includes only the user's finger or a *finger surrogate*. A finger surrogate is a thimble-like or sticklike object with which the user probes the virtual world.

The seminal example of an ROSD is an experimental system by Boeing, Inc. that presents to the user's finger a reconfigurable virtual control panel with appropriate switches. In his paper describing the work, William McNeely [1993] refers to this type of display as "robotic graphics."

Another very creative idea followed from the Cybernetic Systems Laboratory at the University of Tokyo, which used an object containing many types of convex and concave edges and corners positioned to present the appropriate surface to a finger surrogate [Tachi et al. 1994]. The Cybernetic Systems device (FIGURE 4-40) can simulate many shapes by having an assortment of surfaces available, whereas the Boeing display is restricted to the actual devices that the robot has available to present. A more direct approach modifies the surface of the object presented to the user by moving a membrane with pins or rods [Hirota and Hirose 1995].

Components of Robotically Operated Shape Displays

The components of robotically operated shape displays (ROSDs) are simple: a robot, good tracking devices, and a means of probing the virtual world. The robot also needs to be furnished with suitable object(s) to present to the user.

Features of Robotically Operated Shape Displays

The primary advantage of robotic displays is realism. This realism comes from the authenticity of what the user feels. In the Boeing example, as the user reaches for a switch, a robot places an actual switch at the appropriate location on the control panel. Thus, instead of having to build control panels with the controls laid out in

(A)

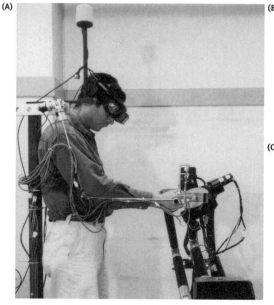

(B)

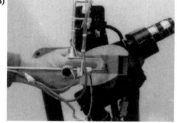

(C)

FIGURE 4-40 *One technique for realistic haptic feedback is to have a robot present actual objects to the participant in the proper place, at the proper time. This technique is effective only when there is a limited number of objects and the participant can't see the real world (Photographs courtesy of Dr. Susumu Tachi (A, B) and Boeing, Inc. (C)).*

many different patterns, different patterns can be designed on the computer, and the robot puts the right device in the right place at the right time. One system can present many different control panel options to the participant to help them evaluate different layouts. *Membrane movement displays* allow the user to touch the virtual object display directly. The surface texture of the object cannot be changed (currently), so the objects take on different shapes but they retain the same surface texture. Membrane displays also act as input devices and can provide a feeling of solidity.

Interface Issues of Robotically Operated Shape Displays

For robotic displays to work, the robot must present the object at the proper location before arrival of the finger or surrogate. The robot will arrive first only if the user's fingers move slowly or the robot moves extremely fast.

A robotic display that moves within reach of the user at rapid speed can be dangerous; therefore, finger tracking must be both fast and accurate for the robot to calculate the display. Glove input devices with magnetic tracking (used in the Boeing experiment) do not meet these requirements, forcing the user to move at an unnaturally slow pace. Using a finger surrogate that is mechanically tracked, Tachi and colleagues [1994] created a system that reacts at an acceptable rate. Also, by using the surrogate, the user's real finger is distanced from the moving robot, thus increasing safety.

This style of display does not work effectively with stationary visual displays or with optical see-through HMDs. Since the robot is only the means of (haptically) displaying the virtual world and is not itself a part of the world, the chosen method of visual display must be one that can hide the robot from view. Hiding the robot is easiest with a fully occlusive HMD, in which the user only sees the virtual world. The video method of see-through HMD filters the real-world visuals to remove the robot from the scene and replaces it with virtual objects [Yokokohji et al. 1996].

Again, safety is a matter of concern with robotic displays. Boeing addressed this issue by placing a Plexiglas shield between the user and the robot. Holes were cut in the shield to allow the switches to protrude onto the user's side. However, the user could accidentally place a finger through the hole and be injured by the robot.

Summary of Robotically Operated Shape Displays

Robotically operated shape displays are interesting in that they can provide highly realistic haptic representations of the virtual world. They render realistic images by placing a real device or surface at the proper position to mimic the object in its virtual world position (if registered properly and displayed quickly enough).

Because the robot itself is not part of the virtual world, this method of haptic display must be combined with a visual display system that occludes some or all of the real world (namely, the robot), and robot noises need to be masked, as well.

Working with robots entails some safety precautions, particularly when using faster robots in combination with haptic displays, since the robot cannot be seen by the user. The primary advantage of using robotic displays as an intermediary to the actual control panel is that the display is readily reconfigurable for alternate scenarios.

3D Hardcopy

A type of "display" that can be considered a haptic display, though it is not particularly interactive, is known as *stereolithography*. Stereolithography is one form of automated creation of physical models based on computer models (FIGURE 4-41). This is done by solidifying a liquid plastic material a portion at a time, building up a complete object. A similar method of rendering physical objects is done by layering adhesive paper and using a laser to score each layer, allowing the excess to break away once the process is complete. The model thus provides a haptic as well as a visual representation of the object, although strictly speaking, the model is a static object and functions only as an output system.

Summary of Haptic Displays

Haptic displays offer tactile and force stimuli to the user, generated by contact with the devices that emulate objects in the virtual world. Most commercially available haptic displays provide either tactile or force stimuli, but not both. Two separate

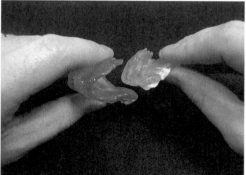

(A)   (B)

FIGURE 4-41 *Stereolithography printers, milling machines, and other rapid prototyping devices can create a real-world, static physical representation of virtual objects (3D hardcopy). Here, we see models of a complex molecular structure (A) and a portion of a monkey's brain (B). The physical models make it easier for a researcher to study how components of a system fit together by physically manipulating them (Models courtesy of professors Klaus Schulten and Joseph Malpeli of the University of Illinois; photographs by William Sherman).*

systems can be combined in a single VR system. Because of the difficulty and expense involved in integrating a haptic display with a virtual reality system, however, they typically are not incorporated unless an application specifically benefits from it.

The requirements of a given application should dictate which type of haptic display is chosen. The following lists summarize the primary benefits of the three main categories of haptic display to aid in making such a determination.

Benefits of Tactile Displays

- Facilitates the fine manipulation of virtual objects
- Can be combined with end-effector displays in some applications
- Body-grounded method is mobile
- Often less expensive than other haptic displays
- Generally portable

Benefits of End-effector Displays

- Can be world- or body-grounded (exoskeletal type is body-grounded)
- Exoskeletal method is mobile
- World-grounded method is less encumbering (nothing to wear)
- Fast and accurate tracking usually built into display

Benefits of Robotically Operated Shape Displays

- Provides very realistic haptic display
- Fast and accurate tracking usually built into display
- Works primarily with head-based visual displays

Due to the limited use of haptic displays in real applications, there is not a lot of data on how helpful they are in performing various tasks. One study comes from Fred Brooks's long-term efforts to investigate the haptic aspects of that *ultimate interface* we've already identified as a primary goal of VR research: a seamless interface that gives the effect of interacting naturally in the real world. In a study based on the GRIP application we discussed earlier—a molecular modeling simulation using a 6-DOF force feedback device—researchers found that the use of haptic display improved a user's ability to quickly perform a simplified task of docking two molecules by a factor of about two [Ouh-Young et al. 1989].

Vestibular and Other Senses

Of the senses we have not yet discussed, vestibular (balance) display is the only other in significant actual use, although there has been some effort made toward an olfactory (smell) display.

Vestibular Display

The vestibular perceptual sense maintains balance. The human organ that provides this perception is located in the inner ear, but it does not respond to aural stimuli. Specifically, it helps humans sense equilibrium, acceleration, and orientation with respect to gravity.

There is a strong relationship between the vestibular and visual systems. Inconsistency between cues such as the horizon line and balance can lead to nausea and other symptoms of simulator sickness.

Vestibular display is accomplished by physically moving the user. Motion base systems, or motion platforms, can move the floor or seat occupied by the user or group of users (FIGURE 4-42). Motion base systems are common in large flight simulator systems used by the military and commercial transport pilots. In these systems, a cockpit platform containing the seats of the pilots surrounded by all the proper instrumentation is moved by a large hydraulic system. Smaller, less expensive systems have also been made available. Other examples of motion base systems can be found in entertainment venues, such as flight and driving arcade systems and group rides.

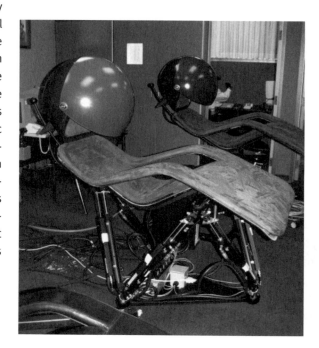

FIGURE 4-42 *Motion base platforms are a common method of providing vestibular information about the virtual world to the user (Photograph courtesy of Brian Park). See color plate 10.*

Another method of vestibular display is a simpler device that shakes, or rumbles, a participant. This motion alone may be insufficient to convey the desired experience, such as a ride on a bumpy road, but it can be very effective when combined with visual information that suggests the cause of the rough ride.

In some VR applications, the only required vestibular sensation is that the participants' perception of gravity is reduced or eliminated. This effect is desirable for simulating low-gravity situations. Although it is not possible to entirely eliminate the sense of gravity, there are methods that can help. One technique, used for many years in training for space travel, is the use of an underwater environment. Obviously, this poses some serious problems for a medium like VR that relies heavily on electronic apparatus. Another method suitable to VR involves placing the user within triconcentric rings that rotate on orthogonal axes or suspending the participant in the air (FIGURE 4-43). Another, simpler technique is to have the participant stand on a dense foam pad into which they slowly sink.

(A)

(B)

FIGURE 4-43 *Techniques for reducing the sensation of gravity include suspending the user in concentric independently movable rings* **(A)** *and suspending the user in the air* **(B)** *(Photographs by David Polinchock and Sheryl Sherman, respectively). See color plate 9.*

Other Senses

Since the time of Morton Heilig's *Sensorama* [Rheingold 1991], very little work has been done on sensory displays other than the visual, aural, and haptic categories we've discussed. Heilig experimented with smell, exposing participants on a simulated motorcycle ride to several aromas, including food smells as one "drove" past a restaurant and exhaust fumes from larger vehicles. Individual identifiable smells that can be perceived by a participant are called *odorants*.

Cater [1992] and Robinett [1992] have postulated several VR and telepresence applications that would benefit from olfactory display. For example, a training application could present specific odors that warn of hazardous materials.

Myron Krueger [1994] and others are investigating presenting and combining odorants to create an olfactory display. One field in which the use of smell is important is surgery. During operations, surgeons use their sense of smell to detect specific substances, such as necrotic tissue within the body.

Some early work has been done by Barfield and Danas [1995], who discuss the basics of olfactory display, including chemical receptors, psychological impacts, and the various parameters of display in a VR experience. They also discuss the current limits of our understanding of olfaction, including our inability to describe the continuum of possible smells.

Display to senses such as taste and magnetoreception has been subject to even less research. Taste display has the obvious obstacle of health concerns, along with a limited number of useful application areas that would benefit from its development. Magnetoreception is the ability to perceive the Earth's magnetic field. It is theorized that this sense is used by birds during migration. Some experiments have also suggested that humans have a limited ability of magnetoreception [Baker 1989]. So little is known about magnetoreception that contemplation of a display of this sense has not been pursued to any extent.

Chapter Summary

VR displays are the means by which participants are physically immersed in a virtual world, replacing or augmenting their sensory input with computer-generated stimuli. Achieving mental immersion is not as simple as physical immersion, but it can be greatly aided by display of the virtual world to multiple senses.

Individual display systems exhibit a variety of qualities and traits. These differences result in tradeoffs among the senses. There are no hard and fast rules signifying which type of display should be used for a particular application. Designers of a VR experience must make choices based on available resources, audience, venue constraints and requirements, and the range of interaction necessary for a successful experience.

Virtual reality experience

User interface

Hardware interface to the user

Input
- Body tracking
  (How the computer "sees" the user)
- Voice/sound recognition
  (How the computer "hears" the user)
- Physical controllers
  (How the computer "feels" the user)

Chapter ❸

Output
- Visual display
  (How the user sees the VW)
- Aural display
  (How the user hears the VW)
- Haptic display
  (How the user feels the VW)

Chapter ❹

Software components

System presentation to the user
- Representation
- Rendering system

Chapter ❺

User interaction with the virtual world
- Manipulation
- Navigation
- Shared Experience

Chapter ❻

Experience design
Chapter ❽

Virtual world
- Immersion
- Point of view
- Venue
- Simulation/physics
- Objects/denizens

Chapter ❼

Life experience
- Memory
- Ability
- Past experience
- Emotional state
- Cultural background

Chapter ❽

Rendering the Virtual World

R*endering* is the process of creating sensory images that depict a virtual world. For virtual reality and other interactive, computer-generated media, new sensory images need to be produced fast enough to be perceived as a continuous flow rather than discrete instances. The ability to create and display images at a realistic rate is referred to as *real-time rendering*.

The creation of sensory images that are displayed to the VR participant can be divided into two stages. The first stage involves choices of how the world will look, sound, and feel to the participant. This is the *representation* stage of creating a world. The second stage is how the chosen representation is implemented in (i.e., performed by) *software and hardware rendering systems*. The two stages are interrelated, of course, as the capabilities of the hardware and software systems affect the type and amount of material that can be represented in real time.

Representation of the Virtual World

An important component of creating a VR experience is choosing how to map thoughts, ideas, and data into the visual, aural, and haptic forms that will be presented to the participant (FIGURE 5-1). How one chooses to represent the virtual world has a significant impact on the effectiveness of the overall experience. Simply put, *representation* is the choice of what to render.

We begin our discussion with the concept of representation, because one must first decide how the virtual world should appear and make decisions about what information needs to be conveyed and how best to do this. Once these decisions have been made, the VR experience creator will have a good idea about what the system requirements will be.

It is not the goal of this book to cover the concept of representation in great detail. However, the topic of this book—understanding virtual reality—relies heavily on the representation of information, so it is important to provide an overview. We can think of the word *representation* as "re-presentation," that is, presenting something again—often in form or manner other than its original. The act of communication is a process of re-presenting. Consider the activity of conveying a simple idea from one person to another using the spoken word as the medium of communication.

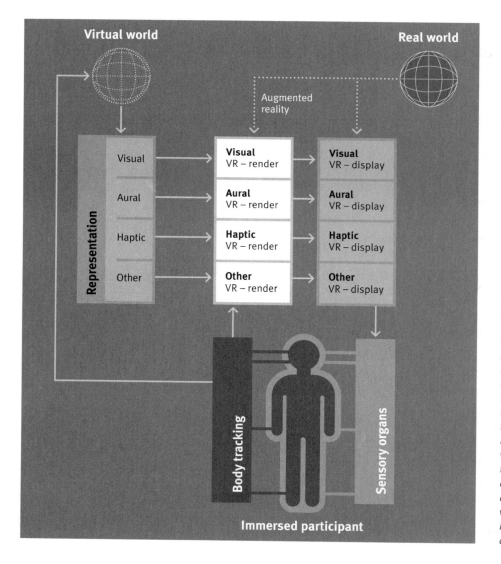

FIGURE 5-1 *An important aspect of any virtual reality application is to provide synthetic stimuli to the participants' senses. To do this, decisions must be made about how to represent the virtual world to the participant (choosing what to display) and how to render the virtual world (choosing how to convert the conceptual virtual world into the signals that are presented by the display devices). This diagram depicts the mapping of the virtual world into visual, aural, haptic, and other sensory components.*

The originator of the message has an idea in mind. This idea cannot be transferred directly into the mind of the receiver, but must be carried via some medium. It becomes necessary, therefore, to re-present the idea in a form suitable for the medium of choice. In our example, the sender represents their idea as a series of sounds. The receiver hears these sounds and translates the aural representation into a mental idea in their own imagination. The received information may not always be interpreted as the transmitted information was intended. Communicating through any medium (including spoken word) requires a common representation and understanding between the parties. Care must be taken to avoid circumstances where each party interprets the same representation differently.

One must remember that ideas, concepts, or physical entities can be represented in a wide variety of ways, and there is not necessarily one *best* representation, although some will be more suitable than others. There may be different suitable representations of the same information based on the goal of the application. For example, a dramatic narrative may be an appropriate choice if the goal is to convey an emotional experience, whereas scientific visualization may be an appropriate choice if the goal is to elucidate complex data. For each of these genres, there may be a desire to represent a severe thunderstorm; however, the way in which we go about representing the storm is drastically different because of what we wish to convey to the audience.

For the dramatic experience, the thunderstorm will be represented with a great deal of visual and aural verisimilitude. As long as the audience comes away with the proper mood—perhaps the foreboding of a tragic event—the goal of the creator is met. However, for scientists trying to visualize their research, verisimilitude is not a concern, but insight into the phenomenon is. So, the scientist may choose to represent the storm with thousands of balloon-like spheres floating through the storm, with arrows showing the flow of the air and a plane of colors intersecting the storm to indicate the temperature at a particular altitude—which would look nothing at all like a real storm.

A similar process is followed when creating entirely new worlds, except the phenomena are created rather than emulated.

The importance of representation is consistent regardless of the subject matter. For example, for both visualization and sonification (i.e., the presentation of information via sound) of scientific data, the focus is on how different representational techniques can help researchers gain insights about their work and how to communicate those insights with others. Cartography is another field of study in which considerable attention has been paid to representional issues. Maps for different purposes (e.g., aviation, geology, driving) are designed with specific goals in mind. In addition, features such as the best orientation for reading maps have long been studied by human factors researchers.

Artists strive to use visual, aural, tactile, and other sensory symbols to evoke emotions and express ideas. For training and education, developers must focus on the representations that will most help the participant learn their task. In particular, developers of VR training experiences must be careful not to include representations that can provide false training, that is, training that cannot be applied outside of the virtual world.

The significance of *misrepresentation* varies by application. For applications with entertainment or artistic goals, misrepresentation may be used intentionally as a narrative device or as a means of inducing the audience to think about the medium itself. For other areas of communication, misrepresentation can be substantially detrimental. Recipients of a representation generally expect to trust the accuracy of the world presented to them, whether they are planning a route on a map, learning to fly in a simulator, or judging a court case based on a re-creation of events. In each instance, the audience is at the mercy of the knowledge, integrity, and skill of the creator (or lack thereof). Misrepresentation may be either the result of insufficient knowledge of how the world works or an intentional attempt to mislead. It may also be a lack of understanding of human perception or of other issues necessary to represent information effectively.

Quantitative and Qualitative Representations

Choosing an appropriate representation depends largely on the *goal* of the task. One major choice is whether to focus on quantitative or qualitative representational forms. In some cases it might be important to be able to accurately perceive *quantitative* information from the data. Displaying information quantitatively requires a representation and a display that allows users to retrieve numeric values from the presentation, either directly (as from a table of numbers) or indirectly (such as from a graph). For other purposes, it might be more important to gain an overall feel for the information, so a high-level *qualitative* presentation may be required. In the best of all worlds, the same representation might be suitable for both applications, but in reality, the designer normally needs to optimize the representation for one goal or the other. Therefore, it is often important to provide a choice of representations.

Often the recipient can perceive only a relatively small percentage of the overall information available from a quantitative display. Qualitative displays provide a means for quickly getting a sense of the big picture. Often, a qualitative display is created by deriving summary information from the full pool of information to give a representative overall view. This can be done using statistical methods or by choosing a representation that focuses on certain aspects of the information. For example, a graph of the Dow Jones average of industrial stocks on the New York Stock Exchange provides an overview of how a certain business segment has fared (FIGURE 5-2). While qualitative information (such as whether the market as a whole is moving up or down) can be gleaned from the Dow Jones average, more detailed information can be garnered by looking at the plots of the individual stocks used to calculate the average.

Another familiar example is the ubiquitous weather chart appearing in newspapers and television news reports (FIGURE 5-3). The meteorologist points out the location of the fronts, "highs," and "lows." We can make some basic determinations from this qualitative information: there will be fewer clouds near the highs, and we can expect wind and showers as certain weather fronts pass, and so on. Of course, the symbology presented in these formats is derived from detailed atmospheric information. A quantitative representation showing isobar contours over the same region can also be used to make the same broad determination about whether tomorrow will be a good day for golf—but not as quickly. If the goal is only to get a

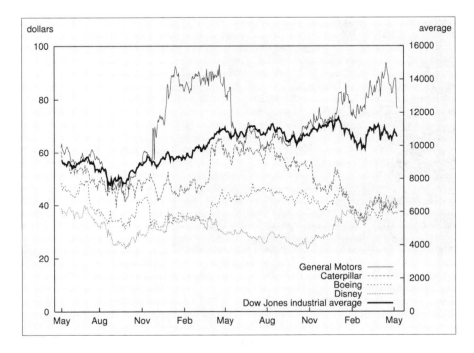

FIGURE 5-2 *Statistical methods can be used to summarize information to an overall big picture. For example, this graph compares the value of the Dow Jones Industrial Average over time with some of the specific stocks that make up the average.*

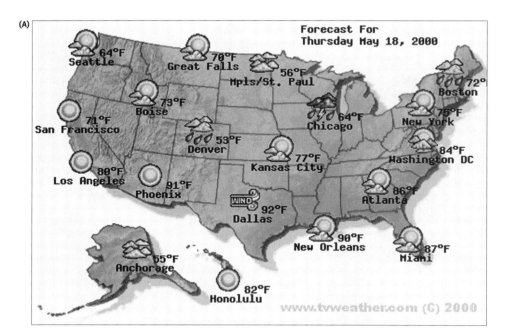

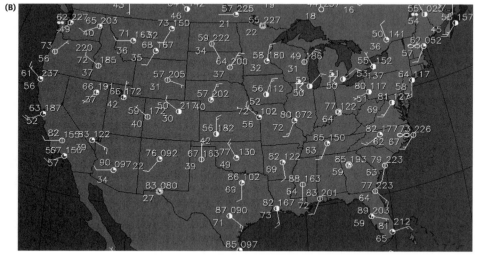

FIGURE 5-3 *Often a more qualitative image is produced for a general audience compared with the more detailed quantitative plots used by scientists.* **(A)** *Here, a qualitative weather map gives overview information that is generally satisfactory for the average viewer (www.tvweather.com).* **(B)** *However, meteorologists and pilots require the additional information provided by the glyphs in this more complex map. (Image courtesy of the University of Illinois at Urbana-Champaign, Department of Atmospheric Sciences).*

general impression of the next day's weather, then the symbolic qualitative representation serves the purpose and is all that is necessary.

Scientists, economists, and indeed anyone who depends on numeric representations of some system often require a quantitative representation of their data, yet also desire some way to see the overall big picture. Both forms of representation are important.

Human Perception

As all representations are eventually filtered through human perception, the application designer must consider human characteristics ranging from the physiological, to the psychological, to the emotional. There have been numerous volumes written on each of these aspects, covering much more than we can include in this book. We do feel it is wise for anyone who is serious about creating compelling representations, visualizations, virtual worlds, and virtual reality applications to take advantage of the available material describing the research and opinions on human perception and cognition.

One particularly interesting aspect of human perception and cognition is our ability to generalize. This is a characteristic that deserves study and exploitation. We can see a telephone of a make and model that one has never seen before yet still know it is a telephone. What are the salient features that are recognized to allow one to know that it is a telephone without ever having seen that particular model before? If we are able to capitalize on the human ability to generalize, we can create images that are accessible to a very wide audience without having to train the participants in every aspect of every symbol. In addition, the ability to generalize can be exploited to save computational complexity by using simplified models of objects that can still be recognized. Generalization can work against us, however, when one generalizes incorrectly or generalizes when indeed it is the specific instance that is intended.

Symbols are an example of how our ability to generalize can be beneficial. One way of creating a representation that will be generalized is to utilize the familiar. If one chooses a symbol with which most people are familiar, many people will understand the meaning. For example, if one were attempting to create a sign that symbolizes "Enter Here," one might utilize a partially open door. Often, it is desirable to use the most generic instance of the object available, since it will likely have the least cultural bias and chance for misinterpretation.

Generalizing allows us to group together objects and concepts with similar characteristics. An analogy extends the relationship between grouped objects or concepts to conclude that other characteristics true of one object are true of the other. So, an analogy can be thought of as a relationship between an original concept and another concept that shares many similar characteristics. Humans are adept at transferring their knowledge of one object or concept to another. This transference can be accelerated if a direct analogy is pointed out between the concept under study and an already understood concept. As patterns of analogous relationships become apparent, the shared concepts can often be generalized into a class of operations (e.g., a mathematical concept).

Verisimilitude

Verisimilitude is the quality of having the appearance of truth or depicting realism. Not all applications strive to appear realistic, and some may choose to deviate from verisimilitude in only very specific instances. Participants can still become mentally immersed if they are able to suspend disbelief regarding the less realistic components.

Experiences can be categorized between those that go beyond what we know to be physically possible ("magical" worlds) and those that attempt to be verisimilar in all respects (the real world). Some of these magical worlds might be straight out of the imagination of a fantasy genre author. Others may be shifts in representation that allow participants to interact with otherwise physically inaccessible concepts, such as the forces between molecules.

Worlds that closely resemble the real world are said to be *mimetic* (i.e., they mimic physical reality). The *mimesis* of a simulated world is the degree to which it mimics the real world or at least responds in a way the participant (audience) can accept as reasonable within the bounds of the rest of the world. In a work of interactive fiction, does it feel as though everything encountered fits with the world, or do some elements seem out of place or overly contrived?

Generally, we expect any world in which we are interacting to be consistent within itself. *Diegesis* connotes the implied consistency within a particular world. The diegesis is the entire world of the experience including those elements that are seen and unseen, encountered and not encountered by the recipient. That is, the diegesis includes events that are presumed to have occurred and places that are presumed to exist [Thompson 1995].

Establishing diegesis is an important role of mental immersion. The participant must have faith that the world is consistent beyond what is immediately presented. Thus, in a consistent world, if the participant encounters a smoldering building surrounded by fire trucks, they can reasonably presume that on the day prior, a fully erect building existed at this location. The specifics of what the build-ing and the fire looked like are thus left to the imagination of the participant. This is referred to as *closure*. McCloud [1993] explains the general concept of closure in a medium: "Closure allows us to *connect* these moments and *mentally construct* a con-tinuous, unified reality."

With specific regard to the medium of comics, McCloud exemplifies how closure is used to make the reader a participant in the story (FIGURE 5-4). This engagement is accomplished by making them use their imagination to "fill in the blanks." Thus, the reader participates in the creation of the world they experience and the actions within it. McCloud calls these actions that occur "off screen" as the events of "the gutter" (the space between the panels of comics): "To kill a man between panels is to condemn him to a thousand [different] deaths."

The Realism Axis (and Beyond)

There is a range that follows along a continuous line proceeding from highly verisim-ilar to highly abstract. Concepts can be mapped into representations that fall any-where along this axis between reality and abstraction. Put another way, the degree to which a display is realistic or abstract is a continuum (FIGURE 5-5A). *Verisimilar* representations strive to be realistic representations of the world: *indexed* repre-sentations map values from some phenomenon onto a new form that can be more easily understood; *iconic* representations use simplified objects to represent parts of the virtual world; and *symbolic* representations map information into forms that signify but do not resemble the original actuality, such as glyphs or words. The further we move toward abstraction, the easier it becomes to use analogy to make infer-ences. However, we also move toward increasingly culture-based representation—for example, $ versus £ versus ¥.

The shift from pictures to words is identified by McCloud [1993] as a shift from *received* information to *perceived* information (FIGURE 5-5 B, C). That is, received information is that which can be absorbed directly, whereas perceived information must be processed. Received representations are immediately obvious to the viewer. Perceived information, on the other hand, requires training the viewer in order for it to be understood. In some abstract representations, many variables may be pre-sented simultaneously (e.g., as glyphs with shapes that encode particular informa-tion). This can be confusing to the novice viewer.

When viewers observe a movie of such glyphs, they are often overwhelmed with the amount of information being unfamiliarly conveyed. However, upon watch-ing the movie multiple times, trends begin to emerge that (the now experienced)

FIGURE 5-4 *In* Understanding Comics *[1993], Scott McCloud points out that what is left out of a scene can greatly affect the level of mental immersion felt by the receiver (Image courtesy of Scott McCloud).*

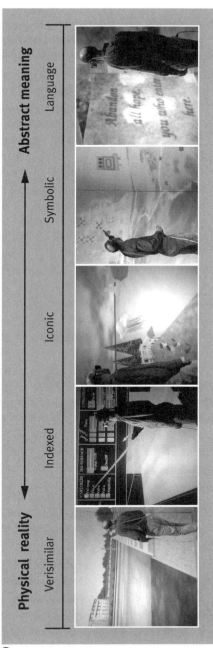

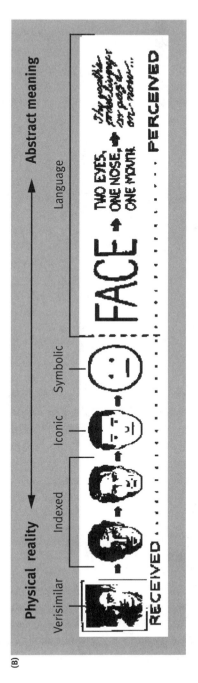

FIGURE 5-5 (A) *Virtual reality applications fall along a realism continuum. From left to right, the StreetCrossing application depicts a real street, the MultiPhase Fluid Flow application shows data indexed to color values, NICE shows iconic representations of sunshine and rain, BattleView incorporates military symbology into the world representation, and Mitologies makes use of language to set the mood (Applications courtesy of NCSA, UIUC, EVL, NCSA, and EVL, respectively; photographs by William Sherman).* **(B)** *Here we map the continuum from (A) to McCloud's representation continuum. The closer we are to physical reality, the more specific we get. The verisimilar representation is a face of a specific person or character. The indexed representations map to a class of people (in this example Caucasian males). The iconic image represents the generic face, and the symbolic representations denote the concept of a face (Adapted from image courtesy of Scott McCloud).*

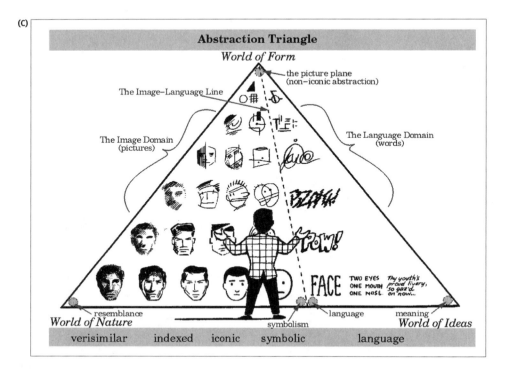

FIGURE 5-5 (CONTINUED)
(C) *In this diagram, also by McCloud, the abstraction triangle is divided at the point where representation shifts from symbols of the object to symbols of the language (i.e., phonetically or semantically based symbols). Worlds represented within the triangle on the right would be those from media such as books or interactive fiction, although this is not exclusively the case (Adapted from image courtesy of Scott McCloud).*

viewers can begin to comprehend. Consequently, a representation that is initially overwhelming due to the large amount of information that must be processed (perceived) can become, with training, a more automatic (received) process. Well-designed glyphs will enable this process to occur more rapidly. Future encounters with the same glyph representation will be more quickly grasped by the viewer.

For some concepts, there is no physical counterpart upon which to build a representation. John Ganter [1989] differentiates between representations tied to some physical (or imagined physical) entities (P-reps) and those that are representations of ideas that we can only conceptualize (C-reps), such as emotions, risk, potential, danger, and the like. Both P-reps and C-reps can be important for virtual reality, where the goal is often to present an experience that is otherwise unseen (e.g., empathizing with another person or manipulating gravitational forces) and put it in context with the physical reality with which we are familiar.

A P-rep embodies some aspect of the *physical* world, something that can be measured, touched, or otherwise experienced. A visualization of a thunderstorm is an example of a P-rep. C-reps objectify some notion for which a physical manifestation does not exist but which can be *conceptualized* in the mind. Artists often work in the C-rep domain, creating poems, songs, and paintings that are representations of some feeling, emotion, or original thought or idea. Of course, some works of art also incorporate P-reps. Indeed, many artworks contain elements of both.

As representations shift from realistic to symbolic, they become increasingly generic and representational of a larger class of objects. McCloud [1993] discusses how this can be used effectively in the medium of comics by choosing a less real, more symbolic representation for the protagonist. Doing so allows a larger group of people to identify with the character.

Semiotics

The human brain is optimized for recognizing patterns. Signs and symbols take advantage of this recognition. Some signs are very closely related to the content that they represent, while others are quite abstract in their construction. A *sign* is something that stands for something else. A *symbol* is the expression of some content. When we are creating representations, we are actually making choices of signs and symbols that will be used to communicate the content of the message. The field of study dedicated to the use of signs and symbols is called *semiotics.*

Signs and symbols are convenient, shorthand representations. In the process of creating these shorthands, the representation often moves along a continuum, becoming more abstract. For example, images that are indexed or iconic may transform into a shorthand notation that crosses the image/language line and becomes a symbol. Two examples of this type of evolution are displayed in FIGURE 5-6, which shows the transformation from an archaic to a modern Chinese character for horse and the evolution of the pictorial bull to the modern letter *A.*

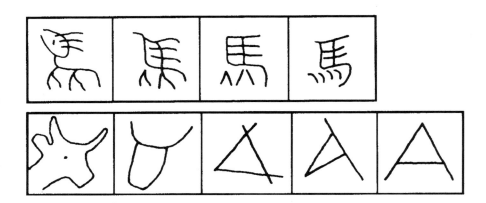

FIGURE 5-6 *Written language has evolved from pictorial to more abstract symbols. In these two examples, the Chinese symbol for horse moves from archaic to modern, and the letter A derives from the symbol for bull* (Signs and Symbols: Their Design and Meaning, *by A. Frutiger, Ebury Press, UK).*

The more abstract a sign, the greater effort required on the part of the receiver to understand its meaning. Of course, some abstract signs can be readily understood if the design is intuitive (FIGURE 5-7). On the other hand, misunderstanding can result if the receiver incorrectly assumes they understand the meaning.

In developing interactive experiences, signs and symbols can be used as part of an interface within the virtual world. The choice of specific signs and symbols is an important part of the design process. In choosing signs and symbols, one must understand the needs and experiences of the intended audience.

Choosing a Mapping

A large part of creating representations is selecting and designing appropriate forms, colors, sounds, textures, and weights and then *mapping* information onto those representations. The most direct example of mapping information is taken from the field of cartography. The work of a cartographer is to collect information about the physical lay of the land and map it to a representation on paper (or, more recently, to digital storage files).

Consider the problem of creating a representation that will allow visitors to effectively navigate the roads of Illinois on their first visit. To accomplish this, the roadmap designer must choose a set of symbols and then map the physical world to the P-rep. To create a visual representation manifested on paper, the designer might color lines in specific hues to represent roads, highways, and interstates. A toll road could be indicated by color or by a symbol associated with money, $. The lines can then be laid out, or mapped, in a configuration that directly corresponds to the spatial layout of the roads in the physical world.

Conversely, the representation could be something entirely different from what one normally considers a roadmap. One could represent the information as a chart of the latitude and longitude of many points along the roads in the state, as well as coordinates for the points at which each of the roads intersect. The required information would be presented, but the recipient would likely find this a rather difficult tool to use, because the representational choices do not facilitate navigating road systems.

Even maps designed for comparable purposes (travel by car versus travel by plane) are tuned for the specific task at hand (FIGURE 5-8). A map designed for use in aviation is based on the same physical data (the physical world) but highlights different features—airports, radio towers, airspace control, navigational beacons, and roads. Aviation maps do not distinguish among the types of roads. The roads work as

FIGURE 5-7 *The creation of compelling signs is important and of practical value. This sign attests to the need for having readily understood visual representations that transcend the boundaries of language and cultural bias. It was designed by Hazard Communication Systems, LLC, using design principles developed by FMC for pictoral display (Image courtesy of HCS, LLC).*

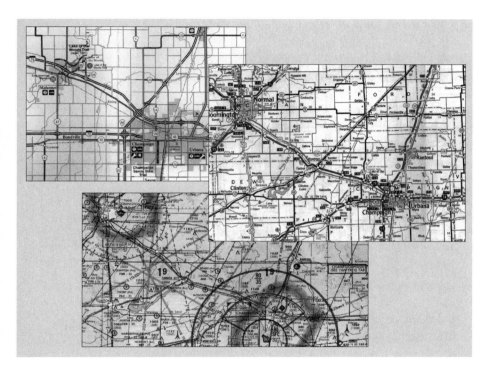

FIGURE 5-8 *Ideally, maps and images are created to be most suitable for the purpose for which they are intended. In this example, a map intended for drivers conveys different information than maps intended for pilots or bicyclists, even though the maps are for the same geographic area (Driving and bicycling maps courtesy of the Illinois Department of Transportation. Aviation map courtesy of National Aeronautical Charting Office).*

a wayfinding aid, so whether or not it is a toll road, for instance, is unimportant to a pilot.

Of course, one can also map information that is not geographic in nature. For example, one could map the historic values of a certain company's stock to a graph that visually depicts the rise and fall in the stock price over time (see FIGURE 5-2). One can also map information that is not inherently numeric. One could map the concept "how well I like the taste of a specific food" to an indication of a smiling face or a frowning face next to each item.

Representation Issues Related to VR

In addition to the global issues of representation, there are a few issues particular to the medium of virtual reality. When considering the level of abstraction for a VR presentation, it is always important to keep in mind the audience and goal of your message. For VR, the experience designer must also consider the implications of real-time rendering, good interactions, user safety, and overall experiential concerns, such as directing attention, providing a narrative within an interactive space, and the added benefits and considerations of having multisensory displays.

A *resource budget* can be established to ensure that scene complexity will remain within the bounds of what can be reliably rendered in real time. In a real-time system, only so much can be done in every visual, aural, or haptic simulation frame. For the visual scene, the design manager can specify how many polygons can be "spent" on the room, the characters, the objects, and the interface. This is especially important if different people are modeling different aspects of the scene. (Level-of-detail and other culling techniques, which we will discuss further in the section Visual Representation in VR, can also be employed to keep down the render resource requirement.)

The same resource constraints apply to the other sensory displays, as well. How many sounds can be combined and/or spatialized in real time? How complicated can the procedural model of air flowing through a French horn be? How precisely can a lump of modeling clay be felt and manipulated? Application designers must pick and choose what is important for the experience or increase the budget for computational resources.

As a medium of multiple sensory (a.k.a. multimodal) display and interaction, virtual reality can explore the conflicts and synergism that arise from a combined display to the senses. In daily life, people use all of their senses to interpret the world around them. Babies exemplify this in their exploration of a new toy. At first they see an object, but to learn more about it, they grab and find out how it feels, they shake it to see what it sounds like, and they bring it to their face to smell and taste it.

Adults are less apt to shake, smell, and taste everything they encounter. However, multimodal sensory input is still very important. Consider the experience of walking into a restaurant. Beyond the visual look of the dining area, information is gathered by other senses—perhaps the sounds of the kitchen or of music playing, the presentation of the food, and, of course, the smells. The inability to smell in such a situation would yield a far less appealing experience.

Not only does our ability for multimodal sensory input make the world seem richer, it provides the brain with a means of determining when things are amiss. To take a particularly convincing example, it has been conjectured [Vince 1995] that if the sense of balance (vestibular) does not match the input from the eyes (i.e., the orientation of the horizon), the possibility of poisoning is inferred, and the person becomes nauseous. That is, the vomiting reflex is induced to rid the body of the probable poison.

A further concern is whether the participant's sensory system will need to re-adapt to operating in the real world at the conclusion of the VR experience—particularly if they will be driving a car. These types of problems have been studied by NASA and the military. Many flight simulation and other VR facilities require users to pass a test that verifies their re-adaptation to the real world before permitting them to leave and drive home [Kennedy et al. 1993]. Another important issue is how much can be reasonably represented from a *safety* perspective. Is it possible for the visual display to become bright enough to damage the eye? Can the sound level be too loud for comfort or worse? Can force displays cause bodily damage? Perhaps sensory substitution can be used to replace a hazardous haptic motion ("Ouch!").

Sensory Substitution

Because of technology limitations, in virtual reality experiences, the amount of sensory information cannot be as abundant and rich as it is in the physical world. To partially compensate for this, VR experiences often use *sensory substitution*. Sensory substitution substitutes one kind of sense display for another—for example, displaying a sound to substitute for the haptic feedback of touching an object.

Sensory substitution is also used in other media. For example, books describe smell and tactile imagery as text: He felt the cold steel of the razor sharp dagger against his throat . . . . However, because many VR experiences purport to mimic the real world, the use of effective sensory substitution in this medium is even more important.

Sensory substitution can be used to substitute perception from any one sense to another. A use of sound to represent haptic information might be a "clunk" or "thud" when the user's avatar collides with an object in the world. Olfaction (smell) might be represented as many icons of the object showing the odor wafting through the "air" emanating from the source—such as hamburgers floating from the grill toward the participant. Or, a canary—a familiar, real-world example—would be used to indicate the presence of dangerous fumes outside the range of human olfactory perception (seeing that your canary dies tells you what your nose cannot detect).

Some substitutions are made between senses that are closely related, such as placing vibrators on the participant's fingers to inform them when they are touching something (one tactile sensation for another). This type of substitution is also exemplified by the use of haptic feedback (e.g., pressure on the skin) to represent vestibular information. One way in which this is done is to have a chair equipped with air bladders that inflate and deflate to give the sensation of pressure due to increased/decreased gravity.

In general, sensory substitution is used whenever the technology to present vital information in its native perceptual form is not available at an acceptable cost or safety level. Sensory substitution is one of the general representation issues in VR. Now that we have discussed the issues common to all the senses, we can move on to specific representational issues, which are further broken down by sensory modality: visual, aural and haptic.

Visual Representation in VR

Visual perception is generally considered to be the primary means of gaining information about physical spaces and objects' appearances. The properties of visual displays summarized in Chapter 4 all affect what can be reasonably presented to the participant. In particular, limitation of the field of view, the resolution quality, and the degree of latency between user motion and world view can affect which representations will work well.

Our visual system provides us with the ability to perceive the world for miles and miles or to focus in on the details of a nearby object. The farther we look, though, the more the details are attenuated, allowing techniques such as *level-of-detail culling* (discussed further in the section on reducing polygon waste) to be applied. The greater the area an object occupies on the retina, the more details that are perceptible.

How Vision Is Used in a VR Experience

A major function of vision in a virtual world is to determine our position relative to various entities. This is useful both to help us find our way through a space and to deal with objects, creatures, and people in the world. A variety of depth cues help us determine the distance and orientation of objects in a scene. In addition to seeing where entities are, we can see their form, color, and other attributes that help us learn more about them. Additional information about the nature of the objects can be inferred. The object might be a vehicle for transportation, a building for shelter, a character with whom to interact, or a button to press.

Sight can be classified as a distant sense in that we can perceive objects beyond our immediate reach. We can look for things not in contact with our bodies, and when we see them, we can assess their size, shape, orientation, and so on. We can also use visual cues from the objects we see to determine their distance from us.

FIGURE 5-9 *When the interface to the virtual world is naturally incorporated into the world itself, the participant can see and interpret the appropriate required action to generate some effect in the virtual world—in a manner, similar to real-world interactions. Here, in Georgia Tech and Emory University's* Fear of Heights *application [Hodges et al. 1995], arrows pointing up and down can be used by the participant to control the elevator within the world (Image courtesy of Rob Kooper, Georgia Tech). See color plate 12.*

Sight is also critical for accessing many of the user interface tools available to the participant (FIGURE 5-9). The participant uses sight to locate and identify buttons to press, dials to rotate, steering wheels to turn.

The virtual world may contain objects visually represented at multiple points on the realism continuum or abstraction triangle (FIGURE 5-5). In one case we know of, using virtual reality for virtual prototyping off-road vehicles, a virtual replica of an object (in this case, a tractor) is rendered realistically. However, the same application may also contain more abstractly rendered information to depict the status of operational parameters like engine speed, wind flow, stress, and/or strain.

Even in the real world, we rely on objects that represent abstract concepts. A frequently seen example (in the United States) is a red octagon with white symbols shaped like *S, T, O,* and *P.* We also use symbols (alphabetic or other) to indicate how to operate doors, elevators, appliances, and a multitude of other everyday things. The same techniques are used in virtual worlds to allow the participant to interpret how the user interface works or to find their way to a desired location (FIGURE 5-10).

We also make inferences about objects by the way they move or change. Not all virtual worlds consist of dynamic objects, but the inclusion of changing objects can make the world both more interesting and better suited for interpreting the relationship between objects in the world. In the real world, the stop sign is often replaced by the more sophisticated (and dynamic) traffic light which also communicates how traffic is allowed to proceed at an intersection.

FIGURE 5-10 *As in the real world, signs provide cues that help us know what choices are available to us in the virtual world (NICE application courtesy of the Electronic Visualization Lab at the University of Illinois at Chicago; photograph by William Sherman).*

Motion is also frequently used for communication between people (and animals and virtual creatures) through body gestures. In a shared virtual world, participants can indicate simple communication gestures via their avatars (FIGURE 5-11). More complicated communications can also be accomplished via a series of body gestures or via sign language. The avatar's range of motion may limit the ability to make some gestures.

FIGURE 5-11 *As in the real world, our words and actions can aid in communication within a virtual world. These avatars in the NICE educational application are using a simple gesture to get the message across (NICE application courtesy of the Electronic Visualization Lab at the University of Illinois at Chicago). See color plate 13.*

Visual displays are also ideal for presenting quantitative information. Numeric displays can be integrated into the visual display through such devices as a temperature readout on a virtual thermometer or heading and speed values displayed on instruments in a virtual vehicle (FIGURE 5-12). Many science and engineering applications accommodate the use of a 3D probe to display specific numeric values within the virtual world.

FIGURE 5-12 *The* Sandbox *application (experienced in a* CAVE *display) investigates different techniques of displaying numeric values within a virtual world. To read the current temperature value for a given location, a thermometer placed at the location shows rising and falling "mercury" and a numeric output. Rainfall can be viewed by placing virtual rain gauges in the terrain. A chart in the scene also plots the temperature and rainfall over time (*Sandbox *application courtesy of Andrew Johnson; photograph by William Sherman).*

Aural Representation in VR

Despite the importance of the visual presentation of a virtual world, the aural presentation is also significant. Sound greatly enhances the participant's ability to become mentally immersed in the world. Sound is compelling. From ambient sounds that give cues to the size, nature, and mood of the setting to sounds associated with particular objects or characters nearby, aural representation is key to user understanding and enjoyment.

Sounds can be attention grabbing. Loud noises or sounds the participant is trained to respond to (such as their name) can be used to call attention to an object or location within the virtual world. Sounds also help determine an object's position relative to the listener. Significantly, sound is also less expensive to produce, relative to the other display modalities used in VR, so the benefits of sound can be added to a VR experience without spending a lot of money.

Features of Sound

Important features of sound include long distance perception (some sounds can be heard for miles), unrestricted field of regard (sounds can be heard no matter which way one faces), and the advantages of a constantly open perceptual channel (we do not have "lids" for the ears, nor can we turn away). The latter feature is useful to VR experience developers, because it guarantees that a signal will be sensed by the participant. On the other hand, this also means that the participant is not able to avoid unpleasant, or even harmful sounds.

The time and space features of sound differ from those of visual perception. Whereas what we see exists in both time and space, we reflect primarily on the spatial countenance of the world. On the other hand, what we hear exists primarily in time (although we are able to localize where a sound comes from, to a degree), so we frequently use sound to attend to aspects of the world related to the passage of time. Because sound exists primarily in time, the rate at which sounds are displayed is even more critical than with the visual system.

We can hear changes in very high-frequency sonic information. Thus, we are able to notice even slight changes in time sequences. As a consequence, sound can be used to identify the relationship between two high-frequency events, if the events have corresponding sonic images. For example, we can tell very precisely if two sonic events occur at the exact same time or if they occur sequentially. Also, if two events create sounds with constant pitch, we can readily discern when the pitch of one of them begins to drift from the original frequency.

The fact that sounds exist in time means that they have a beginning, a middle, and an end. If the beginning of a sound is changed, leaving the middle and end the same, it will have an impact on what is heard. A visual image may be initiated arbitrarily at any time, but a sound usually must be started at its beginning and played out in its proper sequence over time.

How Sound Is Used in a VR Experience

As we discussed generally at the outset of this chapter, there is a range of how sound information can be *represented* in order to enhance a virtual reality experience. Sound can be used to increase the verisimilitude of the experience, supply additional information, help set a mood or indicate a situation, or any combination of these.

Realistic sounds help with mental immersion, but they also provide practical information about the environment. For example, the VR work of Caterpillar Inc. (see

FIGURE 3-15) includes the use of sound to inform the driver of the machine's operating condition. Is the machine idling? How much hydraulic pressure is being created? Has the machine been successfully put into reverse gear? These are all important cues to the driver. In fact, the recent trend of outfitting heavy equipment cabs with the ability to block outdoor noises and to play music may be detrimental to the operator's performance. In the future, perhaps these outdoor cues can be reintegrated into this environment as more pleasing sounds, so the practical data is not lost.

Sonification

In the symbolic region of the realism spectrum lies *sonification*. Sonification is the presentation of information in an abstract sound form. Examples include a sound that varies based on the changing temperature of an object (a machine engine block perhaps) and sounds used to represent levels of carbon dioxide or ozone in the lower atmosphere.

Every sound falls somewhere on the realism continuum. There are general ambient sounds, sounds that mark an event, sounds that continually provide information about the state of something, and sounds that augment or substitute for perceptions made by the other senses.

Ambient Sounds

Ambient sounds (or background sound) are generally used to set the mood of an experience, a technique well understood and used to great effect by playwrights and filmmakers, for instance. Ambient sounds can have the effect of making the experience more compelling, increasing mental immersion. They can be used to guide a participant through an experience. For example, a hostile space might have a menacing sound. Of course, this may attract the curious participant, so to keep them away, an outright annoying sound may be used.

Mood-setting ambient sounds are often musical and fall toward the abstract end of the realism continuum, but they can also be verisimilar. Even if they are associated with the nearby virtual world, as long as they are unresponsive to events in the simulated world, they are classified as ambient rather than interactive sounds. For example, while walking near a stream, a participant might hear a sample loop of flowing water, but if they splash through the stream, the sound does not change to reflect this. Thus, the ambient water sounds are not interactive; they merely change to reflect the user's movement to another region or locale of the virtual environment.

Markers

Markers are sounds that mark the occurrence of some event. The types of events that can be marked include world events, user interface events, sonification events, or sensory substitution events. A world event sonic marker might be the sound of a door closing, an explosion, or the "pluck" of a flower. Interface events are the familiar "bloops" and "beeps" carried over from the computer desktop interface metaphor— pressing a virtual button results in a "click" to acknowledge that user input has been processed. A sonification marker might indicate when some temperature exceeds some threshold. The sensory substitution example of the "clunk" sound representing a user colliding with objects in the world is also a marker.

In addition to the use of a certain sound to mark an event, a change in ambient sounds can serve this purpose. For example, the hum of a collection of bees might change from a light drone while they collect pollen to a louder, angry buzz when the hive has been upset and the bees begin to swarm (FIGURE 5-13). The mood-setting nature of ambient sounds can be used so that a shift in the sound display marks a transition in narrative plot or in location.

FIGURE 5-13 *When aggravated, bees that had been going about their business collecting nectar change their tone from a mild drone to a louder, menacing buzz as they swarm about the cause of the disturbance* (Crayoland *courtesy of Dave Pape; photograph by William Sherman*).

Index Sounds

Index sounds directly map a continuous value (e.g., temperature) to some sonic parameter (e.g., pitch). Unlike marker sounds that denote discrete, fleeting events, index sounds are continuous, and the sound varies to reflect the changing value of whatever it represents, be it temperature, carbon dioxide levels, or other characteristics.

In the real world, we can ascertain that an engine's RPMs are increasing or decreasing by listening to its sounds. We know from experience that the faster it spins, the higher the frequency of the whir. A more abstract example can be found in the *Crumbs* VR visualization tool (Appendix B). One use of *Crumbs* is to annotate a visual representation of scientific data by marking a path through a dataset. The participant can drop virtual markers, or "crumbs," to indicate a path of interest through the volume of data. An example would be to examine a 3D representation of an MRI and mark a path along the spinal cord. After the path is marked, the computer can evaluate the length of the spinal cord. As an aid in dropping the marker points in appropriate locations (in this example, the locations that are the density of the spinal cord), a melody is played that, through changes in orchestration, timbre, and complexity, reflects how close the user is to the desired value. The user quickly learns when they are on target by listening to the sonification.

Combining Sound Techniques

Sound can be used to present quantitative as well as qualitative information. That is, information that relays specific numeric values or that indicates a discrete state from a set of possibilities can be aurally presented. The two basic ways of doing this are through distinct sounds to indicate state information and through vocal output.

Marker and ambient sounds can be used to indicate the general state of the world. For example, the *BoilerMaker* VR application, developed as a collaboration between Argonne National Lab and Nalco Fuel Tech, Inc., indicates whether a user is inside or outside of an industrial boiler by making a marker sound as the user passes through the wall and by changing the ambient sound to indicate their presence inside or outside.

The best way to sonically convey specific numeric values is by speaking the number. For simplicity, this is often done just by speaking the individual digits, with the word *point* indicating decimal placement. It may be easier for the participant if the words used indicate the order of magnitude (hundred, thousand, etc.), as in conversational language.

Sounds can be presented either as unembodied (as part of the background) or as the voice of agents (characters in the world). By assigning different roles to separate agents and giving different vocal qualities to each, the user can make quantitative assessments of incoming messages simply by the sound of the voice. For example, the *MUSE* system has a separate agent for system reports and application reports. An agent's voice may change intonation and amplitude based on the urgency of the message. This is analogous to using the color of text to indicate information about the content, such as red text to indicate an urgent message.

Especially when spatialized, sound can be used to direct the attention of the participant. If the user hears a loud noise, they will instinctively turn their head to investigate. The sound does not have to be loud, of course; there are other ways in which intriguing sounds can lead a person to find out what's happening.

Spatialized sounds that are linked with an object add a sense of permanence to that object. Much like an infant must learn that objects exist even when they cannot be observed, participants in virtual reality experiences seem equally skeptical, turning their head to look at an object after it moves off screen. The designers of Disney's *Aladdin* VR experience [Snoddy 1996] discovered that giving the object a sound that continues to be heard in the proper direction even when out of view helps to subconsciously convince the user that the object is indeed still there.

Haptic Representation in VR

We get a lot of information about physical reality from our sense of touch. This is not currently the case in most virtual reality worlds. The lack of haptic sensation is not detrimental for many types of information gathering; however, when touch *is* an important aspect of an experience, we rely on it heavily.

With haptic displays, the trend is to represent the world as realistically as possible. Abstract haptic representations are seldom used, except for interactions with scaled worlds, sensory substitution, and reduction in danger. When interacting with a scaled world, application designers typically use everyday force interactions to represent interactions that might be experienced at a molecular or celestial scale. For example, in molecular docking, the bonding forces might be displayed in accordance with our day to day experience of magnetic forces. Another example of an abstracted haptic representation is a substitution of a vibration for a force action.

The types of information represented by haptic systems include surface properties, such as texture, temperature, shape, viscosity, friction, deformation, inertia, and weight. Restrictions imposed by most haptic displays preclude the combination of many types of haptic representations. For example, a display that presents forces through a stylus typically does not include a means of temperature display.

While haptic display usually comes from direct physical contact, changes in temperature and air movement can be felt in the air surrounding the skin. Simple representations of environmental conditions like temperature and wind can be controlled via "noncontact" displays such as heat lamps and fans.

Features of Haptics

Perhaps the most important feature of haptic representation is that, when available, the cues it provides about the world are the ones that are most trusted by the cognitive system when confusing or conflicting information is presented to the senses — seeing is believing, but touching is knowing. The human perceptual system, however, is generally governed by the trait of *visual dominance* [Wickens and Hollands 2000]. Perceptually, we attend to and believe our eyes *first*. In a *CAVE* environment, people try to touch objects they see to determine if they are real. For example, you may see a hole in a wall, but once you cannot put your hand through it, you realize it is a painting of a hole in the wall.

Another key feature of haptic display is that perception only happens *local* to the user (i.e., on or near their skin or inside their body). Thus, only the parts of the world that are within reach of the user need to be represented haptically. This is unique to the haptic display, since visual and sonic sensations can be perceived from objects well out of reach.

Since most haptic representations are realistic, a cube should feel like a cube, a warm object should transfer heat to the skin, and so on. However, there are exceptions to this rule of thumb. For instance, an artistic world could break expectation by making glowing embers taken from a fireplace feel ice cold or rough-hewn objects feel smooth. Additionally, haptic representations of potentially injurious situations need to break from realism. Actually, all sensory displays have this safety requirement (light should not be blinding, sounds should not be deafening, smells should not be toxic), but because of the requirement of physical contact, this is usually more of a concern with haptic display.

How the rendering changes representation when the display reaches a known point of harm can be handled in different ways. The force display can just stop at the last position considered to be safe, or it can veer into an abstract representation of the dangerous part of the environment. Haptic displays that produce forces capable of injuring a human are often equipped with a "dead man" switch. A dead man switch is a button, foot pedal, or other trigger that allows the equipment to operate only while pressed. As soon as users are knocked away from the switch or just feel uneasy about the display, they release the switch to cut power to the unit.

Most haptic displays in VR environments are active. That is, to be engaged, the user must reach out and touch the world. Passive haptic sensations are those that always have an effect on the user. Ambient temperature and wind are two examples of passive haptic information.

How Haptic Information Is Used in a VR Experience

Haptic interaction is not used very much in daily human to human communication, with a few obvious exceptions like a handshake, punch, kiss, slap, and the like. More often, humans use haptic information to investigate objects in the world. Haptic information helps us determine features like weight, density, elasticity, and surface texture. We also receive haptic information when we act to exert a force on the real world. The data received helps us to determine the effectiveness of our efforts and to adjust our applied amount of force to bring about the desired effect.

Force displays are used in virtual reality to depict the shape of an object, to push objects (i.e., move them, press a button), and to deform objects (i.e., pushing on immobilized objects with enough force to change their shape). The world simulation must determine whether applied forces will result in displacement or deformation.

Force Display

Force display is very beneficial for interacting with, controlling, or otherwise manipulating objects and is especially useful for delicate and small operations.

Because of the cost and complexity of adding dynamic haptic devices to a VR system, most VR application developers only add them when specifically required by the goals of the application. The two types of applications that most frequently demand haptic display are those for training physical manipulations, such as surgical procedures, and those for exploring complex shapes or forces.

Two medical training applications that make use of force display are the *BDI Surgical Simulator* and the University of Colorado at Denver's *Celiac Plexus Block Simulator*. In both of these applications, the tools used in the procedure are attached to a force display, allowing the operator to manipulate the tools in a manner imitative of the actual procedure. Another use of force display is the University of North

Carolina at Chapel Hill's *GROPE Molecular Manipulation* application [Brooks et al. 1990]; it allows a researcher to explore the force parameters at work between different molecules.

Tactile Display

Tactile display is beneficial when the details and surface features of an object are important as opposed to just the overall shape. Temperature display (a tactile sensation) may be an important part of an experience when training someone to diagnose a problem with a piece of equipment, or to teach children the importance of feeling a door when smoke is flowing from underneath. In the case of equipment diagnosis, the warmth of a particular part may indicate a problem, while other parts may continuously be warm. In the smoke example, children who correctly avoid opening a hot door may be congratulated, and any children who do open the door may be given suggestions for a better course of action.

Braille may be included in a VR experience using appropriate tactile displays. An application for woodworking instruction could allow the student to evaluate the quality of their lathe work or the progress of their carving. Likewise, someone learning to evaluate or merely distinguish among a variety of textiles could benefit from tactile representation.

Passive Haptic Feedback

In addition to active haptic displays, props and platforms provide a passive form of haptic feedback. That is, the user feels something simply by holding or touching a physical object linked to the VR system. By doing so, information about the surface texture, weight, and orientation is imparted to the user—and at a low computational cost to the VR system. For controls such as buttons, the user may also get the direct tactile sensation of the engagement of the physical switch.

In a rescue planning and training application from Sandia National Laboratory [Stansfield and Shawver 1996], a gun prop was used to provide a realistic feel as the participant aimed the prop at targets in the environment. The prop represents the weight and texture of the weapon and indicates the amount of force necessary to fire it. Another case in which a passive prop can provide important haptic information to the participant is putting practice or miniature golf. The use of an actual putter imparts a better sensation of momentum as the participant swings the club.

Representation Summary

How a virtual world is perceived depends on how it is represented. But perception is a result of life experience. The interpretation of icons and other symbols relies on cultural biases. VR experiences that strive for verisimilitude benefit from presenting the world as directly as possible, without cultural biases. If someone without the biases expected by the VR creator participates in an experience that relies on abstraction, then the representation and hence the experience will fail. The closer one remains to the reality corner of the *abstraction triangle,* the less likely one is to be misunderstood. However, this approach does ignore a lot of ways in which information can be communicated. By not venturing out very far along the image or idea axes, an experience developer misses out on many potential content ideas.

The chosen VR medium itself tends to generate biases. As a particular medium evolves, specific representations are formed, providing shortcuts to convey ideas. These shortcuts are language elements of the medium. By using these shortcuts, we can more easily explain an idea via abstract representation. For example, displaying a skull and crossbones quickly informs people who are aware of its meaning that the item so marked is poisonous or otherwise hazardous.

The mass public is consistently being trained in how to observe visual phenomena through watching television and movies. Movie makers are thus able to convey rich information merely from the cinematography of the movie, because viewers become accustomed to understanding the cues provided by the director. People are able to consume more and more information as they grow more tolerant of being fed greater amounts of information simultaneously. In contrast, in the early days of television, a commercial typically had three different cuts or scenes in it. This was about as much as the viewers would tolerate without feeling the commercial was disjointed. Compare this with the modern MTV-style commercials of today, where cuts are made in one-third second intervals or faster. Similar shortcuts (language elements) are evolving for the medium of virtual reality.

Representing information for VR adds both constraints and freedoms beyond other media. Most of the constraints come in the form of the added difficulty in rendering. In particular, rendering must be done in real time and may have the added complication of stereoscopic visuals, spatialized aurals, and haptic sensations of any kind (things that TV/movie makers, for example, do not need to worry about). In return, VR offers the freedom to interactively move about a space and the possibility of manipulating objects in a manner similar to daily life. A wider variety of sensory output is possible, and senses can be substituted across sensory modes. Again, put simply, representation is the choice of what to render.

Rendering Systems

Rendering systems generate the signals that are displayed by the devices we described in Chapter 4. Hardware and software systems are used to transform computer representations of the virtual world into signals sent to the display devices, so they can be perceived by human senses. Because each sense (visual, aural, and haptic) has different display and rendering requirements, they are usually created by different hardware and software systems. The temporal resolution required to create an acceptable illusion of continuous existence varies to a large degree according to each sense. A common visual display rate is 24 Hz (as used in modern motion pictures). Haptic displays require updates at approximately 1,000 Hz [Massie 1993]. Aural display sound quality varies from about 8,000 Hz for telephone-quality voice, to 44,100 Hz for CD-quality music, to 96,000 Hz for DVD-quality sound.

While the goal is to create a cohesive environment for all the available senses, implementation details vary greatly, so we will discuss visual, aural, and haptic rendering independently. In each of the following sections, we begin the discussion with simple and complex rendering methods so that the reader can understand the terminology and gain insight into the requirements of the hardware and software. Then we move into a discussion of the hardware, file formats, and software requirements for the various rendering methods.

Visual Rendering Systems

The craft of generating visual imagery by computer is known as *computer graphics*. This is a well-established field, with many publications available for readers to get a thorough understanding of what can be done and how to do it. Here we will give a basic overview of rendering methods, systems, and data representations and the specific requirements for real-time rendering for a VR experience.

Visual Rendering Methods

The *software rendering system* refers not to the actual application program, but the graphical rendering routines and formats on which the software system is built. This is the component of the VR system that can parse a file containing prebuilt graphical shapes and/or the instructions to generate the shapes that compose the visual image.

There are many different schemes used to describe an environment in programming code so that the VR system can correctly transform that code into a VR display. In the following sections, we describe some schemes for graphics that are geometrically based (polygons, NURBS, and CSG), along with nongeometrically based schemes such as volumetric rendering and particle systems.

Geometrically Based Rendering Systems

Three common geometrically (surface) based graphical representations are the polygonal, non-uniform rational B-splines (NURBS), and constructive solid geometry (CSG) schemes. The polygonal method is perhaps the simplest and can be used to represent shapes described by the other two, although with some loss of information. *Polygons* are planar shapes defined by a series of line segments. Any number of line segments can be used to outline a polygon, although they are often divided into only three- or four-sided shapes for efficiency. Many algorithms designed to speed up polygonal rendering methods have been integrated into hardware geometry engines and, as a result, hardware graphical rendering systems almost exclusively make use of the polygonal method.

NURBS are parametrically defined shapes that can be used to describe curved objects, such as an automobile. *CSG* objects are created by adding and subtracting simple shapes (spheres, cylinders, cubes, parallelepipeds, etc.) together (FIGURE 5-14). For example, a table can be created by adding five parallelepipeds, four as legs and one as the tabletop.

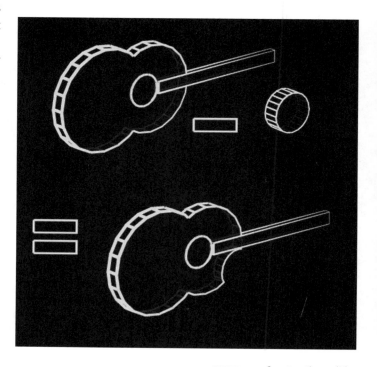

FIGURE 5-14 *Constructive solid geometry (CSG) is one method of constructing shapes within a computer representation. Here, cylinders and a box have been added together to make a simple guitar model. Another cylinder has then been subtracted from the model to make a guitar with a cutaway for reaching the high frets.*

Nongeometric Rendering Systems

Surface-based methods work best with solid, nontransparent objects. When surfaces are transparent, geometric rendering techniques may not be the best choice; this is particularly true when a space is occupied by varying densities of semitranslucent material (e.g., patchy fog or the human body when viewed via X-rays, MRI scans, or CT scans). In such cases, nongeometric methods may offer certain advantages.

Nongeometric (nonsurface) methods of representing objects in a computer-based virtual world include volumetric and particle systems. *Volume rendering* is well suited for rendering semitransparent objects and is frequently used as a visualization tool for datasets created by mapping three-dimensional volumes of material to density and color values to allow the viewer to recognize shapes and patterns within the otherwise opaque material [Drebin et al. 1988]. This technique is often applied to medical, seismic, and other scientific data.

Volume rendering is commonly accomplished using *ray-tracing* (or *ray-casting*) techniques. Ray-tracing and ray-casting techniques operate on the principle of defining rays of light as a light source. The rays behave according to the laws of physics as related to light and optics. The light rays are altered as they reflect off of surfaces of the defined virtual objects, taking into account the nature of the material the surface is supposed to be made of.

The rays are also altered as they pass through semitransparent materials. The final result of this process is often a very realistic computer graphics image of a scene that includes shadows, specular highlights, and other characteristics of real-world scenes (FIGURE 5-15). However, because ray-tracing is implemented in software and the computations are very complex, ray-tracing is not yet generally available as a real-time operation.

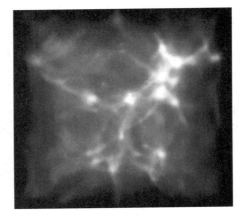

FIGURE 5-15 *This image shows a simulation of the formation of a single cluster of galaxies. Custom volume rendering techniques were implemented as a shading algorithm for the* RenderMan *rendering system to visualize this multiple-grid dataset. Increasing density values vary from dark purple to orange to white (Science: Michael Norman [NCSA], Brian O'Shea [NCSA], and Greg Bryan [MIT]; Visualization: David Bock [NCSA]; Image courtesy of Dave Bock).*

Particle rendering is often used to show complex flow in a visual scene. As the name implies, many small particles are rendered over time, producing visual features that reveal the process of a larger phenomenon [Reeves 1983]. Combustion processes such as fire, explosions, and smoke (FIGURE 5-16) are well suited for particle rendering techniques, as are water flow and animal group behavior (e.g., a flock of birds, a school of fish, or a crowd of people).

FIGURE 5-16 *A particle system was used to render the smoke in this image from* Data Driven *(Image courtesy of Chris Landreth and Dave Bock).*

Rendering Complex Visual Scenes

The complexity of visual scenes can be enhanced by using hardware or software techniques. Complex scenes can profit the viewer by providing a richer visual experience, including a more exacting realism or a more detailed presentation. There are a number of techniques involved.

Shading

The software system can enhance the visual scene by addressing features not handled by hardware, such as shadows. Shadows are just one of many examples of *shading*. Shading includes all aspects of how light is reflected off objects and into our eyes. The shade of an object changes depending on its angle to a given light source; the shadow of an object may affect the shading of some other object. Hardware graphics renderers allow for some forms of shading, but rarely handle shadows.

Reducing Ploygon Waste

Reducing *polygon waste* is another task the software system can perform. Polygon waste exists if you have a 3D object but you are looking at it from only one point of view; the polygons on the back are not seen, not necessary, and drawing them is a *waste* of effort (and therefore of precious time). Other wasted polygons are those occluded by other objects and those inside an opaque object. Some systems can detect and reduce wasted polygons very quickly in hardware.

In a polygonally rendered image, there are many "tricks" that can be applied to maintain a high frame-rate for a complex visual scene. The basic theme of all these tricks is to reduce the number of rendered polygons necessary to produce a rich visual image. These techniques include texture mapping, view culling, level of detail culling, and atmospheric effects. They were developed primarily in the visual simulation arena for military and industrial piloting simulation.

Texture Mapping. *Texture mapping* is "a method of varying the surface properties from point to point (on a polygon) in order to give the appearance of surface detail that is not actually present in the geometry of the surface" [Peachey 1994]. Properties that can be mapped onto a surface include color, transparency, and light reflectivity (bump-maps). The direction of light reflected off bumpy surfaces is what visually reveals the texture, or bumpiness, of the surface. By modifying how light *virtually* bounces off of a surface, it can be made to *appear* bumpy. (To get technical, bump-maps actually map a 2D set of values used to affect how light bounces off a surface, so rendering techniques that use the angle between the surface and the light to determine the reflected color will result in surfaces that look "bumpy.") Thus, a single polygon can appear to contain many detailed objects, such as a wall of coarsely textured bricks (FIGURE 5-17A). Moreover, use of texture mapping has been extended to enable additional polygon-reducing, scene-enriching tricks, which we will cover in more detail shortly.

Texture mapping can also be used to add scientific representations to a polygon (FIGURE 5-17B), such as colors that indicate the temperature at the surface of an object. Texture mapping works well in cases like these, because you may want more than one color on the polygon. You can create a complete range of colors on a single polygon through texture mapping. There is a tradeoff between making a small number of polygons with texture maps versus a large number of colored polygons.

Culling. *Culling* based on view makes use of the fact that not all the polygons in the virtual world are visible at all times. As we just discussed in the section on shading, processing power does not need to be wasted on unseen polygons, such as those of objects off to the side or behind the viewer. Also, if the user is in an

(A)

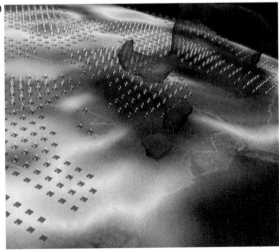
(B)

FIGURE 5-17 *Texture mapping can add detail to polygonal surfaces to add realism, such as a brick appearance to a wall* (A), *or to convey additional information, such as texture mapping rainfall data over a given terrain* (B) *(Images courtesy of William Sherman and Dave Bock, respectively). See color plate 11.*

enclosed virtual location, the walls of the enclosure may enable additional culling. The presence of windows, mirrors, and other reflective surfaces can make accurate culling a difficult task. Culling based on view is not always effective, since some scenes may be presented entirely within the scope of the viewer and would not be conducive to culling (often true in scientific visualization). An example of an inappropriate scenario for culling would be a scene consisting of a single molecule, the entirety of which is directly in front of the viewer.

Another form of culling is *level of detail (LOD) culling*. This technique reduces the number of rendered polygons by choosing between different models of an object based on its size relative to the viewer. A building might consist of several thousand polygons when the viewer stands nearby or inside it, but of only a handful if viewed on the horizon.

Atmospheric effects such as fog, smoke, and haze allow polygon reduction by enabling objects to be culled more quickly than when the user can see for miles and miles. Less detailed objects are more easily disguised when they are seen through a haze, and objects obscured entirely do not require rendering at all.

Advanced Texture Mapping Techniques

Texture mapping polygons with "faux details" is a very good way to reduce the number of polygons required to create a rich scene. As such, it is used in many situations in 3D computer graphics rendering. Simply put, the technique of texture mapping allows one to paste a texture onto a polygon. Textures add the appearance of detail and gradient cues onto what are otherwise simple, flat surfaces. When viewed up close, and especially when viewed stereoscopically, texture-mapped objects begin to reveal their secret of being little more than cardboard cut-outs or the facades of a theatrical set.

A texture can be mapped to complicated shapes made up of many individual polygons, each with a portion of the overall texture. For example, a tree trunk may be modeled as a basic cylinder composed of several flat polygons, but be made to look more realistic by wrapping a texture resembling bark around it.

There are texture map extensions used to help overcome the cardboard cut-out appearance. These tricks include the rotation of textures, multiview textures, stereoscopic textures, and animated textures. The last three are all based on using multiple bitmaps that change with the viewer's direction, view-eye, and view-time.

Distant complicated objects like trees can look very real when rendered as a single, planar polygon with a partially transparent texture map (mapped with a cut-out photograph of a tree). However, as the viewer approaches such a tree, it becomes apparent that the tree is a flat, 2D object positioned in a 3D world. One simple trick to reduce the noticeability of such an object's flatness is to *rotate* the flat polygon to always face the viewer. This gives the appearance of the object being symmetrical (i.e., looking the same from all directions). Limitations of this technique include the requirement that an axis of (near) symmetry exist for the object and that the viewer gaze only on the object orthogonal to that axis. Thus, viewing a 2D tree from above will shatter the illusion. (Of course, the illusion might also be diminished if the viewer notices that the tree looks the same from all directions.)

This rotation technique can be extended to textures with *multiple views*. As we see in FIGURE 5-18, when viewed from different angles, not only is the polygon rotated to face the viewer, but the choice of which image to map onto the polygon also changes [Pausch 1995]. So, a cat can be rendered in the same manner as the tree in the previous example, but when viewed from the front, the face of the cat will be fully visible, and when viewed from behind, the tail will be

FIGURE 5-18 *A three-dimensional object can be mimicked using texture maps by altering the texture map based on the direction from which the object is being viewed. Thus, a complicated object such as the statue depicted here can be mimicked by capturing a handful of images from multiple view-points and choosing/blending those images based on the user's changing perspective (Photographs by William Sherman).*

the prominent feature. Depending on the constraints by which an object will be viewed, the images may vary only about a single axis or from any spherical point of view. Greater texture memory resources are consumed using multiple views as a function of the number of separate viewing angles made available.

Stereoscopic textures can be useful for close-up examination of objects that are too detailed to fully render as numerous individual polygons. In stereoptic displays, stereovision will often indicate to the user that a normal, single-bitmap–textured polygon is a flat surface, regardless of the polygon's detailed appearance. This drawback can be allayed by using separate texture maps for each eye, providing stereoptic cues about the surface of the polygon. However, stereoscopic imagery has a prime viewing location from which the image looks best—the sweet spot—and the same is true for stereoscopic textures. Thus, using stereoscopic textures works best when the user can see the texture only from a location near the sweet spot, or when this technique can be combined with the *rotating texture* technique so that a different stereoscopic texture-pair can be selected based on the direction of view.

Objects that mutate rapidly over time can benefit from the use of *animated texture maps*. Natural processes like fire or falling water look much more realistic when they appear to flow. Another appropriate use of animated texture maps is when a character in the virtual world gives a predetermined speech or action. In an experience created to train people in the proper evacuation procedure from an oil rig, an image of a coworker leads the trainee along the proper escape route (FIGURE 5-19). This image is rendered as an animated texture map created from a video recording of an actor playing the role of the coworker.

FIGURE 5-19 *The man depicted instructing the participant in this application is a changing texture map read from a video file (Image courtesy of Virtuality Group, plc).*

The general term for using images to improve scene rendering time and complexity is *image-based rendering (IBR)*. The main characteristic of IBR is the use of captured or previously rendered images to reduce the time to render an image by avoiding or reducing the geometric complexity of the rendered scene. The more image material available that conforms to the viewing parameters, the less geometric representation is required. Thus, having many images of a scene, from multiple vantage points and in multiple lighting conditions, reduces the geometric rendering work required. IBR requires extensive upfront effort to capture and store the world. Another IBR technique is to make use of the previously rendered scene image and skew it based on the new viewing parameters, filling in any holes using standard geometric rendering.

Taking a picture of a real-world object and placing it on a polygon or on a set of polygons is the simplest form of image-based rendering. Thus, the *advanced* techniques of texture mapping we have discussed so far actually represent the simplest form of IBR currently available to the VR developer!

Visual Rendering Latency

The sense of realism of a virtual world is reduced when the response to user inputs is slow. In VR, slowness is measured in milliseconds. Sixteen milliseconds is a pretty good response time. One hundred milliseconds is generally considered to be the largest acceptable delay. A major benefit of using more expensive graphics engines is that they can render complex visual scenes in a few milliseconds.

The latency between user input and the display's response is a product of many components of a VR system, including tracking, computation of the world's physics (the "laws of nature" of the virtual world), rendering the world, and sending the representation to the display devices. One can measure the total latency by summing together the time required for user input(s) to cause some change in the perception of the world. However, once an image is presented, it continues to age, and just before the next image is presented, the latency between what the user is perceiving and their input may go over the threshold of acceptability. For example, if a participant is gazing at a virtual object and they move their head to see the object from a different perspective, the old perspective will remain until the fresh image is displayed. If the image is not updated quickly enough, the latency between what the user is perceiving and their input (moving their head) may go over that acceptable threshold. This problem is particularly true for the visual rendering system, because the frame rate is measured in tens of hertz.

Reducing the lag time between user interface inputs and image rendering significantly impacts the quality of the user's experience. Put simply, two primary ways to reduce latency are to (1) send information from the input devices to the computer as quickly as possible and (2) reduce the amount of time it takes to generate the computer graphics image. Another technique that does not reduce the minimum latency of the system but can significantly reduce the overall, average latency is through multiplexing multiple renderers into a single display in a technique known as *DPLEX decomposition*. This method reduces the latency caused by the aging of the image by temporally interleaving the images (FIGURE 5-20). Instead of taking the direct (and more expensive) route of using more powerful graphics engines to generate the images faster, the average lag sensed by the user is reduced by having a pipeline of scene renderers that sequentially render the images. DPLEX decomposition does not decrease the latency evidenced by tracking, computation, rendering, or display lag, but it does decrease the latency caused by aging images. The result is that over time, the *average* latency for whatever image the user is seeing is reduced.

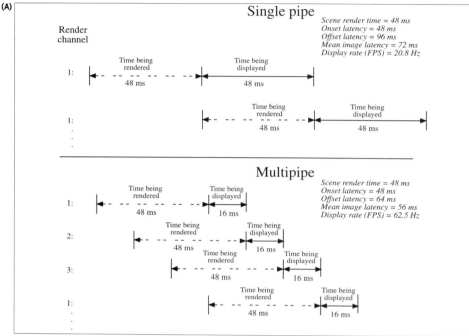

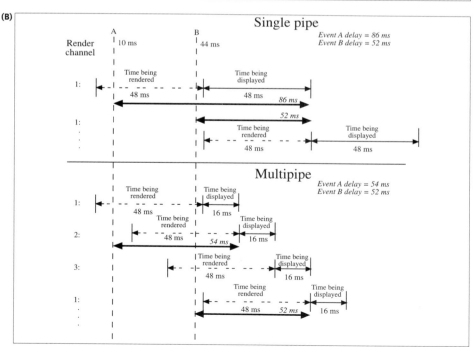

FIGURE 5-20 *DPLEX decomposition reduces the average image latency for each frame. In both diagrams* **(A)** *and* **(B)**, *a single pipe rendering system is compared with a multipipe (in this case a tri-pipe) DPLEX system. All timing values are based on scene rendering time of 48 milliseconds. The single pipe system must display the previous image for as long as it takes to render the next image; thus, just before the next image appears, the information on the screen is almost twice as old as the rendering time. In the tri-pipe system, an image remains visible for only one-third of the time necessary to render the scene, because two other rendering processes are always underway.* **(A)** *Here, we see the effect of DPLEX rendering on the lag time between user input and image rendering. The minimum delay from action to render is the same as the* onset latency. *The maximal delay is the* offset latency *(the maximum age an image achieves prior to disappearing).* **(B)** *Here, two events, A and B, occur early and late during the first rendering cycle. Because event B happened late during one rendering, the delay was only a little longer than the rendering time; thus, the DPLEX method shows no improvement in latency. However, because event A occurred before the second rendering cycle in the tri-pipe system, its results can be seen much earlier than with the single pipe system.*

(C)

Number of multi-plexed pipes	Onset	Offset (milliseconds)	Mean	Frame rate (hertz)
Single pipe	48	96	72	20.8
Dual pipe DPLEX	48	72	60	41.6
Tri-pipe DPLEX	48	64	56	62.5
Quad-pipe DPLEX	48	60	54	83.3
Quint-pipe DPLEX	48	57.6	52.8	104.2

Notes: SRT = scene rendering time; p = number or multiplexed pipes; onset = SRT; offset = SRT+SRT/p; mean = (2*SRT+SRT/p)/2; rate = p/SRT.

FIGURE 5-20 (CONTINUED)
(C) This chart shows how multi-plexing additional pipes to a single screen affects the mean age and frame rate of what is on the screen. In this example, once again, the rendering time is 48 milliseconds, and thus the onset latency of each image is always 48 milliseconds. However, the maximum offset latency and thus the average lag time can be significantly reduced. The general formulas shown in the table notes indicate how to calculate the onset and offset latency from the rendering time of the scene.

Computer Graphics System Requirements

In this section we will discuss the basic system requirements for generating computer graphics images for a VR system. There are two types of computer graphics (CG) rendering: (1) batch-mode rendering in which a series of graphics frames are rendered outside of real time for computer animation and (2) real-time rendering for interactive work. Although computer animations can be produced in real time, the luxury of not being required to do so allows computer animators to employ techniques that produce more refined images—images that cannot be created in real time due to the amount of computation time required to achieve a comparable visual complexity. Real-time images are typically rendered using simpler models and algorithms that can be rendered many times per second, whether by special-purpose hardware or by advanced software on a generic CPU.

Although some interactive computer graphics can be rendered by software on a standard CPU, most complex interactive graphics techniques can be done only using hardware specifically designed for real-time rendering. Gradually, many software rendering features are being integrated into standard hardware renderers. Further, as general-purpose CPUs increase in speed, more complex real-time rendering can be done by software. As the ability to cluster multiple inexpensive personal computers becomes more widespread, the overall computational power for rendering scenes can be increased within the constraints of a moderate budget, although at the cost of somewhat added complexity. Regardless of the methodology, the dual primary goals of the VR visual rendering system are to produce rich and informative images as fast as possible.

Graphics Engines

Rendering engines consist of computer hardware that is optimized to perform the computations necessary for 3D computer graphics operations. Once available exclusively in expensive flight simulators affordable only to the military and large airlines, graphics engines are now available at many different price points. In 1981, Silicon Graphics, Inc. was founded to create graphics hardware at a price/performance ratio affordable to many academic and business research organizations.

Computer graphics techniques that increase the richness of a visual rendering include advanced shading methods, lighting, texture mapping, translucency, and atmospheric effects (e.g., fog and haze). The type and number of effects available to a designer of a real-time experience depend on the computing hardware selected to produce the imagery.

Hardware systems vary widely in cost. Some important variations include the number of polygons rendered per second, texture map memory, antialiasing, stereo buffer (special memory that stores stereo images), genlock (which links and synchronizes multiple screens), special effects like fog and light reflection bump-maps, and many other unique capabilities. Costs for high-end systems can range upward of hundreds of thousand of dollars.

Recent advances driven by the home computer gaming market are bringing many of the benefits of high-end systems into mass-market computer graphics cards. Price per performance ratios are decreasing very rapidly, enabling many sophisticated graphics techniques to be included in low-cost systems. Some features that are desirable for VR (such as stereoscopic rendering) still are not included in the low-price-range graphics cards, but many can be found in midrange computer graphics hardware.

Not all VR applications require complicated visual rendering and can use less powerful and less costly hardware. For example, Boeing's augmented reality application that aids in the creation of wire-bundles requires only very simple line graphics easily rendered (without specialized graphics hardware) on a portable computer system (Appendix C).

Internal Computer Representation

To generate a visual scene, the computer must have some way to internally represent the shape and position of the objects in the world. Currently, the most common method is to represent objects as a collection of polygons, since most hardware rendering engines are optimized for polygonal representation. Files used to store representations also reflect a bias toward polygonal representation.

It is possible for the polygonal shape of an object to be defined directly by the VR application program, thus requiring no file storage. However, it is very common for many (if not all) of the objects in a graphical world to be created a priori using a modeling package. A modeling program allows you to define the 3D geometry of an object as well as the nature of its material composition. You can create those objects in other ways as well—for instance, through the use of a 3D digitizing device (e.g., a mechanically tracked probe or a satellite measurement of terrain elevation) or even by entering the data by hand in the case of very simple objects. Many pre-made objects are available in a variety of formats via the Internet (often at no cost), or they can be purchased from companies that maintain large collections of objects in a variety of formats and resolutions.

A great benefit of file storage formats for polygonal shapes is that shape definitions can be moved from shape creation tools (modelers) to rendering applications. Many file formats are named for the software that created them: *Wavefront, Alias, SoftImage,* and *AutoCAD.* Some formats are associated with programmable graphics libraries: *Inventor* and *Performer.* Others were developed to be software neutral: NFF (Neutral File Format) and VRML (Virtual Reality Modeling Language). Fortunately, there are translators between several formats, and many software packages can read and write descriptions of nonnative objects.

In addition to the location of the vertices of the polygon, the color, texture, and surface parameters must also be correlated with each polygon. Some formats allow parameters to be established for groups of polygons based on simple geometric shapes like cubes, spheres, and cones. These shapes are then converted into a true polygonal representation before being processed by the renderer.

Many file formats allow polygons to be grouped together into related sets. One group might be all the polygons comprising a table and another group may be those of a chair. Grouping allows objects to be easily positioned as a complete entity. Complete entity positioning allows movement of the object as a whole, as opposed to having to move each leg of a table and its top separately, for instance. A tool that provides a more complete and more flexible representation of a graphical virtual world is the scene-graph (FIGURE 5-21). A scene-graph is a mathematical graph that allows objects and object properties to be related to one another in a hierarchical fashion. Scene-graphs specify the relative location and orientation between objects in the virtual world (including geometric objects and sometimes position trackers). Other properties such as the color and texture of objects are also included in the scene-graph. Thus, entire sections of the virtual world can be modified by a single change in the structure of the scene-graph.

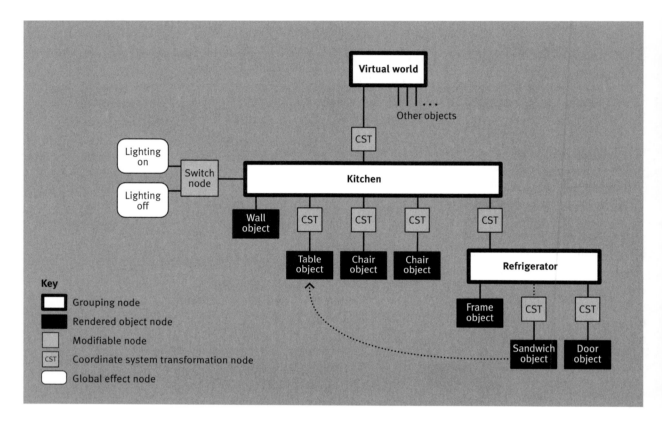

Key

■ (white box) Grouping node
■ (black box) Rendered object node
■ (gray box) Modifiable node
CST Coordinate system transformation node
▢ Global effect node

Until recently, object formats stored only the visible features of the object (e.g., shape and material light reflectivity). Object features like sound, behavior, and scripted motion were not included. These additional features would have to be associated with the object within the application software.

VR Visual Interface Software

Software systems used to convey the description of the virtual world to the VR hardware often make use of a variety of application libraries and toolkits to create, render, and allow interfacing to the virtual world. Each of these different utilities facilitates control of the visual rendering of the virtual world. In the sections that follow, we describe some of the more common software used in virtual reality applications.

A graphics library is a collection of software routines that enable a programmer to execute fairly complex actions by making relatively simple subroutine

FIGURE 5-21 *Scene-graphs are used to group related items together, making it easier for a particular collection of objects to be moved as a whole. In this example, the entire refrigerator and its contents can be moved by changing a single coordinate system. Alternately, the door can be moved relative to the rest of the refrigerator, or an item such as the sandwich can be unlinked from the refrigerator and attached to the table object. At this point, moving the table will also cause the sandwich to go along for the ride.*

and function calls. For example, rather than writing code to draw a line (a trivial amount of code!), a programmer can simply call a line function from the graphics library and specify the start and end coordinates of the line along with other attributes like color, weight, and so on.

OpenGL is a collection of graphics rendering algorithms that provide a standard, cross-platform programming interface that covers the entire line of Silicon Graphics, Inc. (SGI) machines, as well as IBM PCs, PC clones, all manner of Unix workstations, and other platforms. The *OpenGL* library provides easy, convenient access to many tedious and complex functions frequently available in graphics accelerator hardware. It is based around the polygonal form of shape representation.

Libraries can make use of other libraries. Silicon Graphics' *(Open) Performer* library adds programming interface and scene-graph capabilities to the *OpenGL* library. *Performer* uses *OpenGL* for rendering the actual polygons, adding the ability to manipulate groups of polygons from a higher level (cubes instead of six separate polygons) with more geometric calculations, such as testing for intersections between a line and any arbitrary object. *Performer* was designed specifically for the fast rendering of a virtual world scene. Its scene-graph capability adds a hierarchical structure to *OpenGL,* providing an easier programming model.

The initial version was designed for the flight-simulation market, so many of the features work best on virtual worlds based on the concept of flying over a terrain. Scientific databases, such as one describing a complex molecular structure, do not benefit from all of *Performer's* rendering strategies. An exclusive product of Silicon Graphics, Inc., *Performer* is tuned to execute *OpenGL* commands in a way that is optimal for each individual model of graphics hardware available in the SGI product line and in some Linux PCs with particular graphics cards.

The *WorldToolkit (WTK)* from Engineering Animation Inc. provides both an interface to common VR hardware and commands for rendering the virtual world. *WTK* has integrated hardware support, including various models of body trackers, glove interfaces, non–VR desktop devices like the mouse, and 6-DOF input devices. The rendering software interface provides a hierarchical polygonal database structure for producing the virtual world imagery. On some platforms, *WTK* uses *OpenGL* to do the graphics, and on many other platforms it makes use of at least some graphics acceleration hardware models—meaning that *WTK* includes the code to directly access the capabilities of the graphics hardware. A major benefit of *WTK* is its cross-platform functionality. Applications designed for a PC can be quickly ported to higher-end SGI workstations if more speed or a more powerful computer engine is required. Conversely, an application developed on an SGI machine can be ported to a PC when

The VRML File Format

VRML, the so-called *Virtual Reality Modeling Language,* was created out of a desire to share 3D graphical virtual worlds across the Internet via the World Wide Web. The original version was based on the hierarchical, polygonal Silicon Graphics *Inventor* format. Originally, VRML was primarily a shape description language, although it did allow for links to sound files (as well as to all other types of Internet data formats). The later VRML 97 specification included facilities for sound and multiple types of behavioral descriptions.

Although the acronym *VRML* refers to virtual reality, and worlds modeled with VRML can be experienced through a VR interface, it is in fact a virtual *world* specification. This means that the information in a VRML file describes the scenes of a 3D virtual world (which may or may not be experienced in VR). This is not a bad thing, since VR interfaces are not (yet) commonly available on the majority of installed computers. Thus, many more people are able to share and experience these worlds across the Web than if they truly were available only as a virtual reality experience. VRML allows the description of virtual worlds to include shapes, links to other Web entities (including text pages as well as other VRML worlds), animation scripts and other simple behaviors, and audio (FIGURE 5-22A).

Network connection bandwidth limits the amount of complexity that can be quickly transferred from the source to the VRML viewer. Another limitation is the inability for multiple participants to simultaneously occupy the same world. It is technically feasible to create a VRML viewer that is capable of placing more than one participant in the world, but this is not part of the specification, and the application designer would be called upon to determine such details as how a URL selection by one participant would affect the others.

The *Greek Farm* educational experience developed by Learning Sites, Inc. makes extensive use of VRML to present an archaeological database, including the current state of the site, graphical and textual information about its artifacts, and a representation of how the farm may have looked when it was occupied (FIGURE 5-22B).

FIGURE 5-22 **(A)** *Characters in a VRML world are animated via scripted behavior described as code (VRML world courtesy of SGI; photograph by William Sherman).* **(B)** *A VRML-capable Web browser is used to show various levels of information about an archaeological database: a walkthrough of the overall site, a 3D representation of selected objects, and a textual description of the objects (Image courtesy of Learning Sites, Inc.).*

desirable. *WTK* can also support multiple displays and synchronous collaborative experiences.

The *Minimal Reality (MR) Toolkit* developed at the University of Alberta also provides a hardware interface, a shape interface (e.g., the ability to specify cubes and test them for intersections with other shapes, etc.), and some behavioral description of the virtual world. Like the *WTK* library, it is platform-independent. The *MR Toolkit* also provides mechanisms to simultaneously share VR experiences.

The *CAVE* library developed at the Electronic Visualization Laboratory at the University of Illinois at Chicago is primarily a VR hardware interface library. A VR hardware interface library is a collection of routines to support the required communication with different VR hardware devices like gloves, wands, trackers, and the like (as we saw with the *World Toolkit*). Other than the basic graphics routines necessary to create and synchronize the viewing windows, the *CAVE* library leaves the graphics to the application programmer. *OpenGL, IrisGL, WTK, Inventor,* and *Performer* have all been used to render worlds in *CAVE* library applications.

The original *CAVE* library rendered the world only for the *CAVE* VR display device, with a separate desktop simulator version. Later, the library became significantly more adaptable and now allows display to HMDs, *BOOMs,* and handheld displays in addition to a variety of stationary displays like the *CAVE, ImmersaDesk, Responsive Workbench,* and simple fishtank VR displays. The type of VR display does not have to be specified ahead of time; it can be specified at the time you start the application. So a single executable version of an application will work on any VR display or in a mode that emulates position trackers and other inputs for the purpose of code development and testing. The *CAVE* library was designed primarily for applications that run on a variety of SGI workstations.

In addition to communicating with the various tracking devices available, the *CAVE* library also provides the means for applications to communicate with one another. Applications that make use of this feature can more easily be multiparticipant experiences. *CAVE* library applications can also run on specifically configured computers to distribute the rendering task of a single VR display across more than one computer, allowing for more graphics hardware to be used in the rendering process.

There are also a number of open source libraries built by consortia and made available at no cost over the Internet for implementing virtual reality applications. In general, these libraries include the means to display on head-based and stationary displays and can track the user's movements and accept inputs via several different input devices. Three examples are *VR Juggler* from Iowa State University [Just et al. 1998], *Diverse* from Virginia Tech [Arsenault et al. 2001], and *FreeVR,* a grass roots effort [Sherman 2001].

Aural Rendering Systems

Computerized sound generation for virtual reality is also an active area of research. Information about how to create sounds via computer is less readily available than computer graphics information and is spread over many disciplines (including computer graphics, computer music, scientific visualization, and virtual reality). We'll begin our discussion with the basic ways sound can be rendered. From there, we'll cover sound generation hardware, aural software formats, and aural interface systems.

Methods of Aural Rendering

In this section, we discuss three basic methods of rendering aural signals: (1) the playback of recorded waveform samples, (2) synthesis (algorithmic rendering), and (3) the postprocessing of existing sound signals. Sounds are vibrations that travel through the air (or other media) in waves. The *frequency* of the waves, or how many cycles of the wave occur per unit of time, determines whether the sounds are high- or low-pitched. The wave's *amplitude,* the other key feature of sound, determines the loudness of the sound.

Sampling

A common way of producing sounds is through the playback of digitally *recorded samples* of physical world sounds. An analog-to-digital (A/D) converter converts analog signals into digital signals (FIGURE 5-23). The recordings are created by sending the output of a microphone through an A/D converter, which measures the voltage at regular time intervals (sampling rate). The sampling rate and the number of digital bits used to encode the voltage are measures of the resolution of the sound sample. The frequency that the voltage measurements are taken at range from 8,000 Hz for telephone-quality spoken audio to 96,000 Hz for DVD-quality sound. The sound quality for CDs measures at 44,100 Hz. The number of bits available for each measurement determines the dynamic range of the recorded signal. This ranges typically from 8 bits to 48 bits. Standard stereo CDs use 16 bits for each channel. The resulting stream of numbers is processed by the computer and can be stored, edited, or played back as sounds whenever desired. This process is called *sampling,* and the collection of numbers is referred to as both a *waveform sample* and a *sample array.*

The technique of sampling is analogous to the use of digitized photographs to create texture maps (visual bitmaps). It is particularly useful when realistic aural representations are desired. Adding texture enhances the aural environment, but the designer must be mindful to avoid the obvious repetition of the sounds or the listener

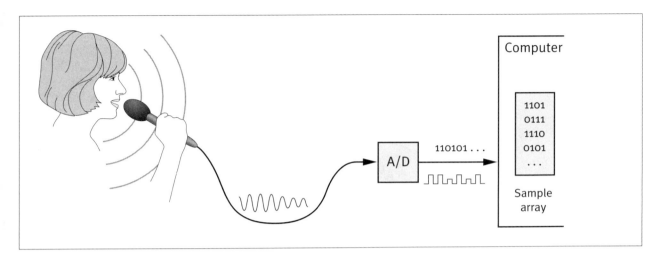

FIGURE 5-23 *Real-world sounds (such as a voice) can be recorded by doing analog-to-digital (A/D) conversion. The resulting digital signals can be processed, stored, or otherwise manipulated by the computer system.*

will become bored or annoyed. Sound repetition can be easily detected by the participant (as can the repetition of patterns caused by visual texture maps). Multiple digitized sound samples can be altered and combined to create a richer, less repetitive environment. They can also be combined with other, algorithmically generated, sounds.

Synthesis

Synthesized sounds are those that are generated by executing an algorithm or some other component of the VR simulation that computes the waveform (FIGURE 5-24). This technique offers extreme flexibility to the experience developer, because creating any sound is possible, yet may require a significant computer engine or specialized synthesizer in order to render the samples in real time.

Synthesizing complex, realistic broadband sounds is difficult. Sound-generation algorithms range in complexity from producing simple sounds like sine waves to sounds created by modeling the properties of a sound-generating object. Methods of sound synthesis can be divided into three subcategories: *spectral methods, physical models,* and *abstract synthesis.*

Spectral Methods. *Spectral methods* of sound synthesis involve observing a sound wave's frequency spectrum (the frequencies and amounts of each of the components that make up the sound) and re-creating that spectrum to mimic the original. Most of the sounds we hear in the real world are broadbanded; that is, they cover a wide variety of frequencies, so it is generally not feasible to create the entire spectrum of

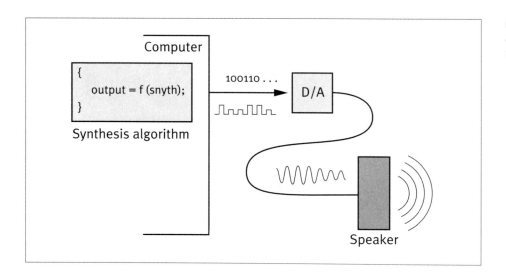

FIGURE 5-24 *Synthesized sounds use algorithms to generate the waveform.*

such sounds in real time. Musical sounds, however, use only a small subset of frequencies. Thus, many spectrally based synthesis methods result in the generation of sounds with musical qualities. Examples of spectral sound-generation methods include sine waves, frequency modulation (modulating one sine according to the frequency of another), and additive synthesis (creating complex sounds by summing sine waves of different frequencies).

Physical Models. *Physical models* are created by computing sounds based on the physics of the object(s) generating the sound. For example, a physical sound model of a flute relies on computing the vibrations that occur as air flows through a tube of specific dimensions. That is, the underlying physical phenomena (air flow, vibration, etc.) are modeled, and the results of those computations are directly used to create the corresponding real-world sound.

With this method, sounds can be made to seem more authentic and integral to the environment. The modeled activity may be continuous, as with the air flow in our flute example, or it may be a discrete event, such as a ping pong paddle striking a ball. Given the proper parameters of the tube and the flow of air through it, a realistic sounding flute can be emulated. Given the proper physical parameters of the paddle and ball (e.g., hardness, force of contact), a realistic sounding ping pong match can be heard.

If the goal were to add realistic car engine sounds to an experience, then one might model the general shape of the engine and exhaust system and determine the air pressure waves generated when rapid explosions are occurring in the piston chambers, as well as other actions that significantly affect the resulting sound. However, unless it is important for the sound to change appropriately with modification to the engine parameters, it is easier (currently) to simply record and play back appropriate engine sounds.

Abstract Synthesis. *Abstract synthesis* of sounds creates sounds from streams of numbers generated by some system and maps the values to sound waveforms by some given function. Rather than re-creating a sound, this technique is used to create sounds that have never been heard before, based on some numerical system. For example, a risk analysis formula could reflect the change of commodity market instruments over time and allow an analyst to become familiar with patterns by listening to their fluctuations.

Any of these synthesized sounds—whether created via spectral methods, physical models, or abstract synthesis—may be combined or filtered to create a more interesting effect. Sound combinations may be created by explicitly scripting a score (event timeline) or by generating the score algorithmically.

Postprocessing

Both sonic waveforms that are generated in real time and those that are preexisting can be further processed into new waveforms. This postprocessing can be applied to sounds created by any of the methods described earlier to modify the sound in some way, yielding a new sound, perhaps similar to the original but with some qualitative differences. The applied effects may be fairly simple, such as adding an echo that gives the impression of coming from a large hall or cavern. Another effect is to reduce the amplitude of the higher frequencies, generating a muffled sound as if emanating from a great distance.

Rendering Complex Sounds

As with visual rendering, there are a variety of useful aural rendering techniques that can enhance the aural environment. In the following sections, we describe such techniques as frequency modulation, algorithmic additive/subtractive techniques, and granular synthesis. Furthermore, a sound can be made more complex through the use of various filtering techniques. In VR systems, such filters are often used to spatial-ize sounds. A complex sonic environment can also be created by combining various elements of ambient sounds, interface sounds, sonifications, spatialized sound, and the like into a coherent presentation.

Sounds are dynamic in complex ways, which makes it difficult to develop effective methods of rendering realistic sounds. It is not just a matter of re-creating a simple wave equation. *Sine waves* (waves that are described by the mathematical sine function) are the fundamental structure of spectral sound synthesis. They are a basic building block of computer-generated sonic imagery, much like polygons are in the visual domain. Just as looking at a single polygon can be boring, an individual sine wave results in a sound that can be annoying to listeners. Sound is temporal, so the equation must change over time. Because the ears and the brain are able to discern slight variations in sound waveforms, the rendering process must be done at very high speed, because the nuances are so fleeting. There is a tradeoff between simple ren-dering equations that can be computed quickly and methods that create more complex (and thus more pleasing or realistic) sounds at the expense of greater pro-cessing resources. We saw this same tradeoff in our discussion of such sophisticated visual techniques as texture mapping, level-of-detail culling, and atmospheric effects.

Frequency Modulation

Frequency modulation (FM) is another, somewhat richer method of spectral sound synthesis. Like sine waves, FM sounds are easy to compute. However, instead of just the two parameters of frequency and amplitude of the sine wave, FM sounds have additional parameters such as the carrier frequency (the frequency of the main sound), carrier/modulator frequency ratio (C/M, or how different the modulating fre-quency is from the carrier frequency), and modulation indices (the ratio of frequency deviation to the modulating frequency). The resultant sounds are more complex and somewhat more gratifying than simple sine waves, but can also cause distress to the listener after a period of time due to listener fatigue. Many of the sounds have bell-like qualities and high-frequency components that can wear on the listener.

Additive and Subtractive Techniques

Additive and *Subtractive* techniques are spectral sound creation methods that allow sounds to be created by combining or subtracting signals of different frequencies. Resultant sounds thus contain a rich combination of selected frequencies. Additive synthesis is basically the summation of many sine waves at different frequencies and phase shifts (differences in signal position with respect to time). Subtractive synthesis is the filtering of frequencies from an already complex sound such as "white noise."

Fourier Analysis is a mathematical technique used to identify the component sine waves that make up a complex waveform. This technique allows one to analyze a real-world sound and determine the frequencies, amplitude, and phases of the underlying sine waves. These sine waves can then be resynthesized, or reconstructed to emulate the original waveform. Only now, the programmer has control over how those waves are combined, allowing great flexibility in how the sound can be altered by the VR program.

Granular synthesis

Granular synthesis is the composition of complex sounds from snippets of sonic bitmaps, FM sounds, sinewaves, and other sources to create a richer, more dynamic sounding environment. The original snippets are not necessarily still recognizable. For example, if we have the sound of a single drop of water falling on a rock, then combining this sound with itself many times over could produce the sound of a waterfall or a flowing river [Scaletti 1997].

Filtering Techniques

Convolution is a mathematical operation that can be applied to a waveform to filter it in interesting ways, such as to make a sound appear to come from a particular location. This very effective sound processing technique is achieved by reproducing how a sound's reception is modified by the listener's head and body (see the discussion on the head-related transfer function, or HRTF, in the section Sound-Generation Hardware). Filters can also cause sounds to seem as though they are being listened to in a room with different acoustical properties like a jazz hall or cathedral. These filters are created by playing an impulse sound (e.g., a gun shot) made at the location where the sound emanates (e.g., a cathedral or orchestra pit) and recording it from various places where a listener might be. The sound is analyzed in the room after the impulse and that analysis leads to a mathematical description of the acoustical properties of the space. The mathematical description can be used to alter any sonic image to sound as though it were being listened to in that space. This technique is used in effects for movies and audio recordings.

HRTFs function similarly, except the space the filter is created for is the space around one's head, and instead of a single location from which sounds are presumed to emanate, recordings of impulse responses are made from many different locations around the head in order to model the effect of emanating from those locations.

Reverberation and *chorusing* are two additional examples of algorithms for processing existing signals to produce effects to give aural clues about a virtual world. A reverberation effect is made by mixing the sound with copies of that sound, which are delayed and filtered to emulate reflections of the sound in a specific enclosed environment. Chorusing mixes the sound with copies of that sound which are shifted in phase, creating a bigger sound. Phase shifting means that two or more sound waves are shifted with respect to each other so that the peaks and troughs are not synchronous with each other. This shifting can have a profound effect on the resulting sound, and the resultant wave is different in nature from any of the component waves.

Combining Effects

Many sound sources rendered in a VR system begin as a monophonic sound image. Rendering techniques like convolution and reverberation are then used to create a stereophonic sound image from these sources. Ambient sounds are sometimes an exception, beginning as a stereophonic sound presented to both ears of the listener. In the real world, sounds are "mixed" naturally in the air; however, the developers of Disney's *Aladdin* VR experience found that electronic sound images of different forms (monophonic, stereophonic spatialized with respect to a fixed sound stage; stereophonic spatialized from a head-based, moving sound stage; and stereophonic non-spatialized sounds) can be directly mixed to create a realistic and compelling sound experience for the participant [Pausch et al. 1996; Snoddy 1996].

Sound-Generation Hardware

A considerable amount of consumer software and hardware is available to aid in music composition and professional audio production. This interest in computer-based audio production has made a wealth of hardware devices available to the consumer, and mass production has allowed prices to drop to a very attractive price/performance point.

Most consumer sound-production devices are focused on creating music, which (generally) uses sounds with specific musical pitches. Most (nonmusical) sounds in the real world are broadbanded sounds—waves crashing on the beach, the rush of the wind, or an engine's rumble. VR systems utilize both musical and broadbanded sounds.

In order to create the different sound forms used in VR experiences, one needs to generate electrical signals that will ultimately be transduced to air pressure variation and delivered to the listener via an aural display device—headphones or speakers. Hardware for generating high-quality audio for virtual environments is relatively low-cost and readily available. Apart from the direct audio output of a personal or workstation computer, sound rendering and filtering hardware includes synthesizers, general-purpose effects processors, and programmable and task-specific digital signal processing (DSP) boxes.

Because the broadcast, film, advertising, and music industries drive the market, most aural rendering hardware is optimized for their specific needs. There are not many general-purpose audio engines available. A general-purpose audio engine is like a general-purpose computer. You can program it to do whatever you want, from reverbs (using custom reverb algorithms) to stereo chorusing; essentially, if you can write the algorithm, you can achieve the sound effect. Due to requirements not met by mass market sound hardware, VR aural rendering systems are often software-based.

Of the hardware systems available, three types are used to create sound for virtual environments: (1) specialized sound renderers (usually called synthesizers), (2) general-purpose sound renderers, and (3) sound postprocessors (or effects boxes). Often, though, some audio-capable computer is used as a general-purpose renderer.

A sound *synthesizer* uses special-purpose hardware to create sounds based on one or more algorithms. The synthesized sounds are fine tuned to various parameters such as pitch, volume, and timbre. Many synthesizers are created with a musical instrument input interface (FIGURE 5-25). In other words, the user interface of the synthesizer is designed to emulate the interface of an instrument, most commonly a piano/organ keyboard. An additional feature of many synthesizers is that they can be controlled by a computer (or other device) via a sequence of commands. By making use of such an interface, a VR application can generate ambient music or trigger the playback of digitally stored sound samples.

Synthesized sounds can be created to represent many different kinds of instruments and sounds that have never been heard before. Collections of recorded sound samples (a digitized sound image) can be stored and played back from many sound synthesizers (FIGURE 5-26). This digitized image of sound is one form of a *sonic bitmap,* analogous to visual texture maps.

A *programmable sound processor* can be used to compute sounds (rather than playing back stored ones). This requires a powerful computer or Digital Signal Processing (DSP) system. The Symbolic Sound *Kyma/Capybara* system consists of *Kyma* software, which allows one to visually design algorithms for computing waveforms, and the *Capybara* hardware, which consists of multiple DSP chips computing

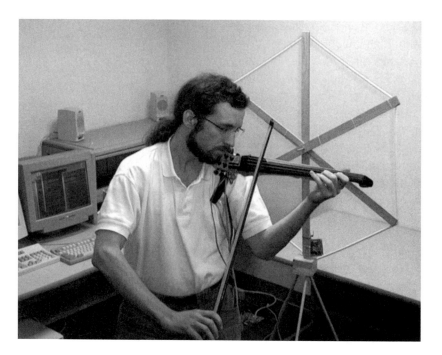

FIGURE 5-25 *Many devices can control synthesized sound. Here, composer Camille Goudeseune plays an electric violin that sends data to a software synthesizer [Garnett and Goudeseune 1999]. Goudeseune's system tracks the position of the violin by means of the antenna shown in the background and a sensor mounted on the violin; software tracks the pitch and amplitude of the signal from the violin's bridge. By means of all this data, the performer controls the parameters of the synthesis in real time (Photograph by William Sherman).*

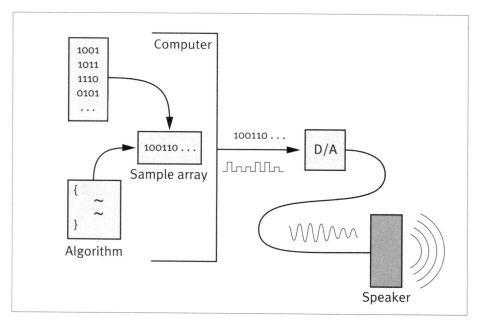

FIGURE 5-26 *This diagram illustrates how digital sounds can be made by playing back a sound file originally created by digitally recording a real-world signal or by using a computer algorithm to create the sound. The digital information is passed through a digital-to-analog (D/A) converter to produce the signal that is transduced by a loudspeaker or headphones.*

in parallel for a display featuring a multitude of complex sounds in real time (FIG-URE 5-27). (We discuss the *Kyma/Capybara* system in greater detail in the section Aural Interface Systems.)

Postprocessors provide a variety of special effects to simulate different listening environments or 3D sounds. These effects and more can be created using software DSP systems or by using commercially available digital signal processing boxes (FIGURE 5-28). Many such processors are available at low cost, and typically allow the parameters of the effects to be controlled via a musical instrument digital interface (MIDI).

One specialized device for producing 3D spatialized sounds is known as the *Convolvotron*. The *Convolvotron*, developed by Crystal Rivers Engineering, can apply an arbitrary transfer function to any sound to filter the sound in some way. The most common transfer functions model the effect of the shape of the individual listener's head. The aptly named head-related transfer function (HRTF) allows the sonic display to seem as if the sound were emanating from a particular direction.

HRTFs are typically created by placing special microphones in the ears of a subject and measuring the waveform of sounds from inside the ear. Very broadband sounds (white noise) are played from several locations around the subject, and the

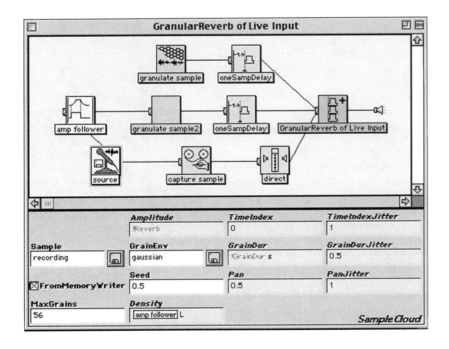

FIGURE 5-27 *The Kyma software system from Symbolic Sound provides a visual interface for constructing and manipulating complex sounds (Image courtesy of Symbolic Sound).*

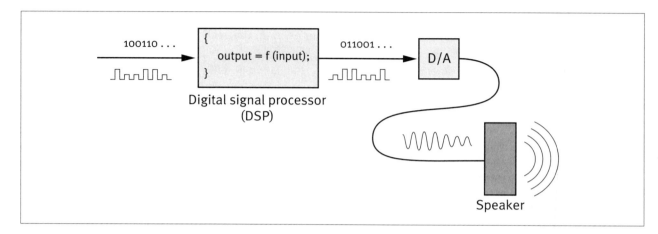

filtering provided by the outer ear, body, and head shadowing is measured. The next step is to load the mathematical description of the filter function into the *Convolvotron*. The result is that the virtual world sounds become spatialized with respect to the listener. In effect the sound display is manipulated in such a way that sounds appear to emanate from particular locations with respect to the listener [Wightman and Kistler 1989].

Internal Computer Representation (Aural Software Formats)

Like visual images, just prior to delivery to the display, aural images consist of a collection of numbers. The numbers for visual images exist in a 2D array that changes over time. Aural images have a single value per channel that changes over time. The frame rate of audio data is typically referred to as *sample rate*.

As we've already discussed, a compact disc uses a sample rate of 44,100 Hz, storing information for two channels (stereophonic). This can use up memory and disk space rapidly, so most audio formats allow for a range of sample rates (again, from 8,000 Hz for telephone quality to the 96,000 Hz of DVDs for audiophile quality) based on a balance between desired quality and available memory. The number of bits used to represent each number also affects the quality. Sixteen bits provide enough dynamic range (96 dB) to cover the range of amplitude of an orchestra playing in a symphony hall. Lower quality audio often uses only 8 bits per number; 20 or 24 bit storage is used in high-end solutions.

FIGURE 5-28 *This diagram illustrates how digital sounds can be processed in the digital domain by using digital signal processing (DSP) techniques. The DSP is a "black box" that executes a computer program to the signal, resulting in a modified signal at the output. Here, the digital signal 1 0 0 1 1 0 enters the DSP and a computation is performed by the DSP unit (e.g., a complex reverberation simulation). The resulting signal comes out the other end as the output 0 1 1 0 0 1. The output signal is sent through a digital-to-analog (D/A) converter and finally through the speaker display.*

The specific formats used in modern computing systems differ in which sample rates, number of bits per sample, number of channels, and compression algorithms can be used to store a sound. Some formats were designed to support only specific values. The audio interchange file format (AIFF) is very flexible, allowing for a variety of sample rates, bits per sample, and encoding. This format is the standard for Macintosh and SGI computers. On PCs, the WAVE audio file format is popular. The WAVE format too is flexible, allowing a choice of sample rate, number of channels, and compression method.

For sounds that are simple event-driven compositions, the musical instrument digital interface protocol (MIDI) provides another file format option. MIDI is a standard protocol for communication between electronic music instruments and/or computers. The MIDI format specifies a sequence of actions or events in a musical score. Adjusting settings for sound qualities (pitch, timbre, amplitude, etc.) modifies the type of sound that will play. Other commands turn sounds on and off and provide other control information. A MIDI-compatible device like a MIDI-equipped synthesizer then generates the actual sound. Using the MIDI protocol to issue control commands uses significantly less bandwidth between the computer and the sound-producing device than sending the actual digital waveform from the computer to the sound-generation device. However, because you are only sending control information via MIDI (rather than the actual sounds), the actual sound produced may differ from system to system, because of inconsistencies between different brands or models of MIDI sound generators.

Typically MIDI signals are sent to music synthesizers and effects boxes. Synthesizers play notes that sound like they come from a variety of instruments, but can also play preloaded sound sample-arrays (sonic bitmaps). With MIDI, the actual sound generation takes place on the synthesizer. A set of MIDI instructions (a MIDI sequence) can be stored in a file and played as a score, or the MIDI instructions can be created in real time by a computer program to control the devices dynamically and in real time. For example, the VR system can issue MIDI instructions to a MIDI-compatible sound device based on the user's position in the virtual world. MIDI commands sent to effects boxes control such features as reverberation or the selection of preset configurations like chorusing, various distortions, volume, and a variety of other features.

Aural Interface Systems

Occasionally, a VR software interface package includes sound-rendering capabilities. Often these packages limit sound generation to the simple playback of sample-files (as with a VRML browser). There are a few different types of software systems available that generate sound in real time: sample-file playback control, general-purpose hardware controllers, and real-time sample-array creation systems. In some circumstances, the application developer must create their own sound-generation algorithms.

Lack of development time for creating a rich sound environment, coupled with limited expertise and availability of real-time sound-creation software tools, lead many application development teams to use the simplest of the sound-generation methods—*sample-array playback*. Some computer systems equipped with built-in hardware for playing sound samples include simple routines for placing samples into an outgoing sound queue. A simple scheme for playing sounds is to put stored sound samples into this queue whenever a specific event occurs. Alternately, notes or sampled sounds can be activated by sending MIDI commands from the computer to a synthesizer.

For VR experience developers interested in creating very complex sounds in real time, hardware devices like the *Capybara* are an option. The *Capybara* is programmed using the *Kyma* language. *Kyma* is a *general-purpose sound creation language*. *Kyma* provides a visual programming language interface that allows a programmer to combine modules into a network that renders (in real time) a sound on a general-purpose audio engine (much like *OpenGL* produces commands to render on a graphics rendering engine). Because the samples are created in real time, any aspect of the sound can be controlled by any data stream. In that the sound is actually being *created* in real time (as opposed to playing some pre-created sound), *any* parameter can be a factor in *how* the sound is created. So data from the tracking system *can* factor into the creation of the sound, or real-world data (like the current temperature) can be used as a factor in creating the resultant sound. The point is that because the sound is actually being created by an algorithm of the VR application developer's design, *anything* can be factored into the sound. Contrast this with using something like a MIDI synthesizer, where you are constrained to the set of sounds it was programmed at the factory to make, along with some minor adjustments.

Our work with Caterpillar Inc. offers an anecdotal example. Commercial synthesizers typically don't make tractor sounds. And, they certainly don't let you make real-time adjustments to the number of pistons in the engine to hear how that sounds. There are commercial synthesizers that let you record a real tractor, but then the sound doesn't change except in simple ways, such as making it louder or softer, shifting the pitch, and the like. With the real-time software synthesis of sounds, we can program the physical characteristics of how the sound is made in the real world (say, diesel fuel exploding in the cylinders) and emulate that in the virtual world. So, if the tractor is operating at a very heavy load, the engine sounds "loaded down" automatically, as opposed to having to make recordings of every possible sound and switching between them in the VR application to suit the situation.

The *Kyma/Capybara* package is capable of synthesis methods such as sample-array playback, Fourier analysis/resynthesis, wavetable synthesis (whereby a wavetable, or sonic bitmap, is constructed by a software algorithm of the programmer's design), subtractive synthesis and filtering, granular synthesis, physically based sound models, and various other processing algorithms. Since the *Capybara* contains multiple DSP processors, the system can generate more simultaneous sounds and sounds of greater complexity in real time than most general-purpose computers. Sound developers can construct new algorithms by combining existing modules, or they can write new algorithms in the assembly language of the DSP chips.

The *Vanilla Sound Server (VSS)* is an example of a general-purpose software audio-rendering system [Bargar et al. 1994]. Currently, *VSS* runs on Silicon Graphics, Linux, and Windows-based workstations. *VSS* is essentially driven by control messages similar to MIDI; however, it is much more flexible than MIDI. *VSS* (the sound *server*) runs on the computer that renders the sounds—which may or may not be the same machine that is computing the rest of the simulation (the *client*). Using functions provided by a companion library, the client application sends commands and data to the server to define, initiate, modify, and terminate sounds. *VSS* feeds directly to the outgoing sound buffer queue on Silicon Graphics or Linux workstations equipped with audio hardware. No hardware accelerators are used.

VSS uses a variety of the sound-generation methods we've discussed, including sample-array playback, sending MIDI commands to a synthesizer, generating sine waves or FM sounds, granular composition, and physically based sound models. In addition to these methods of generating sounds, *VSS* has functions that modify the control parameters of specific sounds or the overall output, that is, the volume of a single sound source or the volume of the entire output. *VSS* can also alter the waveforms themselves by applying filters and effects like reverberation.

The needs of a particular virtual reality experience can call for any of the methods described. However, after analyzing the needs of the application, the best option for sound-generation software may be to write it from scratch and customize it to your particular application.

Haptic Rendering Systems

Of the major senses used in VR systems, the haptic sense is the most difficult to incorporate. One reason for this challenge is that the haptic sense results from direct contact with the environment and thus involves direct two-way communication between the participant and the world. Haptic devices are the only human-computer interfaces that both receive and provide stimuli. A malleable object is rendered so the user can feel its shape, texture, and temperature; in addition, if pushed on with sufficient force, the object's shape will be changed in accordance with its elasticity. It is challenging to create and maintain illusory displays for the haptic sense because of the direct contact required for the stimuli.

Another challenge to successful haptic display is that the human haptic system includes both tactile (skin-based) and kinesthetic (muscle/joint–based) feedback. The two sensations are closely interrelated, but to date VR systems typically address only one or the other. So for practical purposes, our discussion on haptic rendering is divided into two basic techniques: skin-based rendering (temperature and surface texture) and muscle/joint–based rendering (surface texture and force).

In a force display system, a lagging frame rate causes the "feel" of the world to change or can even cause the display to become unstable. This is in direct contrast to the visual system, in which slow frame rates affect only whether images are perceived as a continuous moving scene or as a series of independent images. Either way, each image is still an accurate visual rendering of the world at that moment in time. A brick will still look like a brick, but in a lagging force display, it might *feel* like a lump of clay.

Haptic Rendering Methods

In our discussion of displays in Chapter 4, we covered three types of common haptic displays: (1) tactile devices (attached to the skin), (2) end-effector displays (mechanical force applied to a stylus, finger-grip, etc.), and (3) robotically operated shape displays (mechanism for placing physical objects in the appropriate position). If an application designer is not motivated to design new forms of haptic display, they must use rendering methods that can be accommodated by these devices.

As we've said, haptic perception consists of both skin and kinesthetic (muscle and joint) sensations. Skin stimuli such as temperature, pressure, electric current, and surface texture can all be displayed using tactile display devices. Surface texture can also be rendered using small-scale end-effector (mechanical force) displays. Kinesthetic sensations allow people to determine such features as surface shape, surface rigidity, surface elasticity, object weight, and object mobility. Kinesthetic information can be rendered using either end-effector (FIGURE 5-29) or robotically operated shape displays (ROSDs). The following sections provide an overview of the basic haptic rendering methods currently in use.

FIGURE 5-29 *The Sarcos Dextrous Arm Master provides kinesthetic feedback by applying forces to a handle held by the user (Image courtesy of Sarcos, Inc.).*

Thermal Rendering

Rendering temperature is fairly straightforward. All that is required is to transfer heat to and from an end-effector that is near or touching the skin. Fingertip transducers are end-effector devices used to provide the sensation that virtual objects are hot or cold. Of course, safety is a concern when applying heat or, indeed, extreme cold to the fingertips. The ambient air temperature may also be controlled via the activation of a heat lamp or other climate control device.

Pin-based Rendering

A *tactile feedback array* display renders tactile information by finger movement over small pins arranged to reproduce the sensation of texture. The movement of the pins is varied in accordance with finger motion in order to give the impression of rubbing a surface to feel texture. One rendering method uses pins arranged on a flat surface, rising and falling as the finger moves across the display. Another method uses pins mounted on a cylinder. In this instance the pins rise and fall as the cylinder rotates.

Kinesthetic Display

Object shapes can be rendered using kinesthetic rendering techniques such as a force display. By using robotics to control the movement of an end-effector, the user can "feel" where an object exists by their inability to penetrate the surface. They might also be able to sense qualities such as the object's elasticity and surface texture if that information is rendered. The texture tactile sensation of running a stylus over a surface to feel its texture can be rendered using a force display as illustrated in FIGURE 5-30.

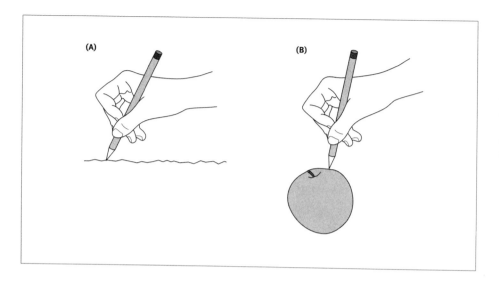

FIGURE 5-30 (A) *The sensation of a textured surface can be produced via a stylus that moves according to the virtual surface texture as a user drags the stylus across that virtual surface.* (B) *A stylus can be used to probe the surface characteristics of a virtual object.*

Robotically Operated Shape Display (ROSD)

Object surfaces can also be rendered using robotic displays as we saw in Chapter 4. A physical surface with an appropriate edge or surface angle is carefully placed in front of the user's finger or finger-surrogate (typically a stylus) to emulate the virtual object. As the user moves the probe, the surface being displayed changes appropriately.

Specific Robotically Operated Shape Display

Specific objects can also be rendered with specialized robotic displays equipped with sample items that serve to represent objects encountered in the virtual world, such as the many switches in an aircraft cockpit as implemented in a VR training application by Boeing [McNeely 1993]. These displays operate by having a robot place actual objects at the appropriate position before the user's finger or stylus arrives at that location. For example, an actual toggle switch can be placed by the robot at a location where a virtual switch is represented in a virtual world.

Physical Object Rendering (3D Hardcopy)

A final alternative is to "render in plastic." This is an intuitive, albeit nonmalleable, technique of actually creating a physical model of a virtual object, bringing it into the real world such that it can be held in the hand and directly experienced. One such technique is stereolithography (see the discussion in Chapter 4; see also FIGURE 4-41). However, this technique does not offer interactive feedback.

Rendering Complex Haptic Scenes with Force Displays

As the field of computer graphics has matured, many techniques that improve the rendering speed of complex scenes have been developed. These hardware and software techniques have made the creation of complex scenes in real time an actuality. The field of computer haptics has not yet reached this level of maturity. For the moment, the type of haptic scenes that can be rendered sufficiently fast to be considered real-time remain fairly simple.

The difficulty of rendering real-time, complex haptic scenes is exacerbated by the fact that a high frame rate is necessary to maintain a consistent feel for rendered objects. If the frame rate is too slow, the time it takes for the system to respond and adjust to supply the appropriate resistance can be noticeable. A hard virtual surface may feel soft for a moment. This potential for low frame rate combined with the lack of sophisticated techniques—comparable to such visual enhancements as texture mapping, for instance—limit the immersiveness of most haptic displays.

The amount of complexity needed for realistic rendering of force information is, in turn, impacted by the type of simulated physical contact allowed in the VR experience (FIGURE 5-31). If only the shape of an object needs to be presented, then a simple stylus poking in the virtual world may be sufficient. A considerably greater amount of information must be passed to the user if they must grasp an object, pick it up, and feel its weight, elasticity, and texture. So prior to discussing the type of information that can be presented with force displays, we will look at the level of contact the user will have with the display. We will address a number of different situations: whether the user manipulates the object at a single point of contact, completely grasps the object with the hand, pinches the object with two fingers, or perhaps holds the object by a handle of some sort.

The level of contact that a user might have with a force display system can vary widely. The type of contact along with the number of degrees of freedom the force display can support impact the level of world simulation required.

Single Point of Contact

A primary form of force interface in VR experiences is at a *single point of contact* with an object. The force display provides stimuli to a fingertip or the tip of a handheld stylus, but no rotational (torque) information is provided. This type of display is often provided by basic end-effectors or robotically operated shape displays. A basic 3-DOF force display is all that is required (FIGURE 5-32A).

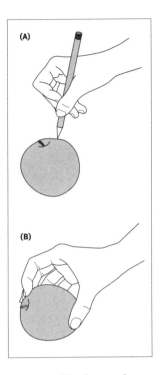

FIGURE 5-31 *The degree of fidelity required by a VR application affects the type of contact that must be reproduced and thus the complexity of the proprioceptive rendering. Compare the level of stimuli required in* **(A)** *versus* **(B).**

FIGURE 5-32 **(A)** *Some haptic displays like this* PHANTOM *device use a generic stylus (or in some devices a thimble) as an interface in a variety of applications (Photograph by William Sherman).* **(B)** *Other displays are designed for a particular application, such as this laparoscopic surgery interface from Immersion, Corp. A companion device emulates a laparoscopic camera that allows movement only up and down within a tube (Photograph courtesy of Immersion, Corp.).*

Single Point of Contact with Torque

Sometimes it is necessary to feel torque in addition to translational forces. For example, this is important in drug design, where it is necessary to feel all the forces between two molecules. These complicated interactions using both 3D movement and 3D torque at a single point require a 6-DOF force output. These displays typically require a more complicated set of linkages in the force display.

Constraint of Movement

Constraining the movement of the user means limiting the possible haptic interactions. For example, a laparoscopic camera allows translational movement in only one dimension, up or down a tube (see FIGURE 5-32B). For this movement, a simple 1-DOF display will suffice. If in addition to translation, it is important to feel forces from twisting the camera, then a 2-DOF device is required to accommodate movement in two dimensions.

Two Points of Contact (Pinching)

Pinching an object is another method for including torque interaction through force displays, in this case, two 3-DOF translational displays (FIGURE 5-33). By combining the two devices, torque is applied at the midpoint of the line between the two contact points. No torque can be driven around the line from one contact point to the other, which yields a 5-DOF display.

Multiple Points of Contact (Grasping)

Grasping an object means that the user and object have multiple points of contact (as we saw in FIGURE 5-31B). Objects not attached within the simulated world allow the user complete 6-DOF freedom in moving them. To provide enough haptic feedback to the user, a device that encompasses the entire hand (such as a glove) is generally used for grasping interfaces.

Summary of Rendering with Force Displays

We use the term *clutch* to indicate that we have enough control over an object to simultaneously reposition it in multiple axes—by more than just pushing the object. In the real world, at least two separate points of contact between the user and the object are needed to clutch it. This rule needn't apply in a VR system. Grabbing with a greater amount of contact can produce higher realism and an increased ability to discern information about an object. However, for systems that include haptic feedback, two points of contact are often used. More than two contacts may be employed, but display and simulation complexity increase with the number of contact points.

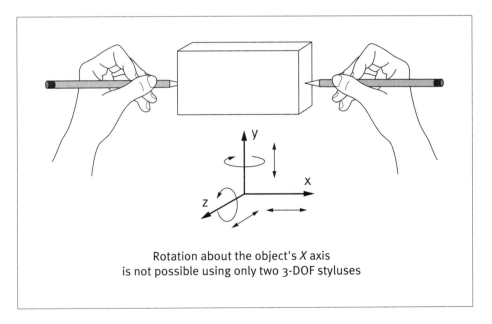

Rotation about the object's *X* axis
is not possible using only two 3-DOF styluses

FIGURE 5-33 *Operated like a pair of chopsticks, two 3-DOF force displays can be combined to create a single 5-DOF display.*

In the virtual world, clutching an object can be implemented with (1) a 3-DOF (or more) end-effector equipped with a switch to allow grasping; (2) two 3-DOF (or more) end-effectors that allow fingers to pinch an object; or (3) a self-grounded device that measures and impedes movement between fingers (such as the *Rutgers Dextrous Master* pictured in FIGURE 4-38).

Self-grounded force displays are only able to render the force exerted by the elasticity of the grasped object; that is, you can squeeze a ball and feel that a virtual ball made of soft rubber squeezes more readily than a virtual ball made of concrete. However, information about object characteristics such as overall weight cannot be conveyed, so you can't feel how heavy either of those balls is.

Haptic Bitmaps

Digital samples (haptic bitmaps) of surface features such as texture and temperature are not yet in common use but are likely to be adopted as haptic rendering systems advance. Much like visual bitmaps, haptic bitmaps will be used to map complex features across a surface to increase the realism of the rendering. Also like visual bitmaps, the texture can be used to affect multiple features. Visually, textures are used to modify color, transparency, and light reflectivity; haptically, textures may be used to affect temperature changes, surface texture, surface friction, and surface shape.

Haptic bitmaps might be applied as a temperature grid mapped to the top of a stove in a kitchen model so the user can feel if the burners are on or off. A bitmap representing the weave of a particular textile could be used to make a surface feel like fabric as the finger moves along it. A friction bitmap could hinder finger or stylus movement over a surface, allowing objects to feel like sandpaper, pumice, or polished marble. Finally, a bitmap can actually add specific shape detail to a surface—the small raised bumps in a Braille pattern, for instance.

Haptic Rendering Techniques

In practice, a computer simulation of haptic interactions, like other rendering systems, can provide only so much detail. Thus, there is a need for simplified computer representations. Essentially, the representation must be simple enough to allow for real-time rendering, yet encompass enough information to permit sensory feedback suitable to the application.

This requirement is especially apparent in force displays that must control a robot at approximately 1,000 Hz. Simulating the complete world at that rate would be ideal, but this is usually not possible so an intermediate representation is used. In the analogous operation in computer graphics, polygons are used as an intermediate step between a higher level description, such as the concept of a "chain," and the ultimate description at the level of individual color pixels. Similarly, an intermediate force (or other haptic) representation might include a description of the forces between a probe and a small number of nearby surfaces. The rendering system then converts this into signals that can be quickly sent to the force display.

However, much like rendering images onto a raster-line display can cause spatial aliasing (jagged edges), force displays can suffer from lag between the world simulation and the force display. Say a probe moves inside a surface before the world simulation can signal the render engine to stop the probe. The rendering system must be able to handle such situations without tipping off the participant that something is amiss.

Due to the amount of information required to adequately represent surface and object characteristics, haptic displays (particularly force displays) require a more complete model of the world than worlds displayed only visually and/or aurally. Visuals and sounds using only simple shapes and waveforms are often adequate to produce a presentable virtual world. Some aspects of tactile haptic display might be achieved in a similar way. For example, an object might be set to a constant temperature and, when virtually touched, reproduce that stimuli at the fingertips. However, force displays used for rendering proprioceptic information and surface texture need some type of physical model to continuously update the stimuli available to the participant.

In other words, it's easier to fake decent visual and audio output. For haptics, not only must the world model be more fully described, but additional information must be known about the objects that occupy the world. Features such as rigidity, elasticity, surface texture, and temperature might also be necessary parts of the world's database.

Haptic rendering often forces the world simulation to perform more computations and the world description to contain more information. For example, a visual-only simulation may compute an estimation of when two objects will intersect to prevent the user from walking through walls. In a VR system with haptic display, the system must determine the amount of force resulting from the collision with the wall and perhaps the temperature and surface texture of the wall. Haptic interactions revolve around when, how hard, and in what manner a participant makes contact with an object.

There are several methods for simplifying the amount of information needed to pass between the world simulation and the haptic rendering:

- Spring and dashpot
- Point and plane
- Multiple plane
- Point to point
- Multisprings
- Inertial and resistant effects
- Vibration
- Error correction

A brief explanation follows for each of these models, but as with our treatment of computer graphic and auditory rendering, the details are best left for other, single-topic treatments. The *GHOST* [SensAble Technologies, Inc. 1997] and *Armlib* [Mark et al. 1996] descriptions and documentation should provide a good starting point.

Spring and Dashpot Model

The *spring and dashpot model* allows the system to control direction, tension, and damping between a probe and surface in the virtual world. The makeup of a physical dashpot is that of a piston in a cylinder, with a small orifice in the end of the cylinder. As the piston moves back and forth within the cylinder, it pushes air in and out through the orifice. This results in viscous losses proportional to the rate of travel of the piston. A dashpot functions as a viscous damping device much like the shock absorbers of an automobile. Thus, some physical interactions can be approximated in the virtual world by using the equations that describe how springs and dashpots interact in the physical world.

Point and Plane and Multiple Plane Models

The *point and plane model* represents the interaction between a probe stylus and a surface by placing a virtual planar surface tangential to (the nearest surface of) the probe's tip. As the probe traces the surface shape, the plane moves along the tangent of the surface to simulate the shape of the virtual object (FIGURE 5-34). However, it is very difficult to simulate the corners of objects and movement through highly

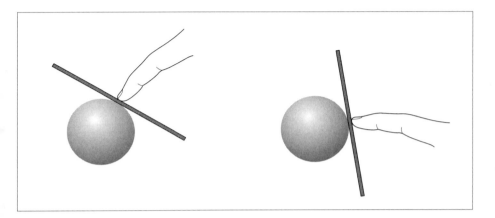

viscous fluids using this model. This model can be implemented using the spring and dashpot physical model.

The *multiple plane* model is an extension of the point and plane model. With the addition of more virtual plane surfaces, this model provides a simplified method of rendering discontinuous corners in the virtual world. As the probe moves toward a corner, additional planes represent the complexity of the shape being depicted (FIGURE 5-35).

Point to Point Model

The *point to point model* uses a basic spring model comprised of the equations that describe the forces of how a spring behaves when it is stretched and compressed between two points. Point to point is often used not as a general model, but as a transitory model to maintain stability in the midst of highly fluctuating forces generated by complicated calculations. For a simulation that may be providing widely divergent forces, perhaps too drastic to be accurately rendered, a spring can be modeled to act between the simulated probe point and the tip of the physical probe. As an analogy, if you were hanging onto the end of an elastic cord, with the other end being tugged by someone else moving in a very erratic fashion, you would experience only a dampened amount of the erratic motion from the other end.

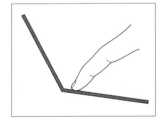

FIGURE 5-35 *The multiple plane representation allows discontinuous surfaces to be rendered.*

Multispring Model

The *multispring model* adds torque simulation. Torque rotation cannot be simulated if contact occurs at only one point. By arranging multiple springs in a pattern around

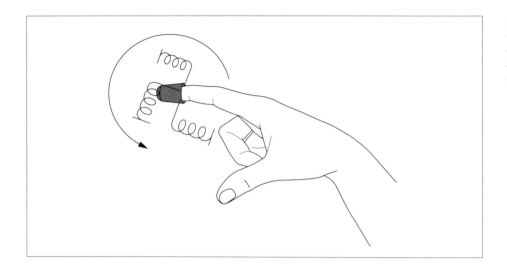

FIGURE 5-36 *Multispring models can be used to add torque to any of the other haptic representations [Adapted from Mark et al. 1996].*

the tip of the display, forces can vary on each side of the tip, resulting in rotational simulation (FIGURE 5-36). A force display must be capable of rendering torque for this model to be effective.

Inertial and Resistant Effects Models

Inertial and resistant effects models add characteristics of friction and viscosity (both resistive forces) and momentum (an inertial force) to the display. Friction is resistance caused by rubbing between surfaces (such as the tip of a stylus and an object). Viscosity is resistance to movement in a fluid (e.g., water, air)—not necessarily on a surface. Surfaces define a shape, but when touched, we also get a sense of features like smoothness, compliance (how it conforms to our hand), and friction. These features are orthogonal. For example, a smooth surface can feel very different depending on the material of which it's composed. Polished marble is smooth to the touch, with low surface friction, and thus has a different feel than a surface made of a high-friction, compliant material like rubber. Some simulated worlds emulate inertial effects. When a user contacts an object with high mass, the user feels resistance against slowing it down or getting it moving.

Vibration Models

Vibration can be modeled on a force display, or it can be rendered directly on a vibrating end-effector. For specialized devices, a signal indicates when the display should vibrate and at what frequency and amplitude. The use of specialized vibrator devices can allow vibration at frequencies greater than those of force display devices, which commonly operate at about 1,000 Hz.

Error Correction Models

Error correction models come into play when the haptic display violates the laws of a virtual world. This situation can occur because the frame rate of the simulation is significantly slower than both the frame rate of the haptic display and the user's speed. It is not uncommon for such errors to occur. The error correction model intervenes to reconcile the discrepancies.

Haptic Rendering Engines

There are not many generally available tactile rendering engines. In fact, not many tactile-based displays have even been developed, merely a modest selection of temperature, vibrator, inflatable bladder, and pin-based displays. Compared with tactile displays, more work has been done on force display and rendering systems. Some early (and continuing) work along these lines has been done at the University of North Carolina at Chapel Hill (UNC-CH). Additional work has been done in the telepresence and robotics industries.

Without specialized haptic rendering hardware to generate the signals needed to drive a haptic display device, the typical solution uses an additional computer system to generate the end-effector display or robotic movements. A common solution off-loads the rendering to a separate, dedicated CPU, allowing the world simulation CPU to focus on higher level operations. In this respect, the computer system dedicated to haptic rendering becomes the *haptic accelerator,* analogous to graphical rendering engines.

Internal Computer Representation (Haptic Formats)

Very little has been done to create common formats for the storage and transmission of haptic information. One exception to this is the format used by the *GHOST* library. *GHOST* uses haptic scene-graph descriptions of the virtual world. The scene-graph is comprised of nodes that describe the structure of the haptic scene. Nodes can indicate the position, shape, and surface features of objects. They can also describe specific effects such as inertia, vibration, or movement constraints, or they can be used to group other nodes. Using a haptic scene-graph that closely resembles a graphical scene-graph allows the two sense displays to blend more easily.

VR Haptic Interface Software

To this point, only a handful of haptic rendering interface software libraries have been produced. All the examples are for the control of force displays (which, again, can be used for rendering kinesthetic forces or surface texture). There are no widely available general-purpose software libraries for temperature, tactile-array, bladder, and other haptic displays.

The University of North Carolina at Chapel Hill has created a software library for the control of force display devices called *Armlib*. The key feature of *Armlib* is that it is a device-independent, 6-DOF force display library freely available from UNC-CH, including the source code. The University's *GRIP* (GRaphical Interaction with Proteins) project developed several generations of *Armlib* for a variety of force devices [Mark et al. 1996].

As a device-independent library, *Armlib* provides a standard set of functionality for a variety of force display devices. Displays for which the *Armlib* has built-in support include the *PHANTOM, Sarcos Dextrous Arm Master,* and the MPB Technologies *Freedom 6* device. However, because the source code is available and designed to be easily extended to include other displays, *Armlib* is very convenient for research labs using devices not supported by other software — particularly if they are involved in a force display hardware development project.

Armlib uses a client/server model to communicate between a PC controlling the force display and the application computer (another PC or a Unix workstation). The client/server model enables the force display to render in parallel with the virtual world simulation. The world simulation needs only to address higher level force models, such as the spring and dashpot model described earlier, sending update information to the "force PC."

Higher level (intermediate) haptic models available in the *Armlib* library include:

- Plane and probe
- Point to point
- Multiple plane
- Multiprobe (or multiprobe contacts)
- Surface texture models
- Error correction

The *GHOST (General Haptics Open Software Toolkit)* software development toolkit was developed by SensAble Technologies, Inc. as a rendering library for their line of force display units including the *PHANTOM*. *GHOST* is primarily a library for force display, although it includes features for other haptic sensations such as vibration.

Information that can be input to the *GHOST* library includes where objects are located, their surface properties, and specific spring and dashpot links to points in space, viscosity models to resist movement through a medium, and vibration models. Collisions between the force display and objects in the scene are reduced to specific rigid spring models that indicate the presence of a surface.

The *GHOST* library also handles the interface between the simulation computer and the haptic rendering computer. The actual force rendering is done at 1,000 Hz, but world simulations rarely run to that specification. Thus, the world simulation specifies to the *GHOST* software changes of the overall world model. *GHOST* in turn specifies a model of how the renderer should behave until the next update.

As mentioned in the section on haptic formats, *GHOST* uses a scene-graph to describe the haptic environment of the VR simulation. Use of a scene-graph is convenient (both in graphics and haptics) in that higher level structures can be described in terms of common scene-elements. It also provides a convenient mechanism by which scenes can be stored and retrieved. A significant feature of *GHOST* is that its scene-graph is reminiscent of *Inventor's* graphical visual scene-graph. This correspondence suggests an opportunity for application designers to more readily relate the simulation, internal description, and rendering of the world between the two senses by combining the two within a single VR system.

The *GHOST* library scene-graph also includes behavioral nodes that can be used to assign dynamic states to objects. Behaviors included with the *GHOST* system include dial rotation, button presses, moving sliders, and full free-body rigid dynamics simulation. Many other VR applications that include a haptic component use libraries developed within the confines of the research group or company developing the application. Since these are not available for use by other groups, we do not discuss them here.

Chapter Summary

The task of rendering is to transform representations of the virtual world into appropriate signals for the display system. In virtual reality, rendering must be done in real time—that is, at a rate that the human brain perceives as a continuous flow.

There are many approaches that one can use when rendering images for a virtual world that appear to achieve the same results. A table might be rendered in software or hardware, using techniques such as polygons, NURBS, CSG, or a flat plane with changing textures based on viewpoint. Aurally, a bird chirp might be rendered as a stored sample or as a physical model of the bird's vocal cord vibrations and echoes in its internal head cavities. In each of these examples, there are trade-offs between render rate and the richness of the presentation. In some cases, there are simply different techniques for achieving the same result (without any significant tradeoffs). In the latter cases, the designers can choose whichever technique they prefer. More often, specific goals lend themselves to certain rendering techniques.

Since the effect of the entire virtual reality experience can fail if rendering is poor, it is important to maintain an appropriate frame rate. It is usually better to simplify the representation than to display a more complicated scene slowly. During the development of a VR experience, however, one may plan with the expectation that both hardware and software rendering technologies will continue to improve rapidly (as with computer technology in general) and prepare to display a world that is incrementally more complex than can be handled with current technology.

Color Plates

PLATE 1 *Early virtual reality systems commonly used low-resolution, head-mounted displays and data input gloves.*

PLATE 2 *Teleoperation allows police officers to interact in dangerous situations from a safe location.*

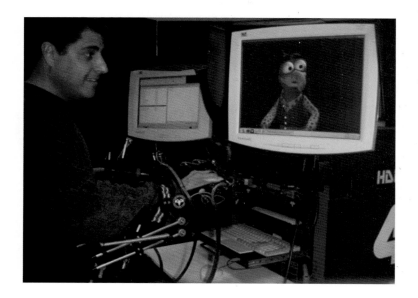

PLATE 3 *A puppeteer uses a* Waldo *hand-input device to control the computer graphics representation of* Gonzo (Henson Digital Performance Studio *and* Gonzo *images courtesy of The Jim Henson Company. © The Jim Henson Company.* The Jim Henson Company, Henson Digital Performance Studio, *and the* Gonzo *characters and elements are trademarks of The Jim Henson Company. All Rights Reserved).*

PLATE 4 *Kem Ahlers tests the* Caterpillar *Virtual Prototyping System in a* CAVE *VR display.*

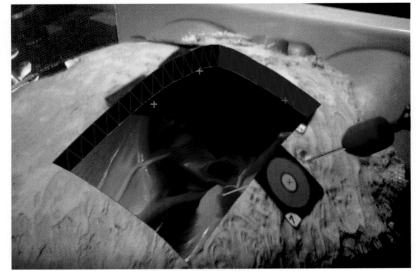

PLATE 5 *In the* Mandala *application, a virtual reality experience with a second person point of view, the participant watches their actions on a screen as their image interacts with the virtual drums.*

PLATE 6 *Fiducial markers, such as the blue and green target seen here, provide a landmark for optical tracking systems. In this augmented reality application, a virtual representation of the patient's internal organs is displayed in registration with their body.*

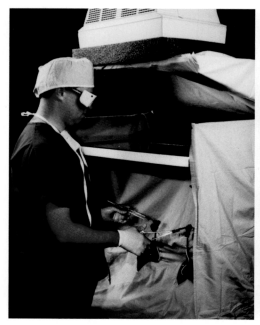

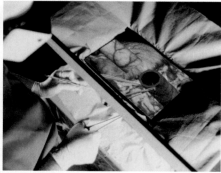

PLATE 7 *A surgeon practices a surgical procedure in a VR trainer that provides both visual and haptic feedback.*

PLATE 8 *A researcher uses a force feed back device to interact with real-world atoms through a virtual reality interface to a scanning tunneling microscope.*

PLATE 9 *Many different methods have been tried to simulate the sensation of flying or of reduced gravity. Here a VR participant is hung from a ceiling in a public electronic art museum.*

PLATE 10 *Vestibular feedback can be provided to individuals seated in the Flogiston chair, which is equipped with a hydraulic motion base.*

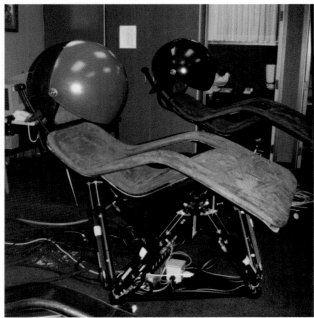

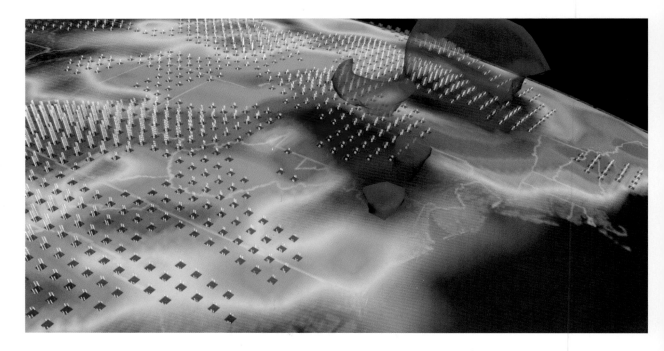

PLATE 11 *The technique of texture mapping allows additional information to be overlaid on a map of the United States. Here, color represents rainfall amounts.*

PLATE 12 *A virtual glass elevator aids therapists in treating patients with a fear of heights.*

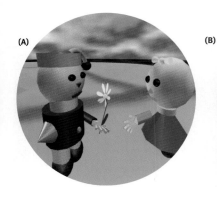
(A)

(B)

Direct User Control

Physical Control

Virtual Control

Agent Control

PLATE 13 *Children use avatars* **(A)** *to collaborate in the* NICE *VR application, despite the fact that they are geographically separated and using different styles of VR systems* **(B).**

PLATE 14 *Operations carried out through a virtual reality interface can be categorized into four basic classifications. Here, a participant moves the virtual table using each of the four classes.*

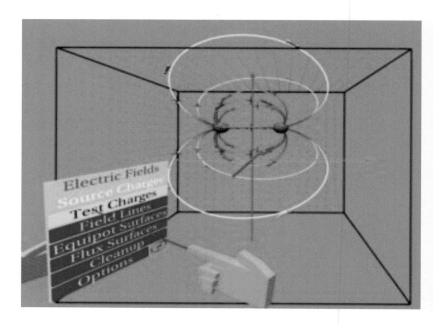

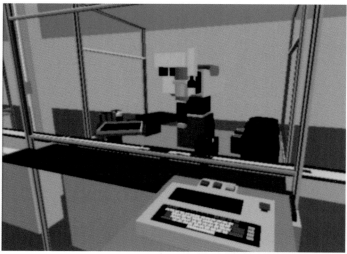

PLATE 15 *Students learn about the 3D nature of electric fields using* MaxwellWorld. *The two-handed interface of this application allows convenient use of a menu system.*

PLATE 16 *Real-world objects, such as this specialized keyboard, are emulated in this assembly line training system at Motorola University.*

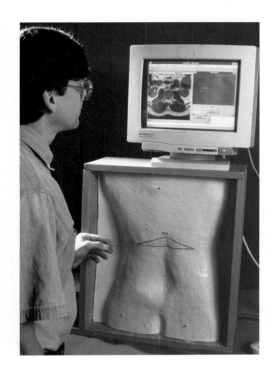

PLATE 17 *A physician practices a procedure requiring a keen sense of touch. This system provides force feedback on the needle as well as a visual display that emulates an X-ray fluoroscope.*

PLATE 18 *A spline indicates the path traveled by a computer animation camera over a visualization of the Chesapeake Bay.*

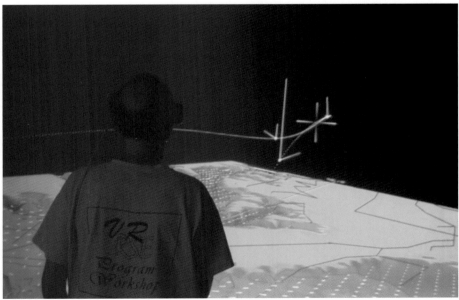

PLATE 19 *In venues such as liquor and grocery stores, customers participate in an advertising campaign by donning head-mounted displays and smuggling Cutty Sark Scots Whiskey during Prohibition.*

PLATE 20 *Disney guests grasp a virtual flying carpet to steer through "Agrabah" in search of hidden treasures.*

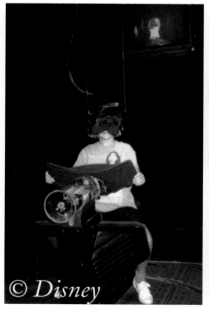

© *Disney*

Virtual reality experience

User interface

Hardware interface to the user

Input
- Body tracking
  (How the computer "sees" the user)
- Voice/sound recognition
  (How the computer "hears" the user)
- Physical controllers
  (How the computer "feels" the user)

Chapter 3

Output
- Visual display
  (How the user sees the VW)
- Aural display
  (How the user hears the VW)
- Haptic display
  (How the user feels the VW)

Chapter 4

Software components

System presentation to the user
- Representation
- Rendering system

Chapter 5

User interaction with the virtual world
- Manipulation
- Navigation
- Shared Experience

Chapter 6

Experience design
Chapter 8

Virtual world
- Immersion
- Point of view
- Venue
- Simulation/physics
- Objects/denizens

Chapter 7

Life experience
- Memory
- Ability
- Past experience
- Emotional state
- Cultural background

Chapter 8

Interacting with the Virtual World

Interaction with a virtual world is a key ingredient of a VR experience. Indeed, if the display of a virtual world does not respond at least to a user's physical movement, then it is not considered virtual reality.

According to Webster's [1989], *interaction* is "reciprocal action or influence." Thus, interacting with a computer-generated environment occurs when user inputs are responded to by corresponding actions of the computer. How we interact with a computer is obviously the result of how the *user interface (UI)* is designed. In fact, our communion with the computer through the interface is so predominant, the UI is how we generally envision the computer itself. (Buxton [1995] analyzed how people's image of what a computer looks like has changed over the years and found that their image consistently reflected the primary means of input and output of the time.)

Sometimes system designers are not mindful of the needs of the user. Because humans are not designed to interface with machines, most interaction interfaces are not natural for the untrained user. Fortunately, humans can be trained and can adapt to new ways of interacting with their environment. However, much anguish can be mitigated if lessons from the fields of human factors psychology and human-computer interaction are integrated into the design.

Not only can individual humans adapt to and learn new user interfaces, but over time some interfaces become integrated into the culture, making them seem natural. For example, the basic interface for most cars is the same. There is a wheel used to steer the car, pedals to control the speed, and two methods of modifying the gear ratio. This interface is so common, it has become ubiquitous—requiring no additional training for each new instance encountered by the user. Most people would probably consider a car with a different type of interface to be unnatural.

In all cases, an interface should be designed to accommodate the needs of its human user. The metaphors and methods reported in this chapter describe only what is possible, not what is best for any particular experience. Case studies such as those in the appendices and elsewhere can help guide the beginning VR content/ system designer based on the positive and negative experiences of these preceding works. However, for VR interfaces to improve, it is vitally important that formal user analysis studies be performed. User interface studies are important both for general knowledge of the medium and for specific knowledge of the efficiency of particular interfaces and representations. User studies during the design and testing phases of development are also a valuable tool for making readily usable experiences.

User Interface Metaphors

As discussed in Chapter 5, the use of metaphors is a very important means of providing the user a context in which they can learn new techniques. By relating a new interface technique to something with which they are already familiar, the user starts with a grasp of what to do. Metaphors take advantage of user knowledge and help make abstract concepts more concrete. If the designer can assume that the user has a familiarity with the play, stop, rewind, and fast forward controls of a VCR, they can implement an interface using virtual buttons to control time in the virtual reality experience (FIGURE 6-1).

The *desktop* metaphor popular on most of today's computer systems provides a set of familiar entities, such as files, folders, and even a trash can. With this set

FIGURE 6-1 *Real-world interface metaphors are often useful in virtual environments. A representation resembling a VCR interface is used in a CAVE display to control time in a VR application that uses a pointer avatar to activate the controls* (Reactor *application* (A) *courtesy of Argonne National Laboratory).*

(A)

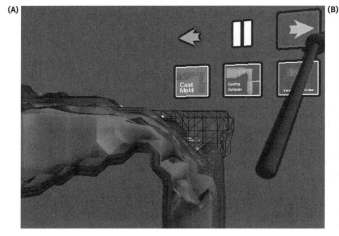

(B)

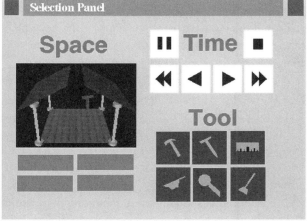

of familiar objects, users can draw on their experience of working in an office as an aid in using their computer. To organize related files requires only that they be placed in a folder. To discard a document, folder, or tool simply requires that it be placed in the trash.

As with representation metaphors, there are some pitfalls associated with using metaphors of interaction. One such pitfall emanates from erroneous mapping of the original concept onto the instantiated interface. Another pitfall arises if the developer and the user have different expectations for how the interface should react based on the metaphor. Unfortunately, the user may learn to use the interface only as suggested by the metaphor, perhaps missing out on other available interactions not immediately suggested by the metaphor. For example, a user of the desktop metaphor may feel constrained to activities allowed on a real desktop. They may spend time looking through individual folders for a particular document, not realizing the interface provides an option to search all the folders.

The concept of the *ultimate interface* uses real-life interactions as the metaphor by which a user interacts with a virtual world. Knowledge of how to move a small object in the physical world enables the participant to move a small virtual object in the virtual world—reach out, grasp it, pick it up, and place it in its new position. Sometimes, however, the justification for using virtual reality is that laws of the physical world need not apply, so the metaphor is expanded for the sake of convenience. For example, when designing a room layout, a user may not want to "travel" to each piece of furniture or object in the room in order to reposition it. They would rather "pick it up" and move it from wherever they are standing, regardless of the distance. And, they would not want to wait for a friend to join the experience to help them move larger objects.

It is useful for new media to adopt the metaphors of previous media if the existing metaphors have become ubiquitous in the society. Even though initial attempts at translating old interfaces to a new medium are often clumsy, they at least provide a familiar place to start. Of course, this could lead to suboptimal interfaces becoming entrenched in the language of the medium, slowing progress toward a more efficient and natural VR interface.

As practitioners gain experience in the new medium and develop new, more appropriate and effective techniques, VR will become more powerful and useful. The techniques described in this chapter reflect the evolution of the VR interface to date, although we are sure there are still many metaphors of existing media to be found and optimized for VR.

Key Interactions: Manipulation, Navigation, and Communication

This chapter is divided into three major sections, each of which focuses on one of the key ways of interacting with a virtual world in the medium of VR. *Manipulation* is one way to interact with the world. Manipulation allows the user to modify the world and the objects that occupy it. *Navigation* allows the user to make their way through the world. In some VR experiences, the *only* interaction available is navigating through the world. In such experiences, the virtual world is static or follows a preprogrammed sequence of events. The final key type of interaction is *communication,* either with other users or with agents within the virtual world.

Manipulating a Virtual World

One of the major benefits of being in an interactive virtual space is the ability to interact with, or manipulate, the objects in that space. The ability to experiment in a new environment, real or virtual, helps one learn how that world works. In the real world, *manipulation* is the application of forces on an object. In the virtual world, we have much more freedom.

In the familiar desktop computer interface metaphor, users are able to manipulate a machine's files and operating system through the use of windows, icons, menus, and pointing devices (known as the *WIMP interface*). Likewise, common manipulation idioms are evolving for virtual reality. Many of these new interface forms are based on principles that are true across media.

In virtual reality, most manipulations operate in two phases: first a *selection* is made and then an *action* is performed. Sometimes these two operations can be performed simultaneously, that is, the selection is inherent in initiating the manipulation. The object the user is "touching" is the one to be manipulated, just as in the physical world; however, in virtual reality, there is a wide array of methods for manipulating virtual objects.

Manipulation Methods

Mark Mine [1995a] lists three ways in which most forms of manipulation can be performed within a VR experience:

1. Direct user control: interface gestures that mimic real world interaction
2. Physical control: devices the user can physically touch
3. Virtual control: devices the user can virtually touch

We would add a fourth category to this list (FIGURE 6-2):

4. Agent control: commands to an entity in the virtual world

Direct User Control

Direct user control is a method of manipulation in which the participant interacts with objects in the virtual world just as they would in the real world. Many direct user interactions combine the object selection process with the actual manipulation. One example is the *grab with fist* interaction, whereby closing the participant's hand into a fist is interpreted as a grab operation and causes the virtual object colocated with the hand to follow the hand's movement as long as the fist posture is maintained.

(A)

(B)

(C)

(D)

FIGURE 6-2 *Manipulations such as "Move table a little to the right" can be accomplished using any of the four forms of manipulation demonstrated here. See color plate 14.*

Most direct user control interactions use either gesture or gaze to make a selection. The grab with fist is an example of gesture selection.

Physical Control

Physical controls are those that control the virtual world via a real-world apparatus. Because of the interface's real-world existence, the participant receives haptic feedback from pressing buttons and performing other actions (FIGURE 6-3). Common types of physical controls include buttons, switches with multiple position settings, slider and dial valuators, 2-DOF valuator controls like joysticks and trackballs, and 6-DOF controls such as the *Magellan* and *Spaceball*.

Controls on a tracked prop can act independently of or in concert with the prop's position. Three buttons on a wand can be used to scroll forward and backward through a menu by clicking on the right or left button and using the middle button to select the desired menu option; this would be an example of acting independently. An example of integrating the prop's position would be to point the prop at an object and press a button to select it.

In the design of an interface that uses physical controls, one needs to pay heed to its association with the virtual object. That is, the design will work better (i.e., more naturally) if there is a real-world metaphor between a joystick, slider, or

FIGURE 6-3 *Physical control mechanisms can be integrated as part of the user interface to control various aspects of a VR experience. Here, the participant controls the virtual vehicle using a physical steering wheel and foot pedals (Photograph by William Sherman).*

FIGURE 6-4 *NASA astronauts and engineers practice extravehicular activity operations in chairs equipped with control devices similar to those found in the actual vehicle (Photograph courtesy of Bowen Loftin).*

other physical control and the manipulation it performs. For example, in astronaut mission training to maneuver an extravehicular activity (EVA) unit, a VR system was equipped with a chair with physical controls mimicking those found on the actual EVA unit [Homan and Gott 1996] (FIGURE 6-4).

Virtual Controls

A *virtual control* is one that is manifested entirely in the virtual world. Many virtual controls are merely computer-generated representations of similar physical counterparts. Buttons, valuators, trackballs, and steering wheels are examples of physical controls sometimes emulated in virtual representations (FIGURE 6-5). Of course, at some point the user must physically do something to activate a virtual control—either through direct, physical, or agent inputs (FIGURE 6-6).

There are many reasons to have virtual controls, even when physical controls are already available. For example, a VR application can be designed to allow a familiar real-world control panel to be placed in the virtual world. Another reason to use virtual controls might be to reduce the number of physical devices needed for an application; on the desktop, the mouse (or trackball) works well for this. The mouse has 2D movement and up to three buttons, yet it can be used to move sliders, rotate dials, press buttons, highlight text—all virtual controls on a standard personal

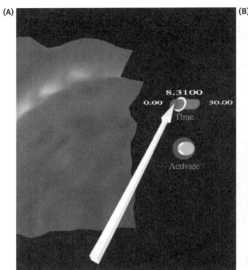

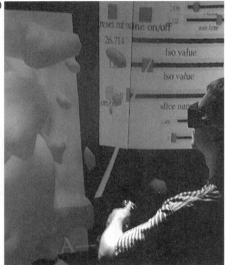

FIGURE 6-5 *These VR-enabled versions of the AVS (Advanced Visualization System)* **(A)** *and VTK* **(B)** *visualization toolkits provide virtual controls that allow the user to control parameters like time and iso-surface values using sliderbars and buttons (Applications courtesy of William Sherman and Paul Rajlich, respectively; photographs by William Sherman).*

FIGURE 6-6 *In this example of a virtual slider, the handheld wand is used to point at the virtual handle (the sphere) and move the slider (Application courtesy of Dan Sandin/EVL; photograph by William Sherman).*

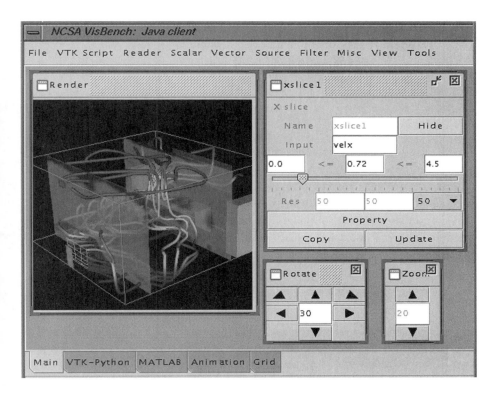

FIGURE 6-7 *Virtual sliders, buttons, and knobs are used in many 2D graphical user interfaces (Image courtesy of Randy Heiland/NCSA).*

computer desktop (FIGURE 6-7). We will discuss how virtual controls can be activated using any of the techniques described in the Item Selection and Direction Selection sections that follow. Because the controls are virtual, their appearance is entirely at the discretion of the application designer. Unlike physical controls, the visibility of a virtual control itself can be governed. Thus, a virtual control can be hidden until specifically requested (via a button press or other event) as with pop-up style menus in the desktop metaphor. Other options for virtual control display are to tone down the appearance when inactive or continue to let them be visible whether active or not.

Another consequence of having *virtual* controls is that there needs to be some way to interact with them. Often, a physical control device will be used to activate virtual controls within a virtual world. This allows a physical device with only a few input signals to have a wider range of uses by creating an interface with numerous virtual controls. This is typically how a desktop mouse is used; the mouse is a physical device used to control many virtual inputs. When implementing such an interface, it is important to keep the physical device interactions consistent across all virtual controls. Because virtual controls are rendered with the rest of the virtual world, their location in the world can vary widely. The six most common places where virtual controls can be found are in the world, in the hand, in front of the view (head up), on the display, through the aperture, and on the panel. We will cover these in detail in the section Control Location later in this chapter.

Agent Controls

Agent controls are those that allow the user to specify commands through an intermediary. That is, the user is in direct communication with an "intelligent" agent who will then perform the requested action (FIGURE 6-8). The agent can be a person or a computer-controlled entity. A human agent would interface with the world via one of the manipulation methods we describe in this chapter, although not necessarily through a physically immersive method. Communication with the agent can take the form of voice (the norm) or gestures. Gesture communication might be simple body language commands, like motioning for someone to approach, or a more formal language, such as naval semaphores or American Sign Language (ASL). Agent controls

FIGURE 6-8 *Here, the user illuminates the light by speaking a command to an agent in the world (Photograph by William Sherman).*

can mimic real-world communication protocols, such as movement orders to a piloting team or commands from the director of a motion picture to a film's crew and actors. In MIT's *Officer of the Deck,* the trainee duplicates submarine protocol to command a virtual piloting team who carry out the actions [Zeltzer et al. 1995].

Properties of Manipulation

Whether using direct, physical, virtual, or agent control methods, there are a number of properties associated with the manipulation of the world. These properties are

- Feedback
- Ratcheting
- Constraints
- Distance
- Pointer beam scope
- Hysteresis
- Frame of reference
- Bimanual interface
- Control location
- Control visibility
- Movement formula (control order and gain)

These property choices affect how the user interfaces with the virtual world. Often a virtual reality manipulation will be based on an analogous operation in the real world; however, there are some interfaces that are purely virtual (such as manipulating an object from a great distance as though holding it in your hand). In the real world, how one interacts with an object is often innate in the object, but in the virtual world, the designer has more freedom and thus more responsibility. It is up to the designer to choose the properties that will work best for a given manipulation and with a particular audience.

In the sections that follow, we address the available property options, focusing on how they affect user experience. These properties apply to the manipulation of objects as well as navigation in the virtual world. Some features will be re-addressed later to discuss their navigational aspects.

Feedback

Feedback from user interactions is very important in VR (and other computer) interfaces. Generating feedback is typically less of a concern with physical devices, because the user can feel when a button depresses or how far they've pushed a joystick. Without physical feedback, it can be difficult to sense whether a direct, virtual, or agent control has been activated. This difficulty can be mitigated by either providing a response through a haptic display device or providing some form of feedback that substitutes for touch. This sensory substitution usually comes in the form of aural or visual cues, such as beeps or flashes, to indicate contact has been made or an event has been triggered.

Ratcheting

Ratcheting is the process of repeating input to create a greater overall effect from the summation of many smaller manipulations. In the desktop metaphor, this would consist of moving the mouse a little, picking it up, placing it in the original position, and continuing the movement; for operations that only occur when a button is pressed, pressing the button, moving the mouse, releasing the button, moving the mouse back to the original position, and repeating would constitute ratcheting.

Constraints

In VR, although complete freedom of movement for travel and object manipulation allows the participant to do a great many things, it comes at a price, and that price is the added difficulty in performing operations. The parameter space of full 6-DOF movement, combined with other controls, make it easy for the user to become disoriented and lost. Thus, *constrained manipulation* can be beneficial to performing operations in a virtual world. Constraints can make it easier for the user to accomplish a task or for the experience creator to control the experience they wish to convey.

Built-in object and travel constraints are useful in controlling how objects are positioned and where users can travel. Object or user movement might be constrained to movement along a specific line or on a certain plane or to rotation about a preset or user-specified arbitrary axis. Two other movement restrictions are (1) the *snap to grid* method for translation and/or rotation, which allows an object to be placed only in positions that are on "the grid," a set of (often invisible) axes at regular intervals, and (2) the *lock to surface* method, which keeps an object attached to a specific surface. In the *BoilerMaker* application for designing large boilers and incinerators, the user can place fuel injection nozzles, but placement is restricted to an exterior wall (which is their only logical location).

Distance

The property of *distance* affects whether one can manipulate objects that are beyond the physical reach of the participant. The ability to perform operations on distant objects is sometimes referred to as *action at a distance (AAAD)* [Mine 1995b]. Feedback is of greater import for AAAD operations due to the added difficulty of determining which object the user is pointing at using solely visual cues.

Pointer Beam Scope

For manipulation operations that use a pointer interface, the shape of the beam at the far end of the pointer can expand, taper, or remain parallel. The two common designs are the *laserbeam,* which is essentially a very thin, straight line emanating from the pointer, and the *spotlight,* which has a graduated, conelike shape. The spotlight allows the user to select distant objects a little more easily because of the broad end of the beam. Distant objects occupy less area on the display and are harder to select with a narrower beam. Despite the increased difficulty in using the laserbeam, many applications utilize this method, because it is much easier to implement.

The scope of the pointer beam can be limited by the beam's length. At the extreme, the beam may be infinite, able to contact objects that are too far for the user to see. Or, the beam may have a fixed range to reach only nearby objects.

Hysteresis

A form of *hysteresis*—a difference in effect between doing and undoing an action—can be used to aid selections by holding an object as a selection candidate for a specified time or amount of movement. The candidate can be chosen even after the pointer beam has moved slightly away from the target object. This helps to compensate for shaky hands or unstable tracking by giving the participant more time in which to trigger an action.

Frame of Reference

In human factors research, the *frame of reference* is the "viewpoint from which the map information is presented" [Wickens and Hollands 2000]. If we consider *map information* to extend to the more general *world representation,* then we can more generally say that frame of reference is the viewpoint from which a world (real or virtual) is presented.

Frame of reference affects our relationship with the virtual world in three ways: perceptual perspective, manipulation, and travel. We will save travel-related aspects of frame of reference for later in the chapter and discuss the other ways here.

In the first of these frame of reference effects, our perception of the world is affected by our relative relationship to that world. Our interpretation of that relationship is influenced by how our viewpoint changes in response to our movements. We can perceive the world as though we were a part of it (inside the world) or as though the world were only a model upon which we can gaze (outside the world). This is the difference between *telepresence* and *teleoperation* discussed in Chapter 1 and exemplified by the view from which a model airplane is controlled. As mentioned there, these two perspectives are often referred to as *inside-out* and *outside-in* frames of reference.

In the field of human factors, the words egocentric and exocentric refer to whether the world is perceived from a personal (first person) point of view (*egocentric*), or from an external point of view (*exocentric*). In an egocentric frame of reference, our viewpoint changes as we move through a space. If instead we see the world from a stable point of view, we have an exocentric frame of reference.

Our perception of where we are in the world differs significantly depending on the frame of reference. From an egocentric point of view, we look around to see what is around us. To see where we are in an exocentric display, the display must include a representation of ourselves, and we must search the view of the world for the representation of our position. We can also relate frame of reference to literary points of view. The first person perspective is clearly an egocentric frame of reference. Second person equates to seeing the world from an exocentric reference, with a representation of "self" in the world. Third person is also an exocentric point of view, but without any inclusion of self in the world.

Manipulating objects in the world is also prejudiced by the reference frame linked to the object or to the operation. If the participant acts to rotate a chosen object, there must be a reference about which the rotation occurs. In mathematics, and thus computer simulation, we reference an object's position from some root position using a system of coordinates. This is called a *coordinate system*. The root position, where all the coordinate values are zero, is referred to as the *origin*. A commonly used coordinate system in computer graphics and simulation is the *Cartesian coordinate system*, which consists of three orthogonal axes in 3D space. Locations are described by distances along each of the axes as an ordered set of three numbers (*x, y,* and *z*).

An alternative is to use a spherical coordinate system in which locations are referenced by a distance and angle from the origin. The world and all entities in the world will each have a coordinate system (and thus frame of reference) of their own affixed to it. So any virtual world that has a participant and one or more objects has at least three coordinate systems (each of which can be specified in Cartesian coordinates, spherical coordinates, or another standard): the world's, the user's, and one for each of the objects. In fact, a user will often have multiple coordinate systems, one for each part of their body that is tracked.

A mathematical operation can be defined that transforms one coordinate system into another. By changing this transformation, we change the relative position between the two entities (or an entity and the world). The three primary transformations are translation, rotation, and scale. The names given to the coordinate axes and types of transformations change depending on whether one is referring to the world's coordinate system (exocentric) or to an object's coordinate system (object-centric, or egocentric if the "object" is a participant). (See the Transformation Names sidebar later in this chapter for examples.)

Every manipulation must be expressed in terms of a coordinate system. If the user rotates their wrist about its longitudinal axis to indicate how an object should be rotated, the position the object will end up in depends on whether the transformation was performed about the object's longitudinal axis, the user's wrist's longitudinal axis, or the world's X axis (longitude). Many operations will have a clear coordinate system axis that can be inferred from how the operation is performed. In the previous example, the user will generally expect rotation of the wrist to cause a rotation of the object based on the longitudinal axis of the wrist's coordinate system. We refer to such obvious links to a particular system as the *canonical axis*. The canonical axis is the preferred frame of reference for a given circumstance. Depending on the task, the canonical axis for a map may be north up (exocentric) or rotated to the direction of travel (egocentric). The preference for how to align a map can change by task and/or person. Someone may make one choice when planning a route (e.g., map oriented north up), and another when driving from one location to the next (e.g., map rotated to the heading of travel). Moving an object or oneself relative to the virtual world can involve relocating (translating) you or it and/or reorienting (rotating) you or it. Either form of repositioning can be performed egocentrically or not.

The same task may have a different canonical axis depending on the style of input. For example, in the *Crumbs* application (Appendix B), the user can rotate the data in two distinct ways. They can grab the object and rotate the handheld wand, or they can use the joystick on the wand. The *grabbing* of the object with the wand

Transformation Names

The names associated with the three orthogonal axes vary depending on the type of transformation being performed and whether they are specified in world or object coordinates. The *axes of translation* refer to the cardinal directions in which a body can move through space. Different names are given to the axes depending on the frame of reference (FIGURE 6-9). In 3D space, the egocentric axes are the longitudinal, lateral, and vertical. Movement along the longitudinal axis is along the fore/aft line as defined by the primary direction of travel. Lateral movement is from side to side, and vertical movement is up and down. Most egocentric forms of travel allow for longitudinal movement through the world, while only a few offer direct lateral and vertical movement. In an exocentric frame of reference, the *x, y,* and *z* Cartesian coordinates are often used. In spherical coordinates, we might also refer to these as the longitude, latitude, and altitude axes, which could potentially be confused with the egocentric terms. (Note that in computer graphics, the convention of whether the *Y* axis or *Z* axis is considered vertical changes depending on the context. Many systems use the *Y*-up convention, but frequently visual simulation applications like flight simulators use the *Z*-up convention.)

The *axes of rotation* specify the directions of rotational movement. In egocentric terms, these rotations are referred to as pitch, roll, and yaw. Pitch is rotation about an object's lateral axis; roll, the longitudinal axis; and yaw, the vertical axis. Depending on context, each of these terms has synonyms that are commonly used in specific situations. For example, an airplane with a steep pitch may rotate about its longitudinal axis (roll), but from the ground a viewer would not see this as a rotation about the world's longitude. Yaw may also be referred to as *heading* or *azimuth*. Pitch may be referred to as *elevation*. And roll is sometimes referred to as *twist*. The terms used for exocentrically defined rotations about the *X, Y,* and *Z* Cartesian axes are more consistently (and more simply) referred to as *rotation about the X axis,* or just *X rotation,* and similarly for *Y* and *Z.*

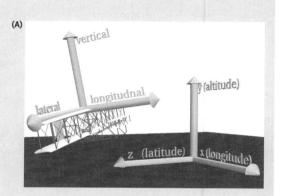

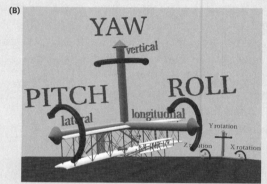

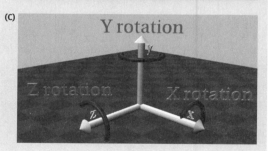

FIGURE 6-9 *The naming conventions of the three axes of the Cartesian coordinate system change depending on whether an exocentric versus an egocentric relationship is being referenced.* **(A)** *A common global naming convention for the X, Y, and Z axes refers to them as longitude, latitude, and altitude. However, when referencing the coordinate system of a particular object, such as an airplane, the terms longitudinal, lateral, and vertical are frequently used.* **(B)** *For egocentric rotations, we use the terms yaw, pitch, and roll.* **(C)** *In referring to global (exocentric) rotations, we use the simple naming convention of stating which Cartesian axis about which to rotate.*

causes the user to mentally link the object to the wand's coordinate system, and thus the user expects that rotations of the wand will cause the object to rotate about it. However, when using the joystick, the user has no mental link with the object, so pushing in the x direction can cause a rotation about the object's origin and seems natural. Note, though, the user still may expect the rotation to be orthogonal to the horizon rather than to the object's X axis.

Bimanual Interface

The use of *bimanual* (two-handed) *interfaces* has not been common in early VR applications. Historically, desktop computer interfaces rarely use more than a single pointer device (i.e., mouse or trackball) to control objects on the screen, so application designers are not accustomed to developing two-handed interfaces. Economically, the added cost of tracking a second appendage is often viewed as an "extra" that can be trimmed. Bimanual interfaces allow the simultaneous specification of multiple parameters. Using both hands to grasp two sides of an object implies an axis of rotation—the center point between the two hands. Thus, the user is immediately able to rotate the object. In a single-handed interface, such an operation requires three steps: the specification of the axis of rotation, changing to rotation mode, and then giving the amount of rotation.

Many bimanual interfaces are asymmetric in that the two hands are used for different purposes in the task. Asymmetric bimanual manipulations can be designed to take advantage of habits that the intended participants have developed through real-world experience. As reported by Guiard [1987], in most manual tasks, the *off* hand generally acts first, defining the frame of reference—that is, setting the context in which the *primary* hand will work. The off hand provides an approximate area in which the primary hand can perform spatially and temporally finer manipulations.

The *BDI Surgical Simulator* simulates a two-handed suturing procedure that illustrates a VR implementation of asymmetric bimanual manipulation (see FIGURE 4-31). The menu system used in the *ScienceSpace* suite of physics education applications uses an asymmetric bimanual method for menu input (FIGURE 6-10). The menu is "held" by the user's off hand, and items are selected via their primary hand. A bimanual interface is more often than not a more usable interface than what have become standard desktop-style interfaces. Many tasks are naturally two-handed; when adapted to a unihand interface, each task must be broken into subtasks that can be sequentially performed by one hand. In such a unihand interface, an additional subtask is required to indicate when each component task is complete.

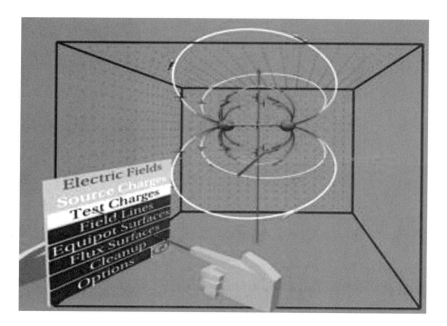

FIGURE 6-10 *In* MaxwellWorld, *a component of the* ScienceSpace *application suite developed by the University of Houston and George Mason University, a user's hands are represented as avatars. In this image a user holds a menu in their left (off) hand while making their selection by gesturing with their right (primary) hand. The student user is able to change parameters of an electromagnetic field and interact with the resulting visualization (Application courtesy of Bowen Loftin). See color plate 15.*

From his research at the University of Virginia, Ken Hinckley [1996] reports that rather than imposing a cognitive burden on the user, a well-designed bimanual interface allows a compound task to be performed undivided, allowing users to better reason about the task and concentrate less on the interface. Hinckley gives five benefits of properly designed bimanual interfaces:

1. Less effort is required to move one hand relative to the other versus moving a single hand relative to an abstract 3D location.

2. Fatigue can be reduced by allowing hands to rest against each other or on a real object.

3. Existing two-handed skills from real-world interactions can be transferred to the computer interaction.

4. A complex spatial relationship can be expressed in a single two-handed interaction.

5. The user can more easily explore the solution space of the task by providing a *dynamic frame of reference* with the nonpreferred hand and working within that frame with the other.

It is important to realize that two-handed input should not be used for performing two tasks simultaneously, but to perform subcomponents of a single task in concert. By working the hands in concert, there is no need for an extraneous mode-changing task.

Control Location

The location of manipulation controls affects when and how the participant is able to use them. Some controls may appear only during particular stages of the experience or may be located in a specific region of the virtual world, while others may be always on hand or at least summonable for use whenever and wherever desired. Of the four manipulation classes, virtual controls and agents have the greatest latitude, because they can be rendered in any location in and around the virtual world.

The placement of direct and physical manipulation forms is constrained to fairly obvious locations given their nature. Direct control of an object must be located at the object itself, by definition. The experience designer can choose what type of contact is required, but it must be associated with the object. Physical controls are mounted on some physical input device such as a prop or platform. The designer may be able to choose the type of prop or platform to which the input is attached and may choose to have many props, giving the user the ability to select the physical tool needed for a particular task. How virtual controls and agents are positioned within the virtual world is also selectable by the experience designer. These input types offer the creator much more flexibility, but the choice does depend, in part, on the type of VR display used. Some forms of agent controls are unembodied, requiring only that the participant speak to an unseen agent. Agents that are embodied in some representation, though, must be placed in some location.

There are six places where virtual controls and embodied agents can be situated: (1) in the world, (2) in the hand, (3) in front of the view (or head up), (4) on the display, (5) through an aperture, and (6) on a panel of interface objects. Each of these techniques can be applied to almost any type of virtual control and embodied agent, although some combinations make more sense than others (a virtual steering wheel will usually be in the world). Menus are an example of a virtual control that can work in most of these placements, so we will use menus to exemplify each respective method.

<control>–**in-world.** The *in the world* (typically shortened to *in-world*) placement option treats the control as a normal object in the world. Some controls have a natural position in the virtual world, such as a virtual button used to activate an

elevator (see FIGURE 5-9). In addition to being placed in a fixed position in the virtual world, a menu or other control can be carried by the participant or be summoned by the participant when needed. An agent can also be summoned, can follow the participant around, or can be stationed at a location where the participant can go to interact with it.

A button or gesture might be used to summon the control to the user's hand. So, a menu that might have been left behind somewhere can be immediately transported to the user. If the participant continuously activates the "summon" trigger so that the menu is constantly at hand, then this method works as a *menu in hand*. Or, if the user summons the menu only when needed, leaving it behind otherwise, then it functions like a menu that is only visible when active (unless the user happens to reencounter the menu where they left it).

An example of a summonable in-world style of virtual control positioning is Caterpillar Inc.'s *Virtual Prototyping System* (FIGURE 6-11). In Caterpillar's application, the menu is normally hidden and pops up to the location in front of the user when activated. If the user moves away without making a selection, then the menu remains in the world at the fixed location until a selection is effected (and it disappears), or the user summons it again.

FIGURE 6-11 *Normally the menu shown in this image is not visible. When needed, the menu may be summoned by pressing a button on a hand-held wand. The menu remains in this location until it is summoned to another location or a menu choice is made (Application courtesy of Caterpillar Inc.).*

<control>–**in-hand.** The *in the hand* placement, again typically shortened to *in-hand,* links a control to the position of a participant's hand, leaving the other hand free to manipulate the controls. For example, in the case of the menu, the free hand is used to point at the desired selection. Typically, this bimanual interface is arranged such that the menu is placed in the off hand, while the primary hand is used to do the selection control.

The in-hand style of interface is a very familiar form of interacting in the modern world. This style is like holding a television remote control and using the other hand to press the buttons. One benefit of this interface mode is that the menu or other virtual control is unobtrusive, yet easily accessible. The participant knows where the control is and can bring it into or remove it from view simply by moving their hand and/or turning their head to look at it. An application that makes use of the menu in hand interface is *ScienceSpace* (see FIGURE 6-10). In *ScienceSpace,* the menu is always attached to the user's off hand, while the primary hand points to possible selections. A physical button press triggers the desired choice.

A shortcoming of in-hand controls is that both hands must be tracked to implement them. Often, two corollary props—a pen and tablet—are used to track the hands and provide a natural interface [Angus and Sowizral 1995]. This metaphor enhances the in-hand interactions by providing passive haptic feedback through the combined use of the props. When the pen touches the tablet, the user can feel the contact. There is no possibility of overshooting the virtual controls. FIGURE 6-15 shows an example of the pen and tablet being used, with virtual controls placed on a panel.

Head up–*<control>*. Real-world *head up displays (HUDs)* reflect data onto a screen located between the user and the world, typically on a helmet or windshield. HUDs can be implemented virtually by creating an information display that is tied to the participant's head motion such that the display always appears in front of them (i.e., in front of the view). The *CALVIN* VR experience implements a virtual head up menu on a stationary VR display (FIGURE 6-12). Menu choices are displayed in front of the participant's gaze. Selections are made by pointing a wand at the desired choice and pressing a button on the wand.

<control>–**on the display.** The *on the display* placement of virtual controls is a technique often implemented on stationary VR displays. In the case of head-based or hand-based displays, this technique simply becomes a head up display. On stationary displays such as the *Responsive Workbench* or the *CAVE,* menus or other virtual

(A)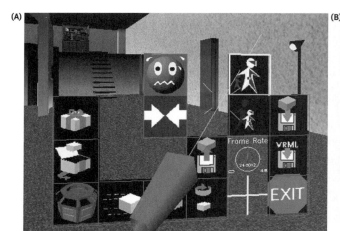
(B)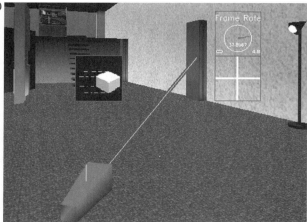

controls can be placed in the virtual world such that their location is fixed to pre-cisely match that of the physical display screen.

Two benefits that arise from this method are that the user knows the location of the menu at all times and that the depth cues of the virtual control object match those of the physical display. Specifically, the depth cues of stereopis and accommo-dation agree, because the user's eyes will focus on the screen, and the stereoptic cues will indicate that the control representation is at the same distance. Having these depth cues match is advantageous, because there is less strain on the eyes and less likelihood of nausea. This is particularly useful for frequently used controls.

An example that places menus on the display is NCSA's *Severe Thunder-storm Visualization* application developed for the *CAVE* (FIGURE 6-13). The creator of this experience implemented a control toolkit that borrows many features from the 2D desktop metaphor, including menus, dials, and buttons. The menus are pull-down style, activated by clicking on a box with the name of the menu. The menus also have a tear-off feature, allowing them to remain visible and be placed anywhere on the surface of the *CAVE*. The ability to move menus and other virtual controls around on the screen allows the user to place them according to their immediate need.

<control>–**through an aperture.** *Through an aperture* interactions are those that use the alignment between the eye and fingers of a participant. The term *aperture* refers to the aperture of a camera, the opening of the lens. In VR, the fingers are one means of defining an aperture through which the participant can peer to sight an object.

FIGURE 6-12 **(A)** *A head up display (HUD) menu that follows the gaze of a partici-pant in the* CALVIN *architec-tural layout application can be summoned by the press of a wand button.* **(B)** *At other times, the HUD shows only the current operational mode. The designers of this application refer to this virtual head up display as a* virtual visor *(Application courtesy of Jason Leigh and Andrew Johnson).*

FIGURE 6-13 *Scientists use the* CAVE *to study the vector fields associated with severe thunderstorms. Interaction with the simulation and visualization is supplemented by menu choices and other virtual controls presented coincidentally on the walls of the* CAVE *(Application courtesy of Bob Wilhelmson; photograph by William Sherman).*

Manipulations performed through an aperture are based on the user's view of the world. Thus, an aperture-based method of moving an object would be done by sighting an object encapsulated by one's fingers and then moving the fingers to another location, thereby moving the object within one's finger-aperture [Pierce et al. 1997]. To use a finger-specified aperture, the fingers obviously must be tracked. Also, because only one of the user's eyes is involved in sighting through the aperture, the user must specify which eye they prefer.

<control>–**on panel.** The *on-panel* (shortened from *on the panel*) option treats a virtual control or group of controls as though they were a GUI panel on a 2D computer screen. A panel is a place where many virtual controls can be grouped together. It is possible to place these virtual control GUI panels in just about all of the places one can place a standalone virtual control: in-world, in-hand, on-display, and head up.

Placing controls on a 2D panel located within the 3D world is frequently done, because of the difficulty of manipulating virtual controls with 6-DOF physical input devices. Users often find it difficult to determine the exact 3D location of objects when experiencing limited and conflicting depth cues. One slightly more effective method allows the user to simply point at the object to interact with it.

However, it can be difficult to judge the spot where the 3D pointing vector intersects with the 2D control.

The primary advantage of a virtual control panel is the implementation of a 2D cursor. Like a cursor on a 2D screen, the user clearly sees when that cursor is on the desired control option. There are two options for moving a 2D cursor. The first is to use a 2D valuator to move it around (a desktop mouse, joystick, or a pen and tablet, for example). The second cursor control option uses a traditional 6-DOF VR input device, perhaps tracking a hand or handheld device, to point at the panel. Of course, this brings back some of the difficulties of 6-DOF control. To improve this interaction method a little, a 2D cursor often replaces or augments the 6-DOF pointer to highlight the location on the panel at which the user is pointing.

The *Solar System Modeler* (FIGURE 6-14), developed at the Air Force Institute of Technology at Wright Patterson Air Force Base, uses panels to allow the user to activate a multitude of controls [Stytz et al. 1997]. Four control panels are located within a virtual vehicle. The 2D panels that seem to float in space before the user are, in fact, an in-world representation of a head up display (part of the vehicle, displaying information on the windshield). The *Solar System Modeler* was designed for a user sitting at a desk, wearing an HMD. So the designers made use of a standard computer mouse. With only one panel active at any time, the active panel is selected by gaze. As the user turns their head, the panel in front of them becomes active, and the mouse movements are mapped to the cursor on the menu in view.

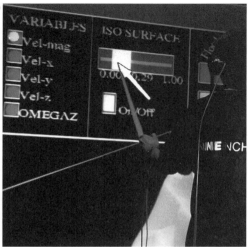

FIGURE 6-14 (A) *In order to avoid the complexities of full 6-DOF control, applications such as the* Solar System Modeler *utilize a menu on a 2D panel to select celestial objects in the virtual world. The user can move their desktop mouse to move the X cursor on the panel in their view.* (B) *In the* Multi-phase Fluid Flow *application, the user points a 6-DOF wand at the panel, and a yellow arrow indicates the intersection of the wand's avatar with the 2D panel. The arrow cursor is constrained to move only in the two dimensions of the menu plane, much like the mouse on a desktop interface (Applications courtesy of Martin Stytz and Eric Loth, respectively; photographs by William Sherman).*

FIGURE 6-15 *In the* Virtual Reality Gorillas Exhibit *application, virtual controls are located on a virtual panel. The panel is then mapped to the location of a tracked physical tablet input device that the user holds in their hand (Images courtesy of Doug Bowman).*

Virtual control panels can also be combined with a physical device to enhance the interface. A physical tablet held by the user can be tracked to the corresponding virtual panel (FIGURE 6-15). The physical tablet can be either a passive sheet of material (such as Plexiglas), or it can be an active electronic tablet that can sense the location of a special pen device. For passive tablets, input to the virtual panel can be specified through a tracked handheld prop. Electronic tablets work with their own stylus and can directly report the participant's written input to the VR system.

One benefit of using a physical tablet to correspond with the virtual panel is the inherent haptic feedback that the tablet provides; the pen stylus cannot overshoot and penetrate the virtual panel because of the physical constraints. In an advanced version of the *Virtual Reality Gorillas Exhibit* application from the Georgia Institute of Technology, users can design the layout of the Gorilla Habitat by using the pen stylus to move objects by their representations on the virtual map. The virtual map is located on a panel mapped to a physical tablet [Bowman et al. 1999].

Control Visibility

A virtual reality experience may have many controls represented in the virtual world. To display them all simultaneously could cause a view that is overly cluttered, hindering efficient exploration of the world. A common solution is to hide many of them until needed or requested. When virtual controls or agents are hidden, the application designers must create an easy way for them to be summoned. This might be done via vocal commands, finger gestures, or by pointing at an object that has specific controls associated with it.

Another consideration to heed with "invisible" virtual controls is that without evidence of a control's presence, the participant may forget, or never learn of its existence, which will render it unused if not unusable. For example, if a walkthrough application has a hidden control that teleports the user directly to another location, the participant may forget where the invisible portal is and be forced to wander through the space until happening through it. Unless the experience is one of exploration and testing memory capacity, some form of markers should be present to denote where controls exist.

Direct and physical controls do not generally impose clutter problems. Physical controls are frequently held in the hand and thus can be held out of view. Direct controls seldom even have a visual representation, since they tend to operate in a way that impersonates the real world. Thus, the major visibility problem for direct controls (and also for agent controls with no in-world avatar) is the problem of the participant potentially not being aware of their existence.

Movement Formula (Control Order and Gain)

Movement through a space can be described by a simple formula as a function of time. The general form of the expression has terms for displacement, velocity, acceleration, impulse, and other input parameters; each input can be further described by a multiplication factor.

The multiplication factor (coefficient) of each term can be thought of as a ratio of the input to the output for that term—the *gain*. The gain for each term of the formula is multiplied by an exponent of time. This order (power) of the exponent is what defines a movement as having displacement (zero order), velocity (first order), acceleration (second order), and so on. This value is referred to as the *control order* of the movement (FIGURE 6-16).

In a typical movement-control expression in a VR application, the coefficient for all the terms but one will be zero, leaving just one gain and one exponent of time (control order), such as velocity. Thus if, for example, the user controls velocity, the gain coefficient for displacement and acceleration are zero, leaving only

$$pos_{new} = gain_{velocity} * time^1 + pos_{old}$$

The movement formula is applicable for both object movement and travel control. However, the type of manipulation (travel or object movement) dictates the default expectation for which control order will have a nonzero gain. For repositioning an object, a direct displacement (zero-order control) is generally assumed. For travel manipulation, a first-order (velocity) control is frequently used to allow the participant to control the speed of their movement.

Control orders higher than first order are seldomly used. This is with good reason, because researchers have found that control systems in which a human has

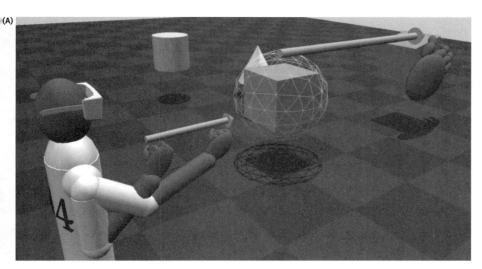

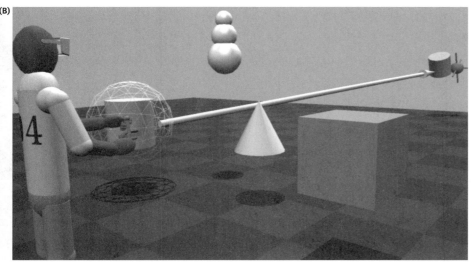

FIGURE 6-16 *User movement can be mapped to object movement or travel with different control order and gain.* (A) *A zero-order control with a gain of five provides a linear mapping from the user's hand movement to the cube. The enlarged hand avatar represents the value of the gain.* (B) *The user's small movements of the joystick are mapped to the velocity (first order) of the cylinder, allowing them to fly it around. The selected object is highlighted by the wireframe sphere enclosure.*

direct control over acceleration (i.e., a constant deflection of the input device produces a constant acceleration) are very unstable and not user friendly; hence, they should be avoided [Wickens and Hollands 2000]. The discrete control of the thrust power on a space capsule as a means to control orientation is an example of this type of acceleration control.

Selection

Regardless of where a control is located in the virtual world or which method of manipulation is chosen, there has to be a way to select the desired object or option in the application. Two categories of selection are choosing a direction (e.g., pointing) or choosing an item. These two categories can be combined, such as when an item selection is carried out by pointing (a direction selection) at the desired choice (e.g., in a menu, on a map, in the world). A third method of selection is via the direct input of numeric or alphabetic values.

Direction Selection

Direction selection is useful as a method of item selection (objects or places) and as a directional indicator for travel control (which we discuss in the next major section, Navigation). Items can be selected whether they are within reach or not. Seven ways of selecting direction are:

1. Pointer-directed

2. Gaze-directed

3. Crosshair-directed

4. Torso-directed

5. Device-directed

6. Coordinate-directed

7. Landmark-directed

Pointer-directed Selection. Selection by *pointing* uses some form of hand posture or gesture to indicate a direction. This can be accomplished either by direct tracking of the hand position or through the use of a prop designed to indicate which way the user is pointing. For travel, the user might point in the direction they want to move and use a separate control to indicate speed of movement (or when to stop). For choosing from a list, an object might be highlighted as the pointer points in its direction, allowing the user to press a button or otherwise signify it as their choice. A visible indicator of a pointer-directed beam showing the scope that is encompassed is useful.

Gaze-directed Selection. *Selection by gaze* depends on the visual attention of the participant, making use of the direction the user is looking (FIGURE 6-17). However, most virtual reality systems do not yet track the actual movement of the eyes. Consequently, it is the direction the nose is pointing that is actually taken into account. As actual eye-tracking becomes more common in VR systems, clarification between nose-directed and true gaze-direction selection will be necessary.

Crosshair-directed Selection. *Selection by crosshair* is created using a combination of pointer-directed and gaze-directed selection (FIGURE 6-18). The vector between the head and a hand-controlled pointer creates an invisible selection beam from one of the participant's eyes through the pointer and toward the direction of interest [Mine 1995a].

FIGURE 6-17 *Gaze-directed selection makes use of the direction the user is looking in as the selection criterion. In this example, the participant merely looks at the object they wish to select. The operation is then activated by some discrete trigger, such as pressing a button, or by a voice command.*

FIGURE 6-18 *Crosshair-directed selection uses the metaphor of looking through a rifle scope to select an object. In this image, the participant uses the tip of their finger as the "crosshair." Note that the computer must know that (in this instance) the right eye is preferred. The object selected will merely be the first one "hit" by the arrow. Note also that the arrow is not actually seen by the participant.*

Crosshair-selection is often an easy technique for novices to master, because they can control the direction with their hand, through a cursor or crosshair in their view. However, because both the hand and head are occupied, using this direction selection method may be found cumbersome by more advanced users. The method of selecting objects for aperture manipulation discussed earlier is essentially a crosshair method of selection. In that case, the sighting is done between the thumb and forefinger rather than with the tip of a finger or prop.

Torso-directed Selection. *Selection by torso* can be a preferred option for indicating direction of travel (FIGURE 6-19). The designers of the *Placeholder* VR

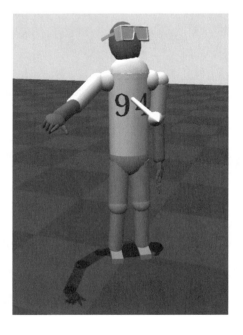

FIGURE 6-19 *In this diagram, the direction the participant will move is determined by the orientation of their torso, not the way they are looking or the direction in which they are pointing. Using the torso for choosing a direction requires that the torso be tracked in addition to the head, hand, and other application-specific components.*

experience felt that using torso direction is a more natural way to select direction of travel (Appendix D). However, it is not often used in VR experiences, because of the additional tracking hardware requirement associated with monitoring the participant's torso. Torso-directed selection is not commonly used as a means of item selection.

Valuator-directed Selection. *Selection by valuator* allows the user to indicate a direction using multiple valuators, such as a joystick (2-DOF valuators), or Spaceball (6-DOF valuators). Because it can be assumed that the valuator is held in some specific orientation with respect to the user's body, the body orientation can be used to determine the orientation of the valuator. The user can then use the valuator to indicate a direction by manipulating it. A selection "beam" is often represented as originating from some location relative to a prop or the body of the participant.

There are several ways a mouse or joystick can be used by the participant to select a direction (FIGURE 6-20). One method is to assume both in which plane the desired direction must lie and where the desired direction vector begins. A direction is then determined by the line passing from the origin through the location indicated by the 2-DOF mouse or joystick. Another method is to use the two degrees of freedom as elevation and azimuth values that indicate the height and angle separating the desired location from the origin. A direction can be specified by giving an elevation (e.g., 45 degrees above the horizon) and an azimuth rotation from your position. For example, if facing north, specify 90 degrees for east, 180 degrees for

FIGURE 6-20 **(A)** *Here the participant selects a direction relative to their body using a simple 2-DOF joystick device. The two degrees of freedom are mapped to azimuth (here 22.9 degrees) and elevation (19.5 degrees). Note that the position of the joystick itself is not tracked, so the user cannot just aim it to make the selection.* **(B)** *The combination of a 2-DOF joystick (and some buttons) mounted on a 6-DOF tracked prop allows for some interesting interface techniques to be implemented (Photograph by William Sherman).*

(A)
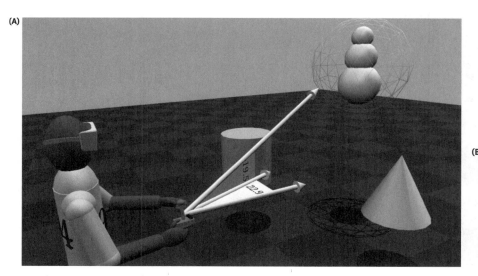

(B)

south. For experiences that limit directions to a single plane, then a 1-DOF input device such as a rudder or other steering device will suffice.

In all cases, a reference point must be determined. The reference point might be an *absolute* direction such as *north,* or it might be *relative* to the direction the torso is facing such as *to the left.* When a relative reference is used for indicating direction of desired travel and the user continues to input a constant value, they will continue to turn because their reference (the user) is turning too. Thus, without a device that automatically returns to the center, input values have the effect of producing a specific rate of turning as opposed to just how far to turn. Sometimes, as with the wand associated with *CAVE* displays, the 2-DOF device is mounted on a 6-DOF tracked device (see FIGURE 6-20B). The information from the 6-DOF tracking and the 2-DOF device can be combined for an effective interface.

Coordinate-directed Selection. If the user has a means of specifying numeric coordinates (e.g., by voice), then they can give azimuth and elevation values to specify a direction relative to some point (FIGURE 6-21). If elevation is not a concern (e.g., when controlling a ground vehicle), then the azimuth is adequate. For example, the user may say "north" to rotate their vehicle to that direction.

FIGURE 6-21 *Speech recognition (voice input) can be used for selecting direction by speaking coordinates that indicate the desired direction. In this case a circular coordinate system based on the hours of the day is used. The coordinate system can either maintain alignment with the world or be rotated as the user rotates.*

Landmark-directed Selection. Given the means of specifying an object in the environment (e.g., voice or a menu), a participant can indicate a direction as being toward some landmark or object.

Item Selection

The use of *item selection* is generally applicable to VR applications of all purposes, but can be customized to meet the needs of a particular application. Item selection methods are basically all ways to select an item from an enumerated list, although this may not necessarily be obvious. The items in a list can appear as individual objects in the world, groups of objects, or even as locations. The latter is particularly useful for the jump to travel method.

The following seven methods of selecting items have been used in various VR applications:

1. Contact-select: the avatar makes contact with the object.

2. Point to select: a pointer indicates the object selected.

3. 3D-cursor-select: a 3D cursor indicates the object selected.

4. Aperture-select: the space between two fingers creates an aperture and objects that appear in the aperture are selected.

5. Menu-select: a list of items is presented for selection.

6. Select in miniworld: selecting items by contact-select in a miniature representation of the world, such as a map.

7. Name to select: speech recognition software allows users to name their selection.

Contact-select. *Selection by contact* is performed by the participant bringing part of their avatar in virtual contact with an object (FIGURE 6-22). The contact itself may automatically activate an action, or the user may need to separately trigger activation. Automatic activation could come from contact with a specific body part (e.g., a fingertip) or from any part of the avatar body (e.g., the head). The user might then be able to change the attributes of the object, move it, or perform whatever type of manipulations are available.

(A)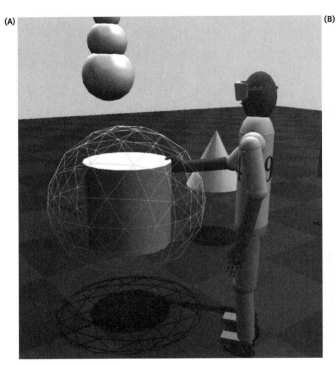

(B)

Object contact feedback can come in many forms: a visual highlight, an aural signal, or kinesthetic resistance. A combination of visual and aural feedback is often used as a substitute for haptic feedback.

In *Placeholder,* voice messages can be stored in designated objects called *voiceholders.* A voiceholder is activated when the participant's avatar makes contact with the object. Travel between regions in the *Placeholder* environment and changes to the user's avatar and persona are also effected by touching specially marked objects.

Point to select. *Selection by pointing* makes use of the already described direction selectors to choose a specific object in the world by pointing directly at it (e.g., point with a prop or via the user's gaze). In effect, the world itself becomes the selection palette. As the selection beam intersects with items, some form of feedback is necessary for the participant to know which item is the current selection candidate. This

FIGURE 6-22 *The contact-select method requires the user to virtually touch an object to indicate it as their choice, which is accomplished as we see here with the participant's avatar. One problem with this selection method is that it may be difficult or impossible to select objects that are beyond the reach of the participant. On the upside, it does not require a separate action to indicate that a choice has been made.*

feedback is often visually presented by surrounding the object in a box or altering one of its properties, such as color. Typically, a second action must be performed by the participant to designate the candidate as their choice.

The *NICE* educational application (Appendix A) uses the point to select technique to allow participants to pick up garden plants or grab and drag a cloud or the sun to a new location. A potential selection is indicated by a translucent yellow sphere surrounding the object, similar to the selection highlight sphere shown in wireframe in FIGURE 6-22A.

3D-cursor-select. *Selection by 3D cursor* is the 3D equivalent of selecting an item on a 2D surface using a mouse or trackball (FIGURE 6-23). In the desktop metaphor, the mouse, trackball, or other device is used to move a cursor around a screen. Activation is then usually accomplished by pushing a button. In a 3D environment, the cursor can be moved through all the dimensions of space. Activation might occur simply by making contact, or it might occur only through a user-activated trigger.

Occasionally the 3D cursor may have some movement constraints that effectively render the 3D-cursor-select operation the same as point to select or contact-select. If the 3D cursor is constrained to be a particular distance from a handheld device, then the operation is similar to contact-select (except the user's reach is extended). If the 3D cursor is constrained to the surface of the nearest object, then the operation reduces to a point to select technique.

The *Crumbs* scientific visualization application (Appendix B) uses the 3D-cursor-select method for grabbing (and moving) tools or breadcrumbs in the data space. The tip of a virtual pointer emanating from the physical wand is the 3D cursor. In the Nalco Fuel Tech *BoilerMaker* application, a pointer-directed drone moves across the inside of the exterior walls of the boiler, highlighting any injector nozzle with which it comes in contact. When the desired nozzle is highlighted, the user presses a button to select it.

Often the 3D cursor is directly attached to a handheld device, but this need not be the case. One technique that allows the user to extend the cursor beyond their physical reach is the *go-go* method described by Ivan Poupyrev and his colleagues [1996]. The go-go technique maps the cursor to the hand (or handheld prop) when it is near the body. As the arm is extended, the cursor drone (a hand avatar in their example) moves away at an exponential rate. The user can make selections from a distance, even when another item is situated between the user and the object being selected.

(A)

(B)

(C)

FIGURE 6-23 *Some VR applications use a 3D cursor analogous to a mouse cursor to make selections.* **(A)** *Here a spherical drone is flown by the user via a joystick until it comes into contact with the desired object in* **(B)**. **(C)** *The* BoilerMaker *application allows for interactive placement and visualization of injectors within a boiler. The user selects injectors by moving a conical object with the wand and pressing a button. The cone is constrained to move only where injector placement is possible in the actual physical boiler (*BoilerMaker *application courtesy of Nalco Fuel Tech and Argonne National Lab).*

Aperture-select. The *aperture selection* technique allows the user to "sight" an object using their hand (FIGURE 6-24). Typically, an object is designated by visually pinching it between the thumb and forefinger. The pinching gesture may trigger the selection, or the selection can be made by voice or other means. Once an object is selected, it may continue to be manipulated using finger gestures, as described in the preceding manipulation section. Similar techniques are common in second person VR displays, where the video image being captured through the actual aperture of the tracking camera is processed using computer vision techniques to determine the gesture being performed.

Aperture-select requires that the VR system be able to determine which object the user is selecting. To determine what the user is seeing through the aperture, the location of both the aperture and the user's eye must be known. In most VR systems, the location of the user's eyes is generally known, although accurate aim requires knowing which eye is doing the sighting (which was also true with the crosshair direction selection). Tracking the aperture may require more effort than is needed in the typical VR setup. If the fingers are used as the aperture, then some device needs to track the position of the fingers; a glove or a camera will work.

Name to select. *Selection by naming* an item provides a means of item selection that doesn't use the hands, allowing the participant to use them for other purposes (or not use them at all). Due to possible ambiguities and the less than 100% accuracy of speech recognition systems, a means of verifying that the computer "understood"

FIGURE 6-24 *This VR participant selects a flower using his fingers as the aperture (Photograph by William Sherman).*

FIGURE 6-25 *The user can select objects by simply speaking their name. Note the wireframe sphere around the "snowman," indicating the selection.*

what was intended is important. For example, the object could be highlighted momentarily before action is taken, allowing the user a chance to cancel the operation (FIGURE 6-25).

One limitation of this method is that the user generally needs to know the exact name of the objects they want to select. However, this method can be combined with the point to select method by using a pronoun to indicate an object in a specified direction—for example, pointing at a particular house and saying "Move that" versus saying "Move the yellow house" (which would be a point to select method with a voice command trigger).

NCSA's *Virtual Director* entertainment production application makes use of vocal instructions to select key frames [Thiébaux 1997]. When the participant verifies that the correct key frame was understood (by saying "Enter"), the participant is then transported to the chosen location and time.

Menu-select. *Selection by menu* is another form of interaction that is derived from the desktop WIMP interface. As with desktop menu systems, the user is presented with a list of choices from which to select an item.

As FIGURE 6-26 shows, the participant can indicate their choice in one of two ways. Using a direction selector, they can *point* at an available option, much like the cursor is used in the desktop metaphor, or they can *scroll* (or use button/gesture triggers to step) through the list of selections until the desired choice is highlighted.

(A)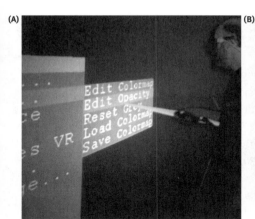

(B)

(C)

(D)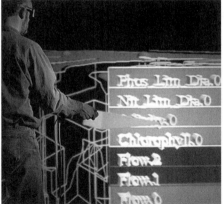

FIGURE 6-26 *A common selection method that emulates 2D interface techniques is the menu-select technique. Here a direction selector is used to point at, scroll through, highlight, and "click" to select various items in the* Crumbs **(A)**, SaraNav **(B)**, BoilerMaker **(C)**, *and* BayWalk **(D)** *applications (Applications courtesy of Rachael Brady/ NCSA, Anton Koning/SARA, William Michels/Nalco Fuel Tech, and John Shalf/NCSA, respectively; photographs by William Sherman).*

We typically think of menus as textual lists of choices, but sometimes pictures might be used to show the selections. In VR, we might even have 3D representations of the object. These representations might be miniature copies of the alternatives or perhaps even the objects within the world itself—*the world is my menu*. However, at this point we've basically shifted to one of the other selection methods, namely, contact-select. So, a primary distinguishing feature of menu-select versus contact-select is that the choices need not be nearby or visible to the user at the moment of selection or even be tangible objects found in the world.

There are many applications that make use of menu selections. Two examples are Caterpillar Inc.'s *Virtual Prototyping System* and the *Crumbs* visualization application (see FIGURE 6-26A). The Caterpillar application uses a wand-waving gesture to step through the menu and a button trigger to indicate selection. *Crumbs* uses a typical desktop-style pop-up menu that appears only when requested by the participant, with one important distinction from the desktop metaphor: to maintain high frame rate during menu operations, the rest of the world is not rendered, temporarily making all of the world invisible except the pointer and the menu. In *Crumbs*, menu selection is used only for tool and mode selection, whereas 3D cursor selection is used for probing and interacting with the virtual world.

Some research has been done on how to use menus in ways that do not originate from the 2D desktop metaphor. Using finger-contact gloves (*PinchGloves* from Fakespace, Inc.), Bowman and Wingrave [2001], researchers at Virginia Polytechnic Institute and State University, have evaluated the usefulness of letting the participant's fingers do the selecting (FIGURE 6-27). In their implementation, the currently available choices are rendered as part of the user's hand avatars.

Select in miniworld. *Selection in a miniature world* can be considered a special case of the menu-select method. As with menu selections, there needs to be some means of indicating a choice, and thus a secondary action of selection must be implemented. Items on the menu may be picked by contact, pointing, naming, and the like. Unlike the direct methods such as contact-select and point to select, select in miniworld provides smaller replicas of objects instead of their primary representations. The smaller world representation might take a form that duplicates the primary world exactly (except for size)—a world in miniature (WIM) [Stoakley et al. 1995] as shown in FIGURE 6-28—or it might be presented as a map. An advantage of using a miniworld

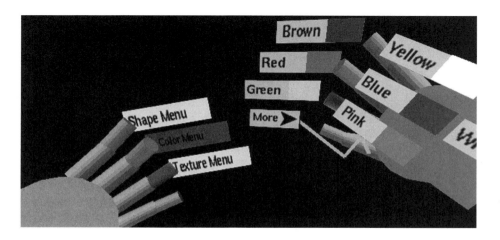

FIGURE 6-27 *A new method of presenting menus that isn't based on a traditional desktop menu uses finger contacts to indicate selections. The thumb is used to select an option by touching the index, middle, or ring finger. Touching the little finger brings up three new choices (Image courtesy of Doug Bowman).*

FIGURE 6-28 *By providing a small-scale representation of the virtual world, or a world in miniature (WIM), participants can indicate their selection on the model, and it will affect the main virtual world.*

for providing the palette of options is that any subset, including distinct regions of the virtual world, can be presented.

In addition to providing a more global context to the user, the scaled-down version can even allow the user to manipulate objects directly in the miniworld. Thus, large-scale manipulations can be performed more easily than is possible in the primary world—for instance, moving a heavy piece of furniture from room to room. In fact, they might even be able to move objects between the miniworld and the primary world [Mine 1996].

Alphanumeric Value Selection

Most virtual reality interactions avoid the necessity of entering specific *numeric or alphabetic information*. However, there are occasions when entering such data is necessary and enhances the VR experience. The direct user method of input for textual data is to use a penlike handheld device that allows handwriting to specify the desired values. Alphanumeric information can also be entered into the system via physical or virtual devices or by voice input.

Physical input of alphanumeric information is most easily achieved via a standard computer keyboard. Another option that may work well in some applications is a tablet and pen interface with appropriate handwriting recognition software. The proliferation of palm computing devices has made this a very reasonable possibility.

Physical input devices work best when the operator can see the device. Touch typists can operate a keyboard without watching their fingers directly, but they need to know where the keyboard is. Thus, keyboard and pen input methods work best when used with devices that do not occlude the real world. A user at a fishtank VR display or a *BOOM* user who can easily look away from the immersive display could be seated with a keyboard directly in front of them. A palm device or small tablet can easily be used while standing, so might work well in a projection VR display. Keyboards and similar devices can also be used by an assistant operator of the VR experience who is not the immersed participant, but this is essentially a form of agent control.

Virtual controls may take the form of something familiar, such as a virtual keyboard or keypad within the virtual world. Although virtual objects such as a keyboard may be more consistent with the virtual world, they can be cumbersome to use, particularly if no touch feedback is provided. However, in some cases it is essential to exactly replicate real-world interfaces. In such cases, the virtual keyboard interface is the best solution. An assembly line trainer developed by Adams Consulting for Motorola University uses a nonstandard keyboard to enter commands to the line. This keyboard is duplicated exactly in the VR experience to enhance the training effectiveness (FIGURE 6-29).

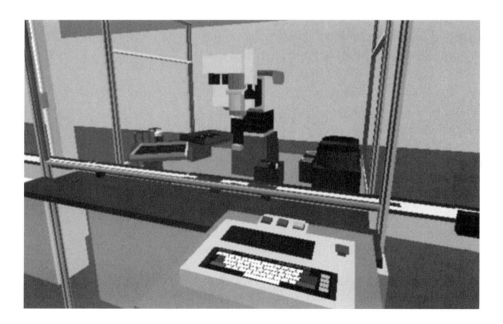

FIGURE 6-29 *The Motorola University assembly line trainer provides a virtual model that is an exact replica of the real-world device being mastered. The participant enters values into a virtual keyboard that resembles its real-world counterpart (Image courtesy of Motorola University). See color plate 16.*

(A)

(B)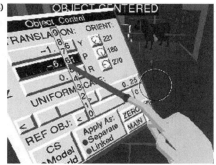

FIGURE 6-30 *At UNC, Mark Mine developed applications that accept numerical input from a virtual counterpart to an old-fashioned mechanical calculator (Images courtesy of Mark Mine).*

A more common input method for specifying numeric values consists of physical or virtual dials or slider controls. However, these methods can be difficult for setting a precise value. Mark Mine [1996] developed a menu-like virtual control for the input of specific numeric values. With this system, the user pulls down a menu of digits and selects a numeral to be input in each place until the desired number is displayed. This is done in a manner similar to mechanical calculators produced in the 1960s and 1970s (FIGURE 6-30). Once all digits are set in this way, the user signifies that the number is complete and its value is used by the application.

Agent controls such as voice input are another intuitive way to give specific numeric or alphabetic input within a VR experience. Depending on the ability of the speech recognition system, the participant may be able to speak the phrase or number or may be required to spell out each letter or digit. Speaking shortcut words such as "hundred" may allow multiple digits to be indicated. This technique is used in the voice control of NCSA's animation creation application *Virtual Director,* in which saying the word "hundred" indicates two zeros are to be entered, completing the number. To specify *101,* the user says "one zero one enter." Otherwise, as soon as the words "one hundred" are spoken, the application interprets this as *100* and ends the numeric input mode. The agent form of numeric input is ideal for applications mimicking vocal directions, such as giving a navigational heading to a crewmember of a ship or submarine.

Manipulation Operations

Many of the selection techniques described in the previous sections provide a means of choosing virtual objects in the world. But once an object is selected, what can the participant do with it? How can it be manipulated?

Manipulation is central to the VR interface. We have classified the types of operations performed in VR experiences into six categories. The two most common classes of manipulation operations are (1) positioning and sizing objects in the virtual world and (2) control of the participant's travel through the world.

The four manipulation methods described earlier—direct, physical, virtual, and agent—can be combined with the various properties of manipulation like gain, control order, ratcheting, constraints, feedback, and so on. Thus, the designer of a VR experience has a variety of interface implementations from which to choose.

Common forms of manipulation include:

- Positioning and sizing objects
- Exerting force on a virtual object
- Modifying object attributes
- Modifying global attributes
- Altering state of virtual controls
- Controlling travel

Manipulation methods of direct, physical, virtual, and agent inputs that are implemented to produce these types of operations, as modulated by a myriad of object properties, result in a large set of potential interface operations. These techniques constitute a set of skills that can be learned through frequent VR participation. Each of these VR skills will be discussed here, except travel controls which will be saved for our discussion on navigation later in the chapter.

Positioning and Sizing Objects

Positioning and sizing an object in a virtual world allows the participant to change the location, orientation, and size of a virtual object. Any of the direct, physical, virtual, or agent control methods of manipulation can be used to affect the object.

Direct user control methods of object movement allow the user to reposition the selected object by simply moving their hand in the same way they would like the object to move. There is an extensive list of ways this interaction can be implemented. The grab with fist interaction is one style of a direct control positioning and sizing operation. Grab with fist implies a one to one mapping of user movement to object movement, restricting how far the user can move an object to how far they can physically move.

When performing rotation and sizing operations, an axis or point (frame of reference) is required about which to center the manipulation. Frequently, the center of the operation is about some part of the object, such as the centroid (center of volume), or it could be specified by the position of the user's hand.

Sometimes (and especially with a unihand interface), the frame is set by an initial action performed by the user. Direct interaction can be greatly enhanced through the use of a bimanual interface. The ability to control rotation and size is more intuitive when two-handed interaction is possible because the two hands help define the frame of reference. For example, the user can virtually grab the object with both hands and rotate the object about the center point of their hands. Or, the user can resize the object with two hands by virtually stretching it (or shrinking it).

Physical or virtual controllers such as sliders can be used to move an object along an axis or to adjust the size of an object. This is a more constrictive and less intuitive way of moving things around, but if there is a need to keep things laid out in an orderly fashion, then this might be a very appropriate method of interaction.

Object positioning can also involve positioning parts of the interface. For example, a user can position streakline release points. Streaklines show the paths taken by all particles that pass through a given location in a vector field. In Brown University's extensions to NASA's *Virtual Windtunnel* [Herndon and Meyer 1994], streakline release points can be positioned in a fluid flow (FIGURE 6-31). NCSA's

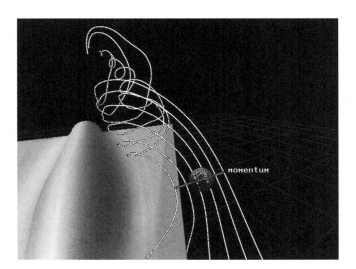

FIGURE 6-31 *This visualization shows streaklines over an airfoil. A virtual control bar (with a ball in the center) can be manipulated to indicate the desired starting position for the streakline visualization. The bar can be moved or it can be stretched or shortened to increase or decrease the number of streaklines (Image courtesy of NASA Ames Research Lab).*

Severe Thunderstorm Visualization allows the user to interactively release weightless particles anywhere they like (see FIGURE 6-13). The particles then flow to indicate the movement of the air current in the storm. The user is also able to reposition the menus in the application. It is especially useful to be able to move the menus when they are blocking something of interest.

When the aperture technique is used, it is frequently used to move and size objects. The ability to virtually grasp an object between the thumb and forefinger and move it by repositioning the hand, or adjust its size by increasing or decreasing the space between the fingers, is an aperture-based manipulation. This adjustment of the distance between the finger aperture and the eyes is another way to scale the size of an object, or it can be used to indicate that an object should be moved nearer to or farther from the viewer. The exact placement of objects when using this technique may be difficult to determine, since the aperture is a 2D plane and the virtual world is presumably 3D.

Exerting Force on a Virtual Object

Exerting force in the virtual world includes interactions such as pushing, hitting, and supporting objects. These are operations that are generally designed to mimic the real world via a VR interface. A haptic interface is often beneficial for such interactions, so the user can tell when they have made contact and have actually begun to exert a force.

Although exerting a force on a virtual object can be used to relocate it, the exertion of force differs from the previous category of manipulation operations. One difference is that exerting a force often will not result in the movement of virtual objects. It may instead be used to hold an object in place or to cut, puncture, or otherwise deform the object.

Examples of hitting objects include hitting a ball with the hand or a virtual golf ball with a virtual putter. Or, the putter could be physical, controlled by a real putter (prop) to give simple haptic feedback. Support of objects in the real world include such instances as lifting an object off of a surface or holding out one's hand avatar (or a virtual stick) and allowing a butterfly to land on it (FIGURE 6-32).

Force exertion is important in training systems in which a primary part of what the user is to learn involves hand manipulation of objects. Training interactions should mimic the behavior and feel of its real-world corollaries. This is exemplified by medical procedure training applications such as the *Celiac Plexus Block Simulator* (FIGURE 6-33) and the BDI *Suture Trainer* (see FIGURE 4-31). In the plexus block

(A)

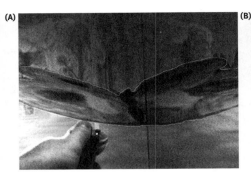

(B)

FIGURE 6-32 *Although no actual support exists, this virtual butterfly is willing to land and be supported by a virtual stick that is positioned by the participant (*Crayoland *application courtesy of Dave Pape; photographs by William Sherman).*

(C)

simulator, the user needs to feel how much force is necessary to puncture certain internal parts of the body. In the suture trainer, the trainee learns how to grasp and manipulate an internal body part while pushing a needle though it.

The ways in which forces are exerted in a virtual world do not need to mimic the real-world interface. This is the case in the *NewtonWorld* portion of the *ScienceSpace* educational suite of applications developed in collaboration between the University of Houston and George Mason University. Forces are applied to a ball using virtual controls, and the movements and collisions of the balls follow the laws of Newton's mechanics, whereas the Newtonian physics do not apply to the user and other entities in the world, such as virtual cameras.

An aperture-based manipulation that exerts a force in a virtual world is exemplified by the ability to destroy or remove an object from the

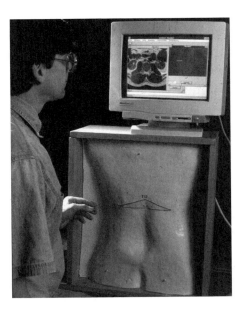

FIGURE 6-33 *A user grasps the end of an actual needle (controlled by a force feedback device inside the "back") to practice the celiac plexus block procedure and can view the results on the nearby virtual fluoroscope display (Photograph courtesy of Karl Reinig). See color plate 17.*

FIGURE 6-34 *Here the participant illustrates the "head crusher" method of terminating one's opponent in* CAVE Quake II *(Photograph by William Sherman).*

virtual world by grasping it and eliminating the distance between the thumb and forefinger. Pierce and colleagues [1997] refer to this as the "head crusher" technique, based on a sketch from *The Kids in the Hall* comedy show (FIGURE 6-34).

Modifying Object Attributes

Modifying object attributes refers to changing the parameters that control how an object is rendered or behaves. Parameters such as transparency, color, light reflectance, sound qualities, firmness, pliability, mass, density, and growth rate can be adjusted. This type of operation might be part of a virtual world design application or perhaps part of a visualization application to view features of objects not immediately visible—for example, making the outer shell of an object transparent or semitransparent.

Operations that fall into this category are typically ones that do not mimic real-world operations, since in the real world, we obviously cannot make such modifications as easily, if at all. In the real world, we can do little more than paint a fence to change its color or paint a window to modify transparency. The basic characteristics such as mass and density cannot be changed without affecting other characteristics of an object (such as size, shape, or strength). In a virtual world, objects can be modified in any way and even created out of "thin air."

Modifying Global Attributes

Similar to object attribute modifications, *global attribute modifications* are methods of adjusting the rendering and/or simulation parameters for the virtual world. But, instead of affecting specific objects, parameter changes are applied to the virtual world as a whole. Some basic global operations include the adjustment of the overall volume of the sounds in the world or the overall lighting, such as setting a time of day that varies the background from dark to bright blue skies and adds shades of orange when the sun is low. Another common global rendering change stipulates how objects will be presented—flat-shaded, wireframe, texture mapped, translucent—or whether objects are solid versus ephemeral and thus block the user's passage or allow the user to pass through them.

Normally, global attribute changes will affect everything in the world at the same time. However, there are possibilities in which the participant can control specific regions in which attribute modifications will take place. One such example of this is the *Magic Lens* interface [Bier et al. 1993]. The Magic Lens interface is primarily applied to views of a 2D desktop computer interface. This interface allows the operator to change the viewing parameters (e.g., render in wireframe) in a specified region of the screen (FIGURE 6-35). This region becomes a "lens" which allows views of a variety of features in the world. This effect can be extended to a 3D virtual world by providing a user-positioned virtual device that changes the viewing (or other) parameters of all the objects seen through the Magic Lens [Viega et al. 1996].

Altering the State of Virtual Controls

Because virtual controls exist inside the virtual world, when they are used in a VR experience, there must be some interface by which the controls can themselves be manipulated. For example, a virtual button or switch might be activated any time it is pointed at, or it may require the user to press a physical button while pointing at the virtual control. Comparable techniques can be applied to virtual sliders and other virtual control devices. Many virtual controls are manipulated just like other objects in the world. For example, a virtual slider may have a handle that the user can grab with a direct grab with fist manipulation and move the handle to a different place on the slider. Other virtual controls may require some form of object selection, along with a physical input that activates the virtual control. Of course, modifying virtual controls is done so the user can select, modify, or travel to some other object/location in the world.

FIGURE 6-35 *A 3D Magic Lens is a tool that allows one to affect the rendering parameters of a specified region of space. Here, a portion of a hand skeleton is magically viewed through the skin and other tissue of the hand (Image courtesy of John Viega).*

Controlling Travel

There are a wide variety of techniques for manipulating the participant's position in the virtual world. These methods of *travel control* are enumerated and discussed in the next section on navigation.

Manipulation Summary

Clearly there are a multitude of ways in which a VR participant can interact with the environment. A myriad of choices provides many possibilities but also requires careful consideration to ensure the participant has the appropriate manipulation mechanisms at their disposal. There is no simple formula for good interface design, but rather a need to clearly understand the medium, the participants, and the goals of the application.

Often the design choices will lean toward mimicking the real world. This may provide a more intuitive, natural interface, but does not guarantee an *effective* interface. An interface that merely mimics the real world does not take advantage of the fact that a nonrealistic interface might provide a better means of interacting with a given virtual world. It is always important to employ the disciplines of good design practice when developing a VR experience.

Of the six types of manipulations that can be performed, most can be implemented using any of the four control methods (direct, physical, virtual, agent) and involve a variety of selection methods and interface properties. However, for many applications, there are choices that are clearly more suitable than others.

Navigating in a Virtual World

Navigation describes how we move from place to place. In the real world, we navigate as we walk, drive, ski, fly, skate, and sail through the world. In a VR experience, there are endless ways of navigating through the virtual environment. The process of navigating a space is a vital part of a participant's experience. How one travels through a world can play a significant role in how it is comprehended. Here we describe critical aspects of navigation and a variety of possible implementations.

Navigation involves two separate components: *travel* and *wayfinding* (FIG-URE 6-36). In day to day conversation (and some literature), these terms are not always used precisely. For clarity, we will use *travel* to discuss how a user moves through space (or time), *wayfinding* to discuss how a user knows where they are and where (and when) they are going, and *navigation* to discuss the combined effort.

FIGURE 6-36 *Navigation is the combination of wayfinding (knowing where you are and how to get where you want to go) and travel (the act of moving through a space).*

Wayfinding

Wayfinding refers to methods of determining (and maintaining) awareness of where one is located (in space or time) and ascertaining a path through an environment to the desired destination. Knowledge of where one is is crucial if one is to profit from an experience. When encountering a new space, one may either wander around aimlessly or deliberately work toward building a mental model of the environment.

Occasionally, there are times when one is moving around without performing any wayfinding. *Maneuvering* refers to a situation in which there is no need for wayfinding, because one is performing movements in a region where the terrain and local objects can quickly be scanned and traversed. Of course, in order to let the user maneuver via physical locomotion, their location must be tracked. Conversely, we might refer to traveling moderate distances without wayfinding as *meandering* (implying no urgent destination) or *wandering*.

The goal of wayfinding is to help the traveler know where they are in relationship to their destination and to be able to determine a path to arrive there. A major step in achieving this is through the development of a cognitive map or mental model of the environment through which one is traversing or plans to traverse. In the domain of human factors studies, knowledge of one's location and surroundings is referred to as one form of *situational awareness* or sometimes as *navigational awareness,* when concerned only with knowledge regarding location. If we don't know where we are, we are lost. *Lostness* refers to a general lack of navigational awareness.

There is a variety of methods and tools that can help in the wayfinding process. Creating a mental model is what the explorer does to be able to find their way around later. Wayfinding aids are objects in the environment or tools carried by the traveler that give information about their position in the environment. These aids can be used to build a mental model and/or relate the current situation to the traveler's current mental model.

Creating a Mental Model

There are many methods that people employ to help them find their way from place to place. Generally, one tries to create a mental model of the space that can be referenced while traversing it. Some methods are more successful than others.

Stasz [1980] describes four common strategies for creating a cognitive map of a space. Ordered from most to least successful, the four strategies are

1. Divide and conquer
2. Global network
3. Progressive expansion
4. Narrative elaboration

The *divide and conquer strategy* is applied by breaking the overall area into subregions, learning the features of individual regions, and then learning (a few) routes between the regions in order to move between them.

The *global network strategy* is based on the use of landmarks (FIGURE 6-37). Here, a person memorizes key, easily identifiable locations (landmarks) and the relationship of subsites with respect to the landmarks. During traversal, this method requires one to remain oriented with regard to one or more of the landmarks.

Progressive expansion is often a less successful strategy whereby one attempts to simply memorize a map of the space. One starts with a small region and expands outward, memorizing more territory.

In the final (typically least successful) strategy, *narrative elaboration,* the wayfarer uses stories to build their mental model. As they travel through a space (or

FIGURE 6-37 *As in the real world, even with a map, one may find oneself lost in a complex virtual world. Through the use of landmarks and other wayfinding aids, the navigation of unfamiliar territory can be improved (*Performer Town *database courtesy of SGI;* Space Needle *model courtesy of Bruce Campbell/Human Interface Technology Lab, University of Washington).*

imagine such travel while viewing a map), a story of events is created including the path taken between events—for example, "I had lunch one block north of the subway stop, and had walked two blocks east when I found the bookstore."

Wayfinding Aids

An interface for navigating through an environment will often include tools to aid in the process of wayfinding. Tools that provide procedural or pathway information (the location of key landmarks, distance measures, and mapping information) can greatly help the user to navigate the space and build a good mental model.

Because different people use different strategies to help them create a cognitive map of their environment, a successful wayfinding system will be able to accommodate different preferences and perhaps include multiple aids.

Some wayfinding aids are built directly into the environment. Others are tools the traveler always has at their disposal to help them discern information about the environment that cannot be directly perceived. Most tools provide ways to visually represent information that is part of the environment. A real-world compass, for example, points north and south, converting magnetic information to a visual stimulus (a sensory substitution).

Here are some common real- and virtual-world aids to improve wayfinding:

- Path following
- Maps
- Landmarks
- Memorable placenames
- Bread crumbs (leaving a trail)
- Compass
- Instrument guidance
- Exocentric view
- Coordinate display and orthogonal grid structure
- Constrained travel

Path Following. Perhaps the easiest wayfinding scheme is to *follow a path* or trail within the environment itself. A path might be marked by a continuous colored line that traces the route, or it might use discrete posts labeled to indicate progression along the path, frequently with an arrow leading to the next waypoint. In the real world, an example of this wayfinding aid can be found in hospitals, where colored lines on the floor indicate travel routes to specific destinations within the building.

Maps. *Maps* are a common (and well studied) form of wayfinding. A map is a graphical representation of any space. The general goal of any map is (or should be) to provide a judicious selection of information that helps with the task at hand; for instance, some maps are used to visualize information as opposed to finding a path from location to location. Both as a visualization tool and a navigation tool, maps have many unique representational challenges, including how information is symbolized as icons and layered with additional information. Books such as *How Maps Work* [MacEachren 1995] and *How to Lie with Maps* [Monmonier 1991] discuss in detail the issues involved in map representation.

Most wayfinding aids can be instantiated in a variety of forms, and this is particularly true with maps. Maps can be displayed in either an exocentric (e.g., north up) or egocentric (e.g., view-direction-up) frame of reference. Maps can be located in the environment by any of the methods available to virtual controls (e.g., map-in-hand, map-in-world, etc.). Maps can even be integrated into the method of travel: the user could point at a location on the map and jump to the specified location.

(A)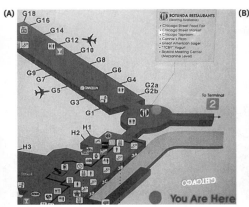

(B)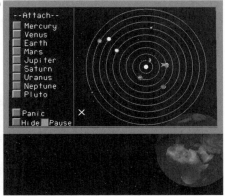

FIGURE 6-38 *In large and small contexts, travelers in virtual and real spaces can use you are here maps to quickly find their way through unfamiliar territory (Solar System Modeller courtesy of Martin Stytz; photograph by William Sherman).*

A familiar map style from real-world experience is the *you are here* map (FIGURE 6-38A). This style of map is usually an exocentric display with an arrow or other symbol that pinpoints where the map (and thus the map reader) is located in an environment. The Wright Patterson Air Force Institute of Technology (AFIT) *Solar System Modeller* has a version of this type of map that indicates which planet the participant is near (FIGURE 6-38B). The planet locations are indicative of where the planets are in their relative orbits, although the distance between orbits is not to scale. The world in miniature display method can also be used as a form of you are here map, with the miniature representation of the world as the map and an avatar representation as the user locator [Pausch et al. 1995].

Landmarks. *Landmarks* can be any obvious and distinct object in an environment that is nonmoving and easy to locate. A good landmark will also be helpful to a user in judging their distance from it. In virtual worlds (as in real environments), objects can be placed in the environment specifically for their function as a landmark.

Audio signals can also be used as landmarks, alone or in conjunction with a visual object. When used alone, a limited number of audio landmarks should be simultaneously audible to avoid overwhelming the user's aural perception. The *Officer of the Deck* experience [Zeltzer et al. 1995] uses a combination of aural cues with visual landmarks (FIGURE 6-39). Buoys in the scene are used to indicate important route information, and as in the real world, they are marked with an identification number and emit a spatialized sound. In the VR experience, sound from only the two nearest buoys is presented.

FIGURE 6-39 *In MIT's Officer of the Deck, participants learn to pilot a submarine into port. Mimicking the real-world task, buoys are used as a navigational aid. Buoys are marked with identification numbers useful for verifying position. Sounds are emitted by the buoys to help the officer determine their location (Image courtesy of David Zeltzer).*

Memorable Placenames. By assigning *memorable place-names* to locations in a world, the place itself can become a landmark. Having a distinguishing object located there helps further, but is not necessary (see *put me there* travel method in the next section). Placenames can also be used in conjunction with a map display to help a participant determine their current location or that of their destination. For named locations, a *name to select* form of item selection can be used to indicate a travel destination.

An example of using memorable placenames in conjunction with a map is the naming of celestial bodies in the *Solar System Modeller* application (FIGURE 6-40). The participant is told what body (typically a planet) they are orbiting or are nearby and can select where they want to travel from a list of objects.

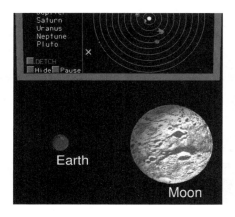

FIGURE 6-40 *One way of remembering where you are is to remember the name of the nearest recognizable feature. In this example, a participant using AFIT's* Solar System Modeller *can remember that they were flying through the solar system and turned left at Earth's moon (Application courtesy of Martin Stytz).*

Bread Crumbs (Leaving a Trail). Dropping *bread crumbs* (or leaving any form of trail markers) can be used as a means of allowing the user to see where they have been and perhaps use the markers to retrace their "steps" to a previously visited location. Hopefully, the markers will be somewhat less ephemeral than actual bread crumbs, although a means of erasing a trail can help to avoid excess clutter in the environment.

One example of the use of leaving a trail is found in the *Virtual Director* camera choreography application (FIGURE 6-41). In this application, the trail serves two purposes. In addition to showing where the user has traveled in the environment, it is also a display of the path of a virtual computer graphics camera. A user can carry the camera through the virtual world virtually filming the world as they travel. The camera records the view as a computer animation. The animation can then be edited by altering the path left by the camera.

Compass. *Compass* indicators in a virtual world can serve the same purpose as those in the real world (FIGURE 6-42). In fact, any form of orientation indicator can be classified in this category, such as an aircraft's artificial horizon indicator. In a computer graphic virtual world, a compass might combine aspects of a magnetic north indicator with those of an artificial horizon. Such a representation is used in

FIGURE 6-41 *Much like Hansel and Gretel left a trail of bread crumbs to allow them to retrace their steps, VR applications can follow the same metaphor. In this image, one can see trails indicating the path through which a computer graphics camera was carried (*Virtual Director *application courtesy of NCSA, Donna Cox, and Robert Patterson; photograph by William Sherman). See color plate 18.*

the *BoilerMaker* visualization shown in FIGURE 6-42C. In this application, a sphere's upper half is white and the lower hemisphere, black. (Each of the four cardinal meridians is marked with a colored line).

Instrument Guidance. The use of *instrument guidance* as a wayfinding aid is common—almost required in the aviation and marine industries. In an aircraft instrument landing system, needles or dials indicate whether the craft is on course or how much adjustment needs to be made to stay on the runway glidepath. Instrument wayfinding systems are now available for road vehicles. A car or truck can be instrumented with a global positioning satellite receiver (GPS) connected to a small computer display (dash-mounted, handheld, or laptop). The display can indicate visually and sonically both the location of the vehicle and route information, such as when the vehicle is approaching a turn.

In a computer-generated virtual world, implementing such features is far easier than in the real world. If the VR application is aware of where the participant wants to go or is being directed to go, a variety of navigation aids can be employed

(A)

(B)

(C)

(D)

FIGURE 6-42 *In real and virtual worlds, stationary and portable compasses help travelers find their way, as we see here in two real-world examples (A, B) and in the VR applications BoilerMaker (C) and GeoView (D) (Applications courtesy of Argonne National Lab and Nalco Fuel Tech, and Doug Johnston/UIUC, respectively; photographs by William Sherman).*

to assist the effort. For example, a large arrow might be located at the participant's feet indicating the direction in which to proceed (FIGURE 6-43).

One method that uses sonification to guide the user was implemented by mathematician George Francis at the University of Illinois at Urbana-Champaign. In his application, called *Optiverse,* users explore 3D topological shapes in a *CAVE* display. Two sounds are emitted to help guide a user to an optimal viewing location. The sounds are of the same timbre, but differ in frequency based on the distance from the destination. The farther the user is from the destination, the greater the difference in frequency. As the user approaches the location, the frequencies begin to converge. The user is able to hear whether they are getting nearer to or farther from the destination and make the appropriate adjustments.

FIGURE 6-43 *At the beginning of this application, the participant is directed where to go by arrows on the floor pointing the way (*The Thing Growing *application courtesy of Josephine Anstey; photograph by William Sherman).*

Exocentric View. A temporary shift in viewpoint from an egocentric view to an *exocentric view* can be used to aid a participant in determining their location within the environment. For example, a user constrained to walking on the ground could be given the ability to have a temporary exocentric view. Their view could shift to a bird's-eye view above and behind them, with an avatar representing their location in the world. In recreational flight and driving simulation software, this is often called the *wingman view.* A world in miniature display containing a mini avatar of the participant is another example of this type of wayfinding aid.

In any instance of moving to an exocentric view, it is important to maintain visual context. One way to maintain context during the shift is to back away from the egocentric point of view to an exocentric view, thereby making a continuous transition. This allows the participant to more easily discern where they are in the global context. There are also other ways to maintain context while assuming the temporary view [Pausch et al. 1995]. For example, a line may be displayed that points from the user's shifted exocentric view to their actual position in the world, or a wedge can be displayed indicating the user's field of view.

Coordinate Display and Orthogonal Grid Structure. *Display of position coordinates* is simply location information presented as text to the user. This can also be used to give one's location to another participant, or it can be stored for future reference

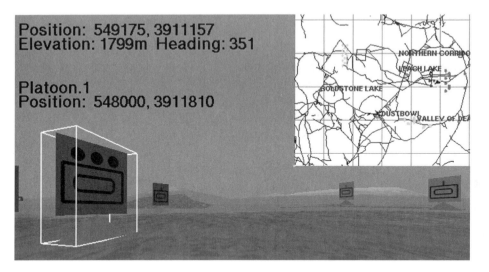

FIGURE 6-44 *Researchers at the National Center for Supercomputing Applications, working in collaboration with the U.S. Army Research Lab, developed the* BattleView *VR application.* BattleView *couples with war game simulations to display terrain, military units, and map and position information. Here, a 2D map and position coordinates are superimposed over the 3D terrain view (Application courtesy of NCSA).*

to help return to the same location. The NCSA *BattleView* military visualization provides a coordinate display in addition to a map locator view (FIGURE 6-44).

In addition to numeric coordinates, another method of text display that helps the traveler ascertain their position is to supply the name of the surrounding regions or nearby markers. For example, the name of the closest town in some direction can appear at the horizon, changing as the user traverses the world.

In order for a coordinate display to hold any meaning, there must be some form of orthogonal grid structure, such as the common Cartesian system. The grid itself is usually not visibly displayed, although it may emerge as a result of how structures and fields are laid out in the world. In some cases, however, the grid *is* visibly rendered to be used as a wayfinding aid. For example, Steve Ellis and colleagues [1987] have researched the effects of adding a grid to cockpit traffic displays to help show current and predicted positions of nearby aircraft.

Constrained Travel. One strategy to prevent or reduce participant *lostness* is to *constrain user travel*. One of the problems with moving freely through multidimensional space is that it can be very disorienting. By restricting the number of ways and places a user can travel, their ability to become lost is reduced. Some methods of travel are restrictive in and of themselves, such as the physical locomotion and ride along methods, which we will discuss with other travel restrictions in the Travel section that follows.

Travel

For any world in which regions of interest extend beyond the virtual reach of the participant, *travel* is the crucial element that accords them the ability to explore the space. Simple VR interfaces that constrain the user to a small range of physical motion or to the manipulation of only those objects within view are not adequate for experiencing most virtual worlds.

In many respects, using physical movement as a means of travel through a virtual space seems quite natural. After all, for many VR developers, the goal is an interface that mimics physical interactions with the real world. However, such physical interactions are many and varied. A young child can learn (even before crawling, walking, or talking) that by pointing in a given direction while riding in a stroller or on a shoulder, they might be taken in that direction. From there, the child progresses through scooters, tricycles, bicycles, and skateboards that translate leg motion to forward or backward movement in a direction controlled by the arms (FIGURE 6-45). This is augmented later in life as various machines allow us to traverse land, sea, and air with relative ease. Some travelers learn to traverse the world via a joystick, riding in a motorized wheelchair. Many more learn to use a joystick, button, or mouse to journey through computer-based worlds.

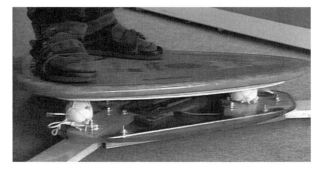

FIGURE 6-45 *Many devices have been developed to enable travel through a virtual world. These photos show a participant using a "surfboard" device to control a virtual surfboard in the virtual world. The participant moves in a manner that imitates an actual surfboard ride. The device was constructed by attaching pressure sensors to three corners of a reduced surfboard (Images courtesy of Peter Broadwell).*

People are capable of learning new interfaces. So, while physical movement may seem the most natural, it need not be considered the only appropriate interface for most experiences. However, VR interface designers still need to develop interfaces based on good design procedures. If an interface is hard to learn or counterintuitive, it will hinder rather than help the user navigate through the world.

One difficulty that faces the designer is that people with different life experiences may have different notions of what is intuitive. A pilot, for example, would attempt pushing forward on a joystick to cause the object in their view to move upward, because they mentally map such an action to descending in flight. Someone else, however, might expect a forward joystick movement to cause the object to descend. If the target audience has a large percentage of pilots (or people who play flight simulator games), then the designer must consider this group.

Properties of Travel Interfaces

Some of the properties of manipulation techniques can also be applied to the various methods of travel (in the same manner as discussed for manipulation):

- Feedback
- Ratcheting
- Bimanual interface

Other manipulation properties have *travel-specific components:*

- Manipulation method (direct, physical, virtual, agent)
- Constraints
- Frame of reference
- Movement formula (control order and gain)

Manipulation Method. The most common manipulation methods used for travel are the physical and virtual. The choice of which method of control to use for travel generally depends on the goal of the experience. *Physical controls* are usually used when attempting to faithfully duplicate the interface of a specific vehicle or other means of locomotion, such as an aircraft, tractor (see FIGURE 3-15), spacewalk (see FIGURES 6-4 and 6-64), or tall ship (see FIGURE 3-11).

Virtual controls can also be used to emulate physical devices like a steering wheel or flight stick to mimic a vehicle interface. More commonly, virtual controls are used to produce an interface without the constraints of a real-world device, such as a point to fly design. Virtual controls can also be more easily reconfigured to implement multiple designs without the need for building a physical version for each situation.

Agent controls are instructions that are spoken or gestured to a real or virtual agent who interprets the instructions as travel commands. The instructions of a ship's captain to the crew on which way to turn and how fast to go are commands to an agent. The *Officer of the Deck* application mimics the role of the officer through the use of a virtual piloting team that interprets and acts on spoken commands through speech recognition [Zeltzer et al. 1995].

Direct user control is not commonly used for travel controls. However, one example of a travel interface that does make use of this technique is the WIM method, in which the participant grasps their own avatar in the miniature world, moves it to a new location, and is taken along a path from their current location to the specified destination. Another example might be to pull yourself along a rope in an environment by making a grasping gesture on the rope and pulling your hand toward you.

Some interface paradigms require a combination of physical and virtual controls. For example, if a physical stair-stepper device is used to give the participant a sense of distance traversed, another (perhaps virtual) form of input would be required to affect the direction of travel.

Constraints. Some of the *constraints* of manipulation methods can also be applied to travel. The use of constraints can define the travel paradigm that is utilized. For example, in a system where travel orientation is constrained to maintain a constant vertical position (i.e., the user remains perpendicular to some virtual ground), the perceived effect is that of traveling on an invisible flat platform.

The idea of constraining the user to certain paths is not limited to following a specific linear path through the data space. Another option limits the user to only a specific plane. So, instead of being able to fly freely through 3D space, the participant can only "walk" on the 2D plane. This is basically a simple type of terrain following.

Terrain following is the movement constraint that maintains a participant (or other agent) at the proper height above the ground or floor of the virtual world. The use of terrain following distinguishes the fly-throughs from the walkthroughs and driving from flying.

Many travel interfaces limit the participant's ability to move laterally. *Lateral movement* is the ability to travel from side to side (the lateral axis), as opposed to in the direction they are facing (the longitudinal axis). Lateral movement can be important in visualization applications where the goal is to explore unknown data. Generic walking/flying interfaces often allow for lateral movement, but many piloted vehicles do not, much like piloting an actual car does not.

Frame of Reference. Travel in a virtual world is the relative motion between the user and the world. How this relative motion is interpreted by the user depends on the implementation of the travel interface. Previously, we discussed the notion of ego-centric versus exocentric reference frames. In general, frame of reference indicates whether one views and acts on the world from an external or internal point of view. When discussing travel, we can frame movement either as referring to a user moving relative to the world or to the user remaining still while the world is moved relative to them (FIGURE 6-46).

Most travel paradigms assume that the participant is moving through the space. In reality, however, the user is remaining (relatively) stationary in the real world, and the world representation is moving past them. For some applications, the goal is to create the illusion of the user moving through the world; for others this is less important.

FIGURE 6-46 *One might specify a rotation, either* **(A)** *exocentrically as north/south or in heading degrees or* **(B)** *egocentrically as left/right or using a clock metaphor.*

(A)

(B)

Movement Formula (Control Order and Gain). Some forms of travel control mimic self-locomotion (walking, flapping wings, etc.). Other forms allow the traveler to jump directly to a specified destination. The most common form of travel control, however, operates as though some vehicle is responsible for propelling the traveler through the world.

Recall from our discussion earlier in the chapter that the choice of control order allows different styles of movement, such as displacement, velocity, or acceleration. For displacement (zero-order movement), movement of the object occurs at the same pace as the control motion, with a button press (or any trigger event) allowing the user to specify when to begin and end motion. However, this is a simple interface, without a means of adjusting gain, so it does not allow them to effect travel with movement any finer than they can achieve through the movement of their own body. For example, it is hard to move oneself 0.5 mm, so movement can be attenuated by a gain factor of less then 1.0, and the user can move 0.5 ft in order to move in the virtual world by 0.5 mm. Setting the velocity (first-order control) allows the user to specify a rate of motion through the space. Similarly, acceleration control (second order) allows the user to begin travel slowly and increase their velocity for regional or global travel.

When we control a vehicle by activating mechanisms that control the speed, velocity, or acceleration of the vehicle, we might be influencing *speed* and/or *direction*. The choice of how much control the user will have over the rate of speed should reflect the object spacing in the virtual world. If all the objects are clustered in one location, then the user will want to be able to move slowly from one spot to another. If the objects are distant, they will generally want to travel at higher speeds. The ability to easily shift between low and high speeds is also desirable, particularly in worlds with a nonuniform distribution of objects, such as a solar system. Setting the *speed* can be done with physical or virtual controls. Examples of physical controls for controlling the speed are foot pedals, slot car controllers, rotating knobs, joysticks, and computer keyboards. Real-world devices can be used to control virtual devices in a manner similar to (or intentionally different from) their real-world function (FIGURE 6-47). Virtual controls can be a virtual slider acting as a throttle, a list of speeds on a menu, or relative distance of the hand from the body (FIGURE 6-48).

Voice can also be used to control travel speed. Commands can give a specific speed or indicate relative changes: "Ahead warp 8," "Faster, faster!" or "Stop." The aforementioned *Officer of the Deck* training experience relies heavily on a voice command interface. In this application, speed (in knots) is spoken by the officer and effected by the virtual helmsman.

Users rarely want to travel in a straight line. Therefore, some means of controlling direction of travel is highly advantageous. Any of the direction selection methods described previously can be used to specify the forward direction of travel. This works well when the user can simply turn their body to face the direction of travel, but that's not always possible when a user is seated or is viewing a stationary display that doesn't allow for shift in body position. There are occasions when the user needs to be reoriented with respect to the virtual world. Like the driver of a car who is fixed relative to the space inside the car, they need to be able to rotate the car relative to the world and change their heading.

In a complete (100%) field of regard display, the developer does not need to include a means of changing the virtual world orientation relative to the real world. In such a display, a user can freely rotate their physical body instead of rotating the world. However, when not using VR visual displays with 100% FOR and on those occasions when a user's freedom of movement is limited (as when seated) or when they want to turn the world upside down, it may be necessary to allow the user to change their virtual orientation as part of the travel interface.

FIGURE 6-47 *Model aircraft controllers can be used to control the speed of a plane in the virtual world or to control a multitude of other functions. For example, the same controller could be used to control the height of a virtual balloon or the translation of a molecular model of caffeine.*

FIGURE 6-48 *In this example of hand control, the user can accelerate, maintain a constant velocity, or decelerate just by moving their hand into one of the three zones [Mine 1995a]. This method may be implemented by allowing the user to accelerate or decelerate faster by moving their hand farther from the constant velocity zone. Both to allow the user to rest their arm and to provide a simple means to stop moving, a separate start/stop trigger mechanism is advantageous. The bar showing the zone divisions is generally invisible to the participant, but could be displayed if found to be beneficial.*

Classes of Travel Methods

The choice of travel method and how to implement it may be based on the genre of the experience, on the I/O devices available to the developer, or on devices known to be available to the user. Applications designed to be readily usable by anyone with a standard *CAVE* installation will make use of only the *CAVE* wand, whereas applications that are designed for sailboat training will likely include physical sail and rudder controls.

Some common travel methods include:

- Physical locomotion
- Ride along
- Towrope (river metaphor)
- Fly-through (walkthrough)
- Pilot-through
- Move the world
- Scale the world
- Put me there
- Orbital viewing

Each travel method might employ multiple interface techniques. Possible interfaces plus other features of these categories will be discussed with each.

Physical Locomotion. The simplest way to travel relies solely on *physical locomotion* (user ambulation). No interface is required, other than tracking of the user's body position and rendering the world appropriately, which are default requirements of virtual reality. By roaming around within the range of the tracking device, the participant has the means to view the world from a variety of positions. The ability to move around also provides proprioceptive feedback that helps give a sense of the relationships of objects in the world. The scope of user movement is limited by the tracking technology; large-area trackers, for example, allow the exploration of larger worlds. User movement can also be scaled up to cover more territory or down for finer view control.

The physical locomotion paradigm is a part of any VR experience in which the user's location is tracked. So, even if their movement is controlled as if on a rollercoaster or other theme park ride, they can still move their head to change their view of the world (the physical movement is effectively added to the primary travel paradigm of the experience). The *Crumbs* visualization application (Appendix B) is an example of an application that uses only physical locomotion as the user's method of travel, although the user does have the ability to reposition individual objects in the world.

A limitation of using only physical locomotion is that the range of the tracking system limits the size of the space the participant can explore. Researchers at the University of North Carolina at Chapel Hill [Razzaque et al. 2001] have developed a technique to fool a user into what amounts to walking in circles (FIGURE 6-49). By altering the visual feedback, participants can be subtly coerced to change their physical direction such that they are aimed at the farthest edge of the tracking system. The physical walking region must be large enough to make the user's circular path imperceptible to them, but not as large as the virtual space. This trick does of course require that the physical world be hidden from the user, so it works only with head-based displays.

(A)

(B)

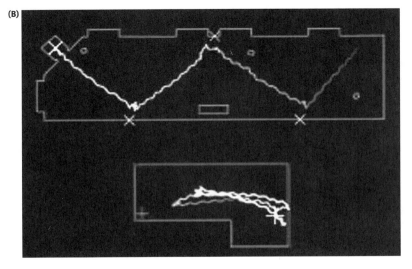

FIGURE 6-49 *With visual rendering trickery, a participant wearing an HBD can be convinced they are walking down a long virtual room* (A), *while in fact they are walking back and forth in a smaller real-world space* (B) *(Images courtesy of University of North Carolina at Chapel Hill).*

FIGURE 6-50 *The spherical view is the simplest form of travel. It places the user's head in the center of a stationary world, allowing them only to change their view by rotating their head. The constraints of this travel interface allow it to be implemented by simply mapping an image of the world onto the inside of a sphere. Here a portion of the sphere is cut away to reveal the user inside.*

In some circumstances, the user might be seated or otherwise stationary, allowing only head movement for looking around. If the virtual world is also static, the experience is reduced to the *spherical view* travel interface (FIGURE 6-50). The name refers to the premise that the entire world can be internally represented by displaying an image of the world on the inside of a sphere with the user's head at the center of the sphere.

Ride Along. Another simple and likewise restrictive travel paradigm is the *ride along*. In the ride along, the user moves through the virtual world on a path controlled by the application. They are free to move their head to change their view, but cannot veer off the furnished route—something like experiencing a factory tour by riding a conveyor belt through the building. Some control may be available to the participant in the way of speed manipulation, or the participant may choose from a selection of routes.

The benefit of the ride along is that the application developer can control the scope of the world that a participant can visit and can concentrate world modeling efforts on portions of the world that are more important to the overall experience. (Less constrained travel paradigms can accomplish a similar effect by providing obstacles or other tricks that prevent the traveler from moving out of bounds.) Another benefit of the ride along is that the interface is much simpler than more flexible travel paradigms, and thus requires less VR skill training. It can also ensure that the participant will visit all the aspects of the world that the experience creator wants them to see.

Some VR games developed by Virtuality Group plc such as *Zone Hunter* use the ride along paradigm primarily to provide more of an arcade game experience that allows customers to start playing right away without the need for skill learning. Rollercoasters and other amusement rides confined to tracks provide real-world examples in which the passenger submits to allowing the ride to direct their movements.

Towrope. The *towrope* travel method is only somewhat less restrictive than the ride along. As the name implies, the towrope paradigm works as though the traveler is being towed through the environment [Pausch 1996]. As with a glider plane, boat, or land vehicle, the participant is able to veer away from the tow vehicle within the constraints of the towrope length. In keeping with the tow analogy, speed is generally controlled by the pulling entity and not the user. This style of travel gives the participant some freedom to move, but retains advantages of the ride along, such as limiting world construction needs and user skill training. (Note that a towrope interface with a "rope" length of zero becomes a ride along interface.)

This method of navigation is also referred to as the *river metaphor* [Weber 1997]. Similar to a towrope, a river also signifies a wide path that must be followed, but with some leeway for lateral motion and adjusting the speed at which the course is traveled. However, while the participants may be able to slow their progress, they cannot entirely overcome the current.

The Cutty Sark Virtual Voyage experience is an example of the towrope method (FIGURE 6-51). In this example, the user pilots a clipper ship using a ship's wheel to steer, but can only move at a fixed speed and in fact cannot veer too far off course from the next, preordained waypoint.

Fly-through (Walkthrough). The *fly-through* paradigm is perhaps the most generic method of travel through a virtual space, allowing movement in three dimensions. The *walkthrough* paradigm is basically the same as a fly-through but with a terrain-following constraint applied to the traveler. There are many interface styles that can fall into these categories. A fly-through (or a walkthrough) refers to any method of travel consisting of a direction selection combined with a speed control. In addition to direction and speed, a fly/walkthrough can also allow orientational movement.

Pointer-directed fly-through was a common early method of VR travel that used pointing to indicate direction and speed of travel. Speed was a simple go/no-go control: go at a set rate when the user pointed, stop when the user stopped pointing.

Gaze-directed fly-through has also been frequently used, because it's simple to use and it can be implemented with just a head tracker. The major disadvantage of the gaze-directed method is that the user cannot look around while traveling without affecting where they are going. Also, when the display is less than 100% field of regard and the user doesn't have the ability to change their orientation relative to the virtual world, there will be occasions when they will not be able to see where they're going.

Torso-directed walk- or fly-through is perhaps a more natural interface style than either gaze- or hand-directed, although it may generally make more sense for the (constrained) walkthrough than the fly-through paradigm. This travel interface method was a particularly important exposition of the *Placeholder* VR experience (Appendix B).

A dual-handed fly-through has been described by Mark Mine [1996] which allows the participant to navigate through 3D space fairly intuitively. In this method, the user specifies a vector from a fingertip in one hand to a fingertip in another or from one prop to another (FIGURE 6-52). The vector provides both a direction and magnitude to travel; to stop, the two fingers are brought together, and to reverse directions, the user reverses the positions of the tracked fingers.

Note that as described, none of the above fly/walkthrough methods prescribes a means for the user to change their orientation (i.e., the relative orientation between the real and virtual worlds). It is as if they were riding on some platform fixed relative to gravity and true north. They can travel in any direction, but will remain facing north. Thus, they may be moving sideways, but they would still be

FIGURE 6-51 **(A)** *In Hiram Walker's* Cutty Sark Virtual Voyage *experience, participants are able to navigate the ship within a channel. However, they are constrained to moving* down *the channel; this is an illustration of towrope travel (Image courtesy of GreyStone Technology, Inc.). See color plate 19.* **(B)** *This water skier demonstrates a real-world example of the towrope metaphor. The boat determines the speed and direction of travel, with the participant (skier) able to enjoy a certain amount of freedom in movement within the envelope imposed by the length of the rope (Chase Jarvis/PhotoDisc).*

FIGURE 6-52 *The travel method shown here uses two hands. The vector from fingertip to fingertip provides both the direction of motion and speed.*

facing north. By introducing orientation control, many problems with travel in displays lacking 100% FOR can be diminished by allowing the user to bring the desired direction of travel into view, and then proceeding normally. An additional input method may be required to alter the rotation.

For example, a common method of travel in many *CAVE* applications is to add yaw rotation to the use of the handheld wand prop for a pointer-directed walkthrough. The built-in joystick on the wand is used to control speed of travel through the world by the amount of fore/aft pressure the user applies. Left/right pressure on the joystick causes the world to rotate about the user. Dave Pape's *Crayoland* was the first *CAVE* application to use this now common method of *CAVE* travel.

Move from reference is an invisible virtual control that makes use of the hand's (or handheld prop's) motion to govern locational and/or orientational movement. It is perhaps the most generic style of fly-through and can be unconstrained in both translation and rotation. This method of travel often uses the relative position between the hand and some known reference. The reference can be fixed in the real world, relative to some tracked real-world entity (such the user's off hand, torso, or head), or can be some point in real-world space that the user can specify before each movement. Notice that if the off hand is used as the reference point, then we have specified the *dual-handed fly-through,* perhaps with orientation control.

A common implementation of the reference-move is to set the reference point at the position of the hand when travel was initialized, and then move the hand relative to this position. Motion of the hand forward from the torso reference point will move the participant forward at a proportional rate. The rate of movement can be directly affected by the distance the hand is moved, it can vary exponentially, or consist of any other type of mapping, such as a scenario where there are several different "zones" defined and each zone corresponds to a specific speed or acceleration. The NCSA *Virtual Director* application [Thiébaux 1997] uses this method of travel because it is very flexible and can be used to perform complex maneuvers such as orbiting about a point of interest while keeping it in view. It is a fully unconstrained method of travel and therefore requires skill to adeptly perform.

Pilot-through. The *pilot-through* paradigm covers any form of travel that is based on the control of some (virtual) vehicle. Although it shares many similarities with the fly-through paradigm, the two paradigms can be differentiated by the immediacy of the control. In a pilot-through interface, controls are ostensibly mediated by the simulation of some vehicle, which can increase the order of control (e.g., acceleration instead of velocity), and direction is changed via some steering control. Fly-through control is more immediate; for example, one can point in the desired direction, specify a speed, and go.

Physical platform interfaces provide a means of vehicle piloting. As physical objects, platforms allow the use of real, physically manipulable objects (e.g., knobs, steering wheels, joysticks) as the control devices. These devices are especially beneficial if they are modeled after control systems from real-world vehicles. The benefit comes from allowing the participant to make use of existing skills. This congruence with the real world can also add to the mental immersiveness of the experience. Additionally, the platforms may impose real-world constraints on the possible manipulations. Examples of using a platform interface pilot-through include Disney's *Aladdin* VR experience (FIGURE 6-53) and the Caterpillar *Virtual Prototyping System* (see FIGURE 3-15).

As discussed previously, virtual controls can also be used to emulate physical control devices or to experiment with new control metaphors. This choice allows the operator of a virtual wheel loader to test-drive it both with a steering wheel and with a joystick without any changes to the physical setup of the VR system—at the cost of either sacrificing haptic fidelity or increasing the cost and complexity of the system by adding a generic haptic display.

Move the World. In some respects, the *move the world* paradigm greatly resembles the fly-through. The user's viewpoint can be manipulated through the environment in a very flexible (6-DOF) manner. However, it is a different outlook on the fly-through paradigm. It is now the world that is flying about the user rather than vice versa. The world is treated as an object that the user moves. Move the world is often used in visualization applications, where the world is generally more abstract and might be scaled relatively smaller than the user, requiring interaction as though the world were a miniature toy.

Despite the similarity in implementation, the difference in mental models is significant. Move the world is an object-centric manipulation method, where the user's input commands are applied to some external object's position with respect to the user. This method is counterintuitive for aircraft pilots (among others), who are more apt to interpret relative position changes between the user and the world as the user flying through the world.

One common interface method of this paradigm is the *world in hand* interface. Here the user moves the world about by repositioning their hand relative to their eyes, as though picking up an object for close examination. This can be done by mapping the movement of the world to a specific prop or to the hand itself. By providing a means of activating and deactivating the mapping, the user can ratchet

FIGURE 6-53 *In Disney's Aladdin's Magic Carpet Ride VR experience, a motorcycle-shaped platform* **(A)** *was designed for the guest to mount while piloting the magic carpet. The rider is able to sit comfortably on the seat, and reach forward to hold onto what feels like the front of a flying carpet. The guest is able to see their hand avatars holding the magic carpet* **(B)** *as they travel through a fantasy world based on the Disney movie* Aladdin *(Images courtesy of Walt Disney Imagineering). See color plate 20.*

through the space. Gain and control order can also be adjusted to allow for coarser or finer movement.

Another move the world interface is to map valuator controls to location and orientation values. So perhaps the world can be rotated about two of its axes via a joystick, and then by activating a switch, joystick control can be mapped to fore/back and left/right movement. Since the latter might also be used as a (user-centric) fly-through interface, it is possible to combine the fly-through and move the world paradigms—one for rotation, the other translation. However, this is generally confusing and not a very efficient interface design.

Scale the World. *Scale the world* treats the world itself as an object that can be manipulated, but is somewhat more user-centric than move the world. Scale the world operates by scaling the world (say, about the user's hand) down in size. The user then moves the reference (their hand) to another location in the now model-sized world, and size is returned to normal. By scaling the size up about a different point in the world, the user is effectively moved to this new location. This method of movement can be performed in any application that allows the user to change the size of the world about a point they specify.

Put Me There. The simplest to implement and perhaps easiest way to travel virtually is the *put me there* method. The user specifies a destination and is taken to that place. There are many ways this can be presented to the participant. Put me there is often available as an alternate means of travel in an expansive experience, allowing the user to travel more quickly between distant locales. It is rarely the only means of travel available.

Put me there travel can occur instantaneously (jump to) or over some length of time (travel to). The method of destination selection can be any type of item selection technique listed in the Manipulation section. Examples include map selection (or miniature world representation), menu selection, voice selection, and entering a portal (with a specific destination).

A simple example of a put me there interface is a virtual elevator that responds to voice-selected destinations. The user enters a chamber, utters the command "Take me to the bridge," and exits the chamber having arrived at the desired location. Another very simple use of the put me there travel paradigm is a *navigation reset* function that repositions the user at their initial position. Many applications provide such an option to allow users to recover after becoming totally lost or to allow a new user to explore the world from the same starting point.

Via the portal interface, put me there is one of the primary means of travel in the *Placeholder* experience (Appendix D). Although physical locomotion, virtual flying, and other means of travel are available to the *Placeholder* participant, portal travel is the only way to move between the different worlds.

Many put me there interfaces can result in momentary disorientation to the user after they arrive at their destination. The world in miniature (WIM) interface uses one form of put me there travel explored by the User Interface Group at the University of Virginia. The user can place their avatar within a miniature copy of the world (the WIM) at a new location as a means of specifying where they want to go [Pausch et al. 1995]. The WIM researchers investigated issues such as the importance of the user becoming cognitively vested (referring to the mental energy the participant has invested in the world) and the effect of different methods of progressing from the user's current location to the destination. Tested methods included immediate jumps, simultaneous movement of the user and a camera view, traveling a path from the current location to the destination in the full-scale world, and moving the user into the model as it scales up to full size.

Two other interesting put me there interfaces that use aperture interface methods to implement put me there modes of travel are *stepping into a picture* [Pierce et al. 1997] and the *head-butt zoom* [Mine et al. 1997]. Stepping into a picture is an operation whereby the frame of the picture defines an aperture. Upon passing the head through the aperture, the participant experiences being placed in the world of the picture. Note that this can be accomplished by the user moving their head through the picture frame or by the picture frame being moved to engulf the user's head. The head-butt zoom is a very similar technique. In this method, an aperture is formed by the participant creating a frame with their two hands and moving their head into the frame thus defined. The latter technique, of course, can only be used to move closer to a location already in view.

Orbital Viewing. *Orbital viewing* is a specialized paradigm for easily viewing small objects or models from any direction [Chung 1992]. It is referred to as *orbital viewing* due to the nature of how an object orbits about a user as they reorient their head (FIGURE 6-54). In this paradigm, the object retains its orientation with respect to the real world, and the user sees a different side of the object as they rotate their head. Consequently, to see the bottom of an object, the user need only look up.

Orbital viewing works best with head-based displays. This correlation is a consequence of lack of full FOR in many stationary displays, which prevents some sides of the object from being viewable. Orbital viewing also works best for relatively small objects that the user could otherwise walk around. An option to view specifically selected objects within a larger virtual world can be integrated into a larger interface. Orbital viewing can also be used in combination with the worlds in miniature technique to provided a more intuitive wayfinding aid. By keeping the WIM aligned with the larger world, the user doesn't lose the relationship between the two, yet can view the WIM from any direction simply by turning their head [Koller et al. 1996].

This paradigm is beneficial in that it provides a very simple user interface. Thus, a potential user can don the VR gear and begin viewing a world quickly and without much training. On the other hand, orbital viewing has problems when used in a VR system that does not provide 100% field of regard. Also, it has been found that when orbital viewing of one object is combined with a world not viewed via this scheme, users are more likely to show signs of simulator sickness [Koller et al. 1996].

FIGURE 6-54 *In the orbital viewing paradigm, the object maintains its orientation but swivels about the user as they turn their head—as if orbiting them. This is a simple interface for users to quickly learn how to examine an object and only requires tracking the head's orientation. However, since location isn't tracked, the user cannot walk around to the other side of the object; to view the object from all sides requires a full FOR VR display like an HMD or a six-sided CAVE.*

Travel through Time

In addition to navigating through space, certain VR applications allow navigational control of time—time travel. In fiction, time travel allows the author to explore a variety of philosophical issues in humorous, tragic, or other veins. However, most VR experiences that allow the user to control *when they are* typically have more mundane goals.

Two uses of time control are to allow a user to peruse a computer simulation of an event and to enable a participant to re-experience the simulation from multiple viewpoints. In a scientific visualization application, the data may encompass hundreds of steps through simulation time (the equivalent of days, microseconds, or millions of years depending on the simulation). By allowing the user to freeze time, let time pass at a given rate, or jump to any time in the simulation, they can study specific phenomena of interest and their relationship to the passage of time. In a mission rehearsal experience, the participant(s) might run through the mission and later return to a stored copy of the episode, being able to observe the actions of all the entities from multiple viewpoints and at any point (and rate) of time.

Controls for navigating through time usually differ from those for navigating through space. This difference begins with the representation of the current value of time (i.e., when you are). A clock-style representation of time—in analog or digital formats—is perhaps the one that is familiar to most users. The analog format is useful for indicating the cyclical repetition of a time sequence. This need not be the passage of a single Earth day, but may be used to represent a single Earth orbit of the sun, for instance.

Another style of clock representation is the time bar. This method of representing the passage of time is done with a (typically horizontal) line or bar, with a marker that moves from left to right (at least in Western culture) as time progresses. Many scientific visualization and animation packages make use of this representation.

As with navigation through space, there are a variety of interface techniques for navigation through time. One such interface is the emulation of standard VCR controls: a play button, a pause button, a stop button, a fast forward, and reverse. To cause simulation time to move forward, the play button is pressed. Another user interface for time control is that of an animation choreography package. In computer animation, the interface is often to jump to a specific point in time (a key frame); set parameters, such as the camera location, object positions, visualization values, and so on; then jump to another time. The package can then interpolate between key frames.

The *Virtual Director* application uses some of the computer animation techniques, but extends them into the inside-out view allowed by the medium of VR. In the *Virtual Director*, the interface specifies the motion of simulation (and animation) time by issuing agent commands and adjusting wand position and other physical/virtual controls as time passes. This control information is then saved as choreography parameters that can be used by an animation renderer. Parameters such as the camera path can also be visualized directly in the virtual world. In the case of the camera path, a trail of points is left behind. As time passes, a time bar represents the position in time, with markers indicating the key frames of the choreography. Many other possibilities exist for the time-control interface (FIGURE 6-55). For example, one might have a world in which the participant takes the hands of a clock and rotates them to cause time to retreat or to advance.

Navigation Summary

Some form of navigation is available in all virtual reality experiences. Therefore, all VR application developers should be familiar with the concepts and methods of navigation possible in the medium. In particular, designers should know that method of

(A)

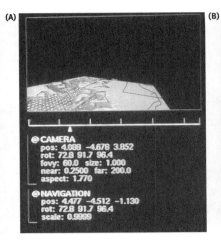

(B)

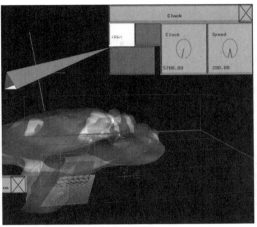

(C)

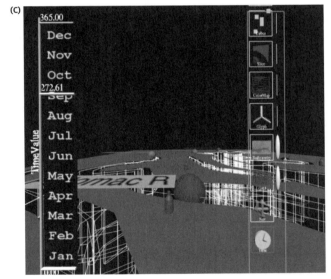

FIGURE 6-55 (A) *Virtual VCR controls,* (B) *virtual clocks, and* (C) *slider bars are only three possible mechanisms that can be used to control travel through time in the virtual world and represent the current position.* (Virtual Director *application courtesy of Donna Cox, Bob Patterson, and NCSA;* BayWalk *application courtesy of John Shalf and NCSA;* Severe Thunderstorm Visualization *courtesy of Bob Wilhelmson and NCSA; photographs by William Sherman*).

travel is only part of the story. Wayfinding is equally important (FIGURE 6-56). Unfortunately, little research has been done on the use of wayfinding for VR, and there is a scarcity of applications that include adequate tools for the task. Of course, wayfinding aid is not consistently done well in the real world, either, but the variety and frequent unfamiliarity of virtual worlds makes wayfinding in virtual reality a more likely problem.

FIGURE 6-56 *Professor Rudy Darken of the Naval Postgraduate School (NPS) conducts research on wayfinding in virtual reality environments [Darken and Banker 1998]. Here, Darken provides a virtual compass that mimics a real-world compass to measure its effectiveness in navigating a virtual world. This data is then compared with data measuring the effectiveness of a physical compass in the real world (Image courtesy of Rudy Darken).*

Because travel control and wayfinding are two components of one task, sometimes both can be manifested in a single interface. For example, a map works as a means of determining where one is in relationship to specific locations in the world. But in VR, a map can also be used to specify where you want to be and can take you there immediately.

When implementing a method of travel, the VR developer should aim for an interface that users will consider natural. However, this should not limit design to only what is possible in the real world.

Interacting with Others

Working together in a virtual environment can also play an important role in an experience. There are many approaches that allow a virtual reality experience to be shared. If the purpose of sharing the experience is to work together to solve a problem (i.e., perform a task), then it is a *collaborative experience*. Participants might also share an experience for competition or other interactions.

Collaborative experiences require a method by which the virtual world is shared. However, the terms *shared* and *collaborative* are not synonymous—not all shared VR experiences are collaborative. Noncollaborative shared experiences include audiences viewing immersed participants as these participants interact with the world, experiences that are captured and replayed, and telling the tale of a past VR experience via some medium other than virtual reality.

There are several concerns that arise with shared experiences. The primary issues involve choosing the methods of how collaborative interaction is to be handled;

how concurrent the experiences must be; who has control over manipulation/ communication operations; how worlds are kept concurrent; and, perhaps most importantly, how coparticipants can communicate with one another.

Shared Experience

The purpose of any communication medium is to share information and experiences with others. VR is no different. In this section, we will look at what it means to share experiences via virtual reality. Before we move on to collaborative experiences later in this chapter, let's first look at sharing in the broader sense and how it can be employed as part of the experience.

Each medium has a different way of allowing an experience to be shared among recipients. A novel is generally read alone and perhaps discussed with others later. Movies and television are often watched by a group, who share the experience as it unfolds. Many virtual reality systems allow only one participant at a time to directly experience an environment. Most of these systems, however, include an auxiliary display such as a computer monitor. On rare occasions, a VR experience may be recorded for later playback. Some VR systems enable multiple participants to share the same virtual world and to interact with each other. Some VR systems enable additional viewers to closely approximate the experience of the active user (e.g., the *CAVE*), facilitating collaborative discussions (FIGURE 6-57). Participants in a projection VR display can easily take turns as the active user by handing the tracked eyewear and controls to one another.

FIGURE 6-57 *Here, two participants interact in a* CAVE *application to examine and discuss weather data presented through a variety of representations (Application courtesy of Andrew Johnson; photograph courtesy of NCSA).*

What Can be Shared?

There are various aspects of a particular experience that might be shared. Let's begin with ideas; ideas can be shared during an experience via a discussion with the people in the physical vicinity or in the cyber-vicinity. If the experience is shared across time, then the participant might be able to make comments that are recorded along with what they are experiencing, such as with the *Placeholder* voiceholder annotation tools (Appendix D). Annotation among users is one method of using a shared experience to aid collaboration. However, the need to collaborate is not a requirement of a shared experience.

The virtual world itself can be shared. In fact, this is almost a requirement. Even if an experience is simply being relayed to a friend in conversation, then enough of the world must be described for the friend to get a good sense of it. More immediate ways of sharing the world include sharing control over the view and taking turns interacting with the virtual world. VR displays that allow a group to partake in an experience together generally make it easy to alternate who wears the tracked glasses and who holds the input device. These elements of control can be passed from one to another either in combination or separately. The more that is shared, the greater commonality participants will have in their respective experiences. Because of differences in life experiences, however, it will never be exactly the same. Each person will bring to the event varying amounts of knowledge on the content and exposure to this and other similar media, along with their own attitude toward the content (see FIGURE 2-3).

Ways of Sharing

The ways of technologically sharing the virtual world can be divided into two categories, based on the consistency of point of view among the participants. Everyone might experience it immersively, in what we would call *full multipresence,* or some viewers could observe nonimmersively. The nonimmersed viewers might be thought of as the audience looking over the shoulders of the participants.

Other people at the venue will also tend to have an effect on how an individual experiences and interacts with a virtual environment, in particular, those people who congregate at or near the VR system. The onlookers may cheer on the participants, offer suggestions, or make snide remarks. The ability of others to watch the happenings provides topics for discussion and thoughts for what to do when they enter the experience themselves.

There are different ways in which the waiting audience can be shown the interactions of the physically immersed participant(s). Of course, one option is to simply show nothing, not even the participant(s). The other extreme is for the participant to be in front of the audience, who can thus witness the immersive display firsthand. This is often the choice when the VR experience is also part of a performance (FIGURE 6-58). Between these extremes is the choice of duplicating for the waiting audience that which is being displayed to the immersed users (FIGURE 6-59). Sharing with an audience is but one way to share the experience.

FIGURE 6-58 *Some VR experiences are developed for the purpose of public performance. Here, an audience watches the interactive world on a large screen, as Jaron Lanier (taking a respite from his HMD) interacts through a musical device (Image courtesy of Jaron Lanier).*

There are a few combinations of shared viewpoints that are somewhat common:

- **One immersed participant with onlookers:** For example, one person wears a head-mounted display with external monitors provided for everyone else to see what is happening.

- **Two (or more) immersed participants:** Each experiences the same virtual world, either using the same paradigm (HMDs) or different paradigms (an HMD and a *CAVE*).

- **Open display:** For example, projection-based displays allow multiple people to view the same screens, with one person at a time being tracked who is physically immersed and who has the ability to share the tracking equipment.

- **Multiperson cockpit:** A common screen represents a window through which everyone within a cockpit can view the outside virtual world.

Each combination influences the amount and type of collaboration possible among everyone involved. In the open display paradigm, the primary viewer can still see the other people, making it easier to share thoughts and express interest in particular aspects of the world.

(A) 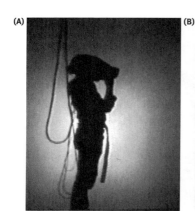 (B)

FIGURE 6-59 *A gallery of viewers is able to passively observe the silhouette of the active participant of the VR application* Osmose. *On the other side of the gallery, the participant's view is projected onto a large screen (Images courtesy of Char Davies).*

Recall that we defined multipresence as many participants simultaneously experiencing the same virtual world through VR, including the representation and activities of the other immersed parties. Multipresence is clearly important when using virtual reality for collaborative work. For example, two design engineers located hundreds of miles apart work in cyberspace on a design project, where each sees a representation of the other person as well as the same virtual objects, including the device they are working on.

Control of the action can also be shared by a number of methods. So far we have just discussed control of the viewpoint. Another option is to share control of the virtual world. In situations where the onlookers can be heard by the primary participant, they can influence the participant to perform specific actions, but there are more direct methods too. Many VR systems have physical devices and voice recognition input that exert influence on the events of the world. This makes it possible for someone other than the primary immersed viewer to have some control of the world. This is particularly useful when someone is being trained in interacting with the application or for doing demonstrations where the immersed viewer(s) are unfamiliar with the controls.

Why Should I Share?

Providing a method to share an experience in a virtual world generally requires an extra programming effort, if not an extra expense for additional equipment. The exceptions to this are when the scene can be viewed off the computer display, and when the VR display paradigm does not restrict the view to only the "immersee." The display can be used to entertain the others waiting to try the experience. This also serves to give some nominal training to those standing in line. Collaboration (discussed in the sections that follow) is a good reason to share views into a virtual world.

If the goal of the experience is marketing of some type, then there are several reasons to have a shared view of the virtual world for those waiting to participate. The first is that it helps to draw people over to the VR system and adds more people who want to try. Second, while people are waiting in line, they can answer a survey for the host of the "free" experience. And third, if the experience is considered an advertisement, then while in line, the viewers are exposed to the ad several times. If something interesting happens to one participant, then they might discuss it with those who were watching vicariously, even after leaving the venue.

Increased throughput is another common reason a shared display might be used in a VR system. The high throughput required in some venues can create situations where there is not enough time for each person to experience the virtual world

Group Control

An interesting approach to control of a virtual world by a group of participants was designed by Loran Carpenter and Rachel Carpenter of Cinematrix, Inc. This system was publicly demonstrated (and used) during the SIGGRAPH 94 and 91 conferences [Carpenter and Carpenter 1993].

FIGURE 6-60 *Hundreds of people participate in a group-oriented, interactive game of the* Pong-*like* Dog N Cat *game. Participants "vote" on how their team should move by holding a paddle prop one direction or the other to control the pong paddle (Image courtesy of Cinematrix, Inc.).*

In this system, each user was given a control by which they could make one of two choices (three if you count abstaining from choosing). Large groups of people were able to provide input into a single virtual world, providing an interesting experiment in group behavior. A few of the worlds implemented and tested include the familiar *Pong* video game, a simple flight simulator, and an "Egg" (the group's avatar) on a pair of skis. In each case, large sections of the group were put in control of a particular aspect of the world, and the percentage of one section making one choice or another was used to control the aspect for which they were responsible (e.g., move the pong paddle up or down). The ability of the groups to cooperate as required to play a reasonable game of *Pong* was quite impressive (FIGURE 6-60).

firsthand. In these cases, a provision for vicarious viewing is part of the venue design. This was done with Disney's *Aladdin's Magic Carpet Ride* VR experience at Epcot Center, where only about 4% of the people who entered the facility were selected to "fly the magic carpet" [Pausch et al. 1996]. This might also happen when a large group visits a VR research facility. In this case, if a projection-based visual display such as a *CAVE* is used, then at least everyone can see what is happening.

Summary of Shared Experience

When people think of VR, it is common to think of being immersed in some world with others. Sharing an experience is part of being human. To do this completely, each immersed participant should have some control of the virtual world, although limits may be placed within the experience, restricting who can interface with certain aspects of the world.

Since the virtual world exists in what we refer to as *cyberspace,* some physical restrictions (such as physical proximity) are removed. Geographic separation of participants can range from being in the same cubicle to being anywhere on—or in orbit about—the same planet. Sometimes an avatar does not represent a real-world being. These computer-generated entities are now generally referred to as *agents* (or sometimes referred to as *intelligent agents* (IAs) or *artificial intelligences* (AIs) when given some form of pseudointelligence).

Ultimately, it is the sharing of ideas that is important. Of course, a kind of sharing of ideas always takes place between the developer(s) and the participants, but more than that, VR allows for a variety of ways for experiences to be shared among participants.

Collaborative Interaction

There are many occupations in which collaborative work is critical for timely task completion. In addition to manual tasks, in which a sufficient amount of physical exertion requires the efforts of multiple people, professionals such as architects, scientists, and medical doctors also engage in projects that require multiple participants to work together to achieve a common goal. Indeed, there is a field of study that investigates general computational tools to aid collaboration—computer-supported cooperative work (CSCW).

The degree to which people can *collaborate* in a virtual space can range from none, to simply coexisting in a shared space, to having special tools available that help immersed participants work together. A simple shared space, where avatar representations of participants are merely added to the scenery of the world, may or may not add interest or usefulness to the application. A skiing experience might be more competitive, and hence more interesting, with other skiers to race, but otherwise doesn't differ from the solitary skiing experience. If there are enough inhabitants in a large information space, the notion that crowds draw crowds might provide for a useful mechanism for participants to find out that something interesting is happening, at least something that is of interest to someone else.

Communication among People

Collaboration requires communication among people. Aside from the handshake and occasional pat on the back, business communication is generally restricted to visual and aural means. Haptic sensation communication is generally important only for applications involving manual tasks requiring the effort of multiple people.

A great deal of communication is done aurally. Information is passed via direct conversation and through the use of voice messages that can be retrieved at a later time. Some applications can take advantage of existing communication technologies to keep the VR system simple. For direct aural communication, the telephone system can be used to relay sounds from one location to another. Integrating the audio communication directly into the computer system is sometimes beneficial. For example, it may be important to synchronize a given communication with a particular action, especially if that communication is stored for later playback.

Also important is information passed via visual means. When we speak, we may augment verbal communications with body gestures. Occasionally the body gestures are the entire message (e.g., waving and pointing), or a person's mere presence may be enough to communicate information. Such gestural communication requires a method of transmitting a visual representation that conveys the actions of the other participant(s).

Simple body gestures can be transmitted using much less bandwidth than even low-quality speech. Thus, body movements can reasonably be integrated into a system, even when there is not enough bandwidth for much of anything else (FIGURE 6-61A).

Video teleconferencing equipment can be used directly or integrated into a VR system when the ability for collaborators to see one another's face is deemed important. This capability can include both visual and aural information. The visual information might be presented as a simple window display of the other parties, or video information might be mapped directly onto a participant's computer graphics avatar, as was implemented by Caterpillar Inc. in their *Virtual Prototyping System* (FIGURE 6-61B).

(A)

(B)

Another form of visual communication is to leave a mark on the world. These can range from dropping markers along a path, to placing directional signs, to putting graffiti on objects to mark one's presence, to writing a message on a virtual paper, to leaving a visual annotation. The participant (or a later participant) may subsequently find that information helpful (FIGURE 6-62).

Of course, the simplest method of collaboration is to occupy the same physical space. This is best done in larger projection-based stationary displays (e.g., a *CAVE*). More than one person can physically occupy the viewing area, and thus these participants can see and hear one another directly. The integration of a multiuser tracked viewing mechanism enhances the collaborative environment even more, (although, currently, this technology is not widely used and can only display independent stereoscopic viewpoints for two people [Arthur et al. 1998].

Synchronous and Asynchronous Communication

An important aspect of collaborative communication is the degree of concurrence in time between the sending and reception of the message. Both ends of communication can occur at the same time (synchronous) or can be separated in time (asynchronous). In *synchronous* communication, the parties are in the virtual (cyber) space together. They can hold live, interactive conversations in real time. In synchronous communication, floor control (i.e., who has the right to talk or act) is a prime determinant of how the interaction will proceed. Another important aspect of synchronous

FIGURE 6-61 (A) *Avatars can be used to communicate visual information. In this image, a fellow player salutes to indicate his willingness to carry out commands issued by the user shown here. In addition, the user can see the orientation and location of the other player from the avatar's position in the world (CAVEQuake II application courtesy of Paul Rajlich; photograph by William Sherman).* **(B)** *Caterpillar Inc. uses video information texture mapped onto a box to provide a realistic representation of a user at a remote site in a collaborative virtual world (Image courtesy of Caterpillar Inc.).*

(A)  **(B)**

FIGURE 6-62 *One of the book's authors leaves his mark in the* Vandal *virtual world so the other author will be able to see where he was (Application courtesy of Dave Pape; photographs by William Sherman and Alan Craig, respectively).*

communication is the extent to which individual participants' worlds are kept congruent. Although this is not exclusive to synchronous communication, the idea of whether the person you are conversing with is experiencing the same world as you is very important.

In *asynchronous* communication, different parties can enter a persistent world, where they can perceive the world as it was left by other participants and, in turn, make changes to the world themselves. In addition to allowing communication among collaborators, participants can leave information in the world for their own retrieval at a later point in time. Also, communication need not be verbal. It can take the form of combined efforts to reshape a world. Two applications developed at the University of Illinois at Chicago's Electronic Visualization Lab, *NICE* (Appendix A) and *CALVIN,* both allow participants to modify a persistent world—in the case of *NICE,* a virtual garden, and with *CALVIN,* a building layout. Both of these examples allow each participant to modify the world for future participants.

Two methods of asynchronous communication are world annotation and experience playback. Annotations (discussed in detail later in this section) are a key method of asynchronous communication. Experience playback is used less often. *Experience playback* refers to the ability to capture and store the actions of participants over time. These actions can then be replayed by the participant(s) themselves or by others. We consider an avatar reliving prior actions as a *ghost,* while the current participant can walk around the same space observing the previous actions from any angle.

A single VR application may provide a method for both synchronous and asynchronous communication. For synchronous communication, the application must provide a means of making the participant heard/seen/felt by other participants in real time. Asynchronous communication requires a persistent world and a means by which participants can leave their mark. The text-based medium of MUDs (multiple-user dungeon/dialog) allows both forms of communication. Users can interact directly through text conversations or through typed commands to combat one another, or users can perform modifications on the world by moving objects from place to place or creating new locations.

The concurrency affects the style of information exchange. For example, synchronous voice communication allows for direct conversation, with the ability for immediate feedback. The asynchronous method of voice communication allows for a voice message style of communication, where participants can be involved at their convenience.

Annotation

The ability to *annotate* a virtual world allows users to explain it, to ask questions about the content, or to give general impressions about what is there. An annotation is a note placed in the world to explain/question/review some aspect of it. A variety of annotations can be manifested and used within virtual worlds.

Regard for how the annotations will be used by the participants must be considered:

- Who is it for?

    The participant—me.

    Other participants—you.

- When is it for?

    While still in the experience—now.

    Post-experience—later.

- What is it for?

    Collaboration—working together to accomplish a task.

    Instruction—trainer/trainee relationship.

Documentation—static information presented to the participant.

This includes the example of real museum walkthroughs that use headsets and push to talk buttons located near a display.

Our focus here will be on the use of annotations for collaboration. Both instruction and kiosk information are one-way forms of communication and assume that the participant has less information about the subject than the content embedded in the kiosk by the experience creator. Collaboration treats participants more equally, allowing anyone to leave notes.

■ How is it manifested?

Voice—annotations that are easy to make in an immersive environment.

Text—annotations that are easier to skim/edit/process outside the experience.

Gestural—annotations that are also easier to enter (and subsequently experience) while immersed in the virtual world.

Pictorial—annotations that can be easy to record within the experience and easy to view outside the experience.

Perhaps the ideal is to simultaneously capture a picture of the world, record a spoken annotation, and later use speech recognition software to convert the input to a text form linked to the picture, which is easy to manipulate and search.

Annotations can be attached to different components of the virtual world: locations/objects, views, time, or a combination of these.

■ Location/Object—allow comments to be made about specific items in the world.

This works well for museum or site walkthroughs. It is also how voice messaging could be implemented in a VR experience. A specific type of object would be designated as performing that task, such as the voice-holders in the *Placeholder* application (Appendix D).

- Point of View—allow comments to be made about a certain view of the virtual world.

  This can be important when trying to address aesthetic issues.

- Time—allow comments about a particular time in a simulation.

  This can be especially important in scientific visualization applications, where an interesting phenomenon occurs only during a particular time in the simulation.

- Combination—possible combinations might be to annotate a location only for a particular time of day or from a particular point of view.

Once created, the user needs to be able to see that an annotation exists and where it is in the virtual world. Thus, a representation is needed to provide information about the annotations themselves. An annotation may be signified by flagged objects that have annotations attached (e.g., changing an object's color when annotated) or by having iconic symbols in the world at the time/view or object that is annotated. A bottle icon is used by the NCSA *BayWalk* collaborative visualization application to annotate a location within a computer simulation of the Chesapeake Bay (FIG-URE 6-63A). The *Placeholder* application (Appendix D) provides specific annotation

FIGURE 6-63 (A) *The NCSA* BayWalk *Application uses the metaphor of a "message in a bottle" as a mechanism for leaving voice annotations in the virtual world. The voice annotations can be retrieved by others in the virtual world, or they can be retrieved later by the person who left the message.* **(B)** *The* Placeholder *application uses voiceholders for a similar purpose. The voiceholders change their appearance depending on their content (BayWalk application courtesy of John Shalf/NCSA; Placeholder image courtesy of Brenda Laurel).*

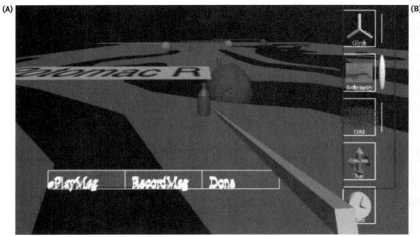
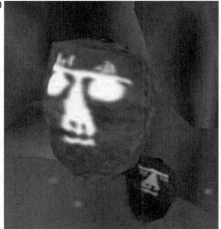

container objects. These objects (called *voiceholders*) have a specific appearance that participants recognize, and slight changes to their appearance indicate the state of the annotation (FIGURE 6-63B). In applications such as a self-guided tour (like walking through a museum), it may be assumed that all objects have an annotation, so no change is necessary to the objects' appearances.

Different annotation icons can be used within a world to indicate some information about the annotation itself. The icon can indicate the state of the annotation as with *Placeholder* (e.g., the voiceholder is full/empty/ready to accept a message). Both the type of annotation (object/time/view) and an indication of who left the annotation can be indicated by the appearance of the annotation icon. It may sometimes be desirable to search through all available annotations for particular information. Searches may be for the type, creator, or creation time of an annotation, or they may be related to the content. It may be burdensome to create an application capable of converting voice annotations into searchable text, but a feature to specify a few keywords for each annotation might be a good compromise. In their paper "The Virtual Annotation System," Harmon and colleagues [1996] describe an annotation system for a VR environment with the ability for users to annotate either objects or views, with different icons for each user and for objects and views. Annotations are manifested vocally, with the name of the user and time of creation stored with each.

Floor Control

In computer-supported collaborative work (CSCW), the notion of who is in charge of a collaborative experience is referred to as *floor control* (i.e., "Who has the floor?"). The question of who has control is only a consideration for applications that provide synchronous communication capabilities. Somewhat analogous to floor control is the issue of permissions. Permission control specifies who is allowed to affect the world in certain ways (moving objects, etc.). This is an issue for both synchronous and asynchronous communication.

The level of floor control can vary from none/simultaneous (a typical conversation between equal partners), to moderated (individuals raise their hand when they would like to speak, and the moderator calls on them when it is their turn), to very formal (Robert's Rules of Order), to hierarchical (a ranking of who can interrupt whom). Different circumstances lend themselves to different methods of control. For permission control, the simple solution may be to allow whoever got there first to have control, but in certain situations other methods may be preferable.

World Congruity

World congruity is the extent to which worlds appear the same to each participant in a shared experience. Fully congruous worlds are those in which each participant can see everything that the other participants can see. Although congruity is important for shared worlds, not all aspects of such worlds need to be consistent. This may involve how object movements are handled; for instance, when a user moves an object, the other participants may see the entire movement sequence or may just see the object "jump" from the old location to the new location. Another minor incongruity would be to have objects that can only be seen by a subset of the participants. For example, participants leave a trail of markers as they travel that only they can see.

World congruity is primarily a concern for synchronous collaborations, but not exclusively. In an asynchronous design experience, one user may keep a separate copy of their design to prevent other users from making changes or judgments on an interim design. Once the user is ready to release the design, they can make it available to all users. Applications in which users must act in concert have a necessity for a higher degree of congruity between worlds. Specifically, operations that require two or more users to lift a single object or to hand off an object from one user to another require that their worlds be kept tightly congruous—at least with respect to the specific objects and users involved. For example, the Hubble Space Telescope repair application (FIGURE 6-64) provides a means for astronauts to practice operations involving two-person tasks, such as one moving an object while the other guides it, the handoff of parts and tools to one another, and other cooperative tasks required by the mission.

Interacting with the VR System (Metacommands)

Sometimes, there is a need to interact not just with the perceptible virtual world or with others within the world, but with the underlying simulation and structure of the world. This includes a range of operations from loading in new scientific data for visualization to the control of a surrogate agent within the world. Commands that operate beneath the surface of the virtual world can be referred to as *metacommands*.

In many VR experiences, someone other than the immersed participant(s) must manipulate the world in some fashion. For example, in a therapy experience to reduce the fear of flying, the therapist may adjust the simulated flight turbulence during a session as a participant becomes able to tolerate the less difficult flight

(A)

(B)

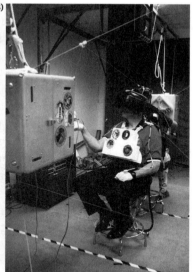

conditions. The therapist interacts via a keyboard rather than a VR interface. A more elaborate example is agent operation within the virtual world. This type of interaction is known as *surrogate agent* control or *Wizard of Oz* agent control, in reference to the film of the same name [Wilson and Rosenberg 1998]. In Georgia Tech's *Virtual Reality Gorilla Exhibit,* a zoologist familiar with gorilla society played the role of the Wizard, directing the gorillas by using keyboard controls (FIGURE 6-65).

Often VR applications designed as tools allow the physically immersed participant(s) to specify metacommands—for example, loading a different model or scientific dataset, changing global parameters, undoing a recent operation, starting the experience over, or terminating the experience program. The ability to affect the world in these ways may be regarded as reducing the mental immersiveness of the experience, so application designers with a goal of an experiential communication generally do not allow the participant to perform such operations.

One application that allows participants to directly give commands to the system is NCSA's *Virtual Director,* which has hundreds of commands available to aid in the creation of computer animation [Thiébaux 1997]. One feature of the *Crumbs* scientific visualization application is the creation of new color palettes to aid in the task of visualization. Users of the application can store and later retrieve palettes they have made using metacommands available via a menu interface.

FIGURE 6-64 **(A)** *Astronauts Story Musgrave and Jeffrey Hoffman practice removing the wide-field planetary camera (WF/PC) unit in the water tank of the Weightless Environment Training Facility (WETF) at Johnson Space Center in Houston, Texas.* **(B)** *A collaborative VR training application for the same task requires careful attention to the congruity of the world that each participant experiences. Astronaut Jerry L. Ross (in the foreground) and his colleague (directly behind) train in a VR system equipped with a haptic display for rendering the manipulation of large masses in a low-gravity environment. This system allows them to practice moving "heavy" objects together while in orbit (Images courtesy of NASA).*

Chapter Summary

To interact is to be involved in reciprocal actions between oneself and another entity. Interaction is a key feature of virtual reality, one that distinguishes it from most other media. When the virtual world responds to our actions, we become more involved with that world, increasing our sense of presence. However, most technologically mediated interaction interfaces are not natural to a human user. A poor interface can make interaction difficult, and thus interfere with a participant's ability to concentrate on the experience—be it for work or play.

FIGURE 6-65 *Gorillas in Georgia Tech's* Virtual Reality Gorilla Exhibit *behave according to a number of predefined action sequences. A gorilla behavior expert can trigger the appropriate action from a keyboard behind the scenes. This Wizard of Oz agent control conveys a realistic experience of gorilla society to the participant (Image courtesy of Don Allison).*

Over time, as people become familiar with new technology, an interface may become part of the culture and even begin to seem natural. One way to expedite this process is to build new interfaces using a metaphor with which the user is likely to be familiar. Another useful strategy that applies to interaction in general is the use of feedback to let the participant know the current state of each interaction event. These metaphors and feedback strategies work well for all forms of interaction: manipulation, navigation, collaboration, and virtual reality system commands.

Some factors that relate to user interaction in the virtual world include the venue, point of view, immersion, world physics, and the substance of the world itself. Chapter 7 will address these aspects of virtual world design and, in particular, how all of these elements work together to form the user's interactive experience.

Virtual reality experience

User interface

Hardware interface to the user

Input
- Body tracking
  (How the computer "sees" the user)
- Voice/sound recognition
  (How the computer "hears" the user)
- Physical controllers
  (How the computer "feels" the user)

Chapter 3

Output
- Visual display
  (How the user sees the VW)
- Aural display
  (How the user hears the VW)
- Haptic display
  (How the user feels the VW)

Chapter 4

Software components

System presentation to the user
- Representation
- Rendering system

Chapter 5

User interaction with the virtual world
- Manipulation
- Navigation
- Shared Experience

Chapter 6

Experience design
Chapter 8

Virtual world
- Immersion
- Point of view
- Venue
- Simulation/physics
- Objects/denizens

Chapter 7

Life experience
- Memory
- Ability
- Past experience
- Emotional state
- Cultural background

Chapter 8

The Virtual Reality Experience

This chapter is about the *experience* of virtual reality. We take a look at the elements that make a successful experience, including mental immersion, physical immersion, and the effect of the presentation venue on the experience. Then we examine the actual components of the world that are available to help shape the experience: What point of view is chosen? Is the user seeing the world as a bug in the grass? A bat in the sky? Or watching their own avatar battle a pirate? We must also consider the physical laws that shape the world: Can you pass through a solid wall? Do heavy objects float in the air? And then there is the substance of the world to think about, its geography, objects, avatars, and the user interface created to access them. We have expressed throughout the book the importance of content in the medium of virtual reality. In this chapter, we will identify the elements of content and briefly discuss them in relationship to each other and to VR applications. There are many different media through which to present virtual worlds; in this chapter, we will focus on how those worlds can be designed for virtual reality.

Immersion

You may recall from Chapter 1 that there are two kinds of immersion. We refer to either mental immersion or physical (sensory) immersion. Much of this chapter focuses on the participant's personal experience with a VR world, and immersion of both types play an important part in creating a successful experience. In this section, we will discuss both aspects of immersion, beginning with the physical.

Physical/Sensory Immersion

Physical immersion is undeniably an important aspect of a virtual reality experience (and system). Indeed, physical immersion is part of our definition of virtual reality and is the element that distinguishes VR from other media.

Physical immersion is accomplished by presenting a virtual world to users based on their location and orientation and providing synthetic stimuli to one or more of their senses in response to their position and actions. The VR system presents perspective-dependent images to each eye, synchronized audio to the ears, and haptic information to the body. The computer "knows" where the user is by *tracking* them.

When the user moves, the visual, auditory, haptic, and other qualities that establish physical immersion in the scene change in response. If they walk closer to an object, it appears bigger, it sounds louder, and they can touch and feel it. When the user turns their head to the right, they can see what is there and react accordingly. If they grab an object, they can manipulate it—turn it around, pick it up, modify it.

In providing synthetic stimuli to the body's senses, virtual reality systems often block out the stimuli provided by the real world. Thus, the participant's mental immersion in the real world is reduced. The extent to which a particular VR experience overrides the natural stimuli with synthetic stimuli and the number of senses that are *fooled* in this way sets the level of physical immersion. This degree of physical immersion does have some effect on *mental* immersion, but there are other influences on mental immersion that are relevant to all virtual world communications.

Mental Immersion

The degree to which mental immersion is desirable for a particular experience varies based on the goals of the experience. If the experience is designed for entertainment purposes and its success is based on how engrossed the participant becomes—thereby wanting to play it more and tell friends about it—mental immersion plays a key role in the experience's fulfillment. Other virtual worlds, such as those described in novels, also depend heavily on mental immersion.

For many applications, however, the goal is to explore information, and a high level of mental immersion may not be necessary, possible, or even desirable. For example, a scientist examining the molecular structure of a protein probably won't believe they are standing next to an actual molecule; in fact, they do not need to believe this for the VR experience to be useful. However, if the experience were of a rollercoaster ride, the participant might lose track of the fact that they are, in reality, standing on an unmoving floor. Certainly in this case, the more mentally immersed the participant becomes, the better the value of their experience.

Effective immersion can be a tool in the communication process. In a fictional work, lack of mental immersion could be viewed as a communication failure.

By contrast, in a documentary piece, information can still be communicated even if the work is not very immersive, although it might not be as effective in causing viewers to modify their behavior or beliefs.

Thus, while mental immersion in virtual reality experiences is often desirable and sometimes critical, its absence does not mean the experience is not VR. But it is important in either case not to be distracted by slow system response and equipment interference. Additionally, in the molecule example, an element of immersion would include trustworthiness of the model; the suspension of disbelief still needs to be engaged. To take an example at perhaps the opposite extreme, a documentary work can certainly be as engaging and immersive as any work of fiction. Immersion denotes a level of engagement, and engagement is a mark of how successful the communication of a virtual world is. It follows, then, that immersion in some form or another is important as an indicator of successful communication.

The Role of Realism in Immersion

A realistic display that includes sight, sound, and touch within an environment can greatly influence the level of mental immersion experienced by the participant. There are two schools of thought on what can and cannot be done in a "realistic" immersive environment. One school states that the experience must be extremely realistic for it to be immersive. This excludes anything *magical* from taking place. This means the ability to point to fly or shrink to molecular size will break the illusion of feeling present in some other place; that is, it excludes anything that demonstrates that you are not in the real world [Astheimer et al. 1994].

The other school allows for magical properties to exist as part of immersive virtual experiences. In fact, it suggests that these magical properties can help the user to be taken away to another world [Slater and Usoh 1994]. The magical elements of an experience include rendering properties, like having a cartoon-like look, and interface properties, such as the ability to fly by pointing a finger. The cartoonishness can allow participants to enter a dream or fantasy state of mind in which anything can happen. Conversely, attempting to render a world in a photo-realistic way can make mental immersion difficult, because any flaw in the realism will spoil the effect.

Psychologists researching the use of VR as a means of phobia treatment have found that the cartoonishness of a world does not prevent engagement in the world. It's been found that the heart rate, perspiration, and respiration rate of patients all respond the same when the patient encounters a cartoon representation of the object they fear in VR as when they encounter the real thing [Rothbaum et al. 1996]. In fact, the cartoonish representation may help to make the therapy more effective by making it seem more approachable.

Of course, there are other factors that affect the degree of realism. The effect of stereoscopic display, for instance, may or may not enhance the realism. If the objects in the world are always presented at a great distance, then only minor depth cues are noticeable by stereopsis. Accurate reproduction of sonic cues, such as reverberation, may enhance realism or may not be a factor (e.g., if the user is on a wide open prairie). As usual, each situation dictates specific requirements for realistic display.

Components of Immersion

In a virtual reality experience, there must be at least some degree of sensory immersion. How much sensory immersion is required to induce mental immersion is still an open question and one that is the focus of current research. What are the necessary components for a user to feel as if they were immersed in the environment and believe that they were actually interacting with the virtual world? In the rest of this section, we'll discuss the content itself, the user's life experience and attitudes, interactivity, and the technological requirements of the display as components of immersion.

Our definition of mental immersion is that the participant is engaged to the point of suspending disbelief in what they are experiencing. Given a compelling presentation, this can be caused by the content of a medium alone. Physical immersion is not necessary when reading a novel, nor is it desired.

Many factors come together in creating the VR experience, and a particular confluence of factors can persuade the participant of the existence of the world. The first of these factors is that the world has to be personally meaningful. If the participant does not find the topic or style in which the content is conveyed absorbing, there is little hope of engagement. A particular point of view from which the world is presented (e.g., first person) might be more effective than another. The amount of suspense in a narrative might heighten the participant's relationship with a protagonist. A participant's mental willingness to believe combines with the other factors to put the person in the world . . . or not.

Interactivity is an element brought to various media through computer technology. After all, if the content were not interactive, then it could generally be presented in some strictly linear medium. However, like some real-world experiences, interactivity may be limited in some respects. A rollercoaster experience is pure sensory input, with no physical interactivity between the ride and the rider, other than the rider's ability to look around by moving their head. In virtual reality, the onus of creating an experience sufficient to allow the participant to achieve mental immersion lies not just with the application's content, but also with the capability of the VR system. A few display qualities that have an impact on immersion include resolution, lag, and field of regard.

Low resolution of one or more of the display modalities (either spatially or temporally) can also result in reduction, or loss, of immersion. Spatial resolution is how much information is presented in a single "image." Each sensory display has its own measurement format: visually we may refer to pixels per inch; sonically to bits per sample or the number of independent channels displayed. Temporal resolution is how fast the display is able to change in terms of the *frame rate,* or sample rate. Again, each sense has a particular range of acceptable rates. The desired rate for each sense is the point at which the brain switches from perceiving several discrete sensory inputs to perceiving continuous input.

Another important factor in providing mental immersion is the amount of sensory coverage. This includes both how many of the sense displays are presented to the user and how much of each particular sense is covered. In the visual sense, the field of regard and field of view of a particular VR system may have variable coverage depending on the particulars of the display hardware.

Probably the most important technological factor that must be addressed for mental immersion is the amount of time between a user's action and the appropriate response by the system—the *lag time*. Each component of the virtual reality system adds to the amount of lag, or *latency*. High latency between an action and its reaction causes several problems for the user. The most problematic is nausea (a not uncommon symptom of simulator sickness). There can also be difficulty dealing with interfaces that rely on body motion to interact with virtual controls.

Transference of Object Permanence

Like young children who don't completely learn the concept of *object permanence* in the real world until the age of 18 months, people entering a virtual world for the first time may have difficulty "believing" in the permanence of objects there. The addition of multiple senses corroborating the existence of an object in the world increases the believability of that object and, by extension, of the world itself.

Developers of virtual reality experiences can take advantage of the *sensory carryover* to increase the impression of realness of the world. This works both to increase the realism of particular objects in the world and of the world as a whole. The more realistic an individual object seems, the more the user will expect it to behave naturally. Adding more sensory displays, such as sound or touch, will likewise increase an object's realism. One way to enhance realism is to make the sonic aspect of an object follow that object through the virtual space—even when it is no longer in view of the participant. The result is that the participant "realizes" that the object has a property of *permanency* [Snoddy 1996].

Likewise, the realism of the world as a whole can be dramatically improved when *some* of the objects are sensorially enhanced. So, when a user encounters one object that seems *very* real to them, the "reality" of the other objects in the world will probably also increase. This can be very useful in helping participants overcome an initial barrier to suspending their disbelief. Thus, participants' expectation of realness becomes heightened, and they begin to trust the world as it is represented without testing it.

Since the haptic sense is very difficult to fool, haptic feedback that corroborates other sensory input can be even more effective. Hunter Hoffman [1998] has taken advantage of this phenomenon by using a simple haptic display to achieve enhanced suspension of disbelief in participants. In his work at the University of Washington Human Interface Technology (HIT) Lab, he mounts a tracker device on a physical dinner plate to produce a (passive) haptic display. The tracker on the real plate is linked to a plate representation in the virtual world. When a user is given the virtual plate and finds that it possesses all the properties of the real counterpart, they are more apt to extend their conception of realness to the rest of the virtual world. This *transference of object permanence* can increase the user's suspension of disbelief to the degree that they won't attempt to walk through a wall and, thus, never discover that the walls are not as fully represented as the plate.

Hoffman takes advantage of this transference in his work on phobia exposure treatment using virtual reality. By increasing the participant's level of immersion, exposure to their object of fear may seem just as real as the real thing and thus increase the effectiveness of the therapy. Hoffman's use of the dinner plate is an example of *passive haptics*.

Recall from Chapter 4 the technique of *passive haptics,* where real objects are used only for their physical properties to convey information about the virtual world. These passive haptic displays do not generate any active forces that react to participant input. More elaborate experiments on transference of object permanence using *passive haptics* have been carried out at the University of North Carolina at

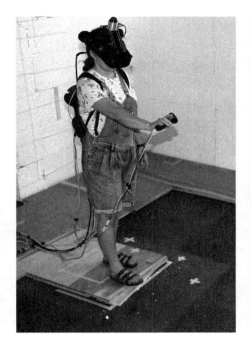 

FIGURE 7-1 *In this image, the participant is given haptic cues about the virtual world using passive objects like plywood to produce a 3-inch ledge and Styrofoam and foamcore to haptically represent brick and stone walls. In her head-mounted display, this partici-pant sees a drop-off of about one story in height. Because she is standing on a surface with an edge, she can feel with her toes that there is indeed a drop-off at this point. Because she is seeing the full story drop off and does not feel the floor at the edge, she is likely to believe that she is indeed standing at the edge of a one-story drop-off (Images cour-tesy of the University of North Carolina at Chapel Hill). See color plate 21.*

Chapel Hill. In research to produce more effective virtual environments, researchers there have used Styrofoam, foamcore, and plywood located coincidentally with visual representations of walls and surfaces in the virtual world to physically mimic a portion of a virtual world (FIGURE 7-1). Thus, as the subjects see a virtual surface, and they reach out and touch it, they can feel the foamcore or plywood in the proper location. The researchers measured the participants' sense of presence by adminis-tering physiological tests; measuring physiological responses such as heart rate, res-piration rate, and other factors; and surveying the subjects on their subjective assessment of how immersed they felt [Insko et al. 2001].

Levels of Immersion

For many VR experiences, full mental immersion is not necessarily required for the application to be useful. Recall that in general scientists visualizing their data do not believe they are standing next to a molecule or looking at the universe from the outside. However, they are often able to make observations about the virtual worlds that represent their data and translate these perceptions to useful insights.

Although there is currently no widely accepted standard measure for mental immersion, it is useful to assign some range for *level of immersion* or *depth of presence* for the purposes of discussion [Slater and Usoh 1993]. Here are some possible rungs on that continuum:

1. **None whatsoever:** The user feels only that they are connected to a computer.

2. **Minor acceptance:** The user believes in certain aspects of the environment. Perhaps they feel as though objects from the virtual world are floating in the user's space, but they do not feel part of the virtual world.

3. **Engaged:** The user doesn't think about the real world. They are concentrating on their interactions with the virtual world. If asked, though, they would be able to distinguish between the real and virtual worlds and would indicate that they are in the real world.

4. **Full mental immersion:** The user feels completely a part of the environment presented via the VR system, perhaps to the point of forgetting they are tethered to a computer and becoming startled when they suddenly encounter the "end of the tether."

There are indicators that can help us qualitatively gauge how immersed a participant is within an experience. One obvious method is to ask the participant. The participant can offer *some* indication of how deeply they were immersed in a virtual world. Questionnaires designed to separate the various parts of an experience are often given to subjects as a means to determine their level of mental immersion and what aspects of the world may have contributed to their impression. Questionnaires cannot be utilized in isolation, though. It is probably a more useful technique to observe the participant while they are involved with the virtual world. Certain reflex behaviors can also indicate the degree to which the participant is immersed. For example, if a (virtual) object flies toward the participant and the participant ducks, this is an indication that they were more fully engaged than if they just stood there and let the object fly "through" their head.

Sometimes a participant's behavior contradicts their verbal assessment. For example, in an informal setting at the University of North Carolina, researchers placed a guest in a virtual kitchen. When the participant was asked if he felt immersed in the world, his response was "no." They then asked him to get down on his hands and knees to judge the height of the countertop relative to the stove. Now, when asked to stand back up, he reached for the virtual counter to help himself up (to no avail, of course) [Bishop 2002].

Although these indicators can help us qualitatively gauge level of immersion, they are no substitute for a rigorous, quantitative measure of immersion. Despite the challenges, some effort has been made to quantify the mental immersion of participants in a VR experience. In particular, Slater and Usoh [1994] measured "presence" in the two ways mentioned: physical reactions to the virtual experience (e.g., danger avoidance) and post-experience questionnaires. These measures were used to analyze the relationship between various virtual world features and mental immersion. Writings by the subjects were examined to determine which sense was dominant for each participant. The researchers looked at what kinds of words were used to describe things.

Some people wrote with a visual (I see . . .) bent, whereas others were more sound dominant (I hear . . .) and others more haptically biased (I feel . . .). Clear relationships between word usage and sensory dominance were discovered. For example, some people are visual learners: they need to see a demonstration. Others are auditory listeners: they need to be told what to do or listen to a lecture. Some people are haptically dominant: they need to actually do something to learn it. Thus the researchers found that depth of immersion is related to the subjects' innate sensory dominance and the type of feedback given in the VR world. If two people, one visually dominant and the other aurally dominant, experience the same VR application, they will likely experience different levels of immersion. For applications focused on visual feedback, the visually oriented person will be more immersed than the auditory oriented person. In a virtual world without sound, aurally dominant subjects were less immersed. For kinesthetically oriented subjects, use of an avatar in the virtual world resulted in higher immersion.

Perhaps the best measure of presence will come from the use of physiological response monitoring. Research on these noncognitive measures of a person's emotional state is increasing. This research is important, because it will offer a more objective mechanism for measuring immersion than relying on a subject's verbal testimony (which has been shown to disagree with what external observers and other measurements record).

Point of View

Content creators in all types of media have at their disposal a variety of literary devices to help them manipulate how their creation will be experienced. One of these devices is the perspective from which the world is perceived, otherwise known as the *point of view (POV)*. There are three points of view from which a situation can be relayed to the communication recipient. The *first person POV* views a world through one's own eyes; *second person* views the world from near the action, such that the reader/viewer/participant shares the same space as the main character; and *third person* views the world from a totally independent viewpoint, which is how desktop interactive graphics are generally viewed.

All of the visual display paradigms can operate with any point of view; however, some combinations are more common than others. Certainly first person POV is the most common, but there is a class of stationary-screen visual displays that frequently use the second person point of view.

First Person POV

First person POV is participating in the world from your own viewpoint. In English prose, the pronoun *I* represents the first person singular form of speech. In motion pictures, adopting a first person POV, the camera (and thus the audience) views the action through the eyes of the character. In virtual reality, the visual display follows the participant's motions; if they look left, they see what's to their left in the world. This is the typical point of view used in most VR experiences.

In VR, the view of the world may be presented from the perspective of another entity. For instance, we might be an insect, where everyday objects take on a whole new scale. Or, we might be the cue ball in a game of pool, as implemented in the arcade application *Cue View* by Virtual Oddesey (FIGURE 7-2). Telepresence applications, where the movement of the user is tracked and the viewpoint changed accordingly, is also a first person experience, from the perspective of some remotely located equipment.

Second Person POV

Once again referring to Webster's, in prose, the *second person* POV is where the speaker or narrator is talking to you and you are a character in the story. In the display of spatial information, the use of second person means that you, as the user, can see yourself or some representation of yourself in the world—sort of an "out of body experience." For example, by adding an avatar of the user to a map signifying

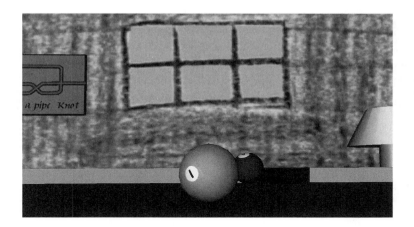

FIGURE 7-2 *This image alludes to the VR application* Cue View, *in which the participant experiences the world from the point of view of a cue ball in a game of billiards.*

their current location, the map is transformed from a third person to a second person POV display. An application designed for a first person POV may include third person POV elements, such as a regular map. While viewing the world from their own perspective, a participant can look to the map to see an icon indicating their position in the world.

There is an entire class of VR systems that rely on the use of second person display for interaction with the world. These systems generally use projection-based displays and track the user with video cameras. The user's image is then placed within the scene, and they watch themselves as they move about. The primary examples of this method are Myron Krueger's *Video Place* and the *Mandala* system discussed in Chapter 4 (FIGURE 7-3).

Another method of second person display is to "tether" the view to the position above and behind where the user is situated (the *wingman view*). The participant can still move wherever the application allows them to move, they just see from behind their avatar. The advantage over regular first person POV is that the participant can more easily see what is happening around them, that is, more of the world can be seen. The user knows where they are in the world, because they can see their avatar in its surroundings. An example would be an application where the participant is training to be a race car driver. From the first person point of view they can see only what they would see if driving the race car. By adopting the wingman view, they can see their own car in the pack of racers. This allows them to get a feel for the herd of cars and where they fit into the herd. Of course, they must then learn to understand where they are in the herd from only a first person point of view for the actual race.

FIGURE 7-3 **(A)** Mandala *second person experiences allow the participant to see themselves interacting in a virtual world.* **(B)** *An example of some of the pioneering work done by Myron Krueger (Images courtesy of The Vivid Group and Myron Krueger, respectively).*

Third Person POV

Third person POV is one in which the user is not part of the action taking place in the world. This is a typical method for presenting worlds in motion pictures and novels—from a distant or even omniscient vantage point. As mentioned earlier, most non-immersive computer graphics are from this perspective, even if the user can interact with the software by changing the vantage point using keyboard or mouse. Since the third person view is entirely unassociated with a participant's location within the environment itself, it is not a form of physically immersed display; that is, it is not virtual reality.

Inside-out versus Outside-in

Another way of describing different points of view is as inside-out versus outside-in. This can be thought of as whether one is seeing the world from within, or whether the world is perceived from an external vantage point [Wickens and Hollands 2000]. An example of an inside-out view would be piloting an airplane. The pilot is within the cockpit and sees the world through the windows of the airplane. Conversely, piloting a radio-controlled model aircraft is typically done from an outside-in perspective. The choice determines the pilot's frame of reference and affects the way in which the pilot perceives the world and controls the plane (see FIGURE 1-11).

Choosing an inside-out or outside-in viewpoint depends on the task and on whether it is more important to see an overall global picture or the internal details of the object of interest. Even when exploring scientific datasets, it is sometimes advantageous to use an outside-in view to gain a feel for the overall system, and then shift to an inside-out point of view to get a sense of what is happening to a particular component of that system. An inside-out point of view often leads to a greater sense of presence in the virtual world; but like walking through a forest, one can easily become lost without something to provide location cues.

Even when emulating a real-world environment that is typically experienced inside-out, it can be advantageous to offer an outside-in point of view. For example, an architect may utilize an inside-out view of a building to get a feel for the emotional impact of walking through the hallways, the mood of the lighting, and so on, but still refer to an overall view for the efficiency of the design from an outside-in perspective.

When switching from the inside-out view to a momentary outside-in view, it is important to maintain visual continuity. In other words, there must be some cue that relates the view from within to the outside view and vice versa. This cue may be a line that connects the current view to the normal view or a gradual shift from the normal view to the current (temporary) view.

Venue

The venue, or setting in which the VR system resides, can have a great impact on how an event is experienced. There are a number of ways in which the venue affects VR application design, including those that pose constraints on the technology, such as the ability to subdue lighting or affect the way in which the experience is perceived. *Officer of the Deck* offers an example in which venue is particularly important. This application was designed to be used on a submarine, an environment that constrains the available space and contains sufficient metal to negatively affect electromagnetic tracking systems. To take another example, part of the experience of going to a haunted house is the setting in which the house is placed and the way in which it is entered (and the fact that it's dark inside!). Likewise in VR experiences, the setting can affect the experience. For example, a VR application experienced in a therapist's office will be perceived differently than the same application presented as a game in an arcade. Venue also plays a significant role in how complex the interface can be, based on whether it will be used in a public or a private venue (and also whether a public venue has docents on hand to help people with the experience). Possible venues where VR has and will increasingly appear include

- Home
- Work
- Museum
- Arcade
- Liquor/grocery store
- Trade show
- Product showroom
- Classroom
- School district facility
- Outdoors
- Submarine
- Corporate meeting room
- Rehabilitation/exercise facility
- Theme park

As the venue can have an effect on the VR experience, so the experience itself can affect the choice of venue. The goal of the experience influences whether the venue or the VR system will dictate the experience. For example, if the goal is to find good educational applications, should one consider only what is now affordable in the classroom? Or should one build good applications now, knowing the technology will become less expensive, allowing higher quality experiences to be brought to students in the near future?

The requirements of the VR system also affect the venues to which an experience can be taken. Many times, an interesting application might be solicited for display in a different venue. Depending on the original venue's type of display and the logistics of the situation, such a transference may or may not be possible. For example, an application designed for a projection-based visual display (e.g., the *CAVE*) might be difficult to move to another venue due to space and lighting requirements.

How the Venue Shapes the VR Experience

In most circumstances, a VR experience will be designed and created for a particular venue or class of venues. There are many practical aspects of system design that need to be taken into consideration based on the expected venue. Of course, an application might wind up placed in a venue for which it was not designed. However, this should not be a major consideration during design, except to plan options that might make the experience work better in an alternate site.

The space available (or cost of the space) will affect the types of VR display paradigms that will fit and the number of participants that can be handled simultaneously. If the system is to be placed in a public space, then the ruggedness of the equipment and cost of maintenance are crucial issues that may restrict what types of interface devices are practical. A data glove, for example, is more fragile than a handheld device with buttons. The expense of various components of the system will also be considerations when choosing what hardware and software to use in public versus private venues.

Time is another variable for determining the acceptability of a particular type of venue. The time an average participant will be immersed has a major impact on the design of the virtual environment and can range from just a couple of minutes in a public space with heavy throughput to many hours in a private research facility, where large blocks of time can be reserved. For venues where prior user exposure to VR will be low and throughput high, the interaction will need to be very simple and easy to learn. Participants waiting for the experience can be given some basic instructions while others are in the experience (and when done well, the learning while waiting can be integrated as a part of the whole experience).

One example of including instructions as part of the experience is the *Magic Edge* dogfighting venue, in which much of the time involved in the overall experience is the briefing and debriefing sessions that bookend the actual time in the simulator. While these are taking place, another group of players can make use of the equipment. Another example is the *Nessy's Egg* location-based entertainment (LBE) application at the Nautilus Science Center in Virginia Beach, Virginia, which has brief/debrief sessions and uses two room displays that switch the real-time graphics hardware from one room to another. As participants enter and exit, prerendered graphics are displayed to the noninteracting room. Often these venues present the current session on monitors outside, where waiting participants glean some idea of what to do and expect from watching the actions of those who go before them. For applications where a good portion of time can be devoted to using the VR system, learning can take place while immersed in the environment.

Venue-imposed time limitations also play a role in the available throughput. If there are not enough stations for everyone to have immersive interaction with the virtual world, then a display that allows those not selected to view the world is needed and must provide enough information to see what is happening in the world. It should be interesting to the onlookers, too! A scenario adopted by the Sapporo Beer Museum, at the Sapporo Brewery in Tokyo, allows one participant using a *BOOM* display to look around the environment while a dozen other viewers watch in nickelodeon-style, stereoscopic PUSH displays (FIGURE 7-4; see also FIGURE 4-20).

How the Venue Shapes the Participatory Experience

The venue itself will shape the way a participant experiences the virtual environment. If the same VR system and application are placed in two different venues, such as an entertainment arcade versus the Guggenheim Museum, there will be a significant difference in the way the experience is perceived. Because the experience is so affected by the state of mind of the participant, anything that affects the participant's subconscious mind may affect how the experience is perceived. For example, when in the Guggenheim, the participant may be in a more serious state of mind than when they are at an arcade. In the museum, they may be less likely to append graffiti to a work of art, even if it were presented as an option; whereas, they may go all out marking up artwork in the same experience placed in an arcade. While the VR system and software are the same, participants may have a very different experience in each venue. One might be thrilling, whereas the other might be frightening. Then, too, an

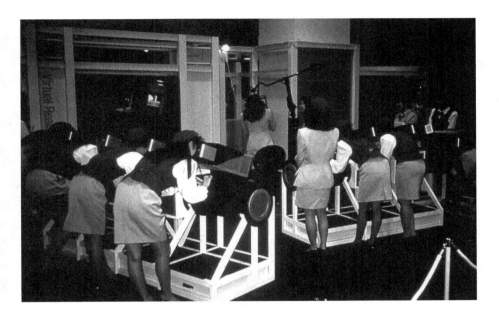

FIGURE 7-4 *At the Sapporo Beer Museum in Tokyo, visitors have the chance to tour a virtual world that explains the beer-making process. In this experience, created by Telepresence, Inc., one visitor controls the experience using a BOOM (center), while many others can follow along through nickelodeon-style stereoscopic viewers (Image courtesy of Scott Fisher).*

individual may experience the same application in the same venue differently on different days.

The location can also affect the credibility of the experience. For example, an application that has the goal of teaching adults about the health effects of smoking cigarettes would be perceived differently if housed in an arcade versus in a laboratory of the National Institute of Health or at a carnival display sponsored by a cigarette manufacturer. A primary effect of venue is the state of mind it puts the participant in when entering the virtual environment. Benjamin Britton, developer of *The VR Cave of Lascaux* experience, speaks of the entire script of events that occur leading up to participating in the VR experience. In the case of his application, the script includes putting on one's coat, driving among the other inhabitants of the town, finding a place to park, rubbing shoulders with other patrons of the museum, viewing/taking part in the experience, relating and sharing one's participatory experience with others, and finally returning home. The script and the participant's frame of mind will be vastly different for virtual worlds experienced at locations such as Disney World, a local liquor store, the research lab down the hall, or one's office (FIGURE 7-5).

In addition to the locations of a VR system, the way in which the venue is adorned affects how one approaches the experience. Does the setting add a sense

FIGURE 7-5 *The venue, or setting, in which VR experiences are placed can contribute a great deal to the overall experience, particularly for entertainment applications.* (A) *Here, the immersed user is engaged in an experience associated with the product being marketed, Cutty Sark Scots Whisky.* (B) *A darkly lit, cavernous space with few adornments suggests a mysterious, otherworldly mood for the* Placeholder *experience. See color plate 22.*

(C) *While the Illinois State Capitol building seems an unlikely place to find a VR display, its presence indicates politicians' interest in discovering the role of virtual reality in serving the public good. See color plate 23. (Photographs and images courtesy of David Polinchock, Brenda Laurel, and William Sherman, respectively).*

of mystery or adventure? For example, an early adopter of the Virtuality PLC arcade system installed a set of four units for a cooperative exploration experience in the style of the popular *Dungeons and Dragons* role-playing game. As part of the venue, the ring platforms were presented in a wooded setting to help create the atmosphere of a medieval English forest (FIGURE 7-6).

All things considered, venue is a very important element of a VR system and should

FIGURE 7-6 *The* Legend Quest *experience is an example of placing an entertainment VR application in an elaborate setting to contribute to the overall mood (Image courtesy of Virtuality Group plc). See color plate 24.*

not be taken lightly or ignored by the application designer. Changing venues might give more people the opportunity to visit a virtual world, but their experience will not be quite what it would be if experienced in the venue for which it was designed.

Rules of the Virtual World: Physics

Objects in the virtual world can contain descriptions of how they interact with each other and the environment at large. Those interactions are described by the *laws of nature,* or *physics,* of the virtual world. The designer can choose to model physical reality or an imaginary world.

Whether the laws are explicitly stated or not, they do exist. That is, the absence of a law governing a certain situation is indeed a law. For example, if there is no stated law of gravity, the law is by default: Objects do not fall. If there is no stated law regarding collisions, the law is Objects never collide; they just pass through one another.

Virtual world physics covers the behavior of objects in space and time. Our discussion of virtual world physics covers various schools of physics, simulation types, collision detection between objects, and the persistence of the world.

Types of Virtual World Physics

There are several common motifs of virtual reality world physics. These include

- The static world
- Cartoon physics
- Newtonian physics
- Aristotelian physics
- Choreographed physics
- Other world physics

The Static World

A *static world* is one in which there are no world physics programmed into the environment. The world consists of fixed objects that the participant has to maneuver around. Many architectural walkthrough applications are of this variety, allowing participants to explore the design of a building or other space but not to manipulate or otherwise interact with it in any way.

Cartoon Physics

Cartoon physics are those that follow or resemble the way things tend to work in many animated films. For instance: "Any body suspended in space will remain in space until made aware of its situation" or "Certain bodies can pass through solid walls painted to resemble tunnel entrances; others cannot" [O'Donnell 1980]. This could be implemented in a VR experience by allowing participants constrained to following terrain to walk off the ledges, applying the terrain-following constraint only when they look down. Of course, even then, gravity doesn't apply for characters who "haven't studied law" (FIGURE 7-7).

Not all VR cartoon physics are as complicated as these examples. A simpler example might be that objects can be picked up and placed anywhere in space without falling or otherwise being displaced. In the *Crumbs* (Appendix B) visualization tool, objects simply hang in space where the user places them. The user may pick them up again to move them or move them into the trash can icon.

Newtonian Physics

Newtonian physics are a good approximation for replicating most circumstances in our physical world. On Earth or in virtual worlds using Newtonian physics, objects fall at 9.8 m/s/s (meters per second per second are the metric units for acceleration).

FIGURE 7-7 *In a virtual world, the laws of nature need not mimic those of the physical world. Like cartoons, entities can behave according to different sets of rules. So, some participants might wonder how another entity accomplishes what seems to them to be an impossible feat. In this case, the agent can soar above other participants due to lack of knowledge about the rules of the virtual world. See color plate 25.*

FIGURE 7-8 NewtonWorld *is an application of the* ScienceSpace *project developed by the University of Houston and George Mason University. It is designed to teach students the concepts of Newtonian physics by allowing them to experience the effects of Newton's laws firsthand. In this image, the student learns about the relationship between kinetic and potential energy. The amount of kinetic energy contained in a ball is visually represented by the amount of compression of the spring attached to the ball (Image courtesy of Bowen Loftin).*

In addition, object collisions transfer momentum from one object to another. Thus, a billiard ball simulation would act as most people would expect, based on their experience with real billiard balls.

The *ScienceSpace* project's *NewtonWorld* application is designed to teach Newtonian mechanics to the participant (FIGURE 7-8). Another example is the Caterpillar Inc. *Virtual Prototyping System,* where a certain degree of real-world emulation is important (FIGURE 7-9). Tractor design engineers create very realistic models of machine systems and their interactions with the ground. Because of the real-time performance needs, a simplified version of Newtonian mechanics is modeled.

Aristotelian Physics

Aristotle also described a set of "rules of nature" based on his observations. His system is less accurate than Newton's, but is often the way people think things work. Consequently, simulations that reflect *Aristotelian physics* may look more natural to many people. For instance, a cannonball fired from a cannon flies in a straight line for a certain distance and then falls straight down to the ground.

FIGURE 7-9 *Because a certain degree of realism is a goal of Caterpillar Inc. VR experiences, their applications are built based on simplified Newtonian physics (Image courtesy of Caterpillar Inc).*

Choreographed Physics

Choreographed physics are laws of nature that consist of preprogrammed (animated) actions chosen by the experience designer. The system is provided with a list of instructions of what to do in each circumstance. Or, the script can dictate that the ball fly in a way that *looks* as if it were behaving according to the laws of physics. As with Aristotelian physics, *choreographed physics* are often used because they can look natural to many people. If a virtual world brick wall crumbled, a Newtonian simulation may be fairly accurate, but may not look as natural as the event portrayed by animators. This may require more up-front effort on the part of the experience creators. Rather than creating a simulation algorithm that handles how the world works under any circumstances, all possible events must now be hand choreographed a priori. The upside is that the real-time simulation of choreographed experiences require less computational resources.

Disney's *Aladdin's Magic Carpet Ride* VR experience uses choreographed physics for most events that take place during the participant's encounter. The *Aladdin* design team felt that a complete world simulation using real physics was impossible (e.g., the movement of individual leaves in the wind), and the world would not look "real" anyway if produced in this way [Snoddy 1996]. Thus, many actions were choreographed, such as the opening of the *Cave of Wonders* and each character's behavior.

Other World Physics

There are other types of physical laws that can be simulated, as well. These laws govern the world at a level beyond our everyday perception. They operate at either a macro or micro scale that Newtonian physics don't adequately describe. Some examples are subatomic particle interactions and relativity theory. These laws are generally in the same vein as the Newtonian model, in which the physics of an observed phenomenon are translated into a computer algorithm to calculate the state of the world over time. Many experiences that intend to replicate the scientific understanding of some phenomenon in the universe are included in this category. These physics simulations must focus on the forces that have the greatest effect at that scale—just as real-world models focus on the forces that have the greatest effect on our world (gravity, properties of light, etc.).

User Interaction with the World Physics

In some applications, the user is allowed to interact with the simulation and modify the laws governing the world. This is typical in many scientific and industrial applications. For example, an ecologist might learn much about the physical world by modifying rules in a virtual world and observing the results of those changes. It is up to the application designer to determine if, and to what extent, the participant is allowed to alter the underlying nature of the world.

Just as these laws of nature govern the objects in the virtual world, so too might the user also be subject to them, although not necessarily. In fact, each object in the world can be treated by its own set of independent laws of nature. The object that represents the user can be treated the same as all other objects, as a member of one class of objects, or entirely separately. Most VR travel schemes have a set of controls that treat the user differently from all other objects in the world.

It is entirely plausible that objects will descend until they come to rest on some surface (another object or terrain), whereas the user can travel in any direction and, when not traveling, remain floating in space. For an oceanographic flow scientific visualization, a scientist may want to observe from a static point of view rather than being swept away by the virtual current.

Simulation/Mathematical Model

Many of the virtual world physics described need to be realized in a virtual reality system through some kind of mathematical model. A mathematical model is a set of equations that describes the possible actions that can take place in the virtual world and when they can occur. The mathematical model is the enforcer of the laws of nature in the virtual world and provides the source of the world physics. These models can sometimes be very complex, and the computations require very fast computers in order to be executed in real time.

Computational scientists also use mathematical models to describe the physical world (universe) in which we exist. This fact can be exploited when using the computer to create virtual worlds. Mathematical formulae can be used to create a virtual object's visual properties (e.g., shape and color), physical properties (e.g., mass), and the laws of nature that govern its behavior (e.g., gravity). Whenever models are based on real-world physical laws, a number of benefits are achieved automatically. For example, if the visual properties of objects are described using real-world optics equations, and the behavior of light and the properties of the materials are all described by the mathematical model, then effects such as shadows, spectral highlights, and correct color interactions between colored lights and objects all happen without further intervention by the VR application programmer. Computational scientists are doing a better job at simulating parts of the real world, and if such computations can be calculated fast enough, then they can be used to help create a more realistic, interactive world, because the virtual world can be governed by the natural laws of (real-world) physics.

Object Co-Interaction

Another feature of home-brewed physics is that the implementer can choose not only what type of physics will affect each object in the world, but also whether those "physical interactions" will work independently or codependently. In other words, is each of the objects in a world of its own, or can it affect the other objects?

As an illustration, a simple cartoon physics world allows the user to pick up a flower or rock. Upon release, the object will fall to the ground. The object can be programmed to stop either when it comes in contact with any object below it or only when it reaches the ground. Or, in a world filled with "rubber" balls, the balls might bounce off all the room surfaces but not off one another.

There are three fundamental reasons why one may choose to create objects that do not interact: artistic expression, difficulty of implementation, and limited computational resources. The latter is often the reason why a "physical" property such as collision interaction is not fully implemented on all objects in larger virtual worlds. It takes a huge amount of resources to monitor and react to all possible ways that an object can collide in a fully realized virtual world. In anything but the very simplest virtual worlds, the computational requirements to determine whether there is a collision between any two objects can be prohibitively expensive. As a result, most virtual worlds have a constrained set of collisions to which the simulation attends. In the previous flower example, the only collisions detected are those between the floor and all movable objects. A flower falling toward the floor will collide with the floor but not with a rock in the falling flower's path.

World Persistence

In many cases, when a participant leaves a virtual world experience, no record is kept of their actions within the world. When that person or another person enters the world again, it is as if no one had ever been there before. The experience starts anew, with the same initial conditions as for all previous participants.

If an experience has the property of *world persistence,* then that is not the case. The world continues to exist in one way or another, whether a participant is engaged with the world or not. In the simplest case, a database stores the conditions of the world when a participant leaves. When the participant reenters the world, they pick up where they left off, with the state of the world reflecting actions they had taken in a previous session.

In a fully persistent world, the world continues to grow and evolve whether anyone is in the world or not. In the *NICE* application (Appendix A), one component in the world is a vegetable garden. The garden is driven by a simulation that models the behavior of growing vegetables. Just as in a real-world garden, those vegetables continue to grow whether anyone is present or not. If the garden is not attended to, it can be overrun by weeds.

Interference from the Physics of the Real World

When modeling your own world laws, you must also concern yourself with how to handle the laws of the real world (such as natural gravity) that cannot be removed in the VR system. For example, if your virtual world has no gravity but you have a virtual object linked to a handheld prop device, when the user lets go of the prop, the prop will fall (because of real-world gravity), causing the virtual object attached to the prop to react to gravity (which breaks the virtual world's laws of nature).

The other side of this coin is that the physical world may not be able to provide the restrictions and restraints that the virtual world requires—for example, when a participant encounters a wall through which they should not be able to pass (FIGURE 7-10). In a system without force feedback, how can the system prevent the user from peeking through the wall? If the experience designer chooses not to allow participants to penetrate hard surfaces, then they must prevent situations where this becomes a possibility. Although it is easy to keep them from virtually traveling to "illegal" locations, in systems without force feedback, there is no way to prevent them from physically moving to "illegal" locations.

Another issue occurs in experiences where the designers have chosen physical locomotion as the only means of travel, and yet they want to convey a space larger than their tracking system can handle or larger than the size of the room in which the system resides. In occlusive visual displays such as HMDs, it may be possible to subtly shift the world, causing the participant to walk in the direction toward the farthest wall without their realization. Researchers at the University of North Carolina at Chapel Hill have met with some success on their research with *redirected walking* [Razzaque et al. 2001].

Substance of the Virtual World

Last, and in no way least, is the "stuff" one interacts with in the virtual world—the substance. The *substance* of the world is made up of the objects, characters, and locations of the experience. It is the stuff you see, touch, and hear. It can be represented in any manner of styles. The world's substance can be rendered and displayed to one or more senses. It is the collection of everything that makes the world the world.

Many people define their physical world as a space through which they move that is filled with objects. A virtual world can be viewed similarly, although we must recognize that the creator can define spaces and objects in ways similar or dissimilar to what is found in the physical world. The space of the virtual world is more or less defined by its contents. This statement does not presuppose that the world is presented visually—a purely audio world does have contents. Although unseen, they are present.

Much like the physical world, objects in the virtual world have properties, such as shape, mass, color, texture, density, and temperature. Certain properties are apparent to specific senses. Color is sensed in the visual domain. Texture can be

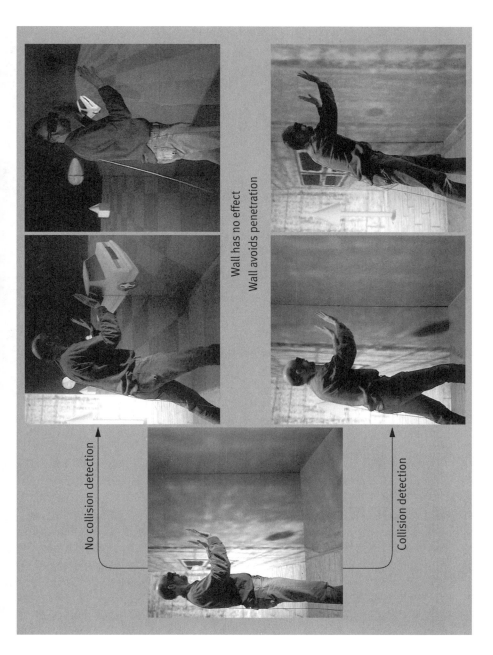

No collision detection

Wall has no effect

Wall avoids penetration

Collision detection

FIGURE 7-10 *For VR systems with no force feedback displays, there are two possible actions the world can have when a participant attempts to pass through solid objects (such as the wall in these photographs). Either the world allows them to pass through the object, or the world must back away from the user (Photographs by William Sherman).*

sensed both in the visual and tactile domains. Objects in the virtual world are associated with a location in the virtual space. Some objects can be moved, while others are fixed. Not all virtual objects have physical attributes—there could be something with *no* physical attributes, like a gust of wind or a spirit. You would know it was there by how it affected other things. Objects can be representations of entities other than real-world objects, such as a floating menu interface that can be manipulated to control various aspects of the virtual world.

We can divide the substance of the world into four primary categories (FIGURE 7-11):

1. World geography
2. Objects
3. Agents
4. User interface elements

World Geography

The *world geography* describes the surfaces upon which the participant travels (the terrain), or it can describe regions of the world that have their own distinct flavor. Borrowing a connotation from the medium of motion pictures, we might refer to the latter as having different *locations* in the world. The *terrain* of the world might be a flat plane or rolling hills, or it might be created from a bizarre mathematical formula. It depends on what the desired effect is and on how much effort the VR creator is willing to expend.

Typically, virtual reality experiences take place in a rather small, consistent region in which the participant can travel. The user is either not permitted to leave this region or will find nothing of interest outside its bounds. A larger virtual world, however, might contain many *locations* of interest. Locations may all be conjoined as if the world were one large location, or locations may be more or less disconnected.

Often, a virtual reality world will be separated into discrete locations. One practical reason to make this division is that it reduces the computational resources required by the application. In a discrete location environment, the application need only display and store the current one within its active memory. Also, the application only needs to calculate the physics for the objects in the limited region rather than for the entire world.

Suppose the virtual world includes leaves blown by the wind. While a participant can only occupy one location at a time, in a nondiscrete world, they can see

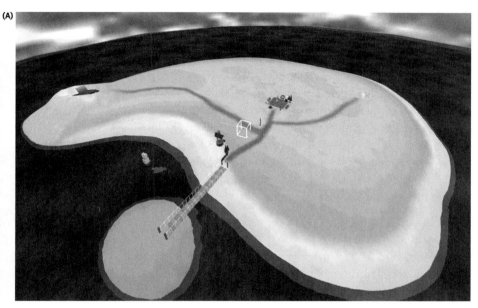

FIGURE 7-11 *VR applications generally include substantive entities of four various types:* **(A)** *geography,* **(B)** *objects,* **(C)** *agents, and* **(D)** *user interface elements (NICE application courtesy of Maria Roussou, EVL).*

(or hear) what is happening in other locations. So, if leaves are blowing down the street somewhere, they may or may not be visible to the participant. Since that is difficult to predict, that possibility should be accounted for. The leaves may eventually blow into view, but if they are in a discrete, independent location, no computation need be done on them.

There are artistic reasons to do this, as well. Each location might have its own distinct representational style, affected by global graphics rendering properties. Each location might have its own interface. The user may learn a different way to travel in each space. Perhaps the way objects are manipulated also differs from place to place. And, finally, there may be a different set of physical laws for each location.

Objects

The *objects* of the virtual world are the "normal" artifacts that occupy the world—the things. That is, objects are the main stuff one finds in the world. Objects are the flowers, trees, fences, Tiki statues, whatever one might encounter in the world. They are the things that one can observe, manipulate, and sometimes destroy or create.

In an architectural walkthrough, the buildings and their contents, the landscaping, streets, and automobiles are the objects. In a scientific visualization application, the representations of the scientific phenomena are the world's objects. Such representations might include a shape representing water vapor content or small balls following the flow of the air. In applications where users are able to create annotations, the annotation markers and the content they contain are also objects of the world.

Agents

The *agents* of a virtual world include the denizens of the world: the autonomous characters, characters controlled through a Wizard of Oz interface, or the avatars of the participants themselves. Visually, the agents may seem to be simply an advanced form of artifact or object. However, if they are animated or exhibit some sort of simulated behavior that seems lifelike, then they are somehow different. They have some sort of intelligence and they seem to be "alive" (embodied).

User Interface Elements

The *user interface element* is the substance that represents the parts of the interface that the user can directly perceive in the virtual world. This includes all virtual controls that require some form of manifestation. Menus and a virtual trash bin are two examples. A simple instructional display that the user might summon is another example. A less clear example includes things that are both an object in the world and can also be used as part of the interface. Specifically, an automobile is clearly a normal object, but if the user enters the car, presses the virtual gas pedal, and turns the virtual steering wheel, it is difficult to classify the wheel and the pedal as "object" versus "user interface representation."

Chapter Summary

A VR experience developer, much like a novelist, a screenwriter, or a painter, considers how to embody the message conveyed through the chosen medium. There are additional concerns specific to virtual reality. Some VR-specific concerns include the types and methods of interaction allowed, the laws of nature by which the objects and people in the world function, what happens to the world when no one is present, and how multiple people can interact within the experience. Even the physical location and setting impact the effect of a VR experience on a participant.

The application designer must consider the goal of the experience and whether or not a sense of mental immersion is necessary, along with how to achieve it when appropriate. In a manner similar to content creators of other media, the VR experience designer has complete control of the virtual world, at least during the design and implementation phases, and must determine all aspects of what *is* or *is not* in the world. They establish all of what can or cannot happen in the virtual world, who can or cannot participate, and what happens to the world at the end of the experience.

Virtual reality experience

User interface

Hardware interface to the user

Input
- Body tracking
  (How the computer "sees" the user)
- Voice/sound recognition
  (How the computer "hears" the user)
- Physical controllers
  (How the computer "feels" the user)

CHAPTER 3

Output
- Visual display
  (How the user sees the VW)
- Aural display
  (How the user hears the VW)
- Haptic display
  (How the user feels the VW)

CHAPTER 4

Software components

System presentation to the user
- Representation
- Rendering system

CHAPTER 5

User interaction with the virtual world
- Manipulation
- Navigation
- Shared experience

CHAPTER 6

Experience design
CHAPTER 8

Virtual world
- Immersion
- Point of view
- Venue
- Simulation/physics
- Objects/denizens

CHAPTER 7

Life experience
- Memory
- Ability
- Past experience
- Emotional state
- Cultural background

CHAPTER 8

8

Experience Design: Applying VR to a Problem

As with other media, if virtual reality does not help solve problems or provide a useful method of conveying messages, ideas, and/or emotions, then it is little more than a technological novelty. Researchers and engineers might find it interesting for a while, but if artists and application designers are not able to cultivate it to create worthwhile experiences, then not many people will want to use it. This chapter looks at how a VR experience is created by bringing together all components of experience discussed in the previous seven chapters.

Will VR Meet Your Goals?

To evaluate whether virtual reality is a medium *you* can apply to a problem, the first step is to determine what outcome you might expect to attain from using VR. There are many potential reasons to use virtual reality, and some projects will have different goals for different participants. Reasons to use VR include:

- Improved ability to examine and explore 3D data
- Cost savings
- Profit
- Improved quality of life
- Conveying ideas as artistic expression
- Conveying ideas as informative expression
- Entertainment or escapism
- Noninvasive experimentation (in a virtual world modeled on a real environment) and other simulation techniques
- Safety
- Marketing

Goals overlap in most projects. If the project is to design a new product in a series of products (e.g., a new engine design), then virtual reality might first be used to analyze the performance of the new unit. This information can then be presented to company executives using VR to communicate the results of the new design (a form of internal marketing).

As the project proceeds, virtual reality can continue to be used in the design simulation, incorporating data recorded by sensors on an early physical, working prototype. Later, when the product hits the market, the use of VR in the design process can be the focus of external marketing, as the newness of the technology often excites the target purchasers, perhaps providing an opportunity for them to interact with the new product in a variety of controlled environments.

If the goal is to entertain, then the fact that VR is perceived as "futuristic" can help draw an audience. But this can only take you so far. More important, the content designers have a whole new, more elaborate medium to work in. Of course, the current expense of good VR systems limits access to the medium and constrains the type of content that is feasible. If profitability is a concern in public venue displays, then high throughput is necessary, requiring the experience to be quick yet provide enough adrenaline flow or other enticement to bring the user back. The feasibility for complicated, longer-lasting experiences will increase as public venue VR becomes cheaper and especially when VR becomes practical for the home.

Virtual reality is not the most appropriate medium for accomplishing all tasks. No medium is. Once the goal of a project is known, one can evaluate how and whether VR can and should be applied. This chapter lays out guidelines for making this determination. Exploring the examples in the appendices will also help to illuminate the practical possibilities.

Is VR the Appropriate Medium?

For any particular concept, there will be some media that are appropriate and some that are not. While virtual reality has a wide range of uses and capabilities, not all forms of communication will benefit from its use. As the underlying technology evolves and improves, the number of appropriate tasks will increase. However, there are many cases where VR *is* the obvious choice. In general, VR is an especially suitable medium for problems that require manipulation of objects in a three-dimensional environment. Usually, the object will also be 3D in nature, although it is not inconceivable to use 2D objects placed in a 3D world. Appropriate uses of applied VR include architectural walkthroughs, design spaces, virtual prototyping, scientific visualization, and medical research, training, and procedures.

Being a graphical task is not enough, however. There are many uses of graphical work most appropriately done in only two dimensions. Architects still use blueprints to convey important details about a building design in a 2D format. In fact, a 3D rendering of the same information might be overly cluttered and convey the information less clearly. Of course, the architect may have other tasks for which immersive 3D presentation is the better choice, such as a customer walkthrough of the finished product, where the details of a blueprint might be less persuasive than a 3D visualization of the space.

Although the best way to experience *Moby Dick* may be by sitting in an armchair with a physical copy of the book, the reader may gain greater insight into the novel through a separate experience in which they can interactively walk about a whaling ship. The best way to experience *Citizen Kane* may be by sitting in a dark room with scores of strangers as the images flicker on a large screen before you. But you may be able to better appreciate Orson Welles's directing and the film's cinematography if you are given a virtual set of the hall of mirrors scene and are asked to duplicate the camera move yourself. The best way to create a document may be to type the characters on a keyboard, but if you are learning the handful of keystrokes necessary to set an assembly line in motion, then learning to type them on a virtual replica of the specialized keyboard used in the actual task may be preferable. Virtual reality is one medium among many options, each of which is appropriate for a particular task.

What Makes an Application a Good Candidate for VR?

There are classes of tasks and goals for which virtual reality is not likely to be an appropriate medium. This may be because the task is not inherently three-dimensional, would require impractical amounts of computer power, or would otherwise be beyond the bounds of current technology (such as precise tracking or lifelike haptic feedback).

Because a key component of VR is that it has a real-time interface, tasks that cannot be computed live in real time using today's technology are not likely to produce satisfactory results in a VR environment. Some tasks can be simplified to be computed in real time, but some cannot. The ones that cannot be modified for real-time computation may become suitable candidates in the future when faster technology is available.

Because virtual reality relies on a three-dimensional environment, tasks that are inherently one- or two-dimensional are not likely to take advantage of VR. For example, very little is likely to be gained by implementing a common *X-Y* plot of stock market prices in a 3D VR environment. However, if one can reconstruct the representation of the data that is driving the plot in a way that takes advantage of the three-dimensionality, such as using the extra dimensionality to relate other factors to a particular stock or perhaps a risk factor over a class of market instruments, then it might become a suitable task for VR.

The imprecision and lag in current tracking methods, as well as relatively slow computation, makes tasks that require a very close registration with the real world (either geographically or temporally) unlikely to be successful VR applications. Because the real world is precise and instantaneous, the technological problems of VR are more apparent than when the VR world needs to be registered only with itself. The need for precise and fast tracking is particularly important for augmented reality applications, although in some AR applications, such as Boeing's wire bundle construction application (Appendix C), the requirements are low enough that even today's technology is adequate.

As we've stated, most VR devices are oriented toward visual and audio display. Because of this, there has been less work done on applications for which haptic display is important. Although there are some counterexamples (see BDI's suture trainer shown in FIGURE 4-31), when the sense of touch is a critical component of the task, current VR systems are less likely to be successful in rendering a satisfactory experience.

Conversely, there are many features of virtual reality that can benefit a project, including the inadequacy of other media, site familiarization, and easier integration with a computer-simulated world. Virtual reality may be considered because there is some aspect of the task for which non–VR technology is inadequate. For instance, if the task is inherently three-dimensional and traditional one- or two-dimensional displays and interfaces are not expressive enough, then VR might be appropriate. The developers of NCSA's *Virtual Director* application [Thiébaux 1997] had such a problem and found a satisfactory solution by moving their three-dimensional problem to VR—a three-dimensional medium. Desktop tools for manipulating an animation camera through 3D space did not offer the type of interface desired by a filmmaker. The way these desktop tools were used often led to unnatural camera moves. These problems were overcome with a virtual reality interface.

Scenarios in which the goal is to explore or familiarize oneself with a physical place (either real or fictitious) are well suited to VR development. Designing buildings and allowing clients to "walk through" them in VR has been successful. VR is a suitable delivery mechanism if the goal is to familiarize a participant with a

FIGURE 8-1 *In the U.S. Navy Research Lab's* Shadwell *VR experience, fire fighting trainees learn about the interior of a ship before taking part in a fire fighting exercise (Image courtesy of David Tate/NRL).*

specific environment. For example, the U.S. Navy Research Lab's (NRL) *Shadwell* fire fighting project [Tate et al. 1997] used a VR experience to help shipboard firefighters plan their route to a fire (FIGURE 8-1). In fact, any application that involves a 3D exploration of a realistic scenario or one in which a change of scale is beneficial could be likely candidates for successful VR applications.

If a task already involves a computed simulation, then VR may be able to augment or take advantage of the many benefits inherent in the simulation process itself, particularly if the simulation can be adequately represented in 3D space and allows for direct/live interaction. There are many problems for which the same benefits and problem solving capabilities of simulation can be extended to the medium of VR, including:

- Problems that cannot be tackled in the physical world (e.g., witnessing the birth of the universe)
- Problems that cannot be studied safely (e.g., witnessing the turmoil within the funnel of a tornado)
- Problems that cannot be experimented with due to cost constraints (e.g., let every student practice docking a billion dollar submarine
- Problems in "What if?" studies (where virtual exploration could lead to better understanding)

Creating a VR Application

When considering constructing a virtual reality system, an important first step is to familiarize yourself with the medium of VR to the greatest extent feasible. Go out and try as many VR experiences and VR hardware devices as you can. By immersing yourself in a variety of VR worlds, on a variety of VR systems, you come to recognize the capabilities, limitations, and attributes of VR. Through a survey of experiences, you will gain an appreciation of the three-dimensional nature of VR and begin to build an intuition of what to expect in VR environments, as well as discern techniques that are helpful or troublesome to users.

If possible, gain access to a VR system and build some simple experiences. Explore different travel interfaces, different manipulation interfaces, and so on. Build experiences with different levels and types of narrative. If possible, spend lengthy periods of time physically immersed in these and other experiences—learn what it's like to live in virtual reality. Learn what types of expectations *you* have as a user and which factors of the experience are important versus which factors are vital.

Do research to discover what others have done in VR and get their impressions of what works and what doesn't. The appendices of this book were designed to be just such a resource, allowing you to learn from a variety of application design experiences. Additional application examples can be found at *www.mkp.com/ understanding-vr.*

After you've spent some time learning about the medium of VR, you may need to reexamine your goal. Chances are high that your goal may change as you become more familiar with the strengths, limitations, and unexpected possibilities of VR. You may find that VR is not (yet) a suitable medium for what you desire to accomplish. You may also find that you can step beyond the scope of the original goal.

Basically, there are three sources from which you may derive your VR experience: (1) from another medium, (2) from an existing VR application, and (3) from scratch.

Adapting from Other Media

If you are deriving work from another medium, it is important to examine the differences between the two media. It often won't work to indiscriminately transfer content from the old medium to VR. In adapting from the original medium, perhaps you can exploit aspects of the content that were neglected in the old medium that can now be implemented spectacularly in virtual reality. In transferring a book to a movie, a screenwriter adapts the narrative from the textual to the visual. They don't just read the book to the audience. New elements of the content emerge as focal points.

Virtual reality is inherently an interactive medium; therefore, the simple transference of content from sequential media makes little sense. For instance, reading a Herman Melville novel does not become more interesting, engaging, or useful if it is done while wearing a head-mounted display (FIGURE 8-2). Watching an Orson Welles film is not enhanced by making the viewer turn their head to follow the action of the film. On the other hand, if the original content is modified for the new medium by adding interactivity, the filmmaker's role of setting the tone and pacing via camera angles, editing, and other techniques is diminished.

FIGURE 8-2 *Some virtual worlds are simply not suitable for adaptation from their existing medium to VR without significant modification!*

Not even all *interactive* tasks are appropriate for VR. Editing a text document involves a lot of input from the user via the computer keyboard, but text documents are one-dimensional, and it is unlikely that a keyboard modeled in a virtual environment will work better than the physical equivalent; thus virtual reality is not an appropriate medium for performing this type of task.

Certain content is especially well suited for presentation in specific media. Presenting a novel such as *Moby Dick* via a virtual reality interface does not enhance the virtual world experience, nor does it offer improvements over the original medium of the written word. On the other hand, derivative works that make use of the special features of VR can create a new, enhanced experience, one that allows exploration of the story in ways not possible in a linear medium. The idea of simply presenting the original novel via a virtual reality interface was parodied by NBC's *Saturday Night Live* television program as a commercial for "Books in VR."

Depending on the media and the content, effective adaptations from one medium to another are possible. Some media adaptations are more straightforward than others; for example, successful VR works have been derived from Disney's *Aladdin* motion picture and the *Pac Man* videogame. Adapting the *Aladdin* screenplay to a 3D interactive, immersive experience required changing from a linear narrative to a goal-oriented, gamelike experience. In addition, the two-dimensional characters and animated sets had to be represented three-dimensionally. The Pac Man videogame was already an interactive experience, in which the player could choose which action to take at any given moment. The 2D maze was extruded into

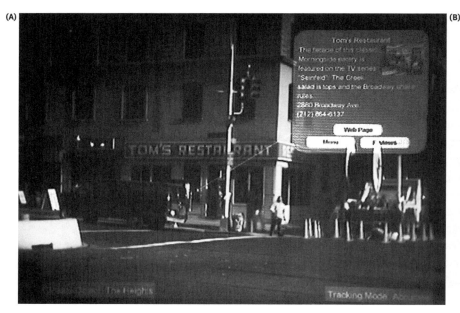

the third dimension, allowing an egocentric player point of view (as opposed to the two-dimensional, God's-eye view of the original arcade game).

Examples of deriving VR experiences from books are less straightforward. Simply putting a virtual copy of the text of *Moby Dick* into a virtual living room obviously doesn't work well. However, putting a reference book into an augmented reality display enables a repair person to reference the manual while performing the task. The reference material may be enhanced to include 3D models of the apparatus, perhaps linking the model with the real world by overlapping the two or using arrows that point to the corresponding feature in each world, real and virtual. A similar example would be to make information from a tourist guidebook available to the user as they walk about town (FIGURE 8-3).

FIGURE 8-3 *One use of augmented reality might be to give a tourist information about places in Manhattan as they walk about the city. As the user looks at a location, pertinent facts are added to their view* **(A)**. *The current prototype is bulky, but will improve as technology advances* **(B)** *(Images courtesy of Steve Feiner/Columbia University).*

Adapting from an Existing VR Experience

Converting an existing VR application into one suitable for your needs is perhaps the easiest way to create a VR application. Say, for instance, someone who has created a scientific visualization tool is willing to share it with you. In this case, you may find that it can be used directly if you simply modify your data to a suitable format. Or, if you have the source code to the application, you may be able to adapt it in small ways to meet your particular needs. The *Crumbs* visualization application (Appendix B) has been used by a variety of scientists in both of these ways.

Creating a New VR Experience

Creating an experience from scratch allows the most flexibility but will require the most effort. The goal must be kept in focus and within a reasonable subset of possibilities. If later it is discovered that the chosen path is going nowhere, then at that point it may be possible to change direction.

The Experience Creation Process

There are courses of action by which one can reduce the amount of wasted effort during the development of a new VR application. For this reason alone, we advocate that the VR experience developer learn about the medium before beginning the project. However, experimenting with possibilities that are ultimately abandoned should not be considered a waste of effort. In fact, it is wise to include some experimentation time in the development schedule. Experimentation can be especially useful when it involves tests with users. Many successful VR experiences and other computer applications have relied on user tests to hone the content and the interface. Include VR application experts as part of the development team. Revisit and critique the application and the progress with these experts during the course of development. Even with these precautions, it may be necessary to abandon a plotline, cool interface idea, or other line of development that doesn't serve the application, but perhaps you can include them in a future endeavor.

As with other technology-based media, such as motion pictures, chances are high that a team of people with various skills will be necessary for anything but the smallest projects. Since VR is a computer-based medium, someone (or a team) who can program is obviously needed—but don't stop there. Content experts—the users themselves or people who know the users—should also be obvious additions to the team. Similarly, include people knowledgeable about user interface design and/or human factors research. Creating experiences with large virtual worlds will probably require set designers, prop creators, and sound effects people. You will also need people skilled in hardware integration and probably an audio/video engineer.

Unless you are adapting an existing system, the next step is to build the hardware/software system. Even if the hardware already exists, it is generally wise to use a software system to simulate the VR experience so that each developer isn't competing for system time during the development process. This can be accomplished by developing or acquiring a software system that emulates your targeted VR hardware platform on a desktop computer. If the software will be written in-house, then debugging tools and a software interface that allows quick turnaround for viewing changes to the virtual world are important. An accessible interface was found to be crucial during the development of Disney's *Aladdin* VR experience [Pausch et al. 1996; Snoddy 1996]. The Disney team found it essential to create their own development language, called SAL, usable by the content creators to allow them to rapidly try new scenarios in the VR environment. It was critical to allow the creative team to make changes in the story without depending on the technical staff for every minor adjustment.

In addition to putting together the team, the hardware components will need to be gathered and integrated (FIGURE 8-4). These components include the displays (visual, aural, haptic), the rendering systems, the primary computer (which may include any or all of the rendering engines), and the user-monitoring hardware (tracking system). A location in which to house the VR system may be needed, at least during development; it may eventually be deployed elsewhere. Space may or may not be a trivial concern, depending on the type of display chosen.

The skills needed in a VR development team provide a clue to the activities necessary to create the virtual world. Objects need to be modeled and painted (texture mapped). Sounds must be recorded, created, or algorithmically modeled. The world rendering must be programmed. The physics simulation for the world needs to be programmed. The user interface must be designed and programmed. The physical hardware must be acquired, integrated, and installed in the venue.

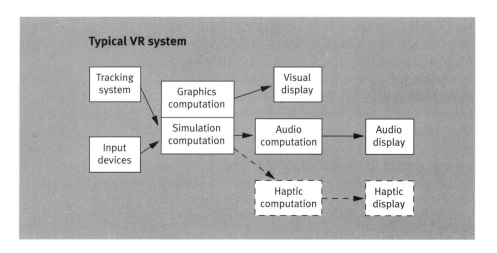

FIGURE 8-4 *A VR system is made up of many components and must be designed from a system perspective. Here we see one way in which the components may be linked. Since haptic interfaces are still rare, they are represented by dashed lines.*

Designing a VR Experience

Unless you are just experimenting with VR to learn the medium, it is wise to approach the creation of a VR experience with good design practices. Just as painters first make a series of sketches of their subject, moviemakers and animators first construct storyboards, architects first lay out buildings as 2D blueprints, and each of these is reviewed and revised through multiple iterations, the same benefits can be reaped in the design of a VR experience. In general, the design process optimizes the overall goal within a given set of constraints. By sketching various possibilities, ideas can be discussed and potential implementations compared with the task requirements. The next sections address some of the highlights of VR experience design, with examples to highlight each point. For a full list of options at key stages of the design, the reader is referred to the appropriate section in the preceding Chapters 3 through 7.

Design Deliberately

Never use methods or program fragments simply because they already exist, or because one way is easier to implement than another. *Choose* your models, software, sounds, and other specifics because they are appropriate for the particular experience. Just because you have some code for flap to fly travel from a previous "pretend you're a bird" experience, don't try to save time by requiring scientists to flap their way around a molecule. Similarly, if a handheld prop with three buttons is provided as a user input device and there are five items from which the user can select, use a menu instead of making the user push a complicated combination of buttons for each choice. In short: *Design to make things easier for the user, not the programmer.*

Design for a VR experience should be constructed looking from the top (global view) down (toward the goal). That is, start by looking at the message you wish to convey, the task you wish to perform, or the emotion you wish to evoke. Of course, the practical challenge is to keep in mind the resources that are available at the same time.

Good design also means to test the experience frequently and evaluate how it is measuring up to the goal. Iterate often and be prepared to throw away a lot of ideas. Don't keep a particular feature because it was difficult to implement and you want to show off your programming skills. If the feature doesn't live up to being good for the user's experience, then it isn't worth keeping. The point of sketching out ideas is to iterate over experimental content. But if we keep the chaff with the wheat, the user's experience may be distasteful. In addition to the goal of the application, keep an eye on the constraints of the system, venue, and audience for which the experience is intended. Then, too, don't forget about the special features that make virtual reality unique as a medium. Virtual reality has more options than day to day reality. This mindset becomes easier as one gains experience using VR and learns to think in terms of what is possible in virtual reality.

Design with the System in Mind

For some applications, the system resources will be known a priori. Such may be the case in business or scientific efforts where the organization maintains a VR facility available to employees within the organization. Under other circumstances, the experience developer may have complete freedom to design and implement the VR system any way they would like. If the system already exists and you know what its capabilities are, then you can design the software with these constraints in mind. If an existing system can be extended or you are creating the system from scratch, then you can choose both hardware and software to accommodate your goals.

If your project will not be deployed to the end user for a considerable amount of time—say, two years—then you can take advantage of the fact that technology is likely to improve considerably in that time. A simple example might be that you intend to render at 30 graphical frames a second when deployed but are willing to accept 20 frames a second during the first phase of development with the expectation that the hardware improvements will fill the gap. If your project will involve large hardware expenditures, then you may also have an advantage in that you could convince the hardware manufacturer to let you test out the next generation of their product before it is released. This can benefit both you and the hardware manufacturer: you get to tune your application specifically for that hardware, and other potential users will more likely be impressed with hardware performance, since the application was optimized for it.

Design with the Venue in Mind

The venue where your virtual reality experience will be deployed will impose some constraints on the type of hardware and displays that can be used, which will in turn affect the experience design. For example, a venue with limited space (or limited space per immersed participant) will likely require a head-based visual display. If the venue is theater-style, requiring a high-resolution display, then a projection-based visual display might be more appropriate. If the venue is a large space in which the participant can roam—an "80-acre" farm, for instance—then a nonocclusive HBD or a hand-based visual display may be the right call. If the venue is in a public space, then throughput and the ability to get people in and out of the experience quickly is important. Providing some form of display that others can view while waiting their turn, or just to see what is going on, can also be a consideration. A large projection display provides one solution to both these concerns by default. Also, if there is a need to limit the amount of sound emitted from the VR system, then the user may wear headphones.

Design with the Audience in Mind

Know your audience is perhaps the most important tenet an experience designer should remember when making any design choice. If the audience is a small, known group of users, then the designer can include them directly in the design process. Let them explain the features they deem important. Perhaps the experience will later be released to a wider audience, but having current users involved in the design can only enhance the experience.

Let's look at another type of audience: a small user community of individuals unfamiliar with VR, that is, people in a particular field who are potential users of the application. In addition to involving members of this community in the design and testing processes, the developer should examine the tools that are already in common use by this group and find out what they like and don't like about these tools. The NCSA's *Virtual Director* application is a VR tool that mimics and extends preexisting desktop tools for computer animation choreography. In this case, a small subset of professionals in computer animation formed both the test group and part of the design team; in fact, they led the project. They then taught others how to use the tool to gather further input and test its robustness.

A general audience is probably the most difficult for which to design. Designing for a general audience means the experience developer needs to find interfaces and representations that are globally understood, can be taught quickly, or can be easily changed to suit each user. This is clearly evident for venues frequented by people who speak a variety of languages. In this case, the first choice may be to avoid language-based messages and choose internationally recognizable sounds and symbols. If there are details that are important to convey textually, then the venue operator may be able to make a quick selection to change the language of the system. Operator selection could also be used to choose a speech recognition database, unless the developers are able to include a multilingual dictionary into the recognition system.

Age, experience, and culture also play significant roles in how an audience interacts with a VR experience. Young children may not have the physical capabilities to hold the same props as adolescents or adults (FIGURE 8-5). Thus, a prop with buttons designed for the adult may require two-handed operation by a child.

Head-based displays and shutter glasses may slip right off a child's head (as the implementors of the child-oriented *NICE* application discovered [Roussos et al. 1999]; see Appendix A). Also, the young child may not be able to quickly correlate how their actions are affecting the virtual world, whereas an adolescent experienced at videogames may be able to instantly manipulate the interface. Depending on life experience, an adult may be able to adapt quickly or may become hopelessly confused.

Audience differences should also be addressed by the navigation interface. Children, adults, or experienced videogame players will have different requirements for travel controls. The videogame player is likely to be able to handle more complicated control systems with several options for different types of movement. An adult may be able to use a car-like steering interface with ease. A young child may like an interface that allows for small, discrete steps. Likewise, there are differences in how people treat their orientation in a three-dimensional space. Some people prefer controls that allow them to change their orientation with respect to the world. Others prefer to orient the world with respect to themselves. These two techniques have opposite control effects. For those who prefer to adjust their orientation to the world, indicating a left turn causes the view of the world to rotate clockwise around the viewer. The preference varies depending on who is using the application; for example, pilots typically prefer to control themselves with respect to the world. There are also group and personal preferences for wayfinding. Different people use different strategies to keep track of where they are in the world. There are even different ways to use the same wayfinding tools. For example, some people prefer to read maps with north always facing up, while others prefer to rotate the map to the direction of travel.

Expectations about a user's life experiences can vary between cultures. It may be safe to assume that most males of a certain age in industrialized nations have had some experience with videogame control, but if the experience is designed to be entirely cross-cultural, this may cause problems. The differences in dress

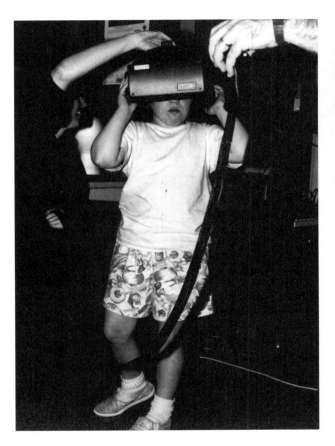

FIGURE 8-5 *Designing applications for children requires special thought. Head-mounted displays are not currently designed for children. Researcher Dorothy Strickland encountered this problem in her studies using VR for teaching children with autism. In this photo, she assists a child who is wearing an HMD that is too big and too heavy for him to wear comfortably (Image courtesy of Dorothy Strickland).*

between cultures may also lead to difficulties. When the *Virtuality* VR arcade system was being deployed in a venue in the Middle East, they discovered that because most men wore a headdress, they could not don the standard HMDs supplied with the units. Part of knowing your audience is understanding and directing their expectations. One way to influence their expectations is through the venue and the pre-immersion part of the experience. Presenting a *backstory* of actions that have come before and what the participant's role in the narrative will be helps to develop a sense of what to expect during the VR part of the experience.

Another way to guide the audience's expectations is through genre. In all other media of human communication, patterns have emerged linking certain types of subject matter with particular styles of presentation, narration, and interface. These patterns are the genres of each medium. By choosing a particular subject matter, you are often linking your application with a genre, which may suggest a particular look and interface to the world. So, part of knowing your audience is to know the conventions they expect from the genre. Along these lines, part of knowing your audience is to make sure the application is promoted to the target audience so those people most likely to understand and appreciate the application will show up. By making the genre evident, participants familiar with it will instantly have an idea of what to expect. Thus, an acquainted participant should quickly become accustomed to the world you present and be able to easily find their way through the interface. Of course, users can become complacent with a genre, often prompting artists to unsettle participants by derailing their expectations.

Consider Design Tradeoffs

Tradeoffs must be made in any design process. The most common tradeoff is between world complexity and the expense required for high computer performance. The amount of world complexity will, in turn, affect how the world designers choose to represent the various aspects of the world. An acceptable representation using highly complex rendering techniques may be totally inappropriate for a system with less graphical rendering power. There are also tradeoffs between the complexity of interaction in the world and the narrative. By limiting the path of travel in the virtual world, the designer doesn't have to create every detail of an entire world. One need only concern oneself with the world that is near the user's path.

A related notion allows the user full freedom to move but keeps them within certain regions of the virtual world through constraints other than limiting their path. For example, in a flight simulation, the designers can keep you in a certain space by ensuring that if you go outside of that space you will be shot down. This allows the world designer to worry about the world only in the places where the user is likely to be, while giving the illusion of total user freedom. Disney's *Aladdin's Magic Carpet Ride* VR experience also takes advantage of this method of constraining how much detail must be developed in the world by creating regions of the world where the user doesn't go because they're uninteresting or impassable (FIGURE 8-6). For example, there is a canyon wall that is too high for the user to go over, so whereas the user feels complete freedom, there are some disguised constraints [Daines 1995].

Constraining travel is one way to create a seemingly complex world that will sustain the interest of the participant by directing them to the important regions. Another method of directing the user's experience is to apply more creation and rendering resources to details of objects and locations in the world that are particularly interesting to the participant. In effect, these are methods of controlling the narrative.

Merely adding lots of polygons to an object to make it look more realistic is not always the answer. Sometimes, extra effort spent in modeling can be used as a tradeoff to lessen the amount of computational effort needed to render an object. The most effective presentation is not always the most complex. As Kathryn Best points out in her book *The Idiots' Guide to Virtual World Design*: "The answer is not to simplify everything, but to emphasize certain features and let the brain fill in the rest" [Best 1993].

FIGURE 8-6 *In Disney's VR experience* Aladdin's Magic Carpet Ride, *the content creators were able to reduce the computation required to simulate and render the world through the creative use of restricted locations that fit the world narrative; thus the participant does not get the impression of limited freedom. Here, the participant can fly around Jafar's laboratory (Image courtesy of Walt Disney Imagineering).*

Design the User Objective

Making the user the focus of the design process is very important. In addition to the hardware, representation, and interface, the way in which the user uses the application must be addressed. The user should feel that the application has a purpose. Applications may be designed to entertain, educate, enlighten, visualize information, and so on, but there must be either a narrative or a task that can be carried out. In *Aladdin's Magic Carpet Ride,* the Disney design team conducted experiments and determined that people only tolerate undirected wandering in an environment for up to about two minutes [Pausch et al. 1996; Snoddy 1996]. After that, they want some direction. The initial hypothesis of the design group was that while people may generally want their entertainment to be packaged, this may not be the case in virtual reality. They found that this hypothesis was incorrect. Left undirected, people got bored and asked what they should do.

The type and amount of user interface needed also depends on the objective. If the experience is primarily a ride along or even a fly-through with little interaction with objects in the world, then a fairly simple user interface can be developed. For applications in which the user must be able to manipulate objects, especially multiple objects in conjunction with one another, the interface becomes more complicated. The more complicated the interactions and the interface, the more user testing must be done—another tradeoff.

Design the End of the Experience

How an experience ends varies greatly, depending on the type of experience. Some experiences are open ended; the user can work or play in the virtual world for an indefinite amount of time. Other experiences come to a definite close. Whether or not an experience has a concrete ending, the time a participant can remain physically immersed may be a fixed amount of time or the user may be allowed to remain in the environment continuously for as much time as desired. Neither open ended nor fixed experiences require a participant to be immersed uninterrupted for the entire duration. After expending their available time for a particular session, many VR applications will allow the participant to return later and pick up where they left off. For some persistent worlds, it may be possible for other participants to have entered and interacted with the world in the meantime.

The quintessential *nonperpetual (fixed)* experiences are the arcade pinball and videogame machines. Each time you experience these games you start at the beginning—zero score, level one—and work your way through as much of the experience as possible. When the last mistake is made (death, ball drop), the experience is over. Going out to a movie is of this same class; it starts at the beginning and after all the information is presented, it ends. If you return to experience it again, it restarts at the beginning. Thus, there are three ways such an experience may end: (1) time expiration (5 minutes are up), (2) terminal event (final ball drops), and (3) early user termination (user leaves from boredom).

Many public venue and demonstration VR applications are nonperpetual, limited-time experiences. The first two publicly exhibited *Aladdin* experiences lasted five minutes, during which time the player tried to accomplish a specific goal to win the game. Extra time was not given to allow the participant a chance to just explore the world. The *Ford Galaxy* VR experience created by Virtuality PLC for marketing automobiles was presented as a fixed-length narrative with a complete story (beginning, middle, and end). The user is prompted to enter the car. As they are driven to a destination, the features of the car are explained. When they reach the end of their journey, they exit the car and the VR system.

Less narratively oriented applications can also be made to work within the confines of a limited-time experience. Char Davies's *Osmose* (FIGURE 8-7) is an artistic application that gives each user 15 minutes with which to explore the experience [Davies and Harrison 1996]. As it winds to a close, the experience shifts to a space designed to gently end the experience. The educational/scientific *Pompeii* application developed at the STUDIO lab at Carnegie Mellon University is another example where the participant is given a fixed amount of time to explore, this particular experience ending with the eruption of Mt. Vesuvius [Loeffler 1995]. The amount of time given (10 minutes) is not enough to explore the entire city, so the participant must choose which parts of the city to visit. In general, experiences for which throughput is important will be of fixed length.

The user can spend extended time in *open ended* experiences. Depending on the genre, this type of experience may or may not have a formal ending. For example, a scientific visualization application can be used over and over, with the scientist trying combinations of tools and exploring new data. Some experiences, particularly those with a strong narrative, may be lengthy but eventually do come to a conclusion. For example, a novel, text adventure (interactive fiction), or role-playing videogames where the player is given a task to accomplish may require 20 or more hours to complete, but eventually the last enigma is solved, the last page turned, and the experience is over. The *Legend Quest* game was a virtual reality experience of this type. There were a set number of quests each participant could undertake, and in each visit to the world they could attempt to accomplish one quest. While each encounter was a one-time event, the overall experience was made to be open

FIGURE 8-7 *The* Osmose *VR application provides an ephemeral, surreal environment for artistic expression (Image courtesy of Char Davies). See color plate 31.*

ended by allowing the participant to store their vital statistics on a card they would keep and insert at the beginning of play each time.

Formal ending or not, these lengthy experiences often allow saving and restoring the state of the experience. The visualization tool parameters can be saved, the novel bookmarked, or the location of adventurer recorded. When the participant returns, they can pick up where they left off. The length of many experiences necessitates the ability to save the state of the world and is almost a defining characteristic of open ended experiences.

Denouement is the wrapping up of a story such that all the story's loose ends are bound up. For many exploratory (scientific or artistic) applications, it is up to the participant to figure out how everything fits together with their model of the world. So, in that respect, the denouement may come sometime significantly after the VR experience has ended. For more story-oriented experiences, it is up to the content creator to tie the ends together.

Document, Deploy, and Evaluate the Experience

Assuming user testing is performed during development, then some documentation will likely be available as the VR experience is readied for deployment. In any event, documentation for the person running the experience will need to be fashioned and polished. A set of common questions and mistakes will come out of the user testing stage of development. A succinct answer/correction should be written for each of these concerns.

If possible, the VR experience can monitor the user's proficiency and either provide subtle hints of how to proceed or for some narrative cases simply nudge them along in the right direction. The hints may be provided by pop-up messages, an agent that speaks some advice, or simply an unembodied voice. These interfaces are interactive ways to access the VR application's documentation.

Once complete, the application is deployed to the venue where the users will come to partake in the experience. The installation effort and amount of personnel training will depend heavily on the type of environment, in particular, on whether it is an existing VR facility. If an existing VR facility is the venue, then perhaps little or no hardware needs to be installed. Also, it is likely that the people running the facility will not require as much training as those at another venue. Care should be taken with VR systems that will be "on tour" in terms of how setup, breakdown, and shipping will be handled. Any system deployed offsite in a public venue should have easily interchangeable spare units for the most fragile and vulnerable components. For example, the *Cutty Sark Virtual Voyage* touring application (see FIGURE 3-11) included extra HMDs.

To *evaluate* the success of your VR experience, the first question you must address is "What is a good measure of success?" The quick answer is "Was the goal attained?" But goal attainment may be hard to measure. It may be easier to appraise success if there is a more concrete measuring stick, such as profit made or money saved, time saved, or increased test scores. Other, less specific measures include whether people did in fact gain new understanding of a concept, whether people became mentally immersed or engaged to some degree in the experience, or whether they are performing better on the job as a result of participating in the experience.

For artist Rita Addison, the measure was both in personal catharsis and conveying her message. After experiencing Rita's work, *Detour: Brain Deconstruction Ahead,* many people comment on the extent to which the piece affected them. For many, it is the first time they are able to truly empathize with someone who has suffered a stroke or brain injury. These anecdotal comments are a measure of the success of *Detour.*

The Future of VR Design

This book enumerates the many options currently available to the VR experience developer. Appendices A through D describe applications that have used virtual reality to attain a goal. We are still in the embryonic stage of the medium. Although much of the hype surrounding it has subsided, VR continues to develop and shows promise as a medium capable of impacting the way we communicate, think, do business, and learn. Designing for the medium will evolve as the medium matures.

Many developments will contribute to the expansion of the medium. First and foremost is the growing acceptance and familiarity of VR. As more VR experiences are produced, the VR community will learn from one another, and successful interface elements will become more common. This, in turn, will allow participants to have a basic knowledge of what to do in a new VR application—they will become VR literate, much as we saw happen with the typical desktop computer interface. Also, the technologies that VR is built on will continue to improve. As this happens, the restrictions making some tasks unlikely candidates for VR will fall by the wayside. Facilitating a collaborative VR work environment is one such challenge that has continued to improve to the point of being more or less solved. Many new VR applications will include the ability to work with collaborators on other systems by default.

VR will also move from the specialized, custom-built application toward mass distribution. Currently, there are software packages designed to ease the burden of writing virtual reality applications. In the future, commercial software vendors will provide predesigned virtual reality applications for areas such as scientific visualization and architectural walkthroughs. One likely type of commercial off the shelf application is VR tools to help design VR experiences. For example, off the shelf packages that allow you to design, build, and walk through your own custom-designed house are available today for home computers. There will be more hardware available at lower cost, enabling more businesses and home experimenters to begin exploring the possibilities of VR, which in turn should lead to a demand for off the shelf VR software. Ultimately, computers may come "VR ready." Finally, more people will be interested in exploring the possible benefits of applying VR to their endeavors. As a result, VR will be used in many new arenas.

Chapter Summary

In summary, virtual reality has already proven to be beneficial for some specific goals. There are many indicators to help evaluate whether virtual reality is appropriate for a given task. Except in cases of marketing and artistic exploration of the medium, it is generally not wise to approach VR looking for a problem to solve. You should have a problem and look to virtual reality as a *possible* solution.

Once a decision is made to explore virtual reality as a means to attain a goal, standard design techniques should be followed. In particular, involve users. Get their ideas up front and get feedback from them at each stage of the development. Iterate over the design. Continually refine the experience by implementing, testing, and analyzing the work as it progresses and be willing to throw away bad ideas, no matter how much effort was put into them. Refer to known sources of information. Reference the fields that study the medium of VR and human computer interaction. Specifically, examine the research done by the human factors and human computer interface communities.

Of course, don't forget the content! When building the content of a VR experience, it is important to consider the same issues involved in creating virtual worlds for any medium. That is, the creator must consider the concept, plot (if any), characters, and setting for the experience. After all, even a compelling VR interface cannot substitute for substantive content. Content producers working with virtual reality for the first time should consider aspects that are not salient in other media, such as ensuring that the user encounters elements critical to the experience. The author might incorporate aids to guide the user through the experience. For those aspects requiring user input, sensible default values should be provided.

Prior to beginning work on a virtual reality application, the designer should ponder a few issues. How would they accomplish the task without VR? What do they expect or hope to gain by using VR? What additional constraints will VR impose on the solution to the task? What are the minimum system requirements? What type of resources will be necessary to achieve such a system? How does the expected gain of using VR compare with the expected resource cost? What tradeoffs can be made to reduce the resource cost without unduly hindering the application performance? What else has been done in VR to accomplish similar goals? What level of success was attained by previous efforts? How much has VR-related technology improved since these efforts? And, finally, how will I evaluate whether virtual reality helped reach the goal?

CHAPTER 9

The Future of Virtual Reality

Although it might seem presumptuous to try to predict the future, it is an important exercise to pursue if one is preparing for a project that will require the latest in technology. Indeed, it behooves any potential virtual reality developer to consider not only today's technology when determining the specifications for a virtual reality application, but to plan for technology that is likely to be available at the time of deployment.

In this chapter we take a look at some of the trends VR is likely to follow in the next five to twenty years in hardware and software technology, in integrated systems, and on the applications front. First, we assess the current state of VR, using a model that outlines typical stages in technology development, and then we'll look at how VR is likely to progress, given this and other models of how a new technology evolves. Once we have an understanding of the state of VR development, we'll discuss what's happening in current research and take a look at development trends in the field. From there, we go on to look at the future of VR technology.

The State of VR

Prior to pursuing virtual reality as a medium in which to work or a field of study, it is imperative to understand where VR stands as a technology. Interest in virtual reality has ebbed and flowed over the past few decades. To those not working directly in the field, it may appear that virtual reality development has subsided to the point of being a mere curiosity, with no long-term economic or leisure benefits. However, there are many indicators that suggest the actual use of VR is rising and, given the advances in hardware and software on the horizon, VR appears to have a healthy future.

One way to examine the state of virtual reality is to compare it with how other technologies have progressed from an interesting concept to an everyday, practical tool. The Gartner Group has observed that other new technologies have followed what they refer to as the "New Technology Hype Cycle" [Fenn 1995]. As seen in FIGURE 9-1, the visibility of developing technologies follows a pattern over time, as measured by how frequently the technology appears in mass media outlets such as news stories, movies, and the like. We can see from the graph that the Gartner Group has identified five phases in the development cycle:

1. Technology trigger

2. Peak of inflated expectations

3. Trough of disillusionment

4. Slope of enlightenment

5. Plateau of productivity

We will explain each phase as it can be applied to a generic technology and briefly identify how each relates to the evolution of virtual reality.

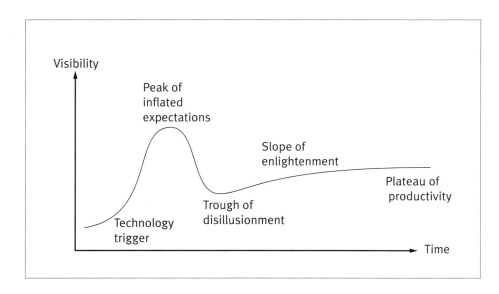

FIGURE 9-1 *The Gartner Group uses this curve to indicate how public awareness of developing technologies shifts over the course of time. (Redrawn from The Gartner Group).*

Technology Trigger

In the VR timeline presented in Chapter 1, there are two dates to which we could ascribe the trigger point of virtual reality's emergence into the public consciousness. The first working head-mounted display connected to a virtual world that responded in a physically immersive fashion was demonstrated and documented by Ivan Sutherland in 1968. While this certainly intrigued a handful of computer scientists, the underlying technology was inadequate to be of high interest to many people.

Despite the lack of visibility after Sutherland's initial foray, the persistent efforts of researchers at the University of North Carolina at Chapel Hill, Wright Patterson Air Force Base, and NASA Ames Research Center, among others, led to a resurgence of interest in VR in the late 1980s. Accordingly, and at least as far as public awareness is concerned, we might better assign the date of *technology trigger* to the year 1989. In that year, VPL Research, Inc. lowered the threshold for researchers to begin developing their own virtual reality experiences by offering affordable hardware on a commercial basis. The year 1989 also saw the introduction of the term *virtual reality* by VPL founder Jaron Lanier.

Peak of Inflated Expectations

To secure funding for new technology research, researchers must raise interest in their work among relevant funding agencies. To do this, researchers will frequently talk about the future promise of the technology. What is often glossed over is how many years it will take to get to that future.

While promoting their work, researchers' efforts will often be featured in newspapers, magazines, and on television. The increased visibility of their work in this great new technology may well lead to funding that will support them for a few years. For virtual reality, this peak of inflated expectations occurred between 1992 and 1995. However, such visibility also often leads to overblown expectations of what the technology can accomplish in the present day. The resulting disappointment leads to the inevitable trough of disillusionment.

Trough of Disillusionment

The spreading disappointment may result in an impression of disillusionment. A drastic falloff in interest stems from this disillusionment. Subsequently, there are fewer funders interested in supporting further development and fewer media outlets interested in covering the technology in their news and entertainment stories. With less funding available, many of the companies that arose to fill the needs of the technology's research community find it difficult to survive this phase. More diversified companies serving other areas of technology or other industries frequently drop their products oriented toward the new technology; this happened in the VR market. In fact, it was difficult for some companies to remain in business even during the peak of VR visibility, as evidenced by VPL's struggle and ultimate demise.

The time of disillusionment for virtual reality fell roughly within the years 1995 to 1998—just as the World Wide Web was taking off. Lest we be accused of presenting only the positive countenance of VR, we should note that some notable business failures of companies that were centered on VR technology and applications occurred at this time. One such example was Virtuality Group plc of Leicester, England. Despite delivering a quality product when VR was highly visible, their machines appeared in only a few general arcades and then quickly disappeared. The hardware was still too expensive to make the experience affordable, and they could not produce real-time imagery that matched public expectation. Later, Walt Disney Imagineering made VR available to the public through the DisneyQuest family arcade venues.

Slope of Enlightenment

If the technology doesn't evaporate in the trough of disillusionment, then chances are that someone found something to keep people inspired about its future. Such inspiration can be generated if sufficient interesting examples exist that hint at what may be possible. Eventually, as more people pursue the technology, new adopters find fresh ways to put it to use. A flourishing community with new practitioners finding innovative uses for the technology is a sign that the community is becoming "enlightened." Many new members will join the community as they begin to see what can actually be accomplished now in addition to the greater possibilities for the future. In part, the assessment of what can be done currently is due to sufficient improvement in support technologies such that more useful and interesting tasks can be performed right away.

Plateau of Productivity

Eventually, a surviving technology will be accepted for the benefits it can provide. It will settle at a level of use that depends on the size of the market it serves. Advances will continue to occur as new generations of products are released.

The Field of VR Research

One indicator that the field of VR is maturing is the shift in focus from developing the technology necessary to implement the medium to studying ways we can communicate through the medium. This study includes both human factors research and the critical analysis and review of existing works of VR.

Another indicator of maturity at the turn of the 21st century is the increasing number of universities offering courses on virtual reality. This increase remains tempered by the limitation of available hardware. Hardware constraints frequently limit class size to a small number of students. Because the current focus of virtual reality has been mostly on developing the technology sufficiently to produce interesting VR, many college VR courses have been offered by computer science departments. However, VR is (or will become) primarily a multidisciplinary endeavor; thus the field may either break from computer science departments or at least spur a significant number of cross-referenced courses. In fact, this trend is already beginning. At the University of Illinois at Urbana Champaign, the computer science department, mathematics, and the school of architecture all offer courses in virtual reality. Students are using virtual reality technology in their fields of study, rather than learning about virtual reality as a "pure" technology.

An important shift in how some universities are treating virtual reality is in the formal study of using the medium. Human factors and usability studies are important aspects of studying the way people interact with new technologies. Although we can name and describe many working examples of VR applications from which we may derive some understanding of the medium, most work thus far leads only to an anecdotal understanding. Formal studies of the contexts in which interface methodologies work the best/worst must continue.

Because most early examples of virtual reality experiences were created before the medium of virtual reality was well established and studied, it is understandable how they may have been created in a mostly ad hoc manner. With the rise in public awareness of virtual reality, many researchers in the field felt pressure to quickly develop the technology to meet rising expectations, so applications were created demonstrating the *potential* usefulness of VR. Less concern was paid to verifying the *actual* usefulness of a particular application. There was little time to perform follow-up studies to measure the actual benefits of using VR. There are of course exceptions to this statement.

At the University of North Carolina at Chapel Hill, researchers measured the performance of subjects using a haptic VR interface to perform a specific task and compared the results to using a traditional computer interface [Ouh-young et al. 1989]. They found that the haptic interface increased task performance speed by a factor of more than two. The advertising agency of Scaros and Casselman studied the effectiveness of making a memorable experience that communicates a desired message. The application was the *Cutty Sark Virtual Voyage,* which presented the user with the opportunity to smuggle Cutty Sark Scots Whiskey during Prohibition. Four months after taking the experience on the road to retail, entertainment, and trade show venues, a follow-up study was conducted to measure how well participants retained the name of the brand. The results indicated it had been quite effective.

As the medium develops, more good research on usability is being done during and preceding application development. Some early work at the University of Virginia includes an effort to use VR technology to improve the visualization interface for neurosurgeons examining patient data [Hinckley et al. 1994] and comparisons of using VR versus non–VR displays in simple search tasks [Pausch et al. 1997]. Work at the Georgia Institute of Technology has explored many interaction techniques, including the ability to access information contained in a complex environment [Bowman et al. 1998] and the ability for virtual reality to cause physiological effects in patients with a fear of flying [Rothbaum et al. 1996].

A collaborative project between the University of Houston and George Mason University compares the effectiveness of virtual reality with traditional textbooks for teaching high school physics [Salzman et al. 1996]. Work at the Electronic Visualization Laboratory at the University of Illinois at Chicago has studied how well two participants immersed in separate *CAVE* displays can manipulate virtual objects in a shared space [Park and Kenyon 1999]. This is not a complete list; however, the work has just begun and there remains a strong need for studies that focus both on the underlying interface design and information presentation. There is also a need to measure the benefits of individual applications as they compare with non–VR solutions. If this research is not done early enough, it is possible that the standard VR interface may just happen to be whatever is popular when VR reaches the plateau of productivity. It can be difficult to change course once an interface has momentum. Because early adopters tend to start with what they know, many early VR applications have adopted interface concepts from the 2D desktop, such as the menu. A suitable VR version or replacement of the menu remains to be created.

In addition to the formal study of how humans can best interact with the medium, it is also important to study the social impact of the medium. One mechanism for beginning such an endeavor is to study how effective the medium is at conveying information to the user. In reviewing a novel or motion picture, one might assess the competence with which the author or director presented their material—whether they did so in an engaging, enlightening way—as well as the impact of the work on the audience. To date, there is no recognized forum for critical review of the societal impact of virtual reality experiences. Reasons for this stem from the fact that the medium has to be pervasive enough for evaluation, sufficient numbers of people need to be knowledgeable about the medium and the language of the medium to initiate a discussion, and enough people must be interested in reading the discourse. Perhaps one day there will be a forum for reviewers to discuss immersion experiences and their impact on society, much as *Film Comment* and other journals serve this purpose for the motion picture industry today.

Trends

In all areas of VR technology, the adage "faster, better, and cheaper" applies. In this section, we will try to address some of the ramifications of this applicable cliché, as well as look at some likely revolutionary changes and evolutionary developments. Many of our specific predictions stem from our observations over years of experience working with VR application developers. Certain overarching themes continually appear as roadblocks to what people want to do in VR and do with ease. We will discuss issues that arise often and that hardware and software vendors frequently try to address. The five main trends in the progress of VR technology are:

1. Less encumbrance

2. Increased use of augmented reality (AR)

3. VR in the home

4. Higher sensory fidelity

5. VR–ready machines

Less Encumbrance

One trend is the evolution of less encumbering VR systems. The weight and movement restriction placed on users wearing bulky, tethered gadgetry lessen the quality of the participant's experience. Head-based displays have been significantly reduced in weight and bulk (FIGURE 9-2). The typical weight of a head-mounted display in 1989 was 8 lbs., whereas the typical weight of a head-mounted display in 2002 is 0.5 lb. Tracking technologies have reduced the number of wires linking the participant to the VR system, as evidenced by modern tracking systems that use computer vision technologies compared with older tracking systems that required bulky transmitting units, marble-sized receivers, and a wire between each receiver mounted on the participant and a box of electronics. In the future we expect a user will pick up a display no larger than a pair of sunglasses, with no attached wires, to become visually and sonically immersed in the medium. Not all advances lead to reduced encumbrances, however. As work continues on haptic displays, many will involve *more* encumbering interface gadgetry during the early stages of development.

Increased Use of Augmented Reality

The feasibility of augmented reality applications will increase due to improvement in tracking and other input technologies. Even when driven by development of potentially useful applications, augmented reality work has focused on identifying and overcoming impractical technological hindrances. Because many AR applications

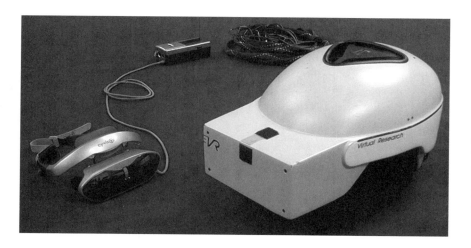

FIGURE 9-2 *As with many technologies, the head-based display has made significant inroads toward being an affordable peripheral for the home computer. In ten years, inexpensive HBDs have come down in cost by a factor of four, increased in resolution by a factor of seven, and significantly decreased in bulkiness as can be seen in this photograph (Photograph by William Sherman).*

make use of "hidden" real-world data (i.e., not apparent to the participant), new technologies with the ability to collect data about the real world will increase the areas where AR can be successfully applied.

VR in the Home

One anticipated future prospect of VR is its appearance in the home. Reduced costs for most of the technology have already made this practical for those who can afford, say, a typical home computer. The major barrier is the lack of available software that would make VR at home appealing. Accompanying the increased pervasiveness of VR will be an interface that will be instantly usable to a large percentage of the population, and this interface will become ubiquitous. These two trends are synergistic: as VR becomes more easily usable through standard interfaces, it will permeate more places and vice versa.

Home computers with sufficient computational horsepower for many VR applications are becoming affordable. The graphics subsystem, however, is a more complicated story. Low-cost, commodity graphics cards are becoming very powerful in terms of numbers of rendered polygons per second, but they are missing features important for full-fledged VR systems. Specifically, inexpensive graphics cards are still missing genlock (synchronizing multiple screens) and stereoscopic rendering. Virtual reality applications that can work with or without these features will give consumers a taste of what is possible and build up a demand for the features required for "true VR." Once the demand is sufficient, manufacturers will begin to provide these features in their home products. Already, companies such as Visbox, Inc. are developing projection VR environments that overcome some of these limitations at price points suitable for small companies, schools, and affluent homes.

The marketplace has occasionally offered HBDs for less than $1,000. However, while this price point is nice for research facilities, it is still too expensive for most home users. In the near future, however, an HBD will be made available that is priced about the same as a standard computer monitor. Of course, there needs to be an application available that makes the HBD worth purchasing. With many open source games becoming available in the Linux market, people will eventually port some of these to work with VR displays, providing the seductive applications for HBDs.

One possible scenario is that a new game will offer camera-based head-tracking to provide a monoscopic fishtank VR display. Players may find that the perception of "looking through a window" gives them a competitive advantage. Once word of this advantage spreads, more and more players will want to use the newly available display modality. Consequently, the technology race will escalate, and players will be using systems with multiple screens to increase their field of view. Some will migrate to larger screens by using their home-theater projection systems, and others will adopt stereoscopic displays in addition to head-tracking (FIGURE 9-3). Eventually, the same course will be pursued with input devices until everyone wants multiple 6-DOF tracked handheld props. Gaming, of course, is not the only potential application area for VR in the home. Other potential applications include virtual travel, educational applications, driver training, exercise enhancement, virtual family gatherings, and applications that support other three-dimensional activities, such as interior design and remodeling.

Virtual reality systems can now be found in the research groups of many companies and universities. Single VR applications have been deployed in just about every venue possible. It won't be long until VR systems will be found commonly in more public venues, from arcades to zoos and everywhere in between (FIGURE 9-4). As VR becomes more widely available and intuitive to use, there will be more applications for synchronously sharing virtual worlds. Games will be a significant driving force in this direction. Real-time, interactive, collaborative worlds are already a rising

FIGURE 9-3 *Lower-cost computer systems and projectors are making it possible to produce VR systems affordable for use in increasingly accessible venues. Here, a single-screen, immersive display from VisBox uses polarized light to produce a stereoscopic image from two projectors fed by a single computer. User tracking is accomplished with a video camera and image processing techniques (Images courtesy of Visbox, Inc.).*

(A)

(B)

FIGURE 9-4 *Virtual reality experiences have already begun to pop up in unexpected venues, such as this educational application at the Atlanta Zoo (Images courtesy of the Georgia Institute of Technology and the Atlanta Zoo). See color plate 26.*

force in gaming environments. Whereas games may be the most popular shared applications, the eventual pervasiveness of VR will mean more people will be using it for other tasks as well, and they too will want to work more effectively together. Shared environments will incorporate competition, master/apprentice relationships, brainstorming sessions, and many other scenarios involving social or professional interaction. Collaborative VR environments will prove invaluable to distance learning.

Higher sensorial fidelity may undergo evolutionary improvements, from greater visual acuity in a head-based screen to revolutionary improvements for displaying tactile sensations. Technology for full-body engagement (particularly the legs) is an area where advances may come with added encumbrances. Providing a treadmill for participants to walk on may enhance the experience, but it will also be more encumbering if it requires them to be tethered as a safety measure.

VR–Ready Machines

The notion of "VR–ready" systems is analogous to purchasing a computer system today that is "multimedia ready" and comes pre-equipped with essential hardware and software components: one will be able to purchase systems that are ready to run shrinkwrapped VR applications.

Turnkey systems combining hardware and software for some special purpose are likely to arise. We have already seen examples of this, such as the BDI suture trainer, Virtuality's game systems, and the therapy treatments by Virtually Better, Inc. Future systems will look less like computers with attached gadgetry; instead, they will be designed as training devices or other special-purpose appliances with all the required hardware and software integrated into the systems.

Technology Futures

As we mentioned at the beginning of this chapter, while it is difficult—no, impossible—to predict the future capabilities of technology, it is nonetheless imperative to make some educated guesses about what is likely to be developed, if one is to plan appropriately. Otherwise, VR applications in research and development today will be hopelessly out of date by the time they are deployed. The descriptions below are some of the thoughts that we believe are likely developments in the somewhat near future. These impressions are based on our discussions with vendors, technology developers, the VR community, and through being otherwise "in touch" with the direction that VR–related technology is headed. There is no doubt that some of the technologies we describe will come into being and some will not, and most likely others that we neither mention nor even conceive of will become pervasive.

Display Technologies

One area in which we are likely to see major changes in the near future is VR display hardware. In the sections that follow, we discuss innovations in the various sensory displays.

Visual Displays

Although not required in every VR application, stereoscopic visual display is generally an important ingredient. Less encumbering are *autostereoscopic displays,* where the display itself provides different images when viewed from different angles; often this is accomplished using a specially designed lenticular screen (i.e., a screen with tiny grooves molded or embossed into its surface). Because the viewer's eyes are slightly offset, each eye sees a different image, resulting in a stereoscopic display. By effectively moving the filtration from the participant's head to the display itself, autostereoscopic displays eliminate the need for wearing special headgear. Current autostereoscopic technology requires that users limit their movement and stay within a specific region. Too much movement causes the eyes to see the wrong image. The movement restrictions make current autostereo displays unfeasible for most VR applications.

   Already, there are commercially available autostereo video monitors that will display preprocessed video signals, and these systems are evolving to eliminate current restrictions (FIGURE 9-5). Developers are making the monitors viewable from a wider and

FIGURE 9-5 *Displays that automatically provide a stereoscopic image without the need for eyewear are now available from commercial manufacturers (Image of SynthaGram monitor courtesy of StereoGraphics Corporation).*

wider range of "sweet spots," reducing the need for users to limit their movements. In the future, we expect to see wall-sized, flat autostereo displays that allow real-time interactive stereoscopic display based on the participant's position. These displays could replace the screens in projection VR environments like the *CAVE,* or could indeed be overlaid on the walls of any given room, making it VR–ready.

Audio Displays

Developments in sound display are happening very rapidly, particularly the ability to present sound from absolute three-dimensional locations regardless of the acoustical environment in which the display is placed. Existing technology already provides a working solution for tracked headphones. However, many VR systems use loudspeakers for aural display in conjunction with large-screen visual displays. Often the screens occlude the speakers, or vice versa. In 100% field of regard projection systems, speakers located on the back sides of the screens will be highly muffled. Transparent speakers are one solution being researched to resolve this issue [Goudeseune 2001] (FIGURE 9-6).

   Advances in sonic rendering techniques also promise to provide a more fulfilling perceptual experience. We can expect significant progress in the ability to render realistic sounds through physically based sound-modeling algorithms. By

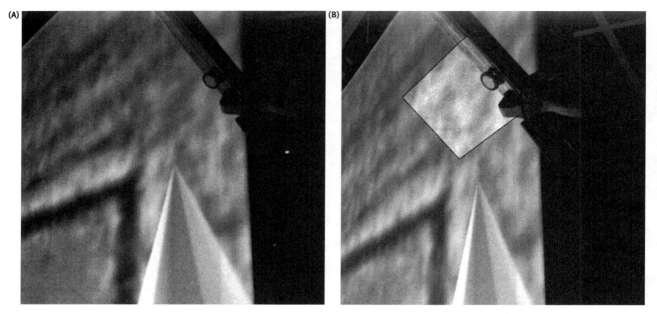

physically modeling the sound, you don't need to know ahead of time what sounds you need, which is a key advantage to this method. Also, if you are computing the sounds, you don't have to store them, and so on: they are fully dynamic. If, for example, an engine is getting bogged down, it will automatically sound like it is getting bogged down. You don't need to have a special "bogged down" sound available. The actual sound will be as it would have been in the real situation. Another sonic algorithm that will be very important is one that provides echo cancellation. Echoes are an issue for large-screen immersive spaces that have sound reflection problems caused by the screens.

Olfactory Displays

Scents are one of the most compelling triggers of emotional memory. The addition of olfactory display will be important for any experience intended to evoke emotional memories. Even for nonemotional applications, smell can be useful, for example, in surgical simulations and in diagnosing problems with electrical systems. Although there have been some experiments with blowing scented air into a virtual reality display space, there are a host of problems that must be addressed before smell can realistically become a common part of virtual reality experiences. Once a smell is

FIGURE 9-6 *This speaker uses a glass membrane to produce sound without visually occluding objects behind it. The glass membrane is vibrated to generate sound waves from a transducer that can be placed out of the line of sight. This device is suitable for projection VR systems that require speakers placed between the participant and the screens. Under normal conditions, only the transducer and mounting apparatus are visible (A). Only by using special lighting and other effects can we see the membrane (B) (Speaker courtesy of Hank Kaczmarski; Photograph by William Sherman).*

introduced into an environment, there is currently no effective way to instantaneously remove it.

At present there is no widely used theoretical model for the creation of scents from "scent primitives" analogous to how colors are produced from combining various amounts of red, green, and blue light (which is how televisions and computer displays work). There is some headway being made toward a usable theory of olfactory display. Not only do we need a good theory, but also technology that implements the theory. That is, we would need to load the display with the smell primitives and have all the different smells produced by combining them. Or, someone may develop a theory that works in some other, completely different way. However, no scent model *exists* (that we know of) with a few basic smells that can be combined to create a multitude of smells. The best today's technology can provide is a cartridge of each smell for introducing scent into the environment. Researchers are working on the problem, but widespread use of such displays is a long way off.

Haptic Displays

The tactile sensation side of haptic display also trails behind most other VR display technologies. Tactile sensations are useful for applications in which the user must piece together small objects or work with instruments that require very sensitive, precise adjustments, such as a surgeon might require. Advances are on the horizon. Displays that allow the participant to sense different surface textures or object edges will be available in the near future. Experimental tactile texture displays use arrays of small pins [Peine et al. 1995] or arrays of miniature electrodes [Kajimoto et al. 2002] that raise or lower as the finger moves across a virtual surface. These pin arrays must be very high resolution to produce the sensation of finely textured surfaces.

Another form of haptic display that will see progress is the class of kinesthetic display focused on locomotion. In order for omnidirectional treadmills and other locomotion displays to become commonplace, a number of improvements must be realized. Current omnidirectional treadmills are large, noisy, and very cumbersome. In order to be useful, they must be small, light, and accurate. Progress is being made in all these areas in a number of labs around the globe. One of the authors has been involved in designing such devices since the early 1990s, has seen numerous improvements, and is optimistic for the day when full-body locomotion is commonplace in virtual environments.

Although there has been minimal effort in developing devices like temperature display gloves and heat lamp and fan controllers, it is inevitable that more comprehensive climate control will be the norm in virtual environments. Because temperature display is relatively easy to do, it can add a lot, and people will probably want it. If one is virtually visiting Niagara Falls, for example, one could feel the temperature of the air drop and the humidity rise as one approaches the falls. This combined with the sound of rushing water could create a more compelling experience than that afforded by visual display alone.

Input Technologies

Innovations in user monitoring and world monitoring may eventually unencumber the participant and lead to the *ultimate interface*. In the next sections, we will focus on less obtrusive tracking devices, potential new input devices, and direct connections.

Unencumbered Input

One step in unencumbering the user is to reduce the wires used to collect input information from the user. Some systems have already been developed that partially eliminate wires from electromagnetic and ultrasonic tracking devices. By using radio communications, these systems eliminate the wires between the user's body and the fixed-position tracking hardware. However, the user must wear a radio pack with wires running to the tracked body parts, so this is not the supreme solution. However, for inputs from buttons and joysticks, commercial, off the shelf wireless devices have recently become available and provide a good solution (FIGURE 9-7).

One of the most significant advances toward unencumbered VR systems is the development of optical tracking. Rather than attaching sensors to the participant's body, video cameras "watch" the participant and convert video signals to tracking information via computer vision algorithms. This optical tracking data conveys position information and interprets gestures made by the participant. Gesture interpretation may reduce the necessity for handheld wand or button input devices.

Besides reporting tracking information, cameras will provide information regarding *who* is in the tracked space, using facial and/or body recognition. The system tailors the experience specifically for the person(s) involved and correctly presents their avatars in shared worlds.

New Input Devices

While gesture recognition may reduce the need for handheld devices, yet another avenue could lead to a vast infusion of specialized input devices. In the future, there may be custom devices for virtually every different type of activity in a virtual environment. It may be possible for some devices to change their shape to better mimic

FIGURE 9-7 *Off the shelf input devices are available that operate without connecting wires, providing a less encumbering interface to the virtual world (Photograph by William Sherman).*

their real-world counterpart; for instance, a golf club prop might change the perceived center of mass to simulate a wood, iron, or putter. This may be particularly useful in training environments, where the participant can interact with the same devices they will use in the real world.

Direct Connections

Human brain research investigates linking sensor devices directly to areas of the brain responsible for seeing and hearing for the goal of curing blindness and deafness. Recipients of devices developed from such research will be given the chance to perceive the real world through technology, and some will even perceive virtual worlds directly in the brain. Once barriers to this kind of technology are crossed, adventurous researchers are likely to bypass sensory organs to provide simulated stimulus directly to the brain, even in cases where sensory functions are not impaired.

Software

VR software can be classified into three groups: hardware interface, world creation, and applications. Current software is sufficient for experienced programmers to create interesting and innovative virtual reality experiences. However, for artists, scientists, educators, and others, a programmer must be hired to deal with all the elements of putting a VR application together. There are software tools available now, but they are still designed only to help programmers avoid some of the lower-level VR programming tasks. Eventually, experience creation software will progress to the point where nonprogrammers can begin to create virtual worlds on their own.

Hardware Interface Software

Presently, there are two types of VR application developers: those that make use of software libraries to handle the hardware interface and those that write applications for exactly the hardware they plan to use. As more inexpensive or free hardware interface libraries become available, more application developers will take advantage of them, ultimately making these applications portable across VR system platforms. The rise in use of open source hardware interface libraries will make it easier for programmers to focus primarily on the task of creating the virtual world.

Application Development Software

When the creation of the codified aspects of a virtual world becomes trivial, we will see a revolution in the creation of VR applications. Application development tools will make it easy for a large number of people to create VR applications and to make those applications available to the masses. The key is that developers must be able to focus on the space and what takes place there rather than on the mathematics necessary to render the world correctly.

Techniques for accomplishing world design tasks have been available for many years. However, systems have not yet approached apotheosis. To become an ideal interface, procedures need to become less tedious, more straightforward, and easier to learn. The experience creator needs to easily and directly convey what they want in the virtual world without the need to hand position each polygon, or to write computer code for each action and interface. This future development environment could be manipulated via a desktop computer interface, but perhaps a virtual reality interface would be more suitable and efficient.

This ideal virtual world creation platform will be able to handle all the components of the virtual world in a comfortable way for the creator. For example, creating a virtual table should not require numerically specifying the location of each vertex. The creator should be able to quickly sketch the shape of the table, with the computer software automatically enhancing the object as much or little as desired [Zeleznik et al. 1996].

Interfaces will be easier to design, because a suite of common and adjustable interface elements will be available. Advances in object behavior simulation (physics models of the world) will allow developers to choose a particular, pre-created object behavior model. Algorithms for generating sounds based on a more comprehensive physics model will reduce the need for tedious sound design and editing. Furthermore, the ideal development platform will need to be modular and provide for hardware device independence.

Modularity allows experience creators to reuse previously created segments of the world, such as a menu system or a travel method. Modularity allows experience creators to share common portions of their creations. For example, developers might share a menu system. Useful modules can be distributed among a community of experience creators.

Hardware independence makes it easier to port virtual reality experiences from one VR platform to another. Of course, some changes, such as from HBDs to *CAVE,* will change the perception of the experience. Hardware independence makes transfers from older hardware to newly updated hardware easier.

Currently VR experience design teams require considerable computer programming and mathematical skills. For the most part, a future VR experience design team should not require people familiar with concepts such as Euler angles, serial protocols, shared memory, message passing, socket interface, head-related transfer functions, or spring and dashpot models. Future design teams should spend almost no time on these concepts and should instead concentrate nearly 100% of their effort on the following issues:

- Story development (storyboarding)
- Representational mapping and aesthetics (what to render rather than how to render)
- Landmarks and other wayfinding aids

- Interactivity between the user and the virtual world
- Effective and entertaining presentation methods
- Problem solving and creativity (meeting the needs of the user)

Likewise, future teams should be more integrally woven around scientists, artists, doctors, teachers, students, homemakers, and writers. That is, VR applications should be designed by and for the people who will use the end result.

Job tasks that are currently critical in the development of virtual reality experiences but will be less critical in the future include electrical engineering, video engineering, code development, computer graphics, and mathematics. VR applications should not be designed by only the infrastructure developers.

Application Futures

Progress in VR is evident in the numerous ways developers have found to make use of the medium. The use of virtual reality for treating psychological disorders was not among the early examples cited for the usefulness of VR. However, in the second half of the 1990s this application of virtual reality flourished (FIGURE 9-8). Other new terrain will open up and be explored as more people bring this medium to bear on problems they face regularly.

The significant step that will herald the arrival of virtual reality as a commonplace tool is the availability of VR–ready applications at local software retailers. Although it is already possible to purchase ready-to-run VR packages with specific applications preinstalled on a VR system, it is not yet possible to purchase the VR system or the VR application at a consumer retailer. There are a handful of VR applications that can be downloaded from the Internet. Soon, one will be able to purchase a package for architectural design and evaluation or, perhaps even sooner, a VR–ready game that you can take home, install on your home computer, and physically immerse yourself into the design space or game arena.

Chapter Summary:
The Future Is Happening Now

The astute reader will recognize that many of the trends we speak of are indeed happening today. Many of the roadblocks to ubiquitous VR are already being overcome. Today, an ambitious programmer with energy and more time than money can assemble a workable fishtank VR system in their own home. For the price of a typical home

FIGURE 9-8 *Researchers at the Georgia Institute of Technology developed a VR application for treatment of individuals suffering from post-traumatic stress syndrome from their experiences in the Vietnam War. The commercial application* Virtual Vietnam *is now available to therapists as a turnkey hardware/software system that can be deployed in their office for use with patients. Virtually Better Inc. provides this and a number of other turnkey systems for phobia treatment, ranging from fear of flying to fear of heights (Image courtesy of the Georgia Institute of Technology). See color plate 27.*

PC with a reasonably priced high-performance graphics card and a low-cost video camera, that same programmer can construct a visual and audio system using off the shelf components and free software to tie the system together. While such a system will probably lack features such as stereoscopic display, it will actually be free from encumbrance due to using video for optical tracking, which requires no connection to the user. As time marches on, such a system can grow in complexity, power, and options for display and interaction devices.

It is just a matter of time before such systems and much more sophisticated systems are available to almost everyone regardless of their computer skills and budget. It only takes a trip to a VR–related tradeshow or a quick browse of the World Wide Web to recognize that manufacturers are providing faster, lighter, less encumbering VR equipment at lower and lower prices.

Because the future is happening now, it behooves us as early VR developers to ensure that the quality of the applications, the user interfaces, and interaction techniques are as appropriate as they can possibly be. What we are developing now is the future. We need to be prepared for a future built on what we are doing today

PART III

Appendices

NICE, An Educational Experience

*N*ICE provides persistent virtual worlds in which children can interact with virtual ecosystems, creating a story from their actions. *NICE* benefits from the ability for virtual reality worlds to contain building blocks with characteristics not possible with physical toys or other learning tools.

Interaction is enhanced by bringing multiple groups of children into the same virtual world using networked collaborative technologies. Each group can see where the other groups are by observing the avatars that represent each group (FIGURE A-1). A single avatar represents the location in the virtual world for each group stationed at a single VR display, typically a projection-based display such as the *CAVE* or *ImmersaDesk*.

Interactions with the objects in the environment and between participating groups become a set of stories of the events that take place in the virtual world. A participant's particular narrative becomes something that can be printed and kept as a reminder of the experience. The ability to produce a physical artifact is something that is felt by constructivists to be an important part of the learning process.

The goals of the *NICE* project lie at two levels. On one level, *NICE* is a research project to investigate the potential of virtual reality as a learning tool for children. The creators state: "NICE aims to create a virtual learning environment based on current educational theories of constructivism, narrative, and collaboration"

(A)  **(B)**  **(C)**

FIGURE A-1 *In the* NICE *environment, children don avatars and explore* The Big Island *virtual world (Image courtesy of Andrew Johnson, EVL).*

[Roussos et al. 1997]. On another level, the application authors wish to create an interesting virtual world that is engaging and fun for kids without diminishing the learning experience.

The theory of constructivism is that assimilation of knowledge can be enhanced from active experiences with the world—or in this case "a" world. Some experiments in distance learning have used text-based virtual worlds to provide an interface between children and classes physically distant from one another. An example of a non–computer-based, contructivist learning activity would be a child building a vehicle or house with LEGO building blocks as part of a story they've imagined—their own imaginary, virtual world. The child may then use the artifacts (house, car, etc.) in support of performing additional narratives about the imaginary (virtual) world they've created in the process.

Other research using VR technology to provide a creative space for children includes work at the Human Interface Technology (HIT) Lab at the University of Washington and the ACM SIGKIDS CitySpace project [Vella et al. 1995]. However, these projects provide a mostly unstructured environment in which children construct objects within an empty virtual world, much as they would use LEGOs to build objects in physical play. Such construction tasks can be made part of a constructivist learning experience, if the activity is guided toward the simultaneous construction of mental models along with the physical ones.

Application Description

NICE combines the use of constructivism with the potential educational benefits from the use of narrative and collaboration in a virtual reality experience. A "living" virtual world is provided that presents the children with a place to explore and study. The world is living in that it has an ongoing, underlying structure (or ecosystem) that continues to exist and evolve as time passes, regardless of whether or not anyone modifies it or is there to witness the gradual change. By manipulating objects in this world, the children can change the evolution of those objects. For example, they can plant a seed and watch as it grows in a garden.

As a child (or small group) explores and manipulates the world, a list of significant events is created—a story. Inspired by ideas developed by Karl Steiner and Tom Moher [1994] in the *Graphical StoryWriter*, a story is constructed detailing their activities. These stories are simple and similar to what a child might produce. A printed copy of the story serves to provide a tangible reminder of the experience. In the printed narrative, some of the nouns are replaced by pictures of the objects, making a much more visually appealing keepsake. (See the *Placeholder* experience in Appendix D for another approach to narrative in a VR experience.) By allowing each group of children to collaborate with other groups using VR displays (often separated by great distances), they have the opportunity to work together within a common world (FIGURE A-2). Thus, they are provided with an environment in which to learn team skills in addition to individual skills.

The virtual world of *NICE* consists of the space in which the activity happens, prototype agents within the space to provide guidance, a persistent ecosystem, and the avatars of the other participants (FIGURE A-3). The prototype world used

FIGURE A-2 *Although distanced from each other in the real world, children interact and collaborate in a shared virtual world (Image courtesy of Andrew Johnson, EVL). See color plate 13.*

(A)

(B)

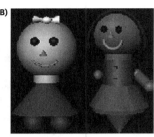

(C)

FIGURE A-3 *Children using the* NICE *application embody an avatar of their choosing, such as the boy in the garden* (A) *or one of the girls* (B). *The experience allows them to interact with other children, also embodied as avatars, and with genies, such as the owl and bird* (C), *who provide aid and instruction during their adventure on* The Big Island. *(Images courtesy of Andrew Johnson, EVL).*

to test *NICE* is called *The Big Island*. Virtual agents (referred to as genies in *NICE*) of varying characteristics help to guide the participants in their exploration.

The Big Island world is limited in scope (it's an island), yet contains distinct places of interest for the exploring mind. Key locations on the island are a vegetable garden, a volcano, a beach, and an area populated by tiki statues. The water surrounding the island can be waded in, and there is a second, smaller island accessible by bridge or by wading through the water. Subterranean catacombs connect an entryway at the volcano to one near the statues.

In the initial prototype version, the vegetable garden provides the most interactive experience. Here the participant can pick up plants, seedlings, a cloud, and sunshine to manipulate the ecosystem of the garden. Bins near the garden supply the seedlings, a raincloud provides the water, a sun the sunshine, and a compost heap a place to deposit weeds and other unwanted plants. Life in the garden continues to evolve whether a participant is there tending it or not.

Information about the world is provided by the genies. Genies can be found in many forms and provide a wide range of help. A talking signpost greets the arriving group and gives directions to interesting locations in the world. The cloud and sun are considered genies that provide required life ingredients for the plants. The developers also experimented with giving some genies *intelligent actions,* which we discuss further in the next sections.

Groups of bees and bunnies swarm and flock toward the closest avatar by using standard computer graphics techniques to create complex looking behavior using simple algorithms (i.e., flocking and object attraction) [Reynolds 1987].

The original concept for *NICE* was to include two agents that exhibit intelligent behavior. These agents were Sofia the owl and a whirligig bird. The plan for Sofia was to have her follow along with participants, sharing wisdom about the world and the possibilities within. The whirligig bird would provide advice on how best to plant and tend the garden. The difficulty in creating reasonably intelligent behavior led to a single avatar, controlled by a single teacher acting as the overall guide to the experience using the Wizard of Oz technique discussed in Chapter 6.

Representation of the Virtual World

Overall, the world is represented in a manner with which kids are familiar: it's cartoon-like. Internally, the objects in the world are VRML models that can easily be transported between machines and software tools (e.g., modeling software packages). This gives the application authors a wider variety of tools with which to create new objects for the world. More importantly, it can make it easier for kids to be able to create their own objects, especially avatars, that can be used within *NICE*.

Visual Representations

Externally, the world is represented in a cartoonish fashion. The plants have eyes and wear sunglasses when they need water and hold umbrellas when they have had too much. The default avatars are iconic, constructed of basic geometric shapes. In this style, cartoonish boy and girl avatars can be chosen to represent any of the groups entering the world. Each group (or pair) of children at a VR display and the agents occupying the world are associated with avatars that allow the other participants to see their location and movement. The avatars are articulated, operating as three separate parts: the torso/body, the right hand, and the head. This method enables gross body gestures, such as shaking the head or waving and pointing with the hand. The lips on each avatar move in conjunction with audio levels originating from the corresponding site, giving a cue as to who is speaking.

Avatars for each group can be selected from a few premade models (e.g., the cartoonish boy or girl), or they can be made by the children before entering the VR system. The avatar need not be in the shape of a human. It can easily be a dinosaur, bird, or whatever can be imagined and modeled by the child. In fact, it might be interesting to study both how the choice of avatar reflects the personality of the child and how an assigned avatar affects the behavior of the child in the virtual world. Does the child alter their behavior based on how they appear to others?

Something that the application authors noticed is that children really enjoy seeing the avatars of the other people. The children also expressed a desire to be able to see what they looked like in the world. In later versions, the application creators added reflection to the water, allowing participants to see themselves. They are also exploring other opportunities for viewing oneself such as "out of body" experiences.

Aural Representations

Sounds are provided both as ambient, environmental sounds and as feedback to interactions with the world. Environmental sounds are based on the proximity of the user to certain elements in the world. When near the beach, one might hear the waves as they roll in or the chirp of birds when near the garden.

Feedback sounds include the "beeps and boops" associated with selecting items in the garden, jumping, or changing size. Footstep sounds also provide feedback as the user moves through the world. The footstep sounds are based on the material of the surface they are trodding on. For instance, if they are walking through water, they will hear small splashes for each "step."

Haptic and Other Sensory Representations

Other than the handheld prop for interacting and moving through the world (the CAVE wand), no haptic feedback devices are employed by *NICE*. The wand itself is not easily used by small hands, which led to other devices being considered for use as passive haptic props.

The use of other haptic, vestibular, or other sensory I/O devices has not been investigated. Keeping the interface kid friendly adds constraints to what can be effectively utilized as interface devices.

Interaction with the Virtual World

Primary interaction with the *NICE* virtual world is in the form of a walkthrough, with abilities to jump and change size and to grab, move, and drop objects. *NICE* is an *interactive narrative* experience, a genre that appears in a range of other applications, including Disney's *Aladdin's Magic Carpet Ride* and the *Placeholder* experience discussed in Appendix D. This type of experience is used almost exclusively in another computer-mediated medium: interactive fiction (e.g., *Colossal Cave* and *Zork*).

Narrative

The application developers emphasize that narrative is a key element of the *NICE* experience. By providing an environment where the narrative evolves from the choices of the participants, the participants become more involved. An important choice in an interactive narrative system is whether to create a *directed* or *undirected* experience. *Directed* interactive narratives are the norm in interactive fiction (IF); these are also known as *text adventures*.

In interactive fiction, the participant makes many choices as they explore a (textual) virtual world. The narrative path traveled may vary, but in the end the story generally culminates in a predetermined ending, no matter what path was taken to get there. Often, IF participants are told up front what their goal (destiny) is. The general view of constructivism, however, is not to provide a predetermined destiny. Rather, a loosely defined goal is given, and the true focus is on the interactions, decisions, connections, and constructions made by the children during the experience.

As builders of a constructivist environment, the authors of *NICE* have elected to provide an open ended space, where children freely experience (and thus construct) their own narrative. The virtual world provides a context for the narrative, while leaving the narrative structure open. The resultant stories might accomplish narrative closure, but often do not. In the case of the educational study performed, children were asked to plot out part of their goal and then to carry out their plan once in the virtual world [Roussos et al. 1999].

The characters of the stories include the children and the objects and agents in the virtual world. Like TV soap operas, the world consists of multiple plotlines with many stories happening simultaneously. Each child's (or group's) path through those stories becomes their specific narrative of the events.

These narratives, generated by the activities of a child, are captured in a simple transcript, which serves as a memento of their experience [Roussos et al. 1997]:

```
Amy pulls a cloud over her carrot patch and waters it.
The tomatoes complain that they didn't get enough water.
Claudio plants his first tree.
```

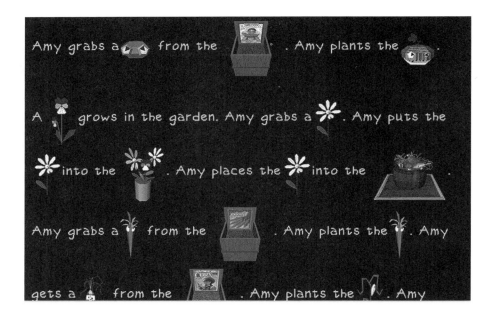

FIGURE A-4 *A written story documenting a child's actions in the virtual world is automatically created to provide a tangible reminder of the experience (Image courtesy of Andrew Johnson, EVL).*

The transcript, which the child can take home, is an important element of contructivist learning. It is made more interesting by replacing the textual representation of some of the nouns with visual representations (FIGURE A-4).

Navigation

Nonintuitive and cumbersome travel interfaces can interfere with the learning experience. Accordingly, the application authors sought to provide an easy, nonintrusive method of traveling through the virtual world. The prototype interface used physical locomotion combined with wand-controlled "walking" (i.e., a walkthrough method of travel). Physically walking within the confines of the *CAVE* provides a 10 ft. × 10 ft. area in which the user can step on objects, including stairs, which virtually raise and lower the child to the correct elevation (terrain following). Traveling beyond the 10 ft. × 10 ft. space is accomplished by pressing on the pressure stick on the wand to move the user in the direction the wand is pointed or to rotate the world about the user.

One problem encountered with this travel scheme is the wand itself. The spacing and layout of the controls on the wand are suboptimal for the small hands of children, who generally had to use two hands to activate some of the controls designed for one-handed input gestures. The application authors sought better solutions, including a new wand design and new travel techniques. Common VR interface devices are not necessarily designed for use by children. A VR system designer might need to put special emphasis on finding suitable input devices for the nonadult user.

In addition to allowing walkthrough travel along the surface of the world, *NICE* users are provided with two other travel options. By pressing the middle wand button, the user springs high into the air. This enables them to see the world from a higher vantage point, as well as allowing them to land on top of very tall objects. The pressure joystick on the wand can still be used to perform regular translational movement while in the middle of a jump. The other special ability is to shrink down to a very small size. While small, the user has the same movement interface, but can now go places where they could not previously fit, such as a tunnel beneath the garden, where the root systems of the plants can be observed. Children had little difficulty using this system and did not experience much fatigue.

If the participant manages to climb or land on top of an object moving through the world, such as the ladybug under the garden, then they can ride the object until they move off or fall off. Thus, the ride along is another method the child can use to travel through the world.

Manipulation

In the prototype *NICE* world, *The Big Island,* the primary venue of interaction is the garden. In the garden, children plant and tend the vegetables. Vegetable seedlings can be "picked" from nearby bins. Picking is done by pointing at an object and pressing a wand button. When the user is holding a plant, it will appear attached to their hand avatar. While holding a plant, the user can place it in the garden by pressing the wand button again.

The buttons and pressure stick of the *CAVE's* wand provide the means for different interactions with the world. To remind the user of the operation of each of these inputs, an instruction sheet moves with the hand portion of the avatar. The hand and instructions move in association with the handheld wand. Seeing the wand represented as their avatar's own hand also provides a connection to the virtual world that helps ground them there (FIGURE A-5).

The developers of *NICE* endeavored to produce an interface that was natural for the child by using visual metaphors to affect the world. The three buttons on the wand are used to create control signals. The functionality of the buttons remains consistent throughout the experience, providing for jumping, picking (i.e., grabbing), and

FIGURE A-5 *In* NICE, *the wand prop is represented as a hand avatar. To improve the usability of the interface, instructions for how to use the wand's buttons and joystick are included as part of the avatar (Application courtesy of EVL).*

changing size (shrinking or growing). Most of the interaction with the objects in the world is done by picking objects and releasing them in a new location.

Plants can be grabbed and moved within the garden. This is also handled by pointing at the plant and pressing a wand button once to grab and again to release. In this way, children can reorganize the garden, move some plants to the compost heap (typically the uninvited weeds), or hand a plant to another participant.

Part of tending the virtual garden includes making sure the plants get the proper amounts of nutrients. In the prototype world, these nutrients are sunshine and rainwater. The source of the nutrients are the sun and cloud genies. These genies can be grabbed in the same manner as the seedlings and then moved and released anywhere within the garden (FIGURE A-6). Given sufficient nutrients, the plants in the garden grow rapidly. If given too much, the plants will react adversely. In this world, the plants pop out an umbrella if too wet or sunglasses if too dry. Although the garden is the primary interactive area of the prototype virtual world, the goal of *NICE's* authors is for everything to be pickable, movable, scalable, and so on.

Selecting an object for picking or other manipulation is done by pointing at it. Although reaching out to an object would be a more natural interface, it doesn't always work well in a VR interface. In the *CAVE,* for example, the user can reach most objects and could thus be required to "touch" them to grab them; however, objects near the extremes of the range of the tracking system can be hard to grab, such as those near the ground, or floor of the *CAVE.* The interface must work within the constraints of all target VR systems. In *NICE,* which uses the *CAVE* and *ImmersaDesk,* objects near the participant's feet cannot always be seen and thus directly manipulated. To resolve this, the method of remotely selecting objects by pointing was included as part of the interface.

FIGURE A-6 *A child tends the plants in the* NICE *garden by dragging the sun over them (Image courtesy of Andrew Johnson, EVL).*

Agents (Genies)

The genies come in a variety of shapes and with a variety of abilities, ranging from simple to very complex. Different methods are used to implement each genie. The actions of the simpler genies are coded into the application software. Difficult to program genies, such as those that exhibit advanced behaviors like discussions with the participants, were implemented by the *Wizard of Oz* technique (see Chapter 6).

Collaboration

Collaborative interactions among the children are an important aspect of the *NICE* experience. Collaboration occurs in two distinct modes: (1) local collaboration among the children in the same physical space and (2) remote collaboration between displays, using avatars to represent the remote groups. Working together locally, the children adopt particular roles. For instance, one child will wear the tracked glasses and control the viewpoint. The wand input device might be controlled by another child to direct the movement and interactions with the virtual world. A third child might take on the role of adviser/manager, directing what the other children should do. Roles can quickly be traded among the children, and exchanges are made several times in the hour-long sessions. Children learn through verbal interactions, collective decision making, and conflict resolution. In the study, one child was randomly chosen as the "leader" and would be the exclusive controller of the wand. This was done to avoid conflicts and reduce the training efforts to a single child.

Computer-mediated collaboration allows the children to interact with other children whom they may never have met in real life. They can communicate between sites by making gestures with the wand, which are reflected by the avatar of their hand. The number of possible gestures is fairly limited: waving hello/goodbye, nodding agreement/disagreement, indicating to come/follow, and pointing at objects and in various directions. The children enjoyed exploring these methods of nonverbal communication between groups. A particularly popular exercise was to pick up a flower and offer it to another avatar, who could then accept it. According to the *NICE* authors, children loved "exaggerating their gestural communication" [Roussos et al. 1997].

The communication channel is broadened by the addition of an audio connection among all the participants. This allows communication to occur more naturally, bringing the separate participants together as if in the same space. Not all the collaborating sites need to use immersive displays. By using the *CAVE* library, the application has the ability to be displayed in nearly any VR paradigm, as well as non-immersive displays. Because the activity in the persistent virtual world is maintained by an independent server program, any application can access the server for information about the world. One such experiment in this direction was done using the NCSA *Habenero* collaborative software system (an internet-based CSCW system). In this particular experiment, the *Habenero* client displayed a 2D representation of the hub of the interactivity, the garden. On a desktop computer screen, users of this client could see and interact with groups in the garden. This was later implemented as a basic Java applet, allowing anyone with a Java-capable Web browser to interact with the garden (FIGURE A-7).

A later addition to *NICE* was an automated Web page showing a picture of the current layout of the garden and the location of anyone in the garden. This turned out to be a very efficient way to monitor a persistent virtual world, since anyone with a Web browser could check on the status of the garden and its visitors. The Web page also includes a chat space that allows all the WWW participants to communicate with one another and with the people in the virtual space. Anything typed in the chat box is displayed in the virtual environment. Additionally, because all the objects in the

virtual world are described in VRML, another option is to view a VRML representation of the current garden over the Web.

World Physics

The physics of the *NICE* virtual world that deal with the participant are somewhat cartoonish. By pressing a button, the user can jump ten times the height of their avatar and slowly float back down to the ground. However, their interaction with the world more or less follows familiar real-world interactions: once airborne, the user doesn't remain aloft, but returns to the ground via simulated gravity. Participants are also unable to walk through walls. Although these interactions are similar to how the real world is experienced, the algorithms that cause them are not based on mathematical models of real-world physics.

The ecological model of the garden is a form of "cartoon" physics; it is a simple ecological model of plants that isn't exactly the way things work in the physical world. In the *NICE* garden, plants need a certain amount of water, sunshine, and spacing. If the plants are given the wrong amounts, they will exhibit specific signals. The donning of sunglasses, popping open of umbrellas, and the rustling activity of the plants when they become too crowded are all examples of such signals.

The ecological model of the garden was designed to be replaceable by other models. This was done to give students the possibility of creating their own ecological models and experiencing the results. The experience creators also wanted to provide a means by which they could incorporate ecomodels of varying complexity based on the age of the children. The application creators did have some rules that they tried to enforce in the interactions between participants and objects in their world. The two major rules are (1) actions in the world should have a cause and effect relationship and (2) the world itself should be persistent, with users able to enter and exit at any time.

Venue

During the analysis phase of the application design, the most common venue for *NICE* was the Electronic Visualization Lab (EVL) at the University of Illinois at Chicago. It has also been demonstrated at multiple sites at SIGGRAPH '96 in New Orleans, at ThinkQuests '96 and '97 in Washington, D.C., and at SuperComputing '97. It is also commonly demonstrated to children at other sites equipped with *CAVE* or *Immersa-Desk* technology, such as the National Center for Supercomputing Applications and the Ars Electronica museum in Linz, Austria.

For the research project, two systems are connected, allowing two groups to interact with each other. The largest single *NICE* collaboration occurred at Super-Computing '97, where 17 different sites participated simultaneously. Those sites included several cities throughout the United States, plus the Netherlands and Fukuoka, Japan [Johnson et al. 1998].

The plan for deploying *NICE* is to make it more readily available for use by children at locations that offer "informal educational" opportunities. Many of these sites—museums, science centers, and cultural centers—have already begun installing projection-based VR systems. A field trip to these locations might now also include a visit to a world within *NICE*.

Up to four children can comfortably participate at each VR display. By keeping the number of participants low, each child has the opportunity to control the experience firsthand. During one study, two children were stationed, one at each display, and allowed to explore for as much time as they pleased. During the analysis phase of *NICE* development, children were allowed to participate as long as they desired. Many kids spent approximately one hour in *NICE,* but several stayed for an extra half hour.

During the controlled experiment, case studies of two children at a time participated, with one in a *CAVE* display and one at an *ImmersaDesk.* Other times, when entire classes would come to experience *NICE,* the children were split into groups of seven or eight. Each group was divided between the two displays, while the rest of the class participated in other related activities.

The provision of a Web-based interface to the persistent *NICE* world lets children continue to be part of the *NICE* experience even after they have left the immersive display. In addition to extending the experience via Internet-based collaborative technologies, other post–VR-experience techniques, such as discussing, drawing, and writing about the experience, can be brought into the classroom.

VR System

NICE is typically displayed on large projection VR displays, such as the *CAVE* and *ImmersaDesk.* Choosing this type of visual display allowed the *NICE* designers to realize such goals as group activity among multiple participants sharing a single display and easy exchange of control between local participants. Working at the EVL at the University of Illinois at Chicago meant that such large-scale, projection-based displays were also a more readily available resource than other display types.

While in general, it is easier for younger children (the target audience) to wear stereo glasses than a typical HMD, they were not ideal. Standard, commonly available shuttering stereo glasses are designed primarily for adult head sizes; thus straps were added to help prevent them from slipping off the children's heads so they could properly view the stereoscopic display. Other possibilities to improve the fit for young children include custom building smaller stereo glasses or using a nonshuttering system for which smaller glasses are available. Despite the steps taken in the *NICE* project, children usually still had to hold the glasses on their heads. This effort was the most significant factor contributing to fatigue in the young participants.

The VR rendering/simulation system is a typical *CAVE/ImmersaDesk* configuration, with the three-button wand with pressure stick, shuttering stereo, and a Silicon Graphics, Inc. (SGI) *Onyx* with *Infinite Reality* graphics hardware (more than one for multiscreened displays). As we've discussed, the *NICE* developers found that the wand buttons were difficult to manipulate in the small hands of children. Some consideration was given to using input devices other than the standard wand, including props such as garden tools. However, the developers felt that adding additional props would increase the complexity of the interface, rather than solve the problems children have manipulating the wand buttons, so they chose to settle with the wand.

Application Implementation

NICE was designed to be a reusable framework for which new educational worlds can be created. The application authors have tried to include as many elements as possible to enable the creation of rich environments suitable for constructivist learning. Many of these elements are demonstrated in *The Big Island* prototype world.

Development of the *NICE* experience was a joint project between the Interactive Computing Environment (ICE) and the Electronic Visualization Lab (EVL), both at the University of Illinois at Chicago. Programming of the application began in January 1996. However, design and brainstorming sessions began several months prior. Some of the ideas implemented in *NICE* came from earlier research projects at the EVL, such as *CALVIN* [Leigh et al. 1996] and the *Graphical StoryWriter*, a nonimmersive system that helps preliterate children to create stories [Steiner and Moher 1994]. *NICE* was first tested with children in July of 1996.

The user interface part of the software system is built on the *CAVE* library, using SGI's *Performer* library. *Performer* provides the advantage of fast graphical rendering on any of the SGI line of computers, enabling the programmers to write a single version that will work well on different levels of hardware. The SGI *Inventor* object format is used to store the models of the objects in the world. It is very similar to the VRML format, so models can be transferred between formats relatively easily.

Without a standard interface within the *CAVE* library, audio communication in *NICE* was implemented by connecting wireless microphones to standard telephone devices.

The programming required part-time work from three graduate students and one postdoctoral staff member at EVL during the year in which the prototype evaluation system was created. The members of the project team were student Maria Roussos (project leader), postdoc Andrew Johnson, students Jason Leigh and Christina Vasilakis, Professor Thomas Moher (Human Computer Interaction and Computer-based Education department), and Professor Mark Gillingham (UIC College of Education, Department of Curriculum, Instruction, and Evaluation), who served as the project advisor. The postdoc and all the students had backgrounds in computer science. Maria and Christina also have a background in art.

Design

The software design includes three components: a behavior module, a networking module, and the display and interaction module. The behavior module uses a client/server model of communication. A *central behavioral server* contains the world database and manages the interactions in the world (FIGURE A-8). Interactions between the participants and the genies and objects of the world follow the rules set for the world and are formatted as story structures by the interaction module.

The networking module was written to be usable by all applications that use the EVL *CAVE* library. This ongoing independent project is called *CAVERNsoft* [Leigh et al. 1997]. For *NICE,* the important feature of this effort was the ability to transfer audio (and video) between VR displays. The display/interaction module is also a client to the behavior server to enable interacting with the rule-based world activities. Independent of this, avatar location is sent via Unix multicasting to all other

FIGURE A-8 *The NICE virtual world is implemented as a persistent server, to which a variety of different clients, with different display devices, can attach (Image courtesy of Andrew Johnson, EVL).*

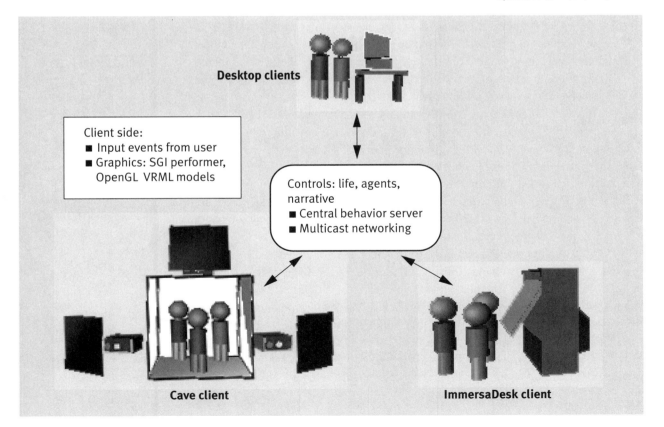

NICE applications running on the network. Clients in addition to the 3D rendering of the world were developed to provide other functions. For example, there is a recording client that saves all the activities that occur during a session so they can be replayed later. The persistent world client/server method also provides the ability for object models to be transferred to *NICE* rendering modules. Thus, when some models have changed since a particular site has last connected, new replacement models will be transferred to the site. Also, models for each user's avatar can be sent to the world server and propagated to the other clients.

Appendix Summary

The application authors have found quantitative assessment of "how much more" children learn in constructivist learning environments to be ineffective. Instead, they have established "a conceptual evaluation framework and a standard evaluation methodology based on observation." Following constructivist research, their theoretical framework takes into account "issues involving technical orientation, affective, cognitive, pedagogical, and behavior aspects." They employed several methods of evaluation, including personal observation, open ended interviews, video recording, computerized tracking of actions in the VR environment, and the use of real people (disguised as avatars) asking questions from "behind the scenes."

The application authors consider the biggest accomplishment of *NICE* to be the combination of many educational practices into a VR environment. With this combination, they have reached their first goal of creating a system that enables the deployment of different, flexible constructivist worlds. The research team has taken many of the lessons learned from their *NICE* experience and applied them to further work in constructivist educational virtual reality applications. Specifically, the *RoundEarth* project was assembled and tested directly in the school environment on a somewhat more portable virtual reality system [Johnson et al. 1998].

NICE was of great interest to many teachers. Many participated by bringing their classrooms to the *CAVE* at the UIC campus to help with project evaluation. Interest has also been shown by community projects in the Chicago area, as well as by educators at conference demonstrations such as ThinkQuest '96 and '97. In their follow-on work, the research team found that working directly inside the school made it much easier to fit within the normal routine of the children's day and also required less effort on their part, because they didn't need to provide a place and activities for those children waiting for their turn. They would just take a few children at a time, while the others remained in the classroom.

Most of the children who participated in the *NICE* evaluation readily became mentally immersed in the virtual world. The amount of a child's experience with videogames seems to be a factor in the degree to which they get involved by physically moving around to accomplish tasks, rather than remaining stationary, moving only the wand. Those *with* videogame experience were *more* likely to physically squat, kneel, and jump in their interactions. The *NICE* application designers are working to include more elements that encourage physical movement, such as walking around the space and physically reaching to grab objects, in upcoming research projects.

One discovery made by the project researchers was that the children learned how to perform the interactions more quickly when instructed by characters in the world, as opposed to a live human standing next to them. By having an avatar of a remote trainer give the instructions, the participant is "immediately pulled into the fantasy because they are talking and gesturing and reacting to the remote user's avatar" [Johnson 1998].

Another *NICE* discovery was the benefit of using a persistent virtual world on a steady, fault-tolerant server. By having the world always available, the VR application would initialize quickly, ready for action. Often there would already be other participants in the world with whom the newcomer could interact. In fact, the researchers would often begin using the application and find users from remote locations exploring the world.

In future efforts, the *NICE* experience authors feel it will be beneficial to provide the element of user programmability. They would like the children to be able to define and manipulate the ecological model (e.g., plant growth rules) and tools within the virtual environment. In the current system, a world is preprogrammed, and the children can explore how the virtual world works but cannot modify the rules.

The application creators believe that exploration into the use of immersive environments as an educational tool has promise for certain types of learning. "Its value in terms of conceptual learning of a subject matter remains to be proven." However, they believe VR is "a unique educational tool [that] can encourage learning through exploration." Finally, Maria Roussos, one of the project leaders, informs us:

> I think that *NICE* had positive outcomes as well as shortcomings. In this sense it was a very successful experiment in that it made us see how difficult a challenge researchers interested in VR learning face. No one technology or application can add learning value if it is not applied to a very important and hard learning goal and informed by contemporary educational research and practice.

A NOTE ON INFORMATION ACQUISITION

The *NICE* application is installed on the VR system run by the National Center for Supercomputing Applications, where the authors work. Thus, we have personally experienced *NICE* on many occasions and have demonstrated it to many visiting individuals. We have attended talks by Roussos and Johnson at conferences and workshops. The application creators reviewed our outline and a late draft and provided us with answers to our questions as we went along.

Crumbs, A Tool for Scientific Visualization

Crumbs is a virtual reality application used for visualizing, exploring, and measuring features within volumetric data sets (FIGURE B-1). *Crumbs* is a robust general-purpose tool that makes use of a variety of display paradigms and data manipulation options, allowing a researcher to explore volumetric data in intuitive and powerful ways. It is designed to "make the visualization and identification of complex biological structures easier" [Brady et al. 1995]. The motivation for developing *Crumbs* stems from the fact that many biological structures are difficult to identify and measure with traditional image analysis techniques and two-dimensional visualization interfaces.

A specific feature of *Crumbs* is a tool to enable the demarcation of linear features by allowing the user to trace fiber structures through a three-dimensional volume. This task is accomplished by dropping virtual "bread crumbs" along the path of a fiber. The crumbs can then be interpolated into a path, which can be further manipulated and analyzed.

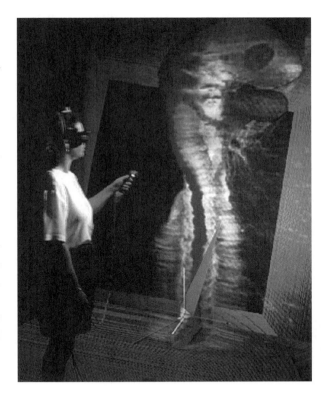

FIGURE B-1 Crumbs *developer Rachael Brady explores a volume representation of a 48-hour-old chicken embryo (Image courtesy of NCSA).*

The *Crumbs* project encompasses three research goals. The first goal is to investigate and develop techniques for real-time rendering of volumetric data in a manner suitable for virtual reality. Second, the developers are interested in exploring navigational and interactive methods to enhance the ability of the user to examine data volumes that have no inherent orientation or horizon. And third, the *Crumbs* team wants to explore the use of this virtual reality interface for controlling remote instruments. All of this is being done in the context of an application that has proved itself useful to a variety of scientists. Plus, according to the developers, a new *Crumbs* user can learn how to perform the basic operations in only 15 minutes.

An impetus for the investigation of using virtual reality for biological data came as a result of a push by then NCSA director Larry Smarr. Smarr sought to have a medical-related, *CAVE*-based virtual reality demonstration in the VROOM venue of the 1994 SIGGRAPH conference on computer graphics. After discussing several possible applications, the NCSA biological imaging group (who were interested in doing more than a onetime demonstration) decided to focus on the needs of scientific visualization of volumetric data sets, such as those produced by CAT (computerized axial tomography) scans, MRI (magnetic resonance imaging), and other medical and scientific instruments.

Although the preliminary application of *Crumbs* was initially focused on biological data, the tool has proved useful in a variety of scientific fields. Other data explored with *Crumbs* include astronomical simulations, fluid dynamic computations, seismic data volumes, and hydrogen state transitions. Prior to the development of the *Crumbs* application, most volume visualization tasks were carried out using conventional computer graphics on desktop workstations. Switching to VR to perform the task of measuring serpentine fibers through a three-dimensional volume proved to be beneficial, relative to the great difficulty of performing the task on a 2D screen.

Application Description

The name of the application refers to the provision for dropping virtual bread crumbs to mark a path through the data set. A handheld wand is used to position and trigger the placement of a crumb. The original name of the application, *HnG,* stood for "Hansel and Gretel," revealing this as a primary focus of the application. However, the application has grown to become useful for visualizing any regularly sampled data volume, with a collection of tools that allows a variety of high-resolution views into the data set.

The ability to communicate interactively in real time with data acquisition systems like MRIs and computational processes running on remote systems (such as for image processing) is also integrated into *Crumbs*. These capabilities enable the remote process or scientific instruments to be "steered" directly within the VR experience. The remote control capability has been demonstrated with the user controlling remote instrumentation and visualizing the results from thousands of miles away [Potter et al. 1996].

Representation of the Virtual World

The virtual world of *Crumbs* consists of the volumetric data set and the collection of tools used to interactively visualize and analyze that data. *Crumbs* can accept data sets that are two- or three-dimensional scalar values sampled on a uniform grid. The data is read from a file or remote connection and is stored internally as a block of bytes. A pink wireframe parallelepiped (box) represents the domain of the data. The user then selects tools to visualize the data via a menu, a virtual tool shelf interface, or speech command.

Visual Representations

Traditionally the type of data for which *Crumbs* was developed (MRI and CAT scan data) is viewed as slices of the volumetric cube, taken from three points of view and displayed as grayscale images on transparent film, much like an X-ray (FIGURE B-2). Currently, the data is frequently viewed on a 2D workstation screen, allowing the researcher to rotate the data set. *Crumbs* extends this trend by providing the ability to view this type of data in a *CAVE* VR display, allowing researchers and medical professionals to walk around and through their data. It also allows them to adjust some viewing parameters and immediately see the results. The location, size, and orientation of the domain of the volumetric data set is indicated by a translucent pink box. A variety of standard visual representation techniques, such as volume rendering, cutting planes, and height meshes (for 2D data), are included.

Isosurface and other polygonal representations are sometimes requested by the users (FIGURE B-3). The developers have accommodated some of these requests. These traditional scientific visualization techniques turned out not to work well with the task of trying to find thin fibers in a dense, noisy material, so they are not part of the general application. However, for some tasks, the addition of certain geometric models provides contextual information that helps the user gain a sense of the

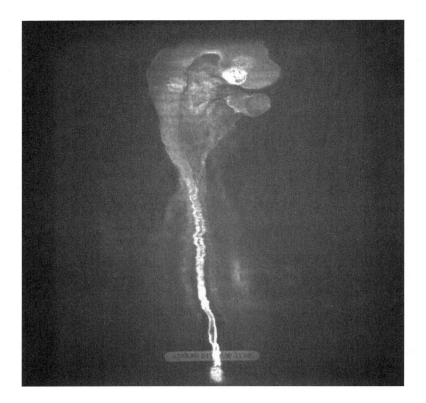

FIGURE B-2 *Physicians traditionally view MRI data as orthogonal slices displayed as grayscale images on transparent film (Photograph by William Sherman).*

structure and topology of the data set. A special version of the application has been developed for these cases.

The volume techniques used in the *Crumbs* system require that a tool such as a volume rendering box cannot be presented obliquely to the viewer. Thus, the rendering box automatically orients itself to be orthogonal to the viewer. Originally this was done by orienting the slices to be orthogonal to the gaze (nose) direction of the participant. However, it was discovered to be much more effective to rotate based on the vector between the user's head and the tool. In other words, it is better if the volume rendering tool always faces the viewer, regardless of the orientation of their head.

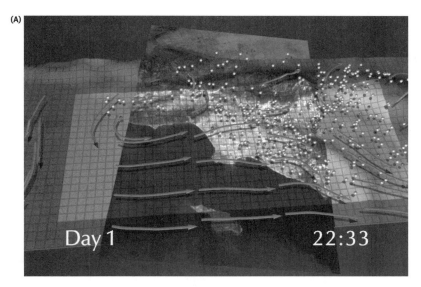

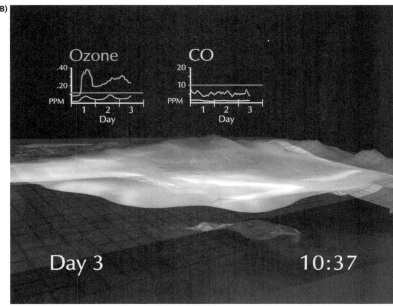

FIGURE B-3 Crumbs *was designed to serve a specific purpose: to allow a researcher to trace a fibrous structure through dense, noisy material. Therefore,* Crumbs *does not include common representational techniques that do not meet this end, such as* **(A)** *streamlines, here used to visualize smog in the Los Angeles Basin and massless particles or* **(B)** *isosurfaces and plot graphs (Images courtesy of NCSA).*

Aural Representations

Audio is used in two ways in the *Crumbs* application. It is used to present feedback to the operator's input requests and to sonify data as the user probes the often murky visual representation. Speech cues are the primary form of feedback to menu selections and other interactions. When a user makes a selection from the menu or interacts with the system in some way, the system unobtrusively speaks a single English word as feedback to the user (e.g., "scaling"). This helps the participant to know the state of the system and when a task has been engaged.

The other way in which aural display enhances the experience is sonification. As the user probes the data set to precisely place bread crumbs along a fibrous thread, the orchestration of a melody changes to reflect the proximity to the optimal placement. A musical melody (rather than simple sine wave tones) was chosen as the form to present this information in order to create a more enjoyable experience for the user [Brady et al. 1996]. Specifically, the brightness and complexity of the orchestration of the music are altered as the voxel (volume element) value of the crumb's location changes.

Other Sensory Representations

Crumbs does not provide an interface to any of the other senses. The application authors may consider the uses of other sensory interfaces (e.g., haptic) in the future, but the VR system for which they designed the application (the *CAVE*) does not inherently include sensory displays other than sight and sound.

Interaction with the Virtual World

The genre of this application is *scientific visualization,* and it is designed in particular for volume rendering. The form of interaction includes a move the world travel interface, menus, a virtual tool shelf with a variety of tools, and, in later incarnations, speech recognition.

Narrative

As a tool meant for scientific exploration, the "narrative" is to explore and interact with data sets and construct visualizations that enable better understanding of the entity being studied. The researcher is generally trying to learn the secrets hidden within the data.

Navigation

For most scientific visualization, there is no natural navigation scheme, especially for worlds through which one doesn't typically walk or fly. Because scientific data sets often lack the intrinsic geometric references of daily life, such as a horizon, the navigational requirements are different than for spaces reminiscent of the real world. The fact that many sciences deal with phenomena that are not appropriate to human scale means the size of the world must be adjusted for the user's perceptual norm.

Early in the design process, the *Crumbs* developers investigated many different forms of travel. The initial travel interface allowed the user to investigate the data set using a metaphor of a car windshield. This pilot-through interface of "driving" through the data set was found to be ineffective. The developers discovered that a much better paradigm was to allow the user to grab the data set via a wand control and move it as desired (i.e., the move the world travel paradigm). Since user location is tracked, they can also use physical locomotion as a natural walk around interface to observe the data set from a variety of views. There are also independent controls for rotating and scaling the data representation.

One of the problems with the driving metaphor was that the user would often drive beyond the edge of the data set and become lost—in spite of the presence of a simple maplike display. The newer move the world travel method of "picking up and moving" offers several advantages. It is nearly impossible to lose the data set, because the user is always consciously manipulating it and can place it wherever they choose. The feedback of watching the data while it is being moved seems natural and intuitive. Finally, the user has fine control over movement, which is important for murky, cloudy environments such as the volume rendered data set.

Although no map of the data set is available with the new technique, a low-resolution volume rendering of the full data set is available and can be used as a wayfinding aid. Selectable as a menu option, this tool displays an overview of the data set, allowing the user to quickly grasp the overall gestalt of the data and begin to focus on regions of interest. Once some marking points ("bread crumbs") have been laid, they too serve as wayfinding landmarks.

Manipulation

There are two basic metaphors used to interface with the *Crumbs* world: tools that can be manipulated directly and global parameter adjustments. The primary interface paradigm is a tool shelf from which the user can select visualization tools to help explore the data. Adjustment of global parameters is done primarily via a menu interface. There are also a handful of operations that are done directly with the hand-held wand.

This dichotomy results in a differentiation that may seem arbitrary to new users because, in some respects, it is. The differentiation is a result of the application authors working in a new medium that is both unfamiliar to them and has few solid works upon which to stand—much like the situation early filmmakers experienced. On the first pass at designing the interface, many decisions were made based on ease of implementation. As we discussed in Chapter 8, this is generally a bad idea. However, the *Crumbs* developers compensate by working closely with many users and implementing changes to refine the interface in accordance with their feedback. In one instance, the developers performed a small experiment to choose a particular interface method from a group of suggested possibilities.

Most design choices were initially made as educated guesses as to what the user might find useful. For example, many options require the selection of a particular number. In the early design, numeric input was via menus. Thus, the particular alternatives available to the user were predetermined by the application. The application designers chose numbers that they thought covered a useful subset of values. The specific values were then refined as new users and new data sets were explored, and a need for a different choice of numbers was shown.

A tool shelf is the location a user goes to grab a tool they would like to use. Some tools are special in that they allow the user to grab a copy of an object. These tools are like a box of nails on a carpenter's tool shelf, where the user can grab an instance of the tool (a single nail), but leaves the box behind, and can grab more later. The developers refer to these special "boxes" from which new "instances" can be retrieved as *icons*.

In *Crumbs,* the whole world is a tool shelf: tools (and tool instances) that are not in use can be placed anywhere in the world. Tools on the tool shelf are treated like any other object in the world. There is no specific single location where a tool shelf exists. Tools can be grabbed and placed anywhere within the reach of the user's wand. Tool orientation can be ratcheted by repeated grab-move-release actions.

Pressing the button when intersecting with an icon or *instance-box tool* results in the creation of a new copy that can then be positioned in the world. The instance-box itself, however, cannot be moved. Another unique feature of the instance-box tools is the ability to summon submenus when pressing the menu button while in contact with the box. The submenu has specific options for how new copies of this tool should be created. For example, the resolution of the textures used for the volume rendering process can be set.

A goal for all the tools was ease of exploration, good insight, and a frame rate of at least 10 frames per second. Should the user wish to change the default parameters for a better view (perhaps at the cost of slower frame rate), they can activate the menu associated with the particular tool to adjust the parameters of how future instances of the tool will be formed.

Menus are used to control both global system settings and individual tool instance-boxes. Menus are always summoned by pressing the left button on the wand. If a tool is selected when the button is pressed, then the menu for that tool is displayed; otherwise, the menu with global choices is brought forth. A menu interface was chosen because it was an existing paradigm with which the programmers were familiar, plus it was one with which many users would also already be familiar. Since they were exploring a new medium, the developers didn't know of any other possibilities.

Similar to pop-up style menus from the desktop metaphor, when a button is pressed (on the wand), the menus are displayed at the tip of the wand pointer (FIGURE B-4). To be more easily readable, menus pop up in a right side up orientation with respect to the floor, regardless of wand orientation. Menu selections are made by releasing the button when pointing at the desired (highlighted) selection.

FIGURE B-4 *Here the user points the wand at an item in the menu to highlight and select it (Photograph by William Sherman).*

When a menu is on screen, the rest of the world is not displayed. This is done to keep rendering speeds high enough for the precise interactivity control needed for menu operation. A common problem with using menus in experiences with low frame rates is that the user may activate the selection thinking they will get the currently highlighted choice. However, when the system response lags, by the time the activation is recognized, the user may be pointing at something else, which the system construes as the desired option.

Hiding the data display when a menu is invoked provides two advantages. First, objects in the scene cannot occlude the view of the menu, which could make the operation difficult. Second, it provides better performance by reducing the number of displayed objects. Low frame rates impede the ability to use menus and other interactive controls effectively.

Many of the options listed in the menus can also be invoked via voice command using an ASCII command protocol over a socket connection between *Crumbs* and a speech recognition system.

In addition to being the physical interface for controlling the menu, the wand is used to accomplish a handful of tasks directly. Foremost among these is the function of grabbing and moving objects in the world. Other tasks include scaling the data set, rotating the data set, and dropping the bread crumbs.

Objects are manipulated using the grab-with-pointer idiom of direct user control. This includes the data set itself, the tool generators, the tool instances, and the crumbs placed in the world, thus providing consistency between travel and navigation and manipulation interaction. When the data set itself is being moved, the move the world travel paradigm is in play.

The object to move is selected using the 3D cursor-select interface (i.e., touching the object with the tip of the wand pointer). If no object is selected, then manipulation actions default to the data set. The scope of selection is direct intersection with an object. For feedback, objects turn red to highlight when they are within range. The user then activates the grab command by pressing a button while the object is highlighted. This is sometimes difficult, because the act of pushing the button can cause the wand to move enough to take the object out of selection scope. Novice users often find it difficult to precisely contact the tip of the wand with the object they wish to grab. With sufficient practice, most users have been able to gain the skill necessary to work with this system, but it does take some time.

Because the data set itself can be captured and moved, there is good reason not to make the range of tool capture too large. This also makes it easier to select individual crumbs, which are often tightly spaced together. The size of the capture area must be small enough that they don't overlap. The tradeoff between having a large, easy to select tool range and the difficulty of having to avoid pointing at a particular tool when grabbing the data set is a matter of preference. The current implementation is thus set to be exactly the dimensions of the object to be grabbed. However, if unpracticed users will be using the system, then perhaps the constraints should be more forgiving. This could be an adjustable feature in the menu system.

Visualization Tools

Crumbs provides the user with access to many visualization tools. Most of these tools are geared toward the demarcation of fibrous paths through the data. The list includes the volume rendering tools to see within the data, the sonification tool for hearing the contents of the data, the crumbs tool, and the fine adjustment tool.

Low-resolution Volume Render

A quick overview of the entire data set can be obtained via a low-resolution volume rendering. Since this is a global setting, this representation is toggled on and off via the main *Crumbs* menu. It can be left on while other operations are in progress if desired. However, for both occlusion and rendering speed issues, its best use is to provide an overview and then the user can switch it off and use other tools appropriate for the specific task (FIGURE B-5).

Volume Rendering Tool

The volume rendering tool allows a user to render a subset of the overall volume using a specialized real-time volume rendering technique. The technique involves rendering several layers of 2D planes through the box (FIGURE B-6). Each plane is texture mapped with an image of the data representing the information through which the plane intersects.

The implementation of this tool treats it like a "box of volume renderers," allowing the user to grab and place as many instances as they desire. A separate menu for this tool has options for adjusting the size and number of planes and the resolution of the texture maps used to present the data, both of which impact the frame rate.

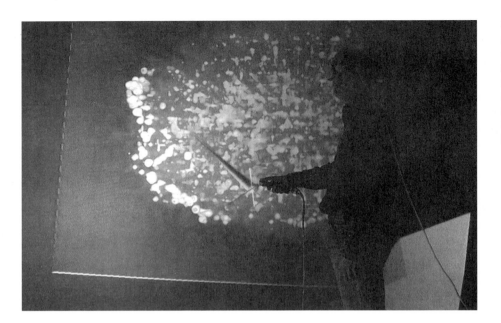

FIGURE B-5 *The* Crumbs *user often begins by examining the entire span of the data with a low-resolution volume renderer. Once they find a region of interest, they can use other tools to fine-tune the visualization (Photograph by William Sherman).*

FIGURE B-6 *In this photograph, the user has placed two copies of the volume rendering tool to follow a fiber through the data set (Photograph by William Sherman).*

Slice Tools

Another representation option is that of the slicing or cutting plane tool. Two methods are provided for visualizing a colored slice arbitrarily positioned within the data. Like the volume rendering tool, a placeable slice tool instance can be grabbed from the "box of slices." Each copy consists of a single plane that can be positioned anywhere within the space. The plane is texture mapped with an image representing any data it intersects (FIGURE B-7). Unlike the volume rendering box, the image is opaque, showing only information on that plane.

Another cutting plane option is a wand slice tool that is permanently attached to the pointer location of the handheld wand. When selected, this tool replaces the normal swordlike representation that emanates from the handheld wand.

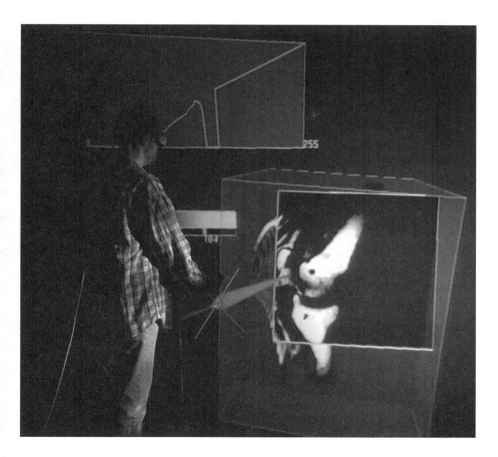

FIGURE B-7 *Here, the user examines an MRI of a horse fetlock by placing a 2D slice plane in the area of interest (Photograph by William Sherman). See color plate 28.*

Since the wand slice tool is not a placeable object, it is activated via the main menu. In addition to remaining permanently attached to the wand, another difference between the wand slice tool and the placeable slice tool is that multiple orthogonal cutting planes are used. Multiple opaque planes are joined together like the corners of a cube. The tool is moved through the data set by moving the wand, providing orthogonal high-resolution 2D views of the data. By reorienting the wand, the wand slice tool may be oriented in any arbitrary direction, providing views previously unavailable to the practicing physician.

The placeable slice tool was added to *Crumbs* as a result of user input. In an early collaboration, scientist Carl Gregory was watching a live MRI scan of earthworms in soil. He found that the handheld cutting plane tool was very useful for watching the worms move, but he grew tired of holding the wand still to watch the worms. He expressed a need for a way to maintain the position of the plane without having to hold one's hand rigidly still. Unlike the computer desktop, where the user can release the computer mouse and it will remain still, and thus the pointer will remain still, the *CAVE* wand will drop to the floor when released, so there must be a method to detach it from the object.

Bread Crumb Marker Tool

One of the original motivations for the development of the *Crumbs* package was to be able to measure complex intertwining fibers within a data set. To accomplish this, the user points to a specific location in the data set and releases a virtual bread crumb. A spline curve automatically connects the crumbs to form a visual connect the dot representation. By following a fiber and dropping bread crumbs along the way, the user creates a representation of the shape of the fiber. The length of the fiber can also be requested and is reported vocally as a spoken sequence of numbers. This measuring tool is unique to the *Crumbs* program and allows researchers to measure fibers that cannot be measured in other ways.

A single activation cue (button press) is used to perform different operations on bread crumbs based on context. When the tip of the wand pointer is in open space, then a new crumb is created and added to the end of the spline. When the tip intersects an existing crumb, that crumb can be grabbed and relocated, and when the tip intersects the spline, a new crumb is inserted along the existing path. When a crumb is relocated to be in the garbage tool (discussed later in the appendix), then it is deleted from the path.

With only this tool, the user has no way to know where the fiber is and thus where to drop the crumbs. A common method for making the fiber perceptible is to place volume rendering tools along the uncharted fiber, drop crumbs, and reposition the volume tool. Slice planes can also be used but are more difficult, because the plane itself obscures any data on the far side of the plane. The sonification capability described below can also be a helpful aid for accurate placement of the crumbs.

Path Adjustment Tool

Once crumbs are dropped, there is a mode for making fine adjustments to crumb positions. In this mode, a slice plane is positioned along and orthogonal to the crumb path. By viewing the data in the plane, the user can more easily see how accurately the crumb path intersects the center of the path of the fiber (FIGURE B-8). If a marker

FIGURE B-8 *Here, the user has dropped a path of crumbs and uses a special version of the 2D slice plane to visualize the data along the path, making adjustments as necessary (Photograph by William Sherman).*

point is off the mark or a new marker is needed, then it can be repositioned or dropped as normal.

Sonification Tool

When in bread crumb mode, a sonification becomes audible whenever the wand button is pressed. Different sonic representations are played when the tip of the wand pointer intersects different values of the data set. The sonification tool helps the user locate the fiber they are demarking by allowing them to use aural cues when their vision is obstructed or when they are having difficulty discerning the visual 3D depth cues.

The application creators felt most prior attempts at sonification of scientific data were hindered by being tiresome to listen to, so they chose to use a musical melody as the sonic representation. The developers believed that users would not use the sonification tool if it were not easy to endure for significant lengths of time. In addition to being fatigue resistant, they also wanted the sound to be familiar yet unobtrusive to the task at hand [Brady et al. 1996].

Four melodies were composed by Robin Bargar and Insook Choi of the NCSA audio development group. Five instruments were used to orchestrate each melody: guitar, piano single register, piano multiple registers, a voicelike synthesized instrument, and flute. Instruments are mixed into the composition based on the data. To enable the listener to more easily discern when instruments enter and exit the composition, the order of introduction was determined by "their unique positions in the frequency domain" [Brady et al. 1996]. The designers feel that a granularity of greater than five is desirable, but have not determined how many discrete sound streams can be easily discerned by the average listener.

Each melody is a repeating sequence of notes; however, separate introduction and exit phrases were also composed to allow the music to begin and end more naturally. The lengths of the introductory and exit pieces had to be adjusted when they discovered that the average time between dropping new crumbs was a fraction of a second, rather than the one or two seconds they had originally estimated.

In their paper "Auditory Bread Crumbs for Navigating Volumetric Data," Rachael Brady and her colleagues [1996] state: "A user can listen to these sounds for several hours without becoming irritated by the auditory signals." There are, however, a few additional constraints on how bearable and useful a melody can be. Keeping the volume relatively soft helps, and having a variety of melodies rather than just one improves listenability. The usefulness of a particular melody is affected by the length of and amount of silence in it. The higher density of notes (less silence) improves the ability to hear when the quality of the data the crumb is in changes. Longer startup and cadence sequences for a particular melody cause problems when the user is fluidly dropping crumbs faster than the melody can resolve. Experienced users can easily drop several crumbs per second, so the melody must be able to respond just as quickly.

Color Mapping/Opacity Tools

Crumbs provides color and opacity tools, giving the user the ability to specify the mapping of data values to color. An MRI data set, for example, is represented by a cube of density values. By choosing colors and opacity appropriately, the researcher can highlight specific matter within the data. For example, bones, nerves, arteries, and skin all have different densities. To more readily differentiate these materials, values for the density of arteries may be represented in red, whereas values for the density of nerves may be represented in blue. The representation is updated immediately as the researcher manipulates the color and opacity tools. This instantaneous feedback allows the researcher to experiment with various mappings and see the results in real time. Color and opacity maps can be saved and reloaded via the main menu.

The color map editor tool is depicted as a three-dimensional cube representing RGB (red, green, and blue) color space. A 7-node spline curve exists in the RGB cube. Nodes are moved with the same manipulation interface as marker crumbs. As the nodes are moved throughout RGB space, the curve connecting them becomes the color described by its location.

The translucency/opacity tool is shown as a 2D graph. The X axis represents data values and the Y axis is the opacity value for a particular data value. This 2D interface is particularly difficult to manipulate in 3D space. It is similar to drawing a line in the air without any physical constraint to guide the wand (as a desk constrains a mouse). Drawing a 1D curve on a 2D XY plot floating in 3D space is much more difficult than when operating on a 2D surface, as with a pen on a desktop or a mouse pointer on a 2D screen. For this reason, *Crumbs* wishes its users a verbal "Good luck" whenever they manipulate the opacity tool (FIGURE B-9). However, without a good 2D input available to the user while standing in the *CAVE* display, the 3D interface is preferable to requiring the user to exit the *CAVE,* make adjustments with a mouse, and then come back to the *CAVE.*

(A)

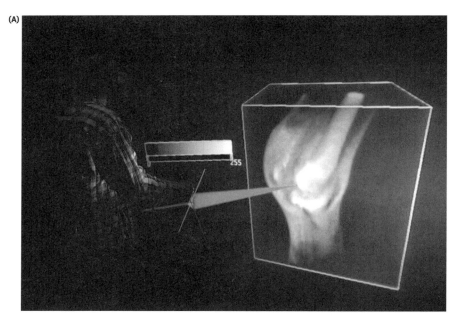

(B)

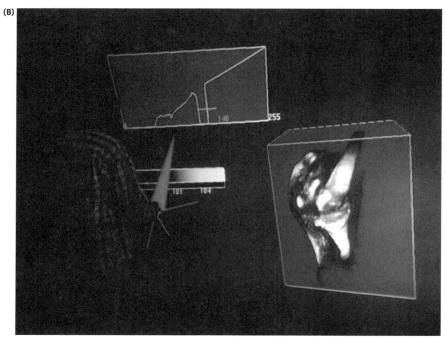

FIGURE B-9 *By carefully manipulating the opacity tool from the default* **(A)***, the user can highlight different aspects of the data set* **(B)** *(Photographs by William Sherman).*

Contrast Enhancement Tool

The contrast enhancement tool can be used to further manipulate how the range of colors specified by the color editor is allocated over the range of data values. When the thresholds are at their extremum values, then the full color map is spread linearly across the maximum and minimum values of the data. By moving the two thresholds lower or higher, the rate of color change is shifted to a smaller region of the values, thus increasing contrast within that range (FIGURE B-10). Values outside the region are clamped to black or white. Above the two sliders is a display of the current color map.

Trash Can Tool

Similar to some computer desktop interfaces, a garbage can represents a tool for deleting certain objects from the world. In the case of *Crumbs,* these objects are the tool instances and bread crumb markers. By relocating a tool instance or an individual crumb into the garbage can, the particular object is removed from the world (FIGURE B-11).

Collaborative Tools

The original version of *Crumbs* had no site to site collaborative features. In day to day use, however, it was common for several researchers to be present, exploring a data set together in a *CAVE.* In 1998, the developers began to integrate a collaborative interface to *Crumbs* based on the *CAVEav* software under development at Argonne National Laboratory.

Argonne's *CAVEav* library is built on the multicast Internet protocol for large group collaboration. Common Mbone tools provide a means for audio and video communication. Audio and visual images of the presenter or user and the audience are controlled externally to *Crumbs.* An additional visual stream can be generated by *Crumbs* under the control of the operator. Multiple streams can be generated with views from virtual cameras placed in the scene or from the vantage point of the user. Because *Crumbs* is built on the EVL *CAVE* library, the application will run on all types of VR visual displays, but cross-geographic collaboration raises additional issues that the developers will need to address. For instance, a method of floor control to specify which user has the authority to modify the visualization parameters must be decided upon and implemented.

The *CAVEav* extended version of *Crumbs* was demonstrated at the 1998 NCSA Alliance Conference in Champaign, Illinois. In this demonstration, Jo Ann Eurell, a

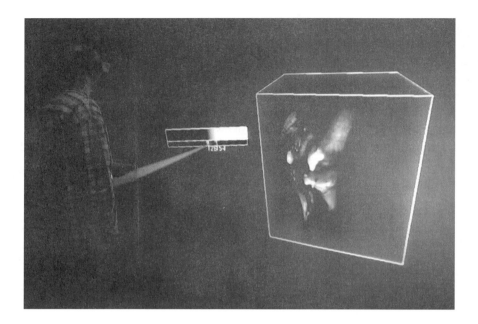

FIGURE B-10 *Adjusting the contrast allows the user to highlight a particular range of data values (Photograph by William Sherman).*

FIGURE B-11 *Borrowing a metaphor from a 2D desktop interface, a user eliminates a "bread crumb" from the visualization by placing it in the trash bin (Photograph by William Sherman).*

University of Illinois associate professor of veterinary biosciences, taught a class to two local high schools via a multicast collaboration over the Internet. The students could see and hear Professor Eurell, and she could see and hear them. From the conference floor, Eurell presented her lecture by placing the (virtual) camera viewpoints at strategic locations in the scene as she spoke. The students and teachers located in their classroom could follow along and ask Eurell questions. Although Eurell operated the demo using a VR display (an *ImmersaDesk*), from the perspective of the students, this was a two-way videoconference lecture and not a virtual reality experience.

The above example was a collaborative experience with a scientist working in a VR interface, displayed to the students as a video image. These audiovisual netcasts of the scientist at work allowed the students to see through a window into the world of the scientist. Such techniques can be used to provide students with the experience of a field trip into a research facility anywhere in the world.

World Physics

The physics within *Crumbs* itself is limited. The data and visualization tools remain floating in space, where they are left, and only move when manipulated by the user. The current version also has no concept of time, resulting in a very limited ability to support time-varying data.

Venue

The *Crumbs* application runs in the *CAVE* at the National Center for Supercomputing Applications (NCSA) at the University of Illinois. The NCSA *CAVE* is a shared resource used by a wide variety of research groups. *Crumbs* has been licensed to other research facilities, often with feature enhancements specific to the particular science under study at that center. *Crumbs* is now freely downloadable through the *CAVE* Users Group (*www.cavernous.org*).

Researchers use *Crumbs* at their own pace, subject to the scheduling constraints of the *CAVE* display. Typical sessions are on the order of one to two hours. The *CAVE* can easily support three researchers working together while exploring a particular data set (larger groups during demos). The *Crumbs* application has also been used as an educational tool. In one instance, an instructor was able to display data of interest to nine or ten students at a time. In another example of educational usage, students viewed MRI data of a developing chicken embryo in conjunction with a much broader educational endeavor known as the *Chickscope* project (*http:// chickscope.beckman.uiuc.edu*).

VR System

Crumbs is built on the CAVE library, so it is primarily run on projection VR systems with the hardware that typically accompanies them; that is, it is powered by a *Silicon Graphics Onyx RE2/iR,* with *CrystalEyes* shuttering glasses, an *Ascension Flock of Birds* tracking system, and a *CAVE* wand. The *CAVE* has proven to be an advantageous choice of VR display, because it is well suited for collaboration among small groups of scientists.

Audio is provided via speakers coupled with a Silicon Graphics workstation equipped with audio and/or MIDI capabilities. The *Crumbs* application originally utilized the MIDI functionality of the NCSA VSS sound server but now uses VSS directly to mix samples in real time under program control. A PC-based voice recognition system has been integrated for remote instrument control, as well as for loading new data sets during a session. Most voice commands duplicate menu-based options but can be performed much more conveniently.

Application Implementation

The *Crumbs* application is undergoing constant development. It is evolving into a general-purpose tool able to accommodate different data sets from a variety of fields. Development began in the spring of 1994, and the basic functionality was demonstrated at the SIGGRAPH '94 VROOM event. Work is continuing, with new features such as the color map editor, the sonification tool, and the integration of *CAVEav* for collaborative capabilities.

Design

The *Crumbs* application goes beyond standard desktop volume rendering programs. It is designed to overcome the limitation inherent in projecting a three-dimensional rendering onto a two-dimensional viewing environment. The initial design concepts came out of the infrastructure of *NewVision,* a biomedical visualization application developed by John Pixton for UIUC Professor Andrew Belmont. The goal was to help him do structural biology research into how chromatin folds to become chromosomes. In *NewVision,* orthogonal views of the data volume are updated on the screen as the user moves a virtual camera through the data set [Pixton and Belmont 1996]. It is interesting to note that the flow of ideas occurred both ways. After adding the grab and drag feature into *Crumbs,* Pixton went back to *NewVision* and added that feature as a means to center the camera on a particular location in the image.

Crumbs is made up of several components. In addition to the primary visualization component, there is a separate transceiver process that communicates with the volume rendering application via shared memory and with other applications via Unix sockets. The transceiver process forwards messages to the remote process and loads received data into *Crumbs's* memory space. These communication interfaces are used in conjunction with the live data acquisition systems and with other data processing resources for such tasks as filtering the noise inherent in many instruments and acquisition systems.

Crumbs is written in C++ using the *CAVE* library for interfacing with the VR input devices and visual display. The graphics routines use *Silicon Graphics IrisGL* and, because of complex usage of texture map routines, has not yet been ported to *OpenGL*. Audio rendering is done using the NCSA VSS audio library, and speech recognition is done using *Dragon Dictate* running on a separate PC.

The Unix socket communication interface was used as a means of reading text input from the speech recognition system, as the interface by which remote instrument control communications are done, and as the means for communicating with data processing servers, such as one for image processing.

The *Crumbs* application was developed in house at NCSA by (primarily) the Biological Imaging Group. The majority of the application is the result of a large programming effort from two primary developers, plus a great deal of consulting and part-time work from several individuals who brought special expertise to the project.

The two main programmers were John Pixton and Rachael Brady, with support and many new ideas from Clint Potter and Bridget Carragher. Brady, now at Duke University, continues to support and enhance *Crumbs* on an ongoing basis. Other contributing programmers include Pat Moran, who worked on the remote program interaction, George Baxter on the implementation of the menuing system, Dennis Strelow on some additional visualization code, and Karla Miller, who wrote a few new pointer representations and conducted a user evaluation study. Other contributions were made by Bridget Carragher, who helped in the design process and in publishing the original paper, and Carl Gregory, who used an early version and critiqued the MRI data visualization interface. The remote MRI interaction interface was implemented by Clint Potter. Andrew Belmont provided the original motivating problem, as well as *NewVision* ideas. Robin Bargar, Incook Choi, and Carlos Ricci helped with the sonification design and implementation.

Appendix Summary

Although no formal evaluation study has been performed, *Crumbs* has been extensively analyzed through real-world use and modified based on the feedback of the scientists who have used it.

The most significant analysis of *Crumbs* comes from its daily usage by a variety of users. On the basis of people using the application and repeatedly returning for more, the application can be deemed successful. Users also provide the means by which the interface is analyzed, as well as the impetus to improve it. For example, Carl Gregory suggested features such as the placeable slice tool and a new pointer implementation to help him locate the active cursor location in 3D space.

The request for a better wand pointer led to an experiment by Karla Miller to implement and evaluate a variety of new location pointer techniques [Miller, Brady, and Potter 1997]. The original *Crumbs* 3D space pointer was a "sword" that emanated from the handheld wand. For her study, Miller implemented volumetric, partially occlusive cursors with four, five, and six sides. The partial occlusion was a visual depth cue for the user. Within the volume cursor, lines are drawn from near the center toward each vertex to allow the user to pinpoint a single location (rather than the entire enclosed volume). The cubic volumetric cursor was compared with the original sword pointer and just the lines surrounding the center. Through a series of user tests, the representation that was appraised as working the best was dependent on the task and level of user experience.

Scientists in a variety of disciplines have used the *Crumbs* application. Professor Tim Karr of the Univeristy of Chicago used *Crumbs* to measure the length of sperm tails in *Drosophila* (fruit flies). This task was difficult before the *Crumbs* application was developed. As we saw earlier in the appendix, another study looked at MRI data of a horse fetlock to examine cartilage structure between joint bones, and the Chickscope project followed MRI data of a chick embryo until the egg hatched. To augment the daily images, a 3D model of a 48-hour-old chick embryo was displayed in the *CAVE* as a field trip for some of the student participants.

The original goal of creating a useful biomedical visualization tool has been met and exceeded. The *Crumbs* application has drawn considerable attention from the biomedical visualization community, as well as from medical instrument developers. However, the goal has become a moving target and thus *Crumbs* is continually evolving. A number of other scientists have extended the application to new areas of scientific research, many modifying the software to add features specific to their applications. For example, physics researcher Burkhard Militzer modified the code himself to add some specific features beneficial to viewing data related to his area of study. Two of the changes implemented by Militzer were to freeze the placeable tools entirely, rather than have them rotated to always face the user, and to add a representational idiom that shows spin states and path integrals of electrons in plasma (FIGURE B-12A).

Another example of working with new scientists and finding new applications for a particular usage comes from a collaborative project with the Lawrence Berkeley National Laboratory in Berkeley, California. Scientists Ken Downing, William Nichols, and Eva Nogales put *Crumbs* to use for viewing EM crystallography data. Some changes they requested were to connect crumb markers with straight lines rather than spline curves, to make the size of the crumbs adjustable, and to allow rendering of the crumbs and the curve to be toggled on and off independently of one another.

It is unlikely that any users of *Crumbs* forget that they are investigating a scientific data set and believe they are standing next to an oversized chick embryo or fruit fly sperm, but *Crumbs* does provide a very compelling view of the data that can be explored in intuitive ways. Mental immersion is not a critical component of this application. The goal is to gain scientific insight from tools that support visualization of volumetric data sets.

Through the course of the development of *Crumbs,* the application authors learned a great deal about user interfaces that allow scientists to explore data in virtual reality systems. Their quest was to find an interface that scientists could learn very quickly and one that was effective for the required tasks.

Among their discoveries was the realization that the use of the grab with wand method of object manipulation—including the primary object, the data set— was a very intuitive method for interfacing with the virtual environment. In contrast, having to switch between different modes of travel was found to be very difficult and was removed from released versions of the software.

The developers encountered a few tradeoffs during the design and implementation of *Crumbs,* as well. For example, greater volume rendering field of view was a tradeoff against rendering times suitable for interactive display. Smaller volume rendering boxes were used to increase the frame rate. As a side benefit, this helps alleviate a common problem in many volume rendering situations where the data is so murky it is difficult to clearly see the structures of interest.

The *Crumbs* developers also pushed the envelope of sonificiation by producing a sonic representation that is fatigue resistant yet provides enough information for the user to more easily position their markers.

(A)

(B)

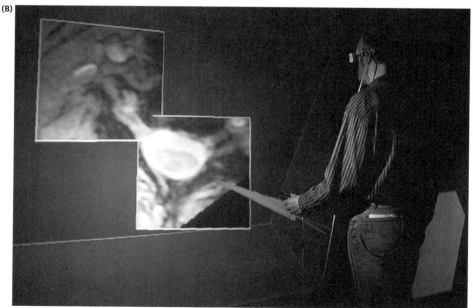

FIGURE B-12 Crumbs *has been used to visualize data sets for researchers in many different fields.* (A) *Here, hot, dense hydrogen is visualized with electron paths, protons, and molecular bonds added to the standard volume visualization. See color plate 28.* (B) *The* Crumbs *application was educational to the authors of this book, as it enabled them to better understand the MRI scan of one of the authors' necks taken during the writing of this book (Photographs by William Sherman).*

Because *Crumbs* is a tool in regular use, new ideas and needs are frequently presented to the developers in the form of user feedback. Current plans to enhance *Crumbs* include increasing the collaborative capability and adding the ability to handle time-varying data so that dynamic data sets can also be visualized. The developers also plan to add tools for modeling 2D and 3D structures (currently only one-dimensional paths through the data can be modeled), plus algorithms for performing semiautomatic segmentation, that is, where the application itself attempts to segregate the data set into specific regions (e.g., the regions of white matter versus gray matter versus bone in a brain data set).

There are also plans to increase the number and functionality of the quantitative tools. Some of the new capabilities the developers plan to incorporate include tools to measure curvature, volume, and area. To enable the researcher to create a time-linear animation (videotape) of a visualization of their work, the developers plan to interface *Crumbs* with NCSA's *Virtual Director,* a VR application for creating animations.

Developer Rachael Brady approached virtual reality skeptically, but is now enthusiastic about the accomplishments and possibilities for VR. The fact that *Crumbs* is actually being used by researchers to do tasks that were previously impossible attests to the potential of VR as a tool in biomedical visualization. Brady has also found that some scientists come to see the *CAVE* just to find out what this new technology is all about and then find that they can see new things in their data. For example, scientist Howard E. Buhse, Jr. of the University of Illinois at Chicago wanted to see the *CAVE* and sent ahead a data set he was researching in preparation of his visit. Buhse was interested in localizing an antibody (OF-1) to the feeding aparatus of *Vorticella convolavia* (a kind of ciliated protozoan). In this way he hoped to trace the pathway of a food particle from capture and ingestion into a food vacuole, where digestion occurs.

After spending some time in the *CAVE* examining his data, Buhse was surprised to find that in addition to localizing to the feeding apparatus, the antibody appeared to localize to *myonemes* (contractile fibers found near the cell membrane). These fibrils initiate cellular contraction upon an increase in calcium levels.

Having seen what can be done with his own data, Buhse says:

By combining the imaging technology of confocal methods with powerful computer graphics, one can view cellular structures in new ways. It's terribly exciting to be able to walk into a cell whose true dimensions are measured in micrometers.

Despite her early skepticism, Brady has found that virtual reality has a role to play as a tool for scientific visualization. In her words:

> VR will never replace desktop scientific visualization, but it augments it and further development is worthwhile. VR is a good technology to encourage scientists to try things they hadn't considered before.

A NOTE ON INFORMATION ACQUISITION

This application was developed at the authors' local VR research facility, so we have seen it many times over the course of development. Most of the information comes from discussions with the developers and users while immersed in the application. We have also read their papers [Brady et al. 1995; Brady et al. 1996], and Rachael Brady and Clint Potter have reviewed drafts of this appendix.

Boeing Wire Bundles, An Augmented Reality Application

In the area of manufacturing, the Virtual Systems Research and Technology group at Boeing Computer Services is exploring augmented reality (AR) as an aid in assembling wiring bundles for aircraft. Making wire bundles is a difficult, tedious task and is different for each individual aircraft. Boeing performed this research in collaboration with CMU, Honeywell, and Virtual Vision, Inc. under a 3-year DARPA TRP project titled "Wearable Computer Systems with Transparent, Head-Mounted Displays," begun in August 1994. In August of 1997, the project culminated in a field study testing the new paradigm with wire shop workers (FIGURE C-1).

FIGURE C-1 *Adam Janin demonstrating the 1993 laboratory prototype, with stereo CRTs and a magnetic tracking system (Image courtesy of David Mizell, Boeing, Inc.).*

Application Description

The traditional way of assembling aircraft wire bundles begins with an engineer designing the bundle on a CAD workstation using the *CATIA* CAD package. Next the 3D CAD model of the bundle gets converted into a 2D schematic—currently a manual process—plus a list of wires at specific lengths. Large plotters then draw the wiring scheme onto mylar printouts. These are then glued to the physical formboards, which are approximately 8 ft. by 3 ft. Before putting the wires on the formboards, connectors are added at one end. The serial number printed on the wire is used to determine which wire goes in a particular slot. Next, they position pegs on the board to support the wires while they are on the formboard. In the final step of the formboard stage, the assembly person procures the correct wires, stands at the board, lays the wires through the proper routes, and sleeves and ties the wire groupings (FIGURE C-2). Following this, the second ends of the connectors are added, the bundles are tested, and then installed.

FIGURE C-2 *The traditional formboard wire bundle assembly process. Hundreds of boards are stored for all the particular wiring harnesses (Image courtesy of David Mizell, Boeing, Inc.).*

One of the issues that makes this task so critical is that there are so many different configurations for these bundles. Each type of aircraft uses different bundles, and each requires many different bundles. For example, a Boeing 747 requires about a thousand bundles. Also, an individual 747 may require bundles that are different from other 747s because of different cabin configurations (the cabin design for large aircraft is sometimes customized for the route it will fly).

While the primary concern is to improve performance of the hundreds of workers "boarding" wire bundles, an additional benefit is that the generic pegboard style formboards used in the augmented reality (AR) system can help reduce the enormous storage space required for the existing racks and racks of boards, each of which only works for a single wire bundle. Boeing is looking to improve this situation. The AR system is one experiment for finding a better solution.

Application Implementation

The AR system they developed provides the wearer with lines superimposed on the real world using a see-through HMD. In the initial, prefunded stage of research, an inexpensive see-around HMD called the *Private Eye* was used; this is a monocular display that takes up only a small fraction of the field of view [Caudell and Mizell 1992].

AR provides an effective means of "annotating" reality. In this case, a single blank pegboard can be annotated for each specific layout. The assembler wears a portable computer around their waist that supplies the computer-generated virtual world superimposed onto the real world.

The net result is that a blank board can be used for assembling a wire bundle. Traditional boards had the pegs prepositioned, with individual boards for each wire bundle. The boards for the augmented reality project have an array of holes in them like a pegboard, so pegs can be placed appropriately for the bundle being constructed. After the pegs are placed as instructed by the system, the wires are run and then bundled. The task is much simpler, because the AR system displays only one wire or a few wires that all route to the same destination at one time. The traditional method of putting the schematic on the board itself produces the negative consequence of the diagram becoming obscured as wires are put in place.

No audio output, voice input, or other modalities are part of this pilot project. However, Boeing is investigating many of these technologies in separate projects, and as applications prove to be effective they will consider adding interface technologies as they mature. The next interface for the formboard application will likely include speech recognition.

The formal study of this pilot project was conducted in August 1997 at the Boeing widebody (747, 767, 777) factory in Everett, Washington. This study was designed to systematically compare three prototype AR systems with the traditional method. Both time and accuracy of bundle assembly were measured. The systems used were built by TriSen Systems, Inc. of Minneapolis, a spin-off of Honeywell. Each system was composed of a wearable PC, a see-through HMD, and a videometric tracking system, all developed by TriSen (FIGURE C-3). Other systems were delivered, but the tracking did not meet the minimal specifications for the work.

Although the formal study demonstrated that a workable augmented reality, formboard system was possible, the particular implementation did not result in increased performance in time to construct a bundle. However, there was no loss of performance, and the workers were able to completely construct wire bundles on the AR formboard. These bundles were then transferred to traditional boards and passed quality-assurance inspection.

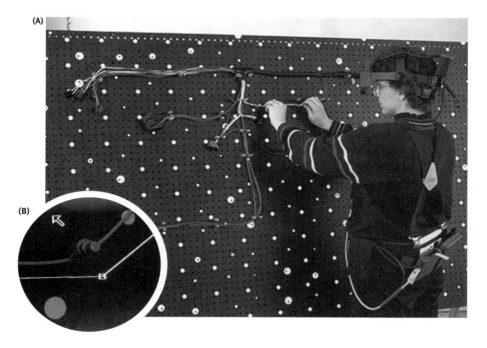

(A)

(B)

FIGURE C-3 *Here, the packaged TriSen system is used to create a wire bundle. The system consists of the light-weight head-based display and a computer worn around the waist* (A). *In the augmented view of the board* (B)*, computer graphic lines indicate where to place the next wire (Image courtesy of TriSen Systems, Inc.) See color plate 29.*

David Mizell, manager of Boeing's Virtual Systems Group, states that they expected the new system to result in faster construction times. In particular, they expected the speed increase to stem from the fact that the old method did not contain all the information directly on the board in the assembler's line of sight. It required the assembler to refer to separate paperwork (the "Shop Aid") for information on how to route each set of wires. The new system was targeted to eliminate this bottleneck by keeping all the information overlaid on the formboard, so the worker would never have to look away from their work.

In analyzing the study, Mizell and his collaborators believe that the lack of improved performance resulted from a poor user interface. The interface used in the study required the worker to use a mouse click paradigm to proceed through the task. Boeing is confident that as they gain experience in working with this new AR display paradigm, they will be able to construct significantly better user interfaces. One specific improvement that they are already integrating is speech recognition. With a better interface, they expect to reduce formboarding time by 10–20%. Mizell added that after exposing factory personnel to augmented reality, the workers have suggested additional ideas of how AR might be useful in a variety of factory tasks.

The DARPA TRP program (under which this project was funded) is designed to integrate military technology into civilian use, which is intended to bring down the cost of the technology by increasing the market size. In this case, Boeing is working with see-through HMD technology created by Honeywell for helicopter pilots. This collaboration helps Honeywell by providing input for the requirements of an AR system.

Augmented reality systems have design constraints that differ from standard virtual reality systems. Whereas in virtual reality, the challenge is to render enough polygons to make a worthwhile world, the world already exists in AR, and only a small amount of information needs to be added. For augmented reality, the challenge comes in producing a self-contained, portable system that still accurately registers the virtual world with the physical world. Environments displayed in VR systems typically allow the user to virtually move through the space. In AR, physical locomotion by the user or a robot (i.e., for telepresence) is generally the only acceptable method of travel.

TriSen Systems, Inc. put together augmented reality systems that met these constraints for Boeing. TriSen themselves manufactured the HMD and tracking system and integrated them with wearable computers from ViA Inc. The wearable computer for the prototype system was a 4 lb., 33 MHz Intel 486. During the 1997 study, the computers were upgraded to a 120 MHz 586 processor. More interesting, though, is the tracking solution provided by TriSen. Their package uses videometric tracking.

Videometric tracking is accomplished by using a camera mounted on the object to be tracked—in this case the HMD—and using the video input to recognize the 6-DOF position of the camera. The incoming video image is analyzed for known landmarks. By finding a sufficient number of landmarks (at least four), the algorithm can determine the camera's location. Typically, artificial landmarks, known as *fiducial markers* (or *fiducial landmarks*) are added to the environment in which the system is to be used. For this system, the fiducial landmarks look like strange polka dots and are placed directly on the formboards in a specific pattern that allows the system to rapidly determine absolute position (FIGURE C-4).

Because the fiducial landmarks are only on the formboards, the system cannot track the user when they look away. However, this poses no problem since the user only needs the augmented information during the time they are facing the formboards. It is important, though, that tracking resume in short order when the user returns to working on the formboards. In this case, the system took less than one second to reacquire position tracking once enough fiducials came into view.

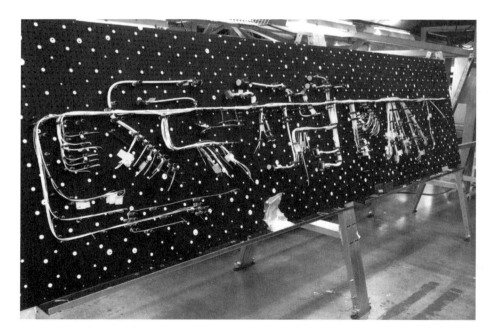

FIGURE C-4 *This bundle, assembled during the 1997 pilot project, shows the special formboards created by TriSen Systems, Inc., with fiducial markers (the light-colored dots) directly integrated into the boards for videometric tracking (Image courtesy of David Mizell, Boeing, Inc.).*

Because the entire videometric tracking system is carried on the user—the camera and the wearable PC—there are no tethers from the user to an external system. This is a major benefit of using this entirely self-contained system. This particular solution is not possible in all augmented reality scenarios. It works perfectly in this scenario because the fiducials can be easily added to the environment and because the processing power to handle the complete task can be contained on a wearable PC.

Appendix Summary

Boeing VR research is conducted within the Virtual Systems group under David Mizell. The AR project was conceived by Tom Caudell (now at the University of New Mexico in the EECS department). Initial development was done by Adam Janin (now a Ph.D. student at the University of California at Berkeley). Current work is now being done by Dan Curtis and Peter Gruenbaum, with Chris Esposito handling much of the prototyping of the wearable PC systems.

Boeing is also involved in non–AR virtual reality work. Due in part to the $100 million cost of building physical, interactive mockups of planes, they are investigating virtual prototyping of aircraft. Visualization of the Boeing 777—the first large aircraft built without the creation of a physical mockup—was done with a package named *FlyThru*, written by Bob Abarbanel and Eric Brechner (now at Microsoft). *FlyThru* was a desktop visualization system and was not designed to work with head-based displays nor at the rendering speeds required by VR.

Following this work, a real-time rendering package, *RealEyes,* was developed. Designed and implemented by Henry Sowizral (now at Sun Microsystems) and Karel Zikan (now at Masaryk University in the Czech Republic), *RealEyes* uses parallel processes to cull hidden polygons, as well as other computer graphics techniques to render large numbers of polygons at real-time rates. *RealEyes* has been interfaced to a Fakespace *BOOM* and demonstrated using partial models of a 777 as a virtual reality application. This work is being carried out at Boeing by Bill Brown and Charkar Swamy.

In addition to the cost savings of not building physical prototypes, virtual prototypes are effective as a tool for maintenance analysis. Boeing research has also produced a series of experiments to analyze the benefits of virtual reality, including its use for maintainability analysis. These experiments have led them to conclude that HBDs are preferable over the *BOOM*-style, handheld method, because they free the hands to reach into spaces. Maintenance aspects of a design can be analyzed by performing collision detection on the hands and arms of the user to determine reachability. TriSen Systems, Inc. now markets a hardware package that combines a wearable PC with head-based display, video camera, and videometric tracking for use in assembling wire bundles and other tasks.

For Mizell, a general point of doing this particular research on augmented reality is that he believes "there are applications all over the factory, for example maintenance and maintenance training." Also, he sees AR as having great benefit for manufacturing, training, and maintenance in both military and civilian aircraft production. The technology is also advancing rapidly to make augmented reality an easy to use interface for workers. As Mizell puts it: "It would be great if one could grab a wearable PC, clip it on, and be tracked in airplane coordinates."

A NOTE ON INFORMATION ACQUISITION

We did not have the opportunity to directly experience the Boeing formboard wire bundling application firsthand. The information in this description comes from a talk by Henry Sowizral, the paper by Caudell and Mizell [1992], and an article by Sara Reese Hedberg [1996] in *Virtual Reality Special Report*. A considerable amount of information and clarifications have been provided through conversations, comments, and interviews with David Mizell, who also reviewed a late draft of this appendix.

D

Placeholder, An Artistic Exploration

The *Placeholder* virtual reality experience is an artistic exploration into new paradigms for interaction and narrative in virtual environments. In this experience two participants don head-mounted displays, embody, or *indwell,* themselves within the body of one of the various "critters" that inhabit the environment, explore the several places that exist in *Placeholder,* and leave their mark on the space for others to encounter (FIGURE D-1). Beyond this, *Placeholder* pushes the common notions about virtual reality, place, play, and self.

The *Placeholder* project was created by multiple developers, each with their own ideas and goals for the project. As in any collaborative work of art, the various developers brought their own skills and interpretations to the table and emphasized their own interests and capabilities. One of the primary goals of the *Placeholder* experience was to explore the nature and possibilities of virtual reality. When *Placeholder* was created in 1993, VR applications were relying heavily on interface design conventions established in other media and early experiments in VR interaction. The *Placeholder* developers questioned whether these conventions were appropriate for use in VR as a medium for narrative, dramatic, or playful activity. The developers also wanted to take advantage of an interface in which the participant could interact with the system naturally, without noticing any constraints placed on them—what is referred to as the *ultimate interface.* Their goal was to maximize naturalness and allow participants to interact directly in the virtual world, while minimizing distractions and cognitive effort.

One of their hypotheses held that VR is more suited as a "play space" than an "entertainment space." So, they attempted to find how best to provide and capture a space for creative play. Other goals included the exploration of (1) various techniques for representing space, time, and distance, (2) how people explore those spaces, and (3) how and why they leave their marks on them.

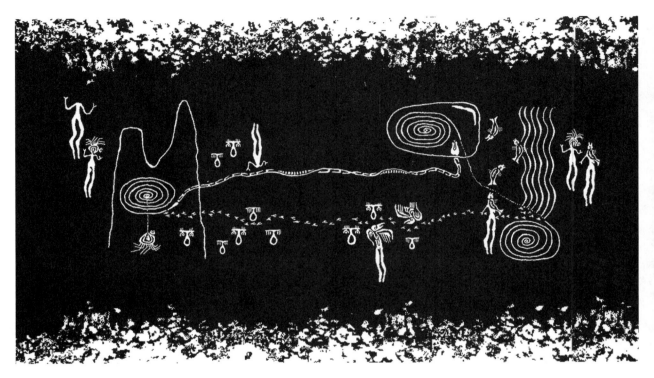

FIGURE D-1 *A map of the* Placeholder *world done in a "primitive" style (Image courtesy of Brenda Laurel).*

This project was also an investigation into the representation of self in a VR experience. By allowing participants to indwell various critters with different characteristics, the participant is able to experience the environment from the perspective and physical capabilities of the critter they embody.

This project was an exploration of a new medium. Thus, there is no direct comparison to how this activity might have been carried out before the advent of VR. In the broader sense, this is a further exploration of many of the same things investigated by artists working in other media. In particular, the creators of *Placeholder* have drawn ideas from those media which revolve around narrative and storytelling.

Application Description

This application visually displays the world in head-mounted displays to two participants simultaneously and provides multiple spaces for the participants to explore. The spaces were constructed of three-dimensional structures by using videographic techniques. The addition of spatialized sounds and animated textures helps to enrich the space. Participants are able to walk, talk, and interact with the world using both hands. The participants each stand within a "magic circle" bordered by rocks. They are free to roam within the circle defined by the rocks (FIGURE D-2).

Representation of the Virtual World

The virtual world consists of three areas modeled loosely after real-life locations near Banff National Park in Alberta, Canada. The first location is a cave, with a sulfur spring. Because the cave is very dark, sound was a very important component in this area of the world. There is also a waterfall location. One of the goals for the waterfall was to give it a visual sense of flow. The third area in the world was named *The Hoodoos,* after the real-world hoodoos, which are rock formations created by erosion. Each of the areas within *Placeholder* has a very different character. The developers hoped to instill very distinct environmental qualities in them.

Another element in the *Placeholder* virtual world are the critters. Participants enter the world without a body (i.e., they have no avatar), so the critters beckon to the participant to enter them and use them as their avatar. The critters are caricatures of real-world animals that reside in Canada's Banff National Park. Each critter has different characteristics, so the participant has a different experience based on the critter they indwell. The application authors refer to the critter avatars as "smart costumes." The critters include a spider, snake, fish, crow, and bear. Ultimately, the bear was

FIGURE D-2 *A* Placeholder *participant wears a head-mounted display within a ring of rocks that defines the area that can be explored by physical locomotion (Image courtesy of Brenda Laurel).*

dropped from the experience as it did not bring new features and did not fit well with the scale of the other critters.

Also residing in the world is an agent known as "the Goddess." The Goddess is not represented visually, only aurally. In *Placeholder,* the Goddess is controlled as a Wizard of Oz agent; that is, the role of the Goddess is controlled by a human being as if they were a part of the virtual world. Voiceholders are another key element in the *Placeholder* world. Voiceholders are a means by which participants in the virtual world can leave their "mark" on the world by leaving a voice message for future participants.

Visual Representation

One of the objectives of the *Placeholder* developers was to capture the essence of real places. Their overriding goal was to find a way to represent the simplest sense of place, rather than a photorealistic duplication of the natural site. One of the techniques they used was to search for places and ways of capturing places that lent themselves to representation from a single point of view. They opted for creating world models by sampling the real places via video and audio recording, rather than synthesizing the entire world (FIGURE D-3). The resulting overall impression in the virtual world is also influenced by stylized icons suggestive of Paleolithic times.

The concept of how participants are embodied in a virtual world was of particular interest to the application authors. They enabled participants to "wear," or indwell, the smart costumes representing the four critters. When participants enter the world of *Placeholder,* they are without a body, able only to see two blue dots representing their hands (FIGURE D-4). They are also able to see the dots that represent the hands of their companion participant. Once a participant has embodied a critter as their own avatar, the other participant can see them represented as a flat, iconic symbol representing the embodied critter. The icon wobbles as a participant moves through the world.

Aural Representation

Placeholder places considerable emphasis on the use of audio to enhance the overall experience. Each location in the virtual world has its own ambient sound. The audio is represented in a high-quality, high-fidelity way. The fidelity of the audio significantly surpasses the fidelity of the visual presentation. The audio is rendered and displayed three-dimensionally, deepening the sense of location and space. For example, an actual waterfall was recorded from four locations creating the effect of

FIGURE D-3 *Many of the world locations, such as the Hoodoos, were modeled using video and audio recordings made in the mountains of Canada (Image courtesy of Brenda Laurel).*

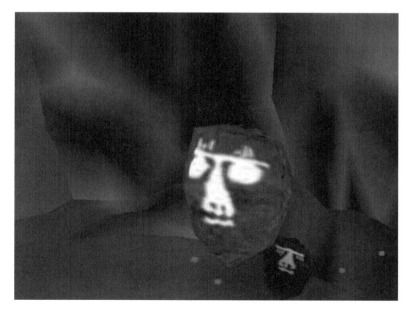

FIGURE D-4 *Until participants don avatars, they are only represented as a pair of small blue dots, a dot for each hand. In this image, two users are interacting with a pair of "voiceholders" (the rocklike objects with facial icons) (Image courtesy of Brenda Laurel).*

a field of sound as opposed to simply a point sound source. Participants commented on the compelling presentation of the water drips, the river, and the wind.

It is also noteworthy that the avatars have an aural as well as a visual representation. This is created by filtering the voice of the participant to give it the quality of their embodied critter. Each critter has its own vocal quality, which is also heard when the unembodied critter calls out to *Placeholder* participants. Thus, participants hear each other via the voice of the crow, the spider, and so forth.

The voices of the participants, voiceholders, and critters are spatialized using a *Convolvotron*. This is particularly useful in being able to precisely locate objects in the world. Participants are more easily able to locate one another by listening to the direction of their voices. More importantly, participants can use the location of sounds to help them make contact with portals (doors into other worlds within *Placeholder*) and unembodied critters with which they are attempting to interact. For example, the Goddess can communicate with the participant, providing suggestions and other guidelines. The Goddess has no visual representation in the world, and her voice seems to emanate from within the participant's own head (FIGURE D-5). This also helps convey the impression of the Goddess as a godlike entity.

The audio is mostly rendered anechoically (i.e., free of echoes and reverberation). To integrate a reflective model would have required additional programming and more processing power. To make the cave world seem natural, however, requires a reflective sonic model. Rather than computing the reflections as fully part of the virtual world, reverberation was simulated using a Yamaha sound-processing box. This proved to be effective for most participants in *Placeholder*. One exception was two professional musicians who felt the reverb was not effective in the cave.

Haptic and Other Sensory Representations

There is no haptic feedback in this application except for that provided by the rocks that indicate when a participant is about to step outside the magic circle. The magic circle was provided to indicate the range of space in which the *Placeholder* application can be experienced.

Interaction with the Virtual World

As a work of art in which the authors specifically set out to explore new forms of interaction within the medium of VR, the choices made are particularly interesting. Of note is the primary reliance on physical movement for travel. This simple form of travel is enhanced by portal jumps (discussed further in the Travel section), flight by gesture, and bimanual interaction for easier object manipulation.

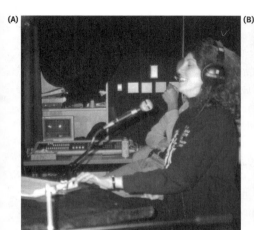

FIGURE D-5 A "Goddess" agent aids participants during their experience by speaking to them. The Goddess is implemented by a performer working outside the VR system through a Wizard of Oz style agent with no visual avatar (Images courtesy of Brenda Laurel).

Narrative

A goal of this project was to investigate ways to combine interactivity with conventional narrative form. In their initial considerations, the application creators looked at other media in which efforts have been made in this direction: including many genres of interactive fiction and multimedia. Unfortunately, none of these proved to be very satisfying in attaining the goal of *interactive* narrative. The developers felt that to achieve an interactive narrative, both the author and the participant must participate in its creation. The *Placeholder* team was very interested in the content of the world as opposed to the technology of the system per se. This is evidenced by the fact that they engaged a professional storyteller to develop motifs from folklore tradition and mythology that could be applied in *Placeholder*.

As an aid in developing the narrative and in constructing sample interactions, the developers enlisted the aid of the Precipice Theatre Society, a Canadian improvisational group who focus on environmental issues. The theater group was largely naïve about VR technology and computers in general, and thus they acted freely without considering the constraints of the technology. Their actions helped determine what elements should be part of the user's interface to the *Placeholder* world. They also performed some of the place and critter voices, became early test users of the system, and were the first participants at the opening of the *Placeholder* experience.

The critters play a key role in the narrative of *Placeholder*. The developers felt that the representation of the body had not been effectively dealt with in virtual reality. Their feeling was that "severed heads" and "disembodied hands" were not an effective representation of self, that the body should be given greater status in the virtual world. To force participants to directly address their need for a representation of self in the virtual world, they are given no body at the onset of the experience. Without a body, participants are able to explore only the world in which they begin the experience, that of the cave. They are not able to see the voiceholders or use the portals to move to other worlds. In order to participate fully in the world, they need to acquire a body.

By providing a selection of smart costumes, or avatars, to fill this need, the developers have been able to explore an additional concept, that of *umwelt*. Jakob von Uexküll [1934] explains *umwelt* as the ability to perceive the world from the perspective and perceptual abilities of another animal. To this end they gave each creature different attributes that would allow them different capabilities in the world.

For their part, the critters also have a simple agentlike quality that they express when not embodied. Each unembodied critter beckons to the participants, advocating themselves as a choice for embodiment. They speak of their capabilities and get more persuasive as a participant gets closer to them. Finally, if the participant's head touches (intersects) the petroglygh (i.e., iconic image) representing the critter, they embody and receive the capabilities of that critter and are seen by the other participants as having that critter's attributes.

In addition to having its own vocal characteristics, each critter has its own method of travel. For example, the crow can fly and the spider can climb vertical surfaces. Each critter also has its own perception of the world, based on natural abilities of their real-world counterpart and a few mythical powers, as well. For example, the crow likes shiny things, so they are visually highlighted for the crow participant. The snake, a "creature of the dark world," can see in the dark. Only the fish can see well underwater. In reality, the developers did not have time to implement all of these visual capabilities and only snake vision was implemented. In practice, "snake vision" does not work particularly well, since it was implemented as a red filter on the world (implying infrared vision) and this makes it even harder to see in the dark.

Audio clips provide much of the narrative of *Placeholder*. In addition to the beckoning of unembodied critters, each world has a story to tell and calls out through portals between the worlds. Narrative is also built up by past participants, who could leave audio clips in voicemarks. Voicemarks and placemarks activate as a participant nears. Voicemarks were created based on the notion that people generally leave marks (usually visual) and trail signs at places they visit. In *Placeholder*, they can mark the world with their voice. Voicemarks are contained in voiceholders, which provide the interface to listen to the voices of past visitors and enable the recording of new marks.

Voiceholders appear as rocklike objects in the world, with iconic representations (glyphs) indicating their current state (FIGURE D-6). One glyph conveys an empty and inactive voiceholder. Touching this voiceholder causes it to go into listen mode. The glyph changes to indicate that it is empty but listening. The participant can then speak to leave a vocal mark. Full but inactive voiceholders can be touched to make them play their contents.

Voiceholders were chosen because the developers felt that voice was the easiest way to mark the environment. They felt it could be more expressive and certainly more immediate than drawing, and they believed people would be less self-conscious about the voice messages. Voiceholders can also be repositioned in the environment. Unfortunately, they proved difficult to use. This difficulty stemmed from the low frame rate of the system. With a significant amount of time passing (i.e., over 100 ms between frames), the user could easily move their hand right through a voiceholder without the world simulation detecting the contact.

FIGURE D-6 *Voiceholders allow participants to leave messages for future visitors. Different glyphs indicate the state of voiceholders. The four states depicted are: empty/inactive, empty/listening, full/inactive, and full/playing (Images courtesy of Brenda Laurel).*

Navigation

The primary mode of travel in *Placeholder* is physical movement. The participant is free to walk anywhere within the magic circle. However, their movement through the virtual world is affected by the specific capabilities of the smart costume they are wearing as their avatar.

Gesture-based movements were developed in a manner somewhat counter to what other VR applications of the time were doing. For example, the *Placeholder* developers chose to use the torso and pelvis as the directional selector, rather than the direction of the nose (which approximates gaze direction). In their opinion, longitudinal orientation of the body gives a better indication of desired direction of movement than gaze. The net result was to "give people back their necks." An additional tracking sensor is required to implement this, which probably explains why few other applications have used this technique.

Their goal was to use more natural interactions as opposed to some of the then commonly used VR interactions, such as the point to fly method of travel. So to determine how to create an interface for flight, they surveyed people and asked them how they fly in their dreams or imagination. They found that there are many different ways in which people imagine self-propelled flight. Some people imagine themselves as Superman, others as though they were swimming through the air like a fish or levitating as if they were a saint; still others pretend to be an airplane, among a variety of other fantasies.

In the end, the method selected for *Placeholder* was that of arm flapping in mimicry of bird flight. This choice turned out to work very well. When costumed as a crow, people who flapped their arms just once found that the motion propelled them into the air. By repeatedly flapping, they found they could fly and steer through the world. Implementing this interface was not entirely trivial. It required determining what constituted a "flap," and what action should be taken based on a flap. However, experiencing this interface was quite natural and required no instruction for most participants. Users found the chosen interface to be an intuitive way to fly in the virtual world.

Another way participants can move in the virtual world is via portal jumping. Based on research of cultural anthropology, mythology, and folklore, portals were selected as a means of transport between worlds. Portals emit sounds indicating the nature of the world to which they were connected. The destination of a portal is not always the same. So, each participant might hear a different sound from the same portal and be transported to a different place. Traveling through a portal takes about

10 seconds before arriving at the new world. While in transit, the participant is in darkness, although they can see the dots indicating their hands and hear the sounds of their destination. Many participants reported that the 10-second transport time was too long for them to wait in darkness during each trip.

Manipulation

One of the goals of *Placeholder* was to provide a natural interface, including the use of bimanual interactions. Thus, the participants are able to handle objects in the virtual world using a natural, two-handed interface. The application authors created simple handheld devices to measure the angle between the thumb and forefinger, calling them *grippees*. Each grippee is tracked and the location of the hands in the virtual space is represented by two blue dots (one for each hand).

Agents

As mentioned previously, the Goddess is an audio-only agent, implemented with a Wizard of Oz interface, meaning that a human controls the behavior of the Goddess from "behind a curtain." The voice of the Goddess performer is filtered through a signal processor to enhance the sound to a Goddess-like quality and spatialize it to be perceived as if inside each participant's head. The person controlling the Goddess is positioned in a booth that enables them to see the real-life bodies of the participants in concert with displays of their points of view.

The role of the Goddess was originally conceived as a playmate or a trickster. Her character was envisioned as a method to enrich the dramatic interaction between the participants and the world, after giving a recorded introduction to the experience. As a human-controlled agent, the Goddess can tailor her role based on the characteristics of the participants and how well they are interacting in the world. If the participants are children, the Goddess plays the role of a friend and helper. With adult couples, the Goddess is more of a Cupid and a tease. The Goddess sometimes offers advice to participants who are having difficulty, suggesting new things to try.

Originally it was planned that the Goddess would have control over many aspects of the world, but development time allowed only implementation of the voice interactions. Even with just the voice interaction, the Goddess had considerable influence over the actions of the participants through suggestions and prodding. In that sense, a great deal of the content and narrative of the virtual world is embedded in the Goddess. Most often, the role of the Goddess was performed by Brenda Laurel or Jennifer Lewis, although on occasion others took on the role, including men.

Collaboration

The *Placeholder* experience was designed to be shared by two simultaneous participants. The participants are able to communicate by voice (filtered by their smart costume). Additionally, the participants are able to see each other represented as their smart costume. The Goddess could be considered a third participant; however, she is a vital source of the narrative and is thus part of the virtual world, rather than a participant in the world.

World Physics

In general, the world physics in *Placeholder* mimicked real-world physics. There is collision detection between the participant and the critter, the portals, and voiceholders. This is, in fact, a major mode of interaction between the participant and these entities.

Venue

The *Placeholder* experience was exhibited in a public venue, the Banff Centre for the Arts. The display housed the magic circles in which the interaction took place. The circles were defined by the maximum distance the tracking system allowed, but equally important, they did so within the context of the experience. Each circle was bordered by rocks such that a participant could detect the edge of the circle by the change in footing. The circles were meant to represent that area in life where "everything falls into place" (FIGURE D-7).

The throughput of the system was very low. Only two people could experience the system about every 15 minutes, resulting in fewer than eight people per hour able to experience *Placeholder*. Spectators were able to witness not only the participants "suited up" but their view of the world displayed on monitors and the sounds of the world played through speakers. During its exhibition, *Placeholder* was experienced by over 50 members of the general public, plus Banff artists and faculty, Interval Research employees, and other guests for an approximate total of 150 people. Regrettably, it was such a complicated system that since the end of the Banff event for which it was created, it has never been reconstructed.

The *Placeholder* developers foresee the ability to include a more cinematic visual presentation in future VR experiences. In such a presentation, the onlooking audience would have the action presented to them via common cinematic camera cuts. Such a system was later described by He, Cohen, and Salesin [He et al. 1996]. The *Placeholder* developers believe that in the future, venues such as theme parks will be embedded in the computer rather than as physical public venues.

(A)

(B)

FIGURE D-7 Placeholder *participants wear head-mounted displays and physically walk within the stone-enclosed "magic ring" (Images courtesy of Brenda Laurel).*

VR System

The system supporting *Placeholder* was designed for two-person interaction. The participants wore Virtual Research's *Flight Helmet,* a head-mounted display with small microphones attached. Stereoscopic images were rendered and presented to each user. Because one of the goals of *Placeholder* was to remove any direct evidence of the participant's natural body, projection VR displays were not a suitable alternative.

The computing system consisted of a Silicon Graphics *Onyx Reality Engine 2* for the graphics and master computing. Sound was provided via a NeXT workstation, a Macintosh II, and two Yamaha sound processors. A PC supported the *Convolvotron* hardware to spatialize the sounds, and a second Mac II handled the input from the grippees. The handling complexity of the multiple computers required three people to run the system (FIGURE D-8).

The grippees were designed and built by Steve Saunders of Interval Research, Inc. They are simple devices created to enable the hand interactions required by *Placeholder.* Grippees are low-tech devices that measure the angle defined by the thumb and forefinger. This is done via a sliding variable resistor. One is placed on each hand with a tracking sensor for location and orientation. The tracking is done using the *Polhemus Fastrak* system. Tracking sensors keep track of the participant's head, pelvis, and both hands. Each of the four sensors were tracked in 6-DOF position tracking.

FIGURE D-8 *The* Placeholder *experience required a team of behind the scene workers to run the heterogeneous set of computers and other technologies (Images courtesy of Brenda Laurel).*

Application Implementation

This experience is a one-off application designed to explore the medium of virtual reality, to develop some new ideas about VR interfaces, and potentially overthrow some of the standing conventions about VR and interactive narrative. It ran over the course of a couple of months and now resides in only the video clips, still images, textual descriptions, and memories of the few people who had an opportunity to experience *Placeholder* firsthand.

Development of the project took place over the summer of 1993. It was a collaborative project between the Interval Research programmers, Banff employees, and the University of Alberta. The project was funded by the Banff Centre and the Interval Research Corporation. Most of the equipment was provided by the Banff Centre. The principal researchers were Brenda Laurel, Rachel Strickland, Rob Tow, John Harrison, Dorota Blaszczak, Michael Naimark, and Glenn Fraser. The team consisted of 10 programmers, a project codirector and filmmaker, a project codirector and game designer/artist, a professional storyteller, and the professional improvisation troupe, Precipice Theatre Society.

Design

One of the key design difficulties encountered was the capture of natural settings in a manner suitable for the *Placeholder* environment. Translation of the real-world models into VR was difficult. The problem was twofold: how to capture all of a space simultaneously rather than sequentially in a time-based medium like video, and how to capture multiple camera perspectives and join the several vantage points. Capturing the world via video is not optimal and requires much offline development to make it useful in an interactive computer graphics experience.

The software support for the system includes custom C code that the project team developed, as well as the M-R Toolkit (a VR development library) from the University of Alberta, with modifications to handle the dual person and dual hand functionality. Alias modeling tools (a commercial software suite for creating 3D computer models) were used for designing the environment. Because things didn't seem to translate well into the VR world, the developers felt it was best to do as much of the design as possible directly in the VR space. The use of the Alias modeler was one source of translation difficulties in that the expected result was not always obtained when models were initially placed in the immersive environment. This made it tedious to design the world. The team's overall summary of the world development process was that because things looked so different in the immersive environment, the world should be built within the virtual reality environment to begin with. Fortunately, they were able to do some of the final object placement, most notably the critters, from within the VR environment.

One of the difficulties of developing this system was that debugging it required three people: one person in the HMD, one to run the graphics system, and one to monitor the audio system. The *ventriloquism effect* made debugging the audio spatialization system difficult. Because this effect causes a listener to perceive sounds from where they are expected rather than from the actual source, it is difficult to judge the accuracy of the spatialized sound. Even when the system was uncalibrated, sound seemed to be good, but when calibrated correctly, it sounded fantastic.

Appendix Summary

The *Placeholder* developers have published considerable informal analysis regarding participant reaction to the experience. Post-experience interviews and surveys were conducted and videotaped. One of the interesting findings was that the participants found sound to be a critical element of the experience. They reported that not only is the quality of the sound higher than that of the visuals, but any necessary trade-offs should be made in favor of sound. This and other information has been published on a CD-ROM technical report available from the abridged *Placeholder* archive at *www.tauzero.com/Placeholder*.

The *Placeholder* developers had many more ideas for their experience than available resources to integrate them all within the time constraints. Thus, *Placeholder* served more as a proof of concept for what could be done in a narrative artistic application. This is not to detract from what they actually accomplished, which is to provide an interesting new way of thinking about the VR interface and of virtual reality as a narrative form.

The application developers felt as though more work needed to be done to find the best way to interface with devices like voiceholders and so on in the virtual world. The experience did allow them to ask many more good questions about VR. The developers came away with the impression that tall vertical objects and other horizon cues help give a strong sense of the body and lead to a sense of immersion. Another important element for immersion is to have something for the participants to do in the space. Overall, they found that mental immersion benefits from a strong cohesion between the display of visual and aural modalities. Cohesion between modalities is even more important than resolution in most if not all of the modalities. Thus, visual resolution can be sacrificed, if it can lead to a more solid tie between senses.

The application authors discovered quite a bit about interface design for VR and interface design in general during the course of producing *Placeholder*. One of the mournful discoveries was that an application relying on a system of such great complexity and requiring many people and many machines to make operate correctly is not likely to be recreated. Other significant discoveries that can benefit future VR experience design include "the importance of body politics as an explicit part of design" and the degree to which "immersion comes from the perception of agency" [Tow 1994].

In summary, it seems as though *Placeholder* has revealed several things about the nature of virtual reality. As we stated at the outset, the developers felt that VR seems to work better as a play space than as an entertainment space, and in the developers' own words: "In VR, one is not done unto, but doing." As investigator Brenda Laurel [Laurel et al. 1994] sums up:

> Working on this piece has demonstrated to me that the art of designing in VR is really the art of creating spaces with qualities that call forth active imagination. The VR artist does not bathe the participant in content; she invites the participant to produce content by constructing meanings, to experience the pleasure of embodied imagination.

A NOTE ON INFORMATION ACQUISITION

We were not among the fortunate few to have the opportunity to directly experience *Placeholder*. Most of our information about this VR experience was obtained through talks by Laurel, papers by Laurel and her colleagues, and the considerable amount of information available online. Additional information came from email correspondence with developer Rob Tow, and developer John Harrison reviewed a late draft of this appendix.

References

CHAPTER 1

[Aviation Week 1985]
Eds. of *Aviation Week & Space Technology*. "Virtual Cockpit's Panoramic Displays Afford Advanced Mission Capabilities," *Aviation Week & Space Technology* 122(2): 143–152, 1985.

[Bly 1982]
Bly, Sara. *Sound and Computer Information Presentation*. Unpublished doctoral dissertation, University of California, Davis, 1982.

[Brooks et al. 1990]
Brooks, Jr, Frederick P., Ming Ouh-Young, James J. Batter, and P. Jerome Kilpatrick. "Project GROPE: Haptic Displays for Scientific Visualization,"*Computer Graphics* (Proceedings of SIGGRAPH 90, Annual Conference Series) 24 (4): 177–185, 1990.

[Comeau and Bryan 1961]
Comeau, C., and J. Bryan. "Headsight Television System Provides Remote Surveillance," *Electronics* 34(45): 86–90, 1961.

[Cruz-Neira et al. 1992]
Cruz-Neira, Carolina, Daniel Sandin, Thomas DeFanti, Robert Kenyon, and John Hart. "The CAVE Audio Visual Experience Automatic Virtual Environment," *Communications of the ACM* 35(6): 65–72, 1992.

[DeFanti et al. 1977]
DeFanti, Thomas A., and Daniel J. Sandin. Final Project Report R60-34-163, U.S. NEA.

[Furness 1986]
Furness, Thomas A. "Fantastic Voyage," *Popular Mechanics* 163(12): 63–65, 1986.

[Grimes 1981]
Grimes, Gary. Digital Data Entry Glove Interface Device. U.S. Patent No. 4414537, Nov. 8, 1983.

[Heilig 1960]
Heilig, Morton. Stereoscopic Television Apparatus for Individual Use. U.S. Patent No. 2955156, 1960. (See also *Computer Graphics* 28(2), 1994.)

[Jacks 1964]
Jacks, E. "A Laboratory for the Study of Man–Machine Communication," *FJCC*64 American Federation of Information Processing Societies' (AFIPS) Fall Joint Computer Conference (FJCC) 25: 343–350, 1964.

[Krueger 1982]
Krueger, Myron W. *Artificial Reality*. Reading, Mass.: Addison-Wesley, 1982.

[Krueger 1991]
———*Artificial Reality II*. Reading, Mass.: Addison-Wesley, 1991.

[Rheingold 1991]
Howard Rheingold. *Virtual Reality.* New York: Summit Books, 1991.

[Schmandt 1983]
Schmandt, Chris. "Spatial Input/Display Correspondence in a Stereoscopic Computer Graphic Workstation," *Computer Graphics* (Proceedings of SIGGRAPH 83, Annual Conference Series) 17(3): 253–259, 1983.

[Sutherland 1963]
Sutherland, Ivan E. "Sketchpad: A Man–Machine Graphical Communication System," *SJCC,* 1963.

[Sutherland 1965]
———"The Ultimate Display," *Proceedings of the 1965 IFIP Congress* 2: 506–508, 1965.

[Sutherland 1968]
———"A Head-Mounted Three-Dimensional Display," American Federation of Information Processing Societies' (AFIPS) Fall Joint Computer Conference (FJCC) 33(Pt. 1): 757–764, 1968.

[Webster 1989]
Webster's New Universal Unabridged Dictionary. New York: Barnes & Noble Books, 1989.

CHAPTER 2

[Adams 1995]
Adams, Mike. Interview with William Sherman and Alan Craig, Leicester, England, July 17, 1995.

[Addison 1995]
Addison, Rita. "Detour: Brain Deconstruction Ahead," *IEEE Computer Graphics and Applications* 15(2): 14–17, 1995.

[Anstey et al. 2000]
Anstey, Josephine, Dave Pape, and Dan Sandin. "The Thing Growing: Autonomous Characters in Virtual Reality Interactive Fiction," *Proceedings of IEEE Virtual Reality 02 Conference,* 2000, pp. 71–78.

[Furness 1995]
Furness, Thomas. "My Forecast for the Future of the VR Industry." Keynote address at Virtual Reality World Conference, San Jose, Ca., May 23, 1995.

[Hinckley et al. 1994]
Hinckley, Ken, Randy Pausch, John C. Goble, and Neal F. Kassell. "Passive Real-World Interface Props for Neurosurgical Visualization," *Proceedings of the ACM CHI 94 Conference on Human Factors in Computing Systems,* 1994, pp. 452–458.

[Laurel et al. 1994]
Laurel, Brenda, Rachel Strickland, and Rob Tow. "Placeholder: Landscape and Narrative in Virtual Environments," *Computer Graphics* 28(2): 118–126, 1994.

[McCloud 1993]
McCloud, Scott. *Understanding Comics: The Invisible Art.* Northhampton, Mass.: Kitchen Sink Press, 1993.

[McLuhan 1964]
McLuhan, Marshall. *Understanding Media: The Extensions of Man.* Cambridge, Mass.: MIT Press, 1964.

[Sherman and Craig 1995]
Sherman, William R., and Alan B. Craig. "Literacy in Virtual Reality: A New Medium," *Computer Graphics* 29(4): 37–42, 1995.

[Stephenson 1992]
Stephenson, Neil. *Snow Crash.* New York: Bantam Books, 1992.

[Wead and Lellis 1981]
Wead, George, and George Lellis. *Film: Form and Function*. Boston: Houghton Mifflin Company, 1981.

[Webster 1989]
Webster's New Universal Unabridged Dictionary. New York: Barnes & Noble Books, 1989.

CHAPTER 3

[Addison et al. 1995]
Addison, Rita, Tom Coffin, Mortez Ghazisaedy, Robert Kenyon, William Reynolds, Joe Reitzer, Marcus Thiébaux, Anthony Tamburrino, Alan Verlo, Margaret Watson, Dave Warner, and Eben Gay. "Synesthesia: Collaborative Biosignal Experience" (Demonstration at the GII Testbed at ACM/IEEE Supercomputing 1995). In *Virtual Environments and Distributed Computing at SC 95*, Holly Korab and Maxine Brown, eds., 1995.

[Fitzmaurice et al. 1995]
Fitzmaurice, George W. Hiroshi Ishii, and William Buxton. "Bricks: Laying the Foundations for Graspable User Interfaces," *Proceedings of the ACM CHI 95 Conference on Human Factors in Computing Systems*, 1995, pp. 442–449.

[Foxlin 1996]
Foxlin, Eric. "Inertial Head-Tracker Sensor Fusion by a Complementary Separate-Bias Kalman Filter," *Proceedings of the IEEE 96 Virtual Reality Annual International Symmposium (VRAIS)*, 1996, pp. 185–194.

[Ghazisaedy et al. 1995]
Ghazisaedy, Morteza, David Adamczyk, Daniel J. Sandin, Robert V. Kenyon, Thomas A. DeFanti. "Ultrasonic Calibration of a Magnetic Tracker in a Virtual Reality Space," *Proceedings of the IEEE 95 Virtual Reality Annual International Symposium (VRAIS)*, 1995.

[Hinckley et al. 1994]
Hinckley, Ken, Randy Pausch, John. C. Goble, and Neal F. Kassell. "Passive Real-World Interface Props for Neurosurgical Visualization," *Proceedings of ACM CHI 94 Conference on Human Factors in Computing Systems*, 1994, pp. 452–458.

[Iwata and Fujii 1996]
Iwata, Hiroo, and Takashi Fujii. "Virtual Perambulator: A Novel Interface Device for Locomotion in Virtual Environment," *Proceedings of the IEEE 96 Virtual Reality Annual International Symposium (VRAIS)*, 1996, pp. 60–65.

[Krüger and Frölich 1994]
Krüger, Wolfgang, and Bernd Frölich. "The Responsive Workbench," *IEEE Computer Graphics and Applications*, 1994, pp. 12–15.

[Leigh et al. 1996]
Leigh, Jason, Andrew E. Johnson, Christina A. Vasilakis, and Thomas A. DeFanti. "Multi-Perspective Collaborative Design in Persistent Networked Virtual Environments," *Proceedings of the IEEE 1996 Virtual Reality Annual International Symposium (VRAIS)*, 1996, pp. 253–260.

[Mapes and Moshell 1995]
Mapes, Daniel P., and J. Michael Moshell. "A Two-Handed Interface for Object Manipulation in Virtual Environments," *Presence: Teleoperators and Virtual Environments* 4(4): 403–416, 1995.

[Sherman et al. 1997]
Sherman, William R., Alan B. Craig, M. Pauline Baker, Colleen Bushell. "Chapter 35: Scientific Visualization," *The Computer Science and Engineering Handbook,* Allen B. Tucker, Jr., ed. Boca Raton, Fla.: CRC Press, 1997.

[Webster 1989]
Webster's New Universal Unabridged Dictionary. New York: Barnes & Noble Books, 1989.

[Welch and Bishop 1997]
Welch, Greg, and Gary Bishop. "SCAAT: Incremental Tracking with Incomplete Information," *Computer Graphics* (Proceedings of SIGGRAPH 97, Annual Conference Series), 1997, pp. 333–344.

[Zeltzer and Pioch 1996]
Zeltzer, D., and Pioch, N. "Validation and Verification of Virtual Environment Training Systems," *Proceedings of the IEEE 96 Virtual Reality Annual International Symposium (VRAIS) I,* 1996, pp. 123–130

CHAPTER 4

[Bajura et al. 1992]
Bajura, Michael, Henry Fuchs, and Ryutarou Ohbuchi. "Merging Virtual Objects with the Real World: Seeing Ultrasound Imagery within the Patient," *Computer Graphics* (Proceedings of SIGGRAPH 92, Annual Conference Series) 26(2): 203–210, 1992.

[Baker 1989]
Baker, Robin R. *Human Navigation and Magnetoreception.* Manchester, England: Manchester University Press, 1989.

[Barfield and Danas 1995]
Barfield, W., and E. Danas. "Comments on the Use of Olfactory Displays for Virtual Environments," *Presence: Teleoperators and Virtual Environments* 5(1): 109–121, 1995.

[Bejczy and Salisbury 1983]
Bejczy, A. K., and J.K. Salisbury. "Controlling Remote Manipulators Through Kinesthetic Coupling," *ASME Computers in Mechanical Engineering* 2(1): 48–60, 1983.

[Bier et al. 1993]
Bier, Eric A., Maureen C. Stone, Ken Pier, William Buxton, and Tony D. DeRose. "Toolglass and Magic Lenses: The See-Through Interface," *Computer Graphics* (Proceedings of SIGGRAPH 93, Annual Conference Series), 1993, pp. 73–80.

[Brooks et al. 1990]
Brooks, Frederick P. Jr., Ming Ouh-Young, James J. Batter, and P. Jerome Kilpatrick. "Project GROPE: Haptic Displays for Scientific Visualization," *Computer Graphics* (Proceedings of SIGGRAPH 90, Annual Conference Series) 24(4): 177–185, 1990.

[Burdea 1996]
Burdea, Grigore. *Force and Touch Feedback for Virtual Reality.* New York: John Wiley & Sons, Inc., 1996.

[Buxton and Fitzmaurice 1998]
Buxton, Bill, and George W. Fitzmaurice. "HMD's, Caves & Chameleons: A Human-Centric Analysis of Interaction in Virtual Space," *Computer Graphics* (Proceedings of SIGGRAPH 98, Annual Conference Series) 32(4): 64–68, 1998.

[Cater 1992]
Cater, John P. "The Noses Have It!" *Presence: Teleoperators and Virtual Environments* 1(4): 493–494, 1992.

[Cutting and Vishton 1995]
Cutting, J., and P. Vishton. "Perceiving Layout and Knowing Distances." In *Perception of Space and Motion,* W. Epstein and S. Rodgers, eds. San Diego: Academic Press, 1995.

[Fitzmaurice 1993]
Fitzmaurice, G. "Situated Information Spaces and Spatially Aware Palmtop Computers," *Communications of the ACM* 36(7): 38–49, 1993.

[Gerzon 1992]
Gerzon, Michael A. *General Meta Theory of Auditory Localisation.* Paper presented at the 92nd Audio Engineering Society Convention, Vienna, March 1992 (Preprint 3306).

[Hirota and Hirose 1995]
Hirota, Koichi, and Michitaka Hirose. "Simulation and Presentation of Curved Surface in Virtual Reality Environment Through Surface Display," *Proceedings of the IEEE 95 Virtual Reality Annual International Symposium (VRAIS),* 1995, pp. 211–216.

[Kennedy et al. 1993]
Kennedy, R. S., N. E. Lane, K. S. Berbaum, M. G. Lilienthal. "Simulator Sickness Questionnaire: An Enhanced Method for Quantifying Simulator Sickness," *International Journal of Aviation Psychology* 3(3): 203–220, 1993.

[Klymento and Rash 1995]
Klymento, V., and C. E. Rash. "Human Performance with New Helmet-Mounted Display Designs," *CSERIAC Gateway* 4(4): 1–4, 1995.

[Krueger 1982]
Krueger, Myron W. *Artificial Reality.* Reading, Mass.: Addison-Wesley, 1982.

[Krueger 1994]
———"Olfactory Stimuli in Virtual Reality Medical Training," ARPA Report, 1994.

[Massie 1993]
Thomas H. Massie. "Design of a Three Degree of Freedom Force-Reflecting Haptic Interface." Thesis submitted for Bachelor of Science degree at the Massachusetts Institute of Technology, May 1993.

[McNeely 1993]
McNeely, William A. "Robotic Graphics: A New Approach to Force Feedback for Virtual Reality," *Proceedings of the IEEE 93 Virtual Reality Annual International Symposium (VRAIS),* 1993, pp. 336–341.

[Ouh-Young et al. 1989]
Ouh-Young, Ming, D. V. Bard, and F. P.Brooks, Jr. "Force Display Performs Better Than Visual Display in a Simple 6-D Docking Task," *Proceedings of IEEE 89 Robotics & Automation Conference,* 1989, pp. 1462–1466.

[Pausch et al. 1996]
Pausch, Randy, Jon Snoddy, Robert Taylor, Scott Watson, and Eric Haseltine. "Disney's Aladdin: First Steps Toward Storytelling in Virtual Reality," *Computer Graphics* (Proceedings of SIGGRAPH 96, Annual Conference Series), 1996, pp. 193–203.

[Reinig et al. 1996]
Reinig, Karl D., Charles G. Rush, Helen L. Pelster, Victor M. Spitzer, and James A. Heath. "Real-Time Visually and Haptically Accurate Surgical Simulation." In *Interactive Technology and the New Paradigm for Healthcare,* S. J. Weghorst, H. B. Sieburg, and K. S. Morgan, eds. No. 29 in Technology and Informatics, Jan. 1996, pp. 542–545.

[Rheingold 1991]
Howard Rheingold. *Virtual Reality.* New York: Summit Books, 1991.

[Robinett 1992]
Robinett, Warren."Comments on a Nose Gesture Interface Device: Extending Virtual Realities," *Presence: Teleoperators and Virtual Environments* 1(4): 493, 1992.

[Rolland et al. 1994]
Rolland, Jannick, Richard Holloway, and Henry Fuchs. "A Comparison of Optical and Video See-Through Head-Mounted Displays," *Proceedings of SPIE Telemanipulator and Telepresence Technologies,* vol. 2351, 1994.

[Shimoga 1992]
Shimoga, Karun B. "Finger Force and Touch Feedback Issues in Dexterous Telemanipulation," *Proceedings of the NASA-CIRSSE International Conference on Intelligent Robotic Systems for Space Exploration,* 1992.

[Snoddy 1996]
Snoddy, Jon. Interview with William Sherman and Alan Craig, July 29, 1996.

[State et al. 1996]
State, Andrei, Gentaro Hirota, David T. Chen, William F. Garrett, and Mark A. Livingston. "Superior Augmented Reality Registration by Integrated Landmark Tracking and Magnetic Tracking," *Computer Graphics* (Proceedings of SIGGRAPH 96, Annual Conference Series), 1996, pp. 429–438.

[Sutherland 1968]
Sutherland, Ivan E. "A Head-Mounted Three-Dimensional Display," American Federation of Information Processing Societies' (AFIPS) Fall Joint Computer Conference (*FJCC* 33(Pt. 1): 757–764, 1968.

[Tachi et al. 1994]
Tachi, Susumu, Taro Maeda, Ryokichi Hirata, and Hiroshi Hoshino. "A Construction Method of Virtual Haptic Space," *Proceedings of the Fourth International Conference on Artificial Reality and Tele-Existence,* 1994, pp.131–138.

[Tan et al. 1994]
Tan, H. Z., Srinivasan M.A., Eberman, B., and Cheng, B. "Human Factors for the Design of Force-Reflecting Haptic Interfaces." In DSC-Vol. 55-1, *Dynamic Systems and Control,* C. J. Radcliffe, ed. Volume 1, ASME 1994, pp. 353–359.

[Webster 1989]
Webster's New Universal Unabridged Dictionary. New York: Barnes & Noble Books, 1989.

[Wickens et al. 1989]
Wickens, Christopher D., S. Todd, and K. Seidler. "Three Dimensional Displays," CSERIAC State of the Art Report (SOAR 89-001), Crew Systems Information and Analysis Center, Wright Patterson Air Force Base, Ohio, 1989.

[Yeh et al. 1999]
Yeh, Michelle, Christopher D. Wickens, and F. Jacob Seagull. "Target Cueing in Visual Search: The Effects of Conformality and Display Location on the Allocation of Visual Attention," *Human Factors* 41: 524–542, December 1999.

[Yokokohji et al. 1996]
Yokokohji, Yasuyoshi, Ralph L. Hollis, and Takeo Kanade. "What You Can See Is What You Can Feel: Development of a Visual/Haptic Interface to Virtual Environment," *Proceedings of the IEEE 96 Virtual Reality Annual International Symposium (VRAIS),* 1996, pp. 46–53.

CHAPTER 5

[Arsenault et al. 2001]
Arsenault, Lance, John Kelso, Ron Kriz, Chris Logie, Fernando das Neves, Sanjiv Parikh, Eric Tester, Chad Wingrave, Robert Hunter, and Alex Kalita. "DIVERSE" website at *www.diverse.vt.edu.*

[Kelso et al. 2002]
Kelso, John, Lance E. Arsenault, Steven G. Satterfield, and Ronald D. Kriz. "DIVERSE: A Framework for Building Extensible and Reconfigurable Device-Independent Virtual Environments," *Proceedings of the IEEE Virtual Reality 02 Conference,* 2002, pp. 183–190.

[Bargar et al. 1994]
Bargar, Robin, Insook Choi, Sumit Das, and Camille Goudeseune. "Model-Based Interactive Sound for an Immersive Virtual Environment," *Proceedings of the 94 International Computer Music Conference,* 1994, pp. 471–474.

[Brooks et al. 1990]
Brooks, Jr., Frederick P., Ming Ouh-Young, James J. Batter, and P. Jerome Kilpatrick. "Project GROPE: Haptic Displays for Scientific Visualization," *Computer Graphics* (Proceedings of SIGGRAPH 90, Annual Conference Series) 24(4): 177–185, 1990.

[Drebin et al. 1988]
Drebin, Robert A., Loren Carpenter, and Pat Hanrahan. "Volume Rendering," *Computer Graphics* (Proceedings of SIGGRAPH 88, Annual Conference Series) 22(4): 65–74, 1988.

[Ganter 1989]
Ganter, John H. "A Comparison of Representations for Complex Earth Volumes," *Auto-Carto 9: Proceedings of the Ninth International Symposium on Computer-Assisted Cartography,* 1989.

[Garnett and Goudeseune 1999]
Garnett, Guy, and Camille Goudeseune, "Performance Factors in Control of High-Dimensional Spaces," *Proceedings of the 99 International Computer Music Conference,* 1999, pp. 268–271. (See also *http://zx81.ncsa.uiuc.edu/camilleg/icmc99.html.*)

[Hodges et al. 1995]
Hodges, Larry F., Rob Kooper, Thomas C. Meyer, Barbara O. Rothbaum, Dan Opdyke, Johannes J. de Graaff, James S. Williford, and Max M. North. "Virtual Environments for Treating the Fear of Heights," *IEEE Computer* 28(7): 27–34, 1995.

[Just et al. 1998]
Just, Christopher, Allen Bierbaum, Albert Baker, and Carolina Cruz-Neira. "VR Juggler: A Framework for Virtual Reality Development," *Procedings of the Second Immersive Projection Technology (IPT) Workshop* (Workshop CD-ROM)," 1998.

[Kennedy et al. 1993]
Kennedy, R. S., N. E. Lane, K. S. Berbaum, and M. G. Lilienthal. "Simulator Sickness Questionnaire: An Enhanced Method for Quantifying Simulator Sickness," *International Journal of Aviation Psychology* 3(3): 203–220, 1993.

[Mark et al. 1996]
Mark, William R., Scott C. Randolph, Mark Finch, James M. Van Verth, and Russell M. Taylor II. "Adding Force Feedback to Graphics Systems: Issues and Solutions," *Computer Graphics* (Proceedings of SIGGRAPH 96 Annual Conference Series), 1996, pp. 447–452.

[Massie 1993]
Thomas H. Massie. "Design of a Three Degree of Freedom Force-Reflecting Haptic Interface." Thesis submitted for Bachelor of Science degree at the Massachusetts Institute of Technology, May 1993.

[McCloud 1993]
McCloud, Scott. *Understanding Comics: The Invisible Art.* Northhampton, Mass.: Kitchen Sink Press, 1993.

[McNeely 1993]
McNeely, William A. "Robotic Graphics: A New Approach to Force Feedback for Virtual Reality," *Proceedings of the IEEE 93 Virtual Reality Annual International Symposium (VRAIS),* 1993, pp. 336–341.

[Pausch 1995]
Pausch, Randy. Presentation of "A Brief Architectural Overview of Alice, a Rapid Prototyping System for Virtual Reality (Course 8: Programming Virtual Worlds)," *ACM SIGGRAPH 95 Conference Course Notes,* August 1995.

[Pausch et al. 1996]
Pausch, Randy, Jon Snoddy, Robert Taylor, Scott Watson, and Eric Haseltine. "Disney's Aladdin: First Steps Toward Storytelling in Virtual Reality," *Computer Graphics* (Proceedings of SIGGRAPH 96, Annual Conference Series), 1996, pp. 193–203.

[Peachey 1994]
Peachey, Darwyn. "Building Procedural Textures." In *Texturing and Modeling: A Procedural Approach,* David S. Ebert, ed. Cambridge, Mass.: Academic Press Professional, 1994, ch. 2.

[Reeves 1983]
Reeves, William T. "Particle Systems: A Technique for Modeling a Class of Fuzzy Objects," *Computer Graphics* (Proceedings of SIGGRAPH 83, Annual Conference Series) 17(3): 359–376, 1983.

[Scaletti 1997]
Carla Scaletti. Telephone communication with Alan Craig, 1997.

[SensAble Technologies, Inc. 1997]
SensAble Technologies, Inc. *Ghost Software Developer's Toolkit Programmer's Guide, Version 1.2.* Cambridge, Mass.: SensAble Technologies, Inc., Sept. 15, 1997.

[Sherman 2001]
Sherman, William R. "FreeVR" website at *http://freevr.org.*

[Snoddy 1996]
Snoddy, Jon. Interview with William Sherman and Alan Craig, July 29, 1996.

[Stansfield and Shawver 1996]
Stansfield, Sharon, and Daniel Shawver. "Using Virtual Reality to Train and Plan Response Actions to Acts of Terrorism," *Proceedings of the SPIE Conference on Enabling Technologies for Law Enforcement and Security,* 1996.

[Tate et al. 1997]
Tate, David L., Linda Sibert, and Tony King. "Virtual Environments for Shipboard Firefighting Training," *Proceedings of the IEEE 97 Virtual Reality Annual International Symposium (VRAIS),* 1997, pp. 61–68.

[Thompson 1995]
Thompson, Reeve S. "The Sprocket Hole Film Glossary" website at *http://hamp.hampshire.edu/~rstF93/glossary.html.*

[Vince 1995]
Vince, John. *Virtual Reality Systems.* Wokingham, England: Addison-Wesley, 1995.

[Webster 1983]
Webster's Ninth New Collegiate Dictionary. Springfield, Mass.: Merriam-Webster, Inc., 1983.

[Wickens and Hollands 2000]
Wickens, Christopher D., and Justin G. Hollands. *Engineering Psychology and Human Performance,* 3rd ed. Upper Saddle River, N.J.: Prentice Hall, 2000.

[Wickens et al. 1989]
Wickens, Christopher D., S. Todd, and K. Seidler. "Three Dimensional Displays," CSERIAC State of the Art Report (SOAR 89-001), Crew Systems Information and Analysis Center, Wright Patterson Air Force Base, Ohio, 1989.

[Wightman and Kistler 1989]
Wightman, Frederic, and Doris J. Kistler. "Headphone Simulation of Free-Field Listening. I: Stimulus Synthesis," *Journal of the Acoustical Society of America* 85: 858–867, 1989.

CHAPTER 6

[Angus and Sowizral 1995]
Angus, Ian G., and Henry A. Sowizral. "Embedding the 2D Interaction Metaphor in a Real 3D Environment," *Proceedings of SPIE, Stereoscopic Displays and Virtual Reality Systems* 2409: 282–293, 1995.

[Arthur et al. 1998]
Arthur, Kevin, Timothy Preston, Russell Taylor, Frederick Brooks, Jr., Mary Whitton, and William Wright. "Designing and Building the PIT: A Head-Tracked Stereo Workspace for Two Users," *Proceedings of the Second International Immersive Projection Technology (IPT) Workshop* (Workshop CD-ROM), 1998.

[Bier et al. 1993]
Bier, Eric A., Maureen C. Stone, Ken Pier, William Buxton, and Tony D. DeRose. "Toolglass and Magic Lenses: The See-Through Interface," *Computer Graphics* (Proceedings of SIGGRAPH 93, Annual Conference Series), 1993, pp. 73–80.

[Bowman and Wingrave 2001]
Bowman, Doug A., and Chadwick A. Wingrave. "Design and Evaluation of Menu Systems for Immersive Virtual Environments," *Proceedings of IEEE Virtual Reality 01 Conference,* 2001, pp. 149–156.

[Bowman et al. 1999]
Bowman, Doug A., Larry F. Hodges, Don Allison, and Jean Wineman. "The Educational Value of an Information-Rich Virtual Environment," *Presence: Teleoperators and Virtual Environments* 8(3): 317–331, 1999.

[Buxton 1996]
Buxton, William. "Absorbing and Squeezing Out: On Sponges and Ubiquitous Computing," *Proceedings of the 1996 International Broadcasting Symposium,* 1996.

[Carpenter and Carpenter 1993]
Carpenter, Loren, and Rachel Carpenter. "Method and Apparatus for Audience Participation by Electronic Imaging." U.S. Patent No. 5210604, 1993.

[Chung 1992]
Chung, J. "A Comparison of Head-Tracked and Non–Head-Tracked Steering Modes in the Targeting of Radiotherapy Treatment Beams," *Proceedings of the 1992 Symposium on Interactive 3-D Graphics,* 1992, pp. 193–196.

[Darken and Banker 1998]
Darken, Rudolph P., and William P. Banker. "Navigating in Natural Environments: A Virtual Environment Training Transfer Study," *Proceedings of the IEEE 98 Virtual Reality Annual International Symposium (VRAIS),* 1998, pp 12–19.

[Ellis et al. 1987]
Ellis, Steve R., Michael W. McGreevy, and R. Hitchcock. "Perspective Traffic Display Format and Airline Pilot Traffic Avoidance," *Human Factors* 29(2): 371–382, 1987.

[Guiard 1987]
Guiard, Yves. "Asymmetric Division of Labor in Human Skilled Bimanual Action: The Kinematic Chain as a Model," *Journal of Motor Behavior* 16(12): 486–517, 1987.

[Harmon 1996]
Harmon, Reid, Walter Patterson, William Ribarsky, and Jay Bolter. "The Virtual Annotation System," *Proceedings of the IEEE 96 Virtual Reality Annual International Symposium (VRAIS),* 1996, pp. 293–245.

[Herndon and Meyer 1994]
Herndon, Kenneth P., and Thomas Meyer. "3D Widgets for Exploratory Scientific Visualization," *Proceedings of the Seventh Annual ACM User Interface Software and Technology (UIST),* 1994, pp. 69–70.

[Hinckley 1996]
Hinckley, Ken. "Haptic Issues for Virtual Manipulation." Doctoral dissertation, University of Virginia, Dec. 1996.

[Homan and Gott 1996]
Homan, Dave J., and Charles J. Gott. "An Integrated EVA/RMS Virtual Reality Simulation, Including Force Feedback, for Astronaut Training," *Proceedings of the 1996 AIAA Flight Simulation Technologies Conference.* NASA reference publication AIAA 96-3498, 1996.

[Koller et al. 1996]
Koller, David R., Mark R. Mine, and Scott E. Hudson. "Head-Tracked Orbital Viewing: An Interaction Technique for Immersive Virtual Environments," *Proceedings of the Ninth Annual ACM Symposium on User Interface Software and Technology (UIST),* 1996, pp. 81–82.

[MacEachren 1995]
MacEachren, A. M. *How Maps Work: Representation, Visualization, and Design.* New York: The Guilford Press, 1995.

[Mapes and Moshell 1995]
Mapes, Daniel P., and J. Michael Moshell. "A Two-Handed Interface for Object Manipulation in Virtual Environments," *Presence: Teleoperators and Virtual Environments* 4(4): 403–416, 1995.

[Mine 1995a]
Mine, Mark R. "Virtual Environment Interaction Techniques." Technical Report TR95-018, University of North Carolina at Chapel Hill, 1995.

[Mine 1995b]
———"ISAAC: A Virtual Environment Tool for the Interactive Construction of Virtual Worlds." Technical Report TR95-020, University of North Carolina at Chapel Hill, 1995.

[Mine 1996]
———"Working in a Virtual World: Interaction Techniques Used in the Chapel Hill Immersive Modeling Program." Technical Report TR96-029, University of North Carolina at Chapel Hill, 1996.

[Mine et al. 1997]
Mine, Mark R., Frederick P. Brooks, Jr., and Carlo H. Sequin. "Moving Objects in Space: Exploiting Proprioception in Virtual Environment Interaction," *Computer Graphics* (Proceedings of SIGGRAPH 97, Annual Conference Series), 1997, pp. 19–26.

[Monmonier 1991]
Monmonier, Mark. *How to Lie with Maps.* Chicago: University of Chicago Press, 1991.

[Pausch 1996]
Pausch, Randy. "Disney's Aladdin: First Steps Toward Storytelling in Virtual Reality." Paper presented at SIGGRAPH 96, Aug. 8, 1996, New Orleans.

[Pausch et al. 1995]
Pausch, Randy, Tommy Burnette, Dan Brockway, and Michael E. Weiblen. "Navigation and Locomotion in Virtual Worlds via Flight into Hand-Held Miniatures," *Computer Graphics* (Proceedings of SIGGRAPH 95, Annual Conference Series), 1995, pp. 399–400.

[Pausch et al. 1996]
Pausch, Randy, Jon Snoddy, Robert Taylor, Scott Watson, and Eric Haseltine. "Disney's Aladdin: First Steps Toward Storytelling in Virtual Reality," *Computer Graphics* (Proceedings of SIGGRAPH 96, Annual Conference Series), 1996, pp. 193–203.

[Pierce et al. 1997]
Pierce, Jeffrey S., Andrew Forsberg, Matthew J. Conway, Seung Hong, Robert Zeleznik, and Mark R. Mine. "Image Plane Interaction Techniques in 3-D Immersive Environments," *Proceedings of the 1997 ACM Symposium on Interactive 3-D Graphics*, 1997, pp. 39–43.

[Poupyrev et al. 1996]
Poupyrev, Ivan, Mark Billinghurst, Suzanne Weghorst, and Tadao Ichikawa. "The Go-Go Interaction Technique: Non-Linear Mapping for Direct Manipulation in VR" *Proceedings of the Ninth Annual ACM Symposium on User Interface Software and Technology (UIST)*, 1996, pp. 79–81.

[Razzaque et al. 2001]
Razzaque, Sharif, Z. Kohn, and Mary Whitton. "Redirected Walking." Technical Report TR01-007, Department of Computer Science, University of North Carolina, 2001.

[Snoddy 1996]
Snoddy, Jon. Interview with William Sherman and Alan Craig, July 29, 1996.

[Stasz 1980]
Stasz, Cathleen. "Planning During Map Learning: The Global Strategies of High and Low Visual-Spatial Individuals." Report N-1594-ONR, Rand Corporation, 1980.

[Stoakley et al. 1995]
Stoakley, Richard, Matthew J. Conway, and Randy Pausch. "Virtual Reality on a WIM: Interactive Worlds in Miniature," *Proceedings of the ACM SIGCHI Human Factors in Computer Systems Conference,* 1985, pp. 265–272.

[Stytz et al. 1997]
Stytz, Martin R., John Vanderburgh, and Sheila B. Banks. "The Solar System Modeler," *IEEE Computer Graphics and Applications* 17(5): 47–57, 1997.

[Thiébaux 1997]
Thiébaux, Marcus. "Steering Scientific Imaging with Virtual Camera Choreography." Masters thesis, University of Illinois at Chicago, 1997.

[Viega et al. 1996]
Viega, John, Matthew J. Conway, George Williams, and Randy Pausch. "3D Magic Lenses," *Proceedings of the Ninth Annual ACM Symposium on User Interface Software and Technology (UIST)*, 1996, pp. 51–58.

[Weber 1997]
Weber, Hans, "Course 29: Programming Virtual Worlds," *ACM SIGGRAPH 97 Conference Course Notes,* 1997.

[Webster 1989]
Webster's New Universal Unabridged Dictionary. New York: Barnes & Noble Books, 1989.

[Wickens and Hollands 2000]
Wickens, Christopher D., and Justin G. Hollands. *Engineering Psychology and Human Performance,* 3rd ed. Upper Saddle River, N.J.: Prentice Hall, 2000.

[Zeltzer et al. 1995]
Zeltzer, D., Pioch, N., and Aviles, W. "Training the Officer of the Deck," *IEEE Computer Graphics and Applications* 15(6): 6–9, 1995.

[Wilson and Rosenberg 1998]
Wilson, J., and D. Rosenberg. "Rapid Prototyping for User Interface Design." In *Handbook of Human-Computer Interaction,* M. Helander, ed. Amsterdam: Elsevier Science, 1998.

CHAPTER 7

[Astheimer et al. 1994]
Astheimer, Peter, Fan Dai, Martin Goebel, Rolf Kruse, Stefan Mueller, and Gabriel Zachmann. "Realism in Virtual Reality." In *Artificial Life and Virtual Reality.* Chichester, England: John Wiley & Sons, 1994, pp. 189–210.

[Bishop 2002]
Bishop, Gary. E-mail correspondence with William Sherman, April 1, 2002.

[Hoffman 1998]
Hoffman, Hunter G. "Physically Touching Virtual Objects Using Tactile Augmentation Enhances the Realism of Virtual Environments," *Proceedings of the IEEE 1998 Virtual Reality Annual International Symposium (VRAIS),* 1998, pp. 59–63.

[Insko et al. 2001]
Insko, Brent E., Michael J. Meehan, Mary C. Whitton, and Frederick P. Brooks, Jr. "Passive Haptics Significantly Enhances Virtual Environments." Department of Computer Science Technical Report 01-010, University of North Carolina at Chapel Hill, 2001.

[Kaufmann and Smarr 1993]
Kaufmann III, William J., and Larry L. Smarr. *Supercomputing and the Transformation of Science.* New York: Scientific American Library, 1993.

[O'Donnell 1980]
O'Donnell, Mark. "O'Donnell's Laws of Cartoon Motion," Quoted in *Esquire Magazine,* June 1980. (Originally published in New York: Random House, *Elementary Education: An Easy Alternative to Actual Learning,* 1985.)

[Pausch et al. 1996]
Pausch, Randy, Jon Snoddy, Robert Taylor, Scott Watson, and Eric Haseltine. "Disney's Aladdin: First Steps Toward Storytelling in Virtual Reality," *Computer Graphics* (Proceedings of SIGGRAPH 96, Annual Conference Series), 1996, pp. 193–203.

[Razzaque et al. 2001]
Razzaque, Sharif, Zac Kohn, and Mary Whitton. "Redirected Walking." Department of Computer Science Technical Report TR01-007, University of North Carolina, 2001.

[Rothbaum et al. 1996]
Rothbaum, Barbara O., Larry F. Hodges, Benjamin A. Watson, G. Drew Kessler, and Dan Opdyke. "Virtual Reality Exposure Therapy in the Treatment of Fear of Flying: A Case Report," *Behavioral Research Therapy* 34(5/6): 477–481, 1996.

[Slater and Usoh 1993]
Slater, Mel, and Martin Usoh. "Presence in Immersive Virtual Environments," *Proceedings of the IEEE 1993 Virtual Reality Annual International Symposium (VRAIS)*, 1993, pp. 90–96.

[Slater and Usoh 1994]
Slater, Mel, and Martin Usoh. "Body Centered Interaction in Immersive Virtual Environments." In *Artificial Life and Virtual Reality.* Chichester, England: John Wiley & Sons, 1994, pp. 125–147.

[Snoddy 1996]
Snoddy, Jon. Interview with William Sherman and Alan Craig, July 29, 1996.

[Wickens and Hollands 2000]
Wickens, Christopher D., and Justin G. Hollands. *Engineering Psychology and Human Performance,* 3rd ed. Upper Saddle River, N.J.: Prentice Hall, 2000.

CHAPTER 8

[Best 1993]
Best, Kathryn. *The Idiots' Guide to Virtual World Design.* Seattle: Little Star Press, 1993.

[Daines 1995]
Daines, Gary. "Designing Virtual Worlds." Presentation at Virtual Reality World Conference and Exposition, May 1995, San Jose, Ca.

[Davies and Harrison 1996]
Davies, Char, and John Harrison. "Osmose: Towards Broadening the Aesthetics of Virtual Reality," *Computer Graphics* 30(4): 25–28, 1996.

[Loeffler 1995]
Loeffler, Carl. "Virtual Pompeii." Presentation at Virtual Reality World Conference and Exposition, May 1995, San Jose, Ca.

[Pausch et al. 1996]
Pausch, Randy, Jon Snoddy, Robert Taylor, Scott Watson, and Eric Haseltine. "Disney's Aladdin: First Steps Toward Storytelling in Virtual Reality," *Computer Graphics* (Proceedings of SIGGRAPH 96, Annual Conference Series), 1996, pp. 193–203.

[Roussos et al. 1999]
Roussos, Maria, Andrew Johnson, Thomas Moher, Jason Leigh, Christina Vasilakis, and Craig Barnes. "Learning and Building Together in an Immersive Virtual World," *Presence Teleoperators and Virtual Environment* 8(3): 247–263, 1999.

[Snoddy 1996]
Snoddy, Jon. Interview with William Sherman and Alan Craig, July 29, 1996.

[Tate et al. 1997]
Tate, David L., Linda Sibert, Tony King. "Virtual Environments for Shipboard Firefighting Training," *Proceedings of the IEEE 1997 Virtual Reality Annual International Symposium (VRAIS)*, 1997, pp. 61–68.

[Thiébaux 1997]
Thiébaux, Marcus. "Steering Scientific Imaging with Virtual Camera Choreography." Masters thesis, University of Illinois at Chicago, 1997.

CHAPTER 9

[Bowman et al. 1998]

Bowman, Doug A., Larry F. Hodges, Jay Bolter. "The Virtual Venue: User-Computer Interaction in Information-Rich Virtual Environments," *Presence, Teleoperators and Virtual Environment* 7(5): 478–493, 1998.

[Fenn 1995]

Fenn, Jackie. "The Microsoft System Software Hype Cycle Strikes Again." *Gartner Research Report,* July 1995.

[Goudeseune 2001]

Goudeseune, Camille. Interview with William Sherman, August 22, 2001.

[Hinckley et al. 1994]

Hinckley, Ken, Randy Pausch, J. C. Goble, and Neil F. Kassell. "Passive Real-World Interface Props for Neurosurgical Visualization," *Proceedings of the IEEE 1995 Virtual Reality Annual International Symposium (VRAIS),* 1994, pp. 179–188.

[Kajimoto et al. 2002]

Kajimoto, Hiroyuki, Naoki Kowakami, and Susumu Tachi. "Optimal Design Method for Selective Nerve Stimulation and Its Application to Electrocutaneous Display," *Proceedings of the Tenth International Symposium on Haptic Interfaces for Virtual Environments and Teleoperator Systems,* 2002, pp. 303–310.

[Ouh-young et al. 1989]

Ouh-young, Ming, David V. Beard, and Frederick P. Brooks, Jr. "Force Display Performs Better Than Visual Display in a Simple 6-D Docking Task," *Proceedings of the IEEE International Conference on Robotics and Automation,* 1999, pp. 1562–1466.

[Park and Kenyon 1999]

Park, Kyoung Shin, and Robert V. Kenyon. "Effects of Network Characteristics on Human Performance in a Collaborative Virtual Environment," *Proceedings of IEEE Virtual Reality 1999 Conference,* 1999, pp. 104–111.

[Pausch et al. 1997]

Pausch, Randy, Dennis Proffitt, and George Williams. "Quantifying Immersion in Virtual Reality," *Computer Graphics* (Proceedings of SIGGRAPH 97, Annual Conference Series), 1997, pp. 13–18.

[Peine et al. 1995]

Peine, William J., Dimitrios A. Koutarinis, and Robert D. Howe. "A Tactile Sensing and Display System for Surgical Applications." In *Interactive Technology and the New Paradigm for Healthcare,* R. Satava, K. Morgan, H. Sieburg, R. Matthews, and J. Christensen, eds. Washington, D.C.: IOS Press, 1995, pp. 283–288.

[Rothbaum et al. 1996]

Rothbaum, Barbara O., Larry F. Hodges, Benjamin A. Watson, and G. Drew Kessler. "Virtual Reality Exposure Therapy in the Treatment of Fear of Flying: A Case Report," *Behavioral Research Therapy* 34(5/6): 477–481, 1996.

[Salzman et al. 1996]

Salzman, Marilyn C., Chris Dede, and R. Bowen Loftin. "ScienceSpace: Virtual Realities for Learning Complex and Abstract Scientific Concepts," *Proceedings of IEEE 1996 Virtual Reality Annual International Symposium (VRAIS),* 1996, pp. 246–253.

[Zeleznik et al. 1996]

Zeleznik, Robert C., K. Herndon, and John F. Hughes. "SKETCH: An Interface for Sketching 3D Scenes," *Computer Graphics* (Proceedings of SIGGRAPH 96, Annual Conference Series), 1996, pp. 163–170.

APPENDIX A

[Johnson 1998]
Johnson, Andrew. Correspondence with William Sherman, September 13, 1998.

[Johnson et al. 1998]
Johnson, Andrew, Maria Roussos, Jason Leigh, Christina Vasilakis, Craig Barnes, and Thomas Moher. "The NICE Project: Learning Together in a Virtual World," *Proceedings of the IEEE 1998 Virtual Reality Annual International Symposium (VRAIS)*, 1998, pp. 176–183.

[Leigh et al. 1996]
Leigh, Jason, Andrew E. Johnson, Christina A. Vasilakis, and Thomas A. De Fanti. "Multi-Perspective Collaborative Design in Persistent Networked Virtual Environments," *Proceedings of the IEEE 1996 Virtual Reality Annual International Symposium (VRAIS)*, 1996, pp. 253–260.

[Leigh et al. 1997]
Leigh, Jason, Andrew Johnson, and Thomas DeFanti. "CAVERN: Distributed Architecture for Supporting Scalable Persistence and Interoperability in Collaborative Virtual Environments," *Virtual Reality: Research, Development, and Applications* 2(2): 217–237, 1997.

[Reynolds 1987]
Reynolds, Craig W. "Flocks, Herds, and Schools: A Distributed Behavioral Model," *Computer Graphics* (Proceedings of SIGGRAPH 87, Annual Conference Series) 21(4): 25–34, 1987.

[Roussos et al. 1997]
Roussos, Maria, Andrew E. Johnson, Jason Leigh, Christina A.Vasilakis, Craig R. Barnes, and Thomas G. Moher. "NICE: Combining Constructionism, Narrative, and Collaboration in a Virtual Learning Environment," *Computer Graphics* (Proceedings of SIGGRAPH 97, Annual Conference Series) 31(3): 62–63, 1997.

[Roussos et al. 1999]
Roussos, Maria, Andrew Johnson, Thomas Moher, Jason Leigh, Christina Vasilakis, and Craig Barnes. "Learning and Building Together in an Immersive Virtual World," *Presence Teleoperators and Virtual Environment* 8(3): 247–263, 1999.

[Steiner and Moher 1994]
Steiner, K. E., and Thomas G. Moher. "Graphic StoryWriter: An Environment for Emergent Storytelling," *Journal of Educational Multimedia and Hypermedia* 3(2): 173–196, 1994.

[Vella et al. 1995]
Vella, Zane, Coco Conn, Jim Thompson, Chris Cederwall, Jim Damiano, and David Goldberg. "CitySpace," *SIGGRAPH 95 Visual Proceedings*, 1995, p. 142.

APPENDIX B

[Brady et al. 1995]
Brady, Rachael, John Pixton, George Baxter, Patrick Moran, Clinton S. Potter, Bridget Carragher, and Andrew Belmont. "Crumbs: A Virtual Environment Tracking Tool for Biological Imaging," *Proceedings of the IEEE Symposium on Frontiers in Biomedical Visualization*, 1995, pp. 18–25.

[Brady et al. 1996]
Brady, Rachael, Robin Bargar, Insook Choi, and Joseph Reitzer. "Auditory Bread Crumbs for Navigating Volumetric Data," *IEEE Visualization,* 1996, pp. 25–27.

[Miller et al. 1997]
Miller, Karla, Rachael Brady, and Clinton S. Potter. "Using Partial Occlusion for Stereoscopic Voxel Selection: Extending the Silk Cursor." NCSA Technical Report 042, Nov. 1997.

[Pixton and Belmont 1996]
Pixton, John L., and Andrew S. Belmont. "NewVision: A Program for Interactive Navigation and Analysis of Multiple 3-D Data Sets Using Coordinated Virtual Cameras," *Journal of Structural Biology* 116:77–85, 1996.

[Potter et al. 1996]
Potter, Clint, Rachael Brady, Pat Moran, Carl Gregory, Bridget Carragher, Nick Kisseberth, Joseph Lyding, and Jason Lindquist. "EVAC: A Virtual Environment for Control of Remote Imaging Instrumentation," *IEEE Computer Graphics and Applications* 16(4): 62–66, 1996.

APPENDIX C

[Caudell and Mizell 1992]
Caudel, Thomas P., and David W. Mizell. "Augmented Reality: An Application of Heads-Up Display Technology to Manual Manufacturing Processes," *Proceedings of the Hawaii International Conference on Systems Sciences,* 1992, pp. 659–669.

[Hedberg 1996]
Hedberg, Sara Reese. "Virtual Reality at Boeing: Pushing the Envelope." Virtual Reality Special Report, Jan.–Feb. 1996.

APPENDIX D

[He et al. 1996]
He, Li-wei, Michael F. Cohen, and David Salesin. "The Virtual Cinematographer: A Paradigm for Automatic Real-Time Camera Control and Directing," *Computer Graphics* (Proceedings of SIGGRAPH 96, Annual Conference Series), 1996, pp. 217–224.

[Laurel et al. 1994]
Laurel, Brenda, Rachel Strickland, and Rob Tow. "Placeholder: Landscape and Narrative in Virtual Environments," *Computer Graphics* (Proceedings of SIGGRAPH 94, Annual Conference Series) 28(2): 118–126, 1994.

[Tow 1984]
Tow, Rob. "Placeholder: Technology and the Senses," Proceedings of the Second ACM International Conference on Multimedia, 1994, pp. 129–132.

[von Uexküll 1957]
Uexküll, Jakob. *A Stroll Through the World of Animals and Men: A Picture Book of Invisible Worlds.* Reprinted in *Instinctive Behavior: The Development of a Modern Concept,* Claire Schiller, trans. New York: International Universities Press, 1957. (Originally published in German in 1934.)

Index

About the Authors

William R. Sherman
National Center for Supercomputing Applications
University of Illinois at Urbana-Champaign

William Sherman leads the virtual reality effort at the National Center for Super-computing Applications (NCSA) at the University of Illinois at Urbana-Champaign. Bill came to NCSA as part of the scientific visualization team in 1989 and took over the reins of the virtual reality facilities in 1992. Bill's primary interests are in exploring the many potential applications of virtual reality, how VR can be beneficial in diverse fields, and how to produce effective VR experiences.

Bill has authored several book chapters and papers on the topics of scientific visualization and virtual reality and has been teaching a graduate-level course on VR at the University of Illinois at Urbana-Champaign. When not writing and lecturing, Bill has spent his time creating virtual reality experiences and computer animations of scientific visualizations, including the award-winning *Smog: Visualizing the Components*.

Alan B. Craig
National Center for Supercomputing Applications
University of Illinois at Urbana-Champaign

Alan Craig currently does research and development in the Visualization and Virtual Environments Group at the National Center for Supercomputing Applications (NCSA) at the University of Illinois at Urbana-Champaign. Alan has been with NCSA since March 1987.

Through his work with the NCSA Virtual Reality Group, Alan has participated in the development of numerous virtual reality applications and visited a large number of VR laboratories, both in the United States and abroad. While working with the NCSA Visualization Group, Alan created the award-winning animation *Landscape Dynamics of Yellowstone National Park.*

Prior to his work in the Visualization and Virtual Environments group, Alan was Manager of the NCSA Training Group, Manager of the NCSA Information Technology Group, and a member of the NCSA Scientific Visualization Group. Before his tenure at NCSA, Alan was employed by Texas Instruments, Inc. in Dallas, Texas.

Alan's areas of expertise include virtual reality applications, multimodal interaction, scientific visualization and sonification, collaborative environments, distance education, information retrieval and mining, and novel I/O devices. In addition to giving numerous presentations, Alan has authored numerous papers and book chapters related to scientific visualization and virtual reality.